에듀윌 토익
실전 LC+RC

시작하라. 그 자체가 천재성이고, 힘이며, 마력이다.

– 요한 볼프강 폰 괴테(Johann Wolfgang von Goethe)

에듀윌 토익
실전 LC+RC를 펴내며

토익은 체계와 유형이 뚜렷한 시험이므로 어느 정도 기본기를 갖추고 실전 문제를 꾸준히 풀어보면서 실전 감각을 높이면 원하는 점수를 획득할 수 있습니다. 그래서 많은 실전 문제를 풀어 보고 틀린 문제들을 복습하면서 약점을 보완해 나가는 것이 중요합니다.

하지만 실전 연습에서 문제를 많이 푸는 것보다 더 중요한 것은 '좋은 문제'를 푸는 것입니다. 기출과 가장 유사한 유형과 적절한 난이도를 갖춘 문제를 풀어야만 내 수준과 약점을 정확히 진단하고 그에 따른 학습 전략을 세울 수 있습니다. 본 책은 최신 기출에 대한 꼼꼼한 분석을 토대로, 토익 베테랑 연구원들과 원어민 집필진이 수차례의 검토와 다양한 수준의 학생 평가를 거쳐 개발한 최상의 문제들만을 수록했습니다. 믿고 정주행하셔도 좋습니다.

본 실전서는 양질의 문제 제공뿐만 아니라 시험 후 복습 효과를 향상할 수 있는 방안에도 남다른 정성을 기울였습니다. 문제를 풀고 난 다음에는 부록으로 실린 '테스트별 핵심 어휘'를 활용하여 중요 어휘 및 몰랐던 표현들을 확실히 익히시기 바랍니다. LC는 실전 적응력을 높일 수 있는 다양한 버전의 음원과, 문제를 제거하고 대화 및 담화만 집중 반복해 들을 수 있게 복습용 음원을 따로 제공합니다. 당장은 기대에 못 미치는 점수가 나왔다 하더라도 이러한 복습용 콘텐츠들을 십분 활용하여 몰랐던 단어와 표현들을 착실히 익혀 나가다 보면 금세 목표로 하는 점수를 얻을 수 있을 것입니다.

에듀윌 토익이 여러분을 응원하겠습니다.

에듀윌 어학연구소 드림

목차

책의 구성 및 특징	005
TOEIC 소개	006
TOEIC 파트별 문제 형태	008
점수 환산표	016
학습 스케줄러	017
TEST 01	018
TEST 02	060
TEST 03	104
TEST 04	146
TEST 05	188

정답 및 해설

TEST 01	002
TEST 02	045
TEST 03	086
TEST 04	127
TEST 05	168
테스트별 핵심 어휘	209

책의 구성 및 특징

최신 기출 경향 완전 분석 및 반영
최신 토익 시험 문제를 밀도 있게 분석하여, 출제 경향과 빈출 유형을 파악한 후 최상의 문제들로만 엄선하여 실었습니다.

실전 모의고사 5회분
과도하게 많은 문제로 중도에 포기하기보다는 부담 없이 알찬 분량 5회분으로 성취감도 느끼고, 실전 훈련도 충분하도록 기획하였습니다.

테스트별 핵심 어휘
해설집의 뒷부분에 각 테스트에 나왔던 핵심 어휘 및 표현들을 모아 다시 한번 확실하게 익힐 수 있게 하였습니다.

다양한 버전의 MP3 파일 무료 제공
리스닝 MP3 파일을 테스트별, 파트별, 문항별로 다운로드할 수 있습니다. 테스트별 MP3 파일은 고속, 매미 소리, 고사장 소음 버전으로도 제공하니 필요한 것으로 골라서 들으세요. 또한 복습 시 불필요한 시간 소모를 최소화하기 위해 파트별 대화문과 담화문 스크립트만 반복해서 들을 수 있는 파일도 제공합니다.

맞힌 문제는 다음에 또 맞히기 위해, 틀린 문제는 또 틀리지 않기 위해 다양한 버전의 MP3 파일을 적극적으로 활용해 보세요. 그러다 보면 실제 시험에서 리스닝 내용이 귀에 쏙쏙 박히는 놀라운 경험을 하게 될 겁니다.

TOEIC 소개

토익이란?
TOEIC은 Test of English for International Communication(국제적인 의사소통을 위한 영어 시험)의 약자로, 영어가 모국어가 아닌 사람들이 비즈니스 현장 및 일상생활에서 필요한 실용 영어 능력을 갖추었는가를 평가하는 시험입니다.

시험 구성

구성	파트		문항 수		시간	배점
LISTENING Comprehension	PART 1	사진 묘사	6	100	45분	495점
	PART 2	질의 응답	25			
	PART 3	짧은 대화	39			
	PART 4	짧은 담화	30			
READING Comprehension	PART 5	단문 빈칸 채우기	30	100	75분	495점
	PART 6	장문 빈칸 채우기	16			
	PART 7	독해	단일 지문 29			
			이중 지문 10			
			삼중 지문 15			
합계	7 PARTS		200문항		120분	990점

출제 범위 및 주제
업무 및 일상생활에서 쓰이는 실용적인 주제들이 출제됩니다. 특정 문화나 특정 직업 분야에만 해당되는 주제는 출제하지 않으며, 듣기 평가의 경우 미국, 영국, 호주 등 다양한 국가의 발음이 섞여 출제됩니다.

일반 업무	계약, 협상, 영업, 홍보, 마케팅, 사업 계획
재무 회계	예산, 투자, 세금, 청구, 회계
개발	연구, 제품 개발
제조	공장 경영, 생산 조립 라인, 품질 관리
인사	채용, 승진, 퇴직, 직원 교육, 입사 지원
사무실	회의, 메모/전화/팩스/이메일, 사무 장비 및 가구
행사	학회, 연회, 회식, 시상식, 박람회, 제품 시연회
부동산	건축, 부동산 매매/임대, 기업 부지, 전기/수도/가스 설비
여행/여가	교통수단, 공항/역, 여행 일정, 호텔 및 자동차 예약/연기/취소, 영화, 전시, 공연

접수 방법

- 한국 TOEIC 위원회 사이트(www.toeic.co.kr)에서 인터넷 접수 기간을 확인하고 접수합니다.
- 시험 접수 시 최근 6개월 이내에 촬영한 jpg 형식의 사진 파일이 필요하므로 미리 준비합니다.
- 시험 11~13일 전부터는 특별 추가 접수 기간에 해당하여 추가 비용이 발생하므로, 접수 일정을 미리 확인하여 정기 접수 기간 내에 접수하도록 합니다.

시험 당일 준비물

신분증	주민등록증, 운전면허증, 기간 만료 전 여권, 공무원증 등 규정 신분증만 인정 (중·고등학생의 경우 학생증, 청소년증도 인정)
필기구	연필, 지우개 (볼펜, 사인펜은 사용 불가)

시험 진행

오전 시험	오후 시험	진행 내용
09:30 - 09:45	02:30 - 02:45	답안지 작성 오리엔테이션
09:45 - 09:50	02:45 - 02:50	쉬는 시간
09:50 - 10:05	02:50 - 03:05	신분증 확인
10:05 - 10:10	03:05 - 03:10	문제지 배부 및 파본 확인
10:10 - 10:55	03:10 - 03:55	듣기 평가 (LC)
10:55 - 12:10	03:55 - 05:10	독해 평가 (RC)

성적 확인

성적 발표	시험일로부터 약 12일 후에 한국 TOEIC 위원회 사이트(www.toeic.co.kr) 및 애플리케이션을 통해 확인 가능합니다.
성적표 수령	온라인 출력 또는 우편 수령 중에서 선택할 수 있고, 온라인 출력과 우편 수령 모두 1회 발급만 무료이며, 그 이후에는 유료로 발급됩니다.

TOEIC 파트별 문제 형태

PART 1 사진 묘사

파트 소개	제시된 사진을 보고, 4개의 문장을 들은 뒤 그중 사진을 가장 잘 묘사한 문장을 고르는 파트
문항 수	6문항
사진 유형	1인 사진, 2인 이상 사진, 사물 및 풍경 사진

문제지 형태

1.

2.

🔊

Number 1.

Look at the picture marked number 1 in your test book.

(A) He's staring at a vase.
(B) He's pouring a beverage.
(C) He's spreading out a tablecloth.
(D) He's sipping from a coffee cup.

PART 2 질의 응답

파트 소개	질문과 3개의 응답을 듣고, 질문에 가장 적절한 응답을 고르는 파트
문항 수	25문항
문제 유형	의문사 의문문, 일반 의문문, 부가 의문문, 선택 의문문, 간접 의문문, 제안 · 요청문, 평서문

문제지 형태

PART 2

Directions: You will hear a question or statement and three responses spoken in English. They will not be printed in your test book and will be spoken only one time. Select the best response to the question or statement and mark the letter (A), (B), or (C) on your answer sheet.

7. Mark your answer on your answer sheet.
8. Mark your answer on your answer sheet.
9. Mark your answer on your answer sheet.
10. Mark your answer on your answer sheet.
11. Mark your answer on your answer sheet.
12. Mark your answer on your answer sheet.
13. Mark your answer on your answer sheet.
14. Mark your answer on your answer sheet.
15. Mark your answer on your answer sheet.
16. Mark your answer on your answer sheet.
17. Mark your answer on your answer sheet.
18. Mark your answer on your answer sheet.
19. Mark your answer on your answer sheet.
20. Mark your answer on your answer sheet.
21. Mark your answer on your answer sheet.
22. Mark your answer on your answer sheet.
23. Mark your answer on your answer sheet.
24. Mark your answer on your answer sheet.
25. Mark your answer on your answer sheet.
26. Mark your answer on your answer sheet.
27. Mark your answer on your answer sheet.
28. Mark your answer on your answer sheet.
29. Mark your answer on your answer sheet.
30. Mark your answer on your answer sheet.
31. Mark your answer on your answer sheet.

Number 7.

When will the landlord inspect the property?

(A) No, it failed the inspection.
(B) I'll e-mail him about it.
(C) Do you like the apartment?

TOEIC 파트별 문제 형태

PART 3 짧은 대화

파트 소개	두 명 또는 세 명의 대화를 듣고, 이와 관련된 3개의 문제에 대해 가장 적절한 답을 고르는 파트
문항 수	39문항(13개 대화문×3문항)
대화 유형	2인 대화(11개)와 3인 대화(2개)로 이루어지며, 2인 대화 중 마지막 3세트(62~70번)는 시각 자료와 함께 제시된다.
문제 유형	주제·목적, 장소, 직업·신분, 세부사항, 제안·요청, 앞으로 일어날 일, 의도 파악, 시각 자료 연계

문제지 형태

PART 3

Directions: You will hear some conversations between two or more people. You will be asked to answer three questions about what the speakers say in each conversation. Select the best response to each question and mark the letter (A), (B), (C), or (D) on your answer sheet. The conversations will not be printed in your test book and will be spoken only one time.

32. Where is the conversation taking place?
    (A) At a bookstore
    (B) At a dry cleaner's
    (C) At a department store
    (D) At a post office

33. What does the man check?
    (A) The available sizes
    (B) The sale price
    (C) The delivery fees
    (D) The shipment date

34. What does the man recommend doing?
    (A) Checking for an item online
    (B) Placing a rush order
    (C) Visiting another branch
    (D) Purchasing a different brand

35. What most likely is the man's job?
    (A) Head of marketing
    (B) Graphic designer
    (C) Repairperson
    (D) Personnel manager

36. What has the woman ordered for the man?
    (A) A uniform
    (B) A desk
    (C) A file cabinet
    (D) A laptop computer

37. What does the woman remind the man to do?
    (A) Sign up for a workshop
    (B) Read a user manual
    (C) Transport an item carefully
    (D) Contact a customer

38. What does the man want his friend's opinion about?
    (A) A payment method
    (B) A reservation time
    (C) A food order
    (D) A seating option

39. Why does the man say, "That's more than I expected"?
    (A)
    (B)
    (C)
    (D)

40.

41.

42.

43.
    (B) A new shipment will arrive.
    (C) The man will conduct an interview.
    (D) Photos will be added to a Web site.

Questions 32-34 refer to the following conversation.

M Welcome to Madison Department Store. Can I help you find anything today?

W I'm wondering if these jeans come in a size fourteen. I didn't see any on the shelf.

M I think twelve is the largest size we carry, but let me look it up on the computer.

W Thanks. I really like this style.

M Hmm... yes, twelve is the largest...

PART 4 짧은 담화

파트 소개	한 사람이 말하는 담화를 듣고, 이와 관련된 3개의 문제에 대해 가장 적절한 답을 고르는 파트
문항 수	30문항 (10개 담화문×3문항)
담화 유형	전화 메시지, 공지, 광고, 방송, 소개, 연설, 회의 등으로 이루어지며, 마지막 2세트 (95~100번)는 시각 자료와 함께 제시된다.
문제 유형	주제·목적, 장소, 직업·신분, 세부사항, 제안·요청, 앞으로 일어날 일, 의도 파악, 시각 자료 연계

문제지 형태

PART 4

Directions: You will hear some talks given by a single speaker. You will be asked to answer three questions about what the speaker says in each talk. Select the best response to each question and mark the letter (A), (B), (C), or (D) on your answer sheet. The talks will not be printed in your test book and will be spoken only one time.

71. How does each workshop tour end?
    (A) An employee answers questions.
    (B) An informative video is shown.
    (C) A group photo is taken.
    (D) A piece of equipment is demonstrated.

72. What does each tour participant receive?
    (A) A piece of jewelry
    (B) A voucher
    (C) A map of the site
    (D) A beverage

73. What do the listeners receive a warning about?
    (A) Which entrance to use
    (B) Where to meet
    (C) What clothing to bring
    (D) How to book in advance

74. Who most likely is giving the speech?
    (A) A factory worker
    (B) A driving instructor
    (C) A gym manager
    (D) A bank employee

75. What have the listeners been given?
    (A) A product sample
    (B) An employee directory
    (C) A daily pass
    (D) A list of classes

76. What does the speaker mean when she says, "You won't see anything like it again"?
    (A) A membership process can be confusing.
    (B) A presentation is worth watching.
    (C) The business is expected to succeed.
    (D) Listeners should take advantage of an offer.

77. What kind of business do the listeners most likely work for?
    (A) A construction company
    (B) An international delivery service
    (C) A newspaper publisher
    (D) A medical facility

78. What does the speaker say he is reassured about?
    (A) A worker's attention to detail
    (B) An investor's future plan
    (C) The responses from a customer survey
    (D) T

79. Wha
    (A) E
    (B) A
    (C) A
    (D) S

80. Why
    (A) It
    (B) It
    (C) T
    (D) T

81. Why indir
    (A) T
    (B) T
    (C) T
    (D) T

82. Wha
    (A) Talk to the speaker
    (B) Show a ticket
    (C) Come back later
    (D) Present a receipt

🔊 Questions 71-73 refer to the following announcement.

Are you tired of the same old tourist sites? Try something new and tour the Lodgevile Jewelry Workshop. You'll get to see each step of the jewelry-making process. And, at the end, you'll have the chance to get your questions addressed by one of our talented jewelry makers. Each participant is given a beautiful bracelet to identify their tour group, and this gift is yours to keep...

TOEIC 파트별 문제 형태

PART 5 단문 빈칸 채우기

파트 소개	빈칸이 포함된 하나의 문장이 주어지고, 빈칸에 알맞은 단어나 구를 4개의 선택지 중에서 고르는 파트
문항 수	30문항
문제 유형	
문법	시제(종종 태, 수 일치와 연계), 대명사, 분사, 한정사, 부정사, 동명사, 능동태/수동태, 그리고 품사 관련 문제가 주로 출제된다. 품사는 명사 및 부사와 관련된 문제가 2~3개 정도 출제되며, 빈도는 낮지만 전치사 관련 문제가 출제되기도 한다.
어휘	같은 품사의 단어들을 제시하고 그중 문맥에 적절한 어휘를 고르는 문제다. 동사, 명사, 형용사, 부사 어휘가 각각 2~3문제씩, 전치사 어휘가 평균 3문제씩 출제된다. 그밖에 접속사나 어구 문제가 출제되기도 한다.

문제지 형태

READING TEST

In the Reading test, you will read a variety of texts and answer several different types of reading comprehension questions. The entire Reading test will last 75 minutes. There are three parts, and directions are given for each part. You are encouraged to answer as many questions as possible within the time allowed.

You must mark your answers on the separate answer sheet. Do not write your answers in your test book.

PART 5

Directions: A word or phrase is missing in each of the sentences below. Four answer choices are given below each sentence. Select the best answer to complete the sentence. Then mark the letter (A), (B), (C), or (D) on your answer sheet.

101. Some officials ------- expressed concerns about the changes to the corporate tax structure.
 (A) privacy
 (B) privatize
 (C) private
 (D) privately

102. The new electric car from Baylor Motors is intended for ------- journeys within an urban environment.
 (A) shortness
 (B) short
 (C) shortly
 (D) shorten

103. Ames Manufacturing developed a packaging method that ------- much less cardboard.
 (A) uses
 (B) using
 (C) to use
 (D) use

104. The building's owner increased the fees ------- parking lot access.
 (A) for
 (B) about
 (C) at
 (D) among

105. Few market analysts ------- predicted the industry effects of the factory's closure.
 (A) locally
 (B) constantly
 (C) kindly
 (D) correctly

106. Customers who wish to ------- us a review on social media are encouraged to do so.
 (A) explain
 (B) say
 (C) give
 (D) have

107. Every weekend ------- the month of August, the hotel's restaurant features live musical performances.
 (A) even
 (B) during
 (C) when
 (D) while

108. Portland Insurance's employees should complete a form with ------- desired vacation days.
 (A) their
 (B) its
 (C) themselves
 (D) it

PART 6 장문 빈칸 채우기

파트 소개	4개의 빈칸이 포함된 지문이 주어지고, 각각의 빈칸에 들어갈 알맞은 단어나 구, 문장을 고르는 파트
문항 수	16문항 (4개 지문×4문항)
문제 유형	4개의 문제 중 문맥에 맞는 문장 고르기 문제가 항상 1개씩 나오며, 평균적으로 어휘 문제가 2개, 품사를 포함한 문법 문제가 1문제씩 출제된다. 지문에 따라서 품사 및 문법 문제가 2개, 어휘 문제가 1개 출제되기도 한다. 문법은 문맥의 흐름을 통해 파악해야 하는 시제 문제가 가장 비중 있게 출제되며, 어휘 문제에서도 문맥을 자연스럽게 연결해 주는 접속부사를 고르는 문제가 자주 등장한다.

문제지 형태

PART 6

Directions: Read the texts that follow. A word, phrase, or sentence is missing in parts of each text. Four answer choices for each question are given below the text. Select the best answer to complete the text. Then mark the letter (A), (B), (C), or (D) on your answer sheet.

Questions 131-134 refer to the following letter.

Georgina Harrison
962 Warner Street
Cape Girardeau, MO 63703

Dear Ms. Harrison,

Thank you for your interest in making a group booking at Westside Hotel. I have attached a comprehensive ------- of our amenities for your convenience. We aim to personalize the guest
                    131.
experience. We are prepared to meet the needs of most guests on short notice. However, if you
have ------- requests, we may need advance notice in order to fulfill them. Once your booking is
     132.
made, you may be charged a fee according to our cancellation policy. -------. Before confirming your
                                                                      133.
booking, please download a copy of the payment details and ------- them carefully.
                                                            134.

Warmest regards,

The Westside Hotel Team

131. (A) describe
(B) describes
(C) described
(D) description

132. (A) unusual
(B) absent
(C) plain
(D) flexible

133. (A) The front desk is open twenty-four hours a day.
(B) You should complete the form with honest feedback.
(C) We appreciate your ongoing patronage.
(D) The terms of this are included on our Web site.

134. (A) reviewing
(B) review
(C) to review
(D) reviewed

TOEIC 파트별 문제 형태

PART 7 독해

파트 소개	지문을 읽고, 지문 내용과 관련된 2~5개 문제에 대해 가장 적절한 답을 고르는 파트	
지문 / 문항 수	단일 지문	10개 (지문당 2~4 문항 ; 총 29문항)
	이중 지문	2개 (지문당 5문항 ; 총 10문항)
	삼중 지문	3개 (지문당 5문항 ; 총 15문항)
지문 유형	이메일 · 편지, 광고, 공지 · 회람, 기사, 양식 (웹페이지, 설문지, 청구서 등), 문자 메시지 대화문 등	
문제 유형	주제 · 목적, 세부사항, 사실 확인, 추론, 문장 넣기, 의도 파악, 동의어 찾기	

총 15개 지문 (54문항)

문제지 형태 (단일 지문)

PART 7

Directions: In this part, you will read a selection of texts, such as magazine and newspaper articles, e-mails, and instant messages. Each text or set of texts is followed by several questions. Select the best answer for each question and mark the letter (A), (B), (C), or (D) on your answer sheet.

Questions 147-148 refer to the following article.

New Library Program Creates "Buzz"

April 30—This summer, Syracuse Library is launching a program to help local bees. The number of local bees has sharply declined, and the library aims to help these creatures. It will have a special section with books about bees and will host lectures about how they benefit the environment. Anyone who attends a lecture will be given a free pack of seeds for flowers that will attract bees.

147. What is the purpose of the program?
(A) To support the bee population
(B) To teach people a new skill
(C) To attract new library members
(D) To raise money for a charity

148. How can participants get a free gift?
(A) By completing a survey
(B) By attending a talk
(C) By making a donation
(D) By showing a library card

문제지 형태 (삼중 지문)

Questions 186-190 refer to the following article and forms.

Oakdale (April 9)—Preparations are underway for Oakdale's 8th Annual Health and Well-Being Expo, which will take place on Sunday, June 19. The expo will feature businesses offering a variety of health-related goods and services. Additionally, local physicians and nurses will provide free screenings for blood pressure and cholesterol levels as well as a basic eye exam.

After many years at Juniper Hall, the expo has been moved to the Bayridge Convention Center this year. "Due to the growing popularity of the event, Juniper Hall could no longer contain the number of vendors interested in participating in the expo," said Ken Exley, one of the event planners. "Visitors can easily find what they're looking for, with vendors of vitamins and health supplements in the main hall, massage therapists and spa representatives in the east wing, and gym representatives and sports-related

To register, visit www.oakdalehealthe
get a twenty percent discount.

**Annual He
Vend

Name:** Anna Pierson
Business/Company: Sunrise S

I was informed about th
Oakdale Business Associat
as a vendor, and I reache
would have liked a larger
spoke to some other vendo
has the same needs, so it
future.

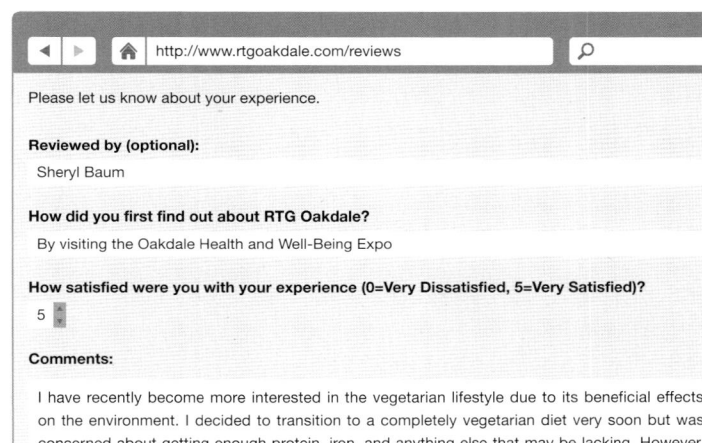

http://www.rtgoakdale.com/reviews

Please let us know about your experience.

Reviewed by (optional):
Sheryl Baum

How did you first find out about RTG Oakdale?
By visiting the Oakdale Health and Well-Being Expo

How satisfied were you with your experience (0=Very Dissatisfied, 5=Very Satisfied)?
5

Comments:
I have recently become more interested in the vegetarian lifestyle due to its beneficial effects on the environment. I decided to transition to a completely vegetarian diet very soon but was concerned about getting enough protein, iron, and anything else that may be lacking. However, I wasn't sure what kind of vitamin supplements I would need. After speaking to Anthony Cress at his business's booth, I felt like I was fully informed. Mr. Cress was knowledgeable and made great recommendations for my specific circumstances. Overall, it was a very positive experience for me.

186. According to the article, why did the event planners use a different site this year?
(A) To ensure more space
(B) To minimize traffic problems
(C) To promote a new building
(D) To reduce travel times

187. What is suggested about Ms. Pierson?
(A) She qualified for early registration.
(B) She recently started her business.
(C) She has participated in past events.
(D) She was eligible for a discount.

188. What does Ms. Pierson recommend for the next expo?
(A) Addressing some noise complaints
(B) Providing more power outlets
(C) Offering booths in various sizes
(D) Advertising the event to more people

189. What is implied about Mr. Cress?
(A) He has lived in Oakdale for a long time.
(B) He worked at a booth in the main hall.
(C) He was an event planner for the expo.
(D) He is considering hiring Ms. Baum.

190. What does Ms. Baum plan to do?
(A) Undertake further research on a topic
(B) Write another online review
(C) Change her daily eating habits
(D) Start a health-related business

점수 환산표

본 점수 환산표는 교재에 수록된 TEST 5회분의 점수 환산을 위해 만든 표입니다.
각 TEST를 마치고 난 후, 본인의 예상 점수대를 가늠해 보세요.

LISTENING RAW SCORE (맞힌 개수)	LISTENING SCALED SCORE (환산 점수)	READING RAW SCORE (맞힌 개수)	READING SCALED SCORE (환산 점수)
96-100	475-495	96-100	460-495
91-95	435-495	91-95	425-490
86-90	405-475	86-90	395-465
81-85	370-450	81-85	370-440
76-80	345-420	76-80	335-415
71-75	320-390	71-75	310-390
66-70	290-360	66-70	280-365
61-65	265-335	61-65	250-335
56-60	235-310	56-60	220-305
51-55	210-280	51-55	195-270
46-50	180-255	46-50	165-240
41-45	155-230	41-45	140-215
36-40	125-205	36-40	115-180
31-35	105-175	31-35	95-145
26-30	85-145	26-30	75-120
21-25	60-115	21-25	60-95
16-20	30-90	16-20	45-75
11-15	5-70	11-15	30-55
6-10	5-60	6-10	10-40
1-5	5-50	1-5	5-30
0	5	0	5

학습 스케줄러

2주 집중 완성 학습

	1일	2일	3일	4일	5일
1주	(월 일)	(월 일)	(월 일)	(월 일)	(월 일)
	TEST 01 풀기	TEST 01 복습	TEST 02 풀기	TEST 02 복습	TEST 03 풀기
	6일	7일	8일	9일	10일
2주	(월 일)	(월 일)	(월 일)	(월 일)	(월 일)
	TEST 03 복습	TEST 04 풀기	TEST 04 복습	TEST 05 풀기	TEST 05 복습

4주 실력 완성 학습

	1일	2일	3일	4일	5일
1주	(월 일)	(월 일)	(월 일)	(월 일)	(월 일)
	TEST 01 LC 풀기	TEST 01 LC 복습	TEST 01 RC 풀기	TEST 01 RC 복습	TEST 02 LC 풀기
	6일	7일	8일	9일	10일
2주	(월 일)	(월 일)	(월 일)	(월 일)	(월 일)
	TEST 02 LC 복습	TEST 02 RC 풀기	TEST 02 RC 복습	TEST 03 LC 풀기	TEST 03 LC 복습
	11일	12일	13일	14일	15일
3주	(월 일)	(월 일)	(월 일)	(월 일)	(월 일)
	TEST 03 RC 풀기	TEST 03 RC 복습	TEST 04 LC 풀기	TEST 04 LC 복습	TEST 04 RC 풀기
	16일	17일	18일	19일	20일
4주	(월 일)	(월 일)	(월 일)	(월 일)	(월 일)
	TEST 04 RC 복습	TEST 05 LC 풀기	TEST 05 LC 복습	TEST 05 RC 풀기	TEST 05 RC 복습

에 듀 윌 토 익 실 전 서

LC+RC

TEST 01

LISTENING TEST

PART 1
PART 2
PART 3
PART 4

READING TEST

PART 5
PART 6
PART 7

LISTENING TEST

In the Listening test, you will be asked to demonstrate how well you understand spoken English. The entire Listening test will last approximately 45 minutes. There are four parts, and directions are given for each part. You must mark your answers on the separate answer sheet. Do not write your answers in your test book.

PART 1

Directions: For each question in this part, you will hear four statements about a picture in your test book. When you hear the statements, you must select the one statement that best describes what you see in the picture. Then find the number of the question on your answer sheet and mark your answer. The statements will not be printed in your test book and will be spoken only one time.

Statement (C), "They're looking at a document," is the best description of the picture, so you should select answer (C) and mark it on your answer sheet.

1.

2.

3.

4.

5.

6.

PART 2

Directions: You will hear a question or statement and three responses spoken in English. They will not be printed in your test book and will be spoken only one time. Select the best response to the question or statement and mark the letter (A), (B), or (C) on your answer sheet.

7. Mark your answer on your answer sheet.
8. Mark your answer on your answer sheet.
9. Mark your answer on your answer sheet.
10. Mark your answer on your answer sheet.
11. Mark your answer on your answer sheet.
12. Mark your answer on your answer sheet.
13. Mark your answer on your answer sheet.
14. Mark your answer on your answer sheet.
15. Mark your answer on your answer sheet.
16. Mark your answer on your answer sheet.
17. Mark your answer on your answer sheet.
18. Mark your answer on your answer sheet.
19. Mark your answer on your answer sheet.
20. Mark your answer on your answer sheet.
21. Mark your answer on your answer sheet.
22. Mark your answer on your answer sheet.
23. Mark your answer on your answer sheet.
24. Mark your answer on your answer sheet.
25. Mark your answer on your answer sheet.
26. Mark your answer on your answer sheet.
27. Mark your answer on your answer sheet.
28. Mark your answer on your answer sheet.
29. Mark your answer on your answer sheet.
30. Mark your answer on your answer sheet.
31. Mark your answer on your answer sheet.

PART 3

Directions: You will hear some conversations between two or more people. You will be asked to answer three questions about what the speakers say in each conversation. Select the best response to each question and mark the letter (A), (B), (C), or (D) on your answer sheet. The conversations will not be printed in your test book and will be spoken only one time.

32. Where is the conversation taking place?
    (A) At a bookstore
    (B) At a dry cleaner's
    (C) At a department store
    (D) At a post office

33. What does the man check?
    (A) The available sizes
    (B) The sale price
    (C) The delivery fees
    (D) The shipment date

34. What does the man recommend doing?
    (A) Checking for an item online
    (B) Placing a rush order
    (C) Visiting another branch
    (D) Purchasing a different brand

35. What most likely is the man's job?
    (A) Head of marketing
    (B) Graphic designer
    (C) Repairperson
    (D) Personnel manager

36. What has the woman ordered for the man?
    (A) A uniform
    (B) A desk
    (C) A file cabinet
    (D) A laptop computer

37. What does the woman remind the man to do?
    (A) Sign up for a workshop
    (B) Read a user manual
    (C) Transport an item carefully
    (D) Contact a customer

38. What does the man want his friend's opinion about?
    (A) A payment method
    (B) A reservation time
    (C) A food order
    (D) A seating option

39. Why does the man say, "That's more than I expected"?
    (A) To make a complaint
    (B) To turn down an offer
    (C) To give an excuse
    (D) To express excitement

40. What does the man inquire about?
    (A) A discount offer
    (B) A chef's recommendation
    (C) The hours of operation
    (D) The parking situation

41. Where do the speakers work?
    (A) At a business institute
    (B) At a library
    (C) At a publishing company
    (D) At a newspaper office

42. What was Jennifer surprised about?
    (A) Attendance at an event
    (B) Some negative reviews
    (C) A proposed contract
    (D) A coworker's transfer

43. What will happen this afternoon?
    (A) Some customers will give feedback.
    (B) A new shipment will arrive.
    (C) The man will conduct an interview.
    (D) Photos will be added to a Web site.

GO ON TO THE NEXT PAGE

44. Where most likely are the speakers?

    (A) At a business school
    (B) At an accounting firm
    (C) At an insurance company
    (D) At a government office

45. How did the woman learn about the job opening?

    (A) By reading a magazine
    (B) By receiving an e-mail
    (C) By speaking to a colleague
    (D) By attending a career fair

46. What accomplishment does the woman mention?

    (A) Training other staff members
    (B) Earning the highest employee rating
    (C) Developing a new software program
    (D) Bringing in the most new customers

47. What is the problem?

    (A) Some equipment was damaged.
    (B) A company is not reliable.
    (C) Some new employees are inexperienced.
    (D) A workspace is too small.

48. Why does the man say, "my friend Felix works in real estate"?

    (A) To suggest getting a recommendation
    (B) To reject a business proposal
    (C) To correct a misunderstanding
    (D) To explain the reason for a decision

49. What does the woman say she will do?

    (A) Visit a neighborhood
    (B) Read some reviews
    (C) Make a phone call
    (D) Prepare some documents

50. Where most likely does the man work?

    (A) At a coffee shop
    (B) At a bank
    (C) At a car rental company
    (D) At a shoe store

51. According to the man, what is the problem?

    (A) Some products are sold out.
    (B) A delivery did not arrive.
    (C) Some software is malfunctioning.
    (D) An employee has made an error.

52. What does the man offer to do for the woman?

    (A) Call her later
    (B) Get a supervisor
    (C) Provide a refund
    (D) Send a catalog

53. Who most likely is the woman?

    (A) A travel agent
    (B) A delivery driver
    (C) A furniture salesperson
    (D) A hotel manager

54. What will the man do next month?

    (A) He will take a trip out of town.
    (B) He will open a new business.
    (C) He will give a talk at an event.
    (D) He will move to a new home.

55. What does the woman suggest?

    (A) Advertising on a Web site
    (B) Viewing some images online
    (C) Hiring a professional decorator
    (D) Downloading a smartphone app

56. In which department do the speakers work?
  (A) Human resources
  (B) Finance
  (C) Marketing
  (D) Shipping

57. What does the woman offer to do?
  (A) Review a company policy
  (B) Call one of Ms. Lee's clients
  (C) Organize a work schedule
  (D) Make preparations for a meal

58. According to the woman, why should the man talk to Tina?
  (A) To contribute to a gift
  (B) To collect a prize
  (C) To express a preference
  (D) To check a report

59. What does the man want to talk about at the meeting?
  (A) Some customer survey responses
  (B) Some employee complaints
  (C) A new supplier of ingredients
  (D) An upcoming sales promotion

60. What problem does Claire mention?
  (A) An ingredient is considered unhealthy.
  (B) The product selection is not large enough.
  (C) Some business hours are inconvenient.
  (D) Some staff members are not fully trained.

61. What are the women asked to do?
  (A) Oversee an ad campaign
  (B) Work some additional shifts
  (C) Create a summary report
  (D) Hire a new employee

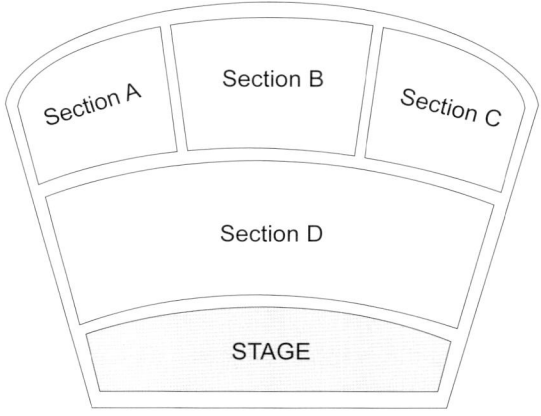

62. Why does the woman express surprise?
  (A) The price of some tickets has increased.
  (B) Some new performance dates have been added.
  (C) A dance group has won an award.
  (D) The man is interested in watching ballet.

63. Look at the graphic. For which section are the man's tickets?
  (A) Section A
  (B) Section B
  (C) Section C
  (D) Section D

64. What will the man's sister do on Friday?
  (A) Go to a party
  (B) Move out of town
  (C) Attend an interview
  (D) Teach a dance class

GO ON TO THE NEXT PAGE

Vehicle Type	Daily Rate
Standard Sedan	$65
Premium Sedan	$70
Luxury Sedan	$85
Elite Sedan	$110

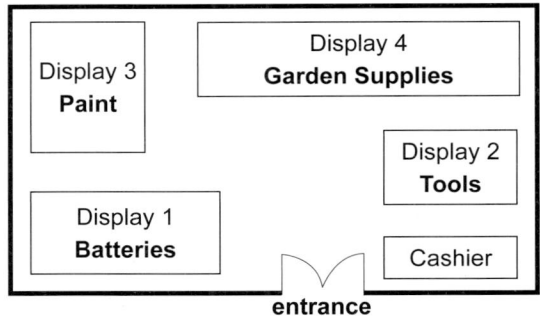

65. Look at the graphic. What will the man be charged per day?
    (A) $65
    (B) $70
    (C) $85
    (D) $110

66. Why is the man visiting Atlanta?
    (A) To sign a contract
    (B) To lead a group discussion
    (C) To attend a conference
    (D) To tour a building

67. What does the woman recommend doing?
    (A) Avoiding a busy road
    (B) Keeping a receipt
    (C) Downloading an app
    (D) Visiting a popular restaurant

68. Where are the speakers?
    (A) At an art institute
    (B) At a repair shop
    (C) At a hardware store
    (D) At a toy store

69. According to the man, what did employees do yesterday?
    (A) Recorded a video
    (B) Completed some training
    (C) Unloaded some new items
    (D) Installed safety equipment

70. Look at the graphic. Where will some paint cans be moved?
    (A) Display 1
    (B) Display 2
    (C) Display 3
    (D) Display 4

PART 4

Directions: You will hear some talks given by a single speaker. You will be asked to answer three questions about what the speaker says in each talk. Select the best response to each question and mark the letter (A), (B), (C), or (D) on your answer sheet. The talks will not be printed in your test book and will be spoken only one time.

71. How does each workshop tour end?
    (A) An employee answers questions.
    (B) An informative video is shown.
    (C) A group photo is taken.
    (D) A piece of equipment is demonstrated.

72. What does each tour participant receive?
    (A) A piece of jewelry
    (B) A voucher
    (C) A map of the site
    (D) A beverage

73. What do the listeners receive a warning about?
    (A) Which entrance to use
    (B) Where to meet
    (C) What clothing to bring
    (D) How to book in advance

74. Who most likely is giving the speech?
    (A) A factory worker
    (B) A driving instructor
    (C) A gym manager
    (D) A bank employee

75. What have the listeners been given?
    (A) A product sample
    (B) An employee directory
    (C) A daily pass
    (D) A list of classes

76. What does the speaker mean when she says, "You won't see anything like it again"?
    (A) A membership process can be confusing.
    (B) A presentation is worth watching.
    (C) The business is expected to succeed.
    (D) Listeners should take advantage of an offer.

77. What kind of business do the listeners most likely work for?
    (A) A construction company
    (B) An international delivery service
    (C) A newspaper publisher
    (D) A medical facility

78. What does the speaker say she is reassured about?
    (A) A worker's attention to detail
    (B) An investor's future plan
    (C) The responses from a customer survey
    (D) The score on an inspection

79. What are the listeners encouraged to do?
    (A) E-mail Ms. Arnold
    (B) Ask for advice
    (C) Attend a training event
    (D) Sample a new product

80. Why is the bus's departure delayed?
    (A) It is being cleaned.
    (B) It is undergoing repairs.
    (C) There is heavy traffic in the area.
    (D) There was a scheduling error.

81. Why does the speaker say, "We do have some indirect routes"?
    (A) To confirm a new schedule
    (B) To explain a policy
    (C) To suggest an alternative
    (D) To make a complaint

82. What are the listeners asked to do?
    (A) Talk to the speaker
    (B) Show a ticket
    (C) Come back later
    (D) Present a receipt

GO ON TO THE NEXT PAGE

83. Where most likely is the speaker calling from?

    (A) A real estate agency
    (B) A dental clinic
    (C) An architecture firm
    (D) A manufacturing facility

84. What qualification does the speaker mention?

    (A) A flexible schedule
    (B) A university degree
    (C) State certification
    (D) Sales experience

85. What does the speaker say she plans to do?

    (A) Send an employment contract
    (B) Arrange an interview time
    (C) Keep some documents
    (D) Check the listener's references

86. Where most likely does the speaker work?

    (A) At a marketing firm
    (B) At a local newspaper
    (C) At a cosmetics company
    (D) At a fashion magazine

87. Why does the speaker say, "our photographer works full time"?

    (A) To explain a problem
    (B) To reject an offer
    (C) To correct a misunderstanding
    (D) To request some help

88. What does the speaker ask the listener to do?

    (A) Inform him of her availability
    (B) Send him some documents
    (C) Confirm a final payment
    (D) Select some photographs

89. What is the speaker mainly discussing?

    (A) A customer complaint
    (B) A staff promotion
    (C) A payment system
    (D) A company policy

90. What are the listeners asked to do?

    (A) Complete an online form
    (B) Work with a partner
    (C) Read a handout
    (D) Attend a training session

91. According to the speaker, what will Olivia do?

    (A) Return some equipment
    (B) Print some materials
    (C) Answer questions
    (D) Create a schedule

92. What will be discussed during the broadcast?

    (A) Online deliveries
    (B) Fruit picking
    (C) Home gardening
    (D) Farmer's markets

93. According to the speaker, why is an activity popular?

    (A) It keeps people in shape.
    (B) It is fun for all ages.
    (C) It saves participants money.
    (D) It is environmentally friendly.

94. Who is Stephanie Lutz?

    (A) A reporter
    (B) A city official
    (C) A farmer
    (D) A radio host

Room 201	Room 202	Room 204
Elevator		
Staff Room	Room 203	Storage Room

Project A	Corporate Sponsorship
Project B	Video Competition
Project C	Free Webinar
Project D	Annual Trade Expo

95. Who is the speaker addressing?
    (A) Potential investors
    (B) Company managers
    (C) Job applicants
    (D) Government inspectors

96. Look at the graphic. Which office will the listeners use for most of the day?
    (A) Room 201
    (B) Room 202
    (C) Room 203
    (D) Room 204

97. Where will listeners go at four-thirty?
    (A) To a conference room
    (B) To a computer lab
    (C) To a cafeteria
    (D) To a security office

98. Why does the speaker thank the team?
    (A) They finished a project on short notice.
    (B) They created a popular product.
    (C) They found some new clients.
    (D) They helped to train new employees.

99. Look at the graphic. Which project will start tomorrow?
    (A) Project A
    (B) Project B
    (C) Project C
    (D) Project D

100. What will Patrick do on Thursday?
    (A) Receive an award
    (B) Give a speech
    (C) Visit a client
    (D) Finalize a budget

This is the end of the Listening test. Turn to Part 5 in your test book.

READING TEST

In the Reading test, you will read a variety of texts and answer several different types of reading comprehension questions. The entire Reading test will last 75 minutes. There are three parts, and directions are given for each part. You are encouraged to answer as many questions as possible within the time allowed.

You must mark your answers on the separate answer sheet. Do not write your answers in your test book.

PART 5

Directions: A word or phrase is missing in each of the sentences below. Four answer choices are given below each sentence. Select the best answer to complete the sentence. Then mark the letter (A), (B), (C), or (D) on your answer sheet.

101. Some officials ------- expressed concerns about the changes to the corporate tax structure.
    (A) privacy
    (B) privatize
    (C) private
    (D) privately

102. The new electric car from Baylor Motors is intended for ------- journeys within an urban environment.
    (A) shortness
    (B) short
    (C) shortly
    (D) shorten

103. Ames Manufacturing developed a packaging method that ------- much less cardboard.
    (A) uses
    (B) using
    (C) to use
    (D) use

104. The building's owner increased the fees ------- parking lot access.
    (A) for
    (B) about
    (C) at
    (D) among

105. Few market analysts ------- predicted the industry effects of the factory's closure.
    (A) locally
    (B) constantly
    (C) kindly
    (D) correctly

106. Customers who wish to ------- us a review on social media are encouraged to do so.
    (A) explain
    (B) say
    (C) give
    (D) have

107. Every weekend ------- the month of August, the hotel's restaurant features live musical performances.
    (A) even
    (B) during
    (C) when
    (D) while

108. Portland Insurance's employees should complete a form with ------- desired vacation days.
    (A) their
    (B) its
    (C) themselves
    (D) it

109. Many construction businesses are nervous about a new ------- on the importation of building materials.
    (A) restrictively
    (B) restrict
    (C) restrictive
    (D) restriction

110. Concert tickets have not been selling well, ------- the event has been advertised heavily for weeks.
    (A) because
    (B) unless
    (C) in addition to
    (D) even though

111. Prices were ------- reduced for the store's summer sale.
    (A) significantly
    (B) significance
    (C) significant
    (D) signify

112. People who are self-employed should keep ------- records of their business's profits and costs.
    (A) accurate
    (B) unfair
    (C) visual
    (D) spacious

113. Attendance at Saturday's community picnic was high ------- the cold weather.
    (A) regarding
    (B) opposite
    (C) despite
    (D) across

114. Soil samples were taken to carry out the ------- testing to check for pollution.
    (A) narrow
    (B) mandatory
    (C) perishable
    (D) obvious

115. Before ------- the air conditioner, Mr. Perkins ordered some replacement parts for the task.
    (A) fixing
    (B) fixed
    (C) fix
    (D) fixes

116. Product sales ------- a setback recently and may not improve without further action.
    (A) to suffer
    (B) have suffered
    (C) suffering
    (D) suffer

117. Business travelers tend to ------- hotel rooms with a large desk.
    (A) apply
    (B) involve
    (C) prefer
    (D) believe

118. Even though ------- than expected, the delivery service was not worth the high cost.
    (A) quick
    (B) quicker
    (C) quickest
    (D) quickly

119. The three tallest ------- in the city, luxury apartment complexes can be seen from most parts of town.
    (A) communities
    (B) streets
    (C) residents
    (D) structures

120. The garage was damaged ------- repair in the storm and had to be rebuilt.
    (A) of
    (B) under
    (C) beyond
    (D) onto

121. Department managers ------- between June 4 and 8 to formally assess employees' work performance.
    (A) will be meeting
    (B) meeting
    (C) having met
    (D) to meet

122. The past few years' favorable market conditions have resulted in more business ------- across most industries.
    (A) invested
    (B) investment
    (C) to invest
    (D) investor

123. All meeting rooms at the VC Conference Hall are ------- with built-in speakers and a projector.
    (A) conducted
    (B) equipped
    (C) activated
    (D) revealed

124. The new shopping center will have a ------- effect on the local economy.
    (A) benefits
    (B) beneficially
    (C) beneficial
    (D) benefit

125. Employees are expected to complete all assigned tasks, ------- difficult they may seem.
    (A) however
    (B) likewise
    (C) indeed
    (D) rather

126. How ------- a candidate answers the questions is an important component of being considered for the role.
    (A) create
    (B) creation
    (C) creative
    (D) creatively

127. Visitors to the national park must be accompanied by a guide ------- the trails can be dangerous.
    (A) than
    (B) given that
    (C) although
    (D) much as

128. The purchase of the restaurant by a corporate chain led to a decline ------- food quality.
    (A) below
    (B) at
    (C) in
    (D) as

129. Mr. McCrae explained that ------- between the two companies has created innovative products.
    (A) confirmation
    (B) consequence
    (C) competition
    (D) commission

130. Southfield Fitness Center ------- closed its main swimming pool for a week while it was being cleaned.
    (A) currently
    (B) perfectly
    (C) adamantly
    (D) temporarily

PART 6

Directions: Read the texts that follow. A word, phrase, or sentence is missing in parts of each text. Four answer choices for each question are given below the text. Select the best answer to complete the text. Then mark the letter (A), (B), (C), or (D) on your answer sheet.

Questions 131-134 refer to the following letter.

Georgina Harrison
962 Warner Street
Cape Girardeau, MO 63703

Dear Ms. Harrison,

Thank you for your interest in making a group booking at Westside Hotel. I have attached a comprehensive ------- of our amenities for your convenience. We aim to personalize the guest
131.
experience. We are prepared to meet the needs of most guests on short notice. However, if you have ------- requests, we may need advance notice in order to fulfill them. Once your booking is
132.
made, you may be charged a fee according to our cancellation policy. -------. Before confirming your
133.
booking, please download a copy of the payment details and ------- them carefully.
134.

Warmest regards,

The Westside Hotel Team

---

131. (A) describe
 (B) describes
 (C) described
 (D) description

132. (A) unusual
 (B) absent
 (C) plain
 (D) flexible

133. (A) The front desk is open twenty-four hours a day.
 (B) You should complete the form with honest feedback.
 (C) We appreciate your ongoing patronage.
 (D) The terms of this are included on our Web site.

134. (A) reviewing
 (B) review
 (C) to review
 (D) reviewed

Questions 135-138 refer to the following information.

Environmental Responsibility at the Kimball Museum

"Waves of Wonder" will be on display throughout the summer at the Kimball Museum. This ------- **135.** features sculptures made from beach glass. The artwork focuses ------- marine animals whose **136.** populations have been severely hurt due to ocean pollution. Interesting facts about each animal will be posted next to the work. Visitors ------- advice on reducing their impact on the oceans, both **137.** locally and worldwide. -------. **138.** "Waves of Wonder" will be available from June 10 to September 5.

---

135. (A) award
 (B) manuscript
 (C) exhibit
 (D) film

136. (A) before
 (B) to
 (C) on
 (D) by

137. (A) are also getting
 (B) can also get
 (C) have also gotten
 (D) also got

138. (A) See how you can make a positive change.
 (B) To become a member, visit our Web site.
 (C) Fortunately, the hours have been extended.
 (D) The glass can be recycled at most locations.

Questions 139-142 refer to the following advertisement.

Verdant Landscaping, founded by brothers John and Jeremy Robles, ------- top-quality landscaping services for residential properties. We can plant a garden from scratch, maintain existing lawns and flowerbeds, trim trees, and remove unwanted garden debris.

-------, your outdoor area will be a beautiful and relaxing place for you to enjoy. -------. We can send a crew of any size, including just one person. If you're unsure whether hiring professionals would be within your budget, call us at 555-4433 for a free ------- of the costs. We look forward to serving you!

139. (A) will provide
 (B) provides
 (C) had provided
 (D) providing

140. (A) For example
 (B) On the contrary
 (C) As a result
 (D) In comparison

141. (A) Other businesses cannot compete with us.
 (B) These techniques are environmentally friendly.
 (C) We are willing to offer training.
 (D) No job is too big or too small.

142. (A) vacation
 (B) estimate
 (C) installation
 (D) pathway

Questions 143-146 refer to the following article.

As a small business owner, Kelly Spencer spends a lot of time researching the best way to improve -------. Her staff was not responding well to her previous methods, but then she found an interesting
143.
piece of software, Pause-Pro. "I was hesitant at first due to the high cost. However, the company was offering free use of the software for thirty days, so I thought I'd give ------- a try."
144.

Pause-Pro allows employers to block access to distracting Web sites, such as social media pages, so employees don't waste time. It wasn't ------- what Ms. Spencer was looking for, but she couldn't
145.
deny the results. She purchased the full version of the software for all of her employees' computers. -------. "With Pause-Pro's help," she said, "we can all focus on the most important tasks."
146.

143. (A) wages
 (B) efficiency
 (C) competition
 (D) education

144. (A) mine
 (B) everyone
 (C) these
 (D) it

145. (A) more original
 (B) originally
 (C) original
 (D) originality

146. (A) She also bought the program for her laptop.
 (B) She has founded a few different businesses.
 (C) She looks forward to meeting them.
 (D) She could not understand the features.

PART 7

Directions: In this part, you will read a selection of texts, such as magazine and newspaper articles, e-mails, and instant messages. Each text or set of texts is followed by several questions. Select the best answer for each question and mark the letter (A), (B), (C), or (D) on your answer sheet.

Questions 147-148 refer to the following article.

New Library Program Creates "Buzz"

April 30—This summer, Syracuse Library is launching a program to help local bees. The number of local bees has sharply declined, and the library aims to help these creatures. It will have a special section with books about bees and will host lectures about how they benefit the environment. Anyone who attends a lecture will be given a free pack of seeds for flowers that will attract bees.

147. What is the purpose of the program?
(A) To support the bee population
(B) To teach people a new skill
(C) To attract new library members
(D) To raise money for a charity

148. How can participants get a free gift?
(A) By completing a survey
(B) By attending a talk
(C) By making a donation
(D) By showing a library card

Questions 149-150 refer to the following invitation.

Please join us for a meet-and-greet session with Adam Jackson, the new Public Relations Director of Watkins Bank.

Monday, December 12, 1 P.M.–2 P.M.
Conference Room A

Adam Jackson handled public relations for CHK Bank for nearly two decades. He will give a brief presentation on his plans for rebranding Watkins Bank and building closer connections with our customers. If you have a question for Mr. Jackson, please send it to the HR team prior to the event.

Coffee and hot tea will be served.

149. What is implied about Mr. Jackson?
(A) He currently works at CHK Bank.
(B) He recently changed his employer.
(C) He will receive an award on December 12.
(D) He founded his own business.

150. What can guests do in advance?
(A) Order hot beverages
(B) View some images
(C) Reserve a seat
(D) Submit their questions

Questions 151-152 refer to the following e-mail.

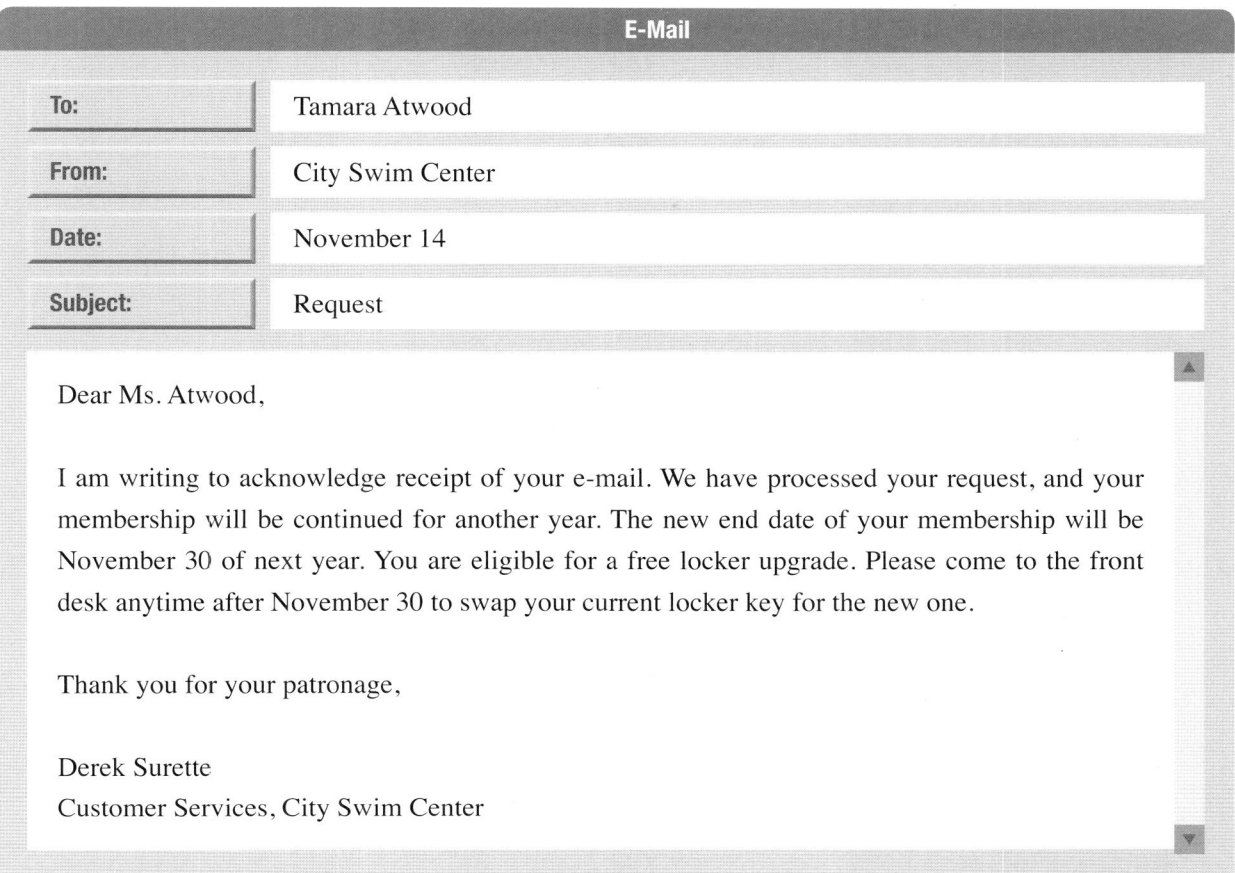

E-Mail

To: Tamara Atwood
From: City Swim Center
Date: November 14
Subject: Request

Dear Ms. Atwood,

I am writing to acknowledge receipt of your e-mail. We have processed your request, and your membership will be continued for another year. The new end date of your membership will be November 30 of next year. You are eligible for a free locker upgrade. Please come to the front desk anytime after November 30 to swap your current locker key for the new one.

Thank you for your patronage,

Derek Surette
Customer Services, City Swim Center

151. Why did Mr. Surette send the e-mail?
(A) To apologize for an error
(B) To introduce a new service
(C) To confirm a renewal
(D) To make a job offer

152. What can Ms. Atwood do after November 30?
(A) Contact Mr. Surette
(B) Receive a refund
(C) Attend a class
(D) Exchange a key

Questions 153-154 refer to the following text-message chain.

Monique Ross [9:21 A.M.]	Good morning. I'm Monique from the Outdoor Gear customer service team. How may I help you?
Eric Harper [9:22 A.M.]	Hello. I ordered a dome tent on August 2 that was supposed to arrive yesterday. However, I still don't have it. I'm wondering when it will get here.
Monique Ross [9:23 A.M.]	I can help with that. What is the order number?
Eric Harper [9:24 A.M.]	It's order #034587.
Monique Ross [9:25 A.M.]	Thank you. Please wait a moment.
Monique Ross [9:28 A.M.]	It looks like there was an issue at the warehouse, and the item is now scheduled to be sent tomorrow. So, it will arrive on Thursday, two days later than originally expected.
Eric Harper [9:29 A.M.]	Since I paid for overnight shipping, I think I should be refunded for the shipping fee.
Monique Ross [9:31 A.M.]	Absolutely. I'll take care of that right now, and it should appear on your account within a few hours. Do you need any other help?
Eric Harper [9:32 A.M.]	Not for now. Thanks.

153. Why did Mr. Harper send a message to Outdoor Gear?

(A) To report damage to a tent
(B) To request a product catalog
(C) To exchange an unwanted product
(D) To check when an item will arrive

154. At 9:31 A.M., what does Ms. Ross most likely mean when she writes, "Absolutely"?

(A) She understands the need for a fast service.
(B) She can open a new account for Mr. Harper.
(C) She enjoyed resolving a problem.
(D) She agrees to issue Mr. Harper a refund.

Questions 155-157 refer to the following Web page.

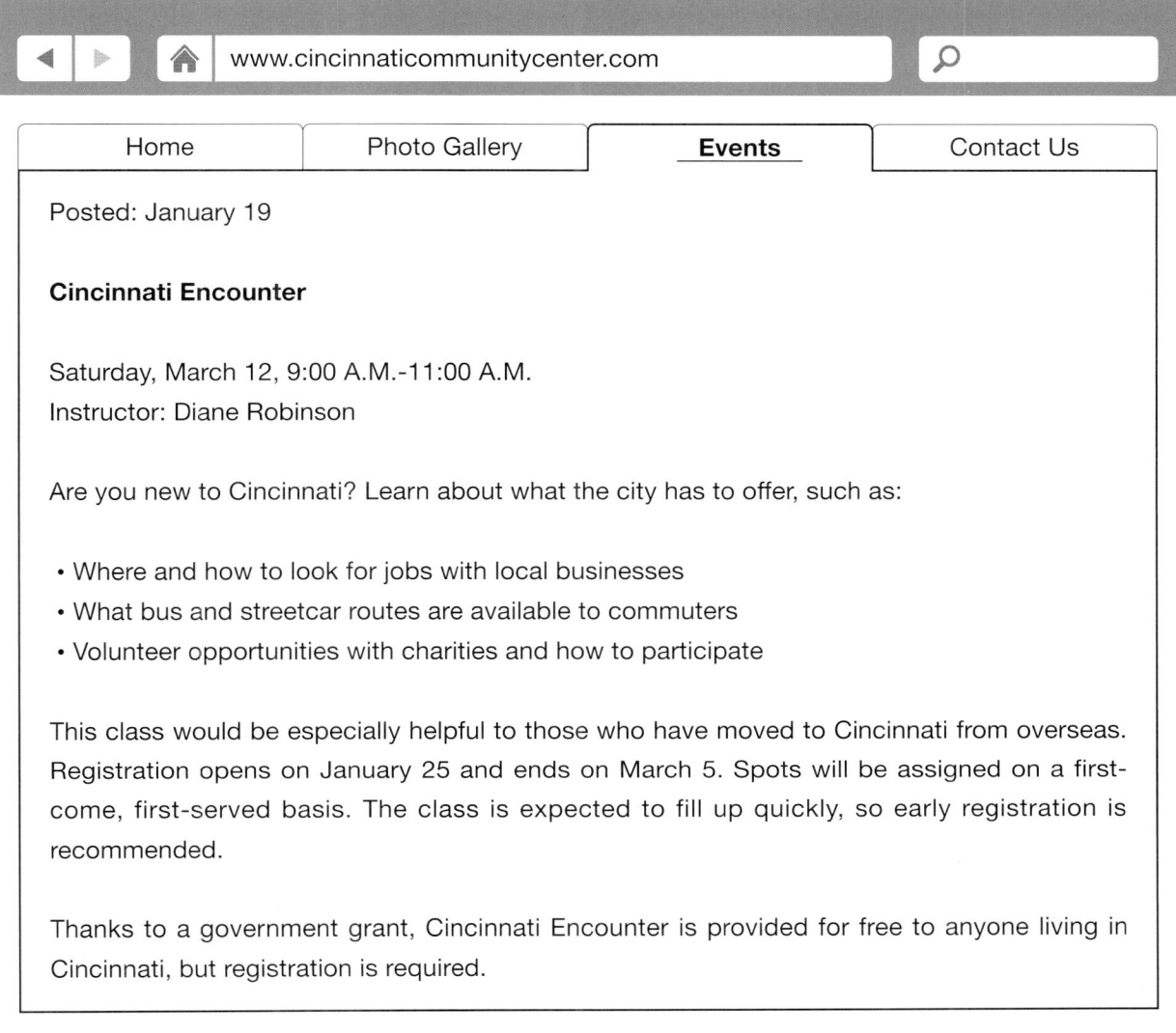

www.cincinnaticommunitycenter.com

Home | Photo Gallery | **Events** | Contact Us

Posted: January 19

Cincinnati Encounter

Saturday, March 12, 9:00 A.M.-11:00 A.M.
Instructor: Diane Robinson

Are you new to Cincinnati? Learn about what the city has to offer, such as:

- Where and how to look for jobs with local businesses
- What bus and streetcar routes are available to commuters
- Volunteer opportunities with charities and how to participate

This class would be especially helpful to those who have moved to Cincinnati from overseas. Registration opens on January 25 and ends on March 5. Spots will be assigned on a first-come, first-served basis. The class is expected to fill up quickly, so early registration is recommended.

Thanks to a government grant, Cincinnati Encounter is provided for free to anyone living in Cincinnati, but registration is required.

155. When will Ms. Robinson teach a class?
(A) On January 19
(B) On January 25
(C) On March 5
(D) On March 12

156. What is NOT indicated as a topic in Cincinnati Encounter?
(A) Using public transportation
(B) Running for local government
(C) Seeking employment in the area
(D) Assisting nonprofit organizations

157. What is stated about Cincinnati Encounter?
(A) It is offered to residents at no cost.
(B) It will last for three hours.
(C) It was developed by a businessperson.
(D) It is part of an ongoing series.

Questions 158-160 refer to the following e-mail.

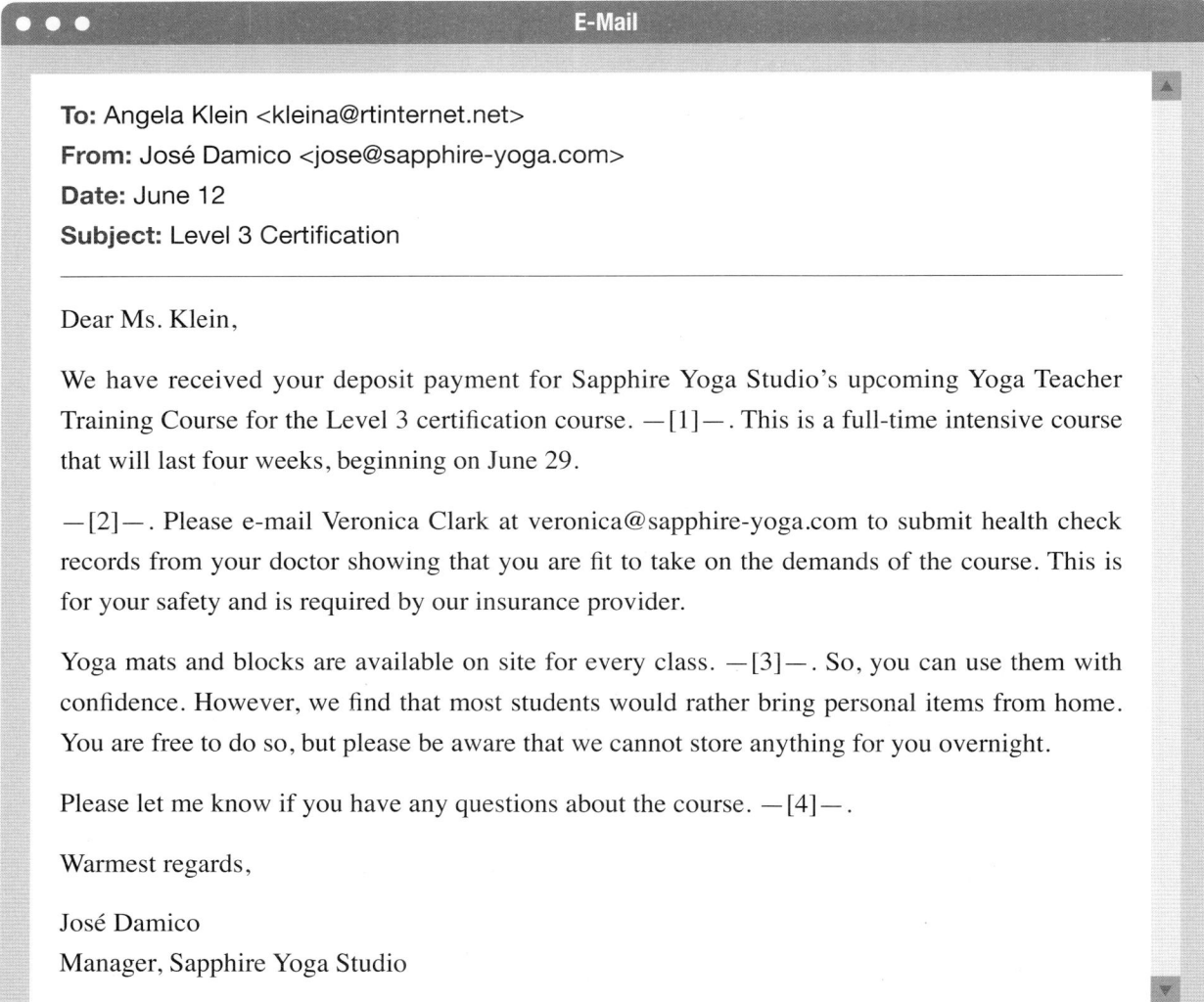

To: Angela Klein <kleina@rtinternet.net>
From: José Damico <jose@sapphire-yoga.com>
Date: June 12
Subject: Level 3 Certification

Dear Ms. Klein,

We have received your deposit payment for Sapphire Yoga Studio's upcoming Yoga Teacher Training Course for the Level 3 certification course. —[1]—. This is a full-time intensive course that will last four weeks, beginning on June 29.

—[2]—. Please e-mail Veronica Clark at veronica@sapphire-yoga.com to submit health check records from your doctor showing that you are fit to take on the demands of the course. This is for your safety and is required by our insurance provider.

Yoga mats and blocks are available on site for every class. —[3]—. So, you can use them with confidence. However, we find that most students would rather bring personal items from home. You are free to do so, but please be aware that we cannot store anything for you overnight.

Please let me know if you have any questions about the course. —[4]—.

Warmest regards,

José Damico
Manager, Sapphire Yoga Studio

158. Why should Ms. Klein e-mail Ms. Clark?

(A) To get a doctor recommendation
(B) To sign up for insurance
(C) To confirm her physical health
(D) To get more course information

159. What does Mr. Damico suggest about students?

(A) They prefer to use their own equipment.
(B) They will do part of the course from home.
(C) They can participate in the class for free.
(D) They have the option of different start times.

160. In which of the positions marked [1], [2], [3], and [4] does the following sentence best belong?

"We implement sanitization practices between each use."

(A) [1]
(B) [2]
(C) [3]
(D) [4]

Questions 161-163 refer to the following contract.

Contract Agreement

This contract is entered into by Adrienne Sales and Oscar Rascon, a freelance graphic designer, on April 22. Mr. Rascon agrees to create an original logo for Adrienne Sales. Mr. Rascon will meet with representatives from Adrienne Sales at the company's headquarters to discuss the intended appearance of the logo. Adrienne Sales will reimburse Mr. Rascon for up to £25 in travel-related expenses for the meeting, provided Mr. Rascon presents receipts of the spending. Mr. Rascon will create and submit three versions of the logo by May 20. Adrienne Sales can ask for up to three additional rounds of revisions to the selected logo. Adrienne Sales agrees to pay Mr. Rascon £750 upon completion of the final image.

Agreed by:

Oscar Rascon	*April 22*
Graphic Designer	Date

Elizabeth Norris	*April 22*
Adrienne Sales	Date

161. What does the contract imply about Mr. Rascon?

(A) He will complete a project by April 22.
(B) He used to work with Ms. Norris.
(C) He is a salesperson at Adrienne Sales.
(D) He will be paid to create a design.

162. The word "presents" in paragraph 1, line 5, is closest in meaning to

(A) publishes
(B) submits
(C) gifts
(D) displays

163. According to the agreement, what is Mr. Rascon required to do?

(A) Give a presentation
(B) Research some industry trends
(C) Make some requested adjustments
(D) Provide professional references

Questions 164-167 refer to the following e-mail.

From:	Nicola Fallaci
To:	All Briarhill Employees
Date:	July 2
Subject:	For your information

Dear Briarhill Employees,

To keep employees better informed, I'll be sending you regular updates about the company's progress. —[1]—. Compared to this quarter last year, our domestic sales have increased by 15%. Though it seems that having some of our goods as part of the *Family Fun* TV show set did not make much difference, it still provided some interesting photos for our Web site.

—[2]—. In Indonesia, we experienced an amazing 63% boost in sales following our participation in the Jakarta Housewares Trade Fair. Sales were steady in Australia, where we saw an increase of just 0.5%. —[3]—. This was not a surprise, as our new line of cotton curtains has been receiving mixed reviews. In Sweden and Norway, sales have been sluggish, down 8% and 6%, respectively. This is due to heavy competition from other businesses.

—[4]—. As you can see, there are some regions that need improvement and others that are doing well. I am sure that the proposal made by Pedro Reid, which targets hotels directly for sales across their entire chain, will yield promising results and grow our sales further.

Sincerely,

Nicola Fallaci

---

164. What type of company most likely is Briarhill?

(A) A chain of supermarkets
(B) A home furnishings retailer
(C) A book publisher
(D) An electronics manufacturer

165. According to Ms. Fallaci, where did people see Briarhill's merchandise in person?

(A) In Australia
(B) In Indonesia
(C) In Norway
(D) In Sweden

166. What does Ms. Fallaci expect will likely lead to increased business?

(A) A customer loyalty program
(B) Association with a TV show
(C) Contracts with hotel chains
(D) Online advertising campaigns

167. In which of the positions marked [1], [2], [3], and [4] does the following sentence best belong?

"Here is an overview of our international performance."

(A) [1]
(B) [2]
(C) [3]
(D) [4]

Questions 168-171 refer to the following article.

BERLIN (September 7)—The Historical Preservation Foundation (HPF) aims to make historical artifacts available to the public as well as provide support for ongoing research. The HPF plans to work on a collection of objects from a 1940s excavation in Western Asia. Fragments of vases and bowls dating back to the 2nd century were acquired by Aldeen University. These will be restored at HPF's main facility in Berlin. "We are honored to have these items under our care," said director Mathias Vogel. "Our track record for dealing with fragile artifacts is unmatched, and we have the resources to give them the attention they deserve."

HPF's staff members are proficient in working with metal objects such as tools, weapons, and jewelry, but they are somewhat new to working with clay items, especially molded ones. "We are forming a partnership with Aldeen University to ensure the work is carried out properly," Vogel said. "We're excited that Jamila Ahmed will travel to our site in Berlin to oversee operations. This project lines up perfectly with her specialized knowledge and extensive experience."

The artifacts are currently housed at Aldeen University. The university's team is starting to examine them to prepare them to be shipped to Berlin, which they are expecting to do on October 2. A date for a public display of the items has not yet been determined.

168. What is the main topic of the article?

(A) The grand opening of a museum
(B) A fundraiser for an excavation
(C) The new discovery of some artifacts
(D) A pottery restoration project

169. What position does Mr. Vogel have?

(A) Maintenance manager
(B) Assistant researcher
(C) Head of Aldeen University
(D) HPF director

170. What is most likely true about Ms. Ahmed?

(A) She is an expert in pottery.
(B) She graduated from Aldeen University.
(C) She grew up in Berlin.
(D) She plans to publish a book.

171. What is implied about the artifacts?

(A) They have been donated by private collectors.
(B) They will be examined for several weeks before transportation.
(C) They will go on display from October 2.
(D) They sustained some damage while being shipped.

Questions 172-175 refer to the following online chat discussion.

Yuhan Gao [9:18 A.M.]	Hi, everyone. Since I canceled yesterday's team meeting, I wanted to check in with how things are going. Lisa, how is your trade show research coming along?
Lisa Timko [9:19 A.M.]	Even better than I expected! I have found one in August, the National Beauty Expo, that I think would be perfect for promoting our natural skincare products. The registration fee is only $1,500.
Yuhan Gao [9:21 A.M.]	Wonderful! Please go forward with that.
George Lainez [9:22 A.M.]	That's great! High-profile events are just what we need.
Ron Fulkerson [9:23 A.M.]	Good job, Lisa! If you send me the details, I can register our company for the event by the end of the day.
Lisa Timko [9:24 A.M.]	I guess we'll be busy preparing for this along with our extensive television campaign on the Mayfair Network.
Yuhan Gao [9:25 A.M.]	Unfortunately, that fell through. We can't afford the prices the station was charging, so we're going to have to promote the new line of lotions in another way.
Lisa Timko [9:27 A.M.]	I see. And I appreciate your dealing with this so quickly, Ron.
Ron Fulkerson [9:28 A.M.]	It's nothing.
Yuhan Gao [9:29 A.M.]	Keep up the good work, everyone!

172. In what industry do the writers most likely work?

(A) Travel
(B) Technology
(C) Clothing
(D) Cosmetics

173. What most likely is Ms. Gao's occupation?

(A) Security advisor
(B) Human resources director
(C) Marketing manager
(D) Research assistant

174. What is true about the Mayfair Network?

(A) It is hosting an annual event.
(B) It will form a partnership with the writers' company.
(C) Its employees have a lot of experience.
(D) Its fees are too high for the writers' company.

175. At 9:28 A.M., what does Mr. Fulkerson mean when he writes, "It's nothing"?

(A) He is pleased that Ms. Timko will resolve a problem.
(B) He is willing to complete a registration process quickly.
(C) He is surprised about the lack of information available.
(D) He is happy to have found an event for the team.

Questions 176-180 refer to the following advertisement and e-mail.

Make your event magical and memorable with Edsel Gardens!

Edsel Gardens, located near Stockton and comprising 4 acres of botanical gardens, features a truly unique and romantic location. You'll love the peaceful backdrop, gorgeous views, and modern amenities offered at our site. We specialize in weddings and anniversary parties and have recently doubled the size of our parking lot to accommodate larger groups. You can hold your event completely outdoors or use our giant tent, which protects against rain and can be heated in cold weather. Our tent seats up to 180 guests, and we have a Food and Liquor License that permits us to serve food and/or drinks from 11 A.M. to midnight on weekdays and 10 A.M. to 1 A.M. on weekends.

Our team will work with you to make sure everything is exactly what you want. With our Premium Package, you can use our in-house photographer and caterer to make planning easy. If you want live music, we can provide a recommendation for bands or singers.

Call us today at 555-8790 to get started. And if you're not sure what kind of theme you'd like for your event, get inspired by visiting our photo gallery at www.edselgardens.com. We look forward to hosting your event!

E-Mail

To: Edsel Gardens <info@edselgardens.com>
From: Ramona Murphy <rmurphy@haven-mail.com>
Date: April 11
Subject: Thank you!

To Whom It May Concern:

I recently held an anniversary party for my parents at your site, and I wanted to thank you for a great experience. I got the Premium Package, which was convenient and affordably priced. I was really impressed with the photos taken by Fred Warren, the professional photographer. I also got a lot of compliments on the band I hired. The beautiful venue was a perfect fit for my parents' style. I plan to highly recommend Edsel Gardens to all my friends and family who are looking for a place to hold an event.

Warmest regards,

Ramona Murphy

176. What is NOT true about Edsel Gardens?

(A) It is now operating under new ownership.
(B) It recently expanded its parking area.
(C) It can provide recommendations for musicians.
(D) It can accommodate different types of weather.

177. When can food be served at Edsel Gardens?

(A) Monday at 10 A.M.
(B) Wednesday at 1 A.M.
(C) Saturday at 11 A.M.
(D) Sunday 9 A.M.

178. Why does the advertisement recommend visiting a Web site?

(A) To view a price list
(B) To read customer comments
(C) To get some inspiration
(D) To make a reservation

179. What is suggested about Fred Warren?

(A) He only took photos inside a tent.
(B) He had excellent reviews on a Web site.
(C) He is a friend of Ms. Murphy's parents.
(D) He is employed directly by Edsel Gardens.

180. In the e-mail, the word "fit" in paragraph 1, line 4, is closest in meaning to

(A) position
(B) match
(C) development
(D) adaptation

Questions 181-185 refer to the following letter and e-mail.

Wanda Milburn
Corbitt Enterprises
4443 Rardin Road
Nashville, TN 37210
January 5

Dear Ms. Milburn,

We are writing to inform you of an increase in the fees for the cleaning services we perform for Corbitt Enterprises at the above address. The current fees you pay will be valid until March 4. As you were one of our customers in the very first month we opened, we have kept the fees at a lower rate for as long as possible.

We are implementing this change to ensure that our workers are compensated fairly, as they always perform a complete and careful cleaning service. This is rare in our industry. Enclosed you will find a breakdown of the new fees.

The change will go into effect on March 5. If you wish to terminate the contract, please inform us of your desired final day of service. We hope to continue serving you for many years to come.

Sincerely,

Grant Berg

Grant Berg
Manager, Shinetime Commercial Cleaning

To:	Grant Berg <grant@shinetimecommcleaning.com>
From:	Wanda Milburn <w.milburn@corbittenterprises.com>
Date:	January 11
Subject:	Cleaning contract

Dear Mr. Berg,

Thanks for informing me about the upcoming changes. We've been satisfied with the level of care provided. I know many business owners have had trouble hiring reliable cleaners, so I feel very lucky. I can't believe it has already been four years since you started working for us. Everyone who has visited us to receive financial advice has been impressed by our office, and your company has played an important role in creating that positive first impression.

In spite of your excellence, we will soon no longer need your services, and we would like the last cleaning day to be February 28. We are moving to a new office building at 579 Ohio Avenue, and the building's maintenance team provides cleaning as part of the monthly fee. I'd be happy to recommend your business to others if the situation arises.

All the best,

Wanda Milburn

181. According to the letter, when will fees for a service increase?

(A) January 5
(B) January 31
(C) March 4
(D) March 5

182. On what point do Mr. Berg and Ms. Milburn agree?

(A) That cleaning should be done regularly
(B) That good cleaners are hard to find
(C) That regulations are becoming tighter
(D) That the cost of cleaning services has risen

183. What type of business does Ms. Milburn most likely work for?

(A) A graphic design firm
(B) A software development company
(C) A commercial construction company
(D) A financial consulting firm

184. What is suggested about Shinetime Commercial Cleaning?

(A) It has been in operation for four years.
(B) It will relocate its head office in March.
(C) It has recently been sold to a competitor.
(D) It plans to recruit more employees.

185. How does Ms. Milburn provide what Mr. Berg has requested?

(A) By giving feedback about a service
(B) By agreeing to some new contract terms
(C) By confirming the desired termination date
(D) By reporting a new business address

Questions 186-190 refer to the following article and forms.

Oakdale (April 9)—Preparations are underway for Oakdale's 8th Annual Health and Well-Being Expo, which will take place on Sunday, June 19. The expo will feature businesses offering a variety of health-related goods and services. Additionally, local physicians and nurses will provide free screenings for blood pressure and cholesterol levels as well as a basic eye exam.

After many years at Juniper Hall, the expo has been moved to the Bayridge Convention Center this year. "Due to the growing popularity of the event, Juniper Hall could no longer contain the number of vendors interested in participating in the expo," said Ken Exley, one of the event planners. "Visitors can easily find what they're looking for, with vendors of vitamins and health supplements in the main hall, massage therapists and spa representatives in the east wing, and gym representatives and sports-related businesses in the west wing."

To register, visit www.oakdalehealthexpo.com. Members of the Oakdale Business Association can get a twenty percent discount.

Annual Health and Well-Being Expo
Vendor Feedback Survey

Name: Anna Pierson
Business/Company: Sunrise Spa

I was informed about the event through my membership in the Oakdale Business Association. This was my first time participating as a vendor, and I reached more people than I expected. However, I would have liked a larger booth to provide massages on-site, and I spoke to some other vendors that needed a smaller one. Not everyone has the same needs, so it would be a good idea to address this in the future.

http://www.rtgoakdale.com/reviews

Please let us know about your experience.

Reviewed by (optional):
Sheryl Baum

How did you first find out about RTG Oakdale?
By visiting the Oakdale Health and Well-Being Expo

How satisfied were you with your experience (0=Very Dissatisfied, 5=Very Satisfied)?
5

Comments:

I have recently become more interested in the vegetarian lifestyle due to its beneficial effects on the environment. I decided to transition to a completely vegetarian diet very soon but was concerned about getting enough protein, iron, and anything else that may be lacking. However, I wasn't sure what kind of vitamin supplements I would need. After speaking to Anthony Cress at his business's booth, I felt like I was fully informed. Mr. Cress was knowledgeable and made great recommendations for my specific circumstances. Overall, it was a very positive experience for me.

186. According to the article, why did the event planners use a different site this year?

(A) To ensure more space
(B) To minimize traffic problems
(C) To promote a new building
(D) To reduce travel times

187. What is suggested about Ms. Pierson?

(A) She qualified for early registration.
(B) She recently started her business.
(C) She has participated in past events.
(D) She was eligible for a discount.

188. What does Ms. Pierson recommend for the next expo?

(A) Addressing some noise complaints
(B) Providing more power outlets
(C) Offering booths in various sizes
(D) Advertising the event to more people

189. What is implied about Mr. Cress?

(A) He has lived in Oakdale for a long time.
(B) He worked at a booth in the main hall.
(C) He was an event planner for the expo.
(D) He is considering hiring Ms. Baum.

190. What does Ms. Baum plan to do?

(A) Undertake further research on a topic
(B) Write another online review
(C) Change her daily eating habits
(D) Start a health-related business

Questions 191-195 refer to the following e-mail, article, and Web page.

E-Mail

To: Armina Giordano <a.giordano@conway-co.com>
From: Rashid Fadel <r.fadel@conway-co.com>
Date: August 21
Subject: Submission

Dear Ms. Giordano,

We appreciate your participation in the Conway Future Growth Initiative here at Conway Co. This is the first time we have requested suggestions for expanding the business, and we were pleased to see so many ideas shared by staff throughout the entire company.

Your submission regarding opening a small-scale version of our usual store in the Brighton Shopping Complex is intriguing. The committee members loved the idea of exposing customers to our most popular items, but we feel like we don't have the big picture. For example, we're wondering what kind of foot traffic could be expected at that site. I understand that the monthly lease fee is quite high, so we would have to make sure it's worth it. In addition, what other businesses are in operation there or plan to do business there? I know that Arcadia has advertised a grand opening at the Brighton Shopping Complex for October. This may be a major issue, as it is our main competitor and carries a very similar inventory to ours. We would like to explore this matter further before making a final decision.

Warmest regards,

Rashid Fadel
Committee Head, Conway Future Growth Initiative

LONGVIEW (October 3)—Later this month, Arcadia, the maker of high-end athletic shoes for basketball, running, and more, will hold a grand opening at its newest branch at the Brighton Shopping Complex. Customers who attend the event will have the opportunity to enter a prize drawing for $5,000 in Arcadia merchandise.

The store will be located next to Golden Apparel and is expected to become one of the company's highest-earning branches. With famous athletes such as basketball player Scott Atkinson and marathon runner Caroline Holmes wearing its products, it is no surprise that Arcadia has grown in popularity over the past few years.

http://www.brightonsc.com/floorplan

HOME | DIRECTORY | **FLOOR PLAN** | CONTACT

Site Map of Brighton Shopping Complex

Unit 101 (Vacant)	Officeland	Home Designs	Unit 107 (Vacant)
Superb Gifts	Food Court		Golden Apparel
	Unit 104 (Vacant)	Unit 106 (Vacant)	

---

191. What is suggested about the Conway Future Growth Initiative?

(A) It targets new staff members.
(B) It will last for one month.
(C) It was suggested by Mr. Fadel.
(D) It was open to all employees.

192. Why did Mr. Fadel send the e-mail?

(A) To suggest merging with a competitor
(B) To request further information about a proposal
(C) To explain the rules of a company program
(D) To recommend improvements to a department's operations

193. In what industry does Conway Co. work?

(A) Footwear manufacturing
(B) Property development
(C) Job recruitment
(D) Media services

194. In what unit of the Brighton Shopping Complex will Arcadia be located?

(A) Unit 101
(B) Unit 104
(C) Unit 106
(D) Unit 107

195. What aspect of Arcadia's products is emphasized in the article?

(A) Its wide range of options
(B) Its affordable price
(C) Its use by celebrities
(D) Its environmentally friendly design

GO ON TO THE NEXT PAGE

Questions 196-200 refer to the following article and e-mails.

FOR IMMEDIATE RELEASE

TORONTO (15 March)—A spokesperson for Millerbrook Enterprises has announced that Salvador Tolentino has been promoted to CEO to replace the outgoing CEO, Mary Gilhurst. He was unanimously selected by the Millerbrook Enterprises board and will take on his new role from May 25 after training with Ms. Gilhurst.

Millerbrook Enterprises provides cutting-edge software for artificial intelligence. Its products and research have led the industry for the past decade, and it has plans to open several international branches in the next few years. As Mr. Tolentino was formerly working as the company's CFO, the company is seeking to fill this position quickly. Duties include analyzing financial data and monitoring company expenditures. The role requires the ability to clearly communicate to the board and investors in both written and spoken form. Further details about the position and the hiring process are posted on www.millerbrook.com.

E-Mail

To: Millerbrook Enterprises Board
From: Walter Vinson
Date: April 4
Subject: CFO Candidate

Dear Fellow Board Members,

I would like to put forth Brianna Chomley as a candidate for the open CFO position. She was a university classmate of mine at Ralston University, and she meets all of the required qualifications for the position. I've spoken to her about applying for the position. However, she is not sure whether it would be right for her. This is because the job description on our Web site only lists the salary and does not include information about the quarterly bonuses, stock options, and housing allowance that we offer. I think we should update this because other candidates probably have the same misconception.

Sincerely,

Walter Vinson,
Vice Chair, Millerbrook Board of Directors

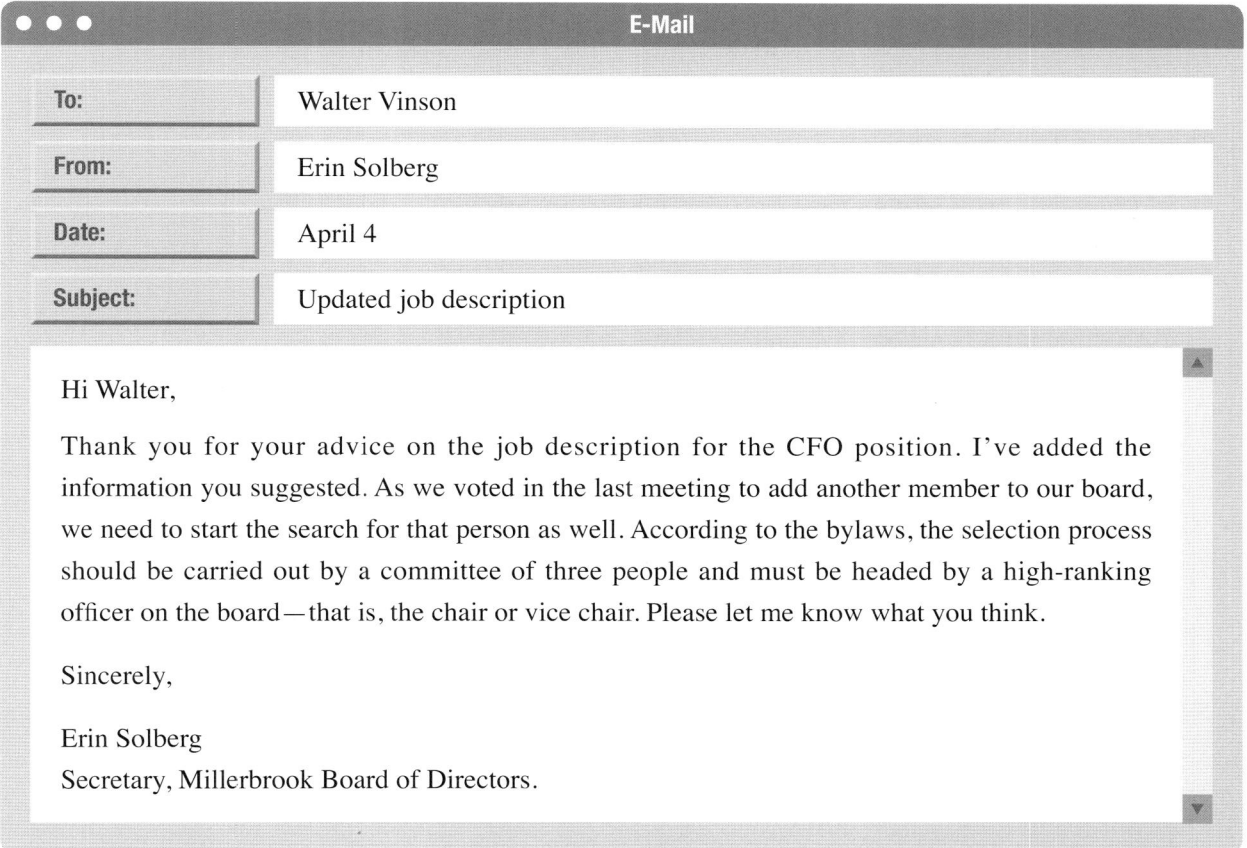

196. What is indicated about Mr. Tolentino in the press release?
(A) He will be given an award from the company.
(B) He is leaving to start his own business.
(C) He had the support of all board members.
(D) He plans to train his replacement.

197. What is suggested about Ms. Chomley?
(A) She plans to relocate to a new city.
(B) She has strong communication skills.
(C) She is Mr. Vinson's former coworker.
(D) She has designed software programs before.

198. According to Mr. Vinson, why is Ms. Chomley unsure about the position?
(A) The job responsibilities are too specialized.
(B) The expected working hours are too long.
(C) The compensation package is not fully described.
(D) The company has a lengthy interview process.

199. In the second e-mail, what is implied about the Millerbrook board?
(A) It will increase in size.
(B) It will meet more frequently.
(C) It will receive larger payments.
(D) It will update the bylaws.

200. What is suggested about Mr. Vinson?
(A) He is the newest member of the board.
(B) He opposed a proposed change.
(C) He will be supervising his friend.
(D) He is eligible to lead a committee.

Stop! This is the end of the test. If you finish before time is called, you may go back to Parts 5, 6, and 7 and check your work.

에듀윌 토익 실전서

LC+RC

TEST 02

LISTENING TEST

PART 1
PART 2
PART 3
PART 4

READING TEST

PART 5
PART 6
PART 7

LISTENING TEST

In the Listening test, you will be asked to demonstrate how well you understand spoken English. The entire Listening test will last approximately 45 minutes. There are four parts, and directions are given for each part. You must mark your answers on the separate answer sheet. Do not write your answers in your test book.

PART 1

Directions: For each question in this part, you will hear four statements about a picture in your test book. When you hear the statements, you must select the one statement that best describes what you see in the picture. Then find the number of the question on your answer sheet and mark your answer. The statements will not be printed in your test book and will be spoken only one time.

Statement (C), "They're looking at a document," is the best description of the picture, so you should select answer (C) and mark it on your answer sheet.

1.

2.

3.

4.

5.

6.

PART 2

Directions: You will hear a question or statement and three responses spoken in English. They will not be printed in your test book and will be spoken only one time. Select the best response to the question or statement and mark the letter (A), (B), or (C) on your answer sheet.

7. Mark your answer on your answer sheet.
8. Mark your answer on your answer sheet.
9. Mark your answer on your answer sheet.
10. Mark your answer on your answer sheet.
11. Mark your answer on your answer sheet.
12. Mark your answer on your answer sheet.
13. Mark your answer on your answer sheet.
14. Mark your answer on your answer sheet.
15. Mark your answer on your answer sheet.
16. Mark your answer on your answer sheet.
17. Mark your answer on your answer sheet.
18. Mark your answer on your answer sheet.
19. Mark your answer on your answer sheet.
20. Mark your answer on your answer sheet.
21. Mark your answer on your answer sheet.
22. Mark your answer on your answer sheet.
23. Mark your answer on your answer sheet.
24. Mark your answer on your answer sheet.
25. Mark your answer on your answer sheet.
26. Mark your answer on your answer sheet.
27. Mark your answer on your answer sheet.
28. Mark your answer on your answer sheet.
29. Mark your answer on your answer sheet.
30. Mark your answer on your answer sheet.
31. Mark your answer on your answer sheet.

PART 3

Directions: You will hear some conversations between two or more people. You will be asked to answer three questions about what the speakers say in each conversation. Select the best response to each question and mark the letter (A), (B), (C), or (D) on your answer sheet. The conversations will not be printed in your test book and will be spoken only one time.

32. How did the woman find out about the sale?
    (A) By reading a banner
    (B) By performing an Internet search
    (C) By receiving a flyer in the mail
    (D) By seeing an ad in the newspaper

33. What does the man recommend buying?
    (A) An electronic device
    (B) Some cookware
    (C) A piece of furniture
    (D) Some clothing

34. Why does the woman want to make a phone call?
    (A) To increase a budget
    (B) To get an opinion
    (C) To confirm an address
    (D) To check another store

35. Where most likely are the speakers?
    (A) At a conference hall
    (B) At a vehicle rental agency
    (C) At a computer repair shop
    (D) At an airport

36. What does the man say he did yesterday?
    (A) Traveled by airplane
    (B) Opened a new business
    (C) Ordered some components
    (D) Gave a presentation

37. What does the woman offer to do for the man?
    (A) Show him a catalog
    (B) Provide a refund
    (C) Consult an expert
    (D) Work extra hours

38. What is the purpose of the man's visit?
    (A) To make a delivery
    (B) To inspect a building
    (C) To introduce a company
    (D) To install security equipment

39. What does the woman plan to do?
    (A) Call the man back
    (B) Keep an entrance locked
    (C) Reschedule a visit
    (D) Put up a sign

40. What does the man inquire about?
    (A) A company invoice
    (B) A parking situation
    (C) An hourly fee
    (D) A road closure

41. What are the men encouraged to do?
    (A) Borrow a company car
    (B) Sign up for a workshop
    (C) Share rides to work
    (D) Reserve a parking spot

42. What will the woman do in the afternoon?
    (A) Meet with managers
    (B) E-mail a plan
    (C) Announce a change
    (D) Launch a program

43. Why does the woman thank Aiden?
    (A) He completed a task ahead of schedule.
    (B) He agreed to attend a meeting for her.
    (C) He volunteered to provide suggestions.
    (D) He will help new employees get settled.

GO ON TO THE NEXT PAGE

44. What does the man need assistance with?
    (A) A film screening
    (B) A retirement party
    (C) A training session
    (D) A recruiting process

45. Why is the woman unable to help the man?
    (A) She has to meet with a client.
    (B) She has interviews with candidates.
    (C) She has to complete a coworker's tasks.
    (D) She has a doctor's appointment.

46. What will the man probably discuss with Ms. Hendricks?
    (A) Changing a due date
    (B) Transferring to another office
    (C) Hiring a temporary worker
    (D) Updating a company policy

47. What has the man recently done?
    (A) Accepted a promotion to a new position
    (B) Introduced new products to a company
    (C) Received negative feedback from employees
    (D) Encouraged the business owner to buy more vans

48. What does the man mean when he says, "it's a lot to ask"?
    (A) He believes a workload is unreasonable.
    (B) He feels bad for needing a big favor.
    (C) He is unable to meet a deadline.
    (D) He needs some time to think about a decision.

49. What does the woman suggest doing?
    (A) Expanding the hours of operation
    (B) Recruiting some drivers
    (C) Finding a new supplier
    (D) Reducing a service fee

50. What is the conversation mainly about?
    (A) Misprints in a catalog
    (B) Images on a Web site
    (C) A product launch
    (D) A customer complaint

51. What does the woman mention about a project?
    (A) It doesn't have enough workers.
    (B) It has been canceled.
    (C) It needs a budget adjustment.
    (D) It is still in progress.

52. What does the man plan to do next week?
    (A) Assess a service
    (B) Replace some images
    (C) Assign a new task
    (D) Repair some equipment

53. Why is the man visiting the business?
    (A) To have a dental checkup
    (B) To get a receipt
    (C) To pick up an item
    (D) To schedule an appointment

54. What did Ms. Michaels do in the morning?
    (A) Processed a credit card payment
    (B) Noticed a billing error
    (C) Filled out some paperwork
    (D) Left a telephone message

55. What will the man most likely do next?
    (A) Speak to a dentist
    (B) Confirm a schedule
    (C) Show an ID card
    (D) Go to an exam room

56. What is the purpose of the call?
 (A) To complain about a damaged item
 (B) To apologize for a delay
 (C) To check on the status of an order
 (D) To inquire about a discount

57. According to the man, what has caused a problem?
 (A) An engine malfunction
 (B) A computer error
 (C) An employee's absence
 (D) A major storm

58. What does the man recommend doing?
 (A) Checking information online
 (B) Calling back later
 (C) Waiting another day
 (D) Providing a tracking number

59. Where most likely are the speakers?
 (A) At an airport
 (B) In a public library
 (C) At a convention center
 (D) In a hotel lobby

60. What does the woman mention about the parking lot?
 (A) It is restricted to guests.
 (B) It is currently full.
 (C) It is under construction.
 (D) It is closed in the evenings.

61. What does the woman imply when she says, "I can't help you"?
 (A) She does not know the directions to a place.
 (B) She is not allowed to make exceptions.
 (C) She has trouble making recommendations.
 (D) She cannot explain the policy's details.

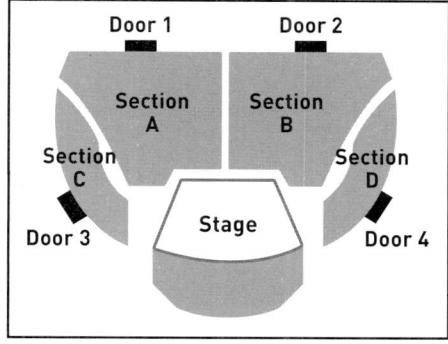

62. Who most likely is the woman?
 (A) A theater employee
 (B) A media critic
 (C) A musical performer
 (D) A stage manager

63. Look at the graphic. In which section will the man probably sit?
 (A) Section A
 (B) Section B
 (C) Section C
 (D) Section D

64. What will the man most likely do next?
 (A) Send a message
 (B) Give the woman his seat
 (C) Exchange a ticket
 (D) Wait for a friend outside

GO ON TO THE NEXT PAGE

778 Crowley Street: Work Schedule	
Week 1	Trim trees
Week 2	Install irrigation system
Week 3	Erect wooden fence
Week 4	Dig flower bed

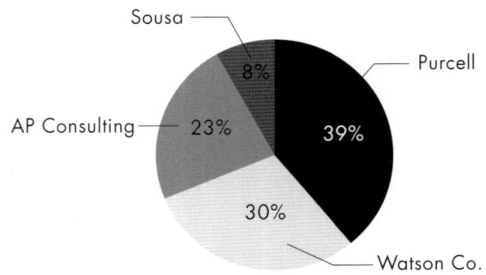

65. What does the woman mention about the permit?

    (A) It has already been approved by the city.
    (B) It is required because of the fence's height.
    (C) It will take several weeks to process.
    (D) It will be valid for eight months.

66. Look at the graphic. What will the speakers do next week?

    (A) Trim trees
    (B) Install an irrigation system
    (C) Erect a wooden fence
    (D) Dig a flower bed

67. What will the woman send to Ms. Kenmore?

    (A) A set of photographs
    (B) An updated schedule
    (C) A final bill
    (D) A list of materials

68. What does the man say happened yesterday?

    (A) A budget proposal was submitted.
    (B) A new branch opened.
    (C) A marketing campaign was launched.
    (D) An award was presented.

69. Look at the graphic. Which company recently changed its CEO?

    (A) Purcell
    (B) Watson Co.
    (C) AP Consulting
    (D) Sousa

70. What is the woman concerned about?

    (A) Losing customers to a competitor
    (B) Spending too much on marketing
    (C) Failing to keep up with demand
    (D) Having dissatisfied staff members

PART 4

Directions: You will hear some talks given by a single speaker. You will be asked to answer three questions about what the speaker says in each talk. Select the best response to each question and mark the letter (A), (B), (C), or (D) on your answer sheet. The talks will not be printed in your test book and will be spoken only one time.

71. What is the main topic of the broadcast?
    (A) A museum tour
    (B) An art contest
    (C) A painting lesson
    (D) A fundraiser

72. How can participants receive a free gift?
    (A) By adding their names to a mailing list
    (B) By making a regular donation
    (C) By being one of the first fifty people to enroll
    (D) By purchasing more than one ticket

73. What does the speaker encourage listeners to do?
    (A) Call the radio station
    (B) Contact Ms. Coleman
    (C) Listen to a program
    (D) Visit a Web site

74. Where most likely does the speaker work?
    (A) At a taxi company
    (B) At an airport
    (C) At a train station
    (D) At a travel agency

75. What will listeners be asked to do?
    (A) Show a receipt
    (B) Take their seats
    (C) Wait for further instructions
    (D) Present their tickets

76. What does the speaker say that employees will do?
    (A) Issue new tickets
    (B) Help to move luggage
    (C) Update safety procedures
    (D) Hang up some notices

77. Why is the speaker calling?
    (A) To accept a task
    (B) To handle a complaint
    (C) To show appreciation
    (D) To request assistance

78. What does the speaker imply when he says, "Tourist season is starting soon"?
    (A) He is concerned about being short-staffed.
    (B) He doesn't understand why profits are low.
    (C) He agrees with the listener's suggestion.
    (D) He thinks the store should advertise more frequently.

79. What does the speaker ask for?
    (A) An access code
    (B) A floor plan
    (C) An authorization form
    (D) A colleague's phone number

80. Who most likely is the speaker?
    (A) A librarian
    (B) A personnel manager
    (C) A marketer
    (D) A teacher

81. Why does the speaker say, "It truly saddens me to say this"?
    (A) To express his regret
    (B) To emphasize his disagreement
    (C) To reject an application
    (D) To show his mood change

82. What does the speaker ask the listener to do?
    (A) Volunteer for a charity
    (B) Provide a document
    (C) Recommend a worker
    (D) Lead a new program

GO ON TO THE NEXT PAGE

83. What is the purpose of the meeting?

(A) To report on a competitor's plan
(B) To announce a leadership change
(C) To explain a new company policy
(D) To congratulate the listeners on an award

84. What kind of company do the listeners most likely work for?

(A) An energy plant
(B) A vehicle manufacturer
(C) A communications company
(D) A construction firm

85. According to the speaker, what has Ms. Melville done?

(A) Ordered replacement parts
(B) Received an award
(C) Analyzed a competitor
(D) Prepared an employee list

86. Where is the introduction taking place?

(A) At a manufacturing plant
(B) At an auto repair shop
(C) At a construction site
(D) At a convention center

87. Who is Gustav Palmer?

(A) A business owner
(B) An engineer
(C) A reporter
(D) A physician

88. What does the speaker ask the listeners to do?

(A) Suggest ideas for a design
(B) Wear protective gear
(C) Refrain from taking pictures
(D) Stay together as a group

89. What is the speaker mainly discussing?

(A) An educational program
(B) A registration fee
(C) A library fundraiser
(D) A community picnic

90. Why is the speaker concerned?

(A) There is a shortage of funding.
(B) A meeting space is not available.
(C) Bad weather is expected soon.
(D) Interest in a project has declined.

91. What does the speaker ask the listeners to do?

(A) Register for an event
(B) Send her property information
(C) Meet in front of a building
(D) Make a financial donation

92. Who most likely is the speaker?

(A) A security guard
(B) A college lecturer
(C) A tour guide
(D) A medical professional

93. What does the speaker mean when he says, "This is really valuable information"?

(A) He encourages the listeners to complete a survey.
(B) He is concerned that some documents will get lost.
(C) He wants some data to be carefully protected.
(D) He is pleased that so much information has been gathered.

94. What are the listeners reminded to do?

(A) Keep their personal items with them
(B) Call later for some test results
(C) Be ready to present an ID card
(D) Fill out a registration form in advance

Customer: Faye Segura	
Order number: 1223389	
Description	Quantity
Daffodil bulbs	35
Tulip bulbs	30
Rose bushes	15
Lavender bushes	6

95. What is the purpose of the call?
    (A) To change an appointment
    (B) To verify an order
    (C) To notify of a delivery error
    (D) To request a payment

96. Look at the graphic. Which quantity does the speaker refer to?
    (A) 35
    (B) 30
    (C) 15
    (D) 6

97. What does the speaker say about Phillip?
    (A) He can issue a refund.
    (B) He can take a message.
    (C) He can design a garden.
    (D) He can pick up some plants.

98. Where do the listeners most likely work?
    (A) At an insurance company
    (B) At a law firm
    (C) At a magazine publisher
    (D) At an environmental agency

99. Look at the graphic. What topic will the company address in June?
    (A) Dress code
    (B) Telecommuting
    (C) Vacation policy
    (D) Free lunch

100. According to the speaker, what is available in the staff lounge today?
    (A) A policy explanation
    (B) Some survey forms
    (C) Some refreshments
    (D) A customer list

This is the end of the Listening Test. Turn to Part 5 in your test book.

READING TEST

In the Reading test, you will read a variety of texts and answer several different types of reading comprehension questions. The entire Reading test will last 75 minutes. There are three parts, and directions are given for each part. You are encouraged to answer as many questions as possible within the time allowed.

You must mark your answers on the separate answer sheet. Do not write your answers in the test book.

PART 5

Directions: A word or phrase is missing in each of the sentences below. Four answer choices are given below each sentence. Select the best answer to complete the sentence. Then mark the letter (A), (B), (C), or (D) on your answer sheet.

101. Most attendees at the conference confirmed that ------- learned a lot of useful information.
    (A) theirs
    (B) their
    (C) them
    (D) they

102. ------- in meeting the delivery demands is an important part of any courier business.
    (A) Relied
    (B) Relying
    (C) Reliable
    (D) Reliability

103. Keller Automotive's mini hybrid is the most affordable ------- among mini hybrids sold in the country.
    (A) such
    (B) one
    (C) what
    (D) each

104. Emerson Railways is interested in ------- its insurance provider in order to save money.
    (A) covering
    (B) emerging
    (C) changing
    (D) obtaining

105. Participants in the marathon will run ------- the Ness River and finish the race at Willow Park.
    (A) along
    (B) onto
    (C) apart
    (D) except

106. The new dryer from Chipley Appliances is designed ------- when the clothes are dry.
    (A) to sense
    (B) senses
    (C) sensing
    (D) sensed

107. The caterer was surprised that the seafood appetizers seemed ------- touched by the guests.
    (A) conveniently
    (B) apparently
    (C) barely
    (D) lightly

108. The peak season for winter wear is coming up, so it is ------- that we find a new manager for the Berka branch soon.
    (A) imperative
    (B) responsive
    (C) exclusive
    (D) persuasive

109. The construction of an additional lane on Highway 27 was delayed ------- a shortage of materials.

(A) because of
(B) since
(C) in case
(D) as a result

110. Community center officials were pleased that course ------- has increased by fifteen percent.

(A) description
(B) enrollment
(C) inventory
(D) attitude

111. Patrons may take out reference books from the library ------- they have received special permission from the head librarian.

(A) or else
(B) so
(C) whereas
(D) provided that

112. After the ticketing machines were installed, it was ------- to handle more passengers at the station.

(A) possible
(B) possibility
(C) possibly
(D) possibilities

113. Dewitt Communications ------- provides customer service training for its employees, so it has built a reputation for excellence.

(A) regularly
(B) firmly
(C) recently
(D) promptly

114. In compliance with regulations, we will give updates to those who are ------- involved in the matter.

(A) more direct
(B) directly
(C) direct
(D) directness

115. The research database maintained by Gyron Pharmaceuticals provides a ------- of information for physicians.

(A) quality
(B) similarity
(C) wealth
(D) mention

116. Once the transaction is complete, the person who requested the transfer will receive a message ------- the deposit.

(A) confirming
(B) confirms
(C) confirmed
(D) confirmation

117. Mr. Lincoln always flies with the same airline ------- he has joined a frequent flyer program.

(A) so that
(B) even if
(C) unless
(D) now that

118. After washing the car, Mr. Howard ------- a thin coat of wax to make the surface shine.

(A) to apply
(B) applying
(C) was applied
(D) applied

119. Ms. Mason forgot to take the fluctuations ------- currency rates into account when making the projections.

(A) often
(B) in
(C) finally
(D) on

120. Many potential customers were discouraged by ------- similar cell phone plans at Fletcher Mobile.

(A) confusing
(B) confusingly
(C) confusion
(D) confused

GO ON TO THE NEXT PAGE

121. Ms. Cheng added her ------- to the contract as a witness to the agreement.

    (A) signed
    (B) signs
    (C) signature
    (D) to sign

122. If you have lost or damaged your boarding pass, please speak to the gate agent, who can verify it and print -------.

    (A) another
    (B) each other
    (C) others
    (D) one another

123. Employees are asked to ------- the model number of the device that needs repairs.

    (A) intensify
    (B) specify
    (C) unify
    (D) testify

124. Lucy Berman has set a number of swimming records ------- her eight-year career as a professional swimmer.

    (A) above
    (B) regarding
    (C) throughout
    (D) of

125. Late for the meeting, Ms. Diaz took a seat in the back of the room to avoid -------.

    (A) noticed
    (B) being noticed
    (C) to notice
    (D) having noticed

126. The town's Independence Day Parade will commence with a brief speech by the newly ------- mayor.

    (A) elected
    (B) elects
    (C) electing
    (D) elect

127. Carla Stenton is an ------- entrepreneur who launched a start-up that expanded quickly across the nation.

    (A) embarrassed
    (B) acceptable
    (C) ambitious
    (D) alarmed

128. The sound quality of Vivico speakers is ------- superior compared to others on the market, but many people cannot afford them.

    (A) markedly
    (B) respectively
    (C) adamantly
    (D) permissibly

129. The first two rows in the auditorium are specially reserved for VIP guests, ------- are presenters.

    (A) the reason why
    (B) as a matter of fact
    (C) most of whom
    (D) on the contrary

130. Many participants in the tour were delighted to discover how ------- learning about the city's history could be.

    (A) considerable
    (B) accountable
    (C) enjoyable
    (D) transferable

PART 6

Directions: Read the texts that follow. A word, phrase, or sentence is missing in parts of each text. Four answer choices for each question are given below the text. Select the best answer to complete the text. Then mark the letter (A), (B), (C), or (D) on your answer sheet.

Questions 131-134 refer to the following advertisement.

During the first week of July, Twinkle Jewelry will hold a special event to celebrate its first anniversary. For one week only, get two items, and we ------- you for only one. For example, if you buy one necklace and one bracelet, you'll pay for the cheaper item only! You can choose any two items you like from our wide ------- of jewelry. This offer applies to all of our products! -------, there is no limit to the number of times a person can benefit from it. However, jewelry will be given out on a first come, first served basis while supplies last. -------. The event starts on July 1.
131. **132.** **133.** **134.**

131. (A) will charge
 (B) will be charged
 (C) were charging
 (D) have been charging

132. (A) select
 (B) selects
 (C) selection
 (D) selected

133. (A) In addition
 (B) As a result
 (C) Therefore
 (D) Accordingly

134. (A) That is why we have agreed to refund your purchase.
 (B) So come early to make sure you don't miss out.
 (C) We will set the items you request aside for you.
 (D) Please complete your payment as soon as possible.

GO ON TO THE NEXT PAGE

Questions 135-138 refer to the following notice.

Public Seminar with Nora Devons
Thursday, May 14, 7 P.M.

Nora Devons, a prominent ------- of eliminating homelessness in Fredrick City, will be presenting a two-hour seminar at the Renner Convention Center. Ms. Devons is the president of the Association of Social Workers, a group with over three hundred members. She ------- efforts to support the homeless community for the past eight years. During the seminar, she will tell the audience about the seriousness of the homeless problem. -------.

The talk is open to audience members of all ages, and there is no entrance fee. -------, donations will be collected at the door to support the Marigold Homeless Shelter. For more information, visit www.assocofsw.org.

135. (A) founder
(B) advocate
(C) candidate
(D) prosecutor

136. (A) had been leading
(B) has led
(C) is leading
(D) will lead

137. (A) She will also mention ways to help resolve it.
(B) The audience asked questions during the break.
(C) At that time, she served as a city council member.
(D) She plans to return to Grayson University to earn a master's degree.

138. (A) Accordingly
(B) Specifically
(C) Apparently
(D) However

Questions 139-142 refer to the following e-mail.

To: Natasha Seymour <nseymour@vicivenues.com>
From: Robert Thornton <r.thornton@hvelectronics.net>
Date: October 3
Subject: Event at Boulevard Hall

Dear Ms. Seymour,

I am part of a committee that is in charge of ------- a retirement dinner for one of my coworkers at HV Electronics. Several of your venues -------, but Boulevard Hall received the most support. This was due to ------- modern facilities and proximity to our office in Blakeley Towers.

139.   140.   141.

This will be our first time holding an event at Boulevard Hall. Could you confirm which dates are available in November? We prefer November 20, so we hope that evening is still free. -------.

142.

Sincerely,

Robert Thornton

139. (A) inspiring
(B) arranging
(C) contributing
(D) visiting

140. (A) will be considered
(B) had considered
(C) were considered
(D) were considering

141. (A) their
(B) it
(C) its
(D) them

142. (A) We think you will be impressed with the spacious room.
(B) Even so, many people can walk from the office.
(C) This fee is within our estimated budget.
(D) If not, we have a few other possibilities in mind.

Questions 143-146 refer to the following e-mail.

To: Travel Times <info@traveltimes-magazine.com>
From: Christopher Venn <c.venn@frequenx.com>
Subject: Subscription #28571
Date: September 3

To Whom It May Concern:

I currently have a subscription to *Travel Times* magazine which is valid until the end of February. I'm wondering ------- it is possible to change the mailing address before the next issue comes out.
          143.
-------. I'm currently receiving the magazine at work, but the new manager ------- that we no longer
144.   145.
have personal mail delivered there. ------- residential address is 798 Trelawney Way, Phoenix, AZ
                                    146.
85010. If there is a fee associated with this change, please e-mail me.

Thank you,

Christopher Venn

---

143. (A) what
(B) if
(C) while
(D) for

144. (A) The information on Spain was particularly interesting.
(B) The monthly bill had charged me for two subscriptions.
(C) I couldn't find any information about doing this through your Web site.
(D) I appreciate your printing the article I submitted.

145. (A) requested
(B) facilitated
(C) acknowledged
(D) canceled

146. (A) Your
(B) Its
(C) Each
(D) My

PART 7

Directions: In this part, you will read a selection of texts, such as magazine and newspaper articles, e-mails, and instant messages. Each text or set of texts is followed by several questions. Select the best answer for each question and mark the letter (A), (B), (C), or (D) on your answer sheet.

Questions 147-148 refer to the following notice.

Warm Hands Warm Hearts (WHWH) is seeking new members for Melville's local group, which knits mittens and gloves to donate to the homeless. Our next meeting will be on Saturday, November 2, from 1 P.M. to 4 P.M. at the Lindale Coffee Shop. To get there, take subway line 5 to Kingstown Arena Station and use exit 5.

Participants should bring their own yarn and knitting needles. In addition, we would like a variety of colors and yarn types, so please let us know what you plan to bring for your project by commenting in the forum at warmhandswh.org/forum.

147. Where most likely would the notice be found?

(A) In a product catalog
(B) On a public bulletin board
(C) On a subway ticket receipt
(D) In a craft instruction book

148. According to the notice, why should people visit the Web site?

(A) To view photos of past projects
(B) To confirm registration for an event
(C) To request instructions by e-mail
(D) To report their choices of materials

Questions 149-150 refer to the following invoice.

Wallace Tools

Invoice Date: October 25
Invoice Number: 8395
Name: Dean Monette
Address: 805 Carriage Drive, Arlington Heights, IL 60005
Contact Number: 555-6950

One-week Rental: $49.99

[Contents]
Hadron-360 electric drill
Plastic carrying case
Charging device for unit battery
One-week insurance coverage (policy information printout)

Tax and Shipping: $8.95
Total: $58.94

Payment has been received in full for the above service. If you would like to keep the item longer, please call us at 555-2900. The device's user manual can be downloaded from our Web site at www.wallacetools.net.

149. What was NOT sent with the rental item?

(A) A user manual
(B) A battery charger
(C) Insurance details
(D) A portable container

150. Why should Mr. Monette call the number provided?

(A) To give feedback about a service
(B) To make a payment
(C) To request instructions
(D) To extend a rental period

Questions 151-152 refer to the following article.

BEIJING (July 5)—The price of raw silk is on the rise again after hitting a four-year low last quarter. This is in part due to trends in China and India, the world's largest producers of silk. Silk suppliers have been accumulating large quantities of the product at cheap prices and storing it rather than putting it on the market. This has led to an increase in price, which is expected to continue for the next few quarters. Clothing producers have enjoyed the low price of silk, but now that a higher cost of raw materials is projected, the fabric is much less attractive. As a result, many such producers are designing clothing made from man-made fabric, such as nylon and rayon, to avoid the unpredictability of the silk market.

151. According to the article, what has affected the price of silk?

(A) Some dealers are stocking up on the material.
(B) The currency value in China and India has dropped.
(C) Production has increased in efficiency.
(D) Customers are starting to prefer other fabrics.

152. How are clothing manufacturers dealing with a change?

(A) By negotiating directly with suppliers
(B) By developing products with alternative materials
(C) By purchasing supplies in bulk
(D) By changing the way goods are advertised

Questions 153-155 refer to the following e-mail.

E-Mail

To: Nina Ezell <n.ezell@prime-cleaning.net>
From: Akash Badal <a.badal@prime-cleaning.net>
Date: April 4
Subject: Cleaning services

Dear Nina,

I am writing to you regarding the professional cleaning services that we will provide for Gilbert & Associates starting from April 10. I was looking over the contract that you wanted me to review, but I'm afraid we can't sign it in its current form because the wrong address was used. I know you met with a Gilbert & Associates representative on April 1 to discuss the contract terms. However, that person should have told you that they were going to relocate their offices two days later. The contract should reflect the new building's address. Since you're the one who has been handling this client, I think it would be best for you to call them to find out the exact new address. We should send the signed version by courier tomorrow, so please take care of this today so we don't get behind schedule on the paperwork.

Sincerely,

Akash

---

153. Why did Mr. Badal send the e-mail?
(A) To recommend a business
(B) To change a cleaning schedule
(C) To send an updated contract
(D) To point out an error

154. When did Gilbert & Associates move to a new building?
(A) March 28
(B) March 30
(C) April 1
(D) April 3

155. What should Ms. Ezell do by the end of the day?
(A) Negotiate some contract terms
(B) Contact the Gilbert & Associates office
(C) Send Mr. Badal a client recommendation
(D) Mail some documents to Prime Cleaning

Questions 156-157 refer to the following text-message chain.

Donald Graham [9:12 A.M.]
I've e-mailed you the estimate from the interior designer for remodeling our lobby.

Wei Lu [9:14 A.M.]
It's more expensive than I was expecting, especially since our lawyers don't even use that area much.

Donald Graham [9:15 A.M.]
Yes, it's slightly over budget, but I think it's worth it.

Wei Lu [9:16 A.M.]
Do you? It doesn't even include the cost of furniture.

Donald Graham [9:18 A.M.]
You have to understand that the lobby is the first thing people see when they arrive. It's essential that they have a good opinion of our business right from the start.

Wei Lu [9:19 A.M.]
You have a point. I guess it will give people more confidence in our services.

156. What are the writers mainly discussing?

(A) Hotel accommodations
(B) Budget limits
(C) Renovation costs
(D) Customer reviews

157. At 9:19 A.M., what does Ms. Lu most likely mean when she writes, "You have a point"?

(A) Attracting new customers is not easy.
(B) The business should be careful about spending.
(C) Making a good impression is important.
(D) The lobby needs to be expanded soon.

Questions 158-160 refer to the following article.

NEW YORK (September 10)—Paula Frederick is known for her trendy and sophisticated fashions both on and off the runway. In addition to her retail business, she has created award-winning costumes for a number of films, most recently the sci-fi blockbuster *Golden Galaxy*. Now Ms. Frederick is lending her talents to a new project—designing warm-up uniforms and performance outfits for the national ice skating team. The team will wear them at the International Ice Skating Tournament, which will take place from January 3 to January 16.

Ms. Frederick was offered the project after meeting the team's coach, Vince Oliero, at an anniversary event for Charlotte Reeves, whose fashion house was Ms. Frederick's first employer after she graduated from design school. When Mr. Oliero mentioned that the team needed to update its look, the idea for the project was born.

Industry insiders are interested to see how Ms. Frederick's elaborate style will translate to the sports world. "I'm looking forward to the challenge," Ms. Frederick said at the debut event for *Golden Galaxy* earlier this week. "With the film, I was able to work with over-the-top designs and lavish embellishments. With my new project, I'll have limited fabric options and will need to prioritize comfort and practicality." *Golden Galaxy* producer Liam Hart, who accompanied Ms. Frederick to the event, also commented on the project, saying that he was certain Ms. Frederick's limitless creativity would help to make it a success.

Fans of Ms. Frederick's work can see *Golden Galaxy* costumes on the big screen and on her Web site. However, to see the uniforms they'll have to watch the tournament in person or live on television.

158. What is true about the *Golden Galaxy* costumes?

(A) They were Ms. Frederick's first project.
(B) They are practical and comfortable.
(C) They received an award.
(D) They are available for sale online.

159. Who most likely is Ms. Reeves?

(A) An ice skating coach
(B) A fashion designer
(C) A film producer
(D) A professional athlete

160. What is suggested about Mr. Hart?

(A) He has worked with Ms. Frederick on several projects.
(B) He recently attended a movie premiere.
(C) He met Ms. Frederick at an anniversary party.
(D) He knows Ms. Reeves personally.

Questions 161-163 refer to the following letter.

March 8

Store Manager Shawn Boyd
Outdoors Plus, Soulard Branch
1009 Ash Avenue
Saint Louis, MO 63146

Dear Mr. Boyd,

As you know, Camping Sphere Inc. is introducing a new lightweight backpack to its product line. For the entire months of April and May, we will hold a special promotion, offering the product at 30% off its suggested retail price. We'll start advertising the sale two weeks in advance. The official launch date will be April 1, and there will be a special launch event at the McKinley Heights branch. I know you also applied to hold the event at the Soulard branch, but we decided to go with a store that had already been in charge of large-scale events such as this. I will visit your store next week to drop off the displays for the new backpacks. These stands should be placed in a prominent area, and I can advise you on the arrangement at that time.

Sincerely,

Justin Dawson
Justin Dawson

161. How long will the discount on the new product be offered?

(A) One week
(B) Two weeks
(C) One month
(D) Two months

162. According to the letter, why was the McKinley Heights branch selected for an event?

(A) It needs the most improvement in its sales figures.
(B) Its employees have hosted similar events.
(C) It is the company's largest store.
(D) Its customers voted to hold the event there.

163. What will happen next week?

(A) A branch manager will print out some promotional material.
(B) Mr. Dawson will recommend some display strategies.
(C) A store will start selling a new line of backpacks.
(D) Mr. Boyd will oversee a product launch event.

Questions 164-167 refer to the following online chat discussion.

Clara Starnes 1:09 P.M.	Hi. I'm going to write about the Lafayette Art Museum for my next exhibit review. I know you've all been there before. Do you have any advice for me?
Radha Pai 1:18 P.M.	The size of the collection is enormous, so you need to plan ahead to see everything.
Clara Starnes 1:42 P.M.	I've heard that visitors aren't allowed to take pictures in some sections of the museum.
Joyce Garza 1:46 P.M.	You're right, Clara. Photos are not permitted in some sections, but signs are prominently displayed to inform visitors.
Clara Starnes 1:59 P.M.	I assume it's really busy on weekends, so I think I'll go on a weekday. Which day is best?
Joyce Garza 2:16 P.M.	It's always packed. But in my experience, Tuesday is the best day to go if you don't want to be around a lot of tourists and school groups.
Clara Starnes 2:25 P.M.	Then I think I'll go there on Tuesday.
Alyssa Verdi 2:37 P.M.	You can get information about their regulations from the Web site, information desk, and signs posted throughout the museum.
Radha Pai 2:51 P.M.	Right. Lafayette is better than the place I visited last week, Timber Museum. Timber Museum should follow its example.
Alyssa Verdi 2:55 P.M.	If you plan on going more than once, it's worth signing up for a membership. It costs $20 for a one-year membership, but you save $7 each time you visit.
Clara Starnes 3:39 P.M.	I appreciate your advice, everyone.

164. What does Ms. Starnes ask for?

(A) Recommendations for tourist sites
(B) Tips for visiting a place
(C) Advice for opening an exhibit
(D) Explanation about a schedule

165. Why does Ms. Starnes decide to make a visit on Tuesday?

(A) Because she wants to avoid the crowds.
(B) Because she can listen to a special lecture.
(C) Because the entrance fee is discounted.
(D) Because a guided tour is being offered.

166. At 2:51 P.M., what does Ms. Pai most likely mean when she writes, "Timber Museum should follow its example"?

(A) The attendance at Timber Museum has gone down significantly.
(B) The entrance fee at Timber Museum is too expensive for tourists.
(C) The policies at Timber Museum are not clearly explained.
(D) The collection at Timber Museum is not very big.

167. What does Ms. Verdi imply about a membership?

(A) It should be purchased online.
(B) It should be renewed annually.
(C) It offers a $20 discount each year.
(D) It allows members to buy a two-day pass.

Questions 168-171 refer to the following e-mail.

E-Mail

To: Aida Mazzanti <a.mazzanti@smindustries.net>
From: Li Zhang <zhangli@metrorealty99.com>
Date: June 10
Subject: From Metro Realty

Dear Ms. Mazzanti,

Thank you for meeting with me last week to tour some of the apartments available through our firm. Please note that the apartments in Elliot Tower and the one in Geo Suites have been rented. —[1]—. The two-bedroom apartment in the HSW Building is still available. I know this is larger than what you wanted. —[2]—. However, it's in the Arleta neighborhood, so you'd be able to walk to your office. —[3]—. The current tenant is moving out on June 20, so you can move in on June 21. If you are interested, I can send you a lease agreement, which should be signed and returned no later than June 14. At that time, we will collect a $200 holding fee. —[4]—. This apartment is in a popular building, so I hope to hear from you soon so that you don't miss your chance.

Sincerely,

Li Zhang

---

168. Why did Mr. Zhang send the e-mail?

(A) To accept a suggestion
(B) To schedule a tour
(C) To send a housing contract
(D) To update property information

169. What is suggested in the e-mail?

(A) Ms. Mazzanti prefers a two-bedroom home.
(B) Mr. Zhang will meet Ms. Mazzanti at her office.
(C) Ms. Mazzanti's workplace is located in Arleta.
(D) Metro Realty is gathering survey information.

170. According to Mr. Zhang, by when should Ms. Mazzanti submit some paperwork?

(A) June 10
(B) June 14
(C) June 20
(D) June 21

171. In which of the positions marked [1], [2], [3], and [4] does the following sentence best belong?

"Additionally, you will be expected to pay a deposit equal to one month's rent when you move in."

(A) [1]
(B) [2]
(C) [3]
(D) [4]

Questions 172-175 refer to the following article.

Cleanup Begins on Carriage Lake *By Jeremy Trigg*

September 9—Plans for an extensive cleanup project at Carriage Lake are finally underway after the city encountered several obstacles. — [1] —. Talks regarding the need to improve the lake's condition began earlier this year, and it didn't take long to gather the public support needed. The city opened the project up for bids from companies in late March. — [2] —. Fortunately, the second round of bids resulted in a suitable contract agreement with Morris Enterprises.

The work, which began last week, involves removing contaminated soil from the bottom of the lake. — [3] —. Crews from Morris Enterprises are using a Preston-680 hydraulic dredge to remove the sediment. This equipment has a pump that is 24 inches in diameter, and Morris Enterprises bought it to replace its Caramillo-55, which would not have been powerful enough for this project.

"While Carriage Lake used to be a major draw for boating and fishing enthusiasts, attendance figures have been on a downward trend for years," said city councilperson Jane Clifton. "This project is costing taxpayers tens of millions of dollars, but the finished result will attract tourists, and the revenue they bring along with them. When you take the environmental impact into account as well, it's a win-win situation for everyone."

Once the work is completed, mercury levels in the water are expected to be reduced by as much as 97%. — [4] —. Because of that, officials will once again permit swimming in the lake, which hasn't been the case for decades. The city will also build an outdoor stage at the site, which will host music concerts, awards ceremonies, and more. To follow the progress of the cleanup, visit www.carriagelakecleanup.org.

172. What is the article mainly about?

(A) A project's progress
(B) A machine's availability
(C) A change in policy
(D) A tourism trend

173. What does Ms. Clifton most likely think about the project?

(A) It should have been started earlier in the year.
(B) The people handling it do not have enough experience.
(C) It will benefit the community despite its high costs.
(D) The final cost should be paid by boaters and fishermen.

174. What is NOT true about Carriage Lake?

(A) It is currently unsuitable for swimming.
(B) Its number of visitors has been steadily declining.
(C) It is the main source of drinking water in the town.
(D) It will be the site of an outdoor performance area.

175. In which of the positions marked [1], [2], [3], and [4] does the following sentence best belong?

"None of the prospective businesses could complete the scope of the work within the proposed budget."

(A) [1]
(B) [2]
(C) [3]
(D) [4]

Questions 176-180 refer to the following letter and survey.

July 3

Anne Stein
414 Fulton Street
Winchester, KY 40391

Dear Ms. Stein,

You recently booked a vehicle rental through the Trivo Rentals mobile phone app. We appreciate your business and would like to get your feedback on the enclosed form about the rental in order to improve our services further. We conduct research such as this regularly because we find that it is the best way to understand our customers.

We hope you will also introduce us to a friend who might be interested in our service. If you do so, your friend will receive a voucher by e-mail for 10 percent off any rental, and you will be given a voucher for a free GPS rental for the next time you rent from us.

Thank you for your participation!

The Trivo Rentals Team

Trivo Rentals

Thank you for taking the time to complete this survey. Your opinion matters to us!

Name: _Anne Stein_   Most Recent Rental Date: _June 25_

Rental Location: _Winchester_   Duration of Rental: _1 week_

1. How often do you use Trivo Rentals and why?
My personal vehicle is a van, so a few times a year I rent a fuel-efficient car to go on business trips out of state.

2. Why did you choose Trivo Rentals?
It's great that Trivo Rentals keeps costs down by using cars that are a few years old, rather than brand-new ones. What really sets the company apart is that it sends a representative to my home to give me a ride to the Trivo Rentals office. This is very convenient because I can't drive there myself without creating a parking issue.

3. How can we improve our services?
I think the added charges for insurance and extra services should be explained more clearly up front.

4. Would you like to recommend our services to a friend or family member? (Y) / N
Name: _Cliff Bower_   E-mail Address: _c.bower@ferrel.com_

176. What is the purpose of the letter?
 (A) To request information about a customer's experience
 (B) To gather feedback about a new product
 (C) To thank a customer for their opinion
 (D) To ask for some research results

177. What is implied about Trivo Rentals?
 (A) It provides special packages to business professionals.
 (B) It operates branches across the country.
 (C) It offers a wide variety of insurance options.
 (D) It has a smartphone application for reservations.

178. In the letter, the word "find" in paragraph 1, line 3, is closest in meaning to
 (A) suggest
 (B) discover
 (C) believe
 (D) acquire

179. What is true about Ms. Stein?
 (A) She can collect reward points for her rental.
 (B) She will be e-mailed a coupon for 10% off.
 (C) She will be entered into a drawing for a GPS device.
 (D) She can receive a free equipment rental.

180. What is one thing that Ms. Stein likes about Trivo Rentals?
 (A) Its convenient location
 (B) Its brand-new vehicles
 (C) Its cheap insurance
 (D) Its pick-up service

Questions 181-185 refer to the following memo and schedule.

To: Cervantes Incorporated Staff
From: Armando Dixon, General Manager
Subject: For your immediate attention
Attachment: Inventory Schedule

February 23

Following last year's merger, we are still downsizing our staff and looking for ways to cut overhead costs. As a result, we will be moving our offices next month from the Rinehart Building to the Werner Building, which has a lower rental fee. Those of you who drive will be pleased to know that the Werner Building has an underground parking lot for employees only, just like our current building does.

We have hired a professional moving company, Guerra Co., whose crew will visit our building on Friday, March 17. You do not need to report to work on that day. Prior to the move, employees will assist with taking inventory of the company's furniture, equipment, and supplies according to the attached schedule. The head of HR will supply boxes, tape, and labels for you to gather your personal belongings.

Inventory Schedule

DATE	LOCATION	DEPARTMENT	MANAGER
Monday, March 13	2nd Floor	Accounting	Naoto Kodama
Tuesday, March 14	3rd Floor	Sales	Troy Concord
		Marketing	Jesse Mateo *
Wednesday, March 15	4th Floor	Human Resources	Alana Templeton
		R&D	Kamal Bakshi
Thursday, March 16	1st Floor	Administration	Joan Pafford

* As Jesse Mateo will be absent that week, Joan Pafford from administration will fill in for him on his department's assigned day.

181. Why did Mr. Dixon send the memo?

(A) To announce a company merger
(B) To explain a relocation procedure
(C) To give an update on a construction project
(D) To ask employees to reduce spending

182. What is indicated about the Rinehart Building?

(A) It has a private parking area.
(B) It will become the Cervantes Incorporated headquarters.
(C) It will be torn down in March.
(D) It is larger than the Werner Building.

183. What is implied about Cervantes Incorporated's employees?

(A) They will be reassigned to different departments.
(B) They should work from home temporarily.
(C) They will be given a day off in March.
(D) They should report inventory problems to Mr. Dixon.

184. What is suggested about Ms. Templeton?

(A) She took a tour of the Werner Building.
(B) She works on the third floor.
(C) She made a suggestion to Mr. Dixon.
(D) She will distribute packing supplies.

185. What is scheduled to happen on March 14?

(A) A company will move to a new building.
(B) Ms. Pafford will assist a department that is not hers.
(C) Employees from Guerra Co. will visit the business.
(D) Mr. Concord will be absent from the office.

Questions 186-190 refer to the following flyer and e-mails.

Wednesday Night Documentary Screenings at Elsberry Hall

Elsberry Hall is pleased to bring you award-winning documentaries followed by a question-and-answer session with the special guests listed.

June 7: *Hourglass* / **Running Time: 2 hrs 21 mins**
Special Guest: Orlando Briggs (director)
This film explores how tourism has affected the small island of Kihoa over the past fifty years.

June 14: *Powering the North* / **Running Time: 2 hrs 18 mins**
Special Guest: Bruce Morrison (Can-Elec Vice President)
This film explores how Canadian energy company Can-Elec has adapted its business model since its inception decades ago.

June 21: *In the Game* / **Running Time: 2 hrs 5 mins**
Special Guest: Shamba Metha (director)
Watch the development of soccer from its humble beginnings in 19th-century England to becoming the world's most popular sport today.

June 28: *Not for Sale* / **Running Time: 1 hr 48 mins**
Special Guest: Erin Hanson (director)
See how politician Benjamin Tribble's career has unfolded from his first election in 1982 to the present day.

Book ahead for big savings! Buy your tickets within the month of May to get $5 off the entrance fee.

E-Mail

To: Elsberry Hall <bookings@elsberryhall.com>
From: Rosie Stiltner <r_stiltner@ravenpost.com>
Date: June 15, 10:33 A.M.
Subject: Tickets

To Whom It May Concern:

I attended last night's screening of *Powering the North*, and I found it to be both entertaining and informative. I'm wondering if there are still tickets available for *In the Game*. I already have one, but I'd like to buy three more, if possible. I understand that the tickets would be $16 this time, instead of the $11 I paid in my original order.

Sincerely,

Rosie Stiltner

To: Rosie Stiltner <r_stiltner@ravenpost.com>
From: Elsberry Hall <bookings@elsberryhall.com>
Date: June 15, 1:41 P.M.
Subject: RE: Tickets

Dear Ms. Stiltner,

Elsberry Hall enjoys a spacious seating area that can accommodate nearly five hundred people, so I'm pleased to inform you that we still have tickets available for the film you requested. However, you should note that the special guest for that date will be screenwriter Kevin Drummond, as the director cannot attend as planned. If you still want the tickets despite this change, you will have to call our box office at 555-3866 to give us your credit card details again, as we do not save information from previous transactions.

Sincerely,

Miles Rahn
Customer Service Agent, Elsberry Hall

186. What characteristic is shared by all of the films?

(A) They last longer than two hours.
(B) They explore a subject over time.
(C) They focus on business-related matters.
(D) They are made by well-known directors.

187. What is implied about Ms. Stiltner?

(A) She wants to exchange her tickets for a different film.
(B) She created a documentary film on her own.
(C) She booked her original ticket before June 1.
(D) She signed up for a theater membership program.

188. Which film's special guest has changed?

(A) *Hourglass*
(B) *Powering the North*
(C) *In the Game*
(D) *Not for Sale*

189. In the second e-mail, the word "enjoys" in paragraph 1, line 1, is closest in meaning to

(A) experiences
(B) possesses
(C) appreciates
(D) welcomes

190. According to Mr. Rahn, why should Ms. Stiltner call the box office?

(A) To verify a change
(B) To get an updated schedule
(C) To cancel a purchase
(D) To provide payment information

Questions 191-195 refer to the following article, Web page, and online review.

McCabe Home Appliances to Trim Its Product Line

August 27—McCabe Home Appliances plans to halt production of its PrimeAir-60 air purifier sometime in September, and stores carrying the product will sell it until it is sold out. Consumers who currently have the PrimeAir-60 are encouraged to stock up on filters, as the filters made for other McCabe air purifiers are a different shape and cannot be accommodated by the device.

A spokesperson for McCabe Home Appliances commented that the decision was made in order to focus on better-selling products. The PrimeAir-60 accounts for less than two percent of the company's revenue, so decision-makers at McCabe believed it was time to start promoting other designs. In addition, the majority of customers who did purchase the device complained about its loud operation. For a complete listing of McCabe Home Appliances' products, visit www.mccabehomeapp.com.

---

www.mccabehomeapp.com

Home » Catalog » Sale Items » Clearance

The following items are on sale until all items are sold. *Updated October 1*

PrimeAir-60 [ADD TO CART]

Regular Price: $169.99   Clearance Price: $75.99

PrimeAir-60 is an air purifier that can be used in rooms up to 1,500 cubic feet. It has low energy usage and operates more efficiently than most air purifiers on the market today. Regular use of the PrimeAir-60 can reduce the presence of bacteria, viruses, and allergens in your home. The device is highly recommended for allergy sufferers and those with respiratory problems. The filter can be cleaned by hand and reused up to ten times.

PrimeAir-60 Replacement Filters 3-Pack [ADD TO CART]

Regular Price: $59.99   Clearance Price: $39.99

PrimeAir-60 Replacement Filters 5-Pack [ADD TO CART]

Regular Price: $89.99   Clearance Price: $55.99

All orders, including those containing clearance items, qualify for free delivery from October 1 to October 31.

www.mccabehomeapp.com

Home » Reviews » PrimeAir-60

Written by: Olivia Densmore **Posted:** October 5

I will be sad to see this product go. I bought mine last year and have enjoyed using it constantly since then. I understand that the company has to take action on the most common complaint, but I've never experienced that problem. Even though the filters can be hand-washed and reused, I bought a 5-pack from the clearance sale today so I could ensure the use of the device for a long time.

191. What is the purpose of the article?

(A) To promote a new product in the line
(B) To notify consumers of a product recall
(C) To commemorate a company achievement
(D) To report the discontinuation of a product

192. In the article, the phrase "accounts for" in paragraph 2, line 2, is closest in meaning to

(A) uses
(B) represents
(C) happens
(D) explains

193. According to the Web page, what can customers receive in October?

(A) An extended warranty
(B) Free replacement filters
(C) An updated catalog
(D) Complimentary shipping

194. What does Ms. Densmore imply about the PrimeAir-60?

(A) She uses it during the daytime only.
(B) She will replace it with a newer model.
(C) She does not think it was too noisy.
(D) She made a complaint about it to the company.

195. What is most likely true about Ms. Densmore?

(A) She bought the PrimeAir-60 for $75.99.
(B) Her living room is less than 1,500 cubic feet.
(C) She spent $55.99 on replacement filters.
(D) Her purchase was delivered by express mail.

Questions 196-200 refer to the following announcement, memo, and e-mail.

Volunteers Needed

Richmond Public Library provides essential educational services to the community, and we are looking for volunteers to assist us with our programs. You must be at least eighteen years old and be available for a minimum of four hours a week. To apply as a volunteer, fill out a form at the front desk by March 20. Please note that all volunteers must go to an orientation workshop at the library before they can begin volunteering. With help from members of the community, we can reach more people and help them to attain their literacy goals. We hope to get at least thirty new volunteers for our programs, so please encourage your family and friends to volunteer as well.

MEMO

To employees,

Thank you, everyone, for taking the time out of your busy schedules to train our new library volunteers. The training session will be held on April 7, starting at 1 P.M. There will be two hours of general library information followed by overviews of individual projects (30 minutes each) by the head of each program as below. At the end of the orientation, volunteers will be given a form on which they can indicate which programs they would like to assist with. I cannot guarantee that all volunteers will be matched with their first choice, but I will do my best.

Program Coordinators:

- Silvano Marchesi, Adult Literacy
- Walter Vance, Children's Storytime
- Elizabeth Lancaster, Homework Help
- Hariti Nayak, Early Readers

We didn't quite make our recruitment goal. However, I'm still pleased with the group's size. I will send a list of the volunteers later this week.

E-Mail

To: Miriam Jarmillo <m.jarmillo@richmondpl.org>
From: Wen Lang <w.lang@richmondpl.org>
Date: April 29
Subject: Programs Update

Dear Ms. Jarmillo,

I'd like to give you an update on how the library programs are going. The new volunteers are settling into their roles nicely, and we've had a lot of positive feedback from the people participating in the programs. Because of the high demand for the Homework Help program, especially among middle school students, the director of that program plans to find a few more volunteers. I am tracking the weekly participation of each program and will have more detailed figures for you next month.

All the best,

Wen Lang
Richmond Public Library Program Coordinator

---

196. What is NOT expected from volunteers?

(A) Working over a certain number of weekly hours
(B) Attending an on-site training session
(C) Meeting a minimum age requirement
(D) Submitting a letter of recommendation

197. In the announcement, the word "reach" in paragraph 1, line 5, is closest in meaning to

(A) equal
(B) stretch
(C) achieve
(D) approach

198. What is suggested about the April 7 training session?

(A) It lasted for two hours in total.
(B) It assessed the volunteers' literacy.
(C) It had fewer than thirty participants.
(D) It got positive feedback from the volunteers.

199. Why will volunteers fill out a form at the training session?

(A) To express their preferences
(B) To rate the speakers' performances
(C) To confirm their schedules
(D) To suggest new programs

200. Who plans to recruit more volunteers?

(A) Mr. Marchesi
(B) Mr. Vance
(C) Ms. Lancaster
(D) Ms. Nayak

Stop! This is the end of the test. If you finish before time is called, you may go back to Parts 5, 6, and 7 and check your work.

▶ 정답 및 해설 p. 45

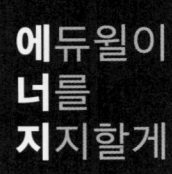

내가 꿈을 이루면
난 다시 누군가의 꿈이 된다.

에듀윌 토익 실전서

LC+RC

TEST 03

LISTENING TEST

PART 1
PART 2
PART 3
PART 4

READING TEST

PART 5
PART 6
PART 7

LISTENING TEST

In the Listening test, you will be asked to demonstrate how well you understand spoken English. The entire Listening test will last approximately 45 minutes. There are four parts, and directions are given for each part. You must mark your answers on the separate answer sheet. Do not write your answers in your test book.

PART 1

Directions: For each question in this part, you will hear four statements about a picture in your test book. When you hear the statements, you must select the one statement that best describes what you see in the picture. Then find the number of the question on your answer sheet and mark your answer. The statements will not be printed in your test book and will be spoken only one time.

Statement (C), "They're looking at a document," is the best description of the picture, so you should select answer (C) and mark it on your answer sheet.

1.

2.

3.

4.

5.

6.

PART 2

Directions: You will hear a question or statement and three responses spoken in English. They will not be printed in your test book and will be spoken only one time. Select the best response to the question or statement and mark the letter (A), (B), or (C) on your answer sheet.

7. Mark your answer on your answer sheet.
8. Mark your answer on your answer sheet.
9. Mark your answer on your answer sheet.
10. Mark your answer on your answer sheet.
11. Mark your answer on your answer sheet.
12. Mark your answer on your answer sheet.
13. Mark your answer on your answer sheet.
14. Mark your answer on your answer sheet.
15. Mark your answer on your answer sheet.
16. Mark your answer on your answer sheet.
17. Mark your answer on your answer sheet.
18. Mark your answer on your answer sheet.
19. Mark your answer on your answer sheet.
20. Mark your answer on your answer sheet.
21. Mark your answer on your answer sheet.
22. Mark your answer on your answer sheet.
23. Mark your answer on your answer sheet.
24. Mark your answer on your answer sheet.
25. Mark your answer on your answer sheet.
26. Mark your answer on your answer sheet.
27. Mark your answer on your answer sheet.
28. Mark your answer on your answer sheet.
29. Mark your answer on your answer sheet.
30. Mark your answer on your answer sheet.
31. Mark your answer on your answer sheet.

PART 3

Directions: You will hear some conversations between two or more people. You will be asked to answer three questions about what the speakers say in each conversation. Select the best response to each question and mark the letter (A), (B), (C), or (D) on your answer sheet. The conversations will not be printed in your test book and will be spoken only one time.

32. Where most likely does the woman work?
 (A) At a hospital
 (B) At a university
 (C) At a museum
 (D) At a restaurant

33. What does the man ask about?
 (A) How much a service costs
 (B) What classes are being taught
 (C) Which day is convenient
 (D) How busy a location is

34. What information will the woman provide next week?
 (A) A business's opening hours
 (B) A detailed schedule
 (C) The topic of a lecture
 (D) The number of visitors

35. Who most likely is the man?
 (A) A manager's assistant
 (B) An applicant for a grant
 (C) The director of a company
 (D) The keynote speaker at a convention

36. What is the woman doing this week?
 (A) Writing up a proposal
 (B) Attending a conference
 (C) Interviewing candidates
 (D) Training at a new company

37. Why does the man want to meet the woman?
 (A) To negotiate a deal
 (B) To prepare a presentation
 (C) To discuss a job opportunity
 (D) To introduce a coworker

38. Where most likely are the speakers?
 (A) At a clothing shop
 (B) At a grocery store
 (C) At a beauty salon
 (D) At a paint retailer

39. What do first-time customers receive?
 (A) A discount
 (B) A free item
 (C) A gift certificate
 (D) A membership card

40. What will the man most likely do next?
 (A) Make a purchase
 (B) Wash some hair
 (C) Choose a color
 (D) Provide a refund

41. Why is the man calling?
 (A) To complain about a rule
 (B) To place an order
 (C) To explain a service
 (D) To ask about a price

42. What problem does the man mention about the lawn mower?
 (A) It wasn't delivered on time.
 (B) It doesn't work properly.
 (C) It is the wrong model.
 (D) It was incorrectly priced.

43. What does the woman say she will do?
 (A) Contact a manager
 (B) Issue a refund
 (C) Organize a sales event
 (D) Repair a device

GO ON TO THE NEXT PAGE

44. What does the woman say she plans to do?
   (A) Go on a cruise
   (B) Write a negative review
   (C) Work some extra hours
   (D) Resign from her position

45. What do the men imply about Gulliver Travel?
   (A) It has poor customer service.
   (B) It offers discounts to its employees.
   (C) It has the cheapest cruises on the market.
   (D) It is more expensive than Blue Green Travel.

46. According to the woman, what happened at the company while the men were away?
   (A) A coworker left her job.
   (B) A customer made a complaint.
   (C) A new person was hired.
   (D) A survey was conducted.

47. What are the speakers mainly discussing?
   (A) An article's contents
   (B) A course's difficulty
   (C) A product's packaging
   (D) A beverage's price

48. Why does the man say, "they went a little too far"?
   (A) He finds a design childish.
   (B) He thinks a product is expensive.
   (C) He wants to relocate a branch.
   (D) He disagrees with a policy.

49. What does the woman say she will do?
   (A) Return an item
   (B) Report a choice
   (C) Create an advertisement
   (D) Contact some customers

50. What are the speakers mainly discussing?
   (A) A new opening
   (B) A job change
   (C) A customer complaint
   (D) An office layout

51. What does the woman say she is looking forward to?
   (A) Talking to people directly
   (B) Working with the man
   (C) Reading some reviews
   (D) Joining a new company

52. What does the man suggest the woman do?
   (A) File a complaint
   (B) Consult a coworker
   (C) Find a different job
   (D) Provide some advice

53. What will happen on August 8?
   (A) A business will be relocated.
   (B) An author will be interviewed.
   (C) A contract will be signed.
   (D) A book signing will be held.

54. What does the woman suggest doing?
   (A) Putting away some items
   (B) Registering for an event
   (C) Waiting in line
   (D) Moving some furniture

55. What does the man say he will do?
   (A) Prepare an advertisement
   (B) Reserve some tickets
   (C) Write a summary
   (D) Visit a venue

56. What has the woman recently done?

(A) Attended a lecture series
(B) Registered for an event
(C) Reviewed a research study
(D) Given a presentation

57. What does the woman think the man should do?

(A) Meet a speaker
(B) Extend a deadline
(C) Submit a study
(D) Choose a topic

58. What does the woman imply about a review she wrote?

(A) It is outdated.
(B) It will be published soon.
(C) It took a long time to make.
(D) It was presented at a conference.

---

59. Who most likely is the man?

(A) A secretary
(B) A dentist
(C) A plumber
(D) A nutritionist

60. Why does the woman say, "Drinking cold water causes it"?

(A) To suggest a possible treatment
(B) To describe a healthy habit
(C) To give details about her diet
(D) To explain when a problem occurs

61. What does the man recommend the woman do?

(A) Follow a personal hygiene routine
(B) Make an appointment with a doctor
(C) Avoid drinking sweet beverages
(D) Take some time off from work

Interview Hours

Time Slot	Day	Time
1	Monday	3:00 P.M.
2	Wednesday	10:30 A.M.
3	Wednesday	5:00 P.M.
4	Friday	1:45 P.M.

62. What was announced in an e-mail?

(A) An employee has been promoted.
(B) A new branch is opening.
(C) A deadline has been extended.
(D) A company is relocating.

63. What is the man hesitating to do?

(A) Accept an offer
(B) Apply for a position
(C) Choose a candidate
(D) Talk to a supervisor

64. Look at the graphic. Which time slot is the man able to attend?

(A) Time Slot 1
(B) Time Slot 2
(C) Time Slot 3
(D) Time Slot 4

GO ON TO THE NEXT PAGE

~ Special Menu ~
Each drink on the special menu
comes with a free pastry!

black coffee ⟶ croissant		$2.50
single latte ⟶ éclair		$3.00
mocha ⟶ Danish		$3.50
cappuccino ⟶ cinnamon roll		$3.50

	Maximum passengers	Transmission
Vehicle 1	5	Manual
Vehicle 2	5	Automatic
Vehicle 3	8	Manual
Vehicle 4	8	Automatic

65. What does the woman ask about?

(A) What food is available
(B) How much an item costs
(C) Which coffee is best
(D) Where a menu is located

66. Look at the graphic. Which pastry will the woman get?

(A) A croissant
(B) An éclair
(C) A Danish
(D) A cinnamon roll

67. Why is the woman surprised?

(A) The prices have been lowered.
(B) The shop closes late.
(C) The menu options have changed.
(D) The coffee is strong.

68. Why does the man prefer renting a car to taking the train?

(A) It is cheaper.
(B) It is more convenient.
(C) It is faster.
(D) It is more reliable.

69. Look at the graphic. Which vehicle will the woman most likely reserve?

(A) Vehicle 1
(B) Vehicle 2
(C) Vehicle 3
(D) Vehicle 4

70. What does the man ask the woman?

(A) Where they will park
(B) How many people will drive
(C) How much the rental will cost
(D) When they should leave

PART 4

Directions: You will hear some talks given by a single speaker. You will be asked to answer three questions about what the speaker says in each talk. Select the best response to each question and mark the letter (A), (B), (C), or (D) on your answer sheet. The talks will not be printed in your test book and will be spoken only one time.

71. What industry does the speaker work in?
    (A) Entertainment
    (B) Fashion
    (C) Automobile
    (D) Marketing

72. According to the speaker, what should the company focus on?
    (A) More comfortable products
    (B) Better customer service
    (C) More competitive prices
    (D) Safer designs

73. What will the listeners most likely do next?
    (A) Look at some designs
    (B) Test-drive some vehicles
    (C) Try on some clothes
    (D) Review some materials

74. What type of business does the speaker work for?
    (A) An insurance company
    (B) A real estate agency
    (C) A law firm
    (D) An accounting business

75. What does the speaker mention about the position?
    (A) Its salary can be negotiated.
    (B) Its location has been changed.
    (C) Its start date is fixed.
    (D) Its duties require advanced skills.

76. What is the listener asked to do?
    (A) Come in for an interview
    (B) Return a phone call
    (C) Submit a job application
    (D) Modify a schedule

77. What department do the listeners most likely work in?
    (A) Human resources
    (B) Marketing
    (C) Accounting
    (D) Customer service

78. What can listeners find in the document the speaker sent last week?
    (A) Contract terms
    (B) Benefit options
    (C) Employee information
    (D) Required qualifications

79. What should listeners do by Wednesday?
    (A) Read about some occupations
    (B) Review job applications
    (C) Advertise a job opening
    (D) Update a Web site

80. What is the speaker preparing for?
    (A) Hosting an event
    (B) Entering a contest
    (C) Moving to a new location
    (D) Installing new equipment

81. Why does the speaker say, "The total is fourteen"?
    (A) To request a payment
    (B) To report the number of participants
    (C) To explain a policy
    (D) To provide the number of lectures

82. What does the speaker offer to do?
    (A) Apply a discount
    (B) Arrange a pickup
    (C) Postpone a meeting
    (D) Send directions

GO ON TO THE NEXT PAGE

83. According to the speaker, what recently happened?

    (A) A branch was opened.
    (B) Two companies merged.
    (C) A product was launched.
    (D) A restaurant changed its menu.

84. What did Mr. Boyle study in graduate school?

    (A) Cooking
    (B) Business administration
    (C) Italian
    (D) Art

85. What is Mr. Boyle currently doing?

    (A) Touring a restaurant
    (B) Designing a menu
    (C) Ordering some food
    (D) Attending a class

86. What type of business has the caller reached?

    (A) A communications provider
    (B) An electronics manufacturer
    (C) A Web design company
    (D) A device repair shop

87. What problem does the speaker mention?

    (A) A service is slow.
    (B) A machine is defective.
    (C) A delivery is delayed.
    (D) A Web site is down.

88. Why should callers press 0?

    (A) To upgrade a plan
    (B) To report an issue
    (C) To cancel an order
    (D) To request a refund

89. Who most likely are the listeners?

    (A) Visiting clients
    (B) Retired employees
    (C) Branch managers
    (D) New workers

90. What is the purpose of the talk?

    (A) To outline some rules
    (B) To announce break times
    (C) To introduce a new manager
    (D) To assess a performance

91. Why does the speaker say, "We work in close proximity to one another"?

    (A) To justify a policy
    (B) To provide directions
    (C) To explain a layout
    (D) To demand respect

92. Who most likely will the speaker interview next week?

    (A) Computer repair technicians
    (B) Sales executives
    (C) Graphic designers
    (D) Laboratory researchers

93. What does the speaker mean when she says, "it was twice what we expected"?

    (A) A job opening got many applicants.
    (B) A company's market share grew significantly.
    (C) A candidate requested a larger salary.
    (D) A hiring process took longer than planned.

94. According to the speaker, what will Timothy do?

    (A) Reserve a conference room for an interview
    (B) Review the résumés of applicants
    (C) Create a vacation schedule for the team
    (D) Find volunteers to give up their workspaces

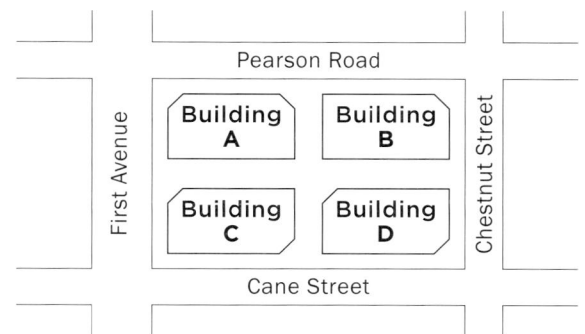

95. Look at the graphic. Which building is under construction?
    (A) Building A
    (B) Building B
    (C) Building C
    (D) Building D

96. What has caused a delay in the construction project?
    (A) Insufficient materials
    (B) A car accident
    (C) Weather conditions
    (D) Financial problems

97. What will take place this afternoon?
    (A) A grand opening
    (B) A sales event
    (C) An anniversary party
    (D) An artisan fair

98. What is the speaker in charge of doing?
    (A) Assuring the quality of goods
    (B) Overseeing the hiring process
    (C) Promoting the company's products
    (D) Repairing production equipment

99. Who most likely are the listeners?
    (A) Safety inspectors
    (B) New employees
    (C) Potential investors
    (D) Department managers

100. Look at the graphic. In which area will the listeners spend the shortest amount of time?
    (A) Zone A
    (B) Zone B
    (C) Zone C
    (D) Zone D

This is the end of the Listening Test. Turn to Part 5 in your test book.

READING TEST

In the Reading test, you will read a variety of texts and answer several different types of reading comprehension questions. The entire Reading test will last 75 minutes. There are three parts, and directions are given for each part. You are encouraged to answer as many questions as possible within the time allowed.

You must mark your answers on the separate answer sheet. Do not write your answers in the test book.

PART 5

Directions: A word or phrase is missing in each of the sentences below. Four answer choices are given below each sentence. Select the best answer to complete the sentence. Then mark the letter (A), (B), (C), or (D) on your answer sheet.

101. You may buy tickets for the May 11 concert in advance ------- at the door.
    (A) for
    (B) so
    (C) or
    (D) nor

102. For her lecture, Bridget Coleman provided ------- of foreign terms commonly used in court.
    (A) translate
    (B) translated
    (C) translator
    (D) translations

103. Most of Margos Electronics' devices are manufactured ------- factories overseas.
    (A) by
    (B) about
    (C) past
    (D) along

104. The team leader is too busy to pick up Colcott's CEO at the airport -------.
    (A) her
    (B) she
    (C) hers
    (D) herself

105. The ------- purpose of this meeting is to review our safety procedures.
    (A) primary
    (B) rigorous
    (C) plentiful
    (D) timely

106. Despite practicing, Peter Bertrand was not ------- prepared for the questions the interviewers asked him.
    (A) suffice
    (B) sufficiency
    (C) sufficient
    (D) sufficiently

107. Before his business trip to Mexico, Mr. Marcus studied Spanish so that he could ------- with the locals.
    (A) state
    (B) communicate
    (C) reserve
    (D) understand

108. ------- attendee will be given a folder with the program and notes about each presenter.
    (A) Every
    (B) Few
    (C) Several
    (D) All

109. Recent ------- in various scientific fields have caused a sudden increase in life expectancy.
    (A) developments
    (B) versions
    (C) timelines
    (D) ranges

110. Ms. Mander added six names to the ------- dinner guest list, bringing the number of expected diners up to twenty-three.
    (A) origin
    (B) originate
    (C) original
    (D) originally

111. The spring line of Vivi Fashion House's leather handbags was ------- at last week's runway show.
    (A) consulted
    (B) relieved
    (C) attempted
    (D) unveiled

112. Volunteers ------- in the lobby of the building at 11:00 A.M. next Saturday to prepare the fundraising event.
    (A) gathered
    (B) have gathered
    (C) will be gathering
    (D) will have been gathering

113. We can meet anytime that is convenient for you since my schedule is more flexible than -------.
    (A) you
    (B) yourself
    (C) your
    (D) yours

114. Gibson Department Store handed out small bags of free samples to customers to thank them for ------- its grand opening event.
    (A) attend
    (B) attending
    (C) attendee
    (D) attendance

115. Passengers traveling in first class are permitted to check in a maximum ------- three suitcases each.
    (A) up
    (B) beyond
    (C) of
    (D) to

116. Strict ------- with the company's policies is expected from employees at all times.
    (A) application
    (B) compliance
    (C) management
    (D) correction

117. Please enter the building through the north door, ------- is located on Sacramento Street.
    (A) who
    (B) what
    (C) where
    (D) which

118. According to the news anchor, the virus infected ------- ten thousand computers in just a few minutes.
    (A) approximate
    (B) approximately
    (C) approximates
    (D) approximation

119. Flucos Clothing plans on making a series of advertisements to appeal to a ------- clientele.
    (A) diverse
    (B) correct
    (C) usual
    (D) descriptive

120. This study indicates that customers would ------- shop online than try on items in a store.
    (A) further
    (B) probably
    (C) rather
    (D) mistakenly

121. The new revelations about the emission of harmful gases by its factories has ------- as an issue for the company.
    (A) become
    (B) emerged
    (C) resulted
    (D) produced

122. Given the complex layout of the city, ------- the location of the Portville branch was difficult.
    (A) choosing
    (B) choice
    (C) choose
    (D) chosen

123. The restaurant manager reviewed food safety ------- with his staff to prepare for the monthly inspection.
    (A) regulating
    (B) regulated
    (C) regulations
    (D) regulates

124. To view a ------- explanation of presidential candidate Ann Lathrup's economic plans, visit her campaign Web site.
    (A) repeated
    (B) customized
    (C) testified
    (D) detailed

125. In order to receive a full refund for a returned item, the receipt ------- to the cashier.
    (A) presented
    (B) has presented
    (C) would be presenting
    (D) must be presented

126. By offering ------- prices, Ergo Supermarkets has become one of the most successful grocery stores in the area.
    (A) competed
    (B) competing
    (C) competitive
    (D) competitively

127. Abigail Hoskins was given a certificate of appreciation by the city ------- her efforts in improving educational standards.
    (A) for
    (B) into
    (C) because
    (D) when

128. Even though Maria's Grill is only ------- closer to the center of town, it gets a lot more customers than Primavera's.
    (A) slightly
    (B) overwhelmingly
    (C) carefully
    (D) popularly

129. The designer used a new type of software ------- the brochure advertising the convention.
    (A) creates
    (B) will create
    (C) to create
    (D) created

130. Management decided to hire Amy Volpert in spite of the ------- in her educational background because of her experience as an intern.
    (A) attainments
    (B) shortcomings
    (C) submissions
    (D) qualifications

PART 6

Directions: Read the texts that follow. A word, phrase, or sentence is missing in parts of each text. Four answer choices for each question are given below the text. Select the best answer to complete the text. Then mark the letter (A), (B), (C), or (D) on your answer sheet.

Questions 131-134 refer to the following e-mail.

To: Margaret Keeble <m_keeble@tysoncomm.com>
From: Juan Torres <j_torres@tysoncomm.com>
Date: November 18
Subject: Keep up the good work!

Dear Ms. Keeble,

I would like to thank you for handling the situation when Ms. Ferona came to our office upset because of a billing error. It is not always easy to know what to do in these situations, but the way you handled it was -------. Pleasing our clients is an important part of the job. -------, we can't give
        131.   **132.**
them everything they demand. This would have a detrimental effect on our finances. By explaining the reason for the error in a calm manner, you resolved the conflict quickly. -------. The other
                                                                                                          133.
managers and I agree that you deserve ------- from your hard work. Therefore, you will be given an
                                          134.
extra day of paid vacation.

Congratulations!

Juan Torres
Office Manager, Tyson Communications

---

131. (A) feasible
(B) appropriate
(C) steady
(D) affordable

132. (A) In addition
(B) Even if
(C) Nonetheless
(D) For instance

133. (A) Ms. Ferona will oversee this area from now on.
(B) We have already reprinted your new bill showing the change.
(C) It was also a good example to set for our junior staff members.
(D) The company will upgrade its billing software soon.

134. (A) to benefit
(B) will benefit
(C) being benefits
(D) it benefitted

Questions 135-138 refer to the following article.

March 16, Narton—A new library ------- in the center of the small town of Narton will be opening its doors next month. The Narton Library will hold a collection of books, magazines, and videos on all topics. In addition, it will offer free Internet access, host regular events, and provide various workshops to ------- the community. "I think this library will be extremely helpful," indicated ------- resident Samuel Prendy. "Narton is isolated in a remote location, and it is difficult for us to stay up-to-date on all the latest information." Mayor Brenkel is scheduled to give a speech at the opening ceremony on April 2. -------. For more information about it, check Narton's official Web site.

135. (A) will be located
 (B) locating
 (C) is located
 (D) located

136. (A) serve
 (B) organize
 (C) request
 (D) visit

137. (A) expert
 (B) dependent
 (C) local
 (D) active

138. (A) All are invited to attend this event.
 (B) It will be announced on that day.
 (C) You can pick up your books at that time.
 (D) He was elected with a large majority.

Questions 139-142 refer to the following notice.

As you know, the company donates to the F&Y homeless shelter every year. This year, instead of money, we have decided to donate various goods that the shelter is in need of. You'll see bins at the entrance of each department head's office. Employees are ------- (139.) to place items in good condition into these bins. When a bin is ------- (140.), it will be picked up by PR staff and taken to the shelter. A list of acceptable items will be posted in the staff lounge. ------- (141.). In particular, note that although clothing is welcome, certain ------- (142.) are not accepted due to common allergies and limited washing options. Thank you in advance for your donations.

139. (A) encouragement
(B) encourage
(C) encouraging
(D) encouraged

140. (A) open
(B) full
(C) finished
(D) consumed

141. (A) Please consult it carefully before placing anything in a bin.
(B) You may take anything that seems necessary to you.
(C) However, entrance is restricted to upper management only.
(D) If you agree with the terms, you may sign below.

142. (A) methods
(B) amounts
(C) materials
(D) payments

Questions 143-146 refer to the following letter.

September 14

Sterling Murray
25 Morocco Drive
Newtown, PA 18777

Dear Mr. Murray,

It is our pleasure to award you first place in the Graper Scientific Research Competition for your paper entitled "Quality Control in Pharmaceuticals: Testing Three Methods." The study you conducted and your findings were fascinating. -------. We trust that the rest of the readers in the scientific community will find your work -------. In addition, you ------- $2,500 for further research. We hope that this will help in your future endeavors. Congratulations, and thank you for your ------- to the field of medicine.

Sincerely,

Richard Nelson
Director, Graper Science

---

143. (A) We highly recommend that you read this study.
(B) Many contestants have entered the competition.
(C) However, most of the information was already well-known.
(D) Your article will appear in next month's *Graper Science News*.

144. (A) inspires
(B) inspire
(C) inspirational
(D) inspiration

145. (A) will grant
(B) would have been granted
(C) would have granted
(D) will be granted

146. (A) distinction
(B) survey
(C) contribution
(D) knowledge

PART 7

Directions: In this part, you will read a selection of texts, such as magazine and newspaper articles, e-mails, and instant messages. Each text or set of texts is followed by several questions. Select the best answer for each question and mark the letter (A), (B), (C), or (D) on your answer sheet.

Questions 147-148 refer to the following e-mail.

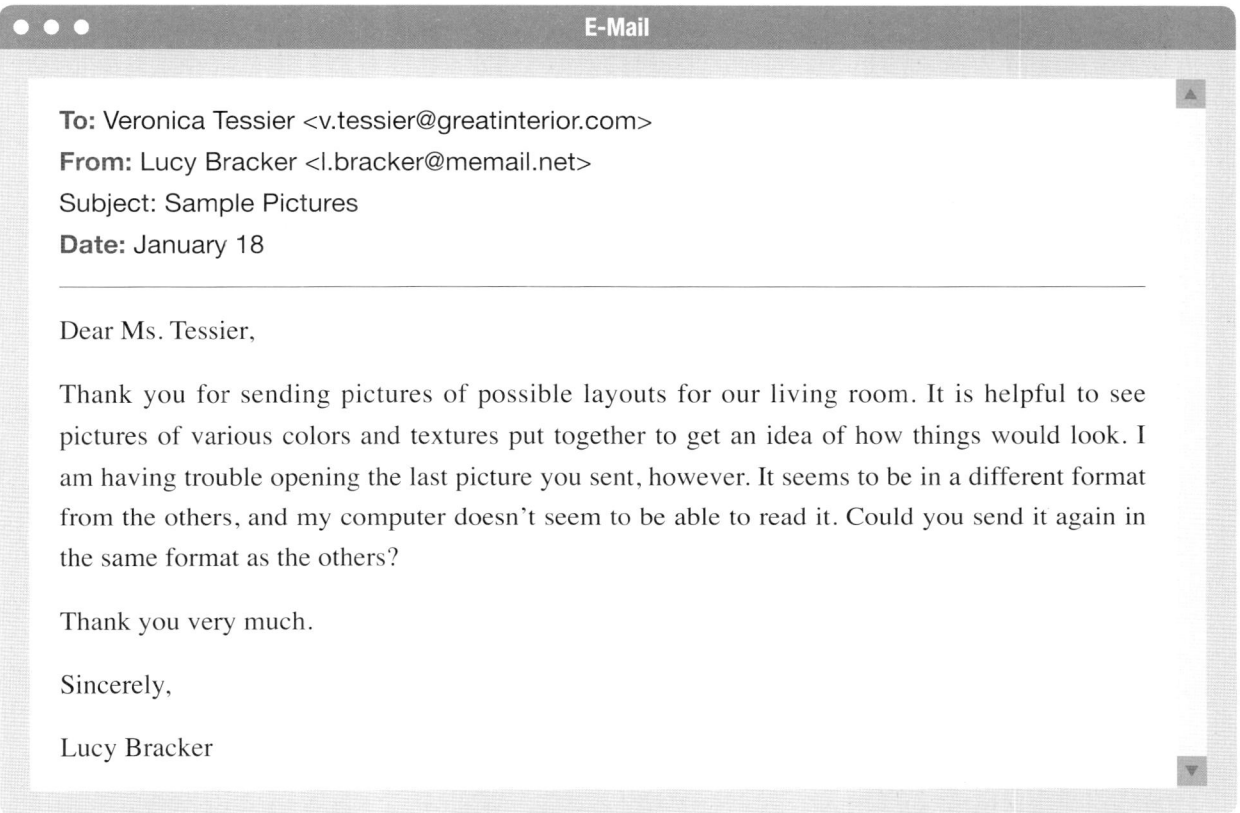

To: Veronica Tessier <v.tessier@greatinterior.com>
From: Lucy Bracker <l.bracker@memail.net>
Subject: Sample Pictures
Date: January 18

Dear Ms. Tessier,

Thank you for sending pictures of possible layouts for our living room. It is helpful to see pictures of various colors and textures put together to get an idea of how things would look. I am having trouble opening the last picture you sent, however. It seems to be in a different format from the others, and my computer doesn't seem to be able to read it. Could you send it again in the same format as the others?

Thank you very much.

Sincerely,

Lucy Bracker

147. Who most likely is Ms. Tessier?

(A) A professional photographer
(B) An interior designer
(C) An IT expert
(D) An art gallery owner

148. What problem is Ms. Bracker having?

(A) She doesn't have enough space.
(B) She doesn't like the color combinations.
(C) She is unable to view a file.
(D) She didn't receive an e-mail.

Questions 149-150 refer to the following calendar.

Mercer Real Estate New Employee Orientation Schedule

AUGUST						
Sunday	Monday	Tuesday	Wednesday	Thursday	Friday	Saturday
	1	2	3	4 OR	5	6
7	8	9	10	11	12	13
14	15	16	17	18	19	20
21	22	23	24 DA	25	26 PRO	27
28	29 FFD	30	31			

OR: First day of orientation. Walk-through of premises

DA: Individual department assignments announced

PRO: Pictures taken and creation of Web site profiles

FFD: First full day compensated as a full-time employee

149. On which day will employees tour the facilities?
    (A) August 4
    (B) August 24
    (C) August 26
    (D) August 29

150. What is indicated about the company's Web site pictures?
    (A) They are required for finding one's department.
    (B) They must be submitted on the first day of work.
    (C) They are taken after departments have been assigned.
    (D) They should be brought to work by employees on August 26.

Questions 151-152 refer to the following text-message chain.

Jimmie Kristof [3:08 P.M.]
Rebecca, have you made arrangements for going to the conference next Monday?

Rebecca Pauly [3:09 P.M.]
I thought the company was taking care of that. Aren't they providing a bus for us?

Jimmie Kristof [3:10 P.M.]
No. They decided not to after all. So most people are taking the subway or driving.

Rebecca Pauly [3:13 P.M.]
Then I guess I'll drive. There aren't any subway stations near my place. But I've never been to that venue. I have no idea how to get there.

Jimmie Kristof [3:14 P.M.]
Well, that's why I contacted you. I was wondering if you'd like me to pick you up.

Rebecca Pauly [3:15 P.M.]
That would be much easier for me. Are you sure you don't mind?

Jimmie Kristof [3:17 P.M.]
Of course not. Your house is on my way. And I've been to that hall many times before.

---

151. What is indicated about the writers' company?

(A) It is not handling transportation for employees.
(B) It has offices located near a subway station.
(C) It is organizing an event for its employees.
(D) It is moving to a new location.

152. At 3:15 P.M., what does Ms. Pauly mean when she writes, "That would be much easier for me"?

(A) She prefers to go by bus.
(B) She would like Mr. Kristof to drive her.
(C) She can pick up Mr. Kristof at the conference.
(D) She doesn't mind taking the subway.

Questions 153-155 refer to the following advertisement.

CLARENCE CO.

Clarence Co. provides the best service in the area for businesses that are relocating. We provide a variety of options so that your transition to the new location is as smooth as possible.

If you sign up for our deluxe package, we will provide the following services:
- Unlimited plastic crates for packing belongings
- Packing of large equipment and furniture
- Special packing by our IT experts for your computers and other electronics
- Loading and unloading of all items
- Special clean-up service from our sister company, Sparkly Clean

Call us today at 553-0295 to schedule a time for us to come take a look at your facilities. We will provide a free estimate for our services.

---

153. What kind of company is Clarence Co.?

(A) A machinery manufacturer
(B) A delivery service
(C) A moving company
(D) A marketing consultant

154. What is indicated about Clarence Co.?

(A) It partners with a cleaning company.
(B) It can fix broken devices.
(C) It has branches in several locations.
(D) It is currently offering free upgrades.

155. What can customers learn if they have a consultation?

(A) How to set up some equipment
(B) How much they will have to pay
(C) Where to relocate their business
(D) When a delivery will be made

Questions 156-158 refer to the following online review.

Hotel Review: Bashiva Hotel, 1882 Hummingbird Way

Rating: ★★★★☆
Name: Stella Manning
Date(s) of stay: January 18–20 **Room type:** Regular Single Room

I stayed at Bashiva Hotel for two nights. I was on a business trip to meet some clients. Bashiva Hotel was ideal for my purposes. The rooms are comfortable, and the breakfast buffet is nice and well worth the price. — [1] —. Most importantly, despite being in a busy area of the city, I didn't hear much noise at night.

I chose this hotel because of its proximity to the downtown area. It was convenient for finding restaurants and getting to my meetings. — [2] —. I was supposed to catch a train early in the afternoon. I asked the front desk to call a taxi. I had to wait about fifteen minutes for it to arrive. — [3] —. Then, although the hotel staff said it would take about twenty minutes to get to the train station, it took closer to forty-five minutes. — [4] —. Fortunately, I managed to make it on time for my train because I had left early. However, all of this hassle could have been avoided had there been a bus from the hotel. The hotel already offers rides to and from the airport, but I think many of its guests come by train. Offering rides to the station as well would be very helpful.

---

156. What does Ms. Manning indicate about the hotel?

(A) It provides free breakfast.
(B) It is very noisy during the night.
(C) It is located near the city center.
(D) It is twenty minutes away from an airport.

157. In which of the positions marked [1], [2], [3], and [4] does the following sentence best belong?

"The only issue I had was when I was leaving."

(A) [1]
(B) [2]
(C) [3]
(D) [4]

158. What does Ms. Manning want the hotel to do?

(A) Add a shuttle service
(B) Adjust a timetable
(C) Clean its facilities
(D) Hire more staff

Questions 159-160 refer to the following notice.

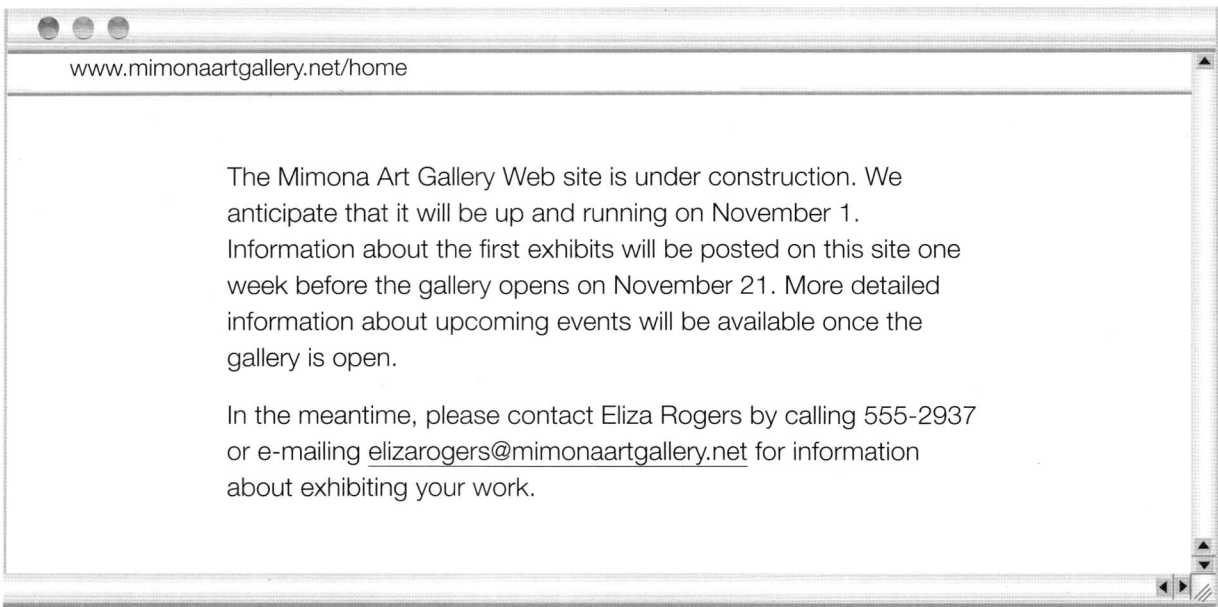

www.mimonaartgallery.net/home

The Mimona Art Gallery Web site is under construction. We anticipate that it will be up and running on November 1. Information about the first exhibits will be posted on this site one week before the gallery opens on November 21. More detailed information about upcoming events will be available once the gallery is open.

In the meantime, please contact Eliza Rogers by calling 555-2937 or e-mailing elizarogers@mimonaartgallery.net for information about exhibiting your work.

159. What is the purpose of the notice?

(A) To request reviews of an exhibit
(B) To announce the opening of a gallery
(C) To advertise artwork available for sale
(D) To provide a timeline for a new Web page

160. Why should Eliza Rogers be contacted?

(A) To make an appointment for a visit
(B) To purchase a work of art
(C) To ask about displaying artwork
(D) To register for an event

Questions 161-163 refer to the following e-mail.

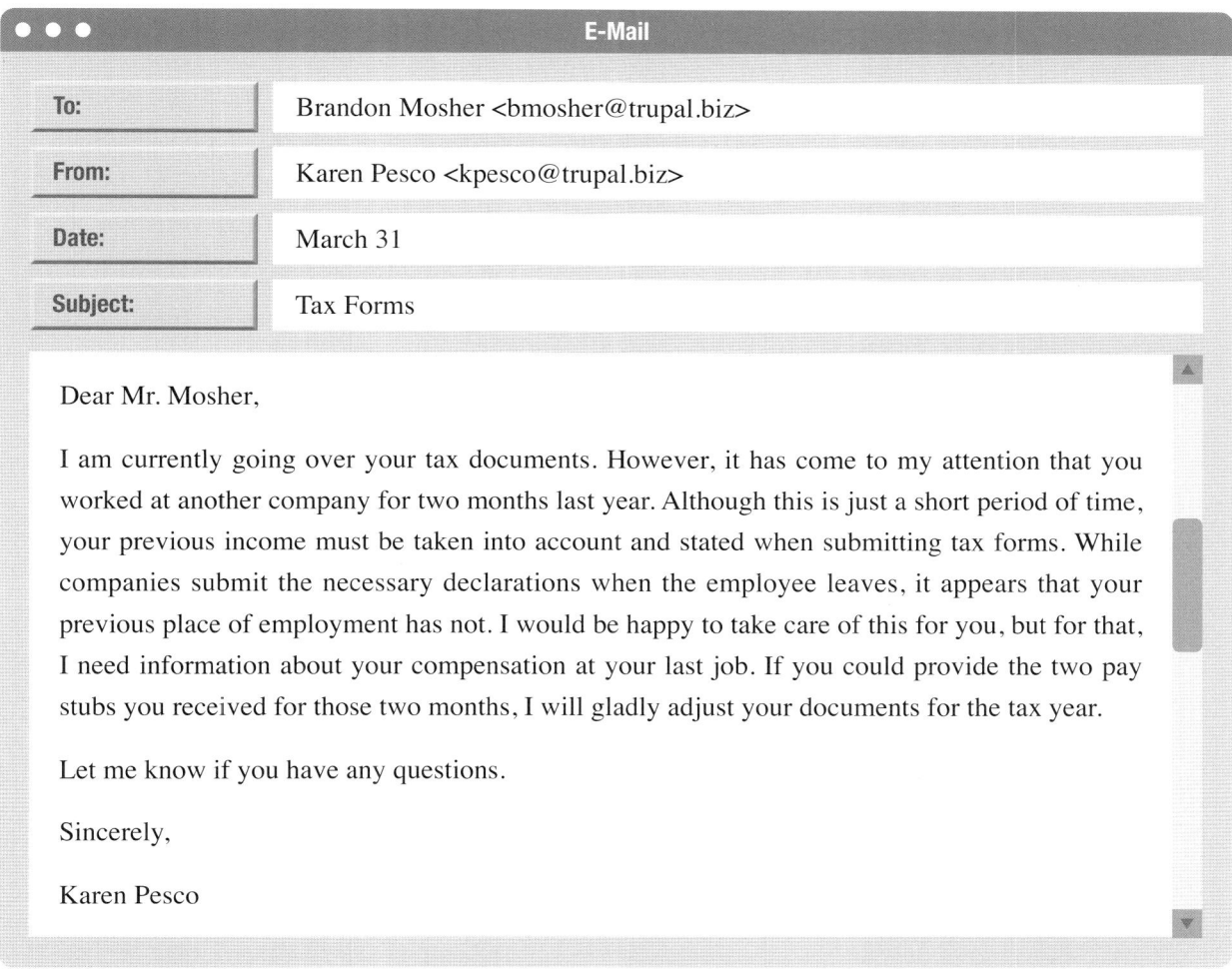

To: Brandon Mosher <bmosher@trupal.biz>
From: Karen Pesco <kpesco@trupal.biz>
Date: March 31
Subject: Tax Forms

Dear Mr. Mosher,

I am currently going over your tax documents. However, it has come to my attention that you worked at another company for two months last year. Although this is just a short period of time, your previous income must be taken into account and stated when submitting tax forms. While companies submit the necessary declarations when the employee leaves, it appears that your previous place of employment has not. I would be happy to take care of this for you, but for that, I need information about your compensation at your last job. If you could provide the two pay stubs you received for those two months, I will gladly adjust your documents for the tax year.

Let me know if you have any questions.

Sincerely,

Karen Pesco

161. In what department does Ms. Pesco most likely work?
(A) Accounting
(B) Marketing
(C) Customer service
(D) Research and Development

162. What problem does Ms. Pesco mention?
(A) Some income must be declared.
(B) A payment has been rejected.
(C) A tax rate has increased.
(D) Lots of employees have quit.

163. What does Ms. Pesco ask Mr. Mosher for?
(A) A job description
(B) Salary records
(C) Proof of employment
(D) Tax schedules

Questions 164-167 refer to the following online chat discussion.

	Clyde Mortensen [10:40 A.M.]	Hi, Jennifer and Henry. I want to get started on the design for the April issue's cover. Do you know who we are interviewing for the main article?
	Jennifer Sydnor [10:41 A.M.]	It's going to be Jeff Blasio, a chef from an upcoming cooking show. I'll be writing that article, actually. I'm interviewing him next Tuesday.
	Henry Tessor [10:42 A.M.]	And I'm the photographer for this one. So I'll be there on Tuesday as well to do the photo shoot of Mr. Blasio.
	Clyde Mortensen [10:44 A.M.]	Oh, let me know when you're done. It would help to know what topics will be covered in the article and what the pictures will look like.
	Jennifer Sydnor [10:45 A.M.]	How about we all meet on Wednesday? Henry, you can show us your pictures, and I can tell you both about the interview.
	Clyde Mortensen [10:47 A.M.]	That works for me. I think the covers work best when the designers collaborate with the writers and photographers.
	Henry Tessor [10:48 A.M.]	I couldn't agree more. Wednesday works for me too. Morning or afternoon? I can meet at any time.
	Clyde Mortensen [10:49 A.M.]	The morning would be much better for me. Let's say at ten.
	Jennifer Sydnor [10:50 A.M.]	Ten is good. I'll see you two then.

164. Where do the writers most likely work?

(A) At a photo studio
(B) At a restaurant
(C) At a design firm
(D) At a magazine publisher

165. What is indicated about Mr. Blasio?

(A) He owns a popular restaurant.
(B) He will be on television.
(C) He writes for a magazine.
(D) He applied for a new job.

166. What will Mr. Tessor do on Tuesday?

(A) Create an advertisement
(B) Take some pictures
(C) Write an article
(D) Choose a menu

167. At 10:48 A.M., what does Mr. Tessor most likely mean when he writes, "I couldn't agree more"?

(A) He doesn't like the design of one of the projects.
(B) He believes pictures are the most important element.
(C) He thinks people from different departments should work together.
(D) He isn't sure what topics will be covered in the interview.

Questions 168-171 refer to the following article.

Broken Pearls to Be Performed at the Marina Theater

January 21—*Broken Pearls*, a play in three acts, will be performed at the Marina Theater in Dresdon on February 13, 14, and 15. The script was written by Maria Deluz, who also directed the play. It will be the Marina Theater's first modern-era play. — [1] —.

Because of a limited marketing budget and a rather low-profile cast, the premiere, which was at the Golden Volcano Theater in Henryville, did not attract a large audience. However, the performance received such good reviews that the troupe was encouraged to start a tour of the region and perform at various local venues. — [2] —. What sent the play's popularity skyrocketing was one review in particular, by notorious critic Joshua Corbett. Mr. Corbett, who is known for his strict and often scathing reviews, called *Broken Pearls* "a jewel of modern theater" in a long-form article. Thus, the play suddenly went from obscure piece to famous work. — [3] —.

"We never expected *Broken Pearls* to become such a hit," lead actor Jeremy Moriah explained. "It is all very exciting. I look forward to performing at new venues. I hope to even travel overseas for a show someday." — [4] —. Indeed, several venues around Europe have contacted production manager Isabelle Morton about possible future events.

168. What is implied about the Marina Theater?

(A) It usually shows performances of older works.
(B) It has already hosted *Broken Pearls* several times.
(C) It has become Dresdon's most popular theater.
(D) It received a lot of negative reviews in the past.

169. What is indicated about the play's troupe?

(A) It spent a lot of money on advertising.
(B) It is composed of little-known actors.
(C) It is used to performing in renowned venues.
(D) It has performed in a variety of countries.

170. According to the article, who contributed the most to the play's popularity?

(A) Maria Deluz
(B) Joshua Corbett
(C) Jeremy Moriah
(D) Isabelle Morton

171. In which of the positions marked [1], [2], [3], and [4] does the following sentence best belong?

"This dream might just become a reality."

(A) [1]
(B) [2]
(C) [3]
(D) [4]

Questions 172-175 refer to the following information.

Langda Goods Terms and Conditions

Thank you for choosing Langda Goods to carry your luggage on your next trip. All Langda luggage is covered by our one-year warranty. Please inspect your parcel carefully upon receiving it. If any part of the product is damaged, do not throw away any part of the product or its packaging. Immediately inform the delivery company. They will pick up the damaged goods and provide you with a claim form to fill out and a claim number. You may then follow the progress of your request on our Web site. It may take up to three weeks to review a claim.

A replacement will be sent to the customer if any of the following cases is reported within one year of purchase:
– Flaws in workmanship or material
– Tearing of the material
– Broken part
– Wearing of the wheels
– Color fading

Please note that in case of the following events, the customer is fully liable for the article and is entitled to no compensation:
– Unreasonable usage
– Staining
– Loss or theft

172. What is suggested about the recipients of the information?

(A) They have tried to return an item.
(B) They have recently purchased some luggage.
(C) They have just signed a contract with Langda Goods.
(D) They have posted a negative review of Langda Goods.

173. What does Langda Goods ask customers NOT to do if they receive a damaged item?

(A) Discard broken parts
(B) Notify the deliverer
(C) Complete a document
(D) Wait for a response

174. What can customers do on the Langda Goods Web site?

(A) Request faster delivery service
(B) Fill out a complaint form
(C) Check the status of a claim
(D) Extend the warranty of an item

175. In which case can a customer get a replacement?

(A) If the item is stolen.
(B) If the product has defects.
(C) If the material becomes stained.
(D) If the luggage is overused.

Questions 176-180 refer to the following flyer and form.

Arnett Co.

Arnett Co. has been providing high-quality services for the past five years. From May 1 to October 31, we're here to help you keep your yard and garden in excellent condition. We can provide mowing, tree-trimming, and weeding on a weekly or biweekly basis. If you are interested in having trees, flowers, or bushes planted, we can get you a discount with our partners at the Pineway Greenhouse, a reliable local business.

We have lots of returning customers every season, but slots are still available even if you've never used our services before. Please note that we do not serve corporate properties. If you'd like advice about the best way to care for your yard, we'll send one of our technicians to your home for a consultation at no charge. The monthly charge* for our basic service (mowing and cleanup only) is $425 for weekly visits or $250 for biweekly visits. There is also a premium service (the basic service plus weeding, bush trimming, and fertilizer treatments) for $675 for weekly visits or $450 for biweekly visits. Call us today at 555-5588.

*Applies to standard lots only. For oversized lots, please call to inquire about our rates.

Arnett Co. – New Customer Information

Customer: Vickie Warnick
Property: 226 Sunburst Drive, Portland, OR 97221
Lot Type: Standard
*Equipment: Lawnmower (model: Duncan-440)
Type of Service requested: [ ] Basic   [X] Premium
                               [ ] Weekly   [X] Biweekly
Start Date of Service: June 2

- -

Consultation Date: May 26   **Property Assessed by:** Robert Cass

* If the customer prefers to use his/her own equipment, list the type and model name above.

176. What is the purpose of the flyer?

(A) To announce a change in ownership
(B) To promote a gardening care business
(C) To advertise a sales event
(D) To introduce a new service

177. What is indicated about Arnett Co.?

(A) It collaborates with a greenhouse.
(B) It accepts bookings by e-mail.
(C) It sells several varieties of plants and flowers.
(D) It offers services year-round.

178. What is NOT mentioned about Arnett Co.?

(A) It only caters to residential properties.
(B) It is not currently accepting new customers.
(C) It has different prices for standard and oversized lots.
(D) It offers a free consultation.

179. What is suggested about Ms. Warnick?

(A) She will receive a discount for the first month.
(B) She wants her own equipment to be used.
(C) She was referred to Arnett Co. by a friend.
(D) She has a property that is larger than average.

180. How much will Ms. Warnick be charged per month?

(A) $250
(B) $425
(C) $450
(D) $675

GO ON TO THE NEXT PAGE

Questions 181-185 refer to the following e-mails.

To: Gladwell Finance <info@gladwellfinance.com>
From: Keith Angulo <k.angulo@irvinemail.net>
Date: November 17
Subject: Transfer issue

To Whom It May Concern:

I tried to send money to my cousin in Vancouver using your online money transfer service. I applied a $5 credit toward the fees, which I got from signing up for your newsletter. He was able to pick up the cash at the Vancouver branch. However, after the transaction was completed, I noticed that I had been charged the full amount for the transfer fee. I looked over my account history to make sure I hadn't already used the credit, and I confirmed that I hadn't. However, the credit is no longer listed on my account. Please let me know why there was a problem with this transaction, request #45960, and what can be done to resolve it.

Thank you,

Keith Angulo

To: Keith Angulo <k.angulo@irvinemail.net>
From: Gladwell Finance <info@gladwellfinance.com>
Date: November 18
Subject: RE: Transfer issue

Dear Mr. Angulo,

On behalf of Gladwell Finance, I would like to apologize for the inconvenience you experienced. You did not mention the date that you sent the funds, but I was able to find it by using the number you provided. We were experiencing some problems when our internal server went down for a brief period on November 16, and this affected some customers. I have reissued you a credit of $5 to make up for the discount you should have gotten. My manager, Patrick Ogden, has also given me authorization to issue you a further $10 credit due to your inconvenience. This credit can be used toward our processing fees. You can verify that these amounts have been credited to you by clicking on the My Balance link after logging into your online account. You can use the credit anytime at your discretion. Should you have any further problems, you can call 555-3940, extension 31, rather than our customer service hotline. That way, you can get straight through to me.

Sincerely,

Brielle Stewart

181. What did Mr. Angulo do before contacting Gladwell Finance?

    (A) He heard about the problem from his cousin.
    (B) He received an invoice in the mail.
    (C) He checked his past transactions.
    (D) He reviewed his credit card bill.

182. What did Ms. Stewart use to look into Mr. Angulo's complaint?

    (A) His transaction code
    (B) His account number
    (C) His request date
    (D) His credit balance

183. In the second e-mail, the phrase "went down" in paragraph 1, line 3, is closest in meaning to

    (A) deflated
    (B) malfunctioned
    (C) decreased
    (D) lost

184. How can Mr. Angulo confirm that a credit was received?

    (A) By reviewing an online page
    (B) By checking a printed receipt
    (C) By requesting a paper statement
    (D) By e-mailing Ms. Stewart's manager

185. What is Mr. Angulo told to do if he has more issues?

    (A) Call a customer service hotline
    (B) Request a contract termination
    (C) File a formal complaint online
    (D) Contact Ms. Stewart directly

Questions 186-190 refer to the following summary, flyer, and review.

Portrait Pro

Portrait Pro is a four-part series for people who have already mastered the basics of oil on canvas and want to move on to more advanced methods of painting. In these videos, renowned designer Gloria Hutton guides you through four steps to take your painting skills to the next level. In the first tutorial, you will learn how to choose the best brushes for various types of projects. The second video focuses on several advanced techniques. Third, you will create a portrait based on a provided model. Finally, you will learn how to paint your own ideas instead of using a model. The videos are available for download from all major Web sites.

Special Seminar at Hacksburg Museum of Arts and Crafts

On October 30, come to the Hacksburg Museum of Arts and Crafts for a special master class on painting. Artist Gloria Hutton will be giving a lecture based on the first video of her recently released four-part series, *Portrait Pro*.

Gloria Hutton is a prominent painter who created hundreds of breathtaking works that have been displayed in museums and festivals worldwide. Her natural talent has allowed Ms. Hutton to make a living off of her art early on, so money was not the motivation for making the videos. But she was receiving repeated requests for tips and private lessons and didn't have time to give regular classes. So she finally decided to release her tutorial series, which immediately became a bestseller.

Time: October 30, 3:00 P.M.
Place: Hacksburg Museum of Arts and Crafts, Shalandra Room
Fee: $35.00

Seating is limited for this event. Please register in advance by calling 555-8874.

Portrait Pro

Review by Margaret Jones

I highly recommend the *Portrait Pro* series to anyone passionate about art. I've been painting for several years now, and I thought all I could do to improve was to keep practicing. I never thought I'd learn so much simply by watching some videos. However, I've improved my skills tenfold by following Ms. Hutton's tutorials. She manages to explain complicated techniques in simple terms, and I was amazed by what I could accomplish by the time I finished watching these.

The only complaint I have is with the video about creating a project from scratch without referring to anything. I've watched that video dozens of times and still can't understand what Ms. Hutton is saying. However, because the three other videos were so helpful, I still think this series is worth the purchase.

---

186. According to the summary, who is the intended audience for the series?

(A) Professional artists with expert skills
(B) Beginners who never painted before
(C) People with experience in painting
(D) Collectors looking for artwork

187. What will attendants do at the seminar on October 30?

(A) Participate in filming a video
(B) Learn how to select utensils
(C) Create a portrait
(D) Practice some brushstrokes

188. According to the flyer, why did Ms. Hutton create the series?

(A) She needed more income.
(B) She wanted to advertise her classes.
(C) She was often asked for advice.
(D) She enjoyed her teaching experience.

189. In the review, the word "following" in paragraph 1, line 4, is closest in meaning to

(A) modifying
(B) coming after
(C) using
(D) testing

190. Which video of the *Portrait Pro* series does Ms. Jones say she watched many times?

(A) The first
(B) The second
(C) The third
(D) The fourth

GO ON TO THE NEXT PAGE

Questions 191-195 refer to the following advertisement, e-mail, and text message.

Divine Delights Caterer

For the best service in the area and the highest-quality food, choose Divine Delights Caterer! Summer is over, and our fall premium menus are here! See our Web site www.divinedelightscaterer.com for beverages and many other types of menus.

Premium Menu 1 ($50 per person)

Appetizer (choose one)
☐ Pumpkin soup
☐ Caesar salad

Main dish (choose one)
☐ Parmesan chicken
☐ Broccoli cream pasta

Dessert
Apple pie

Premium Menu 2 ($75 per person)
Includes one glass of wine

Appetizer (choose one)
☐ Onion soup
☐ Cobb salad

Main dish (choose one)
☐ Beef tenderloin
☐ Stuffed mushrooms

Dessert
Blueberry crumble

* Prices include service. Reservations for premium menus must be made at least one month in advance. A minimum of twenty people are required. Only one type of premium menu is possible per event. Please indicate each guest's dish preference at the time of reservation.

From: Rooter, Phil <prooter@glypha.com>
To: Stacker, Lindsay <lstacker@glypha.com>
Date: September 15
Subject: Corporate Dinner

Hi. I think your suggestion of holding a corporate dinner to celebrate the merger of Glypha Corp. and Baller Inc. is an excellent idea. You mentioned October 20 as a possible date. I've checked with everyone, and it seems to be a good day to hold the event. As requested, I've attached a flyer for a catering company I told you about. I know we want to have a nice meal, so I think we should get a premium menu. But I'm not sure what our budget is. Let me know which one you think would be best. I will then pass the menu around the office so that everyone can select their dish choices.

From: Tracy Meloy
To: Phil Rooter

Since Stephanie is out on vacation this week, I chose her dish preferences for her for the corporate dinner. I told you that she and I would both be having the same thing. However, I just found out that she is a vegetarian, so could you switch her selection to the broccoli cream pasta? Sorry about the change.

191. What is suggested about Divine Delights Caterer?

(A) It is closed in the winter and spring.
(B) It adapts its menus to the seasons.
(C) It offers only two types of menus.
(D) It has an online reservation system.

192. What is the purpose of the planned event?

(A) To congratulate a colleague
(B) To celebrate a successful quarter
(C) To impress a potential client
(D) To mark a new partnership

193. When should Glypha Corp. make the catering reservation by?

(A) September 15
(B) September 20
(C) October 15
(D) October 20

194. What is Mr. Rooter asked to do?

(A) Postpone a vacation
(B) Modify a meal choice
(C) Reschedule an event
(D) Add a guest to an attendance list

195. What main dish will Ms. Meloy most likely have at the corporate dinner?

(A) Parmesan chicken
(B) Broccoli cream pasta
(C) Beef tenderloin
(D) Stuffed mushrooms

Questions 196-200 refer to the following Web pages and e-mail.

---

www.kikilafabrics.com/about

| HOME | ABOUT | PRODUCTS | CLEARANCE | CART |

Kikila Fabrics is famous for having the widest selection of fabrics. You can find any texture and color you need for all of your projects right here on our site.

Make sure you check out the CLEARANCE page, where all items are 50 percent off. There, you'll find the best value for your money. In addition, if you order more than 10 meters of any fabric, you are eligible for free delivery.

Fabric is cut to the size indicated in the order form. Please check your measurements carefully as we do not grant returns or exchanges if you entered the wrong numbers.

---

www.kikilafabrics.com/clearance

| HOME | ABOUT | PRODUCTS | CLEARANCE | CART |

SEPTEMBER CLEARANCE ITEMS

Flannel – print
  Available prints: owls, cats, bears
  Description: This single layer flannel is wonderful for quilts and children's apparel.
  Washing: machine wash/tumble dry
  Price: $9.50 per meter

Wool Blend
  Available colors: green, red
  Description: This is the perfect material for coats, jackets, blankets, and other winter favorites.
  Washing: machine wash cold/tumble dry low; Note: do NOT iron
  Price: $12.00 per meter

Faux leather
  Available colors: brown, black
  Description: This heavyweight imitation leather is great for luxurious pillows and other home decor elements.
  Washing: wipe down with damp rag
  Price: $6.00 per meter

To: Frances Olsen <folsen@pozmail.net>
From: Kikila Fabrics <cs@kikilafabrics.com>
Subject: Order Number 201483
Date: September 21

Dear Mr. Olsen,

We have received your request to exchange the faux leather you purchased. Please accept our sincerest apologies for sending you the wrong color. We have verified your original order and confirmed that you had in fact requested black. Your order of 6 meters of faux leather in black has been shipped. You can expect to receive it by Friday afternoon. In addition, we've included 5 meters of red wool blend as an apology. It can be easily combined with the faux leather to create a variety of winter apparel.

As for the material we originally sent, we kindly request that you send it back to us and we will refund you for its shipping.

Thank you for your patience and understanding.

Sincerely,

Kikila Fabrics

---

196. According to the first Web page, what is Kikila Fabrics known for?

(A) Its low prices
(B) Its fast delivery
(C) Its variety of items
(D) Its return policy

197. How should the flannel material be washed?

(A) By wiping it with a wet piece of cloth
(B) By taking it to a dry cleaner
(C) By putting it in a washing machine
(D) By using cold water only

198. What color material did Mr. Olsen originally receive?

(A) Green
(B) Red
(C) Black
(D) Brown

199. What is implied about Mr. Olsen?

(A) He received a discount on his purchase.
(B) He provided the wrong measurements.
(C) He tried to exchange some apparel.
(D) He did not pay a delivery fee for his order.

200. What does Kikila Fabrics offer as an apology to Mr. Olsen?

(A) Complimentary fabric
(B) A refund for his purchase
(C) An article of winter clothing
(D) Free shipping on a future order

Stop! This is the end of the test. If you finish before time is called, you may go back to Parts 5, 6, and 7 and check your work.

에듀윌 토익 실전서

LC+RC

TEST 04

LISTENING TEST

PART 1
PART 2
PART 3
PART 4

READING TEST

PART 5
PART 6
PART 7

LISTENING TEST

In the Listening test, you will be asked to demonstrate how well you understand spoken English. The entire Listening test will last approximately 45 minutes. There are four parts, and directions are given for each part. You must mark your answers on the separate answer sheet. Do not write your answers in your test book.

PART 1

Directions: For each question in this part, you will hear four statements about a picture in your test book. When you hear the statements, you must select the one statement that best describes what you see in the picture. Then find the number of the question on your answer sheet and mark your answer. The statements will not be printed in your test book and will be spoken only one time.

Statement (C), "They're looking at a document," is the best description of the picture, so you should select answer (C) and mark it on your answer sheet.

1.

2.

3.

4.

5.

6.

PART 2

Directions: You will hear a question or statement and three responses spoken in English. They will not be printed in your test book and will be spoken only one time. Select the best response to the question or statement and mark the letter (A), (B), or (C) on your answer sheet.

7. Mark your answer on your answer sheet.
8. Mark your answer on your answer sheet.
9. Mark your answer on your answer sheet.
10. Mark your answer on your answer sheet.
11. Mark your answer on your answer sheet.
12. Mark your answer on your answer sheet.
13. Mark your answer on your answer sheet.
14. Mark your answer on your answer sheet.
15. Mark your answer on your answer sheet.
16. Mark your answer on your answer sheet.
17. Mark your answer on your answer sheet.
18. Mark your answer on your answer sheet.
19. Mark your answer on your answer sheet.
20. Mark your answer on your answer sheet.
21. Mark your answer on your answer sheet.
22. Mark your answer on your answer sheet.
23. Mark your answer on your answer sheet.
24. Mark your answer on your answer sheet.
25. Mark your answer on your answer sheet.
26. Mark your answer on your answer sheet.
27. Mark your answer on your answer sheet.
28. Mark your answer on your answer sheet.
29. Mark your answer on your answer sheet.
30. Mark your answer on your answer sheet.
31. Mark your answer on your answer sheet.

PART 3

Directions: You will hear some conversations between two or more people. You will be asked to answer three questions about what the speakers say in each conversation. Select the best response to each question and mark the letter (A), (B), (C), or (D) on your answer sheet. The conversations will not be printed in your test book and will be spoken only one time.

32. What does the woman want to buy?
    (A) A card
    (B) A desk
    (C) A computer
    (D) A shelf

33. What does the man say about the items?
    (A) Not all of them are discounted.
    (B) Most of them are out of stock.
    (C) Many of them are outdated.
    (D) Some of them are mislabeled.

34. What will the man most likely do next?
    (A) Verify a product's price
    (B) Speak to a manager
    (C) Check an account history
    (D) Print out a coupon

35. What is the purpose of the woman's call?
    (A) To make an appointment
    (B) To extend a deadline
    (C) To report some test results
    (D) To change work hours

36. What does the man mention about the company?
    (A) Its workers' shift schedules are flexible.
    (B) Its major tasks are done before noon.
    (C) Its medical office isn't open in the morning.
    (D) Its productivity is particularly high this week.

37. What does the man say he will do?
    (A) Inform a manager of a change
    (B) Reduce the workload for employees
    (C) Postpone a dental checkup
    (D) Promote the woman to a higher position

38. Why is the man calling?
    (A) To schedule the delivery of an item
    (B) To notify of a document's availability
    (C) To update his personal information
    (D) To request directions to a location

39. What does the man say is required?
    (A) Picture identification
    (B) Contact information
    (C) A local mailing address
    (D) A payment receipt

40. Why can't the woman meet the man today?
    (A) She forgot her passport.
    (B) She didn't make an appointment.
    (C) She is stuck in traffic.
    (D) She lives too far away.

41. Where most likely is the conversation taking place?
    (A) At a train station
    (B) At a bookstore
    (C) At a print shop
    (D) At a library

42. What does the woman ask Mr. Clayton?
    (A) Where a facility is located
    (B) Whether an exception can be made
    (C) How a process should be executed
    (D) How much an item costs

43. What will need to be paid on Friday?
    (A) An overdue fine
    (B) A transportation fee
    (C) A lost item charge
    (D) A luggage delivery bill

GO ON TO THE NEXT PAGE

44. What are the speakers mainly talking about?
   (A) An audience review
   (B) A musician's performance
   (C) An advertisement design
   (D) An informational handout

45. What problem does the woman mention?
   (A) A show's break time is too short.
   (B) A piece of music was poorly interpreted.
   (C) An entertainer is running late.
   (D) A schedule printout is incomplete.

46. What does the man mean when he says, "How is that possible"?
   (A) He doesn't understand how to do a task.
   (B) He wants the woman to explain a change.
   (C) He is surprised to notice an error.
   (D) He disagrees with the woman's statement.

47. What most likely is the woman's job?
   (A) Subway ticket vendor
   (B) Interior designer
   (C) Real estate agent
   (D) Taxi driver

48. What does the man ask about?
   (A) A meeting time
   (B) A place's location
   (C) Property values
   (D) Ticket prices

49. What will the woman most likely do next?
   (A) Find a property for the man
   (B) Help the man locate a place
   (C) Drive the man to a station
   (D) Send a document to the man

50. Where most likely is the conversation taking place?
   (A) At a fire station
   (B) At a real estate agency
   (C) At a jewelry store
   (D) At an interior designer's

51. What characteristic do Maria and Clyde want?
   (A) An old-fashioned appearance
   (B) A contemporary look
   (C) A traditional system
   (D) A high energy production

52. What is mentioned about the Windsor Gold?
   (A) It has sold out.
   (B) It's a customer favorite.
   (C) It has a gold finish.
   (D) It's in a modern style.

53. Who most likely is the man?
   (A) A hotel manager
   (B) A restaurant worker
   (C) A private caterer
   (D) An event organizer

54. What does the woman plan on doing after work tomorrow?
   (A) Going straight home
   (B) Dining with colleagues
   (C) Shopping for groceries
   (D) Meeting her friends

55. What does the woman ask the man to do?
   (A) Cancel her request
   (B) Add items to her order
   (C) Meet her at her office
   (D) Make a reservation

56. What is the purpose of the woman's call?
    (A) To ask for directions
    (B) To schedule a meeting
    (C) To inquire about a package
    (D) To report a missing item

57. What does the man mean when he says, "I should have been clearer"?
    (A) He needs to explain a new strategy.
    (B) He thinks the woman went the wrong way.
    (C) He is going to provide a status update.
    (D) He is confused by the woman's statement.

58. What does the woman say about the intersection?
    (A) She has already passed it.
    (B) She used to work in an office near it.
    (C) She doesn't know where it is.
    (D) She has found a post office by it.

59. Who most likely is the man?
    (A) A pastry chef
    (B) A business consultant
    (C) A newspaper reporter
    (D) A fitness expert

60. What are the speakers mainly discussing?
    (A) A business strategy
    (B) A product launch
    (C) A shortage of materials
    (D) A training event

61. What does the woman say will happen next month?
    (A) Free refreshments will be served.
    (B) A new location will be opened.
    (C) A class will be offered.
    (D) More employees will be hired.

WEEKDAY TRAIN SCHEDULE

Train Number	Destination	Departure Time	Arrival Time
105	Atlanta	6:20 A.M.	7:40 A.M.
207	Atlanta	10:30 A.M.	11:50 A.M.
482	Atlanta	2:20 P.M.	3:40 P.M.
553	Atlanta	5:50 P.M.	7:10 P.M.

62. What type of company do the speakers most likely work at?
    (A) A travel agency
    (B) A clothing store
    (C) A transportation company
    (D) A food producer

63. What will the man do tomorrow?
    (A) Depart for Atlanta
    (B) Attend an event
    (C) Search for a hotel
    (D) Leave the office early

64. Look at the graphic. Which train will the man most likely take?
    (A) Train 105
    (B) Train 207
    (C) Train 482
    (D) Train 553

GO ON TO THE NEXT PAGE

**Amateur Art Contest
Call for entries**

Submission period: February 3-5
Awards Ceremony: February 7 at 6 P.M.
Show opens to the public: February 8
Show closes: February 20

Willow Art Museum

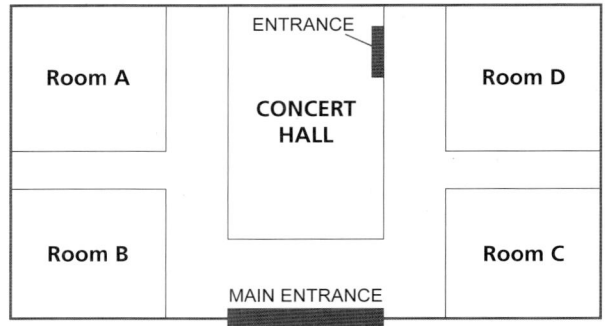

65. What will the man do tomorrow?

(A) Write an article
(B) Meet with a reporter
(C) Tour a museum
(D) Purchase some artwork

66. Look at the graphic. When does the man need extra help?

(A) February 3
(B) February 5
(C) February 7
(D) February 20

67. What does the woman say she will do?

(A) Move to a new home
(B) Submit an original painting
(C) Come to the museum early
(D) Create a registration form

68. Who most likely is the man?

(A) A conductor
(B) A musician
(C) A ticket agent
(D) An audience member

69. What does the man mention about the lecture?

(A) It costs extra to attend.
(B) It doesn't have any more seats available.
(C) It started a few minutes ago.
(D) It will be about tonight's music.

70. Look at the graphic. Where will the woman most likely go next?

(A) Room A
(B) Room B
(C) Room C
(D) Room D

PART 4

Directions: You will hear some talks given by a single speaker. You will be asked to answer three questions about what the speaker says in each talk. Select the best response to each question and mark the letter (A), (B), (C), or (D) on your answer sheet. The talks will not be printed in your test book and will be spoken only one time.

71. Where is this talk most likely being heard?
    (A) At a museum
    (B) At a department store
    (C) At a concert hall
    (D) At a souvenir shop

72. What will the speaker do at eleven thirty?
    (A) Host an auction
    (B) Play a song
    (C) Explain a device
    (D) Start a guided tour

73. What does the speaker recommend the listeners do at twelve o'clock?
    (A) Meet with a specialist
    (B) Attend a lecture
    (C) Observe a specific item
    (D) Exit the building

74. Why does the speaker apologize?
    (A) There is a lack of seats.
    (B) A machine malfunctioned.
    (C) A meeting is starting late.
    (D) A location has changed.

75. What is the purpose of the meeting?
    (A) To introduce an employee
    (B) To select group members
    (C) To explain a new policy
    (D) To review a project's goals

76. According to the speaker, why should the questions be written down?
    (A) They should be reviewed by a supervisor.
    (B) They will be read aloud for a recording.
    (C) They need to be sorted by category.
    (D) They are limited to one per person.

77. What kind of product does the report describe?
    (A) Athletic shoes
    (B) An electronic device
    (C) Natural cosmetics
    (D) A home appliance

78. According to the speaker, what is special about the product?
    (A) Its safety features
    (B) Its recyclable materials
    (C) Its compact size
    (D) Its lightweight design

79. What does the speaker recommend doing?
    (A) Comparing prices
    (B) Testing products
    (C) Visiting a Web site
    (D) Calling with questions

80. Who most likely are the listeners?
    (A) Tour guides
    (B) Job applicants
    (C) Beach visitors
    (D) Hotel guests

81. What are the listeners asked to do?
    (A) Explain a problem
    (B) Fill out a survey
    (C) Find a partner
    (D) Do a role-play activity

82. What will the listeners most likely do next?
    (A) Pick up a handout
    (B) Follow the speaker
    (C) Take a break
    (D) Sign up for a session

GO ON TO THE NEXT PAGE

83. Where is this announcement most likely being heard?

    (A) At a grocery store
    (B) At an airport
    (C) At a daycare center
    (D) At a zoo

84. Why does the speaker say, "This will only slow the process"?

    (A) To prevent rude behavior
    (B) To clarify an estimate
    (C) To encourage purchases
    (D) To announce a delay

85. What does the speaker offer some young visitors?

    (A) Priority seating
    (B) Free entry
    (C) A toy animal
    (D) Photographs of animals

86. What is the purpose of the message?

    (A) To modify an order
    (B) To make an apology
    (C) To explain a process
    (D) To request a payment

87. What is mentioned about *The Grand Hope*?

    (A) It was written by a best-selling author.
    (B) It is less expensive than *Agents and Foes*.
    (C) It is currently out of stock.
    (D) It was given as a birthday present.

88. What does the speaker ask the listener to do?

    (A) Provide a refund
    (B) Use a fast delivery service
    (C) Update a Web site
    (D) Return a phone call

89. What task are the listeners expected to do?

    (A) Taste some beverage samples
    (B) Record some music performances
    (C) Review some advertisements
    (D) Assess some job candidates

90. What does the speaker imply when he says, "Don't pay attention to them"?

    (A) The company wants independent opinions.
    (B) Some handouts contain an error.
    (C) The listeners were given the wrong instructions.
    (D) Some employees will be monitoring the activity.

91. What will the listeners most likely do next?

    (A) Print some documents
    (B) Write down questions
    (C) Put on name tags
    (D) Form small groups

92. What is the purpose of the talk?

    (A) To introduce an author
    (B) To advertise a book
    (C) To criticize an idea
    (D) To request nominations

93. What does the speaker imply when she says, "Trust me"?

    (A) She has read the book.
    (B) She will write a novel.
    (C) She plans on answering questions.
    (D) She has won several awards.

94. What will most likely happen next?

    (A) A book will be signed.
    (B) A passage will be read.
    (C) Some questions will be asked.
    (D) An award will be presented.

EMERALD PARK TOUR SCHEDULE

DEPARTURE TIME	GUIDE
11:00 A.M.	Cindy
12:30 P.M.	Sandra
2:00 P.M.	Josh
3:30 P.M.	Richard

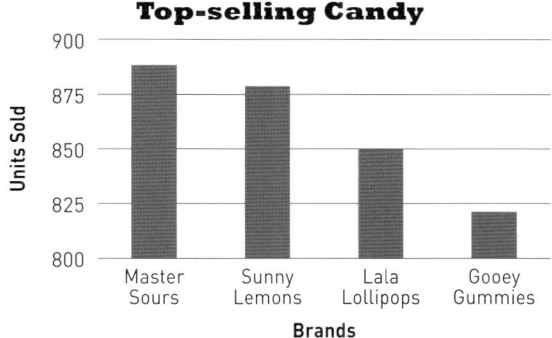

95. Why has one of the tours been canceled?
    (A) Weather conditions are unfavorable.
    (B) An employee was injured.
    (C) An area needs renovations.
    (D) Not enough people registered.

96. Look at the graphic. At what time was the canceled tour supposed to leave?
    (A) At 11:00 A.M.
    (B) At 12:30 P.M.
    (C) At 2:00 P.M.
    (D) At 3:30 P.M.

97. What are the visitors prohibited from doing?
    (A) Leaving children unattended
    (B) Entering without a guide
    (C) Running in the park
    (D) Joining several tours

98. According to the speaker, how can the company increase profits?
    (A) By selling a new product
    (B) By changing suppliers
    (C) By purchasing more goods
    (D) By targeting different customers

99. Look at the graphic. What will the company buy less of?
    (A) Master Sours
    (B) Sunny Lemons
    (C) Lala Lollipops
    (D) Gooey Gummies

100. What will the speaker most likely do next?
    (A) Place an order
    (B) Finalize a plan
    (C) Give out documents
    (D) Negotiate a price

This is the end of the Listening Test. Turn to Part 5 in your test book.

READING TEST

In the Reading test, you will read a variety of texts and answer several different types of reading comprehension questions. The entire Reading test will last 75 minutes. There are three parts, and directions are given for each part. You are encouraged to answer as many questions as possible within the time allowed.

You must mark your answers on the separate answer sheet. Do not write your answers in the test book.

PART 5

Directions: A word or phrase is missing in each of the sentences below. Four answer choices are given below each sentence. Select the best answer to complete the sentence. Then mark the letter (A), (B), (C), or (D) on your answer sheet.

101. Ms. Anita always ------- participates in fundraisers by baking cookies and selling them.
    (A) active
    (B) acts
    (C) actively
    (D) activity

102. The parade for the town festival is ------- to start at 1 P.M. tomorrow.
    (A) scheduled
    (B) remained
    (C) considered
    (D) celebrated

103. Once the door opened, the usher showed the audience members to their ------- seats.
    (A) respective
    (B) respect
    (C) respectful
    (D) respecting

104. All of the furniture sold in our store comes with easy-to-follow ------- for fast assembly.
    (A) estimates
    (B) instructions
    (C) comforts
    (D) refunds

105. Mr. Crob had to wait fifteen minutes for an ------- when he called customer service.
    (A) answer
    (B) answering
    (C) answered
    (D) answers

106. Being fluent in at least two languages is a necessary qualification ------- working as a concierge at the Summertime Resort.
    (A) about
    (B) through
    (C) by
    (D) for

107. Technicians must turn off the power to the entire building when ------- the electrical system.
    (A) repair
    (B) repaired
    (C) repairing
    (D) repairs

108. The video ------- various ways in which the software can help a business to organize its data.
    (A) inquires
    (B) focuses
    (C) terminates
    (D) demonstrates

109. Recommend a friend of ------- to join our gym, and we will provide a discounted membership fee.
    (A) you
    (B) your
    (C) yourself
    (D) yours

110. The manager ------- asked that Ms. Nicola be the one to lead the negotiations with Cinta Corp.
    (A) utterly
    (B) specifically
    (C) broadly
    (D) gradually

111. Many candidates ------- applications for the sales associate position, so it will take time to go over all of them.
    (A) to submit
    (B) were submitted
    (C) submission
    (D) have submitted

112. It is impossible to get a shuttle bus from the airport to the hotel ------- any reservations.
    (A) unless
    (B) without
    (C) except
    (D) besides

113. Mr. Moss expressed interest in ------- a workshop to help improve his public speaking skills.
    (A) joined
    (B) join
    (C) joining
    (D) to join

114. The airline's new policy increases the baggage ------- from one suitcase per passenger to two for international flights.
    (A) claim
    (B) involvement
    (C) allowance
    (D) acquisition

115. Patrons of the Mencer Public Library can renew ------- checked-out books online and thus avoid overdue fines.
    (A) their
    (B) theirs
    (C) they
    (D) them

116. Not only senior staff members but also new employees will benefit ------- the revisions to the pay scale.
    (A) of
    (B) among
    (C) from
    (D) to

117. The branch supervisor decided to close the store early to let the staff go home ------- the snowstorm started.
    (A) so as to
    (B) before
    (C) ahead of
    (D) rather than

118. The date and venue for the convention have been chosen, but the program ------- needs to be finalized.
    (A) still
    (B) lately
    (C) once
    (D) exactly

119. Colleagues will offer to give money for gas to ------- who volunteer to drive them to the annual picnic.
    (A) them
    (B) those
    (C) other
    (D) anyone

120. The price of gold was rising steadily for a few months, but it started ------- at the end of June.
    (A) to impede
    (B) to decline
    (C) to spend
    (D) to eliminate

121. In response to severe ------- concerning its high pollution levels, the factory took measures to protect the surrounding environment.
    (A) critical
    (B) criticizes
    (C) critically
    (D) criticism

122. Now that the bookstore's Web site has been updated, regular customers can get reading recommendations ------- their purchase history.
    (A) on behalf of
    (B) such as
    (C) based on
    (D) in spite of

123. Pearly White Toothpaste, though ------- recommended by dentists nationwide, is not as popular among buyers as its main competitor.
    (A) strong
    (B) strength
    (C) strongest
    (D) strongly

124. Engineers must have a master's degree or ------- work experience to be considered for senior management openings.
    (A) deliberate
    (B) lucrative
    (C) equivalent
    (D) systematic

125. To alleviate traffic congestion in the downtown area, the city planner ------- some roadways to one-way streets.
    (A) has been converted
    (B) are converted
    (C) is converting
    (D) convert

126. While the final winners will be kept secret, the top ------- for the talent awards will be revealed two weeks before the ceremony.
    (A) subscriptions
    (B) confidences
    (C) congratulations
    (D) nominations

127. Denny Marlow became more and more ------- about his chances of getting the accounting job as the interview progressed.
    (A) hope
    (B) hopefully
    (C) hopeful
    (D) hoping

128. Guests are expected to reply to the invitation by the end of the month ------- they plan on attending the event or not.
    (A) either
    (B) whether
    (C) since
    (D) though

129. Chef Francis Gales opened a restaurant ------- menu changes daily depending on the best fish and produce available each morning.
    (A) that
    (B) when
    (C) whose
    (D) while

130. The directors of Hencer Inc. are very ------- about who they allow into the biannual meeting for setting the company's objectives.
    (A) selective
    (B) prominent
    (C) accessible
    (D) ambitious

PART 6

Directions: Read the texts that follow. A word, phrase, or sentence is missing in parts of each text. Four answer choices for each question are given below the text. Select the best answer to complete the text. Then mark the letter (A), (B), (C), or (D) on your answer sheet.

Questions 131-134 refer to the following e-mail.

To: All members <memberlist@bettermegym.com>
From: Dennis Primus <dprimus@bettermegym.com>
Subject: New Weekend Hours
Date: August 4

Dear members,

Thank you to all who ------- our survey to share ideas concerning Better Me Gym. We strive to keep
            131.
our gym the most modern and convenient for our clients, so feedback such as yours is highly -------
                                                                                              132.
to us. While we cannot reply to each of you individually, we are happy to make changes to address

the most common -------. The first of these was about our closing times. Many of you complained
                 133.
about our short weekend hours. -------. We hope that you will enjoy these added hours.
                                134.

See you at the gym!

Dennis Primus
Manager, Better Me Gym

131. (A) completing
    (B) completes
    (C) are completing
    (D) completed

132. (A) values
    (B) value
    (C) valuable
    (D) valuing

133. (A) demands
    (B) schedules
    (C) routines
    (D) patrons

134. (A) Unfortunately, we cannot extend our hours of operation.
    (B) In response, we have decided to stay open until 9 P.M. on Saturdays.
    (C) Members are free to work out as many hours as they wish.
    (D) These are described in detail in your gym membership contract.

GO ON TO THE NEXT PAGE

Questions 135-138 refer to the following advertisement.

Secure your house with Houseguard! Our ------- security system has all the latest features you need
                                              135.
to feel safe and comfortable in your own home. We will set up security cameras, motion sensors,
and an alarm system that will cover all areas of your property. -------, we will equip your home with
                                                                136.
our smart control robot, which constantly monitors your appliances to eliminate any danger. -------.
                                                                                              137.
For example, should you leave the gas on when you leave, it will ------- turn it off for you, thus
                                                                 138.
preventing a potential fire. Make your home safer today! Visit www.houseguard.com today to
schedule an installation.

135. (A) second-hand
(B) ill-equipped
(C) out-of-date
(D) state-of-the-art

136. (A) Therefore
(B) Nonetheless
(C) In addition
(D) On the other hand

137. (A) Indeed, burglaries have been on the rise lately.
(B) The Houseguard robot could save your house.
(C) There are many control systems to choose from.
(D) You can now cook amazing meals from your own kitchen.

138. (A) automatic
(B) automates
(C) automation
(D) automatically

Questions 139-142 refer to the following letter.

November 25

Eric Closter
2957 Marisol Avenue
Willows, PA 18765

Dear Mr. Closter,

We are writing to inform you that the latest payment for your subscription to *Monthly Talks* was declined. Thus, we were unable to process the transaction. -------. If you cannot determine the cause of the error after ------- all of your information, contact your bank.
                                                                              139.   **140.**

Since your payment did not go through, we have ------- shipment of the latest issue to your address.
                                                141.
In order to receive the December issue, you must ------- provide valid payment information as we
                                                 142.
will be sending out the last issues soon.

If you have any questions about your *Monthly Talks* subscription, please call us at 555-3548.

Sincerely,

The *Monthly Talks* Staff

---

139. (A) However, we do not have the correct credit card information.
(B) A cancelation fee of $12.99 will be deducted from your account.
(C) Attached is a form for renewing your subscription to our magazine.
(D) This problem may be due to an address change or card expiration.

140. (A) verifying
(B) verification
(C) verify
(D) verified

141. (A) timed
(B) refunded
(C) canceled
(D) measured

142. (A) incorrectly
(B) surely
(C) promptly
(D) temporarily

Questions 143-146 refer to the following article.

Local Companies Commit to Change

BETHOS (January 22)— ------. According to this potential contract, Frester Corp., Alphet Inc., and Proga Corp. would commit to limiting their factories' energy consumption and emission levels. Such changes could cost each company a large amount of money by slowing their production rates. ------, the directors agreed that focusing on environmentally friendly methods would be beneficial in the long run. "If all three companies ------ to the agreement, then no one will lose too much, and the environment will gain," argued a director of Frester Corp. ------ of the sixteen directors volunteered any details about the logistics of the plan, but they did confirm that an agreement was reached and will be made public soon.

143. (A) A recent study shows that pollution levels in Bethos are at an all-time high.
(B) Several local companies are currently seeking to hire entry-level workers.
(C) The directors of three large companies met yesterday to discuss an agreement.
(D) Solar energy is just one example of renewable energy that is easy to harvest.

144. (A) Furthermore
(B) Nevertheless
(C) Similarly
(D) Otherwise

145. (A) propose
(B) follow
(C) compare
(D) adhere

146. (A) Those
(B) Any
(C) None
(D) Neither

PART 7

Directions: In this part, you will read a selection of texts, such as magazine and newspaper articles, e-mails, and instant messages. Each text or set of texts is followed by several questions. Select the best answer for each question and mark the letter (A), (B), (C), or (D) on your answer sheet.

Questions 147-148 refer to the following receipt.

Tina's Treasures

Date: 11/15
Member number: 194538838

Silk Tie	$22.99
Leather belt	$39.99
Linen shirt	$45.00
Subtotal	$107.98
Tax (6%)	$6.48
Total	**$114.46**
Cash	$120.00
Change	-$5.54

Member points earned	110
Total member points	1,005

Congratulations! You have reached more than one thousand member points and have earned this coupon:

> **Good for $5.00 at Tina's Treasures**
> Coupon Code: A2225SG56

Find us online at www.tinastreasures.com, where you can browse our merchandise, write product reviews, and place orders. You can also sign up for our newsletter to receive special promotions by e-mail.

---

147. What kind of store most likely is Tina's Treasures?

(A) A fabrics distributor
(B) A clothing outlet
(C) A hardware store
(D) A jewelry shop

148. According to the receipt, how did the buyer receive a coupon?

(A) By winning a contest
(B) By reviewing a product
(C) By being a loyal customer
(D) By subscribing to a newsletter

Questions 149-150 refer to the following text-message chain.

Laura Fisher [6:58 P.M.]
Thomas, are you still at the office by any chance?

Thomas Volpert [6:59 P.M.]
Yes, I'm still here, but I was just about to leave for Jarrod's retirement party.

Laura Fisher [7:00 P.M.]
I was supposed to bring Jarrod's gift to the restaurant, but I just noticed that I left it at the office. I'm almost at the restaurant already.

Thomas Volpert [7:01 P.M.]
No problem. Just tell me where it is, and I'll bring it.

Laura Fisher [7:02 P.M.]
Oh, that's such a relief. You'll see a box under my desk. It's blue and black. It has a label from Galinda's Collection Shop on it.

Thomas Volpert [7:03 P.M.]
Okay, hold on. Let me check.

Thomas Volpert [7:07 P.M.]
Got it. The invitation says seven thirty, right? I'd better get going.

Laura Fisher [7:08 P.M.]
Yes. Thank you so much! You're a lifesaver.

---

149. At 7:07 P.M., what does Mr. Volpert mean when he writes, "Got it"?

(A) He found the present.
(B) He understands the directions.
(C) He received a party invitation.
(D) He has a gift receipt.

150. Where is Mr. Volpert most likely going next?

(A) To the office
(B) To Ms. Fisher's home
(C) To a restaurant
(D) To a store

Questions 151-152 refer to the following e-mail.

E-mail

To: Sooyeon Baek <baeksooyeon@harligen.net>
From: Gerald Finn <finngerald@harligen.net>
Date: January 18
Subject: Urgent

Dear Ms. Baek,

I need your help. The foreman at the 171 Dutton Street property has informed me that his team has nearly run out of the gravel for the water barrier. They need more as soon as possible not to fall behind schedule. I'll be away from the office the rest of the day performing safety checks at our other sites, so I can't take care of this myself. Would you please call the supplier and ask for more gravel to be delivered? The type we're using is listed in the database under that property's name. It should be easy to find.

Thank you!

Gerald Finn

---

151. For what kind of business does Mr. Finn most likely work?

(A) A construction company
(B) A manufacturing facility
(C) A hardware store
(D) A real estate firm

152. What is Ms. Baek asked to do?

(A) Meet a potential customer
(B) Place an order
(C) Update a database
(D) Pick up a delivery

Questions 153-154 refer to the following Web page.

To the Clouds was established over fifteen years ago and has continuously strived to create the most innovative climbing gear and apparel around. Contact us today to become an official To the Clouds distributor. We are one of the top-selling brands on the market, and you will want to have our products in your store to attract the climbing community. By selling To the Clouds equipment, you will gain a reputation as a trustworthy store that sells excellent gear and apparel. Moreover, all of our products come with lifetime warranties to reassure customers that they are buying superior equipment. And we supply high-quality posters, banners, and leaflets. Our merchandise is thus simple to market and always sells out quickly.

153. Who should contact To the Clouds?

(A) Sporting goods retailers
(B) Professional athletes
(C) Climbing club leaders
(D) Equipment manufacturers

154. What is NOT mentioned about To the Clouds products?

(A) Their warranty doesn't expire.
(B) They are sold at affordable prices.
(C) They are popular among climbers.
(D) They are easy to advertise.

Questions 155-157 refer to the following notice.

Employee Notice: Annual Juny Fundraising Gala

The annual fundraising gala for Juny Children's Organization will be held at the Sarcona Convention Center on Sunday, April 30, from 6 P.M. to 8:30 P.M. Attendance for Dream Voyages employees is optional but strongly encouraged. As usual, our company will be sponsoring the event. However, instead of donating money as we have every other year, we are donating prizes for the raffle. For those of you who have not been to this event before, please note the dress code.

Dress code

Men do not need to wear tuxedos but must wear dark-colored suits, with a white shirt and solid-color tie. Please avoid loud prints and patterns.

Acceptable attire for women includes long gowns and pantsuits. Please do not wear short-cut dresses. If you decide to wear high heels, make sure you can comfortably stand in the shoes for a long period of time.

Prize donations

Dream Voyages will be donating one all-inclusive tour package to Europe, three vacation packages to resorts in Mexico, and ten weekend spa packages. Please note that anyone affiliated with Dream Voyages is not eligible to win any of these prizes.

---

155. What has Dream Voyages changed?
 (A) Its dress code for employees
 (B) Its contribution to the organization
 (C) Its policy on attendance to the event
 (D) Its type of rewards for customers

156. What are women NOT allowed to wear?
 (A) Dark-colored dresses
 (B) High-heel shoes
 (C) Long pants
 (D) Short skirts

157. What is suggested about the prizes donated by Dream Voyages?
 (A) They may not be won by Dream Voyages employees.
 (B) They do not include expenses related to plane tickets.
 (C) They will be awarded to the best-performing workers.
 (D) They are the most expensive gifts at the fundraiser.

Questions 158-160 refer to the following e-mail.

To: Garfield, Anna <annagarfield76@peoplesnet.com>
From: Customer Service <cs@featherflights.com>
Date: July 12
Subject: Flight reservation – Action needed

Dear Anna Garfield,

We are writing to inform you that payment for your flight to Los Angeles has not been processed. Please make a payment through our Web site in the amount of $636.88. — [1] —. Your reservation will not be complete until this amount has been received. If payment is not submitted within twenty-four hours after the request was made, the seats will be forfeited. — [2] —.

For your reference, you have requested two seats for a round-trip flight to Los Angeles departing from Austin on Saturday, August 7, at 3:20 P.M. and returning on Sunday, August 29, at 10:10 A.M. — [3] —.

Please note that the price you were originally quoted for the tickets may no longer be available after today. This is why we urge you to complete the reservation as soon as possible. If you require assistance, you may call our customer service line at 555-293-5892 between 9 A.M. and 5 P.M. on weekdays. — [4] —.

Thank you for choosing with Feather Flights. We look forward to serving you.

Regards,

The Feather Flights Customer Service Team

---

158. What is the purpose of the e-mail?
(A) To confirm a reservation
(B) To explain a flight change
(C) To acknowledge a cancelation
(D) To notify a customer of a due payment

159. In which of the positions marked [1], [2], [3], and [4] does the following sentence best belong?

"Thus, you will have to start the reservation process again."

(A) [1]
(B) [2]
(C) [3]
(D) [4]

160. What is indicated about the ticket price?
(A) It might change in the future.
(B) It is temporarily discounted.
(C) It includes only one way.
(D) It is payable only by phone.

Questions 161-164 refer to the following article.

January 30—After an unprecedented successful fourth quarter, it was rumored that Habbart Corp. would be giving large year-end bonuses to all of its employees. — [1] —. Habbart Corp. spokesperson Mr. Bryan Caster announced that the company would instead be making a large donation to Enviro First, an environmental foundation.

The revelation came as a surprise, as Habbart Corp. has a reputation for ignoring environmental issues. — [2] —. Controversy was especially intense after one of Habbart's plants had a small explosion that caused a chemical leak, contaminating a nearby river. Although the leak was quickly contained, local residents took to the streets to protest, denouncing the company's lack of care for ecological concerns. — [3] —.

Yet Habbart Corp.'s latest decision seems to contradict those claims. Mr. Caster emphasized that the company took matters related to sustainable production very seriously. "We want to support and work in collaboration with organizations that fight to protect the environment," Mr. Caster declared. — [4] —. The total amount of the donation has not been revealed, but it is expected to be the largest one Enviro First has yet received. Mr. Caster insisted that all of Habbart Corp.'s extra profits would go to the organization.

161. What is the purpose of the article?
(A) To criticize a corporation's approach to environmental issues
(B) To advocate stronger measures against natural disasters
(C) To announce a company's contribution to a nonprofit
(D) To report an accident that happened at a local factory

162. What is indicated about Habbart Corp.?
(A) It is known for its environment-friendly methods.
(B) It will be giving extra compensation to its employees.
(C) It had an exceptionally profitable fourth quarter.
(D) It is planning on building a new plant near a river.

163. According to the article, what caused people to protest against Habbart Corp.?
(A) Its neglect of the environment
(B) Its employee benefits packages
(C) Its frequent explosion accidents
(D) Its small charitable donations

164. In which of the positions marked [1], [2], [3], and [4] does the following sentence best belong?

"However, this was denied at a press conference held yesterday."

(A) [1]
(B) [2]
(C) [3]
(D) [4]

Questions 165-167 refer to the following advertisement.

Boca Chocolates is seventy-five years old, and to celebrate, the factory will be opening its doors to the public for one week, from May 6 to May 12. This is your chance to visit the premises and find out how Boca Chocolates makes its delicious sweets!

First, you will take a guided tour that will show you every step of the process from the bean to the box. You will see our workers operating the machinery, and our chocolate artists decorating the final products.

After you learn all about how chocolate is made, you can taste special samples of upcoming products, enjoy our magical chocolate fountain, and purchase gift baskets at a discount. In addition, every visitor will go home with a box of chocolates as a gift.

For security purposes, the number of visitors is limited, so make your reservation early! Tours are $45 for adults, $30 for students, and $20 for children under twelve. Call 555-9963 to schedule a time.

165. What is being advertised?

(A) A new kind of chocolate
(B) A special anniversary tour
(C) A sales event at a grocery store
(D) An innovative candy-making machine

166. What will be given out for free?

(A) Gift baskets
(B) Fountains
(C) Decorations
(D) Boxes of sweets

167. What are readers encouraged to do?

(A) Reserve a time slot
(B) Place an order
(C) Taste a product
(D) Try a piece of equipment

Questions 168-171 refer to the following online chat discussion.

Selam Habte [4:26 P.M.] I know you two had to miss my announcements at the end of the weekly staff meeting, so I wanted to fill you in.

Anna Morgan [4:28 P.M.] Thanks. What did we miss?

Selam Habte [4:29 P.M.] Our company is going to release a new long-lasting lipstick.

Kikuyo Tsuruta [4:30 P.M.] That's great news. I'm glad the R&D department took my advice about adding another product to the line.

Anna Morgan [4:31 P.M.] When will we start advertising the new lipstick?

Selam Habte [4:32 P.M.] Mr. Catteneo is putting together a marketing plan now.

Kikuyo Tsuruta [4:34 P.M.] Wouldn't this be a better job for a senior marketing executive?

Anna Morgan [4:35 P.M.] Yeah. Mr. Catteneo is new to our company and doesn't know much about our products.

Selam Habte [4:39 P.M.] I realize that, but he has a marketing background in cosmetics.

Anna Morgan [4:41 P.M.] I see. Well, it wouldn't hurt for him to see some of our previous work. I could send him a portfolio of previous projects.

Kikuyo Tsuruta [4:42 P.M.] And I'd be happy to review his work.

Selam Habte [4:43 P.M.] I don't think that'll be necessary, Kikuyo, but I like your idea, Anna.

Anna Morgan [4:44 P.M.] Okay. I'll do that now.

168. What is mainly being discussed?
    (A) A policy update
    (B) A new client
    (C) A schedule change
    (D) A product launch

169. What is implied about Ms. Tsuruta?
    (A) She thinks the company needs to control spending.
    (B) She made a suggestion about the company's goods.
    (C) She asked Mr. Habte for some advice.
    (D) She developed a new line of cosmetics.

170. At 4:41 P.M., what does Ms. Morgan most likely mean when she writes, "I see"?
    (A) Mr. Catteneo is too busy to work on a project.
    (B) Mr. Catteneo cannot help Ms. Morgan with a problem.
    (C) Mr. Catteneo has already reviewed a portfolio.
    (D) Mr. Catteneo may be qualified for a task.

171. What will Ms. Morgan most likely do next?
    (A) Review documents prepared by Mr. Catteneo
    (B) Send information about previous projects
    (C) Set up a meeting with Mr. Catteneo
    (D) Recommend a new marketing director

Questions 172-175 refer to the following e-mail.

E-Mail

To: Katrina Simon <ksimon@presslerlibrary.org>
From: Nora Yales <nyales@presslerlibrary.org>
Date: November 30
Subject: Opening tomorrow

Dear Ms. Simon,

I was told that you were willing to open the library in my place tomorrow morning and work my shift. I wanted to send you a quick reminder to help you out with the opening procedure. It's been a while since you last did this, and there are several steps, so I thought it would be helpful.

First, I wanted to make sure you know the code to disarm the alarm: 0358. Remember to pick up the mail, including the newspapers. You can leave the mail on my desk. Stamp the newspapers with the library stamp, and display them on the news shelf in the journals section. Make sure you take off yesterday's papers and classify them with the other past newspapers.

The key to the cash register is in the top drawer of my desk. Double check that there is $48 in it to start the day.

After you turn on the lights on every floor, you should be ready to unlock the front doors. The keys for that are in the key cabinet in my office.

The weather forecast says there will be a huge snowstorm, and since I live far away, I'd rather not drive in that weather, so I'm taking the whole day off and not leaving the house. But if you run into any trouble or have any questions, feel free to call me. I will also be available to chat online if you need my advice.

I am very thankful that you live close enough to be able to walk to the library. Thank you for being willing to do this.

Good luck!

Nora Yales
Library Assistant

172. What is the purpose of the e-mail?

(A) To warn of weather conditions
(B) To recommend a schedule change
(C) To offer a position
(D) To outline a procedure

173. What is suggested about Ms. Simon?

(A) She has opened the library before.
(B) She will drive to work tomorrow.
(C) She reads the newspaper every day.
(D) She usually closes the library.

174. What is NOT something Ms. Simon is expected to do?

(A) Disable a security system
(B) Open the front doors
(C) Read the mail
(D) Count money

175. What will Ms. Yales do tomorrow?

(A) Retire from her job
(B) Drive Ms. Simon to work
(C) Stay home for the day
(D) Handle customer questions

Questions 176-180 refer to the following e-mail and voucher.

To: Cage, Peter <pcage@jaysmail.net>
From: Topher, Edward <etopher@sapphireflowers.com>
Date: May 8
Subject: Free Voucher

Dear Mr. Cage,

We are very sorry for the late delivery of your floral arrangement on May 5. We understand that because of this delay, the celebration of your daughter's acceptance into Boston University was not as special as it could have been.

Unfortunately, we ran out of roses on that day and had failed to set some aside for your afternoon delivery. We placed another order, but since our supplier is located in Stratton, it took time to get the flowers. We are in the process of switching to a more modern inventory management program, and we can assure you that this kind of mistake will not happen again. We hope that you will continue to choose Sapphire Flowers for your future special occasions.

To express our regret, we are offering you a voucher for a complimentary bouquet of your choice to be delivered at any address in the area. You will find it attached to this e-mail. Please print it and fill it out when you wish to order a delivery.

Sincerely,

Edward Topher
Sapphire Flowers

~ Sapphire Flowers ~

Voucher Code: XS564813

Good for one floral arrangement and its delivery within Jayville.

Choose from the following selection:

☐ Classic Roses ■ Blue Bunch ☐ Dream Bouquet ☐ Spring Special

Delivery date: Monday, May 18   **Delivery time:** 10 A.M.
Address: Janice Richards
Frontier Corp. finance department
514 Enterprise Drive

Message(Optional):

Dear Janice,

I am sad to see you go. It was great working with you all these years. I hope you enjoy your new job in Bendertown!

Regards,
Peter Cage

176. What is the purpose of the e-mail?

    (A) To notify of a delay
    (B) To offer an apology
    (C) To report a system error
    (D) To congratulate a coworker

177. What does Mr. Topher indicate happened on May 5?

    (A) His store's inventory was mismanaged.
    (B) His daughter was accepted into college.
    (C) His supplier was replaced.
    (D) His flowers were all delivered late.

178. In the e-mail, the word "assure" in paragraph 2, line 4, is closest in meaning to

    (A) convince
    (B) remind
    (C) guarantee
    (D) compensate

179. Who most likely is Janice Richards?

    (A) Mr. Cage's colleague
    (B) Mr. Topher's supervisor
    (C) Mr. Cage's customer
    (D) Mr. Topher's supplier

180. Where most likely is Mr. Topher's store located?

    (A) Boston
    (B) Stratton
    (C) Jayville
    (D) Bendertown

Questions 181-185 refer to the following letter and e-mail.

July 31

Jerome Madison
2675 Chenoweth Drive
Nashville, TN 37214

Dear Mr. Madison,

I heard that you are searching for a new assistant manager for the marketing team. As you know, I have been the manager of Gamma Motors' design team for eleven years. Ms. Skye Armand started working on my team six years ago and has proven to be a strong asset. She has informed me of her intention to apply for the position of assistant manager with the marketing team, and I offered to write a reference letter.

I believe that Ms. Armand's transfer could be beneficial to the company. Her understanding of design strategies and how to appeal to customers is evident in her work, and this talent would be of high value in the marketing team. Moreover, her experience within Gamma Motors and her intimate knowledge of its various models would contribute greatly to creating effective marketing campaigns. I know that you will soon be focusing on preparing for the launch of the new Gamma SUV 6. Ms. Armand has been involved in several aspects of the vehicle's design, and I think she will have some great ideas about how to present it in its best light.

If you have any questions about Ms. Armand's work, feel free to contact me.

Sincerely,

Melanie Yoder
Melanie Yoder, Design Manager

To: Marketing employees <marketingteam@gammamotors.com>
From: Jerome Madison <jmadison@gammamotors.com>
Date: September 2
Subject: Marketing Campaign

The campaign for our newest model has proven highly successful. Our teaser video has been shared all over social media and has reached millions of views. A reporter for a popular car magazine has even asked to interview one of our managers.

Congratulations to everyone, but especially to Ms. Armand. This was her first campaign, and we were able to come up with the best features to highlight in our advertisements thanks to her experience in developing its design. We already have a high number of test drive requests, and we expect the launch to be even more successful than our minivan's.

Regards,

Jerome Madison, Marketing Manager

181. Why did Ms. Yoder write to Mr. Madison?

(A) To recommend a worker
(B) To submit her résumé
(C) To offer him a position
(D) To advertise a product

182. In the letter, the word "intimate" in paragraph 2, line 4, is closest in meaning to

(A) private
(B) detailed
(C) objective
(D) faithful

183. What is mentioned about the teaser video?

(A) Many people have watched it.
(B) It features a talk with a Gamma employee.
(C) It became a top-rated movie.
(D) It was released by Gamma's competitor.

184. What is Mr. Madison congratulating his team about?

(A) A minivan's advertisement
(B) An SUV's marketing
(C) A member's promotion
(D) A magazine's popularity

185. What is suggested about Ms. Armand?

(A) She turned down a job offer.
(B) She has been promoted to manager.
(C) She recently switched teams.
(D) She wrote an article for a magazine.

GO ON TO THE NEXT PAGE

Questions 186-190 refer to the following Web page, log sheet, and e-mail.

Help Center

What can we help you with?

I have   ☐ a Question   ■ a Request/Problem   ☐ a Comment

My Message to Fuchsia Foods:

I've been receiving Fuchsia Foods' organic food delivery boxes for three months now. I really enjoy receiving my package each afternoon, so I wish to upgrade my plan to the next level. When you make the switch, please keep in mind that I am a vegetarian and continue to send me the packages that don't include meat or eggs. If this change is possible, please bill me accordingly.

Thank you very much.

Sebastian Palmer

Do you expect a reply?
■ Yes   ☐ No

If yes, please provide your e-mail address:
sebpalmer@yourmail.net

SUBMIT

Thank you for contacting us.
If you requested a reply, we will be in contact with you shortly regarding your inquiry.
If you have a question that requires immediate assistance, please call us at 352-555-2948.

March 15 Deliveries

	Basic	Deluxe	Basic vegetarian	Deluxe vegetarian	Delivery Time
86 Tassen Road			✓		11:35 A.M.
15 Jordan Drive				✓	11:50 A.M.
56 Preston Avenue		✓			2:12 P.M.
12 Mesca Street				✓	2:26 P.M.

To: Sebastian Palmer <sebpalmer@yourmail.net>
From: Customer Service <cservice@fuchsiafoods.com>
Date: March 15
Subject: About your upgrade request

Dear Mr. Palmer,

This is to confirm that we have switched your package delivery plan. Your first package of the new plan was delivered this afternoon. The credit card that we have on record for your account was billed accordingly.

Please note that we do not customarily allow plan switches before the end of a month since we preschedule our orders ahead of time. However, another member asked to change to your original plan, so we were able to simply switch your two deliveries. This was a lucky coincidence, but please note that if you wish to make future changes, you will have to wait until the end of a month to do so.

Thank you for your understanding, and enjoy your new food deliveries!

Sincerely,

Rebecca Lars
Customer Service Representative

---

186. Why did Mr. Palmer post on the Web page?
(A) To cancel an erroneous payment
(B) To ask for a non-vegetarian option
(C) To stop receiving packages
(D) To modify his current plan

187. What kind of package was Mr. Palmer originally receiving?
(A) Basic
(B) Deluxe
(C) Basic vegetarian
(D) Deluxe vegetarian

188. Where does Mr. Palmer most likely live?
(A) 86 Tassen Road
(B) 15 Jordan Drive
(C) 56 Preston Avenue
(D) 12 Mesca Street

189. In the e-mail, in paragraph 2, line 1, the word "customarily" is closest in meaning to
(A) normally
(B) fairly
(C) naturally
(D) rarely

190. According to the e-mail, why was Mr. Palmer's request granted?
(A) He waited until the end of the month.
(B) He asked to switch in advance.
(C) Another customer requested a plan switch.
(D) The desired plan is more expensive.

Questions 191-195 refer to the following invitation, article, and text message.

OFFICIAL INVITATION

Dear Mr. Pratt,

As a longtime investor of Barton Electronics, you are invited to Barton's Future and Progress Event on April 24. I will be making a major announcement that you do not want to miss.

Date: April 24
Time: From 2 P.M. to 4 P.M.
Location: Falcon Room (third floor), Hiver Hotel
Entrance: Free (must present this card)

Looking forward to seeing you,

Vin Vecino

Barton Electronics' Upcoming Announcement

Barton Electronics will be holding a special event on April 24. The company is to make what its CEO called a "major announcement" in the invitations that were sent out. It has since then been confirmed that Barton Electronics will be presenting a new device. Yet the type of device is still unconfirmed, and rumors have been flooding the Internet.

It all started when photos of a new laptop design were leaked on social media last week. However, the source of these leaks is unknown, and their authenticity has not been verified.

Mr. Vecino was also caught on camera meeting with Ms. Beatrix Starling, the famous fitness expert who created a popular series of training videos. Fitness trackers have recently seen a surge in popularity, so this meeting sparked rumors about a possible Barton fitness tracker. When asked about his reason for meeting with Ms. Starling, Mr. Vecino refused to comment.

Finally, it is likely that Barton Electronics will announce their new smartphone model. The company has released a new phone every year for the past four years, and their last model, the Barton 44, is close to a year old.

From: Vin Vecino
To: Steven Parker

Ms. Starling sent me a copy of the speech she intends to give. In it, she explains the advantages of the device's main features. Originally, we were going to have her present at the end, but I think it would be better if she went before we show the pictures of the device. So I've decided to save the pictures for last to build up anticipation. I'll e-mail her speech to you now. Take a look at it and tell me if you agree.

191. What is Mr. Pratt required to do for the event?

    (A) Show the invitation
    (B) Bring a device
    (C) Reserve the room
    (D) Prepare a presentation

192. Who is Vin Vecino?

    (A) A special guest
    (B) A company CEO
    (C) A fitness expert
    (D) A private investor

193. In the article, the word "caught" in paragraph 3, line 1, is closest in meaning to

    (A) recorded
    (B) scheduled
    (C) arrested
    (D) expected

194. What new device is Barton Electronics most likely launching?

    (A) A smartphone
    (B) A camera
    (C) A laptop
    (D) A fitness tracker

195. When will people see pictures of the new device?

    (A) Before the event
    (B) At the start of the event
    (C) At the end of the event
    (D) After the event

Questions 196-200 refer to the following advertisement, online form, and review.

Yula School Programs

Yula School provides the most comprehensive programs for event decorators. Learn how to design a space to create the best customized environment. Our programs take just one year to complete! At Yula, you will take several core courses before moving on to your two specialty courses, which depend on the curriculum you choose. The specialty courses included in each curriculum are listed below.

Curriculum A: Weddings and Showers
– Draping and Fabrics
– Using Plants and Trees

Curriculum B: Private Holiday Celebrations
– Choosing a Color Scheme
– Mood Creation with Lighting

Curriculum C: Corporate Events
– Choosing a Color Scheme
– Creating a Stage

Curriculum D: Themed Children's Parties
– Balloon Sculptures
– Creating a Stage

*The deadlines for applying are August 15 for the fall semester and November 15 for the spring semester. Submit a résumé, motivation letter, and letter of recommendation to admissions@yula.com to apply.

Questions & Comments

STUDENT
Jeremy Forester

I am in my last class to complete my Yula event decorator program. However, I was wondering if it would be possible to take one more class after this semester. My friend Kelly Leonard is in the Private Holiday Celebrations program, and she is really enjoying her current course, which is not offered in any other curriculum. Is it possible to add just this class without following the entire curriculum? If so, how much would it cost?

SUBMIT

Review: ★★★★★
Name: J. Forester

Shortly after I completed the curriculum, I was contacted by a company to decorate their venue for a new product launch party. Everyone was praising the decorations, and the company was so pleased with my work that they asked me to deal with their tenth anniversary celebration. I never expected to be so quickly hired for such a big event. Thanks to all the hands-on experience I received at Yula School, everyone thought I'd been in the business for years! Yula really prepares you well by giving you excellent tips and training you in everything you'll need for your decorating business. I highly recommend Yula to anyone who wants to become a professional decorator.

196. What is NOT mentioned about Yula School's programs?

(A) How to submit an application
(B) What the specialty courses are
(C) How long a program lasts
(D) When each semester begins

197. Which class is Ms. Leonard currently taking?

(A) Draping and Fabrics
(B) Choosing a Color Scheme
(C) Mood Creation with Lighting
(D) Creating a Stage

198. In the review, the phrase "deal with" in paragraph 1, line 3, is closest in meaning to

(A) handle
(B) touch
(C) inform
(D) compensate

199. What is suggested about Mr. Forester?

(A) He has not worked as a decorator for very long.
(B) He now teaches courses at Yula School.
(C) He recently designed a new product.
(D) He will start a new program at Yula School.

200. Which curriculum did Mr. Forester most likely study?

(A) Curriculum A
(B) Curriculum B
(C) Curriculum C
(D) Curriculum D

Stop! This is the end of the test. If you finish before time is called, you may go back to Parts 5, 6, and 7 and check your work.

에 듀 윌 토 익 실 전 서

LC+RC

TEST 05

LISTENING TEST

PART 1
PART 2
PART 3
PART 4

READING TEST

PART 5
PART 6
PART 7

LISTENING TEST

In the Listening test, you will be asked to demonstrate how well you understand spoken English. The entire Listening test will last approximately 45 minutes. There are four parts, and directions are given for each part. You must mark your answers on the separate answer sheet. Do not write your answers in your test book.

PART 1

Directions: For each question in this part, you will hear four statements about a picture in your test book. When you hear the statements, you must select the one statement that best describes what you see in the picture. Then find the number of the question on your answer sheet and mark your answer. The statements will not be printed in your test book and will be spoken only one time.

Statement (C), "They're looking at a document," is the best description of the picture, so you should select answer (C) and mark it on your answer sheet.

1.

2.

3.

4.

5.

6.

PART 2

Directions: You will hear a question or statement and three responses spoken in English. They will not be printed in your test book and will be spoken only one time. Select the best response to the question or statement and mark the letter (A), (B), or (C) on your answer sheet.

7. Mark your answer on your answer sheet.
8. Mark your answer on your answer sheet.
9. Mark your answer on your answer sheet.
10. Mark your answer on your answer sheet.
11. Mark your answer on your answer sheet.
12. Mark your answer on your answer sheet.
13. Mark your answer on your answer sheet.
14. Mark your answer on your answer sheet.
15. Mark your answer on your answer sheet.
16. Mark your answer on your answer sheet.
17. Mark your answer on your answer sheet.
18. Mark your answer on your answer sheet.
19. Mark your answer on your answer sheet.
20. Mark your answer on your answer sheet.
21. Mark your answer on your answer sheet.
22. Mark your answer on your answer sheet.
23. Mark your answer on your answer sheet.
24. Mark your answer on your answer sheet.
25. Mark your answer on your answer sheet.
26. Mark your answer on your answer sheet.
27. Mark your answer on your answer sheet.
28. Mark your answer on your answer sheet.
29. Mark your answer on your answer sheet.
30. Mark your answer on your answer sheet.
31. Mark your answer on your answer sheet.

PART 3

Directions: You will hear some conversations between two or more people. You will be asked to answer three questions about what the speakers say in each conversation. Select the best response to each question and mark the letter (A), (B), (C), or (D) on your answer sheet. The conversations will not be printed in your test book and will be spoken only one time.

32. What are the speakers discussing?
    (A) A product description
    (B) A seating chart
    (C) An entrance code
    (D) A supplies order

33. What does the man give the woman?
    (A) A product catalog
    (B) An ID badge
    (C) A new form
    (D) A training manual

34. What does the man recommend doing?
    (A) Canceling an order
    (B) Directing questions to a coworker
    (C) Viewing an example online
    (D) Getting approval in advance

35. Who most likely are the speakers?
    (A) Salespeople
    (B) Researchers
    (C) Lecturers
    (D) Photographers

36. What does the man ask the woman to do?
    (A) Contact a supplier right away
    (B) Put some information on display
    (C) Finish a project ahead of schedule
    (D) Make some suggestions for improvements

37. What does the woman say she wants to do?
    (A) Check the inventory
    (B) Adjust a fee
    (C) Arrange a meeting
    (D) Confirm the attendance

38. What problem does the man mention?
    (A) A board member hasn't arrived yet.
    (B) A sales promotion didn't go well.
    (C) A document is missing some information.
    (D) A branch is performing more poorly than expected.

39. What does the woman ask about?
    (A) The topic of a report
    (B) The cost of a service
    (C) The number of board members
    (D) The start time of a meeting

40. What does the woman suggest doing?
    (A) Hiring a different printing service
    (B) Contacting the Fletcher branch
    (C) Changing the meeting date
    (D) Completing a task on site

41. What is the woman interested in buying?
    (A) A refrigerator
    (B) A television
    (C) A smartphone
    (D) A software program

42. Why does Barrett recommend the Stinson brand?
    (A) It has the widest selection.
    (B) It is currently on sale.
    (C) It is the most popular brand.
    (D) It has long-lasting products.

43. What will the woman probably do next?
    (A) Watch a demonstration
    (B) Ask for a discount
    (C) Extend a warranty
    (D) Fill out a registration form

GO ON TO THE NEXT PAGE

44. What are the speakers mainly discussing?
    (A) A hiring decision
    (B) An employee evaluation
    (C) A registration process
    (D) A business trip

45. Why was the man unable to read some materials?
    (A) He had a problem with his computer.
    (B) He recently returned from a vacation.
    (C) He had to visit an important client.
    (D) He was working on a coworker's task.

46. What does the woman imply when she says, "You shouldn't have to do that alone"?
    (A) She will help train the new employees.
    (B) She can assign an extra task to Liam.
    (C) She can help the man finish a report.
    (D) She will speak to the man's supervisor.

47. What kind of business do the speakers probably work for?
    (A) A delivery service
    (B) A printing company
    (C) A clothing outlet
    (D) An insurance agency

48. According to the man, what is the problem?
    (A) There is a shortage of supplies.
    (B) An order form contained an error.
    (C) There are not enough workers.
    (D) A client has made a complaint.

49. What do the speakers decide to do?
    (A) Work additional hours
    (B) Purchase some equipment
    (C) Cancel a project
    (D) Request a deadline extension

50. What does the man say he likes about the store?
    (A) Its wide selection
    (B) Its friendly employees
    (C) Its convenient hours
    (D) Its member rewards

51. Why is the man unable to use his coupon?
    (A) It has already expired.
    (B) It has a minimum purchase amount.
    (C) It is for a different store.
    (D) It cannot be used with other offers.

52. What does the woman mean when she says, "I'll go there shortly"?
    (A) She can drop off some paperwork for the man.
    (B) She will help the man carry his items.
    (C) She plans to take a break soon.
    (D) She will try to find some merchandise for the man.

53. What field does the man most likely work in?
    (A) Tourism
    (B) Ecology
    (C) Construction
    (D) Agriculture

54. What kind of project will the man explain?
    (A) A local cleanup
    (B) A building renovation
    (C) A marketing campaign
    (D) A company picnic

55. What is the woman concerned about?
    (A) Staying within a budget
    (B) Getting official approval
    (C) Finding enough volunteers
    (D) Starting a study on time

56. Where most likely is the conversation taking place?

(A) At a bus terminal
(B) At an airport
(C) At a hotel
(D) At a theater

57. According to the man, what is the additional fee for?

(A) A transportation service
(B) A room upgrade
(C) A cancellation fee
(D) A deposit

58. What will Alexandra most likely give Ms. Brooks next?

(A) A ticket
(B) A receipt
(C) A schedule
(D) A business card

59. What are the speakers mainly discussing?

(A) Vacation plans
(B) An opening celebration
(C) An end-of-year event
(D) A catering service

60. What will the woman ask her coworkers?

(A) What type of venue they want
(B) When their vacations are
(C) Who they plan to invite
(D) Which date they prefer

61. What does the man say he will do?

(A) Select menu items
(B) Reserve a restaurant
(C) Prepare a meal
(D) Contact guests

Dark Tan Shades

Brand	Product Code
Bridgeport	147
Lancaster	295
Reiser	466
Saldana	803

62. Why did the man change his mind?

(A) He asked a colleague's opinion.
(B) He tested some free samples.
(C) He found a cheaper item.
(D) He reviewed a product catalog.

63. Look at the graphic. Which product will the man purchase?

(A) Product 147
(B) Product 295
(C) Product 466
(D) Product 803

64. What is the man asked to do?

(A) Call back again later
(B) Provide room measurements
(C) Update an order form online
(D) Return some unused goods

GO ON TO THE NEXT PAGE

INTERPRETATION RATES	
Number of Hours	Price per Hour
1 hour	$80
2-4 hours	$75
5-6 hours	$70
More than 6 hours	$65

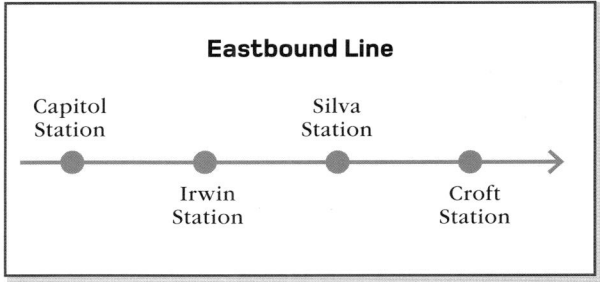

65. Who most likely is the man?
    (A) An event organizer
    (B) A language specialist
    (C) An information technology expert
    (D) A chemistry professor

66. What information does the woman ask for?
    (A) The date of the event
    (B) The address of a venue
    (C) The languages needed
    (D) The registration fee

67. Look at the graphic. How much will the man most likely pay per hour?
    (A) $80
    (B) $75
    (C) $70
    (D) $65

68. What does the man want to do?
    (A) Find a sports facility
    (B) Pick up a map
    (C) Change a train ticket
    (D) Get to a theater

69. Look at the graphic. To which stop is the man told to go?
    (A) Capitol Station
    (B) Irwin Station
    (C) Silva Station
    (D) Croft Station

70. What is the man concerned about?
    (A) Having to buy another ticket
    (B) Moving his luggage by himself
    (C) Missing the next train
    (D) Walking through a crowded station

PART 4

Directions: You will hear some talks given by a single speaker. You will be asked to answer three questions about what the speaker says in each talk. Select the best response to each question and mark the letter (A), (B), (C), or (D) on your answer sheet. The talks will not be printed in your test book and will be spoken only one time.

71. Where most likely are the listeners?
    (A) At a fashion show
    (B) At an art institute
    (C) At a hardware store
    (D) At a community center

72. According to the speaker, what can be found in the west wing?
    (A) A promotional video
    (B) A demonstration
    (C) Some free samples
    (D) Some paintings

73. What does the speaker encourage listeners to do?
    (A) Enroll in a rewards program
    (B) Share their feedback
    (C) Make some suggestions
    (D) Sign up for a workshop

74. Where most likely does the speaker work?
    (A) At a construction company
    (B) At a property management firm
    (C) At an insurance agency
    (D) At a plumbing company

75. What is the call mainly about?
    (A) Arranging a repair
    (B) Scheduling a tour
    (C) Announcing renovations
    (D) Signing a lease

76. Why should the listener call the speaker back?
    (A) To pay for a service
    (B) To register a complaint
    (C) To approve a charge
    (D) To change an appointment

77. Who is Jackie Galvani?
    (A) A radio host
    (B) A researcher
    (C) A painter
    (D) An art critic

78. What did Ms. Galvani recently do?
    (A) Started a school
    (B) Gave a lecture
    (C) Opened a gallery
    (D) Reviewed a sculpture

79. What does the speaker ask listeners to do?
    (A) Register for a class
    (B) Buy a painting
    (C) Speak with the guest
    (D) Submit questions

80. Who is this advertisement intended for?
    (A) Job seekers
    (B) Business owners
    (C) New employees
    (D) Professional recruiters

81. What field does the speaker's company specialize in?
    (A) Pharmaceuticals
    (B) Journalism
    (C) Fashion
    (D) Computer science

82. What are listeners asked to send?
    (A) A description of their facilities
    (B) A selection of preferred candidates
    (C) An explanation of their needs
    (D) A list of interview questions

GO ON TO THE NEXT PAGE

83. Why is the business closed?
    (A) An emergency happened.
    (B) Renovations are being made.
    (C) A dentist recently retired.
    (D) Workers are on vacation.

84. What does the speaker imply when he says, "Otherwise, tell us if you have a preferred dentist"?
    (A) New customers may choose a dentist.
    (B) A new dentist will be hired.
    (C) Patients can write reviews of their dentists.
    (D) Regulars may select a new dentist.

85. When will the clinic reopen?
    (A) On July 30
    (B) On July 31
    (C) On August 8
    (D) On August 9

86. Why did the speaker schedule the meeting?
    (A) To give a demonstration of a product
    (B) To make corrections to a sales report
    (C) To provide information about an industry event
    (D) To request volunteers for a trade fair booth

87. What recently changed about the Kenosha-50?
    (A) Its battery weight was reduced.
    (B) Its warranty period was extended.
    (C) Its processing speed was improved.
    (D) Its screen size was increased.

88. What does the speaker mean when she says, "it's currently just under five hundred grams"?
    (A) The price is too high for the weight.
    (B) A device does not meet the industry standard.
    (C) Supplies are running out faster than expected.
    (D) The product is inconvenient to carry around.

89. Who does the speaker introduce?
    (A) An author
    (B) A history professor
    (C) A director
    (D) A movie producer

90. What does the speaker apologize for?
    (A) A leaflet has an error.
    (B) A presentation is delayed.
    (C) A movie screening is canceled.
    (D) A guest cannot come.

91. What does the speaker imply when he says, "I hope you brought your own"?
    (A) Items will not be available on site.
    (B) Listeners need an entrance ticket for the talk.
    (C) Mr. Stroud will answer some prepared questions.
    (D) Listeners may suggest their own ideas.

92. Why does the speaker congratulate the listeners?
    (A) They improved their work efficiency.
    (B) They exceeded a sales goal.
    (C) They hired a hard-working employee.
    (D) They attracted a new client.

93. According to the speaker, what was the most impressive part of a presentation?
    (A) Its simple explanations
    (B) Its variety of photographs
    (C) Its accompanying handout
    (D) Its helpful charts

94. What will the speaker probably do next?
    (A) Introduce a coworker
    (B) Present some awards
    (C) Write a list of companies
    (D) Assign the listeners to teams

Elliot Bay Ferries

Seattle → Bainbridge Island

Departure: 9:20 A.M.   Arrival: 10:10 A.M.

Ticket Type: Walk-on Passenger
Ticket Fee: $8.20

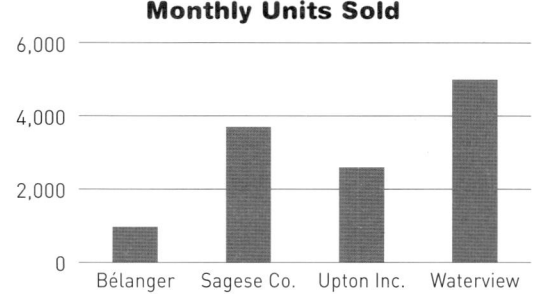

95. What does the speaker remind listeners to do?
    (A) Direct questions to terminal employees
    (B) Keep their belongings with them
    (C) Check the departure dock
    (D) Have their tickets ready

96. Look at the graphic. When should the ticket holder board the ferry?
    (A) At 8:50 A.M.
    (B) At 9:00 A.M.
    (C) At 9:20 A.M.
    (D) At 10:10 A.M.

97. What will be given to listeners soon?
    (A) A ticket receipt
    (B) A safety briefing
    (C) A terminal map
    (D) A seat assignment

98. What did the speaker do on Tuesday?
    (A) Met with a consultant
    (B) Tested product samples
    (C) Checked the inventory
    (D) Processed an order

99. What is causing a change in product supplies?
    (A) A building expansion
    (B) A business closure
    (C) An inventory error
    (D) A training event

100. Look at the graphic. Which brand will have more items added?
    (A) Bélanger
    (B) Sagese Co.
    (C) Upton Inc.
    (D) Waterview

This is the end of the Listening Test. Turn to Part 5 in your test book.

READING TEST

In the Reading test, you will read a variety of texts and answer several different types of reading comprehension questions. The entire Reading test will last 75 minutes. There are three parts, and directions are given for each part. You are encouraged to answer as many questions as possible within the time allowed.

You must mark your answers on the separate answer sheet. Do not write your answers in the test book.

PART 5

Directions: A word or phrase is missing in each of the sentences below. Four answer choices are given below each sentence. Select the best answer to complete the sentence. Then mark the letter (A), (B), (C), or (D) on your answer sheet.

101. Mr. Wexler bought lunch for ------- team as a way of showing appreciation.
    (A) he
    (B) him
    (C) his
    (D) himself

102. ------- the past three months, the number of members at Slate Gym has doubled.
    (A) Under
    (B) While
    (C) At
    (D) Over

103. The letter to the editor was written by Janice Reeves, a ------- to *National Gardening Magazine*.
    (A) subscribed
    (B) subscribes
    (C) subscriber
    (D) subscription

104. Bothell Manufacturing will ------- be streamlining its production line with modern equipment.
    (A) quite
    (B) soon
    (C) else
    (D) ever

105. Now that the bakery has brought in a long-term investor, it is in good shape -------.
    (A) finances
    (B) finance
    (C) financial
    (D) financially

106. Benz Athletics was able to increase sales thanks to the ------- of a new line of clothing designed for children.
    (A) delivery
    (B) suggestion
    (C) content
    (D) addition

107. Consumers can save a lot of money on furniture if the components ------- at home.
    (A) assembling
    (B) to be assembled
    (C) have assembled
    (D) are assembled

108. Nature enthusiasts enjoy taking hikes ------- the woods located at the northern section of Derby National Park.
    (A) through
    (B) onto
    (C) regarding
    (D) except

109. The guests seated at the VIP table at the company's banquet include ------- for the annual employee awards.
   (A) nominated
   (B) nominations
   (C) nominees
   (D) nominate

110. Security guards at Mayfair International Airport need to be ------- of the rules and regulations for travelers.
   (A) alert
   (B) precise
   (C) aware
   (D) strict

111. Since the director was not available that day, the members of the sales team gave the product presentation to the buyers by -------.
   (A) themselves
   (B) them
   (C) they
   (D) theirs

112. Shobe Utilities ------- the information on its Web site to Spanish and Chinese so that it can be understood by more customers.
   (A) is translated
   (B) have translated
   (C) has translated
   (D) be translated

113. The current IT department is indeed the most ------- group in the company's history.
   (A) diversely
   (B) diversification
   (C) diverse
   (D) diversify

114. The manuscript for Ms. Colby's award-winning bestseller was ------- rejected by the publisher.
   (A) rather
   (B) nearby
   (C) yet
   (D) almost

115. Ms. Simpson, who is the Carolina branch's top salesperson, requested that ------- be promoted to team leader.
   (A) herself
   (B) she
   (C) her
   (D) hers

116. EZ Couriers will purchase three more vans for its fleet in an effort to ------- the rise in demand for its services.
   (A) predict
   (B) accommodate
   (C) attribute
   (D) generate

117. Tourists and locals alike visit the farmers' market because the produce there is very ------- priced.
   (A) reason
   (B) reasoned
   (C) reasonably
   (D) reasonable

118. ------- arriving at their final destination, the airline passengers waited for their belongings at the luggage carousel.
   (A) Along
   (B) Upon
   (C) Unlike
   (D) During

119. The newly trained cook forgot two of the ------- ingredients in the soup, so it did not turn out right.
   (A) essential
   (B) inherent
   (C) equal
   (D) reliable

120. The company's image is built on trust, ------- employees are expected to be open and honest with customers at all times.
   (A) never
   (B) so
   (C) what
   (D) then

121. Mr. Vaughn wants to prepare a working model of the prototype ------- collaborating on the details with others.
    (A) even so
    (B) before
    (C) so that
    (D) instead

122. Lavola Restaurant is almost always filled to capacity and has earned a ------- for excellent food and service.
    (A) clarification
    (B) statement
    (C) commitment
    (D) reputation

123. The department store provided sample bottles of perfume ------- allow customers to try them.
    (A) by far
    (B) as a result of
    (C) in order to
    (D) above all

124. As its expansion project is completed, Lintz Hotel will ------- more staff members to handle the higher volume of guests.
    (A) forfeit
    (B) recruit
    (C) dedicate
    (D) delegate

125. The quality of the first draft of the report was not -------, so the manager asked for it to be rewritten.
    (A) accepting
    (B) acceptably
    (C) acceptable
    (D) acceptability

126. Event planners selected the Ingram Center for the software convention due to its ------- to major highways.
    (A) publicity
    (B) proximity
    (C) regularity
    (D) locality

127. Dr. Kapadia, who has conducted ------- research in the field of genetic engineering, is a highly respected biologist.
    (A) furnished
    (B) extensive
    (C) perishable
    (D) punctual

128. ------- gently the criticism of a staff member is made, it could still cause offense to a sensitive person.
    (A) Somewhat
    (B) However
    (C) Entirely
    (D) Seldom

129. Gabriel Falcone created a fully automated system that allowed the pharmaceutical company to more ------ evaluate a medical test's accuracy.
    (A) narrowly
    (B) increasingly
    (C) partially
    (D) efficiently

130. A number of board members questioned ------- Mr. Woodworth had the right qualifications for the position.
    (A) both
    (B) unless
    (C) because
    (D) whether

PART 6

Directions: Read the texts that follow. A word, phrase, or sentence is missing in parts of each text. Four answer choices for each question are given below the text. Select the best answer to complete the text. Then mark the letter (A), (B), (C), or (D) on your answer sheet.

Questions 131-134 refer to the following advertisement.

Jacobs Interiors

Why move when you can just upgrade for a fraction of the cost? Our experienced designers have ------- homes, offices, and even television studios! They will help you every step of the way, starting
131.
with the selection of materials. -------. Nevertheless, we are willing to get items imported or shipped
132.
to get you exactly what you want. We will also keep your safety in mind, as we have engineers inspect structures ------- to the building's support system before making any changes. Visit our Web
133.
site at www.jacobsint.com to see photos of past projects and read testimonials about how we fulfilled customers' -------.
134.

131. (A) related
(B) transformed
(C) invested
(D) toured

132. (A) The business offers a money-back guarantee on the work.
(B) Don't hesitate to share your project ideas with the designer.
(C) Some colors remain popular from year to year.
(D) We try to use locally sourced supplies as often as we can.

133. (A) vitally
(B) vital
(C) vitalize
(D) vitality

134. (A) orders
(B) relations
(C) behaviors
(D) forms

Questions 135-138 refer to the following memo.

To: All Haynes Airlines Ticket and Gate Agents
From: Crystal Lecuyer
Date: October 25

In preparation for the busy holiday travel season, we will be ------- two extra lines in our check-in area. We believe this will help us to reduce the long wait times for check-in.
135.

Under this new plan, part-time workers will have additional shifts ------- January 5. You may also
136.
------- to work at the gate, as boarding is an important factor in on-time departures. Your supervisors
137.
plan to set a schedule soon. -------.
138.

Thank you for your hard work and cooperation.

135. (A) opening
(B) relocating
(C) decorating
(D) suspending

136. (A) within
(B) until
(C) during
(D) following

137. (A) assigning
(B) be assigned
(C) assigned
(D) having assigned

138. (A) Gate numbers should be posted as soon as possible.
(B) A copy of it is attached to this memo.
(C) Travelers are expected to request this service.
(D) Please notify them of any potential scheduling conflicts.

Questions 139-142 refer to the following article.

Golf Club to Raise Funds for Local Museum

HOLTONVILLE, August 7—The Holtonville Golf Club will hold its first-ever tournament at Greenway Golf Course to raise money for the Contemporary Art Museum. -------. Winners will take home a trophy as well as gift cards. The club hopes that participants will not only have a good time but will also become ------- informed about the importance of art in the community. -------, the event provides a great opportunity for young golfers to play in a friendly competition. All ------- from the event will go toward making urgent roof repairs at the museum.

139. (A) The city's mayor praised organizers for their focus on the environment.
(B) Golf lessons are offered at the site throughout the summer months.
(C) The prizes for the competition will be announced at a later date.
(D) The competition will grant participants prizes donated by local businesses.

140. (A) full
(B) fullness
(C) fuller
(D) fully

141. (A) Otherwise
(B) Thus
(C) Furthermore
(D) In fact

142. (A) interest
(B) proceeds
(C) materials
(D) separation

Questions 143-146 refer to the following e-mail.

To: Pamela Rardin <p.rardin@montoyainc.net>
From: Aarom Communications <info@aaromcomm.com>
Date: September 4
Subject: Aarom-6 Phone

Dear Ms. Rardin,

Our records show that you recently made a ------- (143.) of an Aarom-6 smartphone from Aarom Communications. We are delighted to offer you our noise-canceling wireless headphones for just $89.99. ------- (144.). These headphones provide premium sound quality, a comfortable fit, and a long battery life.

If you are interested, please ------- (145.) to this e-mail no later than September 10 with your preferred mailing address. We will then make a charge to your Aarom customer account. ------- (146.) will appear on your monthly statement as "Aarom Headphones." We hope you will take advantage of this great deal, and we look forward to serving you.

Sincerely,

Sharon Kearney
Customer Service Agent, Aarom Communications

143. (A) review
(B) repair
(C) purchase
(D) profit

144. (A) This special price reflects a thirty percent discount.
(B) They come as a standard accessory at no extra charge.
(C) You can read more about this in your product warranty.
(D) We appreciate your notifying us of the issue promptly.

145. (A) respond
(B) subscribe
(C) disregard
(D) feel free

146. (A) Those
(B) Few
(C) Another
(D) It

PART 7

Directions: In this part, you will read a selection of texts, such as magazine and newspaper articles, e-mails, and instant messages. Each text or set of texts is followed by several questions. Select the best answer for each question and mark the letter (A), (B), (C), or (D) on your answer sheet.

Questions 147-148 refer to the following notice.

Crestar Maintenance Project

From June 3 to July 18, we will be working on several maintenance projects on our network. This work may affect your departure time and/or journey duration. Signs are posted throughout the station to inform you of the changes to the timetable for each day. Please be sure to view this posted information to ensure that you know what to expect. Thank you for your patience.

147. For whom is the notice most likely intended?
(A) Safety inspectors
(B) Travel agents
(C) Construction workers
(D) Train passengers

148. What does the notice instruct people to do?
(A) Check an adjusted schedule
(B) Provide feedback about a service
(C) Report problems to the company
(D) Make a payment in advance

GO ON TO THE NEXT PAGE

Questions 149-150 refer to the following invoice.

Barrington Roofing
305 Acres Lane, Brentwood, TN 37027
(615) 555-8483

Customer: Leonard Harper
Property Site: 4651 Guevara Street, Brentwood, TN 37027
Description of Work: Replace roof on residential property

Original Quote	$7,500	Issue Date	May 3
Updated Quote	$6,300	Issue Date	May 7

Notes: The original quote included the entire roof replacement process. Now the client will remove the old shingles before the project begins and handle their disposal separately.

Start Date	May 15	End Date	May 16
Deposit and first payment received			$300 on May 7

* Half of the balance ($3,000) is due as a second payment on the first day of work. The final payment is due one week after the completion of the work. Please note that payments must be made in accordance with this schedule regardless of weather delays.

149. Why has a charge on the invoice been changed?
 (A) The price of materials has increased.
 (B) The customer presented a coupon.
 (C) The permit had to be paid for separately.
 (D) The customer will take care of some of the work.

150. When should Mr. Harper make his second payment?
 (A) On May 15
 (B) On May 16
 (C) On May 22
 (D) On May 23

Questions 151-152 refer to the following text-message chain.

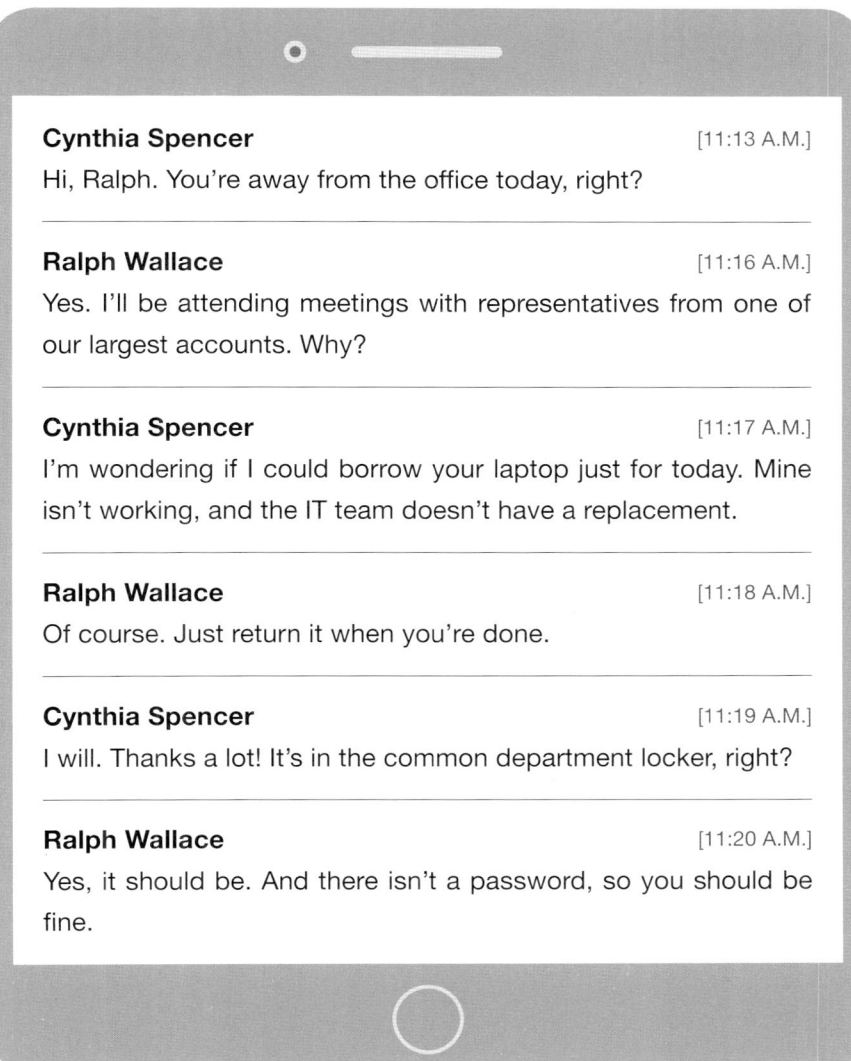

Cynthia Spencer [11:13 A.M.]
Hi, Ralph. You're away from the office today, right?

Ralph Wallace [11:16 A.M.]
Yes. I'll be attending meetings with representatives from one of our largest accounts. Why?

Cynthia Spencer [11:17 A.M.]
I'm wondering if I could borrow your laptop just for today. Mine isn't working, and the IT team doesn't have a replacement.

Ralph Wallace [11:18 A.M.]
Of course. Just return it when you're done.

Cynthia Spencer [11:19 A.M.]
I will. Thanks a lot! It's in the common department locker, right?

Ralph Wallace [11:20 A.M.]
Yes, it should be. And there isn't a password, so you should be fine.

151. What is Mr. Wallace doing today?

(A) Meeting some clients off-site
(B) Training some IT workers
(C) Setting up a meeting room
(D) Giving some customers a tour

152. At 11:18 A.M., what does Mr. Wallace mean when he writes, "Of course"?

(A) He will call the IT team to make a request.
(B) He does not mind lending some equipment to Ms. Spencer.
(C) He can help repair Ms. Spencer's malfunctioning laptop.
(D) He will order a replacement item for Ms. Spencer.

Questions 153-154 refer to the following memo.

To: All Osage Consulting Employees
From: Carla Watson, Branch Supervisor
Date: October 17
Subject: Employee break room

Now that the employee break room is open again following the renovations, we want to make sure that this area is kept clean and tidy for all who use it. Therefore, from now on, we are changing the policy on the usage of the refrigerator. Whenever you put something in the refrigerator, it must have your name and the date marked on it clearly. Every Friday afternoon, the refrigerator will be cleaned out, and items that have expired and those that do not have names on them will be thrown out. This will ensure that the refrigerator does not get too full and does not have any spoiled food in it. Thank you in advance for your cooperation.

153. Why did Ms. Watson write the memo?
(A) To notify staff of a renovation
(B) To explain a break schedule
(C) To report a room closure
(D) To announce a new rule

154. What are readers of the memo asked to do?
(A) Refrain from eating food in the office
(B) Empty the refrigerator every Friday
(C) Label their food and drink items
(D) Volunteer for a weekly cleanup job

Questions 155-157 refer to the following Web page.

The Bloomfield Public Library is proud to be one of the venues for the city's first-ever Spring Literary Festival, which runs from April 16 to 20. The event will feature talks all over the city from professional writers who have had their works published recently, including Jiang Li, Linda Atchison, Yamuna Bose, and Patrick Corona. Ms. Atchison's talk, which will be held at our library, is expected to be a particularly big draw, as her latest mystery novel, *Onward North*, has spent thirty weeks on the bestseller list. The book also took home the prestigious Larochelle Prize last month.

Tickets for the event can be purchased at the Bloomfield Community Center.

155. What is NOT true about the Spring Literary Festival?

(A) It has never been held before.
(B) It will last for less than a week.
(C) It includes an author awards ceremony.
(D) It will take place in several locations.

156. Who has recently won an award?

(A) Jiang Li
(B) Linda Atchison
(C) Yamuna Bose
(D) Patrick Corona

157. What is mentioned about Bloomfield Public Library?

(A) It will be closed in preparation for the festival.
(B) It organizes the literary festival every year.
(C) It will host a lecture by a professional writer.
(D) It is seeking volunteers to assist with the festival.

Questions 158-160 refer to the following e-mail.

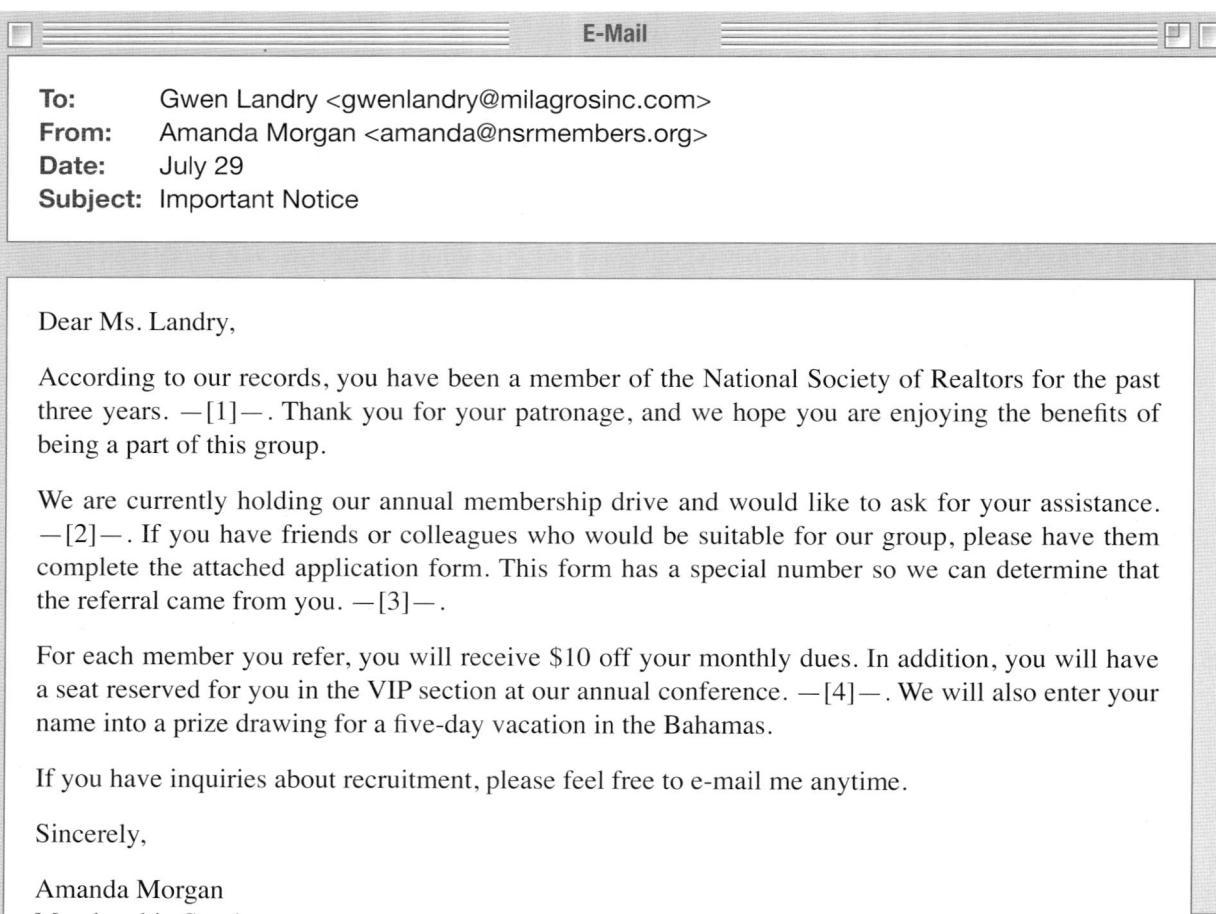

158. Who most likely is Ms. Landry?

(A) A group founder
(B) A real estate agent
(C) A homeowner
(D) A bank teller

159. What is NOT an advantage of referring members?

(A) A chance to win a trip
(B) Priority seating at an event
(C) A reduction in membership fees
(D) Discounted tickets to a conference

160. In which of the positions marked [1], [2], [3], and [4] does the following sentence best belong?

"It can be found at the bottom of the page."

(A) [1]
(B) [2]
(C) [3]
(D) [4]

Questions 161-163 refer to the following letter.

Aiden Holt
739 Kessler Way
Syracuse, NY 13202

Dear Mr. Holt,

We hope you have enjoyed the free one-month trial of our Premium Sports Package. Your access to the four international football channels, two basketball channels, and two mixed sports channels will end on April 30 if you take no further action. To make sure you don't miss any of the sports coverage you love, sign up for a one-year subscription to the Premium Sports Package, which will add just $7.95 to your monthly bill. You can do so by changing the settings on your online account with Chapman Cable through our Web site. There you can also check your user agreement for details about how to add or discontinue premium packages.

Enclosed you will also find a postage-paid postcard, on which you can share your suggestions, ideas, and complaints. We'd love to hear how you are finding your Chapman Cable experience so far.

Warmest regards,

The Chapman Cable Accounts Team

161. What is the purpose of the letter?
(A) To encourage a customer to continue a service
(B) To announce which channels will be added next month
(C) To introduce a new package of sports channels
(D) To remind a customer to make a payment on his account

162. What will happen on April 30?
(A) A free trial will expire.
(B) A sports event will take place.
(C) A discount will be applied.
(D) An online account will be disabled.

163. What is enclosed with the letter?
(A) A discount coupon
(B) A broadcast schedule
(C) An updated user agreement
(D) A comment card

Questions 164-167 refer to the following online chat discussion.

	Latika Nair 1:23 P.M.	Renovations on our office will not start next week as planned.
	Chet Matthews 1:25 P.M.	I heard that the company we were supposed to use went out of business unexpectedly.
	Latika Nair 1:26 P.M.	Right. So I'm looking for another construction firm, preferably one endorsed by someone I know. Any ideas?
	Diane Perdue 1:27 P.M.	I was very pleased with the work done by Norris Construction at my house last year.
	Chet Matthews 1:28 P.M.	But that business was sold to another person last month, so the quality might not be the same.
	Diane Perdue 1:29 P.M.	I didn't know that. We'd better not take any chances.
	Chet Matthews 1:30 P.M.	The dental clinic across the street recently had its interior redesigned, and it looks great.
	Latika Nair 1:31 P.M.	We should try to find out the address and contact number of their contractor.
	Motoshi Tenno 1:32 P.M.	I actually have an appointment there on Friday, so I'll do that during my visit.

164. Why did Ms. Nair start the online chat?

(A) To get a business recommendation
(B) To introduce a new contractor
(C) To review some contract terms
(D) To approve a renovation schedule

165. What is indicated about Norris Construction?

(A) It was endorsed by a dental clinic.
(B) It canceled a contract unexpectedly.
(C) It is under new ownership.
(D) It has lower prices than its competitors.

166. At 1:29 P.M., what does Ms. Perdue most likely mean when she writes, "We'd better not take any chances"?

(A) She wants to retract her suggestion.
(B) She thinks they should do a safety check.
(C) She plans to do further research.
(D) She needs more time for a decision.

167. What will Mr. Tenno do on Friday?

(A) Contact Norris Construction
(B) Gather information about a business
(C) Reschedule an appointment
(D) Visit a new contractor

Questions 168-171 refer to the following e-mail.

To: Gregory Pearlman <g.pearlman@oakway.com>
From: Tibbs Inc. <inquiries@tibbsinc.com>
Date: August 26
Subject: RE: Inquiry

Dear Mr. Pearlman,

I received your message about your recent participation in our sightseeing boat ride around Nieves Bay. I've checked our lost-and-found box, and there are indeed a few men's watches in there, one of which might be yours. Unfortunately, I cannot provide you with a photograph of these items as requested, as our company regulations do not allow it. To claim a lost item, you should come to our office at the harbor and give a description of the item. If possible, showing the ticket from your boat ride will make the process faster. That's because we will be able to determine exactly which boat you were on, and our found items are cataloged by date and boat.

There is no need to book an appointment in advance. Simply stop by during our office hours, which are 9 A.M. to 6 P.M. daily. Please note that we are a seasonal business, and the season is wrapping up at the end of the month. Therefore, you only have a few days to visit us before the office closes for the low season, so please do so if you can, as returning your item will become a lot more complicated after that.

Sincerely,

Lucy Wooldridge

Administrative Assistant, Tibbs Inc.

168. What kind of service does Tibbs Inc. most likely provide?
 (A) Event photography
 (B) Swimming lessons
 (C) Group tours
 (D) Hotel bookings

169. Why was Ms. Wooldridge unable to send Mr. Pearlman a picture?
 (A) A Web site is not working.
 (B) It is against company policy.
 (C) Some equipment is missing.
 (D) The image needs to be edited.

170. According to the e-mail, how can Mr. Pearlman expedite a process?
 (A) By avoiding the peak times
 (B) By paying an additional fee
 (C) By booking an appointment
 (D) By presenting a ticket

171. What does Ms. Wooldridge recommend doing?
 (A) Purchasing a season pass
 (B) Contacting her manager
 (C) E-mailing a description
 (D) Taking action quickly

Questions 172-175 refer to the following article.

Investment at GT Communications

March 3—GT Communications has confirmed its plans to invest heavily in technology for its facilities. Customers have shifted away from landlines, which previously made up GT Communications' entire business, and started using mobile phone networks and the Internet. Therefore, the company is adapting its business model by changing its infrastructure. — [1] —.

The smallest of the company's facilities—located in Nashville—already received the new machines so that the plan could be tried out on a small scale before rolling out the changes companywide. — [2] —. GT Communications is taking measures to ensure that its staff members are not negatively affected by the upgrades. "During the transition at Nashville, we looked for areas where we could retrain our people instead of laying them off," said company spokesperson Katherine Coyle. "— [3] —. We expect similar figures at the rest of our facilities."

GT Communications is now ready for Phase 2 of its transition, which is installing the state-of-the-art equipment at all sites. — [4] —. The work will begin with the Detroit site later this year, followed by the Kansas City branch early next year, and the Houston branch late next year. Once all of the upgrades have been completed, the final site will be open for public tours so that people can see the operations for themselves.

172. According to the article, what caused GT Communications to transform its business plan?

    (A) A new government regulation
    (B) A complaint from the workforce
    (C) A change in consumer behavior
    (D) An increase in shareholders

173. What is mentioned about the company's facility in Nashville?

    (A) It was used as a testing site.
    (B) It received a technology award.
    (C) It is the first factory opened by GT Communications.
    (D) It was the meeting place of investors.

174. Where does GT Communications plan to offer public tours of a site?

    (A) Nashville
    (B) Detroit
    (C) Kansas City
    (D) Houston

175. In which of the positions marked [1], [2], [3], and [4] does the following sentence best belong?

    "We were thus able to keep ninety percent of staff members at that location."

    (A) [1]
    (B) [2]
    (C) [3]
    (D) [4]

Questions 176-180 refer to the following information and e-mail.

Four intense workshops are being made available to employees of HTT Corp. Employees must choose one of the four courses below. Each course comprises three three-hour sessions unless otherwise specified. The sessions will be held on Fridays (March 14, 21, and 28) from 2 P.M. to 5 P.M.

Exchange Rates Risk Management
❏ Instructor: Frederic Masker
This course will look closely at how exchange rates affect markets, explain how predictions are made, and go over the best strategies for investing in an international context. This course has one additional two-hour session on April 4.

International Capital Flows
❏ Instructor: Lydia Benson
This course will explain how capital flows globally, introduce a few key relationships among countries, and go over the major effects of these flows on the global economy.

Multinational Corporations
❏ Instructor: Sylvia Glazkova
This course will introduce three major multinational corporations and give an in-depth analysis of their functioning and budget management.

Case Studies
❏ Instructor: Trenton Blair
This hands-on course will have students work in groups to analyze a case and determine the best strategy for the sample corporation to take. Each group will present their findings in the last session.

To: Linda Kay <lindakay@httcorp.com>
From: Peter Moreno <petermoreno@httcorp.com>
Subject: Friday Afternoon
Date: Thursday, March 27

Dear Ms. Kay,

Ms. Benson has changed the last session for the workshop from tomorrow to next Tuesday. I am thus free to work tomorrow afternoon. However, I was wondering if it would be acceptable for me to watch the presentations from Mr. Blair's class. Several coworkers taking that course have told me about their work, and I am highly interested in seeing the results. Of course, if I am needed in the office at that time, I will be available to work.

Thank you for your consideration.

Sincerely,

Peter Moreno
Budget Analyst, HTT Corp.

176. Where will the information most likely appear?

(A) In a brochure
(B) On a bulletin board
(C) In a magazine
(D) On a flyer

177. When will Ms. Glazkova's last class be held?

(A) March 14
(B) March 21
(C) March 28
(D) April 4

178. Which instructor will have students collaborate on a project?

(A) Frederic Masker
(B) Lydia Benson
(C) Sylvia Glazkova
(D) Trenton Blair

179. Which course has Mr. Moreno been attending?

(A) Exchange Rates Risk Management
(B) International Capital Flows
(C) Multinational Corporations
(D) Case Studies

180. What is NOT true about Mr. Moreno?

(A) He has already attended several classes.
(B) He wants to see his coworkers' projects.
(C) He is scheduled to give a presentation.
(D) He is able to come to the office on Friday.

Questions 181-185 refer to the following memo and schedule.

To: MMH Law Firm Employees
From: Tamara Caudill, Attorney
Subject: Re: Building for Sale

April 16

As discussed in the weekly meeting, the owner of Midland Tower will put the building up for sale next month, and we will relocate our offices. Aldridge Co., the realtor handling the sale of the building, would like professionals to take photos for the property listing on its Web site. This photo shoot will take place on April 24 and will be carried out in all parts of the building. I have attached a schedule with the offices that are going to be photographed. In preparation for the photographers' visit, all items must be cleared from your desk except your computer and phone. We will provide plastic bins for you, and you should put your items in them for the short duration of the shoot. A maintenance worker will visit you ten minutes before your appointed time to collect these bins with a cart. Furniture might be rearranged in your office, but it will be returned to its original placement before you get back. The entire process will take about twenty minutes maximum, during which time you can take a break in the staff lounge. This does not count toward your usual daily break time.

Thank you for your cooperation, and we apologize for any inconvenience this may cause.

[Attachment: Final Schedule]

Aldridge Co. Schedule: April 24

TIME	OFFICE	OCCUPANT(S)
9:00 A.M.	201	Harriet Duncan
9:20 A.M.	202	Ranjan Singh
9:40 A.M.	203	Dale Mumford, Michael Bellamy
10:00 A.M.	204	Shirley Swain
10:20 A.M.	205	Brandon Parra, Huan Ren

Brandon Parra will handle room 202 because the occupant won't be in the office that day.

181. What is the purpose of the memo?
 (A) To introduce a new building owner to employees
 (B) To explain how an office relocation will occur
 (C) To distribute a schedule for a renovation project
 (D) To announce a plan for photographing a building

182. What does Ms. Caudill advise the memo recipients to do?
 (A) Direct their questions to Aldridge Co.
 (B) Use containers to temporarily move items
 (C) Contact her regarding their availability on April 24
 (D) Leave their personal belongings at home

183. What can the memo recipients do on April 24?
 (A) Take an additional break
 (B) Work part of the day from home
 (C) Leave work early
 (D) Have an extended lunchtime

184. At what time will a maintenance worker arrive at Ms. Swain's office on April 24?
 (A) 9:40 A.M.
 (B) 9:50 A.M.
 (C) 10:00 A.M.
 (D) 10:10 A.M.

185. What is implied about Mr. Singh?
 (A) He will move to office 203.
 (B) He shares an office with Mr. Parra.
 (C) He will be absent on April 24.
 (D) He requested a change in the schedule.

Questions 186-190 refer to the following product description, online review, and online response.

The Bag of the Future: Zimmer-40

The Zimmer-40 will revolutionize the way you think about backpacks. It features a fold-out solar panel that can be used to charge your personal electronics. The advanced battery ensures that you always have the power you need on the go. The outer section is fully resistant to water, so your devices are always protected. In addition, all plastic parts on the backpack come from recycled plastic.

The Zimmer is sold at department stores and sporting goods outlets. Sign up for our monthly newsletter at the time of purchase to get a free second battery.

www.ucanreview.net/customer_reviews/accessories

Brand: Zimmer
Reviewer: Tyson Quintero
Item: Zimmer-40
Post Type: New

After researching several technology-enabled backpacks on the market, I selected the Zimmer-40 because of Zimmer's solid reputation. The color of the bag was darker than it appeared in the catalog, but that wasn't a problem for me. I'm impressed with how long the battery holds its charge, and I'm glad to have the second free one. The only thing that disappointed me was that my 15-inch laptop does not fit inside the bag. Despite this, I highly recommend this product, and I intend to buy it as a gift for several friends.

Brand: Zimmer **Item:** Zimmer-40
Commenter: Phillip Sandoval **Post Type:** Reply

As a Zimmer customer service agent, I'm sorry you were not completely satisfied with your purchase. Based on your needs, you might want to consider the Zimmer-40B. It has a special charging compartment on the inside that can accommodate up to a 17-inch laptop. It has the same gel-filled shoulder straps as the Zimmer-40, so you can still wear it comfortably even if it is loaded with heavy items. Since you already have the Zimmer-40, there isn't any point in buying a new battery because the same one can be used in all of our bags. I hope this resolves your issue.

186. What is NOT indicated about the Zimmer-40?

(A) It has a waterproof exterior.
(B) It makes use of renewable energy.
(C) It is partially made from recycled materials.
(D) It is light enough to use during sports.

187. What can be inferred about Mr. Quintero?

(A) He will receive monthly updates from Zimmer.
(B) He purchased the bag at a department store.
(C) He doesn't like the color of the bag.
(D) He mainly uses the bag for outdoor activities.

188. What is suggested in the online review?

(A) Zimmer is a relatively new company.
(B) Mr. Quintero plans to purchase more bags.
(C) Zimmer sells a line of laptop computers.
(D) Mr. Quintero noticed some damage on his bag.

189. Why does Mr. Sandoval recommend the Zimmer-40B to Mr. Quintero?

(A) It is the only bag with gel-filled straps.
(B) It can charge items more quickly.
(C) It has a larger carrying capacity.
(D) It is more durable than the Zimmer-40.

190. In the online response, the word "point" in paragraph 1, line 6, is closest in meaning to

(A) opinion
(B) reason
(C) aspect
(D) spot

Questions 191-195 refer to the following e-mails and information.

E-Mail

To: Kimberly Garrett <kgarrett@saezinc.net>
From: Marietta Convention Center <info@mariettacc.com>
Date: February 19
Subject: Information

Dear Ms. Garrett,

Thank you for taking a tour of the Marietta Convention Center on February 18. I hope you enjoyed viewing our technology-enabled facilities, including the expansion of the west wing. Based on your description of the banquet your company plans to hold, I believe we would be the perfect site. Each room comes equipped with a stage, which could be used to present awards to your art instructors and give speeches, and there are a variety of amenities to suit your needs. Furthermore, I can confirm that we currently have no reservations booked for your desired date of March 31. Attached, please find the detailed information you requested about each room. If you would like to make a booking, or if you have any further questions, do not hesitate to contact me at 555-6677, extension 21. I hope to hear from you soon.

Sincerely,

Ralph Shelby
Guest Services Representative, Marietta Convention Center

Marietta Convention Center Room Descriptions

Daisy Room—Maximum Capacity: 50 / Rental Fee: $2,600
4 x 8 m stage, podium, projector, pull-down video screen

Sunflower Room—Maximum Capacity: 50 / Rental Fee: $2,900
4 x 8 m stage, podium, projector, pull-down video screen, exterior doorway to garden

Peony Room—Maximum Capacity: 100 / Rental Fee: $3,500
6 x 10 m stage, podium, projector, flat-screen built-in television, full-service bar

Orchid Room—Maximum Capacity: 100 / Rental Fee: $4,800
6 x 12 m stage, podium, projector, flat-screen built-in television, full-service bar, view of Lochmere Bay

Various seating arrangements are available. Guests may use south or west parking lot for a nominal fee.

E-MAIL MESSAGE

To: Amina Jeffries, Dean McGraw, Kimberly Garrett, Bai Tan
From: Amil Rao
Date: February 20
Subject: Banquet plans

Hi Everyone,

It seems like we are making progress on our committee's plans for the upcoming banquet for our staff and their families. Thank you, Kimberly, for taking over the Marietta Convention Center visit for me, since I had to fly to Toronto that day for an unexpected business matter. I'm still waiting for the reports from the rest of you regarding the caterers you were assigned to research. Please e-mail that information to me by Thursday afternoon.

As for the venue options, I'd love our ninety guests to be able to overlook Lochmere Bay as they dine, but I don't think this will be feasible, given our limited budget. Instead, I think it would be best to rent the cheaper room that fits our size needs. We can discuss this further at Friday's meeting. See you then!

Amil

191. Where does Ms. Garrett most likely work?
(A) At a technology company
(B) At a fitness center
(C) At an art institute
(D) At a performance venue

192. Which room amenity is indicated in the information?
(A) Special lighting for the stage area
(B) A view of the city skyline
(C) Complimentary parking for guests
(D) Access to an outdoor space

193. What is implied about Mr. Rao?
(A) He joined the committee at the last minute.
(B) He visited several meeting venues.
(C) He wrote a review of a caterer.
(D) He took a business trip on February 18.

194. What can be inferred about Mr. McGraw?
(A) He is in charge of the committee's budget.
(B) He is gathering information about caterers.
(C) He is unable to attend Friday's meeting.
(D) He visited the Marietta Convention Center.

195. Which room would Mr. Rao most likely want to rent?
(A) Daisy Room
(B) Sunflower Room
(C) Peony Room
(D) Orchid Room

Questions 196-200 refer to the following article, Web page, and review.

Theater Fundraiser a Success

Last night's charity banquet to raise funds for the Gilcrest Theater was deemed a remarkable success by event planners, who reported proceeds of nearly $12,000, approximately $2,000 over the goal. The money will be used for the installation of a cutting-edge sound system in the theater, which will serve as a much-needed replacement for the outdated system currently being used.

The work will be completed just in time for the Regional Film Festival, of which the Gilcrest Theater is a hosting site. While the facility usually presents live theater performances, it is equipped with a large projection screen for movies. Other theaters across the region will also participate, but Gilcrest Theater has the highest seating capacity among them, more than double that of the second-largest one, Corinth Theater.

Tickets for the film festival go on sale next week. Movie fans can take in intense dramas by critically acclaimed directors. Or for those looking for something light, there are plenty of films with comedic writing.

---

www.regionalfilmfestival.com/schedule

| HOME | ABOUT | **SCHEDULE** | SEATING | DIRECTION |

Regional Film Festival

| Thursday, September 6 | Friday, September 7 | **Saturday, September 8** | Sunday, September 9 |

Venue / Phone Number	Film	Start Time	
24th Street Theater / 555-4102	*Underground*	7:00 P.M.	[More Info]
Corinth Theater / 555-0578	*A Summer's Day*	7:30 P.M.	[More Info]
Gilcrest Theater / 555-5855	*The Tale of Marco*	7:05 P.M.	[More Info]
Palacios Theater / 555-9360	*Wilson's Army*	8:10 P.M.	[More Info]

Customers should select the seat number and row when purchasing tickets, so please review the map of the venue's seating sections, downloadable at www.regionalfilmfestival.com/seating, before calling to order tickets. This will speed up the ordering process.

Underground: Best Thriller of the Year
★★★★
By Casey Ashton

If you're looking for a thriller that will keep you guessing until the very end, look no further than *Underground*, the latest masterpiece by director Mia Camacho. I recently saw it at the Regional Film Festival, and I was extremely impressed with the character development, intriguing plot, and fantastic acting. This film is a must-see!

---

196. In the article, the word "deemed" in paragraph 1, line 2, is closest in meaning to

(A) considered
(B) expected
(C) admired
(D) caused

197. How will the raised funds be used at Gilcrest Theater?

(A) To launch an advertising campaign
(B) To purchase a projection screen
(C) To upgrade an outdated Web site
(D) To install new audio equipment

198. When will the largest theater start its screening event on September 8?

(A) At 7:00 P.M.
(B) At 7:05 P.M.
(C) At 7:30 P.M.
(D) At 8:10 P.M.

199. What are ticket purchasers advised to do?

(A) Download a digital receipt
(B) Check a seating chart in advance
(C) Read some online movie reviews
(D) Receive tickets by express mail

200. Where did Mr. Ashton watch a film?

(A) 24th Street Theater
(B) Corinth Theater
(C) Gilcrest Theater
(D) Palacios Theater

Stop! This is the end of the test. If you finish before time is called, you may go back to Parts 5, 6, and 7 and check your work.

에듀윌이 너를 지지할게

ENERGY

삶의 순간순간이
아름다운 마무리이며
새로운 시작이어야 한다.

– 법정 스님

ANSWER SHEET
ACTUAL TEST

(Answer sheet bubbles for LISTENING (Part I ~ IV), items 1–100, and READING (Part V ~ VII), items 101–200)

ANSWER SHEET
ACTUAL TEST

ANSWER SHEET
ACTUAL TEST

LISTENING (Part I ~ IV)

NO.	ANSWER A B C D	NO.	ANSWER A B C D	NO.	ANSWER A B C D	NO.	ANSWER A B C D	NO.	ANSWER A B C D
1	ⓐ ⓑ ⓒ	21	ⓐ ⓑ ⓒ ⓓ	41	ⓐ ⓑ ⓒ ⓓ	61	ⓐ ⓑ ⓒ ⓓ	81	ⓐ ⓑ ⓒ ⓓ
2	ⓐ ⓑ ⓒ	22	ⓐ ⓑ ⓒ ⓓ	42	ⓐ ⓑ ⓒ ⓓ	62	ⓐ ⓑ ⓒ ⓓ	82	ⓐ ⓑ ⓒ ⓓ
3	ⓐ ⓑ ⓒ	23	ⓐ ⓑ ⓒ ⓓ	43	ⓐ ⓑ ⓒ ⓓ	63	ⓐ ⓑ ⓒ ⓓ	83	ⓐ ⓑ ⓒ ⓓ
4	ⓐ ⓑ ⓒ ⓓ	24	ⓐ ⓑ ⓒ ⓓ	44	ⓐ ⓑ ⓒ ⓓ	64	ⓐ ⓑ ⓒ ⓓ	84	ⓐ ⓑ ⓒ ⓓ
5	ⓐ ⓑ ⓒ ⓓ	25	ⓐ ⓑ ⓒ ⓓ	45	ⓐ ⓑ ⓒ ⓓ	65	ⓐ ⓑ ⓒ ⓓ	85	ⓐ ⓑ ⓒ ⓓ
6	ⓐ ⓑ ⓒ ⓓ	26	ⓐ ⓑ ⓒ ⓓ	46	ⓐ ⓑ ⓒ ⓓ	66	ⓐ ⓑ ⓒ ⓓ	86	ⓐ ⓑ ⓒ ⓓ
7	ⓐ ⓑ ⓒ ⓓ	27	ⓐ ⓑ ⓒ ⓓ	47	ⓐ ⓑ ⓒ ⓓ	67	ⓐ ⓑ ⓒ ⓓ	87	ⓐ ⓑ ⓒ ⓓ
8	ⓐ ⓑ ⓒ ⓓ	28	ⓐ ⓑ ⓒ ⓓ	48	ⓐ ⓑ ⓒ ⓓ	68	ⓐ ⓑ ⓒ ⓓ	88	ⓐ ⓑ ⓒ ⓓ
9	ⓐ ⓑ ⓒ ⓓ	29	ⓐ ⓑ ⓒ ⓓ	49	ⓐ ⓑ ⓒ ⓓ	69	ⓐ ⓑ ⓒ ⓓ	89	ⓐ ⓑ ⓒ ⓓ
10	ⓐ ⓑ ⓒ ⓓ	30	ⓐ ⓑ ⓒ ⓓ	50	ⓐ ⓑ ⓒ ⓓ	70	ⓐ ⓑ ⓒ ⓓ	90	ⓐ ⓑ ⓒ ⓓ
11	ⓐ ⓑ ⓒ ⓓ	31	ⓐ ⓑ ⓒ ⓓ	51	ⓐ ⓑ ⓒ ⓓ	71	ⓐ ⓑ ⓒ ⓓ	91	ⓐ ⓑ ⓒ ⓓ
12	ⓐ ⓑ ⓒ ⓓ	32	ⓐ ⓑ ⓒ ⓓ	52	ⓐ ⓑ ⓒ ⓓ	72	ⓐ ⓑ ⓒ ⓓ	92	ⓐ ⓑ ⓒ ⓓ
13	ⓐ ⓑ ⓒ ⓓ	33	ⓐ ⓑ ⓒ ⓓ	53	ⓐ ⓑ ⓒ ⓓ	73	ⓐ ⓑ ⓒ ⓓ	93	ⓐ ⓑ ⓒ ⓓ
14	ⓐ ⓑ ⓒ ⓓ	34	ⓐ ⓑ ⓒ ⓓ	54	ⓐ ⓑ ⓒ ⓓ	74	ⓐ ⓑ ⓒ ⓓ	94	ⓐ ⓑ ⓒ ⓓ
15	ⓐ ⓑ ⓒ ⓓ	35	ⓐ ⓑ ⓒ ⓓ	55	ⓐ ⓑ ⓒ ⓓ	75	ⓐ ⓑ ⓒ ⓓ	95	ⓐ ⓑ ⓒ ⓓ
16	ⓐ ⓑ ⓒ ⓓ	36	ⓐ ⓑ ⓒ ⓓ	56	ⓐ ⓑ ⓒ ⓓ	76	ⓐ ⓑ ⓒ ⓓ	96	ⓐ ⓑ ⓒ ⓓ
17	ⓐ ⓑ ⓒ ⓓ	37	ⓐ ⓑ ⓒ ⓓ	57	ⓐ ⓑ ⓒ ⓓ	77	ⓐ ⓑ ⓒ ⓓ	97	ⓐ ⓑ ⓒ ⓓ
18	ⓐ ⓑ ⓒ ⓓ	38	ⓐ ⓑ ⓒ ⓓ	58	ⓐ ⓑ ⓒ ⓓ	78	ⓐ ⓑ ⓒ ⓓ	98	ⓐ ⓑ ⓒ ⓓ
19	ⓐ ⓑ ⓒ ⓓ	39	ⓐ ⓑ ⓒ ⓓ	59	ⓐ ⓑ ⓒ ⓓ	79	ⓐ ⓑ ⓒ ⓓ	99	ⓐ ⓑ ⓒ ⓓ
20	ⓐ ⓑ ⓒ ⓓ	40	ⓐ ⓑ ⓒ ⓓ	60	ⓐ ⓑ ⓒ ⓓ	80	ⓐ ⓑ ⓒ ⓓ	100	ⓐ ⓑ ⓒ ⓓ

READING (Part V ~ VII)

NO.	ANSWER A B C D	NO.	ANSWER A B C D	NO.	ANSWER A B C D	NO.	ANSWER A B C D
101	ⓐ ⓑ ⓒ ⓓ	121	ⓐ ⓑ ⓒ ⓓ	141	ⓐ ⓑ ⓒ ⓓ	161	ⓐ ⓑ ⓒ ⓓ
102	ⓐ ⓑ ⓒ ⓓ	122	ⓐ ⓑ ⓒ ⓓ	142	ⓐ ⓑ ⓒ ⓓ	162	ⓐ ⓑ ⓒ ⓓ
103	ⓐ ⓑ ⓒ ⓓ	123	ⓐ ⓑ ⓒ ⓓ	143	ⓐ ⓑ ⓒ ⓓ	163	ⓐ ⓑ ⓒ ⓓ
104	ⓐ ⓑ ⓒ ⓓ	124	ⓐ ⓑ ⓒ ⓓ	144	ⓐ ⓑ ⓒ ⓓ	164	ⓐ ⓑ ⓒ ⓓ
105	ⓐ ⓑ ⓒ ⓓ	125	ⓐ ⓑ ⓒ ⓓ	145	ⓐ ⓑ ⓒ ⓓ	165	ⓐ ⓑ ⓒ ⓓ
106	ⓐ ⓑ ⓒ ⓓ	126	ⓐ ⓑ ⓒ ⓓ	146	ⓐ ⓑ ⓒ ⓓ	166	ⓐ ⓑ ⓒ ⓓ
107	ⓐ ⓑ ⓒ ⓓ	127	ⓐ ⓑ ⓒ ⓓ	147	ⓐ ⓑ ⓒ ⓓ	167	ⓐ ⓑ ⓒ ⓓ
108	ⓐ ⓑ ⓒ ⓓ	128	ⓐ ⓑ ⓒ ⓓ	148	ⓐ ⓑ ⓒ ⓓ	168	ⓐ ⓑ ⓒ ⓓ
109	ⓐ ⓑ ⓒ ⓓ	129	ⓐ ⓑ ⓒ ⓓ	149	ⓐ ⓑ ⓒ ⓓ	169	ⓐ ⓑ ⓒ ⓓ
110	ⓐ ⓑ ⓒ ⓓ	130	ⓐ ⓑ ⓒ ⓓ	150	ⓐ ⓑ ⓒ ⓓ	170	ⓐ ⓑ ⓒ ⓓ
111	ⓐ ⓑ ⓒ ⓓ	131	ⓐ ⓑ ⓒ ⓓ	151	ⓐ ⓑ ⓒ ⓓ	171	ⓐ ⓑ ⓒ ⓓ
112	ⓐ ⓑ ⓒ ⓓ	132	ⓐ ⓑ ⓒ ⓓ	152	ⓐ ⓑ ⓒ ⓓ	172	ⓐ ⓑ ⓒ ⓓ
113	ⓐ ⓑ ⓒ ⓓ	133	ⓐ ⓑ ⓒ ⓓ	153	ⓐ ⓑ ⓒ ⓓ	173	ⓐ ⓑ ⓒ ⓓ
114	ⓐ ⓑ ⓒ ⓓ	134	ⓐ ⓑ ⓒ ⓓ	154	ⓐ ⓑ ⓒ ⓓ	174	ⓐ ⓑ ⓒ ⓓ
115	ⓐ ⓑ ⓒ ⓓ	135	ⓐ ⓑ ⓒ ⓓ	155	ⓐ ⓑ ⓒ ⓓ	175	ⓐ ⓑ ⓒ ⓓ
116	ⓐ ⓑ ⓒ ⓓ	136	ⓐ ⓑ ⓒ ⓓ	156	ⓐ ⓑ ⓒ ⓓ	176	ⓐ ⓑ ⓒ ⓓ
117	ⓐ ⓑ ⓒ ⓓ	137	ⓐ ⓑ ⓒ ⓓ	157	ⓐ ⓑ ⓒ ⓓ	177	ⓐ ⓑ ⓒ ⓓ
118	ⓐ ⓑ ⓒ ⓓ	138	ⓐ ⓑ ⓒ ⓓ	158	ⓐ ⓑ ⓒ ⓓ	178	ⓐ ⓑ ⓒ ⓓ
119	ⓐ ⓑ ⓒ ⓓ	139	ⓐ ⓑ ⓒ ⓓ	159	ⓐ ⓑ ⓒ ⓓ	179	ⓐ ⓑ ⓒ ⓓ
120	ⓐ ⓑ ⓒ ⓓ	140	ⓐ ⓑ ⓒ ⓓ	160	ⓐ ⓑ ⓒ ⓓ	180	ⓐ ⓑ ⓒ ⓓ

NO.	ANSWER A B C D
181	ⓐ ⓑ ⓒ ⓓ
182	ⓐ ⓑ ⓒ ⓓ
183	ⓐ ⓑ ⓒ ⓓ
184	ⓐ ⓑ ⓒ ⓓ
185	ⓐ ⓑ ⓒ ⓓ
186	ⓐ ⓑ ⓒ ⓓ
187	ⓐ ⓑ ⓒ ⓓ
188	ⓐ ⓑ ⓒ ⓓ
189	ⓐ ⓑ ⓒ ⓓ
190	ⓐ ⓑ ⓒ ⓓ
191	ⓐ ⓑ ⓒ ⓓ
192	ⓐ ⓑ ⓒ ⓓ
193	ⓐ ⓑ ⓒ ⓓ
194	ⓐ ⓑ ⓒ ⓓ
195	ⓐ ⓑ ⓒ ⓓ
196	ⓐ ⓑ ⓒ ⓓ
197	ⓐ ⓑ ⓒ ⓓ
198	ⓐ ⓑ ⓒ ⓓ
199	ⓐ ⓑ ⓒ ⓓ
200	ⓐ ⓑ ⓒ ⓓ

* 문제를 다 풀고 채점한 후 점수로 환산해 봅니다. 점수 환산표는 16페이지에 있습니다.

자르는 선

ANSWER SHEET
ACTUAL TEST

ANSWER SHEET
ACTUAL TEST

ANSWER SHEET
ACTUAL TEST

ANSWER SHEET
ACTUAL TEST

에듀윌 토익 실전 LC + RC

발 행 일	2022년 3월 14일 초판 ｜ 2023년 4월 24일 5쇄 ｜ 2024년 3월 20일 9쇄
저　　자	에듀윌 어학연구소
펴 낸 이	양형남
펴 낸 곳	(주)에듀윌
등록번호	제25100-2002-000052호
주　　소	08378 서울특별시 구로구 디지털로34길 55 코오롱싸이언스밸리 2차 3층

* 이 책의 무단 인용 · 전재 · 복제를 금합니다.

www.eduwill.net

대표전화　1600-6700

여러분의 작은 소리
에듀윌은 크게 듣겠습니다.

본 교재에 대한 여러분의 목소리를 들려주세요.
공부하시면서 어려웠던 점, 궁금한 점,
칭찬하고 싶은 점, 개선할 점, 어떤 것이라도 좋습니다.
에듀윌은 여러분께서 나누어 주신 의견을
통해 끊임없이 발전하고 있습니다.

에듀윌 도서몰 book.eduwill.net
- 부가학습자료 및 정오표: 에듀윌 도서몰 → 도서자료실
- 교재 문의: 에듀윌 도서몰 → 문의하기 → 교재(내용, 출간) / 주문 및 배송

꿈을 현실로 만드는
에듀윌

공무원 교육
- 선호도 1위, 신뢰도 1위! 브랜드만족도 1위!
- 합격자 수 2,100% 폭등시킨 독한 커리큘럼

자격증 교육
- 7년간 아무도 깨지 못한 기록 합격자 수 1위
- 가장 많은 합격자를 배출한 최고의 합격 시스템

직영학원
- 직영학원 수 1위, 수강생 규모 1위!
- 표준화된 커리큘럼과 호텔급 시설 자랑하는 전국 51개 학원

종합출판
- 4대 온라인서점 베스트셀러 1위!
- 출제위원급 전문 교수진이 직접 집필한 합격 교재

어학 교육
- 토익 베스트셀러 1위
- 토익 동영상 강의 무료 제공
- 업계 최초 '토익 공식' 추천 AI 앱 서비스

콘텐츠 제휴·B2B 교육
- 고객 맞춤형 위탁 교육 서비스 제공
- 기업, 기관, 대학 등 각 단체에 최적화된 고객 맞춤형 교육 및 제휴 서비스

부동산 아카데미
- 부동산 실무 교육 1위!
- 상위 1% 고소득 창업/취업 비법
- 부동산 실전 재테크 성공 비법

공기업·대기업 취업 교육
- 취업 교육 1위!
- 공기업 NCS, 대기업 직무적성, 자소서, 면접

학점은행제
- 99%의 과목이수율
- 15년 연속 교육부 평가 인정 기관 선정

대학 편입
- 편입 교육 1위!
- 업계 유일 500% 환급 상품 서비스

국비무료 교육
- '5년우수훈련기관' 선정
- K-디지털, 4차 산업 등 특화 훈련과정

에듀윌 교육서비스 **공무원 교육** 9급공무원/7급공무원/경찰공무원/소방공무원/계리직공무원/기술직공무원/군무원 **자격증 교육** 공인중개사/주택관리사/전기기사/경비지도사/검정고시/소방설비기사/소방시설관리사/사회복지사1급/건축기사/토목기사/직업상담사/전기기능사/산업안전기사/위험물산업기사/위험물기능사/도로교통사고감정사/유통관리사/물류관리사/행정사/한국사능력검정/한경TESAT/매경TEST/KBS한국어능력시험/실용글쓰기/IT자격증/국제무역사/무역영어 **어학 교육** 토익 교재/토익 동영상 강의/인공지능 토익 앱 **세무/회계** 회계사/세무사/전산세무회계/ERP정보관리사/재경관리사 **대학 편입** 편입 교재/편입 영어·수학/경찰대/의치대/편입 컨설팅·면접 **공기업·대기업 취업 교육** 공기업 NCS·전공·상식/대기업 직무적성/자소서·면접 **직영학원** 공무원학원/경찰학원/소방학원/군간부학원/공인중개사 학원/주택관리사 학원/전기기사학원/세무사·회계사 학원/편입학원/취업아카데미 **종합출판** 공무원·자격증 수험 교재 및 단행본/월간지(시사상식) **학점은행제** 교육부 평가인정기관 원격평생교육원(사회복지사2급/경영학/CPA)/교육부 평가인정기관 원격 사회교육원(사회복지사 2급/심리학) **콘텐츠 제휴·B2B 교육** 교육 콘텐츠 제휴/기업 맞춤 자격증 교육/대학 취업역량 강화 교육 **부동산 아카데미** 부동산 창업CEO과정/실전 경매 과정/디벨로퍼과정 **국비무료 교육(국비교육원)** 전기기능사/전기(산업)기사/소방설비(산업)기사/IT(빅데이터/자바프로그램/파이썬)/게임그래픽/3D프린터/실내건축디자인/웹퍼블리셔/그래픽디자인/영상편집(유튜브)디자인/온라인 쇼핑몰광고 및 제작(쿠팡, 스마트스토어)/전산세무회계/컴퓨터활용능력/ITQ/GTQ/직업상담사

교육문의 1600-6700 www.eduwill.net

에듀윌 토익 실전 LC+RC
정답 및 해설

고객의 꿈, 직원의 꿈, 지역사회의 꿈을 실현한다

펴낸곳 (주)에듀윌　**펴낸이** 김재환　**출판총괄** 오용철
개발책임 김기임, 박호진　**개발** 정상욱, 김기상, 김상미, 박은석, Julie Tofflemire
주소 서울시 구로구 디지털로34길 55 코오롱싸이언스밸리 2차 3층
대표번호 1600-6700　**등록번호** 제25100-2002-000052호
협의 없는 무단 복제는 법으로 금지되어 있습니다.

에듀윌 도서몰 book.eduwill.net
- 부가학습자료 및 정오표: 에듀윌 도서몰 → 도서자료실
- 교재 문의: 에듀윌 도서몰 → 문의하기 → 교재(내용, 출간) / 주문 및 배송

정답 및 해설

- [ ] **as a result of** ~의 결과로서
- [ ] **above all** 무엇보다도
- [ ] **allow** 허용하다
- [ ] **ask for** ~을 요청하다
- [ ] **proximity** 근접성
- [ ] **major** 주요한
- [ ] **extensive** 광범위한
- [ ] **pharmaceutical** 약학의, 제약의
- [ ] **evaluate** 평가하다
- [ ] **accuracy** 정확성
- [ ] **a number of** 다수의
- [ ] **board member** 이사, 임원
- [ ] **qualification** 자격, 자질

PART 6

- [ ] **selection** 선택
- [ ] **inspect** 점검하다, 검사하다
- [ ] **vital to** ~에 필수적인
- [ ] **fulfill** 이행하다, 만족시키다
- [ ] **transform** 변형시키다
- [ ] **check-in** (공항의) 탑승 수속(대)
- [ ] **urgent** 시급한
- [ ] **no later than** 늦어도 ~까지는

Please submit all expense reports no later than February 15.
늦어도 2월 15일까지 모든 비용 보고서를 제출해 주세요.

- [ ] **shift** 교대 근무 (시간)
- [ ] **assign** 맡기다, 배정하다
- [ ] **raise funds** 기금을 모으다
- [ ] **contemporary** 현대의

PART 7

- [ ] **maintenance** 유지 보수
- [ ] **affect** 영향을 미치다
- [ ] **duration** (지속) 기간, 지속
- [ ] **property** 건물, 부동산
- [ ] **quote** 견적(가)
- [ ] **disposal** 폐기, 처분
- [ ] **balance** 잔액, 잔고

- [ ] **inform A of B** A에게 B를 알리다

The store sent an e-mail to customers informing them of the upcoming holiday sale.
그 상점은 다가오는 연휴 세일을 알리는 이메일을 고객들에게 보냈다.

- [ ] **regardless of** ~에 상관없이
- [ ] **representative** 담당자, 대표
- [ ] **account** 거래처, 고객
- [ ] **renovation** 보수
- [ ] **from now on** 이제부터
- [ ] **break room** 휴게실
- [ ] **expire** 만료되다, 기한이 지나다
- [ ] **spoil** 상하게 하다, 망치다
- [ ] **prestigious** 명망 있는, 일류의
- [ ] **patronage** 후원, 애용
- [ ] **drive** (모집 등의) 운동
- [ ] **suitable** 적합한
- [ ] **referral** 소개, 위탁
- [ ] **enter** 참가시키다, 기입하다
- [ ] **drawing** 추첨, 제비뽑기
- [ ] **inquiry** 문의, 질문
- [ ] **recruitment** 모집
- [ ] **take action** 조치를 취하다
- [ ] **enclose** 동봉하다
- [ ] **go out of business** 폐업하다
- [ ] **preferably** 가급적이면
- [ ] **endorse** 보증하다, 지지하다
- [ ] **take a chance** 모험을 하다, 운에 맡기다
- [ ] **contractor** 계약자, 도급업자
- [ ] **lost-and-found** 분실물 취급소
- [ ] **claim** 요구하다, 주장하다
- [ ] **description** 묘사, 설명
- [ ] **wrap up** 마무리 짓다

Let's wrap up the marketing meeting.
마케팅 회의를 마무리합시다.

- [ ] **complicated** 복잡한
- [ ] **administrative** 관리의, 행정상의
- [ ] **previously** 이전에
- [ ] **adapt** 조정하다, 맞추다

- [ ] **transition** 변천, 전환
- [ ] **lay off** 해고하다
- [ ] **phase** 단계
- [ ] **operation** 운용, 작동
- [ ] **comprise** ~으로 구성되다
- [ ] **specify** 명시하다
- [ ] **in-depth** 심도 있는, 면밀한
- [ ] **take place** 일어나다, 발생하다
- [ ] **maximum** 최고, 최대
- [ ] **wing** 부속 건물
- [ ] **amenity** 편의 시설
- [ ] **suit** ~에 맞다
- [ ] **extension** 내선, 구내전화
- [ ] **make progress** 진행하다, 진전하다
- [ ] **overlook** 내려다보다
- [ ] **feasible** 실현 가능한
- [ ] **remarkable** 놀랄 만한, 주목할 만한
- [ ] **proceeds** 모금액, 수익금
- [ ] **cutting-edge** 최첨단의

The company provides cutting-edge software for artificial intelligence.
그 회사는 최첨단 인공지능 소프트웨어를 공급한다.

- [ ] **outdated** 구식의
- [ ] **in time** 시간 맞춰, 늦지 않게

- in the meantime 그동안에
- in advance 사전에
- place an order 주문하다
- take a look at ~을 보다
- width 가로, 폭
- make arrangements for ~을 준비하다

> Please make your own arrangements for accommodation.
> 숙소 준비는 본인이 직접 해주세요.

- upcoming 곧 있을, 다가오는
- interpret 통역하다
- fit 꼭 맞다
- profile 인물 개요
- arena (원형) 경기장[공연장]

PART 4

- commemorate 기념하다
- throughout ~의 전체에 걸쳐, ~ 도처에
- demonstrate (사용법을) 보여 주다, 설명하다
- enroll in ~에 등록하다
- pressure 압력
- representative 대표자, 담당 직원
- let in ~을 들어오게 하다
- expect (오기로 되어 있는 대상을) 기다리다
- in addition to ~일 뿐 아니라, ~에 더하여
- perform 성취하다, 수행하다
- innovative 혁신적인
- organize 조직하다, 구성하다
- well-suited 적합한, 적임의
- hire (신규) 입사자, 채용자; 고용하다
- count on ~을 믿다[의지하다]
- job posting 구인 광고
- potential 잠재적인
- job description 직무 기술(서)
- reach (특히 전화로) 연락하다

- currently 현재, 지금
- emergency 비상(사태), 응급
- hang up 전화를 끊다
- schedule an appointment 예약을 하다
- applicable 해당[적용]되는
- fully booked 예약이 꽉 찬
- resume 재개하다, 다시 시작하다
- regular hours 정상 영업시간
- offer 제공하다
- warranty (품질 등의) 보증, 보증서
- intend to do ~하기를 의도하다
- average 평균의, 보통의
- characteristic 특징, 특질
- attractive 매력적인
- excerpt 발췌 (부분)
- last-minute 마지막 순간의
- entrance (출)입구, 문
- achievement 업적, 성취
- sign a contract 계약을 맺다
- factor 요인, 인자
- impressive 인상 깊은
- support (사실임을) 뒷받침하다
- memorable 기억할 만한
- approach 접근하다
- hold onto 꼭 잡다, 손을 떼지 않다
- on board 승선[승차/탑승]한

> You can bring two pieces of luggage on board the train.
> 기차에 수하물 두 개를 들고 탑승할 수 있습니다.

- on-time 시간을 어기지 않은, 정시의
- announcement 안내 방송, 발표
- regarding ~에 관하여
- inventory 물품 목록, 재고(품)

PART 5

- appreciation 감사, 감상
- subscriber 구독자
- production line 생산 라인

- long-term 장기적인
- addition 추가
- athletics 운동 경기
- component (구성) 요소, 부품
- enthusiast 애호가, 열광적인 팬
- banquet 연회, 만찬
- include 포함하다
- nominee 후보, 지명된 사람
- be aware of ~을 알고 있는

> Everybody is aware of the hazards of smoking.
> 모든 사람이 흡연의 위험성을 알고 있다.

- regulation 규정
- precise 정확한
- translate 번역하다
- indeed 정말, 확실히
- diverse 다양한
- reject 거부하다, 거절하다
- courier 택배 회사, 배달원
- fleet (한 회사 소유의) 전 차량
- reasonably priced 합리적으로 가격이 매겨진
- destination 목적지, 도착지
- belongings 소지품, 소유물
- luggage carousel 수하물 컨베이어
- ingredient 재료, 성분
- at all times 항상, 언제나
- expansion 확장, 확대
- volume 양, 부피
- detail 세부 사항
- reputation 명성
- field 분야
- cause 초래하다, 일으키다
- sensitive 예민한, 세심한
- efficiently 효율적으로
- be filled to capacity 꽉 차다, 만원이다

> The theater was filled to capacity for the opening of the new play.
> 극장은 새로운 연극의 개막으로 만원사례를 이루었다.

테스트별 핵심 어휘 **223**

TEST 05

PART 1

- [ ] **put on** ~을 착용하다
- [ ] **pay for** ~의 값을 지불하다
- [ ] **for sale** 팔려고 내놓은
- [ ] **intersection** 교차로
- [ ] **stack** 쌓다, 포개다
- [ ] **kneel down** 꿇어 앉다
- [ ] **set up** ~을 놓다[세우다], 마련하다
- [ ] **hold** 들다, 잡다
- [ ] **hand out** 나누어 주다
- [ ] **dock** (배를) 부두에 대다; 부두
- [ ] **port** 항구
- [ ] **occupied** 차 있는, 사용 중인

PART 2

- [ ] **update** 업데이트하다, 가장 최근의 정보를 알려 주다
- [ ] **regular customer** 단골(손님)
- [ ] **issue** 발행(물), (정기 간행물의) 호
- [ ] **depend** (~에) 달려 있다, 의존하다
- [ ] **industry** 산업, 공업
- [ ] **candidate** 후보자, 지원자
- [ ] **refreshing** 신선한
- [ ] **attendee** 참석자
- [ ] **attendance** 참석(률), 참석자 수
- [ ] **user manual** 사용 설명서
- [ ] **assemble** 조립하다
- [ ] **respondent** 응답자
- [ ] **market research** 시장 조사
- [ ] **treatment** 관리, 치료
- [ ] **produce** 초래하다, 일으키다
- [ ] **treat** 대접, 한턱; 치료하다
- [ ] **worth** ~을 할 가치가 있는, ~을 해 볼 만한
- [ ] **opinion** 의견, 견해
- [ ] **delivery** 배달
- [ ] **recommendation** 추천
- [ ] **make a donation** 기부하다

- [ ] **stray** 길 잃은
- [ ] **household** 가정의; 가정
- [ ] **recyclable** 재활용할 수 있는
- [ ] **package** 용기, 포장
- [ ] **a wide range of** 다양한, 광범위한
- [ ] **fill out a form** 서식을 작성하다, 서식에 기입하다
- [ ] **directory** (건물 내의) 안내판
- [ ] **auction** 경매
- [ ] **sculpture** 조각품
- [ ] **invitation** 초대장, 초대
- [ ] **out of focus** 초점이 맞지 않는
- [ ] **adjust** 조정[조절]하다
- [ ] **focus on** ~에 중점을 두다, ~에 초점을 맞추다
- [ ] **oversee** (작업·활동 등을) 감독하다
- [ ] **merger** 합병
- [ ] **negotiation** 협상, 교섭
- [ ] **market share** 시장 점유율
- [ ] **replacement** 교체[대체]물
- [ ] **brand-new** 아주 새로운, 신품의
- [ ] **counter** 판매대, 계산대
- [ ] **contain** ~이 들어 있다
- [ ] **inspector** 검사관, 감독관
- [ ] **safety gear** 안전 장비[장치]
- [ ] **rate** 요금
- [ ] **affordable** (가격이) 알맞은, 적당한
- [ ] **handle** 처리하다, 다루다
- [ ] **residential** 주거의, 주택에 알맞은

PART 3

- [ ] **submit** 제출하다
- [ ] **supplies** 비품, 공급품
- [ ] **miss** 빠뜨리다, 누락하다
- [ ] **available** 구할[이용할] 수 있는
- [ ] **post** (안내문 등을) 게시하다, 공고하다
- [ ] **put up** 내붙이다, 게시하다
- [ ] **statistics** 통계, 통계표
- [ ] **count** 총수, 총계
- [ ] **participant** 참가자

- [ ] **board** 이사회; 탑승하다
- [ ] **leave out** ~을 빼다
- [ ] **sales figure** 매출액
- [ ] **express** 신속한, 급행의
- [ ] **bind** 묶다, 매다
- [ ] **supplementary** 보충의, 추가의
- [ ] **stop by** (~에) 잠시 들르다
- [ ] **specific** 특정한, 구체적인
- [ ] **deal with** ~을 다루다[처리하다]
- [ ] **quite a few** 상당수(의)
- [ ] **performance** 성능, 실적
- [ ] **be familiar with** ~에 익숙하다
- [ ] **feature** 기능, 특징
- [ ] **interpersonal** 대인 관계에 관련된
- [ ] **as far as** ~하는 한, ~에 관한 한
- [ ] **promotional** 홍보의
- [ ] **expense** 비용
- [ ] **look over** ~을 살펴보다
- [ ] **find out** (~을) 알아내다
- [ ] **appreciate** 고마워하다, 감사하다
- [ ] **insurance** 보험
- [ ] **work on** ~을 작업하다
- [ ] **in stock** 비축되어, 재고로
- [ ] **at the moment** 지금
- [ ] **due** ~하기로 되어 있는[예정된]

When is the quarterly report due?
분기별 보고서는 언제까지 제출해야 하나요?

- [ ] **in a hurry** 서둘러, 급히
- [ ] **loyalty program** 회원 혜택 프로그램
- [ ] **on behalf of** ~을 대표[대신]하여
- [ ] **environmental** 환경의, 환경과 관련된
- [ ] **commission** 위원회, 위원단
- [ ] **pollution** 오염, 공해
- [ ] **plenty of** 많은
- [ ] **resident** 거주자, 주민
- [ ] **owe** (돈을) 빚지고 있다
- [ ] **process** 처리하다; 과정, 절차
- [ ] **reimburse** 환급하다, 상환하다
- [ ] **reserve** 예약하다

- [ ] **routine** 일상; 일상적인
- [ ] **secure** 지키다, 안전하게 하다
- [ ] **constantly** 끊임없이
- [ ] **eliminate** 제거하다, 없애다
- [ ] **potential** 잠재적인
- [ ] **state-of-the-art** 최신의
- [ ] **inform** 알리다
- [ ] **subscription** 구독(료)
- [ ] **transaction** 거래, 매매
- [ ] **determine** 알아내다, 밝히다
- [ ] **verify** 확인하다
- [ ] **go through** 통과되다, 진행되다
- [ ] **valid** 유효한
- [ ] **attach** 첨부하다
- [ ] **expiration** 만료
- [ ] **promptly** 지체 없이
- [ ] **be committed to** ~에 전념하다

We are committed to maintaining the highest level of customer satisfaction.
우리는 최고 수준의 고객 만족을 유지하기 위해 최선을 다하고 있습니다.

- [ ] **consumption** 소비, 소모
- [ ] **beneficial** 유익한
- [ ] **gain** 이득을 얻다, 이익을 보다
- [ ] **argue** 주장하다, 논쟁하다

PART 7

- [ ] **subtotal** 소계
- [ ] **place an order** 주문하다
- [ ] **sign up for** ~을 신청하다

How do I sign up for the workshop?
워크숍은 어떻게 신청하나요?

- [ ] **promotion** 판촉물, 판촉
- [ ] **newsletter** 소식지
- [ ] **subscribe** 구독하다
- [ ] **by any chance** 혹시라도
- [ ] **run out of** ~을 다 써 버리다, ~이 없어지다
- [ ] **real estate** 부동산
- [ ] **establish** 설립하다

- [ ] **distributor** 유통 업체, 배급사
- [ ] **warranty** 품질 보증(서)
- [ ] **leaflet** 전단
- [ ] **retailer** 소매업자
- [ ] **equipment** 장비
- [ ] **sponsor** 후원하다
- [ ] **raffle** (모금용) 복권
- [ ] **attire** 복장, 의복
- [ ] **be eligible to do** ~할 자격이 있다

He is eligible to receive a higher salary.
그는 보다 높은 급여를 받을 자격이 있다.

- [ ] **make a payment** 지불하다
- [ ] **process** 처리하다
- [ ] **reference** 참고, 참조
- [ ] **quote** 견적을 내다
- [ ] **urge** 촉구하다, 권고하다
- [ ] **unprecedented** 전례 없는
- [ ] **revelation** 공개, 폭로
- [ ] **controversy** 논란
- [ ] **intense** 거센, 극심한
- [ ] **sustainable** 지속 가능한
- [ ] **advocate** 옹호하다
- [ ] **exceptionally** 예외적으로, 매우
- [ ] **premises** 부지, 구내
- [ ] **make a reservation** 예약하다
- [ ] **senior** 선임의, 상급자의
- [ ] **executive** 임원, 경영진
- [ ] **launch** 출시; 출시하다
- [ ] **be qualified for** ~에 적임이다, 자격이 있다

She is qualified for a job.
그녀는 그 일에 적임이다.

- [ ] **procedure** 절차, 방법
- [ ] **classify** 분류하다, 구분하다
- [ ] **outline** 개요를 말하다
- [ ] **voucher** 상품권, 쿠폰
- [ ] **set aside** 따로 떼어 두다
- [ ] **inventory** 재고(품)
- [ ] **assure** 보장하다, 확인하다
- [ ] **complimentary** 무료의

- [ ] **notify** 알리다
- [ ] **supplier** 공급업체, 공급자
- [ ] **replace** 변경하다, 대체하다
- [ ] **asset** 자산, 재산
- [ ] **intention** 의사, 의도
- [ ] **evident** 분명한, 눈에 띄는
- [ ] **intimate** 깊은, 상세한
- [ ] **contribute to** ~에 기여하다
- [ ] **aspect** 측면, 양상
- [ ] **detailed** 상세한
- [ ] **keep in mind** 명심하다
- [ ] **accordingly** 그에 따라서
- [ ] **shortly** 얼마 안 되어, 곧
- [ ] **modify** 수정하다
- [ ] **source** 근원, 출처
- [ ] **authenticity** 진실성
- [ ] **comprehensive** 포괄적인, 종합적인
- [ ] **curriculum** 교육 과정
- [ ] **hands-on** 직접 해 보는

- disassemble 분해하다, 해체하다
- fascinating 대단히 흥미로운, 매력적인
- dress code 복장 규정
- no longer 더 이상 ~ 아닌[하지 않는]
- manner 방식, 태도
- trade expo 무역 박람회
- cosmetics 화장품
- electronics 전자 제품
- set ~ apart ~을 돋보이게[다르게] 만들다
- previous 이전의
- pass out 나누어 주다
- refreshments 다과
- take a stroll 산책하다
- queue up 줄을 서다
- respectful 예의 바른, 공손한
- cut in line 줄에 새치기하다
- proceed 나아가다, 이동하다
- apology 사과, 사죄
- be in stock 재고가 있다
- original 원래의
- expedite 더 신속히 처리하다
- panel 패널, 토론인단
- flavor 맛
- comment 의견, 논평
- pay attention to ~에 유의[주목]하다
- be in disagreement 의견이 맞지 않다
- identify (신원 등을) 확인하다, 알아보다
- recognize 표창하다, 인정하다
- astonish 깜짝 놀라게 하다
- critic 비평가, 평론가
- impress 깊은 인상을 주다, 감명을 주다
- intricate 복잡한
- philosophical 철학적인, 철학에 관련된
- explore 탐험하다, 살펴보다
- sign up 신청하다, 등록하다
- apologize for ~에 대해 사과하다
- be accompanied by ~와 동행하다, ~을 동반하다

- stock 재고(품)
- run out of ~을 다 써 버리다
- adjust 조절하다, 조정하다
- simply (부정문에서) 전혀, 단순히
- profitable 수익성이 있는
- hand out 나누어 주다

I have to pick up the promotional materials that will be handed out to attendees.
나는 참석자들에게 나누어 줄 홍보물을 가지러 가야 한다.

- outline 개요, 윤곽

PART 5

- fundraiser 모금 행사
- be scheduled to do ~하기로 되어 있다

Jenny is scheduled to work at the information desk on Sunday.
제니는 일요일에 안내 데스크에서 일하기로 되어 있다.

- audience 관객
- respective 각자의
- come with ~이 딸려 있다
- assembly 조립
- instructions 설명서
- fluent 유창한
- qualification 자격, 자질
- turn off 차단하다, 끄다
- demonstrate 보여 주다
- provide 제공하다
- negotiation 협상, 협의
- submit 제출하다
- application 지원서, 지원
- sales associate 영업 사원
- go over ~을 검토하다
- reservation 예약
- baggage allowance 수하물 허용량
- policy 정책, 방침
- patron 이용자, 후원자
- renew 갱신하다

- revision 수정, 정정
- ahead of ~ 앞에
- supervisor 관리자
- steadily 꾸준히
- decline 하락하다
- in response to ~에 대응하여

In response to consumer complaints, assembly instructions have been simplified.
소비자 불만에 대응하여 조립 설명서가 간소화되었다.

- severe 극심한
- criticism 비판
- concerning ~에 관한
- take measures 조치를 취하다
- environment 환경
- based on ~을 바탕으로 한
- on behalf of ~을 대표하여
- in spite of ~에도 불구하고
- now that ~이기 때문에
- recommendation 추천
- purchase 구매; 구매하다
- competitor 경쟁자
- work experience (근무) 경력
- opening 빈자리, 공석
- deliberate 의도적인
- traffic congestion 교통 혼잡
- convert 전환시키다
- reveal 드러내다, 밝히다
- ceremony 의식, 식
- progress 진행되다; 진보
- produce 농산물; 생산하다
- prominent 눈에 잘 띄는
- accessible 접근 가능한
- director 임원
- objective 목표; 객관적인

PART 6

- survey 설문 (조사)
- strive to do ~하려고 노력하다
- valuable 소중한, 매우 유익한

TEST 04

PART 1

- [ ] **fill A with B** A를 B로 채우다
- [ ] **pot** 주전자
- [ ] **make a copy** 복사하다
- [ ] **pile up** 쌓다, 쌓이다
- [ ] **take measurements** 치수를 재다
- [ ] **gaze at** ~을 응시하다
- [ ] **place** 놓다, 두다
- [ ] **in a row** 일렬로
- [ ] **rooftop** 옥상, 지붕
- [ ] **traffic jam** 교통 체증

PART 2

- [ ] **delay** 지연시키다
- [ ] **test drive** 시승, 시운전
- [ ] **manual** 안내서, 설명서
- [ ] **out of** ~을 다 써 버린, ~이 떨어진
- [ ] **plumber** 배관공
- [ ] **rest** 쉬다, 휴식을 취하다
- [ ] **bike lane** 자전거 전용 도로
- [ ] **alongside** ~ 옆에, 나란히
- [ ] **be willing to do** ~할 의향이 있다
- [ ] **fill in for** ~을 대신하다
- [ ] **display** 표시되다, 전시하다
- [ ] **properly** 제대로, 적절히
- [ ] **format** 포맷, 서식
- [ ] **serve** (음식을) 내다, 상을 차리다
- [ ] **in the mood for** ~할 기분[생각]인

I'm not in the mood for jokes.
나는 농담할 기분이 아니다.

- [ ] **check out** (도서관 등에서) 대출하다, 확인하다
- [ ] **at a time** 한 번에, 한꺼번에
- [ ] **meet** (기한 등을) 지키다
- [ ] **deadline** 기한
- [ ] **lend** 빌려주다
- [ ] **conference** 학회, 회의
- [ ] **definitely** 틀림없이, 분명히

- [ ] **speaker** 연사, 발표자
- [ ] **handle** 처리하다, 다루다
- [ ] **on one's own** 혼자서, 단독으로
- [ ] **analysis** 분석
- [ ] **sales figure** 매출액, 매출 수치
- [ ] **author** 작가
- [ ] **inspiration** 영감
- [ ] **article** 기사
- [ ] **committee** 위원회
- [ ] **offer** 제공하다
- [ ] **complete** 완성하다, 끝마치다
- [ ] **out of service** 사용이 불가능한
- [ ] **in a minute** 곧, 즉시
- [ ] **print out** 출력하다, 인쇄하다
- [ ] **malfunction** 제대로 작동하지 않다
- [ ] **membership** 회비, 회원 자격[신분]
- [ ] **pile** 더미, 쌓아 올린 것
- [ ] **restock** 재고를 다시 채우다
- [ ] **section** 구역, 구획
- [ ] **on sale** 할인 판매 중인, 판매되는
- [ ] **out of stock** 품절되어, 매진의

PART 3

- [ ] **shame** 아쉬운[애석한] 일
- [ ] **trade A for B** A를 B로 교환하다
- [ ] **come in** 들어오다, 도착하다
- [ ] **instead of** ~ 대신에
- [ ] **rather** 꽤, 약간
- [ ] **strict** 엄격한
- [ ] **behind schedule** 예정보다 늦게
- [ ] **in person** 직접, 몸소
- [ ] **make it** (어떤 곳에 간신히) 시간 맞춰 가다

Mr. Li made it to the engineering conference on time.
리 씨는 엔지니어링 총회에 제시간에 도착했다.

- [ ] **extend** 연장하다, 넓히다
- [ ] **due date** 만기일
- [ ] **make an exception** 예외로 하다
- [ ] **contact** 연락하다
- [ ] **late fee** 연체료

- [ ] **give out** ~을 나누어 주다
- [ ] **tenant** 세입자, 임차인
- [ ] **property** 건물, 부동산
- [ ] **go for** ~에 해당되다
- [ ] **come by** 잠깐 들르다
- [ ] **have ~ in mind** ~을 염두에 두다
- [ ] **feature** 특징; ~을 특별히 포함하다
- [ ] **energy-efficient** 연료 효율이 좋은
- [ ] **suggestion** 제안, 제의
- [ ] **coworker** 동료
- [ ] **in that case** 그런 경우에는, 그렇다면
- [ ] **intersection** 교차로
- [ ] **a while ago** 조금 전에
- [ ] **subscriber** 독자, 구독자
- [ ] **option** 선택(할 수 있는 것)
- [ ] **strategy** 전략
- [ ] **a great deal** 상당히, 많이
- [ ] **come up with** ~을 내놓다[제시하다]
- [ ] **bring in** 가져오다, 들여오다
- [ ] **host** 주최하다
- [ ] **nutrition** 영양
- [ ] **organize** 개최하다, 조직하다
- [ ] **ingredient** 재료, 성분
- [ ] **creativity** 창의성, 창조성
- [ ] **submission** 제출(물)
- [ ] **speaking of which** 말이 나온 김에, 얘기가 나왔으니 말인데
- [ ] **spare** 할애하다, 내다
- [ ] **entry** 출품작
- [ ] **performance** 공연, 연주
- [ ] **include** 포함하다
- [ ] **lecture** 강연, 강의
- [ ] **brief** 간단한, 간략한
- [ ] **introduction** 소개
- [ ] **directly** 똑바로, 곧장
- [ ] **face** ~을 마주 보다[향하다]

PART 4

- [ ] **artifact** 공예품
- [ ] **exhibit** 전시(회)

PART 6

- [ ] **keep up** ~을 계속하다
- [ ] **upset** 화난, 속상한
- [ ] **manner** 태도, 방식
- [ ] **conflict** 갈등, 충돌
- [ ] **benefit from** ~으로부터 혜택을 받다
- [ ] **appropriate** 적절한
- [ ] **resident** 주민, 거주자
- [ ] **isolated** 외떨어진
- [ ] **remote** 외진, 먼
- [ ] **up-to-date** 최신의
- [ ] **in addition** 또한
- [ ] **in need of** ~을 필요로 하는

We're in need of people to help out with the beverage booths.
우리는 음료 부스를 도와줄 사람이 필요하다.

- [ ] **in particular** 특히, 특별히
- [ ] **material** 직물, 재료
- [ ] **award** 수여하다
- [ ] **entitle** 제목을 붙이다
- [ ] **inspirational** 고무적인, 영감을 주는
- [ ] **grant** 수여하다, 승인하다
- [ ] **endeavor** 노력, 시도

PART 7

- [ ] **put together** 한데 모으다, 합치다
- [ ] **have trouble doing** ~하는 데 어려움을 겪다
- [ ] **expert** 전문가
- [ ] **real estate** 부동산
- [ ] **premises** 구내, 부지
- [ ] **compensate** 보수를 지불하다, 보상하다
- [ ] **make arrangements for** ~을 준비하다

She will make all the arrangements for the company retreat next month.
그녀는 다음 달 회사 야유회를 위한 모든 준비를 할 것이다.

- [ ] **after all** 결국에는

- [ ] **relocate** 이전하다
- [ ] **transition** 이동, 과도기
- [ ] **load** 짐을 싣다
- [ ] **set up** 설치하다
- [ ] **ideal** 가장 알맞은, 이상적인
- [ ] **be supposed to do** ~하기로 되어 있다

It's supposed to rain all day today.
오늘은 하루 종일 비가 내리기로 되어 있다.

- [ ] **manage to do** 간신히 ~하다,
- [ ] **on time** 정각에, 시간을 어기지 않고
- [ ] **timetable** 시간표
- [ ] **anticipate** 예상하다
- [ ] **exhibit** 전시회; 전시하다
- [ ] **come to one's attention** ~을 알게 되다
- [ ] **take ~ into account** ~을 고려하다

You must take the environmental impact into account.
환경에 미치는 영향을 고려해야 합니다.

- [ ] **compensation** 보수, 보상(금)
- [ ] **declare** 신고하다
- [ ] **collaborate with** ~와 공동으로 작업하다
- [ ] **skyrocketing** 치솟는
- [ ] **notorious** 악명 높은
- [ ] **obscure** 무명의, 잘 알려져 있지 않은
- [ ] **be composed of** ~로 이루어지다
- [ ] **a variety of** 다양한
- [ ] **warranty** 보증, 보증서
- [ ] **progress** 진행, 경과
- [ ] **flaw** 결함
- [ ] **in case of** ~의 경우에
- [ ] **be liable for** ~에 대해 책임이 있다

You will be liable for any damage caused.
야기되는 모든 손상에 대해 당신이 책임을 지게 될 것입니다.

- [ ] **be entitled to do** ~을 할 권리가 있다
- [ ] **sign a contract** 계약서에 서명하다

- [ ] **reliable** 신뢰할 수 있는
- [ ] **at no charge** 무료로
- [ ] **apply to** ~에 적용되다
- [ ] **temporary** 일시적인
- [ ] **internal** 내부의
- [ ] **make up for** ~에 대해 보상하다
- [ ] **balance** 잔고, 잔액
- [ ] **at one's discretion** 재량에 따라
- [ ] **file a complaint** 민원을 제기하다
- [ ] **release** 공개하다, 발매하다
- [ ] **prominent** 유명한
- [ ] **limited** 한정된
- [ ] **by the time** ~할 때까지
- [ ] **from scratch** 아무런 사전 준비 없이
- [ ] **preference** 선택, 선호
- [ ] **apparel** 의복, 의류
- [ ] **luxurious** 고급의, 호화로운
- [ ] **verify** 확인하다, 입증하다
- [ ] **as for** ~에 대해서 말하자면

As for the flight, it is delayed for two hours.
항공편에 대해 말하자면, 그것은 2시간 연착되었다.

- [ ] review 보고서, 논평
- [ ] relevant 유의미한, 적절한
- [ ] shut down 문을 닫다
- [ ] checkup 건강 진단, 검사
- [ ] sensitive 민감한
- [ ] overall 전반적으로; 전체의
- [ ] necessarily 반드시, 필연적으로
- [ ] stay away from ~을 멀리하다
- [ ] symposium 심포지엄, 학술 토론회
- [ ] get around 돌아다니다
- [ ] hassle 번거로운[귀찮은] 일
- [ ] criterion 기준

PART 4

- [ ] call a meeting 회의를 소집하다
- [ ] perform 해내다, 공연하다
- [ ] retail store 소매점
- [ ] grab 움켜쥐다, 낚아채다
- [ ] rarely 드물게, 좀처럼 ~ 않고
- [ ] visually 시각적으로
- [ ] appealing 매력적인
- [ ] itchy 가렵게 하는
- [ ] concentrate on ~에 집중하다
- [ ] to start with 우선
- [ ] fabric 옷감, 직물
- [ ] advantage 강점
- [ ] legal 법률과 관련된
- [ ] consultant 컨설턴트, 고문
- [ ] at the latest 늦어도
- [ ] urgent 긴급한
- [ ] case 소송, 사건
- [ ] negotiable 협상의 여지가 있는
- [ ] time frame 기간
- [ ] benefits package 복지 혜택, 복리 후생 제도
- [ ] qualify for ~의 자격이 있다
- [ ] consult 참고하다, 찾아보다
- [ ] status 지위
- [ ] lead 이끌다, 지도하다
- [ ] equipped with ~을 갖춘

- [ ] familiarize oneself with ~을 익히다, ~에 익숙해지다

It needs time to familiarize yourself with the office procedures.
사무실 절차를 익히는 데는 시간이 필요합니다.

- [ ] ride 탈것
- [ ] graduate (대학의) 졸업생
- [ ] cuisine 요리(법)
- [ ] obtain 획득하다, 얻다
- [ ] business administration 경영학
- [ ] combination 결합
- [ ] confident 확신하는
- [ ] reach 연락하다, 닿다
- [ ] connection 접속, 연결
- [ ] resolve 해결하다
- [ ] normal 정상, 보통
- [ ] connect 접속하다, 연결하다
- [ ] manufacturer 제조 회사, 제조업자
- [ ] general 전반적인
- [ ] safety guideline 안전 지침
- [ ] safety glasses 보안경
- [ ] task 작업, 일
- [ ] threatening 위협하는, (나쁜 일이) 닥칠 듯한
- [ ] agenda 안건
- [ ] concerned 염려하는
- [ ] pool 이용 가능 인력
- [ ] under construction 건설[공사] 중인
- [ ] congested 혼잡한, 붐비는
- [ ] project 프로젝트; 예상하다
- [ ] push back 미루다
- [ ] take a detour 우회하다
- [ ] disturbance 소란, 방해
- [ ] quality control 품질 관리
- [ ] make an investment 투자하다
- [ ] various 여러 가지의, 다양한
- [ ] except for ~을 제외하고
- [ ] safety gear 안전 장비
- [ ] throughout ~ 동안 내내

PART 5

- [ ] term 용어, 말
- [ ] manufacture 제조하다
- [ ] purpose 목적
- [ ] safety procedure 안전 수칙
- [ ] business trip 출장
- [ ] diner 식사하는 사람
- [ ] line (상품의) 종류
- [ ] leather 가죽
- [ ] volunteer 자원봉사자
- [ ] gather 모이다
- [ ] flexible 탄력적인, 유연한
- [ ] grand opening 개점, 개업
- [ ] passenger 승객
- [ ] check in (짐을) 부치다
- [ ] maximum 최대(량), 최고(점)
- [ ] suitcase 여행 가방
- [ ] compliance 준수
- [ ] strict 엄격한
- [ ] policy 정책, 방침
- [ ] a series of 일련의

We are designing a series of online advertisements for them.
우리는 그들을 위한 일련의 온라인 광고를 디자인하고 있다.

- [ ] clientele 고객, 의뢰인
- [ ] try on ~을 입어 보다
- [ ] complex 복잡한
- [ ] layout 배치, 설계
- [ ] location 장소
- [ ] inspection 점검, 조사
- [ ] campaign 선거 운동, 캠페인
- [ ] full refund 전액 환불
- [ ] receipt 영수증
- [ ] present 제시하다, 수여하다
- [ ] grocery store 식료품점
- [ ] management 경영(진)
- [ ] shortcomings 결점

TEST 03

PART 1

- [ ] **tie** 묶다, 매다
- [ ] **apron** 앞치마
- [ ] **kitchen counter** 부엌 조리대
- [ ] **be located** 위치해 있다
- [ ] **be crowded with** ~으로 붐비다
- [ ] **pedestrian** 보행자
- [ ] **section** 구획, 구역
- [ ] **plaza** 광장
- [ ] **pave** 포장하다
- [ ] **luggage** 수하물, 짐
- [ ] **unload** 짐을 내리다
- [ ] **walkway** 통로, 보도
- [ ] **lecturer** 강사
- [ ] **point at** ~을 가리키다
- [ ] **examine** 검토하다
- [ ] **hang** 걸다, 매달다
- [ ] **empty** 비우다; 비어 있는

PART 2

- [ ] **speech** 연설
- [ ] **recent** 최근의
- [ ] **election** 선거
- [ ] **store** 보관하다; 상점
- [ ] **client** 고객
- [ ] **order** 순서; 주문하다
- [ ] **forecast** 예보, 예측
- [ ] **lane** 차선
- [ ] **performance** 공연
- [ ] **best-selling** 베스트셀러의
- [ ] **parking garage** 주차장 건물
- [ ] **after hours** 근무 시간 후에
- [ ] **pass** 출입증; 통과하다
- [ ] **fee** 요금, 수수료
- [ ] **cancel** 취소하다
- [ ] **postpone** 연기하다
- [ ] **profit** 수익
- [ ] **increase** 증가하다
- [ ] **dramatically** 급격하게, 극적으로
- [ ] **profitable** 수익성이 있는
- [ ] **pick up** ~를 (차에) 태우러 가다
- [ ] **land** 도착하다, 착륙하다
- [ ] **be likely to do** ~할 것 같다

The demand for the new product is likely to be high.
신제품에 대한 수요는 높을 것으로 보인다.

- [ ] **organizer** 주최자, 조직자
- [ ] **original** 원본; 원래의
- [ ] **charitable** 자선의
- [ ] **organization** 단체, 조직
- [ ] **business card** 명함
- [ ] **reserve** 예약하다
- [ ] **retire** 퇴직하다, 은퇴하다
- [ ] **cost** (값이) ~이다
- [ ] **make a copy of** ~을 복사하다
- [ ] **be about to do** 막 ~하려는 참이다

The movie is about to start.
영화가 막 시작하려고 한다.

- [ ] **flight** 항공편, 비행
- [ ] **tenant** 세입자
- [ ] **lease** 임대차 계약
- [ ] **rent** 임대료
- [ ] **due** (돈을) 지불해야 하는

PART 3

- [ ] **normally** 보통은, 일반적으로
- [ ] **the public** 일반 사람들, 대중
- [ ] **exactly** 정확히
- [ ] **assistant** 비서, 조수
- [ ] **a couple of** 몇 개의, 두서너 개의
- [ ] **proposal** 제안
- [ ] **wonder** ~할까 생각하다, 궁금하다
- [ ] **convention** 협의회, 대회
- [ ] **make time** 시간을 내다
- [ ] **offer** 제안, 제의
- [ ] **detail** 세부 사항
- [ ] **reach an agreement** 합의에 도달하다
- [ ] **dye** 염색하다
- [ ] **newcomer** 새로 온 사람
- [ ] **lawn mower** 잔디 깎는 기계
- [ ] **misunderstand** 오해하다
- [ ] **accept** 받아들이다, 받다
- [ ] **defective** 결함이 있는
- [ ] **shortly** 곧, 얼마 안 되어
- [ ] **cruise** 유람선 여행
- [ ] **terrible** 형편없는, 끔찍한
- [ ] **reputation** 평판
- [ ] **would rather** (차라리) ~하고 싶다
- [ ] **worth** ~의 가치가 있는
- [ ] **quit** 그만두다
- [ ] **cover for** ~의 일을 대신 처리하다
- [ ] **replacement** 후임자, 대체
- [ ] **font** 서체
- [ ] **appeal to** ~의 관심을 끌다

The commercials are designed to appeal to younger consumers.
그 광고들은 젊은 소비자들의 관심을 끌기 위해 만들어졌다.

- [ ] **target** 목표의; 목표
- [ ] **demographic** (상품의) 고객층, 구매층
- [ ] **go too far** 도를 넘다
- [ ] **ultimately** 결국, 궁극적으로
- [ ] **make a decision** 결정을 내리다
- [ ] **transfer** 이동하다, 옮기다
- [ ] **look forward to doing** ~하기를 고대[기대]하다
- [ ] **interact** 소통하다, 상호 작용하다
- [ ] **stressful** 스트레스가 많은
- [ ] **complaint** 항의, 불평
- [ ] **positive** 긍정적인
- [ ] **to be honest** 솔직히 말하면
- [ ] **nervous** 긴장되는, 불안해하는
- [ ] **crowd** 사람들, 군중
- [ ] **line up** 줄을 서다
- [ ] **publicize** 홍보[광고]하다, 알리다
- [ ] **healthcare** 건강 관리, 의료
- [ ] **presenter** 발표자
- [ ] **send in** 제출하다, 내보내다

- [ ] **mailing address** 우편 주소
- [ ] **come out** (책이) 출판되다, 나오다

His new novel is coming out in October.
그의 새 소설은 10월에 출간될 것이다.

- [ ] **residential address** 집 주소
- [ ] **associated with** ~과 관련된

PART 7

- [ ] **donate** 기부하다
- [ ] **comment** 의견을 말하다, 주석을 달다
- [ ] **invoice** 청구서, 송장
- [ ] **rental** 대여료, 임대
- [ ] **unit** (작은) 기구, 장치
- [ ] **coverage** (보험) 보장 범위
- [ ] **policy** 보험 증권
- [ ] **printout** 인쇄(물)
- [ ] **in full** 전부
- [ ] **on the rise** 상승 추세에 있는
- [ ] **in part** 부분적으로는
- [ ] **supplier** 공급자, 공급 회사
- [ ] **accumulate** 모으다, 축적하다
- [ ] **store** 비축하다, (창고에) 보관하다
- [ ] **lead to** ~으로 이어지다
- [ ] **project** 예상하다
- [ ] **unpredictability** 예측 불가능
- [ ] **associate** (일·사업 등의) 제휴자, 동료
- [ ] **representative** 대표자, 담당자
- [ ] **relocate** 이전하다
- [ ] **reflect** 반영하다
- [ ] **paperwork** 서류 작업
- [ ] **estimate** 견적
- [ ] **budget** 예산
- [ ] **worth** ~을 할 가치가 있는
- [ ] **have a point** 일리가 있다
- [ ] **confidence** 신뢰, 자신감
- [ ] **sophisticated** 세련된
- [ ] **outfit** 복장
- [ ] **prioritize** 우선순위를 매기다
- [ ] **accompany** 동행하다, 동반하다

- [ ] **introduce** 내놓다, 도입하다
- [ ] **large-scale** 대규모의
- [ ] **drop off** 내려 주다, 갖다 주다
- [ ] **assume** (사실일 것으로) 추정하다
- [ ] **follow one's example** ~을 본받다
- [ ] **sign up for** ~을 신청[가입]하다
- [ ] **realty** 부동산
- [ ] **lease agreement** 임대 계약(서)
- [ ] **collect** 징수하다, 모으다
- [ ] **obstacle** 장애(물)
- [ ] **bid** 입찰
- [ ] **contaminated** 오염된
- [ ] **revenue** 수익
- [ ] **conduct** 실시하다, 수행하다
- [ ] **regularly** 정기적으로
- [ ] **voucher** 할인권, 쿠폰
- [ ] **matter** 중요하다, 문제가 되다
- [ ] **set ~ apart** ~을 돋보이게 만들다

Her creativity sets her apart from other candidates.
그녀의 창의성은 그녀를 다른 후보자들보다 눈에 띄게 한다.

- [ ] **give ~ a ride** ~를 태워 주다
- [ ] **convenient** 편리한
- [ ] **immediate** 즉각적인
- [ ] **attachment** 첨부
- [ ] **downsize** 줄이다, 축소하다
- [ ] **underground** 지하의
- [ ] **report to work** 출근하다
- [ ] **prior to** ~에 앞서
- [ ] **take inventory of** ~의 목록을 만들다

They took inventory of the company's furniture, equipment, and supplies
그들은 회사의 가구와 장비, 비품의 목록을 작성했다.

- [ ] **administration** 경영, 관리
- [ ] **absent** 결근한, 결석한
- [ ] **humble** 보잘것없는, 겸손한
- [ ] **unfold** 펼쳐지다, 펴다
- [ ] **entertaining** 재미있는

- [ ] **informative** 유익한
- [ ] **spacious** 널찍한
- [ ] **trim** 잘라 내다
- [ ] **halt** 중단시키다
- [ ] **be encouraged to do** ~하도록 장려되다
- [ ] **stock up on** ~을 비축하다
- [ ] **account for** (부분·비율을) 차지하다
- [ ] **majority** 대다수
- [ ] **operation** 작동
- [ ] **clearance** (재고) 정리
- [ ] **qualify for** ~의 자격이 있다, ~의 대상이 되다

All orders qualify for free delivery from October 1 to October 31.
모든 주문은 10월 1일부터 10월 31일 까지 무료 배송 대상이 됩니다.

- [ ] **constantly** 끊임없이, 계속
- [ ] **take action** 조치를 취하다
- [ ] **minimum** 최소한도
- [ ] **attain** 달성하다, 이루다
- [ ] **overview** 개관, 개요
- [ ] **indicate** 명시하다, 나타내다
- [ ] **coordinator** 책임자, 진행자
- [ ] **track** 추적하다, 탐지하다

- [ ] **put together** (이것저것을 모아) 만들다
- [ ] **qualified** 자격이 있는
- [ ] **take on** (일을) 맡다
- [ ] **remind** 다시 한번 알려 주다, 상기시키다
- [ ] **literacy** 읽고 쓰는 능력
- [ ] **registration** 등록자 수, 등록
- [ ] **venue** 장소
- [ ] **accommodate** 수용하다
- [ ] **screening** 검사, 심사
- [ ] **specific** 구체적인
- [ ] **concern** 걱정, 관심사
- [ ] **valuable** 귀중한
- [ ] **quantity** 수량, 양
- [ ] **place an order** 주문하다
- [ ] **be dedicated to** ~에 전념하다
- [ ] **pleasant** 쾌적한, 기분 좋은
- [ ] **provide A with B** A에게 B를 제공하다
- [ ] **reassess** 재평가하다

PART 5

- [ ] **confirm** 확인해 주다, 확증하다
- [ ] **reliability** 신뢰성, 신뢰할 수 있음
- [ ] **demand** 수요
- [ ] **provider** 공급자
- [ ] **appliance** 가전제품, 기기
- [ ] **sense** 감지하다
- [ ] **caterer** 출장 요리업자
- [ ] **peak season** 성수기
- [ ] **come up** 다가오다
- [ ] **additional** 추가의
- [ ] **shortage** 부족
- [ ] **community center** 지역 문화 회관
- [ ] **official** 공무원, 직원
- [ ] **patron** (도서관의) 이용자, 고객
- [ ] **take out** 가지고 나가다, 꺼내다
- [ ] **reference book** 참고 도서
- [ ] **build a reputation** 명성을 쌓다

- [ ] **in compliance with** ~에 따라

In compliance with regulations, we will give updates to those who are directly involved in the matter.
규정에 따라, 우리는 그 문제에 직접적으로 관련된 사람들에게 최신 정보를 제공할 것이다.

- [ ] **update** 최신 정보
- [ ] **involved in** ~에 관련[연루]된
- [ ] **pharmaceuticals** 약, 제약
- [ ] **physician** 내과 의사
- [ ] **transaction** 거래, 매매
- [ ] **transfer** 이체
- [ ] **deposit** 예금, 입금
- [ ] **apply** 바르다, 신청하다
- [ ] **surface** 표면
- [ ] **take ~ into account** ~을 고려하다, 계산에 넣다

Ms. Mason took the fluctuations in currency rates into account when making the projections.
메이슨 씨는 예측을 할 때 환율의 변동에 대해 고려했다.

- [ ] **make a projection** 예측하다
- [ ] **potential** 잠재적인
- [ ] **discouraged** 의욕을 잃어버린, 낙담한
- [ ] **confusingly** 혼란스럽게
- [ ] **add** 추가하다, 덧붙이다
- [ ] **contract** 계약(서)
- [ ] **boarding pass** 탑승권
- [ ] **agent** 직원, 대리인
- [ ] **verify** 확인하다, 입증하다
- [ ] **set a record** 기록을 세우다
- [ ] **professional** 프로의, 전문적인
- [ ] **take a seat** 자리에 앉다
- [ ] **notice** 주목하다, 알아채다
- [ ] **commence** 시작되다
- [ ] **brief** 짧은
- [ ] **elect** 선출하다
- [ ] **entrepreneur** 기업가, 사업가
- [ ] **launch** 시작하다, 착수하다; 출시, 발매
- [ ] **start-up** 신규 업체
- [ ] **expand** 확장하다

- [ ] **on the market** 시중에 나와 있는

The sound quality of Vivico speakers is markedly superior compared to others on the market.
비비코 스피커의 음질은 시중에 나와 있는 다른 스피커들에 비해 눈에 띄게 우수하다.

- [ ] **afford** (~을 살) 여유가 되다
- [ ] **row** 줄, 열
- [ ] **auditorium** 객석, 강당
- [ ] **reserve** 지정하다, 예약해 두다
- [ ] **presenter** 발표자
- [ ] **as a matter of fact** 사실상
- [ ] **on the contrary** 반대로
- [ ] **discover** 깨닫다, 발견하다

PART 6

- [ ] **charge** (요금·값을) 청구하다, 충전하다
- [ ] **pay for** 대금을 지불하다
- [ ] **a wide selection of** 다양하게 구비된

You can choose any two items you like from our wide selection of jewelry.
여러분은 다양하게 구비된 저희의 보석류 중 어느 것이든 마음에 드시는 것 두 개를 고르실 수 있습니다.

- [ ] **offer** 할인, 제안
- [ ] **limit** 제한
- [ ] **supply** 재고(량), 공급(량)
- [ ] **prominent** 유명한, 현저한
- [ ] **association** 협회, 연상
- [ ] **support** 후원하다; 지지
- [ ] **donation** 기부(금)
- [ ] **shelter** 쉼터, 피난처
- [ ] **be in charge of** ~을 맡다[담당하다]
- [ ] **retirement** 은퇴
- [ ] **facility** 시설
- [ ] **proximity** 근접성, 가까움
- [ ] **subscription** 구독
- [ ] **valid** 유효한
- [ ] **wonder** 궁금하다

TEST 02

PART 1

- [ ] **groceries** 식료품류
- [ ] **stroll** 거닐다, 산책하다
- [ ] **on display** 진열된
- [ ] **put away** ~을 치우다
- [ ] **operate** 조작하다, 가동하다
- [ ] **remove** 벗다, 없애다
- [ ] **hard hat** 안전모
- [ ] **be lined up** 줄지어 있다
- [ ] **lawn** 잔디(밭)
- [ ] **install** 설치하다
- [ ] **unoccupied** 비어 있는

PART 2

- [ ] **on the other side of** ~의 반대편에
- [ ] **depart** 출발하다, 떠나다
- [ ] **recommend** 추천하다
- [ ] **book** 예약하다
- [ ] **plenty of** 넉넉한, 많은
- [ ] **promote** 승진시키다, 촉진하다
- [ ] **branch** 지사, 분점
- [ ] **vending machine** 자동판매기
- [ ] **unplug** (전기) 플러그를 뽑다
- [ ] **take a break** 잠시 휴식을 취하다
- [ ] **electrical** 전기의
- [ ] **reach** (목적 따위를) 달성하다, ~에 이르다
- [ ] **fundraising** 모금
- [ ] **charity** 자선
- [ ] **short** 부족한, 모자란
- [ ] **restore** 재건[복구]하다
- [ ] **sales figure** 판매 수치
- [ ] **accurate** 정확한
- [ ] **evaluation** 평가
- [ ] **cover** 다루다, 포함시키다
- [ ] **fill a prescription** (처방) 약을 조제하다

- [ ] **be out of town** (출장 등으로) 도시를 떠나 있다
- [ ] **present** 발표하다, 보여 주다
- [ ] **give a lecture** 강연하다
- [ ] **renew** 갱신하다, 연장하다
- [ ] **release** 발매하다, 발표[공개]하다
- [ ] **translate** 번역하다
- [ ] **trade agreement** 무역 협정
- [ ] **take apart** 분해하다
- [ ] **relief** 안도, 안심
- [ ] **instructions** (사용) 설명서
- [ ] **approve** 승인하다
- [ ] **package** 소포, 포장한 상품
- [ ] **in transit** 운송 중에
- [ ] **advanced** 고급[상급]의
- [ ] **minor** 가벼운, 심각하지 않은
- [ ] **calculate** 계산하다
- [ ] **cut back** 줄이다, 삭감하다
- [ ] **notice** 알아채다; 공고문, 통지

PART 3

- [ ] **flyer** 전단
- [ ] **discontinue** (생산을) 중단하다
- [ ] **work overtime** 초과 근무를 하다
- [ ] **on schedule** 예정대로
- [ ] **permit** 허가(증)
- [ ] **lot** (특정 용도의) 부지
- [ ] **assignment** 임무, 과제
- [ ] **take care of** ~을 처리하다
- [ ] **upset** 당황한, 화난
- [ ] **make a delivery** 배달하다
- [ ] **make a purchase** 구매하다
- [ ] **make an adjustment** 조정하다

I'd like to make an adjustment to the current policy.
현재의 방침을 조정하고 싶습니다.

- [ ] **take part in** ~에 참여하다
- [ ] **get together with** ~와 만나다
- [ ] **oversee** 감독하다
- [ ] **screen** 거르다, 가려내다

- [ ] **be out sick** 아파서 결근하다
- [ ] **complete** 완료하다; 완전한
- [ ] **under control** 통제[제어]되는
- [ ] **leave behind** ~을 두고 가다
- [ ] **get in touch with** ~와 연락하다
- [ ] **have no choice** 선택의 여지가 없다
- [ ] **strict** 엄격한
- [ ] **look forward to** ~을 기대[고대]하다
- [ ] **property** 토지, 부동산
- [ ] **regulation** 규정
- [ ] **switch A with B** A와 B를 바꾸다
- [ ] **progress** 진행, 진척
- [ ] **prestigious** 명망 있는
- [ ] **bring up** (화제를) 꺼내다

PART 4

- [ ] **raise funds** 기금을 모으다
- [ ] **operating expense** 운영비
- [ ] **exclusive** 독점적인
- [ ] **exit** 나가다
- [ ] **require** 필요로 하다
- [ ] **assistance** 도움
- [ ] **transport** 이동시키다, 실어 나르다
- [ ] **throughout** 도처에
- [ ] **set up** ~을 놓다[설치하다]

How many chairs need to be set up for the reception?
리셉션 장소에 의자를 몇 개 설치해야 하나요?

- [ ] **for a while** 잠시 동안
- [ ] **volunteer** 자원봉사로 하다; 자원봉사자
- [ ] **rewarding** 보람 있는
- [ ] **participate in** ~에 참여하다
- [ ] **replacement** 후임자, 대체(물)
- [ ] **on short notice** 갑자기, 충분한 예고 없이
- [ ] **distribute** 나누어 주다, 배포하다
- [ ] **step down** 사직하다, 물러나다
- [ ] **enormous** 거대한, 막대한
- [ ] **select** 선정하다

- [ ] **worldwide** 전 세계적으로
- [ ] **available** 이용 가능한
- [ ] **found** 설립하다
- [ ] **residential** 주거의, 주택용의
- [ ] **from scratch** 맨 처음부터

We have to do the whole thing again from scratch.
우리는 모든 걸 맨 처음부터 다시 해야 합니다.

- [ ] **existing** 기존의
- [ ] **unwanted** 원치 않는, 불필요한
- [ ] **distracting** 주의를 산만하게 하는
- [ ] **waste** 낭비하다

PART 7

- [ ] **launch** 시작하다
- [ ] **attract** 유인하다, 끌어들이다
- [ ] **public relations** 홍보 (활동)
- [ ] **prior to** ~에 앞서
- [ ] **acknowledge** (편지·소포 등을) 받았음을 알리다
- [ ] **be eligible for** ~에 대한 자격이 있다
- [ ] **patronage** (상점 등의) 단골, 애용
- [ ] **warehouse** 창고
- [ ] **overnight shipping** 익일 배송
- [ ] **registration** 등록
- [ ] **on a first-come, first-served basis** 선착순으로

Spots will be assigned on a first-come, first-served basis.
자리는 선착순으로 배정될 것입니다.

- [ ] **grant** 보조금
- [ ] **required** 필수인
- [ ] **certification** 증명, 인증
- [ ] **fit** 건강한
- [ ] **provider** 제공자, 제공 기관
- [ ] **on site** 현장에서
- [ ] **overnight** 하룻밤 동안
- [ ] **enter into a contract** 계약을 체결하다

- [ ] **headquarters** 본사
- [ ] **reimburse** 변제하다, 배상하다
- [ ] **provided** ~라는 조건으로
- [ ] **completion** 완성, 완료
- [ ] **keep ~ informed** ~에게 계속해서 알려 주다

Keep me informed of any developments.
진전이 생기면 제게 계속 알려 주세요.

- [ ] **houseware** 가정용품
- [ ] **sluggish** 부진한
- [ ] **respectively** 각각
- [ ] **target** 겨냥하다, 대상으로 삼다
- [ ] **yield** (결과를) 내다
- [ ] **promising** 유망한, 전망이 좋은
- [ ] **ongoing** 계속 진행 중인
- [ ] **date back to** ~까지 거슬러 올라가다

The college dates back to 1870s.
그 대학의 역사는 1870년대로 거슬러 올라간다.

- [ ] **fragile** 부서지기 쉬운
- [ ] **unmatched** 타의 추종을 불허하는

Our track record for dealing with fragile artifacts is unmatched.
부서지기 쉬운 유물들을 다뤄온 저희의 실적은 타의 추종을 불허합니다.

- [ ] **operation** 작업 (과정), 공정
- [ ] **line up** 한 줄로 서다, 줄을 이루다
- [ ] **house** 소장하다
- [ ] **come along** (원하는 대로) 되어가다
- [ ] **promote** 홍보하다, 판매를 촉진하다
- [ ] **high-profile** 세간의 이목을 끄는
- [ ] **register for** ~에 등록하다
- [ ] **along with** ~와 함께
- [ ] **fall through** 불발되다, 실패로 돌아가다
- [ ] **specialize in** ~을 전문으로 하다
- [ ] **in-house** (회사) 내부의
- [ ] **affordably priced** 저렴한 가격의
- [ ] **compliment** 칭찬

- [ ] **venue** 장소
- [ ] **underway** 진행 중인
- [ ] **take place** 개최되다
- [ ] **screening** 검사
- [ ] **vendor** 상인, 판매 회사
- [ ] **supplement** 보충(물)
- [ ] **be informed** 통보 받다
- [ ] **on-site** 현장의
- [ ] **address** 고심하다, 다루다

Many issues were addressed at the meeting with board members.
이사진들과의 회의에서 많은 사안들이 다뤄졌다.

- [ ] **beneficial** 이로운
- [ ] **transition** 이행[변천]하다; 변경
- [ ] **be concerned about** ~에 대해 걱정하다
- [ ] **knowledgeable** 아는 것이 많은, 잘 아는
- [ ] **circumstance** 상황, 환경
- [ ] **submission** 제출, 제안
- [ ] **initiative** 계획
- [ ] **carry** (가게에서 품목을) 취급하다
- [ ] **high-end** 고급의, 고가의
- [ ] **replace** 교체하다, 대신하다
- [ ] **outgoing** 떠나는
- [ ] **expenditure** 지출, 경비
- [ ] **qualification** 자격요건
- [ ] **list** 나열하다, 목록화하다
- [ ] **quarterly** 분기별
- [ ] **misconception** 오해
- [ ] **head** 이끌다
- [ ] **high-ranking** 고위직의
- [ ] **chair** 의장

PART 4

- [ ] **tourist site** 관광지
- [ ] **workshop** 작업장
- [ ] **process** 과정, 절차
- [ ] **talented** 재능 있는
- [ ] **identify** 확인하다, 식별하다
- [ ] **extra** 여분의, 추가의
- [ ] **be delighted to do** ~해서 기쁘다
- [ ] **membership** 회원 자격[신분]
- [ ] **reach a goal** 목표를 달성하다
- [ ] **fitness** 건강
- [ ] **special deal** 특가 상품
- [ ] **keep up with** ~을 따르다
- [ ] **demand** 요구
- [ ] **medical** 의료의
- [ ] **proper** 적절한
- [ ] **inspect** 점검하다
- [ ] **feel reassured** 마음이 놓이다
- [ ] **thorough** 빈틈없는
- [ ] **guidance** 지도
- [ ] **knowledgeable** 아는 것이 많은
- [ ] **fix** 수리하다, 고치다
- [ ] **operate** 운영하다
- [ ] **current** 현재의
- [ ] **due to** ~ 때문에
- [ ] **impressed** 깊은 인상을 받은
- [ ] **essential** 필수의, 없어서는 안 될
- [ ] **cover letter** 자기 소개서
- [ ] **résumé** 이력서
- [ ] **in case** ~할 경우에 대비해서
- [ ] **available** 시간이 있는
- [ ] **short-staffed** 직원이 부족한, 일손이 모자란
- [ ] **serve** (손님을) 접대[응대]하다
- [ ] **from now on** 이제부터
- [ ] **fill out** 작성하다
- [ ] **preferred** 선호하는
- [ ] **guarantee** 보장하다
- [ ] **keep A up to date** A에게 최신 소식을 알려주다
- [ ] **interest** ~의 관심을 끌다
- [ ] **trend** 추세, 경향
- [ ] **harvest** 수확하다, 거둬들이다
- [ ] **applicant** 지원자, 신청자
- [ ] **be interested in** ~에 관심이 있다
- [ ] **invite** 초대[초청]하다
- [ ] **across from** ~의 맞은편에
- [ ] **personality** 인성, 성격
- [ ] **move on to** ~으로 넘어가다
- [ ] **annual** 연례의
- [ ] **trade expo** 무역 박람회
- [ ] **quite a few** 상당수
- [ ] **consider** 고려하다
- [ ] **task** (부과된) 일, 직무
- [ ] **in detail** 상세히

PART 5

- [ ] **express** 표현하다
- [ ] **corporate** 기업의, 법인의
- [ ] **structure** 구조, 체계
- [ ] **be intended for** ~을 위해 만들어지다[의도되다]

> The new car is intended for short journeys within an urban environment.
> 그 신차는 도시 환경 내에서의 짧은 이동을 위해 만들어졌다.

- [ ] **manufacturing** 제조업
- [ ] **parking lot** 주차장
- [ ] **access** 이용, 접근
- [ ] **analyst** 분석가
- [ ] **predict** 예측하다
- [ ] **effect** 영향
- [ ] **closure** 폐쇄
- [ ] **review** 평가, 비평
- [ ] **feature** 특별히 포함하다, 특징으로 삼다

> The hotel's restaurant features live musical performances.
> 그 호텔 레스토랑은 라이브 음악 공연을 선보인다.

- [ ] **complete** (서식을 빠짐없이) 작성하다
- [ ] **restriction** 제한, 규제
- [ ] **reduce** 줄이다, (가격 등을) 낮추다
- [ ] **self-employed** 자영업을 하는
- [ ] **profit** 이익, 수익
- [ ] **cost** 비용
- [ ] **carry out** ~을 실행[수행]하다

> Soil samples were taken to carry out the testing to check for pollution.
> 오염 여부 확인을 위한 실험을 실행하기 위해 토양 표본이 채취되었다.

- [ ] **replacement** 대체, 교체
- [ ] **setback** 차질
- [ ] **further** 더 이상의, 추가의
- [ ] **garage** 차고
- [ ] **damage** 피해를 주다, 훼손하다
- [ ] **rebuild** 다시 짓다, 재건하다
- [ ] **department** 부서
- [ ] **formally** 공식적으로
- [ ] **assess** 평가하다
- [ ] **favorable** 유리한, 순조로운
- [ ] **condition** 상황, 사정
- [ ] **result in** ~의 결과를 낳다

> The favorable market conditions resulted in more business investment.
> 유리한 시장 상황은 더 많은 사업 투자라는 결과를 낳았다.

- [ ] **built-in** 붙박이의, 내장의
- [ ] **have an effect on** ~에 영향을 미치다
- [ ] **complete** 완료하다

PART 6

- [ ] **for one's convenience** ~의 편의를 위해

> An order form is enclosed for your convenience.
> 귀하의 편의를 위해 주문서가 동봉되어 있습니다.

- [ ] **personalize** (개인의 필요에) 맞추다
- [ ] **meet the needs** 요구를 충족시키다
- [ ] **short notice** 촉박한 통보

테스트별 핵심 어휘

TEST 01

PART 1

- [ ] **pour** 따르다, 붓다
- [ ] **water** 물을 주다
- [ ] **pile** (물건을 차곡차곡) 쌓다
- [ ] **put away** 치우다
- [ ] **fold** 접다
- [ ] **position** ~에 두다, 배치하다
- [ ] **stack** 쌓다
- [ ] **arrange** 정리하다, 배열하다
- [ ] **wait in line** 줄을 서서 기다리다
- [ ] **instrument** 악기, 도구
- [ ] **copy** (책·신문 등의) 한 부, 사본
- [ ] **store** 저장하다, 보관하다
- [ ] **place** 두다, 놓다

PART 2

- [ ] **landlord** 집주인, 임대인
- [ ] **property** 건물, 부동산
- [ ] **new employee** 신입 직원
- [ ] **give a tour** 견학[구경]을 시켜 주다
- [ ] **site** 장소, 현장
- [ ] **prefer** 선호하다
- [ ] **thirsty** 목이 마른, 갈증이 나는
- [ ] **on sale** 할인 중인
- [ ] **attend** 출석하다, 참석하다
- [ ] **sustainable** 지속 가능한
- [ ] **sign up** 신청하다, 등록하다
- [ ] **give a ride** 태워 주다
- [ ] **go on a business trip** 출장을 가다
- [ ] **trim** 다듬다
- [ ] **lot** 지역, 부지
- [ ] **sign** 표지판, 간판
- [ ] **leftover** 남은
- [ ] **promotional** 홍보의

- [ ] **recycle** 재활용하다
- [ ] **laboratory** 실험실
- [ ] **summary** 요약, 개요
- [ ] **take notes** 메모하다, 필기하다
- [ ] **full-time position** 정규직
- [ ] **details** 세부 정보
- [ ] **no later than** 늦어도 ~까지
- [ ] **check** (수하물을) 부치다
- [ ] **streamline** 간소화하다
- [ ] **by oneself** 혼자, 스스로
- [ ] **copy** (신문·책의) 한 부
- [ ] **take a day off** 하루 쉬다, 휴가를 내다

If you need to take a day off, ask your manager for approval.
하루 휴가를 내야 한다면 관리자에게 승인을 요청하세요.

- [ ] **video conference** 화상 회의
- [ ] **performance** 성과
- [ ] **lock** 잠그다
- [ ] **turn in** 제출하다
- [ ] **portable** 휴대용의
- [ ] **give a speech** 연설하다
- [ ] **awards ceremony** 시상식

PART 3

- [ ] **wonder** 궁금하다
- [ ] **shelf** 선반
- [ ] **look up** 찾아보다
- [ ] **stop by** (~에) 잠시 들르다
- [ ] **matter** 문제
- [ ] **so far** 지금까지
- [ ] **work from home** 재택근무를 하다
- [ ] **be responsible for** ~을 책임지다
- [ ] **damage** 손상, 피해
- [ ] **device** 기기, 장치
- [ ] **protective** 보호하는
- [ ] **from place to place** 여기저기

- [ ] **patio** 테라스
- [ ] **job opening** (직장의) 빈자리
- [ ] **alert** 알림, 경보
- [ ] **firm** 회사
- [ ] **rather than** ~보다는
- [ ] **individual** 개인
- [ ] **focus A on B** A를 B에 집중시키다
- [ ] **base** 기반
- [ ] **register** 등록하다
- [ ] **be out of** ~을 다 써서 없다, 바닥나다
- [ ] **move to** ~로 이사하다
- [ ] **in stock** 재고가 있는
- [ ] **renovate** 개조하다
- [ ] **be promoted to** ~로 승진하다

She was recently promoted to marketing director.
그녀는 최근에 마케팅 본부장으로 승진했다.

- [ ] **accomplishment** 성과, 성취
- [ ] **schedule** 일정을 잡다
- [ ] **be pleased with** ~에 만족하다, 기쁘다
- [ ] **business hours** 영업 시간
- [ ] **sell out** 다 팔리다
- [ ] **plan on** ~할 계획이다
- [ ] **out-of-town** 다른 도시의, 다른 시에서 하는
- [ ] **job interview** 취업 면접
- [ ] **select** 선택하다
- [ ] **standard** 일반적인, 보통의
- [ ] **earn** 얻다, 벌다
- [ ] **regional** 지역의
- [ ] **make sure** 확실히 하다
- [ ] **meet** 충족시키다
- [ ] **quota** 할당량
- [ ] **work on** ~에 노력을 들이다

테스트별 핵심 어휘

아주 흥미로운 plot 줄거리, 구성   acting 연기   must-see 꼭 보아야 할 것

196. 기사에서, 첫 번째 단락 두 번째 줄의 "deemed"와 의미상 가장 가까운 단어는?

(A) 여기다
(B) 예상하다
(C) 감탄하다
(D) 야기하다

해설 동의어 문제

문맥상 '자선 만찬이 놀라울 정도로 성공적이었다고 여겼다'는 의미이므로 이와 유사한 의미의 어휘를 골라야 한다. 따라서 정답은 '여기다, 생각하다'라는 의미의 (A).

197. 모금된 기금이 길크레스트 극장에서 쓰이게 될 용도는?

(A) 광고 캠페인을 시작하기 위해
(B) 영사막을 구매하기 위해
(C) 구식 웹사이트를 개선하기 위해
(D) 새 음향 장비를 설치하기 위해

해설 특정 정보 확인 문제

기사의 단서 (197)에서 기금은 극장의 최첨단 음향 시스템 설치에 사용될 것이라고 했으므로 정답은 (D).

패러프레이징 [단서] for the installation of a cutting-edge sound system in the theater → [정답] To install new audio equipment

198. 9월 8일에 가장 큰 극장의 상영 행사가 시작될 시각은?

(A) 저녁 7시
(B) 저녁 7시 5분
(C) 저녁 7시 30분
(D) 저녁 8시 10분

해설 두 지문 연계 문제_특정 정보 확인 문제

기사의 단서 (198-1)에서 길크레스트 극장이 영화제 장소 중 좌석 수가 가장 많은 곳임을 알 수 있고, 웹페이지상 일정표의 단서 (198-2)에서 9월 8일에 길크레스트 극장의 영화 상영은 저녁 7시 5분에 시작한다는 것을 알 수 있다. 따라서 정답은 (B). 지문의 Gilcrest Theater has the highest seating capacity among them이 문제에서는 the largest theater로 패러프레이징되었다.

199. 입장권 구매자들에게 하도록 권하는 것은?

(A) 디지털 영수증 다운로드하기
(B) 미리 좌석 배치도 확인하기
(C) 온라인 영화 후기 몇 개 읽어 보기
(D) 속달 우편으로 입장권 받기

해설 특정 정보 확인 문제

웹페이지의 지역 영화제 일정표 하단에 입장권 구매 시 유의 사항이 나와 있다. 단서 (199)에서 고객들은 입장권 구매 시 좌석 번호와 열을 선택해야 하기 때문에 미리 다운로드 가능한 좌석 구역 지도를 확인하라고 했으므로 정답은 (B).

패러프레이징 [단서] review the map of the venue's seating sections / before calling to order tickets → [정답] Check a seating chart / in advance

200. 애슈턴 씨가 영화를 본 장소는?

(A) 24번가 극장
(B) 코린트 극장
(C) 길크레스트 극장
(D) 팔라시오스 극장

해설 두 지문 연계 문제_특정 정보 확인 문제

후기의 단서 (200-1)에서 애슈턴 씨가 미아 카마초 감독의 최신 걸작 〈지하〉를 최근 지역 영화제에서 봤다고 했고, 웹페이지상 일정표의 단서 (200-2)에서 영화 〈지하〉는 24번가 극장에서 상영했음을 알 수 있으므로 정답은 (A).

아 준 킴벌리 씨에게 감사를 표했다. 첫 번째 이메일의 단서 (193-2)를 보면 킴벌리 씨가 마리에타 컨벤션 센터를 방문한 날짜는 2월 18일이므로, 라오 씨가 2월 18일에 출장을 갔다는 것을 추론할 수 있다. 따라서 정답은 (D).

패러프레이징 [단서] I had to fly to Toronto that day for an unexpected business matter → [정답] He took a business trip on February 18.

194. 맥그로 씨에 대해 추론할 수 있는 것은?
(A) 위원회의 예산을 담당하고 있다.
(B) 출장 요리업체들에 대한 정보를 모으고 있다.
(C) 금요일 회의에 참석할 수 없다.
(D) 마리에타 컨벤션 센터를 방문했다.

해설 추론 문제

단서 (194)에서 라오 씨는 개릿 씨를 제외한 나머지 이메일 수신자들이 조사하기로 되어 있는 출장 요리업체 관련 보고서를 기다리고 있다고 했다. 이를 토대로 이메일 수신자들 중 한 명인 맥그로 씨가 현재 출장 요리업체들을 조사하고 있음을 추론할 수 있으므로 정답은 (B).

패러프레이징 [단서] the caterers you were assigned to research → [정답] gathering information about caterers

195. 라오 씨가 대여하고 싶어 할 것 같은 연회장은?
(A) 데이지 룸
(B) 선플라워 룸
(C) 피어니 룸
(D) 오키드 룸

해설 두 지문 연계 문제_추론 문제

두 번째 이메일의 단서 (195-1)에서 라오 씨는 러크미어 만이 내려다 보이는 연회장 대신에 그보다 저렴하면서도 90명이라는 인원에 맞는 연회장을 빌리는 것이 가장 좋겠다고 했다. 정보문의 단서 (195-2)를 통해 러크미어 만이 보이는 오키드 룸보다 저렴하면서도 90명의 인원을 수용할 수 있는 곳은 피어니 룸이라는 것을 알 수 있고, 이를 통해 라오 씨가 피어니 룸을 대여하고 싶어 할 것임을 추론할 수 있으므로 정답은 (C).

196-200 기사 & 웹페이지 & 후기

성공을 거둔 극장 모금 행사

행사 기획자들은 지난밤 길크레스트 극장 기금 마련을 위해 열린 자선 만찬이 놀라울 정도로 성공적이었다고 ¹⁹⁶여겼는데, 이들은 목표액보다 약 2,000달러 상회하여 거의 12,000달러의 모금액이 모였다고 전했다. ¹⁹⁷기금은 극장의 최첨단 음향 시스템 설치에 사용될 예정으로, 현재 사용되고 있는 구식 시스템에 꼭 필요한 교체 작업에 쓰일 것이다.

작업은 길크레스트 극장이 주최 장소가 될 지역 영화제에 딱 맞춰 완료될 것이다. 이 시설은 주로 실황 극장 공연을 상영하기는 하지만, 영화를 위한 대형 영사막도 갖추고 있다. 지역 전역에 있는 다른 극장들도 참여할 예정이지만, ¹⁹⁸⁻¹길크레스트 극장이 그중에서 좌석 수가 가장 많은데, 이는 두 번째로 큰 코린트 극장의 두 배가 넘는 것이다.

영화제의 입장권은 다음 주에 판매에 들어간다. 영화 팬들은 비평가의 극찬을 받은 감독들의 열정적인 드라마들을 보러 갈 수 있다. 아니면 가벼운 것을 찾는 사람들에게는 코미디 각본의 영화들도 많이 있다.

어휘 fundraiser 모금 행사 charity 자선 (단체) remarkable 놀랄 만한, 주목할 만한 proceeds 모금액, 수익금 cutting-edge 최첨단의 outdated 구식의 in time 시간 맞춰, 늦지 않게 projection screen 영사막 seating capacity 좌석 수, 수용력 take in (영화 등을) 보러 가다 critically acclaimed 비평가들의 극찬을 받은

---

www.regionalfilmfestival.com/schedule

| 홈 | 소개 | **일정** | 좌석 | 오시는 길 |

지역 영화제

| 9월 6일 목요일 | 9월 7일 금요일 | **9월 8일 토요일** | 9월 9일 일요일 |

장소 / 전화번호	영화	시작 시간	
²⁰⁰⁻²24번가 극장 / 555-4102	〈지하〉	저녁 7시	[추가 정보]
코린트 극장 / 555-0578	〈어느 여름날〉	저녁 7시 30분	[추가 정보]
¹⁹⁸⁻²길크레스트 극장 / 555-5855	〈마르코 이야기〉	저녁 7시 5분	[추가 정보]
팔라시오스 극장 / 555-9360	〈윌슨의 군대〉	저녁 8시 10분	[추가 정보]

¹⁹⁹고객들은 입장권을 구매할 때 좌석 번호와 열을 선택해야 하니 입장권 주문을 위해 전화하기 전에 www.regionalfilmfestival.com/seating에서 다운로드할 수 있는 극장의 좌석 구역 지도를 확인해 주십시오. 이것으로 주문 과정을 더 빨리 진행할 수 있을 것입니다.

어휘 speed up 속도를 높이다

〈지하〉: 올해 최고의 스릴러물

★★★★

케이시 애슈턴 작성

마지막 순간까지 계속해서 추측을 하게 하는 스릴러물을 찾고 있다면, ²⁰⁰⁻¹미아 카마초 감독의 최신 걸작 〈지하〉만한 것이 없습니다. 저는 최근 지역 영화제에서 그것을 봤고 캐릭터의 발전 과정, 흥미로운 줄거리, 그리고 환상적인 연기에 대단히 감명받았습니다. 이 영화는 꼭 봐야 해요!

어휘 thriller 스릴러물 very (강조하여) 맨, 가장 masterpiece 걸작, 명작 extremely 대단히, 극도로 development 발달, 전개 intriguing

즐겁게 둘러보셨기를 바랍니다. 귀사가 개최하고자 하는 연회에 대한 설명을 토대로, 저는 저희가 완벽한 장소가 될 것이라고 생각합니다. ¹⁹¹각각의 연회장에는 귀사의 미술 강사들에게 상을 수여하고 연설을 하는 데 사용될 수 있는 무대가 갖춰져 있고, 귀사의 필요에 맞는 다양한 편의 시설이 있습니다. 게다가, 귀하께서 원하시는 날짜인 3월 31일에는 현재 예약된 건이 없음을 확인해 드릴 수 있습니다. 요청하신 각 연회장의 세부 정보를 첨부해 드리오니 확인해 주시기 바랍니다. 예약을 원하시거나, 혹은 더 궁금하신 사항이 있으시면 주저 마시고 555-6677번에 내선 21번으로 제게 연락해 주십시오. 귀하로부터 곧 답변을 듣게 되기를 바랍니다.

마리에타 컨벤션 센터, 고객 서비스 담당자
랠프 셸비 드림

어휘 wing 부속 건물   equipped with ~을 갖춘   present 수여하다   amenity 《보통 복수형》 편의 시설   suit ~에 맞다   make a booking 예약을 하다   hesitate 주저하다, 망설이다   extension 내선, 구내전화

마리에타 컨벤션 센터 연회장 설명

데이지 룸 – 최대 수용 인원: 50명 / 대여료: 2,600달러
4×8미터 무대, 연단, 프로젝터, 접이식 영상 스크린

선플라워 룸 – 최대 수용 인원: 50명 / 대여료: 2,900달러
4×8미터 무대, 연단, 프로젝터, 접이식 영상 스크린, ¹⁹²정원으로 통하는 외부 출입구

¹⁹⁵⁻²**피어니 룸** – 최대 수용 인원: 100명 / 대여료: 3,500달러
6×10미터 무대, 연단, 프로젝터, 붙박이식 평면 스크린 텔레비전, 풀 서비스 바

오키드 룸 – 최대 수용 인원: 100명 / 대여료: 4,800달러
6×12미터 무대, 연단, 프로젝터, 붙박이식 평면 스크린 텔레비전, 풀 서비스 바, 러크미어 만이 보이는 전망

다양한 좌석 배치가 가능합니다. 손님들은 아주 적은 요금으로 남측 또는 서측 주차장을 이용하실 수 있습니다.

어휘 capacity 수용력[량]   podium 연단, 지휘대   pull-down (끌어당겨 펼쳐서 쓸 수 있도록) 접는 식의   exterior 외부의   doorway 출입구   built-in 붙박이의   arrangement 배치, 정리   nominal (금액이) 얼마 안 되는, 미미한

수신: 아미나 제프리스, ¹⁹⁴딘 맥그로, 킴벌리 개릿, 바이 탄
발신: 아밀 라오
날짜: 2월 20일
제목: 연회 계획

안녕하세요, 여러분.

우리는 곧 있을 직원 및 직원 가족들을 위한 연회에 관한 우리 위원회의 계획을 잘 진행하고 있는 것 같습니다. ¹⁹³⁻¹그날 제가 예기치 못한 사업 문제로 토론토에 가게 되는 바람에 저를 대신해 마리에타 컨벤션 센터 방문을 맡아 주셔서 고맙습니다, 킴벌리.

¹⁹⁴저는 아직 나머지 분들이 조사를 맡은 출장 요리업체들에 관한 보고서를 기다리고 있습니다. 목요일 오후까지 그 자료를 저에게 이메일로 보내 주세요.

행사 장소 후보지들에 관해 이야기하자면, ¹⁹⁵⁻¹90명의 우리 손님들이 식사하는 동안 러크미어 만을 내려다볼 수 있다면 정말 좋겠지만, 우리의 한정된 예산을 고려할 때 이는 가능할 것 같지 않습니다. 대신에, 우리의 인원 규모상의 요구에 맞는 더 저렴한 연회장을 빌리는 것이 가장 좋을 것 같습니다. 금요일 회의에서 이것에 대해 좀 더 논의할 수 있을 겁니다. 그때 뵙겠습니다!

아밀 드림

어휘 make progress 진행하다, 진전하다   committee 위원회   take over (남을 대신하여) 떠맡다, 인계받다   overlook 내려다보다   dine 식사를 하다   feasible 실현 가능한   given ~을 고려해 볼 때

---

191. 개릿 씨가 근무할 것 같은 곳은?
(A) 기술 회사
(B) 피트니스 센터
(C) 미술 교육 기관
(D) 공연장

해설 추론 문제

단서 (191)에서 각 연회장에는 개릿 씨가 소속된 회사의 미술 강사들에게 상을 수여할 수 있는 무대가 갖춰져 있다고 했다. 이를 통해 개릿 씨가 근무하는 곳이 미술 교육 기관임을 추론할 수 있으므로 정답은 (C).

192. 정보문에 시사된 연회장의 편의 시설은?
(A) 무대 공간을 위한 특수 조명
(B) 도시의 지평선이 보이는 전망
(C) 손님들을 위한 무료 주차
(D) 야외 공간으로 연결되는 입구

해설 Not/True 문제

단서 (192)에서 정원으로 통하는 외부 출입구가 언급되었으므로 정답은 (D). 러크미어 만이 보이는 전망은 언급되었지만 특수 조명이나 지평선 전망에 대한 언급은 없으며, 아주 적은 주차 요금을 받는다고 했으므로 나머지는 오답.

패러프레이징 [단서] exterior doorway to garden → [정답] Access to an outdoor space

193. 라오 씨에 대해 암시된 것은?
(A) 막판에 위원회에 합류했다.
(B) 회의 장소 몇 군데를 방문했다.
(C) 출장 요리업체에 대한 후기를 작성했다.
(D) 2월 18일에 출장을 갔다.

해설 두 지문 연계 문제_추론 문제

두 번째 이메일의 단서 (193-1)에서 라오 씨는 당일에 예기치 못하게 토론토로 출장을 가게 된 자신을 대신해 마리에타 컨벤션 센터 방문을 맡

www.ucanreview.net/customer_reviews/accessories

브랜드: 짐머 제품: 짐머-40
작성자: 필립 샌도벌 게시글 유형: 답변

짐머 사의 고객 서비스 담당자로서 저는 고객님께서 구매하신 제품에 완전히 만족하지는 못하셔서 유감입니다. ¹⁸⁹⁻²고객님의 요구를 본다면, 짐머-40B를 고려해 보시는 게 좋을 것 같습니다. 그것은 내부에 17인치 노트북까지 수용할 수 있는 특별 충전용 칸을 가지고 있습니다. 짐머-40과 동일한 젤 충전 어깨끈이 있어서 무거운 물건들로 채워져 있어도 편안하게 메실 수 있습니다. 이미 고객님께서 짐머-40을 갖고 계시기 때문에 새 배터리를 구매할 ¹⁹⁰이유도 전혀 없습니다. 같은 것을 저희의 모든 가방에 사용할 수 있기 때문입니다. 이것이 고객님의 문제를 해결해 드리기를 바랍니다.

어휘 be satisfied with ~에 만족하다 completely 완전히, 전적으로 based on ~에 근거하여 compartment (물건 보관용) 칸 accommodate 수용하다, 충분한 공간을 제공하다 up to ~까지 comfortably 편안하게, 편리하게 load (짐·사람 등을) 싣다 resolve 해결하다

186. 짐머-40에 대해 시사되지 않은 것은?
(A) 방수 외장재로 되어 있다.
(B) 재생 가능한 에너지를 이용한다.
(C) 부분적으로 재활용 소재로 만들어졌다.
(D) 운동 중에 쓰기에 충분히 가볍다.

해설 Not/True 문제

(A)는 단서 (186A)에서 외부가 완전히 방수가 된다는 것을 알 수 있고, (B)는 단서 (186B)에서 전자 기기를 충전하는 데 사용 가능한 태양 전지판을 특징으로 한다고 나와 있으므로 재생 가능한 에너지를 이용함을 알 수 있으며, (C)는 단서 (186C)에서 배낭의 플라스틱 부품은 모두 재생 플라스틱으로 만들어진 것이라고 했다. 그러나 운동 중에 배낭을 사용하는 내용이나 배낭의 무게에 대한 내용은 나와 있지 않으므로 정답은 (D).

187. 킨테로 씨에 대해 추론할 수 있는 것은?
(A) 짐머 사로부터 매달 소식을 받게 될 것이다.
(B) 백화점에서 가방을 구매했다.
(C) 가방의 색상을 마음에 들어 하지 않는다.
(D) 주로 야외 활동을 위해 가방을 사용한다.

해설 두 지문 연계 문제_추론 문제

온라인 후기의 단서 (187-1)을 통해 킨테로 씨는 무료 보조 배터리를 받은 것을 알 수 있는데, 제품 설명서의 단서 (187-2)에서 구매 시에 짐머 사의 월간 소식지 구독 신청을 하면 무료 보조 배터리를 준다고 했으므로 킨테로 씨가 짐머 사의 월간 소식지를 신청했고, 이에 따라 짐머 사로부터 매달 소식을 받게 될 것임을 추론할 수 있다. 따라서 정답은 (A).

패러프레이징 [단서] our monthly newsletter → [정답] monthly updates from Zimmer

188. 온라인 후기에서 암시된 것은?
(A) 짐머 사는 비교적 신생 업체이다.
(B) 킨테로 씨는 가방을 더 구매할 계획이다.
(C) 짐머 사는 노트북 컴퓨터 제품군을 판매한다.
(D) 킨테로 씨는 자기 가방에서 손상된 부분을 발견했다.

해설 추론 문제

단서 (188)에서 킨테로 씨는 자기 친구 몇 명에게 선물로 짐머-40을 사줄 생각이라고 했으므로 정답은 (B).

패러프레이징 [단서] I intend to buy it as a gift for several friends → [정답] Mr. Quintero plans to purchase more bags.

189. 샌도벌 씨가 킨테로 씨에게 짐머-40B를 추천하는 이유는?
(A) 젤 충전 끈이 있는 유일한 가방이다.
(B) 더 빨리 물건들을 충전할 수 있다.
(C) 물건을 넣을 수 있는 공간이 더 크다.
(D) 짐머-40보다 내구성이 더 강하다.

해설 두 지문 연계 문제_특정 정보 확인 문제

온라인 후기의 단서 (189-1)에서 킨테로 씨는 가방에 15인치 노트북이 맞지 않는다는 문제점을 언급했고, 이에 대해 온라인 답변의 단서 (189-2)에서 샌도벌 씨는 17인치 노트북까지 들어갈 수 있는 짐머-40B를 고려해 보라고 했으므로 정답은 (C).

패러프레이징 [단서] It has a special charging compartment on the inside that can accommodate up to a 17-inch laptop. → [정답] It has a larger carrying capacity.

190. 온라인 답변에서, 첫 번째 단락 여섯 번째 줄의 "point"와 의미상 가장 가까운 단어는?
(A) 의견
(B) 이유
(C) 측면
(D) 점

해설 동의어 문제

문맥상 '새 배터리를 구매할 이유가 전혀 없다'는 의미이므로 정답은 (B). 지문의 there isn't any point에서처럼 not any point라는 표현이 쓰인 경우, point는 '이유'라는 의미를 나타낼 수 있다는 것을 알아 두자.

191-195 이메일 & 정보문 & 이메일

수신: 킴벌리 개릿 〈kgarrett@saezinc.net〉
발신: 마리에타 컨벤션 센터 〈info@mariettacc.com〉
날짜: 2월 19일
제목: 정보

개릿 씨께,

¹⁹³⁻²2월 18일에 마리에타 컨벤션 센터를 돌아보러 와 주셔서 감사합니다. 확장된 서쪽 부속 건물을 포함한 저희의 기술 기반 시설들을

단서 (181)에서 사진 촬영이 4월 24일에 있을 것이고 건물 전체에서 이루어질 것이라고 했으므로 정답은 (D). 사무실이 이전할 예정이라고는 했지만 구체적인 이전 방식은 메모에서 밝히고 있지 않으므로 (B)는 오답.

패러프레이징 [단서] This photo shoot ~ in all parts of the building. → [정답] a plan for photographing a building

182. 코딜 씨가 회람 수신자들에게 하도록 조언하는 것은?
(A) 질문을 앨드리지 사에 보내기
(B) 임시로 물품을 옮기기 위해 용기 사용하기
(C) 4월 24일 그들의 근무 가능 여부와 관련하여 자신에게 연락하기
(D) 개인 소지품을 집에 두기

해설 특정 정보 확인 문제

단서 (182)에서 메모 작성자인 코딜 씨는 수신자들에게 촬영이 진행되는 동안 제공받은 플라스틱 통에 본인의 물품들을 넣어 놓아야 한다고 했으므로 정답은 (B).

패러프레이징 [단서] plastic bins / put your items in them for the short duration of the shoot → [정답] containers / temporarily move items

183. 4월 24일에 회람 수신자들이 할 수 있는 것은?
(A) 추가 휴식 시간 갖기
(B) 당일 일부 재택근무 하기
(C) 일찍 퇴근하기
(D) 연장된 점심시간 갖기

해설 특정 정보 확인 문제

단서 (183)을 종합해 보면 4월 24일에 직원들은 촬영이 진행되는 동안 직원 휴게실에서 쉬어도 되는데 통상적인 휴게 시간에 이 시간이 포함되지 않는다고 했으므로, 직원들이 이날 평상시의 휴식 시간 외에 추가적인 휴식 시간을 더 가질 수 있다는 것을 알 수 있다. 따라서 정답은 (A).

184. 4월 24일에 관리 직원이 스웨인 씨의 사무실에 도착할 시각은?
(A) 오전 9시 40분
(B) 오전 9시 50분
(C) 오전 10시
(D) 오전 10시 10분

해설 두 지문 연계 문제_특정 정보 확인 문제

회람의 단서 (184-1)에서 관리 직원이 지정된 시각 10분 전에 사무실을 방문할 것이라고 했으므로 스웨인 씨의 사무실이 지정된 시각을 일정표를 통해 확인해야 한다. 일정표의 단서 (184-2)에서 4월 24일에 스웨인 씨가 배정받은 시각이 오전 10시이므로 그보다 10분 앞선 9시 50분에 관리 직원이 그녀의 사무실에 도착할 것임을 알 수 있다. 따라서 정답은 (B).

185. 싱 씨에 대해 암시된 것은?
(A) 203호로 이동할 것이다.
(B) 파라 씨와 사무실을 같이 쓴다.
(C) 4월 24일에 자리를 비울 것이다.
(D) 일정 변경을 요청했다.

해설 추론 문제

단서 (185)를 보면 싱 씨는 202호 사무실 이용자인데, 일정표 아래 설명에서 '그날 사무실 이용자의 부재로 202호는 파라 씨가 맡아 줄 것'이라고 했다. 따라서 202호 사무실 이용자인 싱 씨가 그날, 즉 4월 24일에 자리를 비울 것임을 추측할 수 있으므로 정답은 (C).

패러프레이징 [단서] the occupant won't be in the office that day → [정답] He will be absent on April 24.

186-190 제품 설명서 & 온라인 후기 & 온라인 답변

> **미래의 가방: 짐머-40**
>
> 짐머-40은 당신이 배낭에 대해 생각하는 방식에 혁신을 일으킬 것입니다. [186B]이 제품은 여러분의 개인 전자 기기를 충전하는 데에 사용될 수 있는 접이식 태양 전지판을 특징으로 합니다. 최신 기술의 배터리는 여러분이 이동 중에 필요로 하는 전력을 항상 보유할 수 있게 합니다. [186A]바깥 부분은 완전히 방수가 되어서 여러분의 전자 기기는 항상 보호됩니다. [186C]이 밖에도, 배낭에 있는 모든 플라스틱 부품은 재생 플라스틱에서 온 것입니다.
>
> 짐머는 백화점과 스포츠용품 전문 매장에서 판매됩니다. [187-2]구매 시에 저희 월간 소식지를 신청하셔서 무료 보조 배터리를 받으세요.

어휘 revolutionize 혁신을 일으키다 fold-out 접이식의, 접는 방식의 solar panel 태양 전지판 charge 충전하다; 충전 advanced 최신의, 선진의 on the go 이동하여 resistant to ~에 잘 견디는, ~에 강한

> www.ucanreview.net/customer_reviews/accessories
>
> 브랜드: 짐머 제품: 짐머-40
> 후기 작성자: 타이슨 킨테로 게시글 유형: 신규
>
> 시중에 나와 있는 기술 활용 배낭 몇 개를 조사해 본 후, 저는 짐머의 탄탄한 명성 때문에 짐머-40을 선택했습니다. 가방의 색상은 카탈로그에 나온 것보다 더 어두웠지만, 그건 저한테 문제가 되지 않았어요. 저는 배터리의 충전 전력이 얼마나 오래 가는지에 감명받았고, [187-1]무료 보조 배터리를 갖게 되어서 기쁩니다. [189-1]단 하나 저를 실망시킨 것은 제 15인치 노트북이 가방 안에 맞지 않는다는 것입니다. 그럼에도 불구하고 저는 이 제품을 적극 추천하고, [188]친구 몇 명에게 이것을 선물로 사줄 생각입니다.

어휘 technology-enabled 기술이 활용된 solid 탄탄한, 믿음직한 be impressed with ~에 감명받다 hold 유지하다, 수용하다 disappoint 실망시키다 fit (들어가기에) 맞다, 적합하다 intend to do ~할 작정이다

177. 글래즈코바 씨의 마지막 강의가 열릴 날짜는?
(A) 3월 14일
(B) 3월 21일
(C) 3월 28일
(D) 4월 4일

> 해설   특정 정보 확인 문제

단서 (177)에서 달리 명시되지 않았다면 강의는 3월 14일, 21일, 28일에 진행된다고 했고, 글래즈코바 씨의 강좌 설명에 별도의 언급이 없으므로 정답은 (C).

178. 학생들에게 공동으로 프로젝트를 수행하게 할 강사는?
(A) 프레더릭 매스커
(B) 리디아 벤슨
(C) 실비아 글래즈코바
(D) 트렌턴 블레어

> 해설   특정 정보 확인 문제

단서 (178)에서 사례 연구 강좌는 실습 강좌로 학생들이 조를 이루어 사례를 분석하고 전략을 찾게 될 것이라고 했다. 해당 강좌를 맡은 강사는 트렌턴 블레어이므로 정답은 (D). 지문의 work in groups가 문제에서는 collaborate으로 패러프레이징되었다.

179. 모레노 씨가 수강해 온 강좌는?
(A) 환율 위기 관리
(B) 국제 자본 흐름
(C) 다국적 기업
(D) 사례 연구

> 해설   두 지문 연계 문제_특정 정보 확인 문제

이메일의 단서 (179-1)에서 벤슨 씨가 마지막 강의를 내일에서 다음 주 화요일로 바꿔서 내일 오후에 일할 수 있다고 했으므로 모레노 씨가 벤슨 씨의 강좌를 듣고 있다는 것을 알 수 있다. 정보문의 단서 (179-2)에서 벤슨 씨는 '국제 자본 흐름' 강좌의 담당 강사임을 확인할 수 있으므로 정답은 (B).

180. 모레노 씨에 대해 사실이 아닌 것은?
(A) 이미 몇 개의 강의에 참석했다.
(B) 동료들의 프로젝트를 보고 싶어 한다.
(C) 발표를 할 예정이다.
(D) 금요일에 사무실에 나올 수 있다.

> 해설   Not/True 문제

(A)는 단서 (180A)에서 내일로 예정되어 있던 마지막 강의를 언급했으므로 앞선 두 강의를 수강했을 것으로 추측할 수 있고, (B)는 단서 (180B)에서 동료들의 작업 결과를 확인하는 것에 관심이 있다고 했으므로 작업을 보고 싶어 한다는 것을 알 수 있으며, (D)는 단서 (180D)에서 이메일을 발송한 요일이 목요일인데 그 다음 날 오후에 일할 수 있다고 했으므로 선택지와 지문 내용이 일치한다. 하지만 발표를 참관하고 싶다고 했지 본인이 발표를 할 것이라는 말은 없으므로 정답은 (C).

181-185 회람 & 일정표

수신: MMH 법률 사무소 직원

발신: 변호사, 타마라 코딜

제목: 회신: 건물 매매

4월 16일

주간 회의에서 논의된 대로, 미들랜드 타워의 소유주는 다음 달에 건물을 팔려고 내놓을 예정이고, 우리는 사무실을 이전할 것입니다. 이 건물의 매매를 맡고 있는 부동산업체인 앨드리지 사는 업체 웹사이트의 부동산 목록에 올릴 사진들을 전문가들이 찍게 하고 싶어 합니다. ¹⁸¹ ¹⁸³이 사진 촬영은 4월 24일에 진행될 것이고 건물 전체에서 시행될 것입니다. 촬영될 사무실들의 일정을 첨부했습니다. 사진 기사들의 방문에 대한 준비로, 본인의 컴퓨터와 전화를 제외한 모든 물품을 책상에서 치워야 합니다. ¹⁸²저희가 여러분에게 플라스틱 통을 드리면, 여러분은 촬영하는 잠시 동안 본인의 물품을 거기에 넣어야 합니다. ¹⁸⁴⁻¹관리 직원이 지정된 시각 10분 전에 방문해서 카트로 이 통들을 수거할 것입니다. 여러분의 사무실에 있는 가구들이 재배치될 수도 있는데, 여러분이 돌아오기 전에 원래의 배치로 되돌려 놓을 것입니다. ¹⁸³전체 과정은 최대 20분 정도 걸릴 것이고, 이 시간 동안 여러분은 직원 휴게실에서 휴식을 취해도 됩니다. 이것은 통상적인 일일 휴게 시간에 포함되지 않습니다.

협조해 주셔서 감사드리고, 이로 인해 생길 수 있는 모든 불편에 대해 사과드립니다.

[첨부 파일: 최종 일정]

> 어휘   put ~ up for sale ~을 팔려고 내놓다   relocate 이전하다, 이동시키다   photo shoot 사진 촬영   take place 일어나다, 발생하다   carry out 수행하다, 이행하다   appoint (시간·장소 등을) 정하다   placement 놓기, 배치   maximum 최고, 최대   count toward ~에 포함되다[가산되다]

앨드리지 사 일정: ¹⁸⁴⁻² ¹⁸⁵4월 24일

시간	사무실	사무실 직원(들)
오전 9시	201호	해리엇 던컨
오전 9시 20분	¹⁸⁵202호	란잔 싱
오전 9시 40분	203호	데일 멈퍼드, 마이클 벨러미
¹⁸⁴⁻²오전 10시	204호	셜리 스웨인
오전 10시 20분	205호	브랜든 파라, 후안 런

¹⁸⁵사무실 직원이 그날 부재 예정이어서 브랜든 파라 씨가 202호실을 맡아 주실 것입니다.

> 어휘   occupant 사용자, 입주자

181. 회람의 목적은?
(A) 새 건물 소유주를 직원들에게 소개하기 위해
(B) 사무실 이전이 어떻게 될지 설명하기 위해
(C) 보수 공사 일정표를 배포하기 위해
(D) 건물의 사진 촬영 계획을 알리기 위해

> 해설   목적 문제

174. GT 통신이 일반인 대상의 현장 견학을 제공하려고 계획하는 장소는?

(A) 내슈빌
(B) 디트로이트
(C) 캔자스시티
(D) 휴스턴

해설 특정 정보 확인 문제

단서 (174)에서 전환 작업이 마지막으로 진행되는 현장이 일반인 대상 견학용으로 개방될 것이라고 했으므로 각 현장들의 전환 시점이 언급된 부분을 살펴보아야 한다. 내년 말에 전환되는 휴스턴 지점이 가장 마지막으로 업그레이드되는 현장이므로 정답은 (D).

175. [1], [2], [3], [4]번으로 표시된 위치들 중 다음 문장이 들어가기에 가장 적절한 곳은?

"우리는 그렇게 해서 그곳 직원의 90%를 유지할 수 있었습니다."

(A) [1]
(B) [2]
(C) [3]
(D) [4]

해설 문장 위치 찾기 문제

주어진 문장은 어떤 지역에서 직원의 일자리가 대부분 유지될 수 있었다는 내용이다. 단서 (175)에서 그 지역이 어디인지에 대한 내용과 직원을 해고하는 대신 재교육시키고자 했다는 내용을 언급했고, 주어진 문장의 ninety percent가 다음 문장에서 similar figures로 연결되는 것이 자연스러우므로 정답은 (C).

176-180 정보문 & 이메일

> [176]HTT 사 직원들에게 4개의 집중 워크숍이 제공될 예정입니다. 직원들은 아래 4개 강좌 중 하나를 선택해야 합니다. [177]달리 명시되지 않았다면, 각 강좌는 3시간짜리 강의 3개로 구성되어 있습니다. 강의는 금요일마다(3월 14일, 21일, 28일) 오후 2시부터 5시까지 열릴 예정입니다.
>
> **환율 위기 관리**
> 강사: 프레더릭 매스커
> 이 강좌에서는 환율이 시장에 어떻게 영향을 주는지 면밀히 살펴보고, 예측이 어떻게 이루어지는지 설명하며, 국제적인 맥락에서의 투자를 위한 최고의 전략들을 살펴보게 될 것입니다. 이 강좌는 4월 4일에 2시간짜리 강의 하나가 추가로 있습니다.
>
> [179-2]**국제 자본 흐름**
> 강사: 리디아 벤슨
> 이 강좌는 자본이 전세계적으로 어떻게 흐르는지 설명하고, 몇 가지 핵심적인 국가 간 관계들을 소개하며, 이러한 흐름이 세계 경제에 미치는 주요 영향들을 살펴볼 예정입니다.
>
> **다국적 기업**
> [177]강사: 실비아 글래즈코바
> 이 강좌는 3개의 주요 다국적 기업을 소개하고 그들의 기능 및 예산 관리에 대해 심도 있는 분석을 할 예정입니다.
>
> [178]**사례 연구**
> 강사: 트렌턴 블레어
> 이 실습 강좌는 학생들이 조를 이루어 사례를 분석하고 샘플 기업이 취할 최적의 전략을 찾게 할 것입니다. 각 조는 마지막 강의에서 연구 결과를 발표할 것입니다.

어휘 intense 집중적인, 치열한   comprise ~으로 구성되다   specify 명시하다   exchange rate 환율   prediction 예측, 예견   context 맥락   capital flow 자본 흐름, 자본 회전   multinational 다국적의   in-depth 심도 있는, 면밀한   functioning 기능, 작용   case study 사례 연구   hands-on 실습의, 직접 해 보는   finding (보통 복수형) (조사·연구 등의) 결과, 결론

> 수신: 린다 케이 〈lindakay@httcorp.com〉
> 발신: 피터 모레노 〈petermoreno@httcorp.com〉
> 제목: 금요일 오후
> [180D]날짜: 3월 27일 목요일
>
> 케이 씨께,
>
> [179-1 180A]벤슨 씨가 워크숍의 마지막 강의를 내일에서 다음 주 화요일로 바꿨습니다. [179-1 180D]저는 그래서 내일 오후에 일할 수 있습니다. 그런데, 저는 제가 블레어 씨의 강의에서 하는 발표를 참관해도 되는지 궁금합니다. [180B]그 강좌를 듣는 동료들 몇 명이 그들의 작업에 대해 이야기해 줬고, 저는 그 결과를 확인하는 것에 매우 관심이 있습니다. 물론, 만약 그 시간에 사무실에서 저를 필요로 한다면 저는 일을 할 수 있을 겁니다.
>
> 배려해 주셔서 감사합니다.
>
> HTT 사, 예산 분석가
> 피터 모레노 드림

어휘 acceptable 용인되는, 받아들여지는   consideration 배려, 이해   analyst 분석가

176. 이 정보문이 있을 것 같은 장소는?

(A) 안내 책자
(B) 게시판
(C) 잡지
(D) 전단

해설 출처 문제

단서 (176)에서 HTT 사 직원들에게 4개의 집중 워크숍이 제공될 예정이라는 것으로 보아, 이 정보문은 회사 직원들이 확인하는 게시판에 있을 것으로 추론할 수 있으므로 정답은 (B).

(C) 어떤 장비가 없어졌다.
(D) 이미지는 편집이 필요하다.

해설 특정 정보 확인 문제

단서 (169)에서 회사 규정이 허용하지 않기 때문에 고객이 요청한 사진을 줄 수 없다고 했으므로 정답은 (B). 지문의 I cannot provide you with a photograph of these items가 문제에서는 Ms. Wooldridge unable to send Mr. Pearlman a picture로 패러프레이징되었다.

패러프레이징 [단서] our company regulations do not allow it
→ [정답] It is against company policy.

170. 이메일에 따르면, 펄먼 씨가 절차를 신속하게 처리할 수 있는 방법은?
(A) 바쁜 시간대를 피함으로써
(B) 추가 요금을 지불함으로써
(C) 예약을 함으로써
(D) 티켓을 제시함으로써

해설 특정 정보 확인 문제

단서 (170)에서 탑승했던 배의 티켓을 보여 주는 것이 절차를 더 빠르게 해 줄 것이라고 했으므로 정답은 (D). 지문의 make the process faster가 문제에서는 expedite a process로 패러프레이징되었다.

패러프레이징 [단서] showing the ticket from your boat ride
→ [정답] presenting a ticket

171. 울드리지 씨가 하기를 권하는 것은?
(A) 시즌권 구매하기
(B) 그녀의 상사에게 연락하기
(C) 상세 설명을 이메일로 보내기
(D) 빨리 조치를 취하기

해설 특정 정보 확인 문제

권유하는 내용은 지문의 후반부에 주로 등장하므로 이 부분을 살펴봐야 한다. 단서 (171)에서 업체가 며칠 뒤면 비수기로 인해 문을 닫을 것이고 그 이후에는 물건을 돌려주는 일이 더 복잡해지므로 가능하면 그 전에 사무실을 방문해 달라고 했다. 즉, 펄먼 씨가 빨리 행동을 취할 것을 권하는 것이므로 정답은 (D).

패러프레이징 [단서] to visit us before the office closes for the low season → [정답] Taking action quickly

172-175 기사

GT 통신에서의 투자

3월 3일—GT 통신은 자사 설비의 기술에 많은 투자를 할 계획을 확정했다. ¹⁷²고객들은 과거 GT 통신의 사업 전체를 차지했던 일반 전화에서 이동하여, 휴대 전화 통신망과 인터넷을 사용하기 시작했다. 따라서, 이 업체는 기반 시설을 변경하여 사업 모델을 조정하고 있다. — [1] —.

¹⁷³내슈빌에 위치한, 회사에서 가장 작은 시설은 변경 계획을 전사 범위로 펼치기 전에 소규모로 시범 운영할 수 있도록 이미 새 장비들을 받았다. — [2] —. GT 통신은 직원들이 이 업그레이드에 의해 부정적으로 영향받지 않도록 조치를 취하고 있다. ¹⁷⁵"내슈빌에서의 전환 기간 동안, 저희는 저희 직원들을 해고하는 대신 재교육할 수 있는 영역을 찾았습니다."라고 회사 대변인 캐서린 코일 씨가 말했다. "— [3] —. ¹⁷⁵저희는 저희 나머지 시설에서도 비슷한 수치를 기대합니다."

GT 통신은 이제 모든 현장에 최신 장비를 설치하는 두 번째 단계의 전환을 맞이할 준비가 되어 있다. — [4] —. ¹⁷⁴작업은 올해 말 디트로이트 현장에서 시작하여, 내년 초 캔자스시티 지점, 내년 말 휴스턴 지점으로 이어질 예정이다. 일단 모든 업그레이드가 완료되면 마지막 현장은 사람들이 직접 운용 과정을 볼 수 있도록 일반인 대상 견학용으로 개방될 것이다.

어휘 shift 옮기다, 이동하다 landline (지상 통신선으로 연결되는) 일반 전화 previously 이전에 adapt 조정하다, 맞추다 infrastructure 기반 시설, 인프라 roll out 펼치다, 시작하다 take measures 조치를 취하다 negatively 부정적으로 transition 변천, 전환 lay off 해고하다 phase 단계 state-of-the-art 최신의 operation 운용, 작동

172. 기사에 따르면, GT 통신이 사업 계획을 변경하게 된 이유는?
(A) 정부의 새 규정
(B) 직원들의 불만
(C) 소비자 행동의 변화
(D) 주주들의 증가

해설 특정 정보 확인 문제

단서 (172)에서 소비자들이 GT 통신의 기반 사업이었던 일반 전화에서 휴대 전화 및 인터넷으로 이동했기 때문에 GT 통신이 사업 모델을 조정하고 있다고 했으므로 정답은 (C). 지문의 adapting its business model이 문제에서는 to transform its business plan으로 패러프레이징되었다.

패러프레이징 [단서] Customers have shifted away from landlines. ~, and started using mobile phone networks and the Internet. → [정답] A change in consumer behavior

173. 내슈빌에 있는 회사 시설에 대해 언급된 것은?
(A) 시범 현장으로 사용되었다.
(B) 기술 상을 받았다.
(C) GT 통신이 문을 연 최초의 공장이다.
(D) 투자자들의 회합 장소였다.

해설 Not/True 문제

단서 (173)에서 내슈빌에 위치한 시설이 시범 운영을 위해 이미 새 장비를 받았다고 했으므로 정답은 (A).

패러프레이징 [단서] the plan could be tried out on a small scale
→ [정답] testing

에 나오는 네어 씨의 말에 주목한다. 단서 (164)에서 지인이 보증하는 건설업체를 찾으려 한다면서 업체 추천을 요청하고 있으므로 정답은 (A).

패러프레이징 [단서] looking for another construction firm, preferably one endorsed by someone I know → [정답] To get a business recommendation

165. 노리스 건설사에 대해 시사된 것은?
(A) 치과에서 보증했다.
(B) 갑자기 계약을 취소했다.
(C) 소유주가 바뀌었다.
(D) 경쟁사들보다 가격이 낮다.

해설 Not/True 문제
특정 업체에 대해 묻는 문제이므로 해당 고유 명사가 나오는 부분을 집중해서 읽도록 한다. 단서 (165)에서 퍼듀 씨가 노리스 건설사에서 해 준 작업이 마음에 들었다고 하자 매튜스 씨가 그 업체가 지난달에 다른 사람에게 팔렸다고 했으므로 정답은 (C).

패러프레이징 [단서] that business was sold to another person → [정답] It is under new ownership.

166. 오후 1시 29분에, 퍼듀 씨가 "우리가 모험은 하지 않는 게 좋겠죠"라고 한 것에서 그녀가 의도한 것은?
(A) 자기 제안을 철회하려고 한다.
(B) 그들이 안전 점검을 해야 한다고 생각한다.
(C) 추후 연구를 할 계획이다.
(D) 결정을 위해 시간이 더 필요하다.

해설 의도 파악 문제
단서 (166)에서 퍼듀 씨가 노리스 건설사를 추천했으나 매튜스 씨는 그 업체의 소유주가 바뀌어 작업의 질이 같지 않을 수도 있다고 했다. 이에 대해 퍼듀 씨가 그 사실은 몰랐다며 모험은 하지 않는 게 좋겠다고 한 것이므로, 자신이 낸 의견을 철회하고자 했음을 알 수 있다. 따라서 정답은 (A).

167. 텐노 씨가 금요일에 할 일은?
(A) 노리스 건설사에 연락하기
(B) 업체에 대한 정보 모으기
(C) 예약 변경하기
(D) 신규 계약자 방문하기

해설 다음에 할 일 문제
텐노 씨에 대해 묻는 문제이므로 텐노 씨가 하는 말 앞뒤에서 단서를 찾는다. 단서 (167)에서 네어 씨가 작업한 업체의 주소와 연락처를 알아봐야겠다고 하자 텐노 씨가 금요일에 그걸 알아보겠다고 했으므로 정답은 (B).

패러프레이징 [단서] find out the address and contact number of their contractor → [정답] Gather information about a business

168-171 이메일

수신: 그레고리 펄먼 〈g.pearlman@oakway.com〉
발신: 팁즈 주식회사 〈inquiries@tibbsinc.com〉
날짜: 8월 26일
제목: 회신: 문의

펄먼 씨께,

[168]저는 니브즈 만을 따라 운항하는 저희의 유람선 탑승에 고객님께서 최근 참여하신 것에 대한 메시지를 받았습니다. 저희 분실물 보관함을 확인해 보니, 정말 남성용 손목시계가 그 안에 몇 개 있었고, 그중 하나는 고객님의 것일 수 있습니다. [169]유감스럽게도, 저희 회사 규정이 허용하지 않기 때문에 저는 요청하신 대로 이 물품들의 사진을 제공해 드릴 수는 없습니다. 분실물을 수령하시기 위해서는 고객님께서 항만에 있는 저희 사무실로 오셔서 분실물을 묘사해 주셔야 합니다. [170]가능하다면, 탑승하셨던 배의 티켓을 보여 주시는 것이 절차를 더 빠르게 해 줄 것입니다. 이는 저희가 고객님께서 탑승하셨던 배가 정확히 어떤 것인지 확인할 수 있을 것이고, 저희가 발견한 물품들은 날짜와 배에 따라 분류되어 있기 때문입니다.

미리 예약을 하실 필요는 없습니다. 그냥 매일 오전 9시부터 저녁 6시까지인 저희 업무 시간 중에 들러 주십시오. 저희는 특정 시즌에만 진행하는 사업이고, 이번 시즌은 이달 말 마무리된다는 점에 유의해 주십시오. [171]따라서 비수기로 인해 사무실이 문을 닫기 전에 방문하시려면 며칠밖에 남지 않았습니다. 그 이후에는 분실물을 돌려드리는 것이 훨씬 더 복잡해질 것이므로 가능하면 문을 닫기 전에 방문해 주시기 바랍니다.

팁즈 주식회사, 행정 보조원
루시 울드리지 드림

어휘 lost-and-found 분실물 취급소 as requested 요청받은 대로 claim 요구하다, 주장하다 description 묘사, 설명 catalog 분류하다, 목록에 수록하다 seasonal 어느 계절에 한정된 wrap up 마무리 짓다 low season 비수기 complicated 복잡한 administrative 관리의, 행정상의

168. 팁즈 주식회사가 제공할 것 같은 서비스의 종류는?
(A) 행사 사진 촬영
(B) 수영 강습
(C) 단체 관광
(D) 호텔 예약

해설 추론 문제
단서 (168)에서 업체가 니브즈 만 유람선 탑승을 제공하고 있는 것을 알 수 있으므로, 단체 관광 서비스를 제공하는 것으로 추론할 수 있다. 따라서 정답은 (C).

169. 울드리지 씨가 펄먼 씨에게 사진을 보낼 수 없었던 이유는?
(A) 웹사이트가 작동하지 않는다.
(B) 회사 정책에 어긋난다.

161-163 편지

에이든 홀트
케슬러 가 739번지
시러큐스, 뉴욕 주 13202

홀트 씨께,

¹⁶¹ ¹⁶²저희는 고객님께서 저희의 프리미엄 스포츠 패키지의 1개월 무료 체험을 즐기셨기를 바랍니다. 추후 아무런 조치도 취하지 않으시면, ¹⁶¹ ¹⁶²4개의 국제 축구 채널, 2개의 농구 채널, 2개의 혼합 스포츠 채널에 대한 고객님의 접근 권한은 4월 30일자로 종료될 것입니다. ¹⁶¹고객님께서 좋아하시는 스포츠 방송 중 어떤 것도 놓치지 않으시려면 프리미엄 스포츠 패키지 1년 구독을 신청하십시오. 월 이용료에 7.95달러만 추가될 것입니다. 저희 웹사이트를 통해 고객님의 채프먼 케이블 온라인 계정에서 설정을 변경하시면 그렇게 하실 수 있습니다. 그곳에서 프리미엄 패키지를 추가하거나 중단하는 방법에 대한 세부 사항과 관련하여 고객님의 사용자 약관도 확인하실 수 있습니다.

¹⁶³요금 별납 엽서도 동봉된 것을 확인하실 수 있을 텐데, 거기에 고객님의 제안, 아이디어, 불만 사항을 공유해 주실 수 있습니다. 저희는 고객님께서 지금까지 경험하신 저희 채프먼 케이블에 대해 어떻게 생각하시는지 듣고 싶습니다.

채프먼 케이블 계정 팀 드림

어휘 trial 시범 사용, 시도 access 접근 (권한) take action 조치를 취하다 coverage 방송, 보도 subscription 구독 agreement 약관, 합의 discontinue 중단하다 enclose 동봉하다 postage-paid 우편 요금 별납의

161. 편지의 목적은?
(A) 고객에게 서비스를 계속 이용하도록 권장하기 위해
(B) 다음 달에 어떤 채널이 추가될지 안내하기 위해
(C) 새로운 스포츠 채널 패키지 상품을 소개하기 위해
(D) 고객에게 계정에 대금을 지불할 것을 상기시키기 위해

해설 목적 문제
단서 (161)을 종합해 보면 무료 체험으로 이용하던 스포츠 방송을 무료 체험 기간 종료 후에도 계속 시청하려면 1년 구독을 신청하라고 했으므로 정답은 (A).

162. 4월 30일에 일어날 일은?
(A) 무료 체험이 만료될 것이다.
(B) 스포츠 경기가 개최될 것이다.
(C) 할인이 적용될 것이다.
(D) 온라인 계정이 비활성화될 것이다.

해설 특정 정보 확인 문제
단서 (162)에서 프리미엄 스포츠 패키지 1개월 무료 체험을 언급하면서, 이에 대한 접근 권한이 4월 30일자로 종료될 것이라고 했으므로 정답은 (A).

패러프레이징 [단서] end → [정답] expire

163. 편지에 동봉된 것은?
(A) 할인 쿠폰
(B) 방송 편성표
(C) 변경된 사용자 약관
(D) 고객 의견 카드

해설 특정 정보 확인 문제
단서 (163)에서 동봉된 요금 별납 엽서에 고객의 제안, 아이디어, 불만 사항을 적어 공유해 달라고 했으므로 정답은 (D).

패러프레이징 [단서] a postage-paid postcard, on which you can share your suggestions, ideas, and complaints → [정답] A comment card

164-167 온라인 채팅

라티카 네어 오후 1:23	우리 사무실의 보수 공사가 계획대로 다음 주에 시작되지 못할 거예요.
쳇 매튜스 오후 1:25	우리가 고용하기로 했던 회사가 예상치 못하게 폐업했다고 들었어요.
라티카 네어 오후 1:26	맞아요. ¹⁶⁴그래서 저는 다른 건설업체를 찾고 있는데 가급적이면 제가 아는 분이 보증하는 곳이었으면 해요. 의견 있으세요?
다이앤 퍼듀 오후 1:27	¹⁶⁵,¹⁶⁶저는 작년에 노리스 건설사에서 저희 집에 해 준 작업이 굉장히 마음에 들었어요.
쳇 매튜스 오후 1:28	¹⁶⁵ ¹⁶⁶하지만 그 업체는 지난달에 다른 사람한테 팔렸기 때문에 작업의 질이 같지 않을 수도 있어요.
다이앤 퍼듀 오후 1:29	¹⁶⁶그건 몰랐네요. 우리가 모험은 하지 않는 게 좋겠죠.
쳇 매튜스 오후 1:30	길 건너에 있는 치과가 최근에 인테리어를 바꿨는데, 근사해 보이더라고요.
라티카 네어 오후 1:31	¹⁶⁷거기 작업 업체의 주소와 연락처를 알아봐야겠네요.
모토시 텐노 오후 1:32	¹⁶⁷실은 제가 금요일에 거기 진료 예약이 되어 있는데, 간 김에 알아볼게요.

어휘 be supposed to do ~하기로 되어 있다 go out of business 폐업하다 unexpectedly 예상치 못하게, 뜻밖에 look for ~을 찾다[구하다] preferably 가급적이면 endorse 보증하다, 지지하다 take a chance 모험을 하다, 운에 맡기다 contractor 계약자, 도급업자

164. 네어 씨가 온라인 채팅을 시작한 이유는?
(A) 업체 추천을 받기 위해
(B) 새로운 계약자를 소개하기 위해
(C) 계약 조항 몇 개를 검토하기 위해
(D) 보수 공사 일정을 승인하기 위해

해설 목적 문제
네어 씨가 온라인 채팅을 시작한 목적을 묻는 문제이므로 채팅 초반부

유가 그녀의 신작 소설이 베스트셀러로 오래 있었고 지난달 명망 있는 상도 수상했기 때문이라고 했으므로 정답은 (B). 지문의 took home the prestigious Larochelle Prize last month가 문제에서는 has recently won an award로 패러프레이징되었다.

157. 블룸필드 공공 도서관에 대해 언급된 것은?

(A) 축제 준비로 휴관할 것이다.
(B) 매년 문학 축제를 개최한다.
(C) 전문 작가의 강연을 주최할 것이다.
(D) 축제를 보조해 줄 자원봉사자를 찾고 있다.

해설 특정 정보 확인 문제

단서 (157)을 통해 블룸필드 도서관이 전문 작가인 애치슨 씨의 강연을 주최할 것임을 알 수 있으므로 정답은 (C).

패러프레이징 [단서] Ms. Atchison's talk → [정답] a lecture by a professional writer

158-160 이메일

수신: 그웬 랜드리 〈gwenlandry@milagrosinc.com〉
발신: 아만다 모건 〈amanda@nsrmembers.org〉
날짜: 7월 29일
제목: 중요한 안내

랜드리 씨께,

저희 기록에 따르면, ¹⁵⁸회원님께서는 지난 3년간 전국 부동산업자 협회의 회원이셨습니다. ─ [1] ─. 회원님의 후원에 감사드리며, 이 협회의 일원으로서의 혜택을 누리고 계시길 바랍니다.

저희는 현재 연례 회원 모집 운동을 하고 있으며 회원님의 도움을 요청하고자 합니다. ─ [2] ─. 회원님께 저희 단체에 적합한 친구나 동료가 있다면, 그분들께서 첨부된 신청서를 작성하도록 해 주십시오. ¹⁶⁰이 양식에는 특별한 번호가 있어서 저희는 이 소개가 회원님께서 해 주신 것이라는 것을 알 수 있습니다. ─ [3] ─.

¹⁵⁹ᶜ소개해 주신 회원 한 명마다 회원님의 월 회비에서 10달러씩 할인받게 되십니다. ¹⁵⁹ᴮ추가로, 저희 연례 회의의 VIP석에 회원님을 위한 자리가 마련될 것입니다. ─ [4] ─. ¹⁵⁹ᴬ또한 회원님의 성함을 바하마에서 보내는 5일간의 휴가에 당첨될 수 있는 경품 추첨에 넣어 드릴 것입니다.

회원 모집에 대해 궁금한 점이 있으시면 언제라도 저에게 이메일을 보내 주시기 바랍니다.

회원 서비스
아만다 모건 드림

어휘 realtor 부동산업자 patronage 후원, 애용 drive (모집 등의) 운동 suitable 적합한 determine 알아내다, 밝히다 referral 소개, 위탁 reserve ~을 마련해 두다, 예약하다 enter 참가시키다, 기입하다 drawing 추첨, 제비뽑기 inquiry 문의, 질문 recruitment 모집

158. 랜드리 씨의 신분은?

(A) 단체 설립자
(B) 부동산 중개업자
(C) 주택 소유주
(D) 은행원

해설 추론 문제

단서 (158)에서 지난 3년간 전국 부동산업자 협회의 회원이었다고 했으므로 이메일을 받은 랜드리 씨가 부동산 중개업자임을 추측할 수 있다. 따라서 정답은 (B).

패러프레이징 [단서] a member of the National Society of Realtors → [정답] A real estate agent

159. 회원 소개의 혜택이 아닌 것은?

(A) 여행 당첨의 기회
(B) 행사에서의 우대석
(C) 회비 할인
(D) 할인된 회의 입장권

해설 Not/True 문제

회원 추천의 혜택이 세 번째 문단에 나열되어 있으므로 이 부분을 유의해서 살펴보자. (A)는 단서 (159A)에서 바하마에서 보내는 휴가에 당첨될 수 있는 경품 추첨에 이름을 넣어 준다고 했고, (B)는 단서 (159B)에서 연례 회의의 VIP석을 마련해 준다고 했으며, (C)는 단서 (159C)에서 소개한 회원 한 명당 월 회비에서 10달러씩 할인해 준다고 했다. 그러나 회의 입장권 할인에 대한 내용은 언급되지 않았으므로 정답은 (D).

160. [1], [2], [3], [4]번으로 표시된 위치들 중 다음 문장이 들어가기에 가장 적절한 곳은?

"그것은 페이지의 하단에서 찾을 수 있습니다."

(A) [1]
(B) [2]
(C) [3]
(D) [4]

해설 문장 위치 찾기 문제

제시된 문장은 무언가(It)를 찾을 수 있는 위치를 알려 주고 있다. 따라서 지문에서 제시된 문장의 It이 가리키는 특정 정보에 관한 부분을 찾아야 한다. 단서 (160)에서 누가 소개한 것인지 알 수 있게 해 주는 번호가 양식에 있다고 했는데 다음 문장에서 이 번호가 양식의 하단에 있다고 알려 주는 것이 자연스러우므로 정답은 (C).

(B) 스펜서 씨에게 장비를 빌려주는 것에 대해 개의치 않는다.
(C) 스펜서 씨의 고장 난 노트북을 수리하는 데 도움을 줄 수 있다.
(D) 스펜서 씨를 위해 대체품을 주문할 것이다.

해설 의도 파악 문제

윌리스 씨의 Of course는 스펜서 씨의 말에 대한 동의의 표현이므로 바로 앞의 스펜서 씨의 말에 주목해야 한다. 단서 (152)에서 스펜서 씨는 윌리스 씨의 노트북을 빌릴 수 있는지 궁금하다고 했으므로, 이에 대해 '물론이죠'라고 한 것은 자신의 장비를 빌려주는 것에 대해 개의치 않는다는 의미로 볼 수 있다. 따라서 정답은 (B).

153-154 회람

수신: 오세이지 컨설팅 전 직원
발신: 지점장, 칼라 왓슨
날짜: 10월 17일
제목: 직원 휴게실

이제 직원 휴게실이 보수 공사 후 다시 문을 열었으므로, 우리는 휴게실을 이용하는 모두를 위해 반드시 이 공간이 깨끗하고 단정하게 유지되기를 바랍니다. ¹⁵³따라서 이제부터, 우리는 냉장고 사용에 관한 방침을 변경할 것입니다. ¹⁵⁴여러분이 냉장고에 무언가를 넣을 때마다 그 위에 여러분의 이름과 날짜가 분명하게 표시되어 있어야 합니다. 매주 금요일 오후, 냉장고는 깨끗이 비워질 것이며, 유통 기한이 지났거나 이름이 쓰여져 있지 않은 물품은 버려질 것입니다. 이것은 냉장고가 너무 가득 차지 않고, 그 안에 상한 음식이 있지 않도록 해 줄 것입니다. 여러분의 협조에 미리 감사드립니다.

어휘 following ~ 후에   renovation 보수   make sure 반드시 ~하다, ~을 확실히 하다   from now on 이제부터   usage 사용, 용법   expire 만료되다, 기한이 지나다   throw out 버리다   spoil 상하게 하다, 망치다   in advance 미리, 앞서

153. 왓슨 씨가 회람을 작성한 이유는?
(A) 직원들에게 보수 공사를 알리기 위해
(B) 휴식 일정을 설명하기 위해
(C) 공간 폐쇄를 알리기 위해
(D) 새로운 규칙을 발표하기 위해

해설 목적 문제

목적을 묻는 문제의 단서는 보통 지문 앞부분에서 찾을 수 있다. 단서 (153)에서 이제부터 냉장고 사용에 관한 방침을 변경할 것이라고 했으므로 정답은 (D).

패러프레이징 [단서] changing the policy on the usage of the refrigerator → [정답] a new rule

154. 회람을 읽은 사람들이 하도록 요청받은 것은?
(A) 사무실에서 음식 먹는 것 삼가기
(B) 매주 금요일마다 냉장고 비우기
(C) 자기 음식과 음료에 라벨 붙이기
(D) 매주 있는 청소 작업에 자원하기

해설 특정 정보 확인 문제

단서 (154)에서 냉장고에 무언가를 넣을 때마다 이름과 날짜가 분명히 표시되어 있어야 한다고 했는데, 이는 자기 음식과 음료에 이름과 날짜를 쓴 라벨을 붙이라는 말이므로 정답은 (C).

패러프레이징 [단서] it must have your name and the date marked on it clearly → [정답] Label their food and drink items

155-157 웹페이지

http://www.bloomfieldpublib.org/news

| 홈 | 소개 | 서비스 | **소식** | 검색 |

블룸필드 공공 도서관은 자랑스럽게도 ¹⁵⁵ᴮ4월 16일부터 20일까지 열리는 ¹⁵⁵ᴬ시 최초의 춘계 문학 축제를 위한 장소 중 한 곳이 됩니다. ¹⁵⁵ᴰ ¹⁵⁷행사는 지앙 리, 린다 애치슨, 야무나 보스, 패트릭 코로나를 비롯하여 최근에 작품을 출판한 적이 있는 전문 작가들이 도시 전역에서 하는 강연이 특색을 이룹니다. ¹⁵⁶ ¹⁵⁷저희 도서관에서 열릴 애치슨 씨의 강연은 특히 큰 인기를 끌 것으로 기대되는데, 그녀의 신작 미스터리 소설인 〈북쪽으로〉가 베스트셀러 목록에 30주나 있었기 때문입니다. 그 책은 또한 지난달 명망 있는 라로셀 상을 차지하기도 했습니다.

행사 입장권은 블룸필드 지역 문화 회관에서 구매하실 수 있습니다.

어휘 literary 문학의   run (일정 기간 동안) 계속되다   feature 특별히 포함하다, 특징으로 삼다   particularly 특히   draw 인기를 끄는 것[사람]   take home (상을) 차지하다   prestigious 명망 있는, 일류의

155. 춘계 문학 축제에 대해 사실이 아닌 것은?
(A) 이전에 열린 적이 없다.
(B) 일주일이 안 되게 지속될 것이다.
(C) 작가 시상식을 포함한다.
(D) 여러 장소에서 개최될 것이다.

해설 Not/True 문제

Not/True 문제는 지문과 선택지를 하나하나 대조해 가며 풀어야 한다. (A)는 단서 (155A)에서 시 최초의 축제라고 했고, (B)는 단서 (155B)에서 4월 16일부터 20일까지, 즉 일주일이 안 되는 기간 동안 열린다고 했으며, (D)는 단서 (155D)에서 도시 전역에서 진행되는 강연들이 행사의 특색을 이룬다고 했다. 하지만 시상식이 있을 것이라는 언급은 없으므로 정답은 (C).

156. 최근에 상을 받은 사람은?
(A) 지앙 리
(B) 린다 애치슨
(C) 야무나 보스
(D) 패트릭 코로나

해설 특정 정보 확인 문제

단서 (156)에서 애치슨 씨의 강연이 인기가 있을 것으로 기대되는 이

해설 특정 정보 확인 문제

단서 (148)을 보면, 역 도처에 게시된 알림판을 통해 그날그날에 해당하는 시간표 변경 사항을 알 수 있으니 이것을 참고하여 예상되는 일정을 확실히 알아 두라고 했으므로 정답은 (A).

패러프레이징 [단서] view / the changes to the timetable for each day → [정답] Check / an adjusted schedule

149-150 청구서

배링턴 지붕 공사
에이커스 가 305번지, 브렌트우드, 테네시 주 37027
(615) 555-8483

고객: 레너드 하퍼
건물 위치: 게바라 가 4651번지, 브렌트우드, 테네시 주 37027
작업 상세: 주거용 건물 지붕 교체

최초 견적가	7,500달러	발행일	5월 3일
변경 견적가	6,300달러	발행일	5월 7일

참고: [149]최초 견적가는 전체 지붕 교체 절차를 포함했습니다. 지금은 고객이 작업 시작 전에 오래된 지붕널을 제거하고 별도로 폐기 처리할 것입니다.

[150]착수일	5월 15일	완료일	5월 16일
착수금 및 1차 지불금 수령			300달러, 5월 7일

* [150]잔액의 절반(3,000달러)은 2차 지불금으로 작업 첫날 지불되어야 합니다. 최종 지불금은 작업 완료 후 1주 뒤에 지불되어야 합니다. 비용 지불은 날씨로 인한 지연과 관계없이 이 일정에 따라 실행되어야 함을 유의해 주십시오.

어휘 roofing 지붕 공사 property 건물, 부동산 residential 주거의, 주택의 quote 견적(가) replacement 교체, 대체 shingle 지붕널 disposal 폐기, 처분 separately 별도로, 따로따로 deposit 착수금, 보증금 balance 잔액, 잔고 due (돈을) 지불해야 하는; 회비, 요금 completion 완료 in accordance with ~에 따라, ~에 부합되게

149. 청구서에서 청구 금액이 변경된 이유는?
(A) 자재 가격이 인상되었다.
(B) 고객이 쿠폰을 제시했다.
(C) 허가는 별도로 지불되어야 했다.
(D) 고객이 일부 작업을 처리할 것이다.

해설 특정 정보 확인 문제

청구 금액이 변경된 이유를 묻는 질문이므로 청구서에서 금액이 나와 있는 부분에서 단서를 발견할 수 있다. 금액 정보 아래에 있는 단서 (149)에서 최초 견적가에는 전체 절차가 포함되어 있었지만 지금은 작업 시작 전에 고객이 작업의 일부를 진행하기로 되어 있다고 했으므로 정답은 (D).

패러프레이징 [단서] the client will remove the old shingles before the project begins and handle their disposal separately → [정답] The customer will take care of some of the work.

150. 하퍼 씨가 2차 지불금을 내야 하는 날짜는?
(A) 5월 15일
(B) 5월 16일
(C) 5월 22일
(D) 5월 23일

해설 특정 정보 확인 문제

단서 (150)에서 잔액의 절반이 2차 지불금으로 작업 첫날 지불되어야 한다고 했는데, 작업의 착수일은 5월 15일이므로 정답은 (A).

151-152 문자 메시지

신시아 스펜서 [오전 11:13]
안녕하세요, 랠프. [151]오늘 사무실에 안 계시죠, 그렇죠?

랠프 월리스 [오전 11:16]
[151]네, 우리 가장 큰 거래처 중 한 곳의 담당자들과 하는 회의에 참석할 거예요. 왜요?

신시아 스펜서 [오전 11:17]
[152]오늘 하루만 제가 당신의 노트북을 빌려도 될까 궁금해서요. 제 것이 작동하지 않는데, IT팀에는 대체품이 없대요.

랠프 월리스 [오전 11:18]
물론이죠. 다 쓰시고 돌려만 주세요.

신시아 스펜서 [오전 11:19]
그럴게요. 정말 고마워요! 그건 공용 부서 물품 보관함에 있죠, 그렇죠?

랠프 월리스 [오전 11:20]
네, 그럴 거예요. 그리고 비밀번호가 없으니까 괜찮으실 거예요.

어휘 attend 참석하다 representative 담당자, 대표 account 거래처, 고객 common 공동의, 보통의

151. 월리스 씨가 오늘 할 일은?
(A) 나가서 고객들 만나기
(B) IT 직원들 교육하기
(C) 회의실 준비하기
(D) 고객들 견학시켜 주기

해설 특정 정보 확인 문제

단서 (151)에서 오늘 사무실에 없는지를 묻는 스펜서 씨의 질문에 월리스 씨가 그렇다고 답하면서 한 거래처의 담당자들과의 회의에 참석할 것이라고 했으므로 정답은 (A).

패러프레이징 [단서] attending meetings with representatives from one of our largest accounts / away from the office → [정답] Meeting some clients / off-site

152. 오전 11시 18분에, 월리스 씨가 "물론이죠"라고 한 것에서 그가 의도한 것은?

(A) 요청을 하기 위해 IT팀에 전화할 것이다.

143-146 이메일

수신: 패멀라 라딘 〈p.rardin@montoyainc.net〉
발신: 아롬 통신 〈info@aaromcomm.com〉
날짜: 9월 4일
제목: 아롬-6 전화기

라딘 씨께,

저희 기록에 따르면 고객님께서는 최근에 아롬 통신에서 아롬-6 스마트폰을 143구매하셨습니다. 저희는 단돈 89.99달러에 저희의 잡음 제거 무선 헤드폰을 권해 드릴 수 있게 되어 기쁩니다. 144이 특별가는 30% 할인이 반영된 것입니다. 이 헤드폰은 고급 음질, 편안한 착용감, 긴 배터리 수명을 제공합니다.

관심이 있으시면, 늦어도 9월 10일까지는 선호하시는 우편 주소와 함께 이 이메일에 145회신해 주시기 바랍니다. 그러면 저희가 고객님의 아롬 고객 계정에 대금을 청구할 것입니다. 146그것은 고객님의 월 사용 내역서에 '아롬 헤드폰'이라고 나올 것입니다. 저희는 고객님께서 이 좋은 구매 기회를 이용하시길 바라고, 저희가 서비스를 제공하게 되기를 고대합니다.

아롬 통신, 고객 서비스 담당자
샤론 커니 드림

어휘 noise-canceling 잡음 제거의 no later than 늦어도 ~까지는 make a charge 대금을 청구하다 statement 사용 내역(서), 입출금 내역(서) take advantage of ~을 이용하다

143. 명사 어휘 purchase
(A) 비평 (B) 수리 **(C) 구매** (D) 이익

해설 지문은 고객에게 할인된 가격의 제품을 제공하겠다는 내용의 이메일이다. 따라서 빈칸에는 동사 made의 목적어로 할인을 제공할 만한 고객의 행동인 '구매'가 들어가는 것이 적절하므로 정답은 (C). make a purchase는 '구매하다'라는 뜻으로 한 단어처럼 자주 쓰이므로 알아 두도록 하자.

144. 알맞은 문장 고르기
(A) 이 특별가는 30% 할인이 반영된 것입니다.
(B) 그것들은 추가 요금 없이 일반 부속품으로 따라옵니다.
(C) 고객님의 제품 보증서에서 이것에 대해 더 자세히 읽어 보실 수 있습니다.
(D) 저희에게 이 문제에 대해 즉각 알려 주셔서 감사합니다.

해설 알맞은 문장을 고르는 문제의 단서가 되는 대명사나 지시어, 연결어 등에 주목하여 빈칸 주변 문맥을 확인해 보자. 빈칸 앞에서 특정 가격에 헤드폰을 권할 수 있어 기쁘다고 했으므로 빈칸에는 이 가격에 대한 내용이 나오는 것이 적절하다. 따라서 앞서 나온 가격을 This special price라고 하면서 할인 적용에 대해 언급하는 (A)가 정답.

145. 동사 어휘 respond
(A) 회신하다 (B) 구독하다 (C) 무시하다 (D) 거리낌 없이 ~하다

해설 빈칸은 please로 시작되는 명령문의 본동사 자리로, 문맥상 '이 이메일에 회신해 주시기 바랍니다'라는 뜻이 가장 자연스러우므로 (A)가 정답. 참고로, respond는 자동사이므로 목적어를 취할 때 전치사 to와 호응하여 주로 쓰인다. (B)도 목적어를 취하기 위해 전치사 to와 호응하여 쓰이지만 문맥상 적절하지 않고, (C)는 타동사라 전치사 없이 직접 목적어를 취하며, (D)는 to부정사와 함께 쓰이므로 오답.

146. 지시대명사 it

해설 선택지를 보고 알맞은 대명사를 고르는 문제임을 알 수 있다. 빈칸은 문장의 주어로 내용상 빈칸 앞에 언급된 업체가 청구할 대금(a charge)을 가리키는 대명사가 되어야 하므로 3인칭 단수 대명사인 (D)가 정답.

PART 7

147-148 공지

크레스타 유지 보수 프로젝트

6월 3일부터 7월 18일까지 저희는 철도망에 몇 가지 유지 보수 작업을 진행할 예정입니다. 이 작업은 147여러분의 출발 시각 그리고/또는 이동 시간에 영향을 미칠 수도 있습니다. 147 148승객 여러분께 그날그날의 시간표 변경에 대해 알려 드리기 위해 알림판이 역 도처에 게시되어 있습니다. 148꼭 이 게시 정보를 살펴보시고 예상되는 일정을 확실히 알아 두시기 바랍니다. 양해해 주셔서 감사합니다.

어휘 maintenance 유지 보수 network 망, 네트워크 affect 영향을 미치다 journey 이동, 여정 duration (지속) 기간, 지속 throughout ~의 도처에 inform A of B A에게 B를 알리다[통지하다] timetable 시간표 ensure 확실하게 하다, 보증하다 patience 인내력, 인내심

147. 공지의 대상일 것 같은 사람은?
(A) 안전 검사관들
(B) 여행사 직원들
(C) 공사장 인부들
(D) 열차 승객들

해설 대상 문제
단서 (147)에서 출발 시각, 이동 시간에 대해 이야기하고 역 도처에 있는 알림판에 이 정보가 있다고 안내하는 것으로 보아 열차 이용 승객을 대상으로 하는 공지임을 알 수 있으므로, 정답은 (D).

148. 공지에서 사람들에게 하도록 지시하는 일은?
(A) 조정된 일정 확인하기
(B) 서비스에 대한 의견 주기
(C) 회사에 문제 보고하기
(D) 미리 지불하기

135-138 회람

수신: 헤인즈 항공 티켓 및 게이트 담당 전 직원
발신: 크리스털 르퀴예
날짜: 10월 25일

바쁜 휴가 여행철에 대비하여 우리는 탑승 수속 구역에 두 개의 라인을 추가로 ¹³⁵열 예정입니다. 우리는 이것이 탑승 수속을 위한 긴 대기 시간을 줄이는 데 도움이 될 것이라고 생각합니다.

이 새로운 계획에 따라 시간제 직원들이 ¹³⁶1월 5일까지 추가 교대 근무를 하게 될 것입니다. 탑승이 정시 출발에 있어 중요한 요소이므로, 여러분도 역시 게이트에서 근무하도록 ¹³⁷배정될 수 있습니다. 여러분의 관리자들이 곧 일정을 짤 계획입니다. ¹³⁸일정 충돌 가능성이 있다면 그들에게 알려 주시기 바랍니다.

여러분의 노고와 협조에 감사드립니다.

어휘 in preparation for ~의 준비[대비]로   check-in (공항의) 탑승 수속(대)   reduce 줄이다, 축소하다   additional 추가의   shift 교대 근무(시간)   assign 맡기다, 배정하다   boarding 탑승   factor 요인   on-time 정시의, 정각의   departure 출발   cooperation 협조, 협력

135. 동사 어휘 open
(A) 열다 (B) 이전하다 (C) 장식하다 (D) 중단하다

해설 빈칸은 문장의 동사 자리로 빈칸 뒤의 목적어인 two extra lines와 어울리는 타동사가 와야 한다. 문맥상 '두 개의 라인을 추가로 열 예정이다'라고 하는 것이 가장 자연스러우므로 정답은 (A).

136. 전치사 until
(A) ~ 이내에 **(B) ~까지** (C) ~ 동안 (D) ~ 후에

해설 날짜 앞에 가장 어울리는 전치사를 고르는 문제. 특정 날짜까지 시간제 직원들이 추가 교대 근무를 하게 될 것이라는 내용이므로 문맥상 '1월 5일까지'의 의미가 적절하다. 따라서 '~까지'의 의미를 지닌 전치사 (B)가 정답.

137. 조동사+동사원형
해설 빈칸 앞에 조동사 may가 있고, 뒤에는 to부정사구가 이어지므로 빈칸에는 동사원형이 들어가야 한다. 따라서 정답은 (B).

138. 알맞은 문장 고르기
(A) 게이트 번호는 가능한 한 빨리 게시되어야 합니다.
(B) 그것의 사본이 이 회람에 첨부되어 있습니다.
(C) 여행객들이 이 서비스를 요청할 것으로 예상됩니다.
(D) 일정 충돌 가능성이 있다면 그들에게 알려 주시기 바랍니다.

해설 지문은 휴가 여행철을 맞아 업무 조정을 알리는 회람으로 빈칸 앞에 관리자들이 곧 그 일정을 짤 것이라는 내용이 나온다. 따라서 빈칸에는 일정 수립과 관련된 내용이 나와야 하므로 일정 충돌 가능성이 있다면 관리자에게 알려 달라는 내용의 (D)가 정답. 일정은 아직 세워지지 않았으므로 (B)는 오답.

139-142 기사

골프 클럽이 지역 미술관을 위한 기금을 모으다

홀턴빌, 8월 7일—홀턴빌 골프 클럽이 현대 미술관을 위한 기금을 마련하고자 그린웨이 골프장에서 클럽 역사상 최초로 토너먼트를 개최할 예정이다. ¹³⁹대회에서는 참가자들에게 지역 기업들이 기부한 상을 수여할 것이다. 우승자들은 상품권뿐만 아니라 트로피도 집에 가져가게 될 것이다. 클럽은 참가자들이 즐거운 시간을 보내는 것 외에도 지역 사회 내 예술의 중요성에 대해 ¹⁴⁰충분히 잘 알게 되기를 바라고 있다. ¹⁴¹뿐만 아니라, 이 행사는 젊은 골퍼들에게 친선 경기에서 시합을 할 수 있는 아주 좋은 기회를 제공한다. 행사의 모든 ¹⁴²수익금은 미술관의 시급한 지붕 수리에 쓰일 것이다.

어휘 raise funds 기금을 모으다   first-ever 사상 최초의   golf course 골프장   contemporary 현대의   take home (집으로) 가지고 가다, 수상하다   fully 충분히   informed 잘 아는   go toward ~에 쓰이다   urgent 시급한

139. 알맞은 문장 고르기
(A) 시장은 주최자들이 환경에 초점을 맞춘 것에 대해 칭찬했다.
(B) 하계 기간 내내 현장에서 골프 강습이 제공된다.
(C) 대회의 상은 차후 날짜에 발표될 것이다.
(D) 대회에서는 참가자들에게 지역 기업들이 기부한 상을 수여할 것이다.

해설 빈칸 앞에서 골프 토너먼트가 개최될 거라는 내용이 나오고 빈칸 뒤에서는 우승자들에게 수여하는 상에 대한 구체적인 내용이 나오므로, 빈칸에는 대회에서 참가자들에게 상을 수여할 것이라는 내용이 나오는 게 자연스럽다. 따라서 정답은 (D). (C)는 대회의 상과 관련이 있는 내용이지만, 우승자들이 상품권과 트로피를 가지고 돌아가게 될 것이라는 빈칸 뒤의 문장과 내용상 맞지 않으므로 오답.

140. 부사 자리_형용사 수식
해설 빈칸은 that절의 주어 participants를 보충 설명하는 주격 보어로 쓰인 형용사 informed를 수식하는 자리이므로 부사가 들어가는 것이 적절하다. 따라서 부사인 (D)가 정답.

141. 접속부사 furthermore
(A) 그렇지 않으면 (B) 따라서 **(C) 뿐만 아니라** (D) 사실은

해설 빈칸 앞뒤로 대회에 참가함으로써 얻거나 배울 수 있는 것들을 나열하고 있으므로 '뿐만 아니라'라는 추가의 의미를 가지는 접속부사 (C)가 정답.

142. 명사 어휘 proceeds
(A) 관심 **(B) 수익금** (C) 자재 (D) 분리

해설 문맥상 '행사의 모든 수익금이 수리에 쓰일 것'이라는 의미가 가장 자연스러우므로 정답은 (B). (C)는 지붕 수리와 연관성이 있는 어휘이지만 빈칸 뒤 from the event의 수식을 받기에는 문맥상 적절하지 않으므로 오답.

어휘 gently 부드럽게, 약하게 criticism 비판 cause 초래하다, 일으키다 offense 불쾌, 모욕 sensitive 예민한, 세심한

129. 부사 어휘 efficiently
게이브리얼 팰컨 씨는 그 제약 회사가 의료 검진의 정확도를 더 효율적으로 평가할 수 있게 하는 전자동 시스템을 고안했다.
(A) 가까스로 (B) 점점 더 (C) 부분적으로 **(D) 효율적으로**

해설 문맥에 어울리는 부사 어휘를 고르는 문제. 주절에서 전자동 시스템을 고안했다는 내용이 나오므로, 시스템을 수식하는 that 이하의 관계대명사절에서는 '더 효율적으로 평가할 수 있게 해 준다'는 시스템의 목적이 되는 특성을 언급하는 것이 자연스럽다. 따라서 정답은 (D).

어휘 create 고안하다, 창조하다 automated 자동의, 자동화된 pharmaceutical 약학의, 제약의 evaluate 평가하다 medical 의료의, 의학의 accuracy 정확(도)

130. 명사절 접속사 whether
다수의 임원들이 우드워스 씨가 그 자리에 맞는 자격이 있는지 의문을 제기했다.
(A) 둘 다 (B) ~이 아닌 한 (C) ~ 때문에 **(D) ~인지 (아닌지)**

해설 빈칸은 동사 questioned의 목적어가 되는 명사절을 이끄는 접속사 자리로, 문맥상 '자격이 있는지 아닌지'라는 뜻이 되어야 자연스럽다. 따라서 '~인지 아닌지'라는 의미의 명사절 접속사 (D)가 정답.

어휘 a number of 다수의 board member 이사, 임원 question 의문을 제기하다 qualification 자격, 자질 position (일)자리, 직위

PART 6

131-134 광고

제이콥스 인테리어
이사 비용의 일부만 들여서 그냥 개선할 수 있는데 왜 이사를 하세요? 저희의 경험이 풍부한 디자이너들은 주택, 사무실, 심지어 텔레비전 스튜디오까지 131변신시켜 왔습니다! 그들은 자재 선택부터 시작해서 모든 과정의 각 단계마다 여러분을 도와드릴 것입니다. 132저희는 가능한 한 자주 현지에서 공급받을 수 있는 자재를 사용하려고 노력합니다. 그렇기는 하지만, 정확히 여러분이 원하시는 것을 구해 드리기 위해 저희는 기꺼이 자재를 수입하거나 배송받기도 합니다. 어떤 변경 작업이든 하기 전에 엔지니어들에게 건물 하중 지지 시스템에 133필수적인 구조물들을 점검하게 하는 것으로 저희는 여러분의 안전 또한 염두에 둘 것입니다. 저희 웹사이트 www.jacobsint.com에 방문하셔서 이전 작업의 사진들을 보시고 저희가 고객들의 134주문을 어떻게 이행했는지에 대한 추천 글들을 읽어 보세요.

어휘 fraction 부분, 일부 experienced 경험이 풍부한, 숙련된 selection 선택 nevertheless 그럼에도 불구하고, 그렇기는 하지만 be willing to do 기꺼이 ~하다 import 수입하다 keep ~ in mind ~을 마음에 담아 두다 inspect 점검하다, 검사하다 structure 구조(물) vital to ~에 필수적인 support 지지, 버팀대 testimonial 추천의 글 fulfill 이행하다, 만족시키다

131. 동사 어휘 transform
(A) 관련시키다 **(B) 변형시키다** (C) 투자하다 (D) 순회하다

해설 문맥에 알맞은 동사 어휘를 고르는 문제. 빈칸 뒤의 목적어와의 관계를 살펴봐야 한다. 문맥상 '우리 디자이너들은 주택, 사무실, 심지어 텔레비전 스튜디오까지 변신시켜 왔다'는 뜻이 가장 자연스러우므로 정답은 (B).

132. 알맞은 문장 고르기
(A) 그 업체는 작업에 대해 환불 보장을 제공합니다.
(B) 주저하지 말고 디자이너에게 여러분의 작업 아이디어를 공유해 주세요.
(C) 일부 색상들은 해마다 계속해서 인기가 있습니다.
(D) 저희는 가능한 한 자주 현지에서 공급받을 수 있는 자재를 사용하려고 노력합니다.

해설 알맞은 문장 고르기 문제를 풀기 위해서는 빈칸 주변의 문맥을 잘 살펴봐야 한다. 빈칸 앞에 디자이너들이 자재 선택부터 도와줄 거라는 내용이 나오고, 빈칸 뒤에서 자재를 수입하거나 배송받기도 한다는 말을 양보의 접속부사 nevertheless로 연결하는 것으로 보아, 빈칸에는 자재와 관련된 내용이지만 뒷문장과는 반대되는 내용이 나올 것임을 유추할 수 있다. 따라서 현지에서 공급받을 수 있는 자재를 주로 사용하려고 한다는 내용의 (D)가 정답.

133. 형용사 자리
해설 빈칸부터 system까지가 앞에 있는 명사 structures를 뒤에서 수식하는 구조로, 빈칸에는 빈칸 뒤의 전치사 to와 어울려 사용되는 형용사 어휘가 와야 한다. 선택지 중에서 유일한 형용사로, 전치사 to와 어울려 '~에 필수적인'의 의미를 가지는 (B)가 정답. 문맥상으로도 '변경 작업을 하기 전에 엔지니어들에게 건물 하중 지지 시스템에 필수적인 구조물들을 점검하게 한다'는 내용이 자연스럽다.

134. 명사 어휘 order
(A) 주문 (B) 관계 (C) 행동 (D) 양식

해설 빈칸 앞의 동사 fulfilled의 목적어이면서 customers'의 수식을 받는 명사 어휘를 찾아야 한다. 문맥상 '고객들의 주문을 이행했다'라는 의미가 가장 자연스러우므로 정답은 (A).

어휘 build A on B B에 A의 기반을 두다 trust 신뢰, 신임 open 솔직한, 숨김없는 at all times 항상, 언제나

121. 전치사 before
본 씨는 다른 사람들과 세부 사항에 대해 공동 작업을 하기 전에 원형의 운전 모형을 준비하고 싶어 한다.

(A) 그렇기는 하지만 **(B) ~ 전에** (C) ~하도록 (D) 대신에

해설 빈칸 앞에 완전한 문장이 있고 빈칸 뒤에 동명사구가 있으므로, 빈칸에는 동명사구를 이끌어 앞의 문장을 수식하는 품사, 즉 전치사가 와야 한다. 문맥상 '공동 작업을 하기 전에 모형을 준비하고 싶어 한다'는 것이 자연스러우므로 정답은 (B).

어휘 working model 운전[실용] 모형 prototype 원형 collaborate 협력하다, 공동으로 작업하다 detail 세부 사항

122. 명사 어휘 reputation
라볼라 레스토랑은 거의 항상 자리가 꽉 차 있고 훌륭한 음식과 서비스로 명성을 얻어 왔다.

(A) 설명 (B) 진술 (C) 전념 **(D) 명성**

해설 빈칸은 앞에 있는 동사 has earned의 목적어 자리로, 동사 earn과 잘 어울리면서 문맥에 알맞은 명사 어휘가 들어가야 한다. 문맥상 '훌륭한 음식과 서비스로 명성을 얻어 왔다'는 의미가 가장 자연스러우므로 정답은 (D).

어휘 be filled to capacity 꽉 차다, 만원이다 earn a reputation 명성을 얻다

123. to부정사_부사 역할
백화점 측은 고객들이 시향해 볼 수 있게 하기 위해 향수 샘플 병을 제공했다.

(A) 훨씬 (B) ~의 결과로서 **(C) ~하기 위해** (D) 무엇보다도

해설 빈칸 뒤의 allow는 customers를 목적어로 취하는 동사이다. 선택지 중에서 동사원형인 allow 앞에 올 수 있는 것은 (C)뿐이므로 정답은 (C). in order to do는 '~하기 위해'라는 뜻으로 목적의 의미를 분명히 할 때 쓰이는 부사 역할의 to부정사이다. (A)와 (D)는 부사구이고, (B)는 뒤에 명사나 명사구를 취하는 전치사구로 오답. in order to do 뿐만 아니라 so as to do 또한 목적의 의미를 분명히 할 때 사용할 수 있다는 점을 알아 두자.

어휘 provide 제공하다, 공급하다 perfume 향수 allow 허용하다 try 써 보다, 해 보다

124. 동사 어휘 recruit
린츠 호텔은 확장 프로젝트가 끝나는 대로 더 많은 투숙객을 처리하기 위해 직원을 더 모집할 것이다.

(A) 몰수당하다 **(B) 모집하다** (C) 바치다 (D) 위임하다

해설 문맥에 어울리는 동사 어휘를 고르는 문제. 문맥상 '더 많은 투숙객을 처리하기 위해 직원을 더 모집할 것이다'라는 내용이 되어야 가장 자연스러우므로 정답은 (B).

어휘 expansion 확장, 확대 complete 완료하다, 끝마치다 handle 처리하다, 다루다 volume 양, 부피

125. 형용사 자리_주격 보어
그 보고서 초안의 품질은 받아들일 수 있는 수준이 아니어서 팀장은 그것을 다시 쓰도록 요청했다.

해설 빈칸은 주어인 The quality의 성질을 나타낼 수 있는 주격 보어 자리이다. 보어 자리에는 명사나 형용사가 올 수 있으므로 (A), (C), (D)가 정답 후보. 문맥상 '품질이 받아들일 수 있는 수준이 아니다'라는 의미가 자연스러우므로 '받아들일 수 있는'의 의미를 지닌 형용사 (C)가 정답. (A)는 현재분사로 '품질이 받아들인다'는 의미가 되고, (D)는 주어인 The quality와 동격을 이루어 '품질은 받아들일 수 있음이다'라는 의미가 되어 둘 다 문맥상 어색하므로 오답.

어휘 quality 질, 품질 first draft 초안, 초고 acceptable (수준 등이) 받아들일 수 있는 ask for ~을 요청하다 rewrite 다시[고쳐] 쓰다

126. 명사 어휘 proximity
행사 기획자들은 주요 고속 도로와의 근접성 때문에 잉그램 센터를 소프트웨어 대회 장소로 선정했다.

(A) 지명도 **(B) 근접성** (C) 규칙적임 (D) 지역

해설 빈칸 뒤에 to가 나오는 것에 주의한다. proximity는 뒤에 전치사 to를 수반하여 '~와의 근접성'이라는 의미를 가진다. 따라서 '주요 고속 도로와의 근접성'이라는 의미를 나타낼 수 있는 (B)가 정답.

어휘 convention 대회, 협의회 due to ~ 때문에 major 주요한 highway 고속 도로

127. 형용사 어휘 extensive
유전 공학 분야에서 광범위한 연구를 수행해 온 카파디아 박사는 매우 존경받는 생물학자이다.

(A) 가구가 비치된 **(B) 광범위한** (C) 잘 상하는 (D) 시간을 지키는

해설 빈칸 뒤의 명사 research를 수식하는 형용사 어휘를 고르는 문제. 빈칸이 포함된 who부터 engineering까지는 주어인 Dr. Kapadia를 수식하는 관계대명사절로, 문맥상 '유전 공학 분야에서 광범위한 연구를 수행해 왔다'는 뜻이 되어야 가장 자연스러우므로 정답은 (B).

어휘 conduct 수행하다 research 연구, 조사 field 분야 genetic engineering 유전 공학 highly 크게, 매우 respected 훌륭한, 존경받는 biologist 생물학자

128. 복합관계부사 however
직원에 대해 아무리 부드럽게 비판을 하더라도, 이는 예민한 사람에게는 여전히 불쾌감을 줄 수 있다.

(A) 어느 정도 **(B) 아무리 ~해도** (C) 전적으로 (D) 거의 ~ 않다

해설 빈칸에는 두 개의 절을 연결하는 접속사 역할을 하면서 빈칸 뒤의 부사 gently를 수식하는 품사가 와야 한다. 문맥상 '아무리 부드럽게 직원에 대한 비판을 하더라도'라는 뜻이 되어야 자연스러우므로 '아무리 ~해도'라는 양보의 의미를 가지는 복합관계부사 (B)가 정답.

112. 능동태+수 일치
쇼브 유틸리티즈 사는 자사 웹사이트의 정보를 더 많은 고객이 이해할 수 있도록 스페인어와 중국어로 번역했다.

해설 문맥상 쇼브 유틸리티즈 사가 정보를 스페인어와 중국어로 '번역하는' 주체이므로 능동태인 (B)와 (C)가 정답 후보. 주어의 형태가 Shobe Utilities로 복수 명사처럼 보이지만, 회사명은 단수 취급하므로 단수 동사인 (C)가 정답.

어휘 utility (보통 복수형) (수도·전기·가스 같은) 공익사업(체) translate 번역하다 so that ~ can ~가 …할 수 있도록

113. 형용사 자리_형용사+명사
현재의 IT 부서는 정말 회사 역사상 가장 다양한 사람들이 모인 그룹이다.

해설 빈칸 앞의 한정사 the와 형용사를 최상급으로 만들어 주는 부사 most의 수식을 받으면서 빈칸 뒤의 명사 group을 수식하는 품사의 어휘가 빈칸에 와야 한다. 선택지 중에서 명사를 수식할 수 있는 것은 형용사인 diverse뿐이므로 정답은 (C).

어휘 indeed 정말, 확실히 diverse 다양한

114. 부사 어휘 almost
콜비 씨의 수상작인 베스트셀러의 원고는 출판사에서 거의 거절당할 뻔했다.
(A) 꽤 (B) 인근에 (C) 아직 **(D) 거의**

해설 문맥에 어울리는 부사 어휘를 고르는 문제. 문맥상 '원고가 출판사에서 거의 거절당할 뻔했다'는 의미가 가장 자연스러우므로 정답은 (D).

어휘 manuscript 원고 reject 거부하다, 거절하다 publisher 출판사, 출판인

115. 인칭대명사_주격
캐롤라이나 지점의 최고 영업 사원인 심슨 씨는 본인이 팀장으로 승진되어야 한다고 요구했다.

해설 선택지를 보니 인칭대명사의 알맞은 격을 고르는 문제. 빈칸은 접속사 that이 이끄는 명사절의 주어 자리이므로 주격 인칭대명사인 (B)가 정답. 주절의 동사 request는 요구를 나타내는 동사로, 목적어로 취하는 that절의 동사는 〈(should)+동사원형〉의 형태가 되어야 함을 알아 두자.

어휘 branch 지사, 분점 salesperson 영업 사원, 판매원 request 요청[요구]하다 promote 승진시키다

116. 동사 어휘 accommodate
EZ 택배 사는 서비스 수요의 증가에 부응하기 위한 노력의 일환으로 자사 보유 차량에 화물차를 세 대 더 구매할 것이다.
(A) 예측하다 **(B) 부응하다** (C) (결과를) ~에 돌리다 (D) 발생시키다

해설 빈칸 뒤의 the rise를 목적어로 취하면서 의미가 자연스럽게 연결되는 동사 어휘를 찾아야 한다. 문맥상 빈칸 뒤의 목적어 the rise in demand와 가장 잘 어울리는 동사는 요구 등에 '부응하다'라는 뜻의 동사 accommodate이므로 정답은 (B).

어휘 courier 택배 회사, 배달원 fleet (한 회사 소유의) 전 차량 in an effort to do ~하려는 노력으로 rise 증가, 상승 demand 수요, 요구

117. 부사 자리_형용사 수식
관광객들과 지역 주민들 모두 농산물 직거래 장터를 방문하는데 그곳의 농산물은 아주 합리적으로 가격이 매겨져 있기 때문이다.

해설 빈칸 앞의 부사 very의 수식을 받으면서 빈칸 뒤의 과거분사 priced를 수식하는 품사가 빈칸에 와야 한다. 선택지 중에서 과거분사를 수식할 수 있는 것은 부사밖에 없으므로 부사인 (C)가 정답.

어휘 local 지역 주민; 현지의 alike 둘 다, 똑같이 farmers' market (농산물) 생산자 직거래 장터 produce 농산물; 생산하다 reasonably priced 합리적으로 가격이 매겨진

118. 전치사 upon
항공사 승객들은 최종 목적지에 도착하자마자 수하물 컨베이어에서 자기 짐이 나오길 기다렸다.
(A) ~을 따라 **(B) ~하자마자** (C) ~과는 달리 (D) ~ 동안

해설 선택지를 보면 알맞은 전치사를 고르는 문제임을 알 수 있다. 빈칸 뒤의 동명사구와 어울려 '~에 도착하자마자'라는 의미를 나타내는 전치사는 upon이므로 정답은 (B). upon[on] doing은 '~하자마자'라는 뜻의 동명사 관용표현으로 반드시 기억해 두자.

어휘 destination 목적지, 도착지 belongings 소지품, 소유물 luggage carousel 수하물 컨베이어

119. 형용사 어휘 essential
새로 교육받은 요리사가 그 수프에 들어가는 필수적인 재료 중 두 가지를 잊어버려서 수프가 제대로 나오지 않았다.
(A) 필수적인 (B) 타고난 (C) 동일한 (D) 믿을 수 있는

해설 형용사 어휘 문제는 수식하는 명사와의 관계를 따져야 한다. 문맥상 없으면 결과물(수프)이 제대로 나오지 않는 '필수적인 재료'라는 의미가 가장 자연스러우므로 정답은 (A).

어휘 ingredient 재료, 성분 turn out (일·진행·결과가 특정 방식으로) 되다

120. 등위접속사 so
그 업체의 이미지는 신뢰를 기반으로 하기 때문에, 직원들은 항상 고객들에게 솔직하고 정직할 것이 기대된다.

해설 빈칸 앞뒤에 각각 완전한 절이 있으므로 두 절을 연결하는 접속사가 빈칸에 들어가야 한다. 신뢰를 기반으로 하는 것과 고객들에게 솔직하고 정직한 것은 인과 관계이므로 결과의 의미를 나타내는 접속사 (B)가 정답. 여기에서 so는 등위접속사로 두 개의 절을 병렬 구조로 연결해 주고 있다.

103. 명사 자리 + 사람명사 vs. 사물/추상명사

편집자에게 보내진 그 편지는 〈내셔널 가드닝 매거진〉지의 구독자인 재니스 리브스 씨에 의해 작성되었다.

해설 빈칸 앞에는 부정관사 a가, 빈칸 뒤에는 전치사 to가 있으므로 빈칸은 뒤에 있는 전치사구의 수식을 받는 명사 자리이다. 따라서 명사인 (C)와 (D)가 정답 후보인데, 콤마가 있는 것으로 보아 빈칸은 편지를 작성한 주체인 재니스 리브스 씨와 동격이 되어야 하므로 사람을 뜻하는 명사인 (C)가 정답.

어휘 editor 편집장, 편집자 subscriber 구독자 gardening 정원 가꾸기, 원예

104. 부사 어휘 soon

보셀 제조사는 곧 최신 장비로 자사의 생산 라인을 능률화할 것이다.

(A) 꽤 **(B) 곧** (C) 그 밖에 (D) 줄곧

해설 문맥에 어울리는 부사 어휘를 고르는 문제. 미래시제가 쓰인 것으로 보아 미래에 일어날 일을 서술하는 것임을 알 수 있으므로 '곧'을 의미하는 시간 부사 soon이 적절하다. 따라서 정답은 (B). ever는 '줄곧, 영원히'라는 뜻으로 미래시제와 함께 쓰일 수 있지만 여기서는 문맥상 어울리지 않으므로 (D)는 오답.

어휘 streamline 능률화하다, 간소화하다 production line 생산 라인 modern 현대의, 최신의

105. 부사 자리_전치사구 수식

그 제과점은 장기 투자자를 유치했기 때문에 재정적으로 상태가 좋다.

해설 빈칸 없이도 문장이 완전하므로 빈칸은 빈칸 앞의 형용사 역할을 하는 전치사구 in good shape을 수식하는 부사 자리이다. 따라서 부사인 (D)가 정답.

어휘 now that ~이므로, ~이기 때문에 bring in 유치하다, 끌어들이다 long-term 장기적인 investor 투자자 in good shape 상태가 좋은

106. 명사 어휘 addition

벤츠 애슬레틱스 사는 아동용으로 디자인된 새 의류 라인을 추가한 덕분에 매출을 증가시킬 수 있었다.

(A) 배달 (B) 제안 (C) 내용물 **(D) 추가**

해설 문맥상 '새로운 라인의 추가'로 인해 매출이 증대되었다고 하는 것이 가장 자연스러우므로 (D)가 정답.

어휘 athletics 운동 경기 increase 증가시키다, 늘리다 thanks to ~ 덕분에[때문에]

107. 동사 자리 + 수동태

부품이 집에서 조립된다면 소비자들은 가구에 많은 돈을 절약할 수 있다.

해설 빈칸이 포함된 if 이하는 앞에 나온 문장을 수식하는 부사절이고, 빈칸은 그 절의 동사 자리이므로 (C)와 (D)가 정답 후보. 빈칸 뒤에 assemble의 목적어가 없고, 문맥상으로도 부품은 '조립되는' 대상이므로 수동태인 (D)가 정답.

어휘 consumer 소비자 component (구성) 요소, 부품 assemble 조립하다, 모으다

108. 전치사 through

자연 애호가들은 더비 국립 공원의 북쪽 구역에 위치한 숲을 통과하여 하이킹하는 것을 즐긴다.

(A) ~을 통과하여 (B) ~ 위로 (C) ~에 관하여 (D) ~을 제외하고

해설 알맞은 전치사를 고르는 문제가 나오면 전치사의 목적어를 보고 문맥상 적절한 전치사를 고르도록 한다. 빈칸 이하의 목적어는 특정 위치의 숲을 의미하므로 빈칸에는 '~을 통과하여'라는 방향을 나타내는 전치사 through가 들어가야 자연스럽다. 따라서 정답은 (A). (B)도 방향을 나타내지만 내용상 '숲'과 어울리지 않는 전치사이므로 오답.

어휘 enthusiast 애호가, 열광적인 팬 take a hike 하이킹하다 section 구역

109. 명사 자리 + 사람명사 vs. 사물/추상명사

회사 연회에서 VIP 테이블에 앉은 내빈들에는 올해의 직원상 후보들이 포함되어 있다.

해설 빈칸은 동사 include의 목적어 자리로, 명사인 (B)와 (C)가 정답 후보. 문맥상 '내빈들에 후보들이 포함되어 있다'는 뜻이 되어야 자연스러우므로 정답은 (C). '지명, 추천'이라는 의미의 (B)는 문맥상 어울리지 않으므로 오답.

어휘 banquet 연회, 만찬 include 포함하다 nominee 후보, 지명된 사람 annual 연례의, 매년의

110. 관용어구 be aware of

메이페어 국제 공항의 보안 요원들은 여행객 관련 규칙 및 규정을 알고 있어야만 한다.

(A) 경계하는 (B) 정확한 **(C) 알고 있는** (D) 엄격한

해설 문맥에 어울리는 형용사 어휘를 고르는 문제. 빈칸 뒤 전치사 of를 보고 특정 전치사를 동반하는 형용사 관용표현을 떠올릴 수 있다면 쉽게 답을 찾을 수 있다. '~을 알고 있다'라는 뜻의 관용표현 be aware of가 문맥상 가장 알맞으므로 (C)가 정답.

어휘 security guard 보안 요원, 경비원 rule 규칙 regulation 규정

111. 재귀대명사 관용표현 by oneself

팀장이 그날 시간이 되지 않았기 때문에, 영업팀 팀원들은 자기들끼리 구매자들에게 제품 프레젠테이션을 했다.

해설 빈칸 앞에 전치사가 있으므로, 전치사의 목적어로 쓰일 수 없는 주격 인칭대명사 (C)는 오답으로 제외. 문맥상 '다른 사람 없이, 자기들끼리'라는 뜻이 되어야 자연스러우므로 빈칸에는 재귀대명사의 관용표현 by oneself를 이루는 themselves가 와야 알맞다. 따라서 정답은 (A). '스스로, 혼자 힘으로'라는 뜻의 재귀대명사 관용표현 for oneself를 함께 알아 두자.

어휘 available 시간[여유]이 있는 product 제품

객의 승선 시각, (C)는 페리 출발 시각, (D)는 페리 도착 시각이므로 나머지는 오답.

97. 청자들이 곧 받게 될 것은?
(A) 승선권 영수증
(B) 간단한 안전 안내
(C) 터미널 지도
(D) 좌석 배정

패러프레이징 [단서] a short safety announcement → [정답] A safety briefing

미 ㅁ
Questions 98-100 refer to the following excerpt from a meeting and chart.

⁹⁸I'd like to give you all an update regarding the consulting advice provided by Audrey Gordon at Tuesday's meeting. As some of you may know, ⁹⁹Upton Inc. has gone bankrupt and will no longer supply cosmetics to our store. We had considered adding a new brand to our inventory, but ¹⁰⁰Ms. Gordon recommended that we start carrying more products by the most popular brand. So we'll do that as soon as possible, using the display cases that used to house Upton Inc.'s products. You can see our average sales per brand on this chart. I'll be working with managers to place the necessary orders.

⁹⁸저는 화요일 회의에서 오드리 고든 씨에게서 받은 컨설팅 조언과 관련하여 최신 정보를 여러분 모두에게 알려 드리고자 합니다. 여러분 중 일부는 아시겠지만, ⁹⁹업턴 주식회사가 파산하여 저희 매장에 더 이상 화장품을 공급하지 않을 것입니다. 우리는 우리 상품 목록에 새로운 브랜드를 추가할 것을 고려했었습니다만, ¹⁰⁰고든 씨는 우리가 가장 인기 있는 브랜드의 제품을 더 많이 취급할 것을 추천했습니다. 그래서 우리는 업턴 주식회사 제품을 진열하던 진열장을 이용하여 가능한 한 빨리 그렇게 할 것입니다. 이 도표에서 우리 매장의 브랜드별 평균 판매량을 보실 수 있습니다. 저는 매니저들과 함께 필요한 주문을 넣는 업무를 할 것입니다.

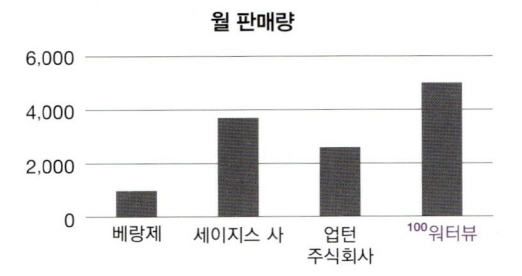

어휘 regarding ~에 관하여 go bankrupt 파산하다 inventory 물품 목록, 재고(품) used to do ~하곤 했다 house 넣어 두다, 보관하다

98. 화자가 화요일에 한 일은?
(A) 컨설턴트를 만났다.
(B) 제품 샘플을 테스트했다.
(C) 재고를 확인했다.
(D) 주문을 처리했다.

패러프레이징 [단서] the consulting advice provided by Audrey Gordon → [정답] Met with a consultant

99. 제품 공급에 변동이 생긴 원인은?
(A) 건물 확장
(B) 폐업
(C) 재고 오류
(D) 교육 행사

패러프레이징 [단서] Upton Inc. has gone bankrupt → [정답] A business closure

100. 시각 자료에서, 물건이 더 추가될 브랜드는?
(A) 베랑제
(B) 세이지스 사
(C) 업턴 주식회사
(D) 워터뷰

해설 단서 (100)에서 컨설턴트인 고든 씨가 가장 인기 있는 브랜드의 제품을 더 많이 취급할 것을 추천했다고 했고 화자의 매장에서 가능한 한 빨리 그렇게 할 거라고 했으므로 도표에서 판매량이 가장 높은 브랜드를 찾아야 한다. 따라서 정답은 (D).

PART 5

101. 소유격
웩슬러 씨는 감사를 표하는 방법으로 자기 팀에 점심을 샀다.

해설 빈칸이 명사 team 앞에 위치하므로 빈칸에는 명사를 수식하는 한정사 역할의 소유격 his가 들어가야 한다. 따라서 정답은 (C).

어휘 appreciation 감사, 감상

102. 접속사 vs. 전치사
지난 3개월 동안, 슬레이트 체육관의 회원 수는 두 배가 되었다.
(A) ~ 아래에 (B) ~하는 동안 (C) ~에 **(D) ~ 동안**

해설 문맥상 '지난 3개월 동안'이 되어야 하므로 기간을 나타내는 접속사 (B)와 전치사 (D)가 정답 후보. 빈칸 뒤에 명사구가 왔기 때문에 전치사인 (D)가 정답.

어휘 double 두 배가 되다

위해 그들이 사용한 다양한 사진들이었습니다. 그것이 정말 프레젠테이션을 기억에 남도록 했습니다. 우리는 이러한 방법으로 더 많은 고객에게 접근할 준비가 되어 있으니, ⁹⁴여러분이 우리 서비스를 이용할 만한 새로운 회사들을 생각해 내시면 좋겠습니다. 큰 소리로 회사를 말씀하시면 제가 칠판에 적도록 하겠습니다.

어휘 achievement 업적, 성취 sign a contract 계약을 맺다 factor 요인, 인자 impressive 인상 깊은 support (사실임을) 뒷받침하다 point 의견, 요점 memorable 기억할 만한 approach 접근하다 shout out ~을 큰 소리로 말하다

92. 화자가 청자들을 축하하는 이유는?
(A) 업무 능력을 향상시켰다.
(B) 매출 목표를 초과했다.
(C) 근면한 직원을 고용했다.
(D) 신규 고객을 유치했다.

패러프레이징 [단서] get Cornell Industries to sign a contract with us → [정답] attracted a new client

93. 화자에 따르면, 프레젠테이션에서 가장 인상 깊었던 부분은?
(A) 간단한 설명들
(B) 다양한 사진들
(C) 동반된 인쇄물
(D) 도움이 되는 도표들

해설 단서 (93)에서 화자는 의견을 뒷받침하려고 사용한 다양한 사진들이 특히 인상 깊었다고 했으므로 정답은 (B).

패러프레이징 [단서] the wide range of photos → [정답] Its variety of photographs

94. 화자가 다음에 할 것 같은 일은?
(A) 동료 소개하기
(B) 시상하기
(C) 회사 목록 적기
(D) 청자들을 팀에 배치하기

패러프레이징 [단서] write them on the board → [정답] Write a list of companies

Questions 95-97 refer to the following announcement and boarding pass.

Good morning, ladies and gentlemen waiting for the ferry to Bainbridge Island. Please remember that lockers are no longer available at this terminal, so ⁹⁵you must hold onto your bags and personal items at all times, both here at the terminal and on board the ferry. ⁹⁶We'll begin boarding shortly, with vehicles boarding at eight fifty and walk-on passengers at nine o'clock. We expect an on-time departure at nine twenty, and with this beautiful weather, our arrival should also be on time. ⁹⁷Please stay in the boarding area, as we'll be presenting a short safety announcement in a few minutes. Thank you.

베인브리지 섬으로 가는 페리를 기다리시는 신사 숙녀 여러분, 좋은 아침입니다. 이 터미널에서는 물품 보관함을 더 이상 이용하실 수 없으니 이곳 터미널에서와 페리 승선 시 둘 다 ⁹⁵가방과 개인 물품을 항상 소지할 것을 기억하십시오. ⁹⁶우리는 곧 승선을 시작할 예정으로, 차량이 있으시면 8시 50분에, 도보 승객은 9시 정각에 승선할 것입니다. 저희는 9시 20분에 정시 출발할 것으로 예상하며, 날씨도 이렇게 맑기 때문에 도착도 제시간에 이루어질 것입니다. ⁹⁷잠시 후에 저희가 짧게 안전 안내를 해 드릴 예정이니, 승선 구역 내에 머물러 주시기 바랍니다. 감사합니다.

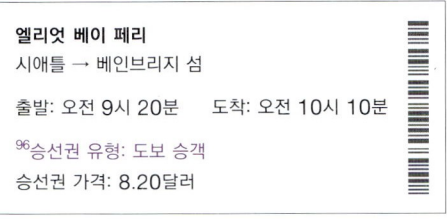

엘리엇 베이 페리
시애틀 → 베인브리지 섬
출발: 오전 9시 20분   도착: 오전 10시 10분
⁹⁶승선권 유형: 도보 승객
승선권 가격: 8.20달러

어휘 ferry 연락선, 페리 hold onto 꼭 잡다, 손을 떼지 않다 personal 개인의, 개인적인 on board 승선[승차/탑승]한 walk-on (차량에 대비하여) 걸어서 탑승하는 on-time 시간을 어기지 않은, 정시의 departure 출발, 떠남 arrival 도착 announcement 안내 방송, 발표

95. 화자가 청자들에게 하도록 상기시키는 일은?
(A) 터미널 직원에게 질문하기
(B) 자기 소지품 가지고 다니기
(C) 출발 부두 확인하기
(D) 자기 승선권 준비하기

해설 단서 (95)에서 가방과 개인 물품을 항상 소지하라고 했으므로 정답은 (B). Please remember that 다음에는 청자가 잊지 않도록 상기시키는 내용이 나온다는 것을 기억해 두자.

패러프레이징 [단서] hold onto your bags and personal items at all times → [정답] Keep their belongings with them

96. 시각 자료에서, 승선권 소지자가 페리에 승선해야 하는 시각은?
(A) 오전 8시 50분
(B) 오전 9시
(C) 오전 9시 20분
(D) 오전 10시 10분

해설 단서 (96)에서 차량이 있으면 8시 50분에, 도보 승객은 9시에 승선한다고 했는데, 승선권을 보면 소지자는 차량을 동반한 승객이 아니라 걸어서 탑승하는 도보 승객이므로 정답은 (B). (A)는 차량 보유 승

(B) 품질 보증 기간이 연장되었다.
(C) 처리 속도가 개선되었다.
(D) 화면 크기가 커졌다.

패러프레이징 [단서] offering a 10-year warranty instead of a 5-year one → [정답] Its warranty period was extended.

88. 화자가 "현재 500그램이 약간 안 되는 수준입니다"라고 말한 의미는?

(A) 무게에 비해 가격이 너무 높다.
(B) 기기가 산업 기준에 맞지 않는다.
(C) 예상보다 빨리 공급품이 떨어지고 있다.
(D) 제품이 들고 다니기에 불편하다.

해설 해당 표현이 쓰인 바로 앞뒤 부분을 통해 화자가 한 말의 의미를 유추할 수 있다. 단서 (88)에서 프린터는 휴대할 수 있도록 의도되었지만 그 무게가 핸드폰의 4배에 가깝다고 한 것으로 보아 휴대하기가 불편하다는 의미로 한 말임을 유추할 수 있다. 따라서 정답은 (D).

Questions 89-91 refer to the following talk.

Good afternoon, ladies and gentlemen. [89]I'm pleased to introduce Nicholas Stroud for this special event at the Ellis Community Center. Mr. Stroud will be reading excerpts from his latest novel, *On the Banks of the Nile*. It's about the history of the Egyptian people in that area, and it will be made into a movie later this year. [90]The director of the movie was going to join us, but I'm sorry to say he's had a last-minute schedule change and won't be here. [91]After the talk, Mr. Stroud will be signing copies of his book at the table near the east entrance. We don't have any for sale, so I hope you brought your own.

신사 숙녀 여러분, 안녕하십니까. [89]엘리스 시민 문화 회관에서 열리는 이 특별한 행사를 위해 제가 니콜러스 스트라우드 씨를 소개하게 되어 기쁩니다. 스트라우드 씨는 본인의 최신작 소설 〈나일 강변에서〉의 발췌문을 낭독할 예정입니다. 이것은 그 지역 이집트인들의 역사에 대한 이야기이며, 올해 하반기에 영화로 만들어질 예정입니다. [90]그 영화의 감독이 저희와 함께할 예정이었으나, 막판에 일정이 변경되어 여기 오지 못하게 되었음을 알려드리게 되어 유감입니다. [91]낭독 후에 스트라우드 씨가 동쪽 출입구 근처의 테이블에서 본인의 책에 사인해 드릴 예정입니다. 판매용으로 준비된 것은 없으니, 여러분이 여러분 본인의 것을 가지고 오셨기를 바랍니다.

어휘 excerpt 발췌 (부분) last-minute 마지막 순간의 entrance (출)입구, 문 own 자기의 것; 자기 자신의

89. 화자가 소개하는 사람은?

(A) 작가
(B) 역사 교수
(C) 감독
(D) 영화 제작자

90. 화자가 사과하는 것은?

(A) 전단에 오류가 있다.
(B) 발표가 지연되고 있다.
(C) 영화 상영이 취소되었다.
(D) 초대 손님 한 명이 오지 못한다.

패러프레이징 [단서] won't be here → [정답] cannot come

91. 화자가 "여러분이 여러분 본인의 것을 가지고 오셨기를 바랍니다"라고 말한 의도는?

(A) 현장에서 물품을 구하지 못할 것이다.
(B) 청자들은 낭독회 입장권이 필요하다.
(C) 스트라우드 씨가 준비된 질문 몇 개에 답변할 것이다.
(D) 청자들은 자신의 의견을 제안해도 된다.

해설 해당 표현의 앞에 있는 단서 (91)에서 작가가 책에 사인해 줄 예정인데 판매용으로 준비된 책이 없다고 하는 것으로 보아 청자들이 자기 책을 가지고 왔어야 한다는 의미임을 알 수 있다. 따라서 정답은 (A).

패러프레이징 [단서] We don't have any for sale → [정답] Items will not be available on site.

Questions 92-94 refer to the following excerpt from a meeting.

To start off today's meeting, [92]I'd like to congratulate you all on your achievement. We've been trying to get Cornell Industries to sign a contract with us for a long time, and it finally happened! The presentation by Mr. Monroe's team was a huge factor in our success. [93]What I found particularly impressive was the wide range of photos they used to support their points. That really made it memorable. We're ready to approach more clients in this way, so [94]I'd like you to think of new companies who could use our services. I'll write them on the board as you shout them out.

오늘의 회의를 시작하면서, [92]여러분 모두에게 여러분의 성취에 대해 축하드리고 싶습니다. 우리는 오랫동안 코넬 산업이 우리와 계약을 맺게 하려고 노력해 왔고, 마침내 그것이 이뤄졌습니다! 먼로 씨의 팀에서 한 프레젠테이션이 우리 성공의 커다란 요인이었습니다. [93]제게 특히나 인상 깊었던 것은 본인들의 의견을 뒷받침하기

you'd like to come in. [84]If applicable, also tell us which dentist usually treats you. Otherwise, tell us if you have a preferred dentist. Note that Dr. Doyle is fully booked until August 8. His next available appointments are on August 9. [85]We will reopen on Monday, July 30 at 8 A.M. and resume regular hours. Dr. Howard, whose off day is Monday, will return on Tuesday, July 31.

안녕하세요. 귀하께서는 브리턴 치과에 전화하셨습니다. [83]저희 치과는 현재 여름 휴가로 인해 문을 닫았습니다. 의료 응급 상황으로 전화하신 것이라면, 지금 전화를 끊고 911로 전화하세요. 진료 예약을 하시려면 성함, 전화번호, 방문하기를 원하는 시각을 메시지로 남겨 주세요. [84]평소 진료받던 선생님이 계시다면 어떤 분인지도 말씀해 주세요. 그렇지 않은 경우, 선호하는 선생님이 있는지 말씀해 주세요. 도일 선생님은 8월 8일까지 예약이 꽉 차 있다는 것을 알아 두세요. 다음으로 가능한 그분의 예약일은 8월 9일입니다. [85]저희는 월요일인 7월 30일 오전 8시에 다시 문을 열어서 정규 진료 시간을 재개할 것입니다. 월요일에 비번인 하워드 선생님은 화요일인 7월 31일에 돌아오실 예정입니다.

어휘 reach (특히 전화로) 연락하다 currently 현재, 지금 medical 의학[의료]의 emergency 비상(사태), 응급 hang up 전화를 끊다 schedule an appointment 예약을 하다 applicable 해당[적용]되는 fully booked 예약이 꽉 찬 resume 재개하다, 다시 시작하다 regular hours 정상 영업시간 off day 비번[쉬는] 날

83. 업체가 문을 닫은 이유는?
(A) 응급 상황이 발생했다.
(B) 보수 공사가 진행 중이다.
(C) 치과 의사 한 명이 최근에 퇴직했다.
(D) 직원들이 휴가 중이다.

패러프레이징 [단서] the summer holidays → [정답] vacation

84. 화자가 "그렇지 않은 경우, 선호하는 선생님이 있는지 말씀해 주세요"라고 말한 의도는?
(A) 새 고객은 치과 의사를 선택할 수 있다.
(B) 새로운 치과 의사가 고용될 것이다.
(C) 환자들은 자신의 치과 의사에 대한 평을 쓸 수 있다.
(D) 단골들은 새로운 치과 의사를 선택할 수 있다.

해설 화자가 한 말의 의도를 문맥을 통해 찾아내는 문제로 해당 표현의 앞뒤를 주의 깊게 들어야 한다. 바로 앞 문장인 단서 (84)에서 평소 어떤 의사에게 진료를 받는지 말해 달라고 하는 것으로 보아, 제시된 문장의 Otherwise는 평소에 담당하는 의사가 없는 경우, 즉 치과에 처음 오는 경우를 의미한다는 것을 알 수 있다. 따라서 처음 오는 고객은 선호하는 의사를 선택할 수 있다는 것을 알려 주려는 의도임을 알 수 있으므로 정답은 (A).

85. 병원을 다시 여는 때는?
(A) 7월 30일
(B) 7월 31일
(C) 8월 8일
(D) 8월 9일

Questions 86-88 refer to the following excerpt from a meeting.

[86]OK. First, let's talk about how things went on at the National Electronics Expo. Our booth was well-positioned, and visitors showed a lot of interest in our new mini printer, the Kenosha-50. [87]We've just started offering a 10-year warranty instead of a 5-year one, and that seems to be helping sales. There are still adjustments that need to be made, however. [88]The printer is intended to be portable, but it's currently just under five hundred grams. [88]That's nearly four times the weight of an average cell phone. I don't think consumers are going to find that characteristic attractive.

[86]좋습니다. 먼저, 이번에 참여했던 전국 전자 제품 박람회 건부터 이야기해 보죠. 우리 부스는 위치가 좋았고, 방문객들이 우리의 새로운 미니 프린터인 케노샤-50에 많은 관심을 보였습니다. [87]우리는 이제 막 5년간의 품질 보증 대신에 10년간의 품질 보증을 제공하기 시작했고, 이것이 판매에 도움이 되고 있는 것 같습니다. 그러나 아직도 조정해야 할 것들이 있습니다. [88]그 프린터는 휴대할 수 있도록 의도되었으나, 현재 500그램이 약간 안 되는 수준입니다. [88]이는 평균적인 핸드폰 무게의 거의 4배에 가깝죠. 저는 소비자들이 그 특징을 매력적이라고 여기지 않을 것 같습니다.

어휘 national 국가의, 전국적인 well-positioned 위치가 좋은 offer 제공하다 warranty (품질 등의) 보증, 보증서 intend to do ~하기를 의도하다 portable 휴대가 쉬운, 휴대용의 average 평균의, 보통의 consumer 소비자 characteristic 특징, 특질 attractive 매력적인

86. 화자가 회의 일정을 잡은 이유는?
(A) 제품을 시연하기 위해
(B) 매출 보고서를 정정하기 위해
(C) 산업 행사에 대한 정보를 제공하기 위해
(D) 무역 박람회 부스에서 일할 자원봉사자를 요청하기 위해

패러프레이징 [단서] how things went on at the National Electronics Expo → [정답] information about an industry event

87. 최근에 케노샤-50에서 변경된 것은?
(A) 배터리 무게가 줄었다.

77. 재키 갈바니 씨의 신분은?
(A) 라디오 진행자
(B) 연구원
(C) 화가
(D) 예술 평론가

78. 갈바니 씨가 최근에 한 일은?
(A) 학교를 시작했다.
(B) 강의를 했다.
(C) 미술관을 열었다.
(D) 조각품을 평가했다.

패러프레이징 [단서] the art school she just opened
→ [정답] Started a school

79. 화자가 청자들에게 하도록 요청한 일은?
(A) 강좌에 등록하기
(B) 그림 구매하기
(C) 초대 손님과 이야기하기
(D) 질문 제출하기

해설 단서 (79)에서 전화해서 갈바니 씨에게 물어봤으면 하는 것을 말해 달라고 했으므로 정답은 (D).

패러프레이징 [단서] tell us what you'd like us to ask Ms. Galvani
→ [정답] Submit questions

영 🎧
Questions 80-82 refer to the following advertisement.

⁸⁰Are you tired of wasting time looking for new employees? Let us do the work for you! ⁸¹Propool has helped hundreds of software companies find well-suited hires. Whether you need full-time staff, part-time staff, or unpaid interns, you can count on us to provide you with a list of IT professionals. We handle everything from the job posting to the preliminary interviews. We then set up final interviews for you to meet the potential candidates. All you have to do is choose the person you prefer. No more sorting through piles of résumés and reading cover letters. ⁸²Send us your job description now and find the perfect worker!

⁸⁰새 직원들을 찾느라고 시간을 낭비하는 것이 지겨우십니까? 여러분을 대신해 저희가 그 일을 하겠습니다! ⁸¹프로풀 사는 수백 군데의 소프트웨어 업체가 적합한 입사자를 찾도록 도움을 드려 왔습니다. 정직원이 필요하시든, 시간제 직원이 필요하시든, 무급 인턴이 필요하시든 간에 저희가 여러분께 IT 전문가들의 명단을 제공할 테니 여러분은 믿고 맡기시면 됩니다. 저희는 구인 광고에서부터 사전 면접까지 모든 것을 처리합니다. 그런 다음 저희는 여러분이 잠재적인 후보자들을 만나 보실 수 있게 최종 면접을 잡아 드립니다. 여러분이 하실 일은 선호하는 사람을 고르는 일뿐입니다. 이력서 더미를 자세히 살펴보는 것도 자기 소개서를 읽는 것도 더 이상 안 하셔도 됩니다. ⁸²지금 저희에게 직무 기술서를 보내 주셔서 완벽한 직원을 찾으세요!

어휘 well-suited 적합한, 적임의 hire (신규) 입사자, 채용자; 고용하다 unpaid 무급의 count on ~을 믿다[의지하다] job posting 구인 광고 potential 잠재적인 sort through (무언가를 찾기 위해) 자세히 살펴보다 job description 직무 기술(서)

80. 이 광고의 대상은?
(A) 구직자들
(B) 사업주들
(C) 신입 사원들
(D) 전문 모집자들

81. 화자의 회사가 전문으로 하는 분야는?
(A) 제약
(B) 언론
(C) 패션
(D) 컴퓨터 과학

해설 단서 (81)에서 소프트웨어 업체들의 입사자 모집을 도왔다는 내용과 IT 전문가들의 명단을 제공하겠다는 내용이 언급된 것으로 보아 화자의 회사는 컴퓨터 과학 분야의 구인 활동을 전문으로 함을 알 수 있다. 따라서 정답은 (D).

패러프레이징 [단서] software / IT → [정답] Computer science

82. 청자들이 보내도록 요청받은 것은?
(A) 그들의 시설에 대한 설명
(B) 선호하는 후보자로 선발된 사람들
(C) 그들이 필요로 하는 인재 조건에 대한 설명
(D) 면접 질문 목록

패러프레이징 [단서] your job description → [정답] An explanation of their needs

미 🎧
Questions 83-85 refer to the following recorded message.

Hello, you've reached the Britton Dental Clinic. ⁸³Our offices are currently closed for the summer holidays. If this is a medical emergency, hang up now and call 911. If you wish to schedule an appointment, leave a message with your name, number, and time

패러프레이징 [단서] one of our staff members will be demonstrating basic drilling techniques → [정답] A demonstration

73. 화자가 청자들에게 하도록 권하는 일은?
(A) 보상 프로그램에 등록하기
(B) 의견 공유하기
(C) 제안하기
(D) 워크숍에 등록하기

패러프레이징 [단서] enroll in our next workshop → [정답] Sign up for a workshop

Questions 74-76 refer to the following telephone message.

Hi, Ms. Griffin. ⁷⁴This is Thomas Collins calling from Whitfield Inc., the company that manages the apartment building you live in. ⁷⁵I got your online request form saying that the water pressure in your bathroom suddenly became low. I can send a plumber today at 4 P.M. One of our representatives can let the person in if you're not there. ⁷⁶Please call me back if you want to change the time. Otherwise, you can expect someone at 4. Thanks.

여보세요, 그리핀 씨. ⁷⁴저는 거주하고 계시는 아파트 건물의 관리 업체인 휫필드 주식회사에서 전화드리는 토머스 콜린스입니다. ⁷⁵저는 욕실 수압이 갑자기 낮아졌다는 귀하의 온라인 요청서를 받았습니다. 제가 오늘 오후 4시에 배관공을 보내 드릴 수 있는데요. 만약에 댁에 안 계시면, 저희 직원이 그 사람을 들여 보낼 수도 있습니다. ⁷⁶시간을 변경하고 싶으시면 제게 다시 전화 주시기 바랍니다. 그렇지 않으면 누군가 4시에 방문할 거라고 알고 계시면 됩니다. 감사합니다.

어휘 pressure 압력 plumber 배관공 representative 대표자, 담당 직원 let in ~을 들어오게 하다 call back (전화해 왔던 사람 등에게) 다시 전화하다 otherwise (만약) 그렇지 않으면 expect (오기로 되어 있는 대상을) 기다리다

74. 화자가 일할 것 같은 곳은?
(A) 건설 회사
(B) 건물 관리 업체
(C) 보험사
(D) 배관 업체

패러프레이징 [단서] the company that manages the apartment building you live in → [정답] a property management firm

75. 전화의 주된 내용은?
(A) 수리 일정 정하기
(B) 견학 일정 짜기
(C) 보수 공사 알리기
(D) 임대 계약에 서명하기

해설 단서 (75)에서 화자가 청자의 수리 요청에 대해 이야기하면서 배관공을 4시에 보내 주겠다고 했고, 이 수리 일정에 관한 이야기가 이어지고 있으므로 정답은 (A).

76. 청자가 화자에게 다시 전화해야 하는 이유는?
(A) 서비스 비용을 지불하기 위해
(B) 불만을 제기하기 위해
(C) 청구 금액을 승인하기 위해
(D) 약속을 변경하기 위해

패러프레이징 [단서] to change the time → [정답] To change an appointment

Questions 77-79 refer to the following radio broadcast.

Good evening. You are listening to *Brush Stroke*. ⁷⁷Today's special guest is Jackie Galvani, whose paintings you can see at the Madison Gallery in Stoneville for the entire month of July. In addition to her artwork, ⁷⁸Ms. Galvani will be talking about the art school she just opened for children with learning disabilities. Ms. Galvani believes that practicing art can help students perform better in school. She will explain why, and she will also talk about how her innovative school is organized. ⁷⁹Give us a call at 555-2020 and tell us what you'd like us to ask Ms. Galvani.

안녕하세요. 여러분은 〈브러시 스트로크〉를 듣고 계십니다. ⁷⁷오늘의 특별 초대 손님은 재키 갈바니 씨인데요. 이분의 그림을 7월 한 달 내내 스톤빌에 있는 매디슨 미술관에서 보실 수 있습니다. 본인의 예술 작품뿐만 아니라, ⁷⁸갈바니 씨는 본인이 얼마 전 학습 장애 아동을 위해 문을 연 미술 학교에 대해서도 이야기해 줄 예정입니다. 갈바니 씨는 미술을 연습하는 것이 학생들로 하여금 학교에서 더 나은 성취를 얻도록 도움을 줄 수 있다고 믿고 있습니다. 그녀는 그 이유를 설명해 줄 것이고, 그녀의 혁신적인 학교가 어떻게 조직되어 있는지도 이야기해 줄 것입니다. ⁷⁹저희에게 555-2020번으로 전화 주셔서 저희가 갈바니 씨에게 물어봤으면 하는 것을 말씀해 주세요.

어휘 in addition to ~일 뿐 아니라, ~에 더하여 artwork 예술 작품, 미술품 learning disability 학습 장애 perform 성취하다, 수행하다 innovative 혁신적인 organize 조직하다, 구성하다

여 아니에요. 역에서 나가지 않으셨으니까 지금 가지고 계신 걸 계속 쓰시면 됩니다.

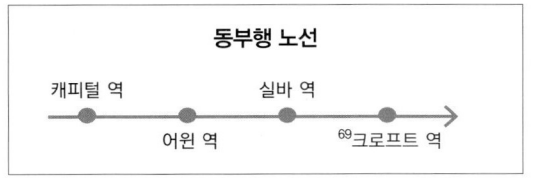

어휘 get to ~에 도착하다, 닿다 arena (원형) 경기장[공연장] get off (탈것에서) 내리다(↔ get on ~에 타다) eastbound 동쪽으로 향하는

68. 남자가 하고 싶어 하는 일은?

(A) 스포츠 시설 찾기
(B) 지도 가져가기
(C) 기차표 변경하기
(D) 극장에 가기

해설 단서 (68)에서 축구 경기를 보러 서니베일 경기장에 가려고 한다고 했으므로 정답은 (A). 대화 중에 map이나 ticket 등이 언급된 것만 듣고 착각하여 (B)나 (C)를 답으로 고르면 안 된다.

패러프레이징 [단서] get to the Sunnyvale Arena to see a soccer game → [정답] Find a sports facility

69. 시각 자료에서, 남자가 가라고 들은 정거장은?

(A) 캐피털 역
(B) 어윈 역
(C) 실바 역
(D) 크로프트 역

해설 지도나 노선도가 나올 경우, 단순히 세부 사항을 확인하는 다른 도표 문제와 달리 설명이 길어질 수 있으므로, 대화를 들을 때 집중력을 유지해야 한다. 단서 (69)에서 현재 있는 어윈 역에서 다시 동부행 열차에 탄 뒤 두 번째 정거장에서 내리라고 했다. 지하철 노선도를 나타내는 도표를 보면 어윈 역에서 화살표 방향으로 두 번째 정거장은 크로프트 역이므로 정답은 (D).

70. 남자가 걱정하는 것은?

(A) 표를 또 사야 하는 것
(B) 혼자 자신의 짐을 옮기는 것
(C) 다음 열차를 놓치는 것
(D) 붐비는 역을 뚫고 걸어가는 것

패러프레이징 [단서] need to pay for another ticket → [정답] Having to buy another ticket

PART 4

미 🎧
Questions 71-73 refer to the following announcement.

May I have your attention, please? Today we are holding a special sales event to commemorate our five-year anniversary. ⁷¹Power tools, paint, and more are on sale throughout the store. In addition, ⁷²one of our staff members will be demonstrating basic drilling techniques in our showroom in the west wing for the next thirty minutes. And ⁷³if you're interested in more do-it-yourself projects, visit our customer service counter to enroll in our next workshop for beginners on March 8. Thank you for choosing Garcia's for all of your hardware needs.

주목해 주십시오, 여러분. 오늘 저희는 5주년을 기념하기 위해 특별 할인 행사를 열고 있습니다. ⁷¹전동 공구, 페인트 및 그 외 많은 상품이 매장 전체에서 할인 판매 중입니다. 게다가, ⁷²저희 직원 중 한 명이 지금부터 30분 동안 건물 서관에 있는 저희 전시실에서 기초 드릴 기술을 시연할 예정입니다. 그리고 ⁷³더 많은 손수 하기 프로젝트에 관심이 있으신 분들은 저희 고객 서비스 카운터에 방문하셔서 3월 8일에 있을 초보자를 위한 저희 다음 워크숍에 등록하시기 바랍니다. 철물이 필요하실 때면 가르시아스를 찾아 주셔서 감사합니다.

어휘 commemorate 기념하다 power tool 전동 공구 throughout ~의 전체에 걸쳐, ~ 도처에 demonstrate (사용법을) 보여 주다, 설명하다 showroom 전시실 wing 부속 건물 do-it-yourself (수리 · 조립 등을) 손수 하기 enroll in ~에 등록하다 hardware 《집합명사》 철물, 장비

71. 청자들이 있을 것 같은 곳은?

(A) 패션쇼
(B) 예술 교육 기관
(C) 철물점
(D) 시민 문화 회관

해설 청자들이 있는 장소, 즉 전반적인 내용을 묻는 문제이므로 도입부를 잘 들어야 한다. 단서 (71)에서 전동 공구, 페인트 등이 매장에서 할인 판매 중이라고 하는 것으로 보아 정답은 (C).

72. 화자에 따르면, 서관에서 발견할 수 있는 것은?

(A) 판촉 영상
(B) 시연회
(C) 무료 샘플들
(D) 그림들

W All right. Let me check if we have someone available. ⁶⁶When is your conference?

M It's on November 3. ⁶⁷We need someone for the whole day, seven hours total. It would be nice if the person had a background in science. There might be a bit of technical language.

W All right. We do have an interpreter who fits that profile. Mr. Yamura has a degree in chemistry and has a lot of experience interpreting for science conferences.

M Perfect. What are your rates?

남 여보세요, 저는 인터그로우스 사의 루크 헤이스팅스입니다. ⁶⁵저는 곧 있을 학회 준비를 담당하고 있습니다. 저희는 영어를 일본어로 통역해 주실 분이 필요합니다.

여 알겠습니다. 가능하신 분이 있는지 확인해 보겠습니다. ⁶⁶학회가 언제인가요?

남 11월 3일입니다. ⁶⁷저희는 온종일, 총 7시간 동안 계실 분이 필요해요. 과학 분야에 배경지식을 가지고 계신 분이라면 좋을 것 같습니다. 전문 용어들이 약간 있을 수 있거든요.

여 알겠어요. 저희에게 그 요건에 꼭 맞는 통역사가 있습니다. 야무라 씨는 화학 학위가 있고 과학 학회에서 통역한 경험이 풍부합니다.

남 완벽하네요. 요금이 어떻게 되나요?

통역료	
시수	시간당 요금
1시간	80달러
2-4시간	75달러
5-6시간	70달러
⁶⁷6시간 이상	65달러

어휘 make arrangements for ~을 준비하다 upcoming 곧 있을, 다가오는 conference 학회, 회의 interpret 통역하다 a bit of 소량의 ~ technical language 전문 용어 fit 꼭 맞다 profile 인물 개요 chemistry 화학

65. 남자의 신분은?
(A) 행사 기획자
(B) 언어 전문가
(C) 정보 기술 전문가
(D) 화학 교수

해설 남자가 자기소개로 한 말을 통해 남자의 신분을 알 수 있다. 단서 (65)에서 곧 있을 학회 준비를 담당하고 있다고 했으므로 정답은 (A). 대화 후반부에 나오는 technical이나 chemistry 등을 단편적으로 듣고 착각하여 (C)나 (D)를 정답으로 고르지 않도록 주의한다.

패러프레이징 [단서] I'm in charge of making the arrangements for an upcoming conference → [정답] An event organizer

66. 여자가 요청한 정보는?
(A) 행사 날짜
(B) 행사장 주소
(C) 필요한 언어
(D) 등록비

패러프레이징 [단서] When is your conference? → [정답] The date of the event

67. 시각 자료에서, 남자가 시간당 지불할 것 같은 금액은?
(A) 80달러
(B) 75달러
(C) 70달러
(D) 65달러

해설 단서 (67)에서 총 7시간 동안 있을 통역사가 필요하다고 했는데 시간당 통역료를 나타내는 도표에서 6시간 이상 통역 시 시간당 요금은 65달러이므로 정답은 (D).

영 미

Questions 68-70 refer to the following conversation and subway map.

W You look a bit lost, sir. Can I help you with anything?

M I'm not sure I'm in the right place. ⁶⁸I'm trying to get to the Sunnyvale Arena to see a soccer game, but I think I got off the subway too early.

W You did. If you look at this map, ⁶⁹you'll see that you're here at Irwin Station. You need to get back on the eastbound train and get off at the second stop from here.

M ⁷⁰Oh, no. Does that mean I need to pay for another ticket?

W No. You can still use the one you have since you didn't leave the station.

여 길을 잃으신 것 같네요. 제가 좀 도와드릴까요?

남 제가 맞는 장소에 있는 건지 잘 모르겠네요. ⁶⁸저는 축구 경기를 보러 서니베일 경기장에 가려고 하는 중인데, 지하철에서 너무 일찍 내린 것 같아요.

여 그러셨네요. 이 지도를 보시면, ⁶⁹여기 어윈 역에 계시다는 걸 아실 수 있을 거예요. 동부행 열차에 다시 타셔서, 여기에서 두 번째 정거장에서 내리셔야 합니다.

남 ⁷⁰아, 이런. 그 말은 제가 표를 또 사야 한다는 말인가요?

61. 남자가 자신이 하겠다고 말한 일은?

(A) 메뉴 품목 고르기
(B) 식당 예약하기
(C) 식사 준비하기
(D) 내빈에게 연락하기

패러프레이징 [단서] choosing what kind of food to order → [정답] Select menu items

호 미 🎧
Questions 62-64 refer to the following conversation and list.

M	Hi. This is Akash Bahri. Is it too late to change an order I placed this morning?
W	Let's see, Mr. Bahri … No, it's okay. Your order hasn't been processed yet.
M	Great. I originally wanted the Lancaster brand, but [62, 63]now that I took a closer look at the catalog, I found one I like better —the Saldana brand.
W	All right. It's a bit more expensive than the Lancaster and Reiser brands, but getting the right color is the most important thing.
M	I agree. I think I need two cans of it, but I'm worried it won't be enough.
W	[64]If you tell me the length and width of your room's walls, I can calculate that for you.
남	여보세요. 저는 아카시 바리입니다. 오늘 아침에 제가 넣은 주문을 변경하기에 너무 늦었나요?
여	어디 볼까요, 바리 씨… 아니요, 괜찮습니다. 고객님의 주문은 아직 처리되지 않았습니다.
남	잘됐네요. 제가 원래는 랭커스터 브랜드를 원했습니다만, [62, 63]이제 카탈로그를 더 자세히 살펴보니, 더 마음에 드는 걸로 샐다나 브랜드를 찾아서요.
여	좋습니다. 그게 랭커스터와 레이저 브랜드보다는 조금 더 비싸지만, 알맞은 색상을 구하는 게 가장 중요한 일이니까요.
남	맞습니다. 제 생각에는 그걸로 2캔이 필요할 것 같은데, 충분하지 않을까 봐 걱정이 되네요.
여	[64]고객님 방에 있는 벽의 세로와 가로 길이를 말씀해 주시면, 제가 고객님께 필요량을 계산해 드릴 수 있습니다.

짙은 황갈색 색조	
브랜드	제품 번호
브리지포트	147
랭커스터	295
레이저	466
[63]샐다나	803

어휘 place an order 주문하다 take a look at ~을 보다 length 세로, 길이 width 가로, 폭 calculate 계산하다, 산출하다

62. 남자가 마음을 바꾼 이유는?

(A) 동료의 의견을 물어봤다.
(B) 무료 샘플을 테스트해 봤다.
(C) 더 저렴한 제품을 찾았다.
(D) 제품 카탈로그를 다시 살펴봤다.

패러프레이징 [단서] I took a closer look at the catalog → [정답] He reviewed a product catalog.

63. 시각 자료에서, 남자가 구매할 제품은?

(A) 제품 147
(B) 제품 295
(C) 제품 466
(D) 제품 803

해설 대화에서는 페인트 브랜드명이 세 가지나 나오지만, 남자가 구매하는 것을 고르는 문제이므로 남자의 말에서 정답을 찾을 수 있다. 단서 (63)에서 샐다나 브랜드의 색상이 더 마음에 든다고 했고 브랜드별 제품 번호를 나타내는 도표에서 해당 브랜드의 제품 번호는 803이므로 정답은 (D).

64. 남자에게 하도록 요청된 일은?

(A) 나중에 다시 전화하기
(B) 방 치수 제공하기
(C) 온라인으로 주문 양식 업데이트하기
(D) 사용하지 않은 제품 몇 개를 반품하기

패러프레이징 [단서] tell me the length and width of your room's walls → [정답] Provide room measurements

미 미 🎧
Questions 65-67 refer to the following conversation and price list.

M	Hello, this is Luke Hastings from Intergrowth Corp. [65]I'm in charge of making the arrangements for an upcoming conference. We need someone to interpret English into Japanese.

여1	그걸 현금으로 내도 되나요?
남	물론이죠. 제가 알렉산드라 씨에게 이것을 처리해 달라고 하겠습니다. 알렉산드라 씨, 브룩스 씨의 셔틀버스에 대해 현금 결제를 처리해 주시겠어요?
여2	그럼요. 그리고 다음 셔틀버스는 15분 정도 후에 출발합니다.
여1	승차권이 필요한가요?
여2	아니요. 그냥 손님의 성함을 제가 승객 명단에 추가해 드릴게요. ⁵⁸영수증이 필요하신가요?
여1	⁵⁸네, 주세요. 회사에서 환급받고 싶거든요.

어휘 owe (돈을) 빚지고 있다 take care of ~을 처리하다 process 처리하다; 과정, 절차 payment 지불, 지급 depart 출발하다, 떠나다 reimburse 환급하다, 상환하다

56. 대화가 이루어지고 있을 것 같은 곳은?
(A) 버스 터미널
(B) 공항
(C) 호텔
(D) 극장

57. 남자에 따르면, 추가 요금의 이유는?
(A) 교통편 서비스
(B) 객실 업그레이드
(C) 해약금
(D) 보증금

패러프레이징 [단서] the airport shuttle → [정답] A transportation service

58. 알렉산드라 씨가 다음에 브룩스 씨에게 줄 것 같은 것은?
(A) 승차권
(B) 영수증
(C) 일정표
(D) 명함

해설 대화 끝부분 여자들의 말에 단서가 있다. 단서 (58)에서 영수증이 필요하냐고 묻는 알렉산드라 씨의 질문에 브룩스 씨가 Yes라고 하면서 영수증을 달라고 했으므로 정답은 (B). 대화 중간에 브룩스 씨가 승차권이 필요한지 묻는 것만 듣고 착각하여 (A)를 정답으로 고르지 않도록 주의하자.

Questions 59-61 refer to the following conversation.

W	Fred, ⁵⁹did you pick the venue for the party yet? We only have a month left. We should reserve a place now.
M	It's going to be at Mariano's Restaurant. But I haven't reserved it yet because I'm still not sure about the date. ⁵⁹We had decided December 20, but many people can't make it that day.
W	Oh, it's true that many people are going on vacation at that time. ⁶⁰Do you want me to send an e-mail asking if people would prefer the first week of December?
M	⁶⁰That would be great. ⁶¹In the meantime, I'll start choosing what kind of food to order. Mariano's will want to know what to prepare in advance.
여	프레드 씨, ⁵⁹파티 장소는 이제 고르셨어요? 우리 딱 한 달밖에 안 남았어요. 이제는 장소를 예약해야 해요.
남	파티는 마리아노스 레스토랑에서 있을 예정이에요. 하지만 아직도 날짜를 잘 모르기 때문에 아직 예약은 안 했어요. ⁵⁹12월 20일로 정했었는데, 많은 사람이 그날 안 된다고 하네요.
여	아, 그때는 많이들 휴가를 가는 게 사실이죠. ⁶⁰제가 사람들이 12월 첫째 주를 선호할지 물어보는 이메일을 보내 볼까요?
남	⁶⁰그거 아주 좋겠네요. ⁶¹그동안에 저는 어떤 음식을 주문할지 고르기 시작할게요. 마리아노스에서 사전에 무엇을 준비해야 할지 알고 싶어 할 거예요.

어휘 pick 고르다 venue 장소 reserve 예약하다 make it (모임 등에) 가다, 참석하다 in the meantime 그동안에 in advance 사전에

59. 화자들이 주로 논의하고 있는 것은?
(A) 휴가 계획
(B) 개업식
(C) 연말 행사
(D) 출장 요리 서비스

해설 단서 (59)를 보면 대화 초반에 여자가 파티 장소를 골랐냐고 물었고, 대화 중반에 남자가 파티의 날짜를 12월 20일로 정했었다고 말했으므로 화자들이 논의하고 있는 것이 12월, 즉 연말에 있을 행사라는 것을 유추할 수 있다. 따라서 정답은 (C).

패러프레이징 [단서] December 20 → [정답] end-of-year

60. 여자가 자신의 동료들에게 물어볼 것은?
(A) 원하는 장소의 종류가 무엇인지
(B) 휴가가 언제인지
(C) 누구를 초대하려고 계획하는지
(D) 어떤 날짜를 선호하는지

패러프레이징 [단서] if people would prefer the first week of December → [정답] Which date they prefer

W   Thank you, Mr. Raja. [53, 54]I think your firm can give us the best advice for solving the pollution problem at Centennial Beach.

M   Yes, I'll walk you through a few options today. [54]We'll focus both on removing trash and other waste from the shoreline as well as cleaning up the picnic facilities. [55]A lot of the work can be done by volunteers.

W   [55]Well, I'm not sure we can get enough people for that.

M   Don't worry. Our preliminary research shows that plenty of residents are willing to share their time.

남   좋은 아침이에요, 커밍스 씨. [53]그린 환경 컨설팅을 대표하여, 자치주 위원회장님을 이곳에 모시게 되어 너무나 기쁘다는 말씀을 드리고 싶습니다.

여   고맙습니다. 라자 씨. [53, 54]귀사에서 저희에게 센테니얼 해변의 오염 문제를 해결하기 위한 최고의 조언을 해 주실 수 있을 것이라고 생각합니다.

남   네, 오늘 제가 몇 가지 선택 사항을 단계별로 설명해 드리겠습니다. [54]저희는 소풍 시설 정화뿐만 아니라 해안가의 쓰레기 및 기타 폐기물 제거 둘 다에 중점을 두려고 합니다. [55]자원봉사자들이 많은 작업을 해 줄 수 있습니다.

여   [55]음, 그 일에 필요한 사람들을 저희가 충분히 구할 수 있을지 모르겠네요.

남   걱정하지 마십시오. 저희 사전 조사에 의하면 많은 주민이 기꺼이 자기 시간을 내어 줄 의향이 있습니다.

어휘 on behalf of ~을 대표[대신]하여   environmental 환경의, 환경과 관련된   county 자치주[군]   commission 위원회, 위원단   pollution 오염, 공해   walk A through B (단계별로 차례차례) A에게 B를 보여 주다   preliminary 예비의   plenty of 많은   resident 거주자, 주민   be willing to do 기꺼이 ~하다

53. 남자가 종사할 것 같은 분야는?
(A) 관광
(B) 생태 환경
(C) 건설
(D) 농업

패러프레이징 [단서] Environmental → [정답] Ecology

54. 남자가 설명할 프로젝트의 종류는?
(A) 지역 정화 사업
(B) 건물 수리
(C) 마케팅 캠페인
(D) 회사 야유회

해설 단서 (54)에서 여자가 남자에게 특정 해변의 오염 문제 해결을 위한 조언을 기대한다고 했고, 남자가 시설 정화와 쓰레기 제거에 중점을 둘 거라고 했으므로 정답은 (A). 단서 앞에 위치한 I'll walk you through ~처럼 앞으로 설명될 내용을 소개할 때 자주 사용되는 표현을 알아 두면 단서를 놓치지 않고 들을 수 있다.

패러프레이징 [단서] removing trash and other waste from the shoreline as well as cleaning up the picnic facilities → [정답] cleanup

55. 여자가 걱정하는 것은?
(A) 예산 범위 내에 머물기
(B) 공식적인 허가 받기
(C) 충분한 자원봉사자 찾기
(D) 제시간에 연구 시작하기

패러프레이징 [단서] get enough people for that → [정답] Finding enough volunteers

🎧 영 미 미

Questions 56-58 refer to the following conversation with three speakers.

W1   Good morning. [56]I'd like to check out. Here is the keycard for my room.

M   All right. Let's see … Ms. Brooks, everything for your room has been paid for, but [57]you owe twenty dollars extra for the airport shuttle.

W1   Can I pay that in cash?

M   Of course. I'll let Alexandra take care of that for you. Alexandra, could you process a cash payment for the shuttle for Ms. Brooks?

W2   Certainly. And the next shuttle departs in about fifteen minutes.

W1   Do I need a ticket?

W2   No, I'll just add your name to the passenger list. [58]Do you need a receipt?

W1   [58]Yes, please. I want to get reimbursed from my company.

여1   좋은 아침이에요. [56]체크아웃을 하고 싶은데요. 여기 제 방 카드 키입니다.

남   좋습니다. 어디 볼까요… 브룩스 씨, 방에 관련된 비용은 모두 지불되었지만, [57]공항 셔틀버스 때문에 추가로 20달러를 지불하셔야 합니다.

47. 화자들이 근무할 것 같은 사업체의 종류는?
(A) 배달 서비스 업체
(B) 인쇄 회사
(C) 의류 직판장
(D) 보험사

> 해설 단서 (47)에서 현수막 작업을 하고 있다고 말한 것으로 보아 화자들은 인쇄 업체에서 일하는 것임을 알 수 있으므로 정답은 (B). 대화 초반에 AR Insurance가 언급된 것만 듣고 착각하여 (D)를 정답으로 고르지 않도록 주의한다.

48. 남자에 따르면, 문제점은?
(A) 물품이 부족하다.
(B) 주문서 양식에 오류가 있었다.
(C) 직원이 충분하지 않다.
(D) 고객이 불만을 제기했다.

> 패러프레이징 [단서] we don't have that many in stock
> → [정답] There is a shortage of supplies.

49. 화자들이 하기로 결정한 것은?
(A) 추가 근무하기
(B) 장비 구매하기
(C) 프로젝트 취소하기
(D) 마감 연장 요청하기

> 패러프레이징 [단서] ask Ms. Evans for more time
> → [정답] Request a deadline extension

영 미 🎧
Questions 50-52 refer to the following conversation.

W Did you find everything you were looking for today?

M Yes, thanks. ⁵⁰I always love shopping at this store. There are so many items to choose from. Oh, and ⁵¹I'd like to use this coupon, please.

W ⁵¹I'm sorry, but you have to purchase at least fifty dollars' worth of goods to use this. Maybe you can use it the next time you come in.

M All right. And I've filled out this form for your loyalty program. ⁵²Do I need to take it to the customer service desk?

W I'll go there shortly. Don't worry about it.

여 오늘 찾으시는 물건은 모두 찾으셨나요?

남 네, 고맙습니다. ⁵⁰저는 항상 이 상점에서 쇼핑하는 게 좋아요. 고를 수 있는 제품이 정말 많거든요. 아, 그리고 ⁵¹이 쿠폰을 사용하고 싶어요.

여 ⁵¹죄송하지만, 이 쿠폰을 사용하시려면 적어도 50달러어치 상품을 구매하셔야 합니다. 아마 이건 다음번에 오실 때 사용하실 수 있겠는데요.

남 알겠어요. 그리고 제가 이 회원 혜택 프로그램 양식을 작성했는데요. ⁵²제가 이걸 고객 서비스 창구로 가져가야 하나요?

여 제가 곧 거기로 갈 거예요. 걱정하지 마세요.

> 어휘 purchase 구매하다 at least 적어도 worth (얼마)어치
> loyalty program 회원 혜택 프로그램 shortly 곧, 얼마 안 되어

50. 남자가 상점에 대해 좋아한다고 말한 것은?
(A) 폭넓은 선택
(B) 친절한 직원들
(C) 편리한 영업시간
(D) 회원 적립

> 패러프레이징 [단서] There are so many items to choose from.
> → [정답] Its wide selection

51. 남자가 자신의 쿠폰을 사용할 수 없는 이유는?
(A) 이미 만료되었다.
(B) 최소 구매액이 있다.
(C) 다른 상점용이다.
(D) 다른 혜택과 함께 사용할 수 없다.

> 패러프레이징 [단서] purchase at least fifty dollars' worth of goods → [정답] a minimum purchase amount

52. 여자가 "제가 곧 거기로 갈 거예요"라고 말한 의미는?
(A) 남자를 대신해 서류를 가져다 놓을 수 있다.
(B) 남자가 물품들을 들고 가는 것을 도와줄 것이다.
(C) 곧 휴식을 취할 계획이다.
(D) 남자에게 어떤 상품을 찾아 주려고 할 것이다.

> 해설 여자가 한 말의 의미를 문맥을 통해 찾아내는 문제로 해당 표현의 앞뒤를 주의 깊게 들어야 한다. 단서 (52)를 보면 해당 표현은 고객 서비스 창구로 회원 혜택 프로그램 양식을 가져가야 하냐고 묻는 남자의 말에 대한 여자의 답변으로, 여자가 남자를 대신해 창구에 해당 서류를 가져갈 것이라는 의미임을 알 수 있으므로 정답은 (A).

> 패러프레이징 [단서] take it to the customer service desk
> → [정답] drop off some paperwork

미 미 🎧
Questions 53-55 refer to the following conversation.

M Good morning, Ms. Cummings. ⁵³On behalf of Green Environmental Consulting, I'd like to say how much of a pleasure it is to have the head of the county commission here.

🎧 미 호
Questions 44-46 refer to the following conversation.

W Hi, Justin. I saw that there's an interpersonal skills workshop coming up. ⁴⁴Do you know how to sign up for it?

M As far as I know, there's a form we need to fill out on the host company's Web site. It's explained in the promotional material, but ⁴⁵I haven't had time to read through it. Liam is on vacation, so I'm trying to complete his expense report for him.

W You shouldn't have to do that alone. ⁴⁶I could look over part of it so we have time to find out more about the workshop together.

M Thanks! I really appreciate that.

여 안녕하세요, 저스틴 씨. 제가 대인 관계 기술 워크숍이 곧 열린다는 것을 봤어요. ⁴⁴어떻게 등록하는지 아세요?

남 제가 알기로는, 주최사의 웹사이트에서 작성해야 하는 양식이 있어요. 홍보 자료에 설명이 되어 있는데, ⁴⁵저는 그걸 자세히 읽어 볼 시간이 없었어요. 리엄 씨가 휴가 중이어서 제가 그를 대신해서 그의 비용 보고서를 마무리하려고 하는 중이거든요.

여 그걸 혼자 하시면 안 되죠. ⁴⁶제가 보고서의 일부를 검토하면 함께 워크숍에 대해 더 알아볼 시간을 가질 수 있을 거예요.

남 고마워요! 정말 감사합니다.

어휘 interpersonal 대인 관계에 관련된 come up (어떤 행사나 때가) 다가오다 sign up for ~에 등록하다 as far as ~하는 한, ~에 관한 한 promotional 홍보의 expense 비용 look over ~을 살펴보다 find out (~을) 알아내다 appreciate 고마워하다, 감사하다

44. 화자들이 주로 논의하고 있는 것은?
(A) 고용 결정
(B) 직원 평가
(C) 등록 절차
(D) 출장

패러프레이징 [단서] how to sign up for it → [정답] A registration process

45. 남자가 자료를 읽을 수 없었던 이유는?
(A) 그의 컴퓨터에 문제가 있었다.
(B) 최근에 휴가에서 돌아왔다.
(C) 중요한 고객을 방문해야 했다.
(D) 동료의 업무를 하는 중이었다.

패러프레이징 [단서] I'm trying to complete his expense report for him → [정답] He was working on a coworker's task.

46. 여자가 "그걸 혼자 하시면 안 되죠"라고 말한 의도는?
(A) 신입 사원 교육을 도울 것이다.
(B) 리엄 씨에게 추가 작업을 맡길 수 있다.
(C) 남자가 보고서를 마치는 것을 도울 수 있다.
(D) 남자의 상사와 이야기할 것이다.

해설 여자가 한 말의 의도를 문맥을 통해 찾아내는 문제로 해당 표현의 앞뒤를 주의 깊게 들어야 한다. 해당 표현 바로 뒤에 있는 단서 (46)에서 여자가 보고서 일부를 검토해서 그 업무를 빨리 끝내면 함께 워크숍에 대해 더 알아볼 시간을 가질 수 있을 거라고 하는 것으로 보아 정답은 (C).

🎧 미 미
Questions 47-49 refer to the following conversation.

M Amy Evans from AR Insurance just called. ⁴⁷We're working on a few banners for her company, and she said she'd like twelve instead of three.

W Twelve? That's great news, isn't it?

M Well, ⁴⁸we don't have that many in stock at the moment, and we can't get more of the size she needs until next week.

W When was this order originally due?

M April 2, but ⁴⁹I can ask Ms. Evans for more time. She didn't seem to be in much of a hurry.

W ⁴⁹Okay, that's a good idea. Let me know what she says.

남 AR 보험사의 에이미 에번스 씨가 방금 전화했어요. ⁴⁷그녀의 회사에서 주문한 현수막 몇 개를 우리가 작업 중인데, 3개가 아니라 12개로 하고 싶다고 하더군요.

여 12개요? 정말 좋은 소식이네요, 그렇죠?

남 글쎄요, ⁴⁸지금 우리가 그렇게 많이는 재고로 갖고 있지 않고, 다음 주까지도 그녀가 필요로 하는 크기를 더 구할 수가 없어요.

여 이 주문은 원래 언제가 마감이었죠?

남 4월 2일인데, ⁴⁹제가 에번스 씨에게 시간을 더 요청할 수 있어요. 많이 급한 것 같지는 않았거든요.

여 ⁴⁹알겠어요, 좋은 생각이네요. 그녀가 뭐라고 하는지 알려 주세요.

어휘 insurance 보험 work on ~을 작업하다 banner 현수막 in stock 비축되어, 재고로(↔ out of stock 품절이 되어) at the moment 지금 originally 원래, 본래 due ~하기로 되어 있는[예정된] in a hurry 서둘러, 급히

(B) 서비스 비용
(C) 임원 수
(D) 회의 시작 시간

패러프레이징 [단서] How much would it be to get the report reprinted using the express service? → [정답] The cost of a service

40. 여자가 하기를 제안한 일은?
(A) 다른 인쇄 업체 이용하기
(B) 플레처 지사에 연락하기
(C) 회의 날짜 변경하기
(D) 현장에서 일을 완료하기

해설 단서 (40)에서 여자가 사무실에 있는 프린터로 추가 페이지를 출력하는 것을 제안하고 있으므로 정답은 (D). 재출력한다는 것만 듣고 착각하여 (A)를 정답으로 고르지 않도록 한다.

패러프레이징 [단서] print out supplementary pages using the printer here at the office → [정답] Completing a task on site

호 미 미

Questions 41-43 refer to the following conversation with three speakers.

M1 Thanks for stopping by the store today, ma'am. Are you shopping for anything specific?

W   ⁴¹I'm in the market for a new smartphone because my current one keeps having problems.

M1 All right. I mainly deal with our large appliances such as refrigerators, so let me check with my coworker. Barrett, this woman wants to replace her current phone.

M2 Hello, ma'am. We have quite a few models to choose from, but ⁴²I recommend the Stinson brand. Its products work well for years with the same level of performance.

W   That's not a brand I'm familiar with, actually.

M2 No problem. ⁴³I can show you the main features on this display model. It'll just take a moment of your time.

W   ⁴³All right. Thank you.

남1 오늘 매장에 들러 주셔서 감사합니다. 고객님. 특별히 찾으시는 것이 있나요?

여   제가 지금 쓰는 스마트폰이 자주 문제를 일으켜서 ⁴¹새 스마트폰을 사는 데 관심이 있어요.

남1 알겠습니다. 저는 주로 냉장고 같은 대형 가전을 담당하고 있어서, 제 동료에게 확인해 보겠습니다. 배릿 씨. 이 여자분께서 현재 쓰시는 전화기를 바꾸고 싶으시대요.

남2 안녕하세요, 고객님. 저희는 선택할 수 있는 기종이 상당수 있습니다만, ⁴²저는 스틴슨 브랜드를 추천해 드립니다. 여기 제품이 몇 년을 써도 같은 수준의 성능으로 잘 작동하거든요.

여   사실, 저한테 익숙한 브랜드는 아니네요.

남2 문제없습니다. ⁴³이 진열 상품으로 주요 기능들을 보여 드릴 수 있습니다. 잠깐의 시간만 내 주시면 됩니다.

여   ⁴³좋아요. 고맙습니다.

어휘 stop by (~에) 잠시 들르다 specific 특정한, 구체적인 be in the market for ~의 구매에 관심이 있다 deal with ~을 다루다[처리하다] appliance 가전제품 quite a few 상당수(의) performance 성능, 실적 be familiar with ~에 익숙하다 feature 기능, 특징

41. 여자가 구매에 관심을 보이는 것은?
(A) 냉장고
(B) 텔레비전
(C) 스마트폰
(D) 소프트웨어 프로그램

해설 단서 (41)에서 새 스마트폰을 사는 데 관심이 있다고 했으므로 정답은 (C). 대화의 in the market for가 문제에서는 interested in buying으로 패러프레이징되었다.

42. 배릿 씨가 스틴슨 브랜드를 권하는 이유는?
(A) 선택의 폭이 가장 넓다.
(B) 현재 할인 판매 중이다.
(C) 가장 인기 있는 브랜드이다.
(D) 오래가는 제품들이 있다.

패러프레이징 [단서] Its products work well for years with the same level of performance. → [정답] It has long-lasting products.

43. 여자가 다음에 할 것 같은 일은?
(A) 시연 보기
(B) 할인 요청하기
(C) 보증 연장하기
(D) 신청서 작성하기

해설 단서 (43)에서 점원인 배릿 씨가 여자에게 진열 상품을 가지고 주요 기능들을 보여 줄 수 있다며 시간을 내 달라고 하자 이에 여자는 좋다고 대답했으므로 시연을 보게 될 것임을 유추할 수 있다. 따라서 정답은 (A).

패러프레이징 [단서] show you the main features on this display model → [정답] a demonstration

W   Sure. ³⁷But first I'd like to get the final count for how many people will be here. That'll affect how I arrange the room.

M   No problem. I'll e-mail you the participant list right away.

여   도너번 씨, ³⁵마케팅 행사를 위한 제품 프레젠테이션은 모두 준비되었나요? 필요한 정보는 모두 가지고 계세요?

남   네, 가지고 있어요. 고맙습니다. ³⁶그런데 회의실 안 여기저기에 포스터를 붙여 주실 시간이 있으신지 궁금해요. 이미지와 통계를 보이게 해 두면 도움이 될 것 같아서요. ³⁵그렇게 하면 제품을 더 많이 파는 데 도움이 될 거예요.

여   물론이죠. ³⁷하지만 우선 여기에 몇 명이나 올 건지 최종 인원 수를 알고 싶어요. 그게 제가 회의실을 어떻게 배치할지에 영향을 줄 테니까요.

남   문제없습니다. 참가자 명단을 이메일로 즉시 보내 드릴게요.

어휘 put up 내붙이다, 게시하다   statistics (항상 복수형) 통계, 통계표   visible (눈에) 보이는, 알아볼 수 있는   count 총수, 총계   affect ~에 영향을 미치다   arrange 배치하다   participant 참가자

35. 화자들의 신분은?
(A) 영업 사원들
(B) 연구원들
(C) 강사들
(D) 사진작가들

해설 단서 (35)를 통해 화자들은 마케팅 행사의 제품 프레젠테이션을 준비하고 있음을 알 수 있고 포스터를 붙여 두면 제품을 더 많이 파는 데 도움이 될 거라고 했으므로 정답은 (A).

36. 남자가 여자에게 하도록 요청한 일은?
(A) 공급 업체에 바로 연락하기
(B) 자료를 전시하기
(C) 일정보다 앞서 프로젝트를 완료하기
(D) 개선을 위한 제안하기

패러프레이징 [단서] put up some posters → [정답] Put some information on display

37. 여자가 하고 싶다고 말한 일은?
(A) 재고 확인하기
(B) 요금 조정하기
(C) 회의 준비하기
(D) 참석자 수 확인하기

패러프레이징 [단서] get the final count for how many people will be here → [정답] Confirm the attendance

---

미 영 🎧
Questions 38-40 refer to the following conversation.

M   Good morning, Evelyn. ³⁸I was just reading over your report for the board meeting this afternoon, but I noticed that you left out the sales figures for the Fletcher branch.

W   Oh, no. Really? I've got the figures saved on my computer. ³⁹How much would it be to get the report reprinted using the express service?

M   Probably around one hundred dollars. They'd need to redo the entire document since the pages are bound together.

W   Hmm... In that case, ⁴⁰how about I just print out supplementary pages using the printer here at the office? It won't look as professional, but I'm sure the board members will understand our situation.

남   좋은 아침이에요, 에벌린 씨. ³⁸제가 오늘 오후에 있을 임원 회의를 위한 당신의 보고서를 막 읽고 있었는데, 당신이 플레처 지사의 매출액을 빠뜨린 것을 발견했어요.

여   아, 안 돼요. 정말이에요? 제가 매출액을 제 컴퓨터에는 저장해 뒀어요. ³⁹빠른 서비스를 이용해서 보고서를 재출력하게 하면 얼마나 들까요?

남   아마 백 달러 정도요. 페이지들이 함께 철해져 있어서 전체 문서를 다시 작업해야 할 거라서요.

여   음… 그렇다면, ⁴⁰제가 그냥 여기 사무실에 있는 프린터를 이용해서 추가 페이지를 출력하는 것은 어떨까요? 전문적으로 보이지는 않겠지만, 임원들도 분명 우리 상황을 이해해 줄 거예요.

어휘 read over ~을 꼼꼼히 읽다   board 이사회; 탑승하다   leave out ~을 빼다   sales figure (보통 복수형) 매출액   express 신속한, 급행의   bind 묶다, 매다   supplementary 보충의, 추가의   professional 전문적인

38. 남자가 언급한 문제점은?
(A) 임원 한 명이 아직 도착하지 않았다.
(B) 영업 판촉이 잘되지 않았다.
(C) 문서에서 어떤 정보가 누락되었다.
(D) 한 지사가 기대보다 더 실적이 나쁘다.

패러프레이징 [단서] your report / left out the sales figures for the Fletcher branch → [정답] A document / missing some information

39. 여자가 문의한 것은?
(A) 보고서 주제

31.

I need to get an anniversary gift at the mall.
(A) Thanks for the thoughtful present.
(B) You could just order one online.
(C) We've been married ten years.

저는 쇼핑몰에서 기념일 선물을 사야 해요.
(A) 사려 깊은 선물에 감사드립니다.
(B) 그냥 온라인으로 하나 주문할 수 있잖아요.
(C) 우리는 결혼한 지 10년이 되었어요.

해설 쇼핑몰에서 기념일 선물을 사야 한다는 말에 온라인으로 주문할 수 있다고 답한 (B)가 정답.

어휘 anniversary 기념일 thoughtful 사려 깊은, 배려심 있는

PART 3

Questions 32-34 refer to the following conversation.

W Hi, Mr. Carlson. ³²You said you wanted to speak to me about the order I submitted for supplies? Was there a problem with it?

M It's missing some data. You need to list the product code for each item that you're ordering. ³³Here is a catalog with pictures of all the available items and their codes. You can keep it.

W Thank you, and sorry about that. I wasn't sure how to complete the form because it was my first time doing it.

M I understand. ³⁴It would probably be helpful for you to check out the example that's posted on the company Web site. Then you can see exactly what to do.

여 안녕하세요, 칼슨 씨. ³²제가 비품 때문에 제출한 주문서에 대해 제게 하실 말씀이 있다고 하셨죠? 거기에 무슨 문제가 있던가요?

남 몇 가지 데이터가 누락되었어요. 주문하려는 물품 각각의 상품 코드 목록을 작성하셔야 해요. ³³여기 주문 가능한 모든 물품의 사진과 상품 코드가 있는 카탈로그예요. 이건 가지셔도 됩니다.

여 감사합니다. 그리고 죄송해요. 제가 처음 해 보는 거라서 양식을 어떻게 작성하는지 잘 몰랐어요.

남 이해합니다. ³⁴회사 웹사이트에 게시되어 있는 예시를 확인해 보는 게 아마 도움이 될 거예요. 그러면 무엇을 해야 할지 정확히 알 수 있거든요.

어휘 submit 제출하다 supplies (항상 복수형) 비품, 공급품 miss 빠뜨리다, 누락하다 available 구할[이용할] 수 있는 complete 작성하다 probably 아마 post (안내문 등을) 게시하다, 공고하다

32. 화자들이 논의하고 있는 것은?
(A) 제품 설명
(B) 좌석 배치도
(C) 출입 비밀번호
(D) 비품 주문

패러프레이징 [단서] the order I submitted for supplies → [정답] A supplies order

33. 남자가 여자에게 준 것은?
(A) 제품 카탈로그
(B) 신분증
(C) 새 양식
(D) 교육 안내서

패러프레이징 [단서] a catalog with pictures of all the available items and their codes → [정답] A product catalog

34. 남자가 하기를 권하는 것은?
(A) 주문 취소하기
(B) 동료에게 질문하기
(C) 온라인으로 예시 열람하기
(D) 미리 승인받기

해설 단서 (34)에서 남자가 여자에게 회사 웹사이트에 게시된 예시를 보는 것이 도움이 될 거라고 했으므로 정답은 (C).

패러프레이징 [단서] to check out the example that's posted on the company Web site → [정답] Viewing an example online

---

Questions 35-37 refer to the following conversation.

W Mr. Donovan, ³⁵is everything ready for the product presentation for the marketing event? Do you have all of the information you need?

M Yes, I do. Thanks. ³⁶But I'm wondering if you have time to put up some posters around the room. I think it would be helpful to have images and statistics visible. ³⁵It would help sell more products.

25. 영 미 🎧

What computer did they buy as a replacement?
(A) **Actually, I'm not sure.**
(B) Yes, that place is popular.
(C) Mine is brand-new.

그들이 교체용으로 무슨 컴퓨터를 샀나요?
(A) **사실, 저는 잘 몰라요.**
(B) 네, 그 장소는 인기가 있어요.
(C) 제 것은 완전 새것이에요.

해설 교체용으로 무슨 컴퓨터를 샀는지 묻는 질문에 잘 모르겠다고 답한 (A)가 정답.

어휘 replacement 교체[대체]물 actually 사실은, 실제로는 brand-new 아주 새로운, 신품의

26. 호 미 🎧

How much did you spend on your business trip?
(A) **Didn't you get the receipts I sent you?**
(B) I just need to meet a few clients.
(C) Five days in Rome.

출장에 비용을 얼마나 쓰셨어요?
(A) **제가 보내 드린 영수증들을 못 받으셨어요?**
(B) 저는 고객 몇 명을 좀 만나야 해요.
(C) 로마에서 5일이요.

해설 출장에서 비용을 얼마나 썼는지 묻는 질문에 자신이 보낸 영수증들을 못 받았냐고 반문한 (A)가 정답. (C)는 출장을 어디로, 얼마나 오래 다녀왔는지 묻는 질문에 적절한 답변이므로 오답.

27. 미 미 🎧

We should wear gloves when using this spray.
(A) Because my hands are cold.
(B) Spray it on the counter.
(C) **It does contain some chemicals.**

우리는 이 스프레이를 사용할 때 장갑을 껴야 합니다.
(A) 제 손이 차갑기 때문입니다.
(B) 판매대 위에 그것을 뿌리세요.
(C) **이것에는 정말 화학 성분이 좀 들어 있네요.**

해설 스프레이를 사용할 때 장갑을 껴야 한다는 말에 그것에 화학 성분이 들어 있다고 답한 (C)가 정답. (B)는 질문의 spray를 반복 사용한 오답으로 질문에서는 '스프레이'라는 의미의 명사로, 선택지에서는 '뿌리다'라는 의미의 동사로 쓰였다.

어휘 counter 판매대, 계산대 contain ~이 들어 있다 chemical 화학 물질

28. 호 미 🎧

Why hasn't the safety inspector arrived yet?
(A) Before it passes the inspection.
(B) **He called to cancel.**
(C) We can put on the safety gear.

안전 검사관은 왜 아직 도착하지 않았나요?
(A) 검사를 통과하기 전에요.
(B) **그 사람이 취소한다고 전화했어요.**
(C) 우리는 안전 장비를 착용할 수 있어요.

해설 안전 검사관이 아직 도착하지 않은 이유를 묻는 질문에 그가 취소한다고 전화했기 때문이라고 직접적인 이유로 답한 (B)가 정답.

어휘 inspector 검사관, 감독관 inspection 검사, 점검 cancel 취소하다 safety gear 안전 장비[장치]

29. 영 미 🎧

Are the rates for the Layton Hotel affordable?
(A) Of course you can stay at my home.
(B) For at least three nights.
(C) **Yes, they're not too expensive.**

레이턴 호텔의 요금은 적당한가요?
(A) 물론 저희 집에서 묵으셔도 됩니다.
(B) 최소 3박 동안이요.
(C) **네, 너무 비싸지는 않아요.**

해설 호텔 요금이 적당한지 묻는 질문에 Yes라고 하면서 너무 비싸지는 않다고 답한 (C)가 정답. (A)와 (B)는 Hotel에서 연상할 수 있는 stay와 three nights를 각각 이용한 오답.

어휘 rate 요금 affordable (가격이) 알맞은, 적당한

30. 미 호 🎧

Does your company handle residential or commercial cleaning?
(A) **Both are possible.**
(B) Jeffrey can handle it.
(C) I saw the commercial on TV.

귀사에서는 가정집 청소를 대행하시나요, 아니면 사업장 청소를 대행하시나요?
(A) **둘 다 가능합니다.**
(B) 제프리 씨가 그것을 처리할 수 있어요.
(C) 저는 TV에서 그 광고를 봤어요.

해설 업체에서 가정집 청소와 사업장 청소 둘 중 어떤 사업을 하는지 묻는 질문에 어느 한쪽을 선택하여 답하지 않고 둘 다 가능하다고 말한 (A)가 정답. (C)는 '상업의'와 '광고'라는 서로 다른 의미와 품사를 지닌 다의어 commercial을 이용한 오답.

어휘 handle 처리하다, 다루다 residential 주거의, 주택에 알맞은

19. 미 호 🎧

How do I get a library card?
(A) A wide range of books.
(B) For a week.
(C) Just fill out this form.

어떻게 도서 대출 카드를 받나요?
(A) 다양한 책들이요.
(B) 일주일 동안이요.
(C) 이 양식을 작성하기만 하세요.

해설 도서 대출 카드를 받는 방법을 묻는 질문에 양식을 작성하라고 답한 (C)가 정답. (B)는 대출 기간을 묻는 질문에 적절한 답변이므로 오답.

어휘 library card 도서 대출 카드 a wide range of 다양한, 광범위한 fill out a form 서식을 작성하다, 서식에 기입하다

20. 미 미 🎧

Could you help me carry this desk to the fourth floor?
(A) Sorry. I hurt my back yesterday.
(B) Did you check the directory?
(C) The flowers haven't been delivered yet.

이 책상을 4층으로 옮기는 것을 도와주시겠어요?
(A) 죄송해요. 제가 어제 허리를 다쳤어요.
(B) 건물 안내판을 확인하셨나요?
(C) 꽃이 아직 배달되지 않았어요.

해설 책상을 4층으로 옮기는 것을 도와달라는 요청에 미안하지만 다쳐서 안 된다고 우회적으로 거절한 (A)가 정답. (B)는 fourth floor에서 연상할 수 있는 directory를 이용한 오답.

어휘 directory (건물 내의) 안내판 deliver 배달하다

21. 호 영 🎧

Why was the meeting cut short?
(A) Tomorrow afternoon at three.
(B) Only for a short period of time.
(C) There wasn't much to discuss.

회의가 왜 갑자기 끝났죠?
(A) 내일 오후 3시요.
(B) 짧은 기간 동안만요.
(C) 논의할 게 많지 않았어요.

해설 회의가 갑자기 끝난 이유를 묻는 질문에 논의할 것이 많지 않았다며 직접적인 이유로 답한 (C)가 정답.

어휘 cut short 갑자기 끝내다, 가로막다

22. 미 미 🎧

When does the art auction begin?
(A) We enjoyed the exhibit.
(B) Paintings and sculptures.
(C) Check the invitation.

미술품 경매는 언제 시작하나요?
(A) 우리는 전시회를 즐겁게 관람했어요.
(B) 회화와 조각품이요.
(C) 초대장을 확인하세요.

해설 미술품 경매의 시작 시간을 묻는 질문에 초대장을 확인하라며 모른다고 우회적으로 답한 (C)가 정답. (A)와 (B)는 art에서 연상할 수 있는 exhibit과 Paintings and sculptures를 각각 이용한 오답.

어휘 auction 경매 exhibit 전시회 sculpture 조각품 invitation 초대장, 초대

23. 호 미 🎧

The camera is out of focus.
(A) I'll try adjusting it.
(B) From a new photo studio.
(C) I'm focusing on the presentation.

카메라가 초점이 맞지 않아요.
(A) 제가 한번 맞춰 볼게요.
(B) 새로 생긴 사진관으로부터요.
(C) 저는 발표에 중점을 두고 있습니다.

해설 카메라가 초점이 맞지 않는다는 말에 자신이 한번 초점을 맞춰 보겠다고 답한 (A)가 정답. (C)는 질문의 focus를 반복 사용한 오답으로 질문에서는 '초점'이라는 의미의 명사로, 선택지에서는 '중점을 두다'라는 의미의 동사로 쓰였다.

어휘 out of focus 초점이 맞지 않는 try doing (시험 삼아) ~해 보다 adjust 조정[조절]하다 focus on ~에 중점을 두다, ~에 초점을 맞추다

24. 미 미 🎧

Who will oversee the merger negotiations?
(A) To gain more market share.
(B) That hasn't been determined yet.
(C) Sometime next month.

누가 합병 협상을 감독할 건가요?
(A) 시장 점유율을 더 높이기 위해서요.
(B) 그건 아직 결정되지 않았어요.
(C) 다음 달 언젠가요.

해설 누가 합병 협상을 감독할 것인지 묻는 질문에 아직 결정되지 않았다고 답한 (B)가 정답.

어휘 oversee (작업·활동 등을) 감독하다 merger 합병 negotiation (보통 복수형) 협상, 교섭 market share 시장 점유율 determine 결정하다

고객 파일도 거기에 보관한다고 답한 (A)가 정답. (B)는 manuals에서 연상할 수 있는 assemble을 이용한 오답.

어휘 user manual 사용 설명서 assemble 조립하다 daily 매일

13. 호 미 🎧

Are you writing the survey, or is Clyde?
(A) **We're doing it together.**
(B) More than a hundred respondents.
(C) By market research.

당신이 설문 조사를 작성하고 있나요, 아니면 클라이드 씨가 작성하고 있나요?
(A) **저희는 그걸 함께 하고 있어요.**
(B) 100명 이상의 응답자들이요.
(C) 시장 조사로요.

해설 설문 조사를 당신과 클라이드 씨 중 누가 작성하고 있는지 묻는 질문에 둘이 함께 작성하고 있다고 답한 (A)가 정답. (B)는 survey에서 연상할 수 있는 respondents를 이용한 오답.

어휘 respondent 응답자 market research 시장 조사

14. 영 호 🎧

Does this skin treatment produce fast results?
(A) This time it's my treat.
(B) Sorry it took me so long.
(C) **Not really, but it's still worth it.**

이 피부 관리는 효과가 빠른가요?
(A) 이번에는 제가 대접할게요.
(B) 너무 오래 걸려서 미안해요.
(C) **그렇지는 않아요, 하지만 그래도 해 볼 만한 가치는 있죠.**

해설 피부 관리의 효과가 빠른지 묻는 질문에 그렇지는 않지만 해 볼 만한 가치는 있다고 답한 (C)가 정답. (A)는 treatment와 발음이 유사한 treat을 이용한 오답.

어휘 treatment 관리, 치료 produce 초래하다, 일으키다 result 결과 treat 대접, 한턱; 치료하다 worth ~을 할 가치가 있는, ~을 해 볼 만한

15. 미 미 🎧

What's your opinion on this restaurant?
(A) Whenever you have time for a meal.
(B) **I wish they had a delivery service.**
(C) We need a recommendation.

이 식당에 대한 당신의 의견은 어떤가요?
(A) 식사할 시간이 있으시면 언제든지요.
(B) **배달 서비스가 있으면 좋겠어요.**
(C) 저희에게 추천 좀 해 주세요.

해설 식당에 대한 의견을 묻는 질문에 배달 서비스가 있으면 좋겠다고 답한 (B)가 정답. (A)와 (C)는 restaurant에서 연상할 수 있는 meal과 recommendation을 각각 이용한 오답.

어휘 opinion 의견, 견해 delivery 배달 recommendation 추천

16. 미 미 🎧

How can I make a donation to the animal shelter?
(A) No, it's closed for the day.
(B) Mostly stray cats and dogs.
(C) **Mr. Frey is in charge of that.**

동물 보호소에 어떻게 기부할 수 있나요?
(A) 아니요, 오늘은 문을 닫았어요.
(B) 대부분 길 잃은 고양이와 개들이에요.
(C) **프레이 씨가 그걸 담당하고 있어요.**

해설 동물 보호소에 기부하는 방법을 묻는 질문에 담당자를 알려 주면서 자신은 모른다고 우회적으로 답한 (C)가 정답.

어휘 make a donation 기부하다 animal shelter 동물 보호소 stray 길 잃은 be in charge of ~을 담당하다

17. 영 미 🎧

Household trash and recyclable items are collected every Wednesday, right?
(A) Look for the symbol on the package.
(B) **Recycling is every other week.**
(C) Yes, I have a collection.

가정 쓰레기와 재활용품은 매주 수요일에 수거되지요, 그렇죠?
(A) 용기에 있는 표시를 찾아보세요.
(B) **재활용은 격주로 해요.**
(C) 네, 저한테 수집품이 있어요.

해설 쓰레기 및 재활용품 수거일이 매주 수요일이라는 말에 동의를 구하는 질문에 재활용은 격주로 한다며 아니라고 우회적으로 답한 (B)가 정답. (C)는 collected와 collection의 파생어를 이용한 오답.

어휘 household 가정의; 가정 recyclable 재활용할 수 있는 symbol 표시, 상징 package 용기, 포장 every other 하나 걸러, 두 ~마다 한 번씩

18. 미 영 🎧

Did you turn the air conditioner on?
(A) By pressing the red button.
(B) **Are you feeling cold?**
(C) Turn left at the next intersection.

당신이 에어컨을 켰나요?
(A) 빨간색 버튼을 눌러서요.
(B) **추우신가요?**
(C) 다음 교차로에서 좌회전하세요.

해설 에어컨을 켰냐는 질문에 추우냐고 반문한 (B)가 정답.

PART 2

7. 미 미 🎧

Where is the list of updated mailing addresses?
(A) Yes, that's the right date.
(B) On Ms. Nelson's desk.
(C) For regular customers.

업데이트된 우편 주소 목록이 어디에 있나요?
(A) 네, 그게 맞는 날짜예요.
(B) 넬슨 씨 책상 위에요.
(C) 단골 고객들을 위해서요.

해설   우편 주소 목록이 있는 위치를 묻는 질문에 구체적인 위치로 답한 (B)가 정답.

어휘   update 업데이트하다, 가장 최근의 정보를 알려 주다   regular customer 단골(손님)

8. 영 미 🎧

Who can answer my questions about the magazine's layout?
(A) That explains it.
(B) One issue a month.
(C) The design team.

잡지의 지면 배치에 관한 제 질문에 누가 답해 줄 수 있나요?
(A) 그래서 그렇군요.
(B) 한 달에 한 번 발행이에요.
(C) 디자인팀이요.

해설   잡지의 지면 배치에 관한 질문에 누가 답해 줄 수 있는지 묻는 질문에 부서명으로 답한 (C)가 정답. (A)는 answer my questions에서 연상할 수 있는 explains를 이용한 오답.

어휘   layout (신문·잡지·광고의) 지면 배치, 레이아웃   issue 발행(물), (정기 간행물의) 호

9. 미 미 🎧

When will the rest of the brochures for the trade expo be ready?
(A) It depends when the printer gets fixed.
(B) For the entire industry.
(C) I'm going to rest for a few minutes.

무역 박람회를 위한 나머지 안내 책자는 언제 준비될 예정인가요?
(A) 프린터가 언제 수리되는지에 달려 있어요.
(B) 산업 전반에 대해서요.
(C) 저는 잠시 동안 쉴 예정입니다.

해설   나머지 안내 책자가 준비될 시점을 묻는 질문에 프린터가 언제 수리되는지에 달려 있다며 모른다고 우회적으로 답한 (A)가 정답. (C)는 '나머지'와 '쉬다'라는 서로 다른 의미와 품사를 지닌 다의어 rest를 이용한 오답.

어휘   brochure 안내 책자   trade expo 무역 박람회   depend (~에) 달려 있다, 의존하다   entire 전체의   industry 산업, 공업

10. 미 호 🎧

Are these refreshments for everyone?
(A) They're for the candidates.
(B) It's very refreshing.
(C) Everyone must attend the training.

이 다과는 모든 사람을 위한 것인가요?
(A) 그건 후보자들을 위한 거예요.
(B) 이건 아주 신선하네요.
(C) 모두 교육에 참석해야만 합니다.

해설   모두를 위해 준비된 다과인지 묻는 질문에 후보자들을 위한 거라며 아니라고 우회적으로 답한 (A)가 정답. (B)는 refreshments와 refreshing의 파생어를 이용한 오답.

어휘   refreshments (항상 복수형) 다과   candidate 후보자, 지원자   refreshing 신선한   attend 참석하다

11. 영 미 🎧

Why don't you make name tags for the attendees?
(A) The attendance was low.
(B) I'm Gerald Stevens.
(C) Sure, I'd be happy to.

참석자들에게 이름표를 만들어 주는 게 어때요?
(A) 참석률이 저조했어요.
(B) 저는 제럴드 스티븐스입니다.
(C) 물론이죠, 기꺼이 할게요.

해설   참석자들에게 이름표를 만들어 주라는 제안에 긍정적으로 답하면서 기꺼이 하겠다고 말한 (C)가 정답.

어휘   attendee 참석자   attendance 참석(률), 참석자 수

12. 미 미 🎧

Isn't this bookshelf for user manuals only?
(A) No, we keep client files there too.
(B) If you can assemble it.
(C) We use them daily.

이 책꽂이는 사용 설명서 전용 아니에요?
(A) 아니요, 우리는 고객 파일도 거기에 보관해요.
(B) 그것을 조립하실 수 있다면요.
(C) 우리는 그것들을 매일 사용합니다.

해설   책꽂이가 사용 설명서 전용인지를 묻는 질문에 No라고 하면서

묘사한 (B)가 정답. 여자는 손에 식료품을 들고 있지만 판매할 물건들을 진열하고 있는 것은 아니므로 (C)는 오답.

어휘 pay for ~의 값을 지불하다   for sale 팔려고 내놓은

3. 미 🎧

(A) A vehicle has stopped at an intersection.
(B) A man is parking a car on a road.
(C) Some boxes have been stacked in a truck.
(D) A man is kneeling down by a cart.

(A) 차량이 교차로에 정차해 있다.
(B) 남자가 차를 도로에 주차하고 있다.
(C) 상자들이 트럭 안에 쌓여 있다.
(D) 남자가 수레 옆에 꿇어앉아 있다.

해설 트럭 안에 상자들이 쌓여 있는 모습이므로 정답은 (C).

어휘 vehicle 차량, 탈것   intersection 교차로   stack 쌓다, 포개다   kneel down 꿇어 앉다

4. 영 🎧

(A) Some people are setting up furniture.
(B) Some people are seated in the lobby.
(C) One of the men is walking up the stairs.
(D) One of the women is moving a stool.

(A) 몇몇 사람들이 가구를 놓고 있다.
(B) 몇몇 사람들이 로비에 앉아 있다.
(C) 한 남자가 계단을 걸어 올라가고 있다.
(D) 한 여자가 의자를 옮기고 있다.

해설 로비에 사람들이 앉아 있는 모습을 바르게 묘사한 (B)가 정답.

어휘 set up ~을 놓다[세우다], 마련하다   stairs (항상 복수형) 계단   stool (등받이와 팔걸이가 없는) 의자, 스툴

5. 미 🎧

(A) The men are clearing a table.
(B) One of the men is holding a folder.
(C) The woman is handing out a document.
(D) One of the men is writing in a notebook.

(A) 남자들이 테이블을 치우고 있다.
(B) 한 남자가 서류철을 들고 있다.
(C) 여자가 문서를 나눠 주고 있다.
(D) 한 남자가 노트에 필기하고 있다.

해설 테이블에 나란히 앉은 두 남자 중 한 명이 노트에 필기하고 있는 개별 동작을 바르게 묘사한 (D)가 정답. 사진에 서류철은 보이지 않으므로 (B)는 오답.

어휘 clear 치우다; 맑은, 분명한   hold 들다, 잡다   hand out 나누어 주다

6. 호 🎧

(A) A path is blocked by a crowd.
(B) There are boats docked at a port.
(C) There's a bridge spanning a river.
(D) The benches are all occupied.

(A) 길이 사람들로 막혀 있다.
(B) 항구에 정박한 배들이 있다.
(C) 강을 가로지르는 다리가 있다.
(D) 벤치들이 다 차 있다.

해설 강을 가로지르는 다리를 바르게 묘사한 (C)가 정답. 벤치들이 다 비어 있으므로 (D)는 오답.

어휘 dock (배를) 부두에 대다; 부두   port 항구   span 가로지르다   occupied 차 있는, 사용 중인

TEST 05

LISTENING TEST

001 (B)	002 (B)	003 (C)	004 (B)	005 (D)
006 (C)	007 (B)	008 (C)	009 (A)	010 (A)
011 (C)	012 (A)	013 (A)	014 (C)	015 (B)
016 (C)	017 (B)	018 (B)	019 (C)	020 (A)
021 (C)	022 (C)	023 (A)	024 (B)	025 (A)
026 (A)	027 (C)	028 (B)	029 (C)	030 (A)
031 (B)	032 (D)	033 (A)	034 (C)	035 (A)
036 (B)	037 (D)	038 (C)	039 (B)	040 (D)
041 (C)	042 (D)	043 (A)	044 (C)	045 (D)
046 (C)	047 (B)	048 (A)	049 (D)	050 (A)
051 (B)	052 (A)	053 (B)	054 (A)	055 (C)
056 (C)	057 (A)	058 (B)	059 (C)	060 (D)
061 (A)	062 (D)	063 (D)	064 (B)	065 (A)
066 (A)	067 (D)	068 (A)	069 (D)	070 (A)
071 (C)	072 (B)	073 (D)	074 (B)	075 (A)
076 (D)	077 (C)	078 (A)	079 (D)	080 (B)
081 (D)	082 (C)	083 (D)	084 (A)	085 (A)
086 (C)	087 (B)	088 (D)	089 (A)	090 (D)
091 (A)	092 (D)	093 (B)	094 (C)	095 (B)
096 (B)	097 (B)	098 (A)	099 (B)	100 (D)

READING TEST

101 (C)	102 (D)	103 (C)	104 (B)	105 (D)
106 (D)	107 (D)	108 (A)	109 (C)	110 (C)
111 (A)	112 (C)	113 (C)	114 (D)	115 (B)
116 (B)	117 (C)	118 (B)	119 (A)	120 (B)
121 (B)	122 (D)	123 (C)	124 (B)	125 (C)
126 (B)	127 (B)	128 (B)	129 (D)	130 (D)
131 (B)	132 (D)	133 (B)	134 (A)	135 (A)
136 (B)	137 (B)	138 (D)	139 (D)	140 (D)
141 (C)	142 (B)	143 (C)	144 (A)	145 (A)
146 (D)	147 (D)	148 (A)	149 (D)	150 (A)
151 (A)	152 (B)	153 (D)	154 (C)	155 (C)
156 (B)	157 (C)	158 (B)	159 (D)	160 (C)
161 (A)	162 (A)	163 (D)	164 (A)	165 (C)
166 (A)	167 (B)	168 (C)	169 (B)	170 (D)
171 (D)	172 (C)	173 (A)	174 (D)	175 (C)
176 (B)	177 (C)	178 (D)	179 (B)	180 (C)
181 (D)	182 (B)	183 (A)	184 (B)	185 (C)
186 (D)	187 (A)	188 (B)	189 (C)	190 (B)
191 (C)	192 (D)	193 (D)	194 (B)	195 (C)
196 (A)	197 (D)	198 (B)	199 (B)	200 (A)

PART 1

1. 미 🎧

(A) He's standing by a stream.
(B) He's looking at a map.
(C) He's pointing at a mountain.
(D) He's putting on a backpack.

(A) 남자가 시냇물 옆에 서 있다.
(B) 남자가 지도를 보고 있다.
(C) 남자가 산을 가리키고 있다.
(D) 남자가 배낭을 메는 중이다.

해설 남자가 산에서 지도를 보고 있는 모습이므로 정답은 (B). 남자는 이미 배낭을 메고 있는 상태이므로 (D)는 오답.

어휘 stream 개울, 시내   put on ~을 착용하다

2. 미 🎧

(A) A woman is paying for an item at a store.
(B) A woman is carrying a basket on her arm.
(C) A woman is displaying items for sale.
(D) A woman is cleaning some vegetables.

(A) 여자가 가게에서 물건값을 지불하고 있다.
(B) 여자가 팔에 바구니를 들고 있다.
(C) 여자가 판매할 물건들을 진열하고 있다.
(D) 여자가 채소를 씻고 있다.

해설 식료품점에서 여자가 팔에 바구니를 들고 있는 모습을 바르게

일로 보내라고 했고, (B)는 단서 (196B)에서 전문 강좌가 아래에 나열되어 있다고 했으며, (C)는 단서 (196C)에서 프로그램을 수료하는 데에 일 년이 걸린다고 했다. 그러나 학기별 지원 마감일만 언급되어 있고 각 학기가 시작하는 시점에 대해서는 언급되어 있지 않으므로 정답은 (D).

197. 현재 레너드 씨가 듣고 있는 강좌는?

(A) 드레이핑 및 직물
(B) 색채 조합 선택하기
(C) 조명으로 분위기 조성하기
(D) 무대 꾸미기

> 해설 두 지문 연계 문제_특정 정보 확인 문제

온라인 양식의 단서 (197-1)에서 레너드 씨가 현재 개인 휴일 기념 행사 프로그램을 수강하고 있으며 그녀가 현재 듣고 있는 강좌는 다른 교육 과정에는 없다고 했다. 광고의 단서 (197-2)에서 알 수 있듯이 개인 휴일 기념 행사 과정의 강좌 중 다른 교육 과정에 없는 것은 '조명으로 분위기 조성하기'이므로 정답은 (C).

198. 후기에서, 첫 번째 단락 세 번째 줄의 "deal with"와 의미상 가장 가까운 단어는?

(A) 맡다, 다루다
(B) 만지다
(C) 알리다, 통지하다
(D) 보수를 지불하다, 보상하다

> 해설 동의어 문제

문맥상 '10주년 기념일 행사를 맡아 달라고 했다'는 의미로, 여기서 deal with는 '다루다, 처리하다'라는 뜻으로 쓰였다. 따라서 가장 유사한 의미의 단어인 (A)가 정답.

199. 포레스터 씨에 대해 암시된 것은?

(A) 실내 장식가로 아주 오래 일한 것은 아니다.
(B) 이제는 율라 스쿨에서 강좌를 가르치고 있다.
(C) 최근에 신제품을 디자인했다.
(D) 율라 스쿨에서 새로운 프로그램을 시작할 것이다.

> 해설 추론 문제

단서 (199)에서 포레스터 씨는 교육 과정을 마친 지 얼마 되지 않아 한 장식 작업을 맡게 되었는데, 그 작업을 보고 모두가 포레스터 씨가 업계에서 수년간 일해 왔다고 생각했다고 했다. 이를 통해 실제로는 포레스터 씨가 실내 장식가로 아주 오래 일한 것은 아님을 추론할 수 있으므로 정답은 (A).

200. 포레스터 씨가 배웠을 것 같은 교육 과정은?

(A) 교육 과정 A
(B) 교육 과정 B
(C) 교육 과정 C
(D) 교육 과정 D

> 해설 두 지문 연계 문제_추론 문제

후기의 단서 (200-1)에서 포레스터 씨가 한 회사로부터 신제품 출시 기념 파티를 위한 장소를 장식해 달라는 요청을 받았다고 한 것으로 보아 포레스터 씨가 기업 행사 관련 교육 과정을 수강했음을 알 수 있고, 광고의 단서 (200-2)를 통해 기업 행사에 관한 과정은 교육 과정 C임을 알 수 있다. 따라서 포레스터 씨가 배운 것은 교육 과정 C라고 추론할 수 있으므로 정답은 (C).

194. 바튼 전자가 출시할 것 같은 신형 기기는?

(A) 스마트폰
(B) 카메라
(C) 노트북
(D) 건강 정보 추적기

해설 두 지문 연계 문제_추론 문제

기사의 단서 (194-1)에서 베시노 씨와 스탈링 씨의 만남이 바튼 전자의 건강 정보 추적기 출시 가능성을 의미할 수 있다고 했고, 문자 메시지의 단서 (194-2)에서는 스탈링 씨가 행사에서 기기의 기능에 대해 설명할 거라고 했다. 따라서 건강 정보 추적기가 출시될 것이라고 추론할 수 있으므로 정답은 (D).

195. 사람들이 신형 기기의 사진을 보게 될 때는?

(A) 행사 전에
(B) 행사 초반에
(C) 행사 마지막에
(D) 행사 후에

해설 특정 정보 확인 문제

문자 메시지의 단서 (195)에서 사진을 마지막 순서로 하기로 했다고 했으므로 정답은 (C).

패러프레이징 [단서] for last → [정답] At the end

196-200 광고 & 온라인 양식 & 후기

율라 스쿨 프로그램

율라 스쿨은 행사 장식가를 위한 가장 포괄적인 프로그램을 제공합니다. 최고의 고객 맞춤 환경을 만들기 위해 공간을 디자인하는 법을 배우세요. ¹⁹⁶ᶜ저희 프로그램은 수료하는 데 일 년밖에 안 걸립니다! 율라에서, 당신은 몇 가지 핵심 강좌를 듣고 나서 ¹⁹⁶ᴮ두 개의 전문 강좌로 넘어가게 되는데, 이는 당신이 선택하는 교육 과정에 따라 다릅니다. 각각의 교육 과정에 포함된 전문 강좌는 아래에 나열되어 있습니다.

교육 과정 A: 결혼식과 선물 파티
- 드레이핑 및 직물
- 식물과 나무 활용하기

¹⁹⁷⁻²**교육 과정 B: 개인 휴일 기념 행사**
- 색채 조합 선택하기
- ¹⁹⁷⁻²조명으로 분위기 조성하기

²⁰⁰⁻²**교육 과정 C: 기업 행사**
- 색채 조합 선택하기
- 무대 꾸미기

교육 과정 D: 테마가 있는 어린이 파티
- 풍선 조각
- 무대 꾸미기

* 지원 마감은 가을 학기는 8월 15일이고 봄 학기는 11월 15일입니다. ¹⁹⁶ᴬ지원하시려면 이력서, 자기 소개서, 추천서를 admissions@yula.com으로 제출하세요.

어휘 comprehensive 포괄적인, 종합적인 decorator (실내) 장식가 customize 주문에 응하여 만들다 core 핵심적인 move on to ~으로 넘어가다[이동하다] depend on ~에 달려 있다 curriculum 교육 과정 motivation letter 자기 소개서(= cover letter)

질문 및 의견

학생
제레미 포레스터

저는 율라 행사 장식가 프로그램을 수료하기 위한 마지막 강좌를 수강하고 있습니다. 하지만, 저는 이번 학기를 마치고 강좌를 하나 더 듣는 것이 가능한지 궁금합니다. ¹⁹⁷⁻¹제 친구 켈리 레너드가 개인 휴일 기념 행사 프로그램을 수강하고 있는데, 그녀는 지금 듣고 있는 강좌에 정말 만족하고 있고, 그것은 다른 어떤 교육 과정에도 제공되지 않습니다. 전체 교육 과정을 듣지 않고 이 강좌만 추가하는 게 가능한가요? 그럴 수 있다면, 비용은 얼마나 들까요?

제출

후기: ★★★★★
이름: J. 포레스터

¹⁹⁹ ²⁰⁰⁻¹교육 과정을 마치고 얼마 안 되어서, 저는 한 회사로부터 신제품 출시 기념 파티를 위한 장소를 장식해 달라는 연락을 받았습니다. 모두가 실내 장식을 칭찬했고, 그 회사는 제 작업에 매우 만족해서 제게 그들의 10주년 기념일 행사를 ¹⁹⁸맡아 달라고 부탁했습니다. 저는 그렇게 큰 행사에 이렇게 빨리 고용될 것이라고는 예상하지 못했습니다. ¹⁹⁹율라 스쿨에서 제가 받은 모든 실습 경험 덕분에, 모든 사람이 제가 업계에서 수년간 일해 왔다고 생각했습니다! 율라는 훌륭한 조언을 해 주고 실내 장식 일을 하는 데 당신이 필요로 할 모든 것을 교육해 줌으로써 당신을 정말 잘 준비시켜 줍니다. 저는 전문적인 실내 장식가가 되기를 원하는 누구에게라도 율라를 적극 추천합니다.

어휘 anniversary 기념일 hands-on 직접 해 보는 tip 조언 professional 전문적인

196. 율라 스쿨의 프로그램에 대해 언급되지 않은 것은?

(A) 지원서를 어떻게 제출하는지
(B) 전문 강좌가 무엇인지
(C) 프로그램이 얼마나 오래 지속되는지
(D) 각 학기가 언제 시작하는지

해설 Not/True 문제

(A)는 단서 (196A)에서 지원하는 데 필요한 서류들을 언급하면서 이메

해설 **특정 정보 확인 문제**

단서 (190)에서 다른 회원이 파머 씨의 기존 식단으로 변경해 달라는 요청을 했기 때문에 두 사람의 배달을 간단히 교체할 수 있었다고 했다. 따라서 정답은 (C).

패러프레이징 [단서] another member asked to change to your original plan → [정답] Another customer requested a plan switch.

191-195 초대장 & 기사 & 문자 메시지

공식 초청

191프랫 씨께,

바턴 전자의 오랜 투자자 자격으로, 귀하를 4월 24일에 열리는 바턴 사의 미래와 진보 행사에 초대합니다. 192-1저는 귀하가 놓치시면 안 될 중대한 발표를 할 예정입니다.

날짜: 4월 24일
시간: 오후 2시부터 오후 4시까지
장소: 팔콘 룸 (3층), 히버 호텔
191**입장료:** 무료 (이 카드를 제시해야 함)

귀하를 뵙기를 고대합니다.

192-1빈 베시노 드림

어휘 investor 투자자 electronics 《항상 복수형》 전자 제품 make an announcement 공표[발표]하다

바턴 전자의 곧 있을 발표

바턴 전자는 4월 24일에 특별한 행사를 개최할 예정이다. 이 회사는 192-2발송된 초대장에 회사의 최고경영자가 '중대한 발표'라고 칭한 것을 공표할 예정이다. 그때부터 바턴 전자가 신형 기기를 출시할 것이 확실시되었다. 하지만 기기 종류는 아직 확인되지 않았으며, 인터넷상에서 유언비어가 넘쳐났다.

이것은 모두 지난주에 신규 노트북 디자인의 사진이 소셜 미디어에 유출되면서 시작되었다. 하지만 이번 유출의 근원지는 알려지지 않았으며, 그것의 진위 여부도 확인되지 않았다.

194-1베시노 씨는 또한 인기 있는 트레이닝 비디오 시리즈를 제작한 유명한 건강 전문가인 베아트릭스 스탈링 씨와 만나는 모습이 카메라에 193잡혔다. 194-1건강 정보 추적기가 최근에 인기가 급증하는 모습을 보였기에, 이 만남은 바턴 사의 건강 정보 추적기의 가능성에 대한 소문을 촉발시켰다. 스탈링 씨와 만난 이유를 질문받았을 때, 베시노 씨는 대답하기를 거부했다.

마지막으로, 바턴 전자는 자사의 신형 스마트폰 모델을 발표할 가능성이 있다. 해당 기업은 지난 4년간 해마다 새로운 휴대폰을 출시해 왔으며, 그들의 가장 최신 모델인 바턴 44가 나온 지 일 년 가까이 되었다.

어휘 send out ~을 발송하다 flood 넘치다, 범람하다 leak 유출하다; 유출 source 근원, 출처 authenticity 진위, 진실성 tracker 추적자

surge 급증 spark 촉발시키다, 유발하다 likely ~할 것 같은

발신: 빈 베시노
수신: 스티븐 파커

194-2스탈링 씨가 저에게 그녀가 하려고 생각하는 연설의 사본을 보내 줬습니다. 거기에서, 그녀는 그 기기의 주요 기능들의 장점을 설명하고 있습니다. 원래, 우리는 그녀가 마지막에 발표하게 하려고 했지만, 제 생각에는 우리가 기기의 사진을 공개하기 전에 그녀가 연설을 하면 더 좋을 것 같습니다. 195그래서 저는 기대감을 고조시키기 위해서 사진을 마지막 순서로 아껴 두기로 했습니다. 지금 당신에게 그녀의 연설문을 이메일로 보내 드리겠습니다. 그걸 보시고 동의하시는지 알려 주세요.

어휘 intend to do ~하려고 생각하다[의도하다] build up ~을 더 높이다 anticipation 기대 take a look at ~을 보다

191. 프랫 씨가 행사를 위해 하도록 요구되는 일은?

(A) 초대장 보여 주기
(B) 기기 가져오기
(C) 방 예약하기
(D) 프레젠테이션 준비하기

해설 **특정 정보 확인 문제**

단서 (191)을 통해 초대장을 받은 프랫 씨는 행사 입장 시 초대장을 보여 줘야 한다는 것을 알 수 있으므로 정답은 (A).

패러프레이징 [단서] present this card → [정답] Show the invitation

192. 빈 베시노 씨의 신분은?

(A) 특별 초대 손님
(B) 기업 최고경영자
(C) 운동 전문가
(D) 개인 투자자

해설 **두 지문 연계 문제_특정 정보 확인 문제**

초대장의 단서 (192-1)에서 빈 베시노 씨는 자신이 중대한 발표를 할 것이라고 했는데, 기사의 단서 (192-2)에서는 초대장에서 '중대한 발표'라는 말을 언급한 사람이 회사의 최고경영자라고 했으므로 정답은 (B).

패러프레이징 [단서] its CEO → [정답] A company CEO

193. 기사에서, 세 번째 단락 첫 번째 줄의 "caught"과 의미상 가장 가까운 단어는?

(A) 녹화하다
(B) 예정하다
(C) 체포하다
(D) 예상하다

해설 **동의어 문제**

문맥상 '카메라에 잡혔다'는 의미로, 여기서 catch는 '목격하다, 포착하다'의 의미로 쓰였다. 따라서 '녹화하다, 기록하다'라는 의미를 가지는 단어인 (A)가 정답.

어휘 organic 유기농의 keep in mind 명심하다 vegetarian 채식주의자 bill 청구서를 보내다; 청구서 accordingly 그에 따라서 be in contact with ~와 연락하다 shortly 얼마 안 되어, 곧

3월 15일자 배달

	기본	고급	¹⁸⁷⁻² 기본 채식	¹⁸⁷⁻² ¹⁸⁸⁻³ 고급 채식	배달 시각
타센 로 86번지				✓	오전 11:35
조던 드라이브 15번지				✓	오전 11:50
프레스턴 로 56번지			✓		오후 2:12
¹⁸⁸⁻³ 메스카 가 12번지				✓	오후 2:26

어휘 deluxe 고급의

수신: 세바스티안 파머 〈sebpalmer@yourmail.net〉
발신: 고객 서비스팀 〈cservice@fuchsiafoods.com〉
날짜: 3월 15일
제목: 고객님의 업그레이드 요청 관련

파머 씨께,

저희가 고객님의 패키지 배달 식단을 변경해 드렸음을 확인해 드리고자 이 이메일을 보냅니다. ¹⁸⁸⁻¹고객님의 새로운 식단의 첫 패키지가 오늘 오후에 배달되었습니다. 이에 따라 고객님의 계정에 등록되어 있는 신용 카드로 요금이 청구되었습니다.

저희는 사전에 주문 일정을 짜기 때문에 ¹⁸⁹관례상 월말 전에는 식단 변경을 허용하지 않는다는 점에 유념해 주세요. 그러나, ¹⁹⁰다른 회원께서 고객님의 원래 식단으로 변경해 달라고 요청하셨고, 따라서 저희는 간단히 두 분의 배달을 교체할 수 있었습니다. 이번에는 운 좋게도 우연이 맞아떨어졌지만, 앞으로 변경을 원하신다면 그렇게 하기 위해 월말까지 기다리셔야 한다는 것을 유념해 주십시오.

이해해 주셔서 감사드리며, 귀하의 새로운 식품 배달을 즐기세요!

고객 서비스팀 직원
레베카 라스 드림

어휘 on record 기록되어, 등록되어 account 계정, 계좌 customarily 관례상, 습관적으로 ahead of time 사전에, 예정보다 빨리 coincidence 우연의 일치 representative 직원, 대표

186. 파머 씨가 웹페이지에 글을 게시한 이유는?
(A) 잘못된 결제를 취소하기 위해
(B) 채식이 아닌 메뉴를 요청하기 위해
(C) 패키지 수령을 중단하기 위해
(D) 자신의 현재 식단을 변경하기 위해

해설 목적 문제

단서 (186)에서 파머 씨가 식단을 다음 단계로 업그레이드하고 싶다고 했으므로 정답은 (D).

패러프레이징 [단서] to upgrade my plan to the next level → [정답] To modify his current plan

187. 파머 씨가 원래 받고 있던 패키지의 종류는?
(A) 기본
(B) 고급
(C) 기본 채식
(D) 고급 채식

해설 두 지문 연계 문제_추론 문제

웹페이지의 단서 (187-1)에서 파머 씨가 식단을 다음 단계로 업그레이드하고 싶은데 본인은 채식주의자이므로 계속해서 채식 패키지를 보내 달라고 했고, 기록지의 단서 (187-2)에서는 채식주의자 식단이 '기본 채식'과 '고급 채식' 두 가지가 있는 것으로 보아 파머 씨의 원래 식단은 아래 단계인 '기본 채식'이었음을 추론할 수 있다. 따라서 정답은 (C).

188. 파머 씨가 살고 있을 것 같은 곳은?
(A) 타센 로 86번지
(B) 조던 드라이브 15번지
(C) 프레스턴 로 56번지
(D) 메스카 가 12번지

해설 세 지문 연계 문제_추론 문제

이메일의 단서 (188-1)에서 파머 씨한테 새로운 식단의 첫 패키지가 오늘 오후에 배달되었다고 했는데, 웹페이지의 단서 (188-2)를 통해 새로운 식단이 상위 단계의 채식 패키지임을 알 수 있다. 기록지의 단서 (188-3)에서 상위 단계의 채식 패키지인 '고급 채식'이 오후에 배달된 곳은 '메스카 가 12번지'임을 알 수 있으므로 정답은 (D).

189. 이메일에서, 두 번째 단락 첫 번째 줄의 "customarily"와 의미상 가장 가까운 것은?
(A) 보통은
(B) 상당히
(C) 당연히
(D) 드물게

해설 동의어 문제

문맥상 '관례상 월말 전에는 식단 변경을 허용하지 않는다'는 의미로, 여기서 customarily는 '관례상'이라는 뜻으로 쓰였다. 따라서 이와 가장 유사한 의미를 가진 단어인 (A)가 정답.

190. 이메일에 따르면, 파머 씨의 요청이 승인된 이유는?
(A) 그는 월말까지 기다렸다.
(B) 그는 사전에 변경을 요청했다.
(C) 다른 고객이 식단 변경을 요청했다.
(D) 원했던 식단이 더 비싸다.

어휘 all over 곳곳에 come up with ~을 생각해 내다 highlight 강조하다 thanks to ~ 덕분에 test drive 시승

181. 요더 씨가 매디슨 씨에게 편지를 쓴 이유는?
(A) 직원을 추천하기 위해
(B) 자신의 이력서를 제출하기 위해
(C) 그에게 일자리를 제안하기 위해
(D) 제품을 광고하기 위해

해설 목적 문제

단서 (181)에서 요더 씨가 아만드 씨를 언급하며 그녀에게 추천서를 작성해 주겠다고 제안했다고 했다. 따라서 요더 씨가 아만드 씨를 매디슨 씨에게 추천하기 위해 편지를 썼음을 알 수 있으므로 정답은 (A).

패러프레이징 [단서] to write a reference letter
→ [정답] To recommend a worker

182. 편지에서, 두 번째 단락 네 번째 줄의 "intimate"과 의미상 가장 가까운 단어는?
(A) 사적인
(B) 상세한
(C) 객관적인
(D) 충실한

해설 동의어 문제

intimate은 '친밀한'이라는 의미뿐만 아니라 '조예가 깊은, 상세한'이라는 의미도 가지고 있다. 위 문맥에서는 '다양한 모델에 대한 깊은 지식'이라는 의미이므로 '상세한'이라는 뜻의 detailed가 이와 유사한 의미를 나타낸다. 따라서 정답은 (B).

183. 티저 영상에 대해 언급된 것은?
(A) 많은 사람이 그것을 보았다.
(B) 감마 사 직원과의 인터뷰를 특별히 포함한다.
(C) 가장 인기 있는 영화가 되었다.
(D) 감마 사의 경쟁사에 의해서 공개되었다.

해설 Not/True 문제

단서 (183)에서 티저 영상이 소셜 미디어 곳곳에 공유되었고 조회 수가 수백만에 달했다고 했으므로 정답은 (A).

패러프레이징 [단서] has reached millions of views
→ [정답] Many people have watched it.

184. 매디슨 씨가 자기 팀원들에게 축하하고 있는 것은?
(A) 미니밴 광고
(B) SUV 마케팅
(C) 팀원의 승진
(D) 잡지의 인기

해설 두 지문 연계 문제_특정 정보 확인 문제

이메일의 단서 (184-1)에서 최신 모델의 캠페인이 매우 성공적이었다고 하면서 모든 팀원에게 축하한다고 했는데, 편지의 단서 (184-2)에서 새로운 감마 SUV 출시를 언급한 것으로 보아 그 최신 모델이 SUV임을 알 수 있다. 따라서 정답은 (B).

패러프레이징 [단서] The campaign for our newest model
→ [정답] An SUV's marketing

185. 아만드 씨에 대해 암시된 것은?
(A) 일자리 제안을 거절했다.
(B) 팀장으로 승진했다.
(C) 최근에 팀을 바꿨다.
(D) 잡지에 기사를 썼다.

해설 두 지문 연계 문제_추론 문제

편지의 단서 (185-1)에서 아만드 씨가 디자인팀에서 일하면서 차량의 디자인에 참여했기 때문에 최상의 방식으로 제품을 보여 주는 아이디어를 낼 수 있을 것이라고 했고, 마케팅팀 팀원을 대상으로 하는 이메일의 단서 (185-2)에서는 특히 아만드 씨가 제품 디자인에 참여했던 경험 덕분에 광고에서 크게 도움이 되었다고 했다. 이를 통해 아만드 씨가 디자인팀에서 마케팅팀으로 이동했음을 추론할 수 있으므로 정답은 (C).

186-190 웹페이지 & 기록지 & 이메일

헬프 센터
무엇을 도와드릴까요?

□ 질문   ■ 요청/문제   □ 의견 이(가) 있습니다.

푸크시아 푸즈에 보내는 메시지:

저는 지금 3개월간 푸크시아 푸즈의 유기농 식품 배달 박스를 받고 있습니다. 저는 매일 오후 제 패키지를 받는 것이 매우 즐겁고, 그래서 186 187-1 188-2제 식단을 다음 단계로 업그레이드하고 싶습니다. 187-1 188-2변경하실 때, 제가 채식주의자라는 점을 명심하시고 계속해서 고기나 달걀을 포함하지 않는 패키지를 보내 주시기 바랍니다. 이러한 변경이 가능하다면, 그에 따라서 청구서를 보내 주세요.

대단히 감사합니다.

세바스티안 파머

회신을 기대하십니까?
■ 네   □ 아니오

'네'라고 하셨으면, 이메일 주소를 제공해 주세요:
sebpalmer@yourmail.net

제출

연락해 주셔서 감사합니다.
회신을 요청하신 경우에는 저희가 고객님의 문의와 관련하여 곧 연락드릴 것입니다.
즉각적인 도움이 필요한 질문이 있으시면, 저희에게 352-555-2948번으로 전화 주십시오.

해설 목적 문제

단서 (176)에서 배달 지연에 대해서 사과하고 있으므로 정답은 (B).

패러프레이징 [단서] We are very sorry → [정답] an apology

177. 토퍼 씨가 5월 5일에 일어났다고 한 일은?

(A) 가게의 재고 관리를 잘못했다.
(B) 딸이 대학에 합격했다.
(C) 공급업체가 변경되었다.
(D) 꽃이 모두 늦게 배달되었다.

해설 특정 정보 확인 문제

단서 (177)에서 5월 5일에 장미가 바닥이 나면서 배달할 장미를 따로 남겨 두지 못했고, 공급업체에서 꽃을 받는 데에도 시간이 걸렸다고 했으므로 정답은 (A).

178. 이메일에서, 두 번째 단락 네 번째 줄의 "assure"와 의미상 가장 가까운 단어는?

(A) 확신시키다
(B) 상기시키다
(C) 보장하다
(D) 보상하다

해설 동의어 문제

문맥상 '이러한 종류의 실수가 다시 일어나지 않을 것이라고 보장할 수 있다'는 의미이므로 이와 비슷한 의미의 어휘를 고른다. 따라서 정답은 (C).

179. 제니스 리처즈 씨의 신분은?

(A) 케이지 씨의 동료
(B) 토퍼 씨의 상사
(C) 케이지 씨의 고객
(D) 토퍼 씨의 공급업자

해설 추론 문제

단서 (179)를 보면 꽃다발과 메시지의 수신자가 리처즈 씨인데, 케이지 씨가 리처즈 씨와 같이 일해서 좋았다고 했으므로 리처즈 씨는 케이지 씨의 직장 동료임을 추론할 수 있다. 따라서 정답은 (A).

180. 토퍼 씨의 가게가 위치해 있을 것 같은 곳은?

(A) 보스턴
(B) 스트래턴
(C) 제이빌
(D) 벤더타운

해설 두 지문 연계 문제_추론 문제

이메일의 단서 (180-1)에서 상품권이 지역 내에서의 무료 꽃 배달에 사용될 수 있다고 했고, 상품권의 단서 (180-2)에서 상품권이 제이빌 내에서의 배달에 유효하다고 했으므로 토퍼 씨의 가게는 제이빌에 있다는 것을 추론할 수 있다. 따라서 정답은 (C).

181-185 편지 & 이메일

7월 31일

제럼 매디슨 씨
체노웨스 드라이브 2675번지
내슈빌, 테네시 주 37214

매디슨 씨께,

당신이 마케팅팀의 새로운 대리를 구하고 있다고 들었습니다. 아시다시피, 저는 11년 동안 감마 자동차 사의 디자인팀장이었습니다. [181] [185-1]스카이 아만드 씨는 6년 전에 저희 팀에서 일하기 시작했고 강력한 자산임을 증명해 왔습니다. [181]그녀는 저에게 마케팅팀의 대리 자리에 지원할 의사를 밝혔고, 저는 추천서를 작성해 주겠다고 제안했습니다.

저는 아만드 씨의 이동이 회사에 이로울 수 있다고 생각합니다. 디자인 전략과 고객들의 관심을 끄는 방법에 대한 그녀의 이해는 그녀의 작업에서 분명하게 드러나며, 이러한 재능은 마케팅팀에서 높은 가치가 있을 것입니다. 게다가, 감마 자동차 사 내에서의 그녀의 경험과 회사의 다양한 모델에 대한 그녀의 [182]깊은 지식은 효과적인 마케팅 캠페인을 구축하는 데 크게 기여할 것입니다. [184-2]저는 당신이 곧 새로운 감마 SUV 6의 출시를 준비하는 일에 집중하시게 될 거라는 것을 알고 있습니다. [185-1]아만드 씨는 그 차량 디자인의 여러 측면에 관여해 왔고, 저는 그녀가 최상의 방식으로 그것을 보여 주는 방법에 대해서 멋진 아이디어가 있을 것으로 생각합니다.

아만드 씨의 작업에 대해 궁금하신 점이 있으시면, 부담 없이 제게 연락 주세요.

디자인팀장, 멜라니 요더 드림

어휘 asset 자산, 재산 intention 의사, 의도 transfer 이동, 이적 appeal to ~의 관심을 끌다 evident 분명한, 눈에 띄는 intimate 깊은, 상세한 contribute to ~에 기여하다 aspect 측면, 양상

[185-2]수신: 마케팅팀 팀원들 〈marketingteam@gammamotors.com〉
발신: 제럼 매디슨 〈jmadison@gammamotors.com〉
날짜: 9월 2일
제목: 마케팅 캠페인

[184-1]우리의 최신 모델 캠페인이 매우 성공적임이 입증되었습니다. [183]우리 티저 영상이 소셜 미디어 곳곳에 공유되었으며 조회 수가 수백만에 달했습니다. 심지어 인기 있는 자동차 잡지의 기자가 우리 팀장 중 한 명과 인터뷰를 하겠다고 요청했습니다.

[184-1]여러분 모두에게 축하드리지만, [185-2]특히 아만드 씨에게 축하를 드리는 바입니다. 이번이 그녀의 첫 캠페인이었고, 이 제품의 디자인을 개발한 그녀의 경험 덕분에 우리 광고에서 강조할 최고의 특징들을 생각해 낼 수 있었습니다. 우리는 이미 많은 수의 시승 요청을 받고 있고, 이번 출시는 우리 미니밴의 출시보다도 훨씬 더 성공적이리라 기대합니다.

마케팅팀장, 제럼 매디슨 드림

(B) 내일 운전해서 출근할 것이다.
(C) 매일 신문을 읽는다.
(D) 평소에 도서관을 닫는다.

해설 추론 문제

단서 (173)에서 사이먼 씨가 이메일 발신자를 대신하여 도서관 문을 열고 일할 것인데, 마지막으로 이것을 한 지 꽤 오래되었다고 했으므로 사이먼 씨는 이 일을 전에 해 본 적이 있음을 유추할 수 있다. 따라서 정답은 (A).

174. 사이먼 씨가 하도록 기대되는 일이 아닌 것은?
(A) 보안 시스템 해제하기
(B) 정문 열기
(C) 우편물 읽기
(D) 돈 세기

해설 Not/True 문제

Not/True 문제의 경우 모든 선택지를 지문과 대조하여 소거하는 방식으로 정답을 찾아야 한다. (A)는 단서 (174A)에서 경보를 해제하는 비밀번호를 알고 있으라는 것으로 보아 보안 시스템을 해제하라는 것임을 알 수 있고, (B)는 단서 (174B)에서 모든 층의 불을 켠 다음에는 정문을 열 준비가 되어 있어야 한다고 했으므로 정문도 열라는 것을 알 수 있으며, (D)는 단서 (174D)에서 금전 등록기 안에 48달러가 있는지 확인하라는 것으로 보아 돈도 세야 한다는 것을 알 수 있다. 그러나 단서 (174C)에서 우편물을 가져와서 책상 위에 올려 두라고 했으나 읽어 보라고는 하지 않았으므로 정답은 (C).

175. 내일 예일즈 씨가 할 일은?
(A) 자기 자리에서 사임하기
(B) 사이먼 씨를 직장까지 차로 데려다주기
(C) 종일 집에 머무르기
(D) 고객 문의 처리하기

해설 다음에 할 일 문제

단서 (175)에서 예일즈 씨는 하루 휴가를 내고 집에서 나가지 않을 것이라고 했으므로 그녀가 온종일 집에 있을 것임을 알 수 있다. 따라서 정답은 (C).

패러프레이징 [단서] taking the whole day off and not leaving the house → [정답] Stay home for the day

176-180 이메일 & 상품권

수신: 케이지, 피터 ⟨pcage@jaysmail.net⟩
발신: 토퍼, 에드워드 ⟨etopher@sapphireflowers.com⟩
날짜: 5월 8일
제목: 무료 상품권

케이지 씨께,

¹⁷⁶ ¹⁷⁷5월 5일에 귀하의 꽃꽂이 배달이 늦은 것에 대해서 진심으로 사과드립니다. 저희는 이 지연으로 인해 따님의 보스턴 대학 합격 축하 행사가 의도하셨던 것만큼 특별하지 못했다는 점을 이해합니다.

¹⁷⁷유감스럽게도, 저희는 그날 장미가 바닥이 났고 귀하에게 오후에 배달할 분량의 장미를 따로 남겨 두지 못했습니다. 저희는 주문을 더 했지만, 저희 공급업체가 스트래튼에 위치해 있기 때문에, 꽃을 받는 데에 시간이 걸렸습니다. 저희는 더 현대적인 재고 관리 프로그램으로 전환하는 과정에 있으며, 이러한 종류의 실수가 다시는 일어나지 않을 것임을 ¹⁷⁸보장해 드릴 수 있습니다. 향후 있을 특별한 행사에 사파이어 플라워즈를 계속해서 선택해 주시기를 바랍니다.

사과의 표시로, ¹⁸⁰⁻¹귀하가 선택하시는 무료 꽃다발을 이 지역 내의 어느 주소로든 배달시킬 수 있는 상품권을 제공해 드립니다. 이 이메일에 그것이 첨부되어 있는 것을 확인하실 수 있을 것입니다. 배달을 주문하시고 싶을 때 그것을 출력하셔서 작성해 주세요.

사파이어 플라워즈
에드워드 토퍼 드림

어휘 voucher 상품권, 쿠폰 floral arrangement 꽃꽂이 acceptance 합격 통지, 받아들임 run out of ~을 다 써 버리다, ~을 바닥내다 set aside 따로 떼어 두다 inventory 재고(품) assure 보장하다, 확인하다 occasion 행사, 경우 complimentary 무료의

~ 사파이어 플라워즈 ~
상품권 번호: XS564813

¹⁸⁰⁻²꽃꽂이 제품 1개와 해당 제품의 제이빌 내 배달에 유효함.

다음 선택 사항 중에서 고르세요:
☐ 클래식 로즈   ■ 블루 번치   ☐ 드림 부케   ☐ 스프링 스페셜

배달 일자: 5월 18일 월요일   **배달 시각:** 오전 10시
주소: ¹⁷⁹제니스 리처즈
        프런티어 사 경리부
        엔터프라이즈 드라이브 514번지

메시지(선택):

¹⁷⁹제니스 씨께,

당신이 떠나신다니 유감입니다. ¹⁷⁹이 몇 해 동안 내내 당신과 일해서 좋았습니다. 벤더타운에서 새로운 일을 즐기시길 바랍니다!

피터 케이지 드림

어휘 following 다음에 나오는, 그 다음의   selection 선택 가능한 것들(의 집합)   bunch 다발, 송이

176. 이메일의 목적은?
(A) 지연에 대해 알리기 위해
(B) 사과하기 위해
(C) 시스템 오류를 보고하기 위해
(D) 동료를 축하하기 위해

169. 츠루타 씨에 대해 암시된 것은?

(A) 회사가 지출을 제한해야 한다고 생각한다.
(B) 회사의 상품에 대한 제안을 했다.
(C) 합테 씨에게 조언을 부탁했다.
(D) 새로운 화장품 라인을 개발했다.

해설   추론 문제

단서 (169)에서 츠루타 씨는 제품 라인에 제품을 하나 더 추가하자는 자신의 조언을 연구 개발 부서가 받아들여 기쁘다고 했다. 이를 통해 그녀가 이전에 회사의 제품 라인에 대한 제안을 했음을 추론할 수 있으므로 정답은 (B).

패러프레이징 [단서] my advice about adding another product to the line → [정답] a suggestion about the company's goods

170. 오후 4시 41분에, 모건 씨가 "그렇군요"라고 한 것에서 그녀가 의도한 것은?

(A) 캐터네오 씨는 너무 바빠서 프로젝트를 수행할 수 없다.
(B) 캐터네오 씨는 문제와 관련하여 모건 씨를 도울 수 없다.
(C) 캐터네오 씨는 이미 포트폴리오를 검토했다.
(D) 캐터네오 씨가 업무에 적임일지도 모른다.

해설   의도 파악 문제

단서 (170)에서 캐터네오 씨가 마케팅 업무를 맡은 것에 대해 모건 씨와 츠루타 씨가 부정적인 반응을 보이자, 합테 씨는 캐터네오 씨가 화장품 마케팅 이력이 있다며 그가 이번 업무에 적임임을 간접적으로 드러냈다. 이에 대해 모건 씨가 I see라며 합테 씨의 말에 수긍한 것이므로 정답은 (D).

패러프레이징 [단서] job → [정답] a task

171. 모건 씨가 다음에 할 것 같은 일은?

(A) 캐터네오 씨가 준비한 서류 검토하기
(B) 이전 프로젝트들에 대한 자료 보내기
(C) 캐터네오 씨와의 회의 잡기
(D) 새로운 마케팅 이사 추천하기

해설   다음에 할 일 문제

단서 (171)에서 캐터네오 씨에게 이전 프로젝트들의 포트폴리오를 보내줄 수 있다는 모건 씨의 말에 합테 씨는 긍정적인 반응을 보였고, 그에 대한 응답으로 모건 씨가 지금 그 일을 하겠다고 했으므로 정답은 (B).

패러프레이징 [단서] send him a portfolio of previous projects → [정답] Send information about previous projects

172-175 이메일

수신: 카트리나 사이먼 〈ksimon@presslerlibrary.org〉
발신: 노라 예일즈 〈nyales@presslerlibrary.org〉
날짜: 11월 30일
제목: 내일 개관

사이먼 씨께,

¹⁷³저는 당신이 기꺼이 내일 아침 저 대신에 도서관을 열고 제가 맡은 근무 시간 동안 일해 주실 거라고 들었어요. ¹⁷²저는 개관 절차와 관련해 당신을 도와드리기 위한 짧은 메모를 보내 드리고 싶었어요. ¹⁷³당신이 마지막으로 이걸 한 지 꽤 오래되었고, 여러 단계가 있기 때문에 제 생각에는 이게 도움이 될 것 같았어요.

¹⁷⁴ᴬ우선, 저는 경보를 해제하는 비밀번호 0358을 당신이 꼭 알고 계셨으면 좋겠어요. ¹⁷⁴ᶜ신문을 포함한 우편물을 가져오시는 것을 기억하세요. 우편물은 제 책상 위에 올려 두시면 됩니다. 신문에는 도서관 도장을 찍으셔서 정기 간행물 구역에 있는 신문 선반에 진열해 주세요. 어제 자 신문은 가져가셔서 다른 과거 신문들과 함께 분류해 놓아야 한다는 것을 명심하세요.

¹⁷⁴ᴰ금전 등록기 열쇠는 제 책상 맨 위 서랍 안에 있어요. 금전 등록기 안에 준비금으로 48달러가 있는지 다시 한번 확인하세요.

¹⁷⁴ᴮ모든 층의 불을 켠 후에는 정문을 열 준비가 되어 있어야 합니다. 그에 필요한 열쇠는 제 사무실에 있는 열쇠 보관장 안에 있어요.

일기 예보에서 거대한 눈보라가 있을 거라고 하고, 또 제가 멀리 살고 있다 보니 그런 날씨에는 운전하고 싶지 않아서, ¹⁷⁵저는 온종일 휴가를 내고 집에서 나오지 않을 예정이에요. 하지만 무슨 문제가 생기거나 질문이 있으시면 마음 놓고 제게 전화하세요. 제 조언이 필요하시면 온라인으로 채팅도 가능할 거예요.

저는 당신이 도서관까지 걸어올 수 있을 정도로 가까이 산다는 걸 정말 다행으로 생각해요. 기꺼이 이 일을 하겠다고 해 주셔서 감사합니다.

행운을 빌어요!

도서관 보조 사서
노라 예일즈 드림

어휘 in one's place ~ 대신에 reminder (할 일 등을) 상기시켜 주는 메모 procedure 절차, 방법 disarm (무장) 해제시키다 journal 정기 간행물, 신문 classify 분류하다, 구분하다 run into (곤경 등을) 만나다[겪다]

172. 이메일의 목적은?

(A) 기상 상황을 경고하기 위해
(B) 일정 변경을 권하기 위해
(C) 일자리를 제안하기 위해
(D) 절차의 개요를 설명해 주기 위해

해설   목적 문제

단서 (172)에서 개관 절차를 도와주기 위한 짧은 메모를 보내 주고 싶었다고 했으므로, 절차의 개요를 설명해 주려고 이메일을 쓴 것임을 알 수 있다. 따라서 정답은 (D).

패러프레이징 [단서] a quick reminder to help you out with the opening procedure → [정답] outline a procedure

173. 사이먼 씨에 대해 암시된 것은?

(A) 전에 도서관을 열어 본 적이 있다.

초콜릿이 어떻게 만들어지는지 모두 알게 된 후에, 여러분은 곧 출시될 제품들의 특별 샘플을 맛보실 수 있고, 저희의 마법 같은 초콜릿 분수를 즐기실 수 있으며, 할인된 가격으로 선물 바구니를 구매하실 수 있습니다. 덧붙여, ¹⁶⁶모든 방문객은 선물로 초콜릿 한 상자를 가지고 가시게 될 것입니다.

보안상의 이유로 ¹⁶⁷방문객의 인원은 제한되니, 일찍 예약해 주세요! 투어는 성인이 45달러, 학생이 30달러, 12세 미만의 어린이가 20달러입니다. ¹⁶⁷555-9963번으로 전화하셔서 시간을 잡으세요.

어휘 premises (항상 복수형) 부지, 구내 sweet 단것, 사탕 및 초콜릿류 upcoming 곧 있을, 다가오는 at a discount 할인하여

165. 광고되고 있는 것은?
(A) 새로운 종류의 초콜릿
(B) 특별 기념일 투어
(C) 식료품점에서의 할인 판매 행사
(D) 혁신적인 사탕 제조기

해설 주제 문제

지문의 주제에 대한 단서는 대부분 지문 초반부에 위치한다. 단서 (165)에서 회사가 75주년을 맞이하여 이를 축하하고자 일반에 공장을 공개하고 가이드 투어를 제공한다고 했으므로 정답은 (B).

패러프레이징 [단서] a guided tour that will show you every step of the process → [정답] A special anniversary tour

166. 무료로 제공될 것은?
(A) 선물 바구니들
(B) 분수들
(C) 장식품들
(D) 초콜릿 상자들

해설 특정 정보 확인 문제

단서 (166)에서 모든 방문객은 선물로 초콜릿 한 상자를 가지고 가게 될 거라고 했으므로 초콜릿이 들어 있는 상자를 무료로 받게 될 것임을 알 수 있다. 따라서 정답은 (D). 지문의 as a gift가 문제에서는 for free로 패러프레이징되었다.

패러프레이징 [단서] a box of chocolates → [정답] Boxes of sweets

167. 독자들이 하도록 권장되는 일은?
(A) 시간대 예약하기
(B) 주문하기
(C) 제품 맛보기
(D) 장비 하나를 시범 사용하기

해설 특정 정보 확인 문제

단서 (167)에서 인원이 제한되므로 일찍 예약하라고 하면서, 특정 전화번호로 전화해서 시간을 잡으라고 했으므로 정답은 (A).

패러프레이징 [단서] schedule a time → [정답] Reserve a time slot

168-171 온라인 채팅

셀람 합테 [오후 4:26] ¹⁶⁸여러분 두 분이 주간 직원 회의 마지막에 있었던 제 공지를 놓칠 수밖에 없었다는 걸 알고 있어요. 그래서 두 분께 보충 설명을 해드리려고요.

애너 모건 [오후 4:28] 고마워요. ¹⁶⁸저희가 놓친 게 무엇인가요?

셀람 합테 [오후 4:29] ¹⁶⁸우리 회사에서 신제품으로 오래 지속되는 립스틱을 발매할 거예요.

기쿠요 츠루타 [오후 4:30] 그거 아주 좋은 소식이네요. ¹⁶⁹제품 라인에 또 다른 제품을 하나 추가하자는 제 조언을 연구 개발 부서가 받아들였다니 기뻐요.

애너 모건 [오후 4:31] 새로운 립스틱의 광고는 언제 시작하나요?

셀람 합테 [오후 4:32] 캐터네오 씨가 지금 마케팅 계획을 짜고 있어요.

기쿠요 츠루타 [오후 4:34] ¹⁷⁰이 일은 선임 마케팅 임원이 맡는 게 더 낫지 않을까요?

애너 모건 [오후 4:35] ¹⁷⁰맞아요. 캐터네오 씨는 우리 회사에 새로 오셔서 우리 제품들에 대해 잘 모르시잖아요.

셀람 합테 [오후 4:39] 그건 알고 있어요. ¹⁷⁰하지만 그분은 화장품 마케팅 경력이 있어요.

애너 모건 [오후 4:41] 그렇군요. 음, 그분이 우리의 이전 작업물을 좀 본다고 해서 나쁠 건 없을 거예요. ¹⁷¹제가 그분께 이전 프로젝트들의 포트폴리오를 보내 드릴 수 있어요.

기쿠요 츠루타 [오후 4:42] 그러면 전 기꺼이 그분의 작업물을 검토할게요.

셀람 합테 [오후 4:43] 그럴 필요까진 없을 것 같아요, 기쿠요 씨, 하지만 ¹⁷¹당신의 생각은 마음에 드네요, 애너 씨.

애너 모건 [오후 4:44] ¹⁷¹알겠어요. 지금 그 일을 할게요.

어휘 announcement 공고, 발표 (내용) fill in (지금까지 있었던 일을) ~에게 들려주다[보충 설명해 주다] long-lasting 오래 지속되는 put together (이것저것을 모아) 만들다, 준비하다 senior 선임의, 상급자의 executive 임원, 경영진 have a background in ~에 이력이 있다

168. 주로 논의되고 있는 것은?
(A) 정책 업데이트
(B) 신규 고객
(C) 일정 변경
(D) 제품 출시

해설 주제 문제

단서 (168)을 종합해 보면, 합테 씨가 주간 직원 회의에서 공지한 신제품 립스틱 발매 계획을 언급하고 있고, 이어서 관련 내용이 논의되고 있다. 따라서 정답은 (D).

패러프레이징 [단서] release a new long-lasting lipstick → [정답] A product launch

161-164 기사

1월 30일—¹⁶²·¹⁶⁴전례 없는 성공적인 4분기 이후에 하바트 사가 전 직원에게 많은 연말 보너스를 지급할 것이라는 소문이 있었다. — [1] —. ¹⁶¹·¹⁶⁴하바트 사의 대변인 브라이언 캐스터 씨는 회사가 그 대신에 환경 재단인 엔바이러 퍼스트에 큰 기부를 할 것이라고 발표했다.

하바트 사는 환경 문제에 소홀한 것으로 유명하기 때문에 그 발표는 뜻밖의 소식으로 여겨졌다. — [2] —. 하바트 사의 공장 중 한 곳에서 발생한 작은 폭발로 인해 화학 물질 유출이 있었고, 이것이 주변의 강을 오염시킨 후에 논란은 특히 거셌다. 유출은 빠르게 억제되었으나, ¹⁶³지역 주민들은 항의 시위를 하러 거리로 나와 회사의 생태 문제에 대한 부주의를 맹비난했다. — [3] —.

그러나 하바트 사의 최근 결정은 이러한 주장을 반박하는 것으로 보인다. 캐스터 씨는 회사가 지속 가능한 생산과 관련된 문제들을 아주 심각하게 여기고 있다고 강조했다. "저희는 환경을 보호하고자 분투하는 단체들을 지지하고 그들과 협력하여 일하기를 원합니다."라고 캐스터 씨는 분명히 밝혔다. — [4] —. 기부금의 총 액수는 밝혀지지 않았으나, 엔바이러 퍼스트가 지금까지 받았던 중에 가장 큰 액수인 것으로 예상된다. 캐스터 씨는 하바트 사의 모든 추가 수익은 해당 단체로 갈 것이라고 강조했다.

어휘 unprecedented 전례 없는 revelation 공개, 폭로 ignore 무시하다 controversy 논란 intense 거센, 극심한 contaminate 오염시키다 contain 억제하다, ~이 들어 있다 take to the streets 가두 시위에 나서다 denounce 맹비난하다, 고발하다 ecological 생태상의, 생태계의 contradict 반박하다, 부정하다 sustainable 지속 가능한 in collaboration with ~와 협력[제휴]하여

161. 기사의 목적은?
(A) 환경 문제에 대한 기업의 접근법을 비판하기 위해
(B) 자연재해를 대비하기 위한 더 강력한 조치를 옹호하기 위해
(C) 비영리 단체에 대한 회사의 기부를 발표하기 위해
(D) 지역 공장에서 발생한 사고를 알리기 위해

해설 목적 문제

단서 (161)에서 하바트 사가 한 재단에 기부를 할 것이라고 발표했다고 했고, 이에 대한 내용이 기사 전반에 걸쳐 다뤄지고 있으므로 정답은 (C).

패러프레이징 [단서] the company would instead be making a large donation to Enviro First, an environmental foundation → [정답] a company's contribution to a nonprofit

162. 하바트 사에 대해 시사된 것은?
(A) 환경친화적인 방식으로 알려져 있다.
(B) 직원들에게 추가 보상을 제공할 것이다.
(C) 4분기에 예외적으로 수익이 좋았다.
(D) 강 주변에 새 공장을 지을 계획이다.

해설 Not/True 문제

단서 (162)를 통해 하바트 사가 전례 없는 성공적인 4분기를 보냈음을 알 수 있으므로 정답은 (C).

패러프레이징 [단서] an unprecedented successful fourth quarter → [정답] an exceptionally profitable fourth quarter

163. 기사에 따르면, 사람들이 하바트 사에 대해서 항의를 하게 된 원인은?
(A) 환경에 대한 소홀함
(B) 직원 복리 후생 제도
(C) 잦은 폭발 사고
(D) 적은 액수의 자선 기부금

해설 특정 정보 확인 문제

단서 (163)에서 지역 주민들은 회사의 생태 문제에 대한 부주의를 맹비난하며 이에 대해 항의하려고 거리로 나왔다고 했으므로, 시위의 원인이 환경에 대한 소홀함 때문이었음을 알 수 있다. 따라서 정답은 (A).

패러프레이징 [단서] the company's lack of care for ecological concerns → [정답] Its neglect of the environment

164. [1], [2], [3], [4]번으로 표시된 위치들 중 다음 문장이 들어가기에 가장 적절한 곳은?

"하지만, 이것은 어제 열린 기자 회견에서 부인되었다."

(A) [1]
(B) [2]
(C) [3]
(D) [4]

해설 문장 위치 찾기 문제

제시된 문장이 '대조'를 나타내는 접속부사 However로 시작하는 것으로 보아, 앞뒤의 내용이 반대되는 관계인 자리에 들어가야 함을 알 수 있다. [1]번 앞뒤의 단서 (164)를 보면, [1]번 앞에서는 회사가 직원들에게 연말 보너스를 지급할 거라는 소문이 있었다고 했고, [1]번 뒤에서는 그 대신 환경 재단에 기부를 할 것이라고 했다. 따라서 앞 문장이 사실이 아닌 것으로 밝혀졌다는 내용의 제시 문장은 [1]번에 들어가는 것이 알맞으므로 정답은 (A).

165-167 광고

¹⁶⁵보카 초콜릿이 75주년을 맞이하여 이를 축하하고자, 공장을 5월 6일부터 5월 12일까지 일주일 동안 일반에 공개할 예정입니다. 이것은 여러분이 공장 부지에 방문하여 보카 초콜릿이 어떻게 맛있는 초콜릿을 만드는지 알 수 있는 기회입니다!

¹⁶⁵우선, 여러분께서는 카카오 열매에서부터 포장 상자에 이르기까지 공정의 전 단계를 보여 줄 가이드 투어를 하시게 될 것입니다. 여러분께서는 저희 직원들이 기계를 작동시키는 것과, 저희 초콜릿 아티스트들이 최종 제품을 장식하는 것을 보시게 될 것입니다.

해설 Not/True 문제

단서 (156)에서 짧은 드레스는 착용하지 말라고 했으므로 정답은 (D).

패러프레이징 [단서] short-cut dresses → [정답] Short skirts

157. 드림 보이지스 사가 기부하는 경품에 대해 암시된 것은?
(A) 드림 보이지스 사 직원들은 받을 수 없을 것이다.
(B) 항공권과 관련된 비용은 포함하지 않는다.
(C) 가장 성과가 좋은 직원들에게 수여될 것이다.
(D) 모금 행사에서 가장 비싼 경품이다.

해설 추론 문제

단서 (157)에서 드림 보이지스 사와 관련된 사람은 누구라도 이 경품들을 탈 자격이 없다고 했으므로, 직원들은 드림 보이지스 사가 기부하는 경품을 받을 수 없다는 것을 유추할 수 있다. 따라서 정답은 (A).

패러프레이징 [단서] anyone affiliated with Dream Voyages is not eligible to win any of these prizes → [정답] They may not be won by Dream Voyages employees.

158-160 이메일

수신: 가필드, 애너 〈annagarfield76@peoplesnet.com〉
발신: 고객 서비스 〈cs@featherflights.com〉
날짜: 7월 12일
제목: 비행편 예약 – 조치가 필요함

애너 가필드 씨께,

¹⁵⁸저희는 고객님의 로스엔젤레스행 비행편에 대한 지불이 처리되지 않았음을 알려 드리기 위해 이메일을 보냅니다. 총액 636.88달러를 저희 웹사이트를 통해 지불해 주십시오. — [1] —. 고객님의 예약은 이 금액이 수령되기 전까지는 완료되지 않을 것입니다. ¹⁵⁸ ¹⁵⁹요청이 이루어진 후 24시간 이내에 지불이 되지 않으면 좌석이 박탈될 것입니다. — [2] —.

참고로, 고객님께서는 8월 7일 토요일 오후 3시 20분에 오스틴에서 로스엔젤레스로 출발하여 8월 29일 일요일 오전 10시 10분에 되돌아오는 왕복 항공편 좌석 2개를 요청하셨습니다. — [3] —.

¹⁶⁰고객님께서 해당 항공권에 대해 최초에 견적을 받으신 가격은 오늘 이후에는 더 이상 이용 가능하지 않을 수 있다는 점을 유념하시기 바랍니다. 이 때문에 저희가 고객님께서 가능한 한 빨리 예약을 완료하시도록 촉구하는 것입니다. 도움이 필요하시면, 평일 오전 9시에서 오후 5시 사이에 저희 고객 서비스 전화인 555-293-5892번으로 전화 주시면 됩니다. — [4] —.

페더 플라이츠 사를 선택해 주셔서 감사합니다. 저희는 고객님을 모시게 되기를 고대합니다.

페더 플라이츠 사 고객 서비스팀 드림

어휘 action 조치, 행동   forfeit 박탈당하다   reference 참고, 참조   originally 최초에, 원래   quote 견적을 내다   urge 촉구하다, 권고하다

158. 이메일의 목적은?
(A) 예약을 확인해 주기 위해
(B) 비행편 변경을 설명하기 위해
(C) 취소를 승인하기 위해
(D) 지불되어야 하는 금액을 고객에게 알리기 위해

해설 목적 문제

목적 문제의 단서는 글의 초반에 있는 경우가 많으므로 이 부분을 주의해서 살펴보자. 단서 (158)에서 비행편에 대한 지불이 처리되지 않았음을 알리기 위해 메일을 보냈다고 했고, 지불 요청액과 지불 기한 또한 언급되고 있으므로 정답은 (D).

패러프레이징 [단서] to inform you that payment for your flight to Los Angeles has not been processed → [정답] To notify a customer of a due payment

159. [1], [2], [3], [4]번으로 표시된 위치들 중 다음 문장이 들어가기에 가장 적절한 곳은?

"그렇게 되면, 고객님께서는 예약 절차를 다시 시작하셔야 할 겁니다."
(A) [1]
(B) [2]
(C) [3]
(D) [4]

해설 문장 위치 찾기 문제

제시된 문장에서 결과를 나타내는 연결어 Thus에 주목하여 이 문장의 원인을 암시하는 문장을 찾아야 한다. '그렇게 되면 예약 절차를 다시 시작해야 한다'고 했으므로, 이 문장은 이메일 수신자가 제시된 조치를 취하지 않아 예약이 취소되는 경우가 언급된 이후에 위치해야 한다. 단서 (159)에서 지불이 기한 내에 이뤄지지 않으면 예약하려고 했던 좌석이 박탈될 것이라고 했으므로, 그 다음 위치인 [2]번에 제시된 문장이 들어가는 게 자연스럽다. 따라서 정답은 (B).

160. 항공권 가격에 대해 시사된 것은?
(A) 향후 변경될 수도 있다.
(B) 일시적으로 할인된다.
(C) 편도만 포함한다.
(D) 전화로만 지불할 수 있다.

해설 Not/True 문제

단서 (160)에서 해당 항공권의 최초 견적가는 오늘 이후에는 더 이상 이용 가능하지 않을 수 있다고 했으므로, 향후 항공권 가격이 변경될 가능성이 있다는 것을 유추할 수 있다. 따라서 정답은 (A).

패러프레이징 [단서] the price you were originally quoted for the tickets may no longer be available after today → [정답] It might change in the future.

153-154 웹페이지

https://www.tothecloudsclimbing.com/about

| 홈 | 소개 | 제품 | 제휴 | 연락처 |

¹⁵³투 더 클라우즈 사는 설립된 지 15년도 더 되었고 시중에서 가장 혁신적인 등산 장비와 등산복을 만들기 위해 끊임없이 애써 왔습니다. 오늘 저희에게 연락하셔서 투 더 클라우즈 사의 공식 유통 업체가 되십시오. ^{154C}저희는 시중에서 가장 잘 팔리는 브랜드 중 하나로, 등산 단체의 관심을 끌기 위해서는 저희 제품을 가게에 구비하셔야 할 것입니다. 투 더 클라우즈 장비를 판매함으로써, 훌륭한 장비와 의복을 판매하는 신뢰할 만한 매장이라는 명성을 얻게 되실 것입니다. 게다가 ^{154A}저희의 모든 제품에는 고객들로 하여금 자신이 우수한 장비를 구매하는 것이라고 안심하게 해 주는 평생 품질 보증서가 딸려 있습니다. 그리고 저희는 고품질의 포스터, 현수막, 전단을 제공합니다. ^{154D}저희 상품은 그래서 홍보하기도 간단하고 항상 빠르게 품절됩니다.

어휘 gear (집합명사) 장비, 복장 apparel (집합명사) 의복, 의류 around 존재하는 distributor 유통 업체, 배급사 gain a reputation 명성을 얻다 trustworthy 신뢰할 수 있는 warranty 품질 보증(서) reassure 안심시키다 superior 우수한 leaflet 전단 market (상품을) 광고하다[내놓다]; 시장

153. 투 더 클라우즈 사에 연락해야 하는 사람은?

(A) 스포츠용품 소매업자들
(B) 전문 운동선수들
(C) 등산 동호회 회장들
(D) 장비 제조업자들

해설 특정 정보 확인 문제

단서 (153)에서 투 더 클라우즈 사는 등산 장비와 등산복을 만드는 업체임을 알 수 있고, 공식 유통 업체가 되기 위해 연락하라고 했으므로 정답은 (A).

패러프레이징 [단서] distributor → [정답] retailers

154. 투 더 클라우즈 사 제품에 대해 언급되지 않은 것은?

(A) 품질 보증이 만료되지 않는다.
(B) 저렴한 가격에 판매된다.
(C) 등산가들 사이에서 인기가 있다.
(D) 광고하기 쉽다.

해설 Not/True 문제

(A)는 단서 (154A)에서 모든 제품에 평생 품질 보증서가 딸려 있다고 했으므로 품질 보증이 만료되지 않는다는 것을 알 수 있고, (C)는 단서 (154C)에서 시중에서 가장 잘 팔리는 브랜드 중 하나라고 했으므로 등산가들에게 인기가 있다는 것을 알 수 있으며, (D)는 단서 (154D)에서 제품을 홍보하기 간단하다고 했으므로 광고하기 쉽다는 것도 알 수 있다. 그러나 가격에 대한 언급은 없으므로 정답은 (B).

155-157 공지

직원 공지: 연례 주니 모금 행사

주니 아동 단체를 위한 연례 모금 행사가 사코나 컨벤션 센터에서 4월 30일 일요일 저녁 6시부터 저녁 8시 30분까지 열릴 예정입니다. 드림 보이지스 사 직원들의 참석은 선택 사항이지만 적극 권장됩니다. 늘 그렇듯이, 우리 회사는 이 행사를 후원할 예정입니다. ¹⁵⁵그러나, 2년에 한 번씩 해 오던 것처럼 돈을 기부하는 대신에 우리는 모금용 복권을 위한 경품을 기부할 것입니다. 이전에 이 행사에 참여한 적이 없으신 분들께서는 복장 규정에 주의해 주세요.

복장 규정

남성분들은 턱시도를 입을 필요는 없지만 흰 셔츠 및 단색 넥타이와 함께 어두운 색상의 정장을 입어야 합니다. 요란한 무늬는 피해 주세요.
여성분들에게 허용되는 복장에는 긴 드레스와 바지 정장이 포함됩니다. ¹⁵⁶짧은 길이의 드레스는 착용하지 말아 주세요. 하이힐을 신으시기로 하셨다면, 오랜 시간 동안 그 신발을 신고 서 계셔도 편안할 수 있도록 해 주셔야 합니다.

경품 기부

드림 보이지스 사는 모든 것이 포함되어 있는 유럽 여행 상품 1종, 멕시코 리조트 휴가 상품 3종, 주말 스파 상품 10종을 기부할 예정입니다. ¹⁵⁷드림 보이지스 사와 관련된 사람은 누구라도 이 경품들을 탈 자격이 없다는 것을 유념해 주세요.

어휘 fundraising 모금 gala 경축 행사, 축제 organization 단체, 조직 attendance 참석, 출석 sponsor 후원하다 donate 기부하다, 기증하다 raffle (모금용) 복권 dress code 복장 규정 loud (색깔·복장이) 화려한 acceptable 허용할 수 있는, 받아들여지는 attire 복장, 의복 all-inclusive 모두를 포함한 affiliate with ~과 관련짓다 be eligible to do ~할 자격이 있다

155. 드림 보이지스 사가 변경한 것은?

(A) 직원들의 복장 규정
(B) 단체에 하는 기부
(C) 행사 참석에 대한 방침
(D) 고객을 위한 보상의 종류

해설 특정 정보 확인 문제

단서 (155)에서 2년에 한 번씩 해 온 것처럼 돈을 기부하는 대신에 모금 목적의 복권을 위한 경품을 기부하겠다고 했으므로, 단체에 기부하는 형태를 변경한 것을 알 수 있다. 따라서 정답은 (B).

패러프레이징 [단서] donating money / donating prizes for the raffle → [정답] contribution

156. 여성들이 착용하도록 허용되지 않은 것은?

(A) 어두운 색상의 드레스
(B) 하이힐 구두
(C) 긴 바지
(D) 짧은 치마

토머스 볼퍼트	[오후 7:01]

문제없어요. 어디에 있는지만 말씀해 주시면 제가 가지고 갈게요.

로라 피셔	[오후 7:02]

아, 정말 다행이에요. ¹⁴⁹제 책상 아래에 상자가 하나 보일 거예요. 파란색이랑 검은색으로 된 거요. 갤린더스 컬렉션 샵의 상표가 붙어 있고요.

토머스 볼퍼트	[오후 7:03]

¹⁴⁹네, 잠시만요. 확인해 볼게요.

토머스 볼퍼트	[오후 7:07]

찾았어요. 초대장에는 7시 30분이라고 되어 있죠, 그렇죠? ¹⁵⁰저는 이제 가 봐야겠네요.

로라 피셔	[오후 7:08]

네, 정말 고마워요! 당신 덕분에 살았어요.

어휘 by any chance 혹시라도 be about to do 막 ~하려는 참이다 retirement 은퇴, 퇴직 be supposed to do ~하기로 되어 있다 relief 다행, 안심 hold on 기다리다 lifesaver 궁지에서 구해 주는 사람

149. 오후 7시 7분에, 볼퍼트 씨가 "찾았어요"라고 한 것에서 그가 의도한 것은?

(A) 선물을 찾았다.
(B) 가는 길을 알고 있다.
(C) 파티 초대장을 받았다.
(D) 선물 영수증을 갖고 있다.

해설 의도 파악 문제

단서 (149)에서 피셔 씨가 자신이 가지고 오기로 했던 선물 상자가 책상 아래에 있다면서 상자의 외양에 대해 설명했고 볼퍼트 씨는 확인해 보겠다고 말한 뒤에 '찾았다'고 했으므로, 피셔 씨가 말한 선물 상자를 볼퍼트 씨가 찾았다는 것을 유추할 수 있다. 따라서 정답은 (A).

패러프레이징 [단서] Jarrod's gift → [정답] the present

150. 볼퍼트 씨가 다음에 갈 것 같은 장소는?

(A) 사무실
(B) 피셔 씨의 집
(C) 식당
(D) 상점

해설 추론 문제

단서 (150)을 종합해 보면 피셔 씨가 식당으로 퇴직 기념 선물을 가지고 오기로 되어 있었는데 이미 식당에 거의 다 왔다고 했으므로 퇴직 기념 파티의 장소가 식당임을 유추할 수 있다. 또한 볼퍼트 씨도 이제 선물을 챙겨서 파티 장소로 가겠다고 했으므로 정답은 (C).

151-152 이메일

수신: 백수연 〈baeksooyeon@harligen.net〉
발신: 제럴드 핀 〈finngerald@harligen.net〉
날짜: 1월 18일
제목: 긴급

백 씨에게,

당신의 도움이 필요합니다. ¹⁵¹더턴 가 171번지 건물의 현장 감독이 제게 알리길, 그의 팀은 수방벽에 사용할 자갈을 거의 다 써 버렸다고 합니다. 그들이 일정에 늦지 않으려면 가능한 한 빨리 더 많은 양이 필요해요. ¹⁵¹저는 다른 현장들에서 안전 점검을 하느라 오늘 남은 시간 동안 자리를 비울 예정이라서, 직접 이걸 처리할 수가 없어요. ¹⁵²당신이 공급업체에 전화해서 자갈을 더 배송해 달라고 요청해 주시겠어요? 우리가 사용하는 종류가 그 건물 이름으로 데이터베이스에 올라가 있어요. 그건 찾기 쉬울 겁니다.

감사합니다!

제럴드 핀 드림

어휘 foreman (공장 · 건설 현장의) 감독 run out of ~을 다 써 버리다, ~이 없어지다 gravel 자갈 water barrier 수방벽 fall (특정 상태가) 되다, 떨어지다 behind schedule 예정보다 늦게 site (건물 · 도시 등의 건설) 현장 take care of ~을 처리하다 supplier 공급 회사, 공급자

151. 핀 씨가 근무할 것 같은 업종은?

(A) 건설 회사
(B) 제조 시설
(C) 철물점
(D) 부동산 회사

해설 추론 문제

단서 (151)의 foreman(현장 감독), property(건물), safety checks(안전 점검), sites(현장) 등의 어휘를 통해 핀 씨는 건설 회사에 근무하고 있음을 추론할 수 있다. 따라서 정답은 (A). property라는 단어 때문에 (D)를 정답으로 고르지 않도록 주의하자.

152. 백 씨가 하도록 요청받은 것은?

(A) 잠재 고객 만나기
(B) 주문 넣기
(C) 데이터베이스 업데이트하기
(D) 배달물 찾아오기

해설 특정 정보 찾기 문제

단서 (152)에서 공급업체에 전화해서 자갈을 더 배송해 달라는 요청을 하라고 했으므로 정답은 (B).

패러프레이징 [단서] call the supplier and ask for more gravel to be delivered → [정답] Place an order

금 막대한 비용을 치르게 할 수도 있다고 했고 빈칸 뒤에서는 임원들이 장기적으로 이익이 될 것이라는 데에 동의했다고 했다. 따라서 서로 반대되는 내용을 연결하는 양보의 접속부사가 빈칸에 들어가는 것이 자연스러우므로 정답은 (B).

145. 구동사 adhere to
(A) 제안하다 (B) 따라가다 (C) 비교하다 **(D) 고수하다**

해설 빈칸 뒤의 전치사 to와 호응하면서 적절한 문맥을 이루는 동사 어휘를 찾아야 한다. 빈칸이 포함된 절 뒤에 세 업체가 협약을 따름으로써 얻게 되는 결과들이 나오므로, 빈칸에는 to와 호응하여 '고수하다, 충실히 지키다'라는 의미를 나타내는 adhere가 오는 것이 알맞다. 따라서 정답은 (D). (B)는 타동사로 뒤에 전치사 없이 바로 목적어를 취하므로 오답.

146. 부정대명사 none

해설 빈칸에 알맞은 대명사를 찾는 문제이다. 빈칸은 문장의 주어이면서 문맥상 임원 중 아무도 내용을 자진해서 말하지 않았다는 부정의 의미가 자연스러우므로 (C)와 (D)가 정답 후보. 빈칸은 뒤의 전치사구 of the sixteen directors의 수식을 받는데 (D)는 둘 중에서 어느 쪽도 아니라는 의미로 쓰이므로 오답. 따라서 셋 이상 중에서 아무도 아니라는 의미를 나타내는 (C)가 정답. 지시대명사 (A)는 those of로 쓰일 경우 '~의 것들'을 의미하고, 부정대명사 (B)는 any of로 쓰일 경우 '~중 무엇이나[누구나]'를 의미하여 문맥상 적절하지 않으므로 오답.

PART 7

147-148 영수증

티나스 트레저스

날짜: 11/15
회원 번호: 194538838

¹⁴⁷실크 넥타이	22.99달러
가죽 벨트	39.99달러
리넨 셔츠	45.00달러
소계	107.98달러
세금 (6%)	6.48달러
합계	**114.46달러**
현금	120.00달러
거스름돈	-5.54달러
¹⁴⁸적립 회원 포인트	110
총 회원 포인트	1,005

축하드립니다! ¹⁴⁸회원 포인트 1,000점 이상에 도달하셨고 이 쿠폰을 발급받으셨습니다:

티나스 트레저스에서 사용할 수 있는 5달러권
쿠폰 코드: A2225SG56

www.tinastreasures.com에서 저희를 온라인으로 찾아 주시면, 거기에서 저희 상품을 살펴보시고, 제품 후기를 작성하시고, 주문을 하실 수 있습니다. 저희 소식지를 신청하셔서 이메일로 특별 판촉물을 받아 보실 수도 있습니다.

어휘 subtotal 소계 good for ~과 같은 가치를 지니는 place an order 주문하다 sign up for ~을 신청하다 promotion 판촉물, 판촉

147. 티나스 트레저스의 매장 종류일 것 같은 것은?
(A) 원단 유통 회사
(B) 의류 직판점
(C) 철물점
(D) 귀금속 매장

해설 추론 문제

물건을 구매한 영수증의 단서 (147)에서 구매 항목이 실크 넥타이, 가죽 벨트, 리넨 셔츠인 것으로 보아, 의류를 판매하는 매장의 영수증임을 유추할 수 있다. 따라서 정답은 (B).

148. 영수증에 따르면, 구매자가 쿠폰을 받은 방법은?
(A) 대회에서 입상함으로써
(B) 제품을 평가함으로써
(C) 단골 고객이 됨으로써
(D) 소식지를 구독함으로써

해설 특정 정보 확인 문제

단서 (148)에서 회원 포인트 1,000점 이상에 도달해서 쿠폰을 받았다고 했고 회원 포인트는 구매에 따라 누적되는 것으로 보이므로 지속적인 구매를 통해 쿠폰을 받게 되었다는 것을 유추할 수 있다. 따라서 정답은 (C). 지문의 earned가 문제에서는 receive로 패러프레이징되었다.

패러프레이징 [단서] have reached more than one thousand member points → [정답] being a loyal customer

149-150 문자 메시지

로라 피셔 [오후 6:58]
토머스, 혹시 아직 사무실에 계세요?

토머스 볼퍼트 [오후 6:59]
네, 아직 여기 있긴 한데, 재러드 씨의 퇴직 기념 파티에 가려고 막 나가려던 참이었어요.

로라 피셔 [오후 7:00]
¹⁴⁹ ¹⁵⁰제가 식당으로 재러드 씨의 선물을 가져오기로 되어 있었는데, 그걸 사무실에 두고 왔다는 걸 방금 알아차렸어요. ¹⁵⁰저는 이미 식당에 거의 다 왔어요.

139-142 편지

11월 25일
에릭 클로스터
마리솔 로 2957번지
윌로우스, 펜실베이니아 주 18765

클로스터 씨께,

저희는 귀하의 〈먼슬리 토크스〉 지의 구독에 대한 최근 지불이 거부되었다는 것을 알려 드리기 위해 편지를 드립니다. 이에 따라, 저희는 거래를 진행할 수가 없었습니다. [139]**이 문제는 주소 변경이나 카드 만료 때문일 수 있습니다.** 귀하의 정보를 모두 [140]**확인하신** 후에도 오류의 원인을 알아낼 수 없으시면, 귀하의 은행에 연락하십시오.

귀하의 지불이 진행되지 않았으므로 저희는 귀하의 주소로 보내질 최근 호의 배송을 [141]**취소했습니다**. 12월 호를 받으시려면, 저희가 마지막 발행물들을 곧 발송할 예정이므로 [142]**지체 없이** 유효한 지불 정보를 제공해 주셔야 합니다.

귀하의 〈먼슬리 토크스〉 지 구독에 관한 질문이 있으시면 555-3548번으로 저희에게 전화해 주십시오.

〈먼슬리 토크스〉 지 직원 드림

어휘 subscription 구독(료) decline 거절하다 process 처리하다 transaction 거래, 매매 determine 알아내다, 밝히다 verify 확인하다 go through 통과되다, 진행되다 valid 유효한

139. 알맞은 문장 고르기
(A) 그러나, 저희는 정확한 신용 카드 정보를 가지고 있지 않습니다.
(B) 12.99달러의 취소 수수료는 귀하의 계좌에서 공제될 것입니다.
(C) 첨부된 것은 귀하의 저희 잡지 구독 갱신을 위한 양식입니다.
(D) 이 문제는 주소 변경이나 카드 만료 때문일 수 있습니다.

해설 빈칸 앞에 업체에서 거래를 처리할 수 없었다는 문제점이 언급되었으므로 빈칸에는 문제의 원인에 대한 내용이 오는 것이 적절하다. 따라서 (A)와 (D)가 정답 후보. 빈칸 뒤에서 오류의 원인을 알아내지 못할 가능성이 언급되었고, 또한 앞뒤로 연결되는 내용이 비슷한 내용들이므로 대조의 접속부사 However로 연결하는 것은 어색하다. 따라서 정답은 (D).

140. 명사 자리+동명사 vs. 명사
해설 빈칸에 알맞은 품사를 고르는 문제로, 빈칸은 전치사 after의 목적어 자리이므로 동명사 (A)와 명사 (B)가 정답 후보. 명사는 뒤에 목적어를 취할 수 없지만, 동사의 성질을 가지고 있는 동명사는 뒤에 있는 명사구 all of your information을 목적어로 취할 수 있으므로 동명사인 (A)가 정답.

141. 동사 어휘 cancel
(A) ~의 시간을 정하다 (B) 환불하다 **(C) 취소하다** (D) 측정하다

해설 문맥에 알맞은 동사 어휘를 고르는 문제. 빈칸을 포함한 문장의 다음 문장에서 12월 호를 받기 위해 클로스터 씨가 해야 하는 일이 나오는 것으로 보아, 빈칸을 포함한 문장에는 클로스터 씨에게 최신 호인 12월 호가 배송되지 않도록 조치가 취해졌음을 알리는 내용이 오는 것이 자연스럽다. 따라서 업체 측이 최신 호의 배송을 '취소했다'는 의미가 가장 적절하므로 정답은 (C).

142. 부사 어휘 promptly
(A) 부정확하게 (B) 확실히 **(C) 지체 없이** (D) 임시로

해설 문맥에 어울리는 부사 어휘를 고르는 문제로, 문맥상 '발행물을 곧 발송할 예정이므로 지체 없이 유효한 지불 정보를 제공해 줘야 한다'고 하는 것이 가장 자연스러우므로 정답은 (C).

143-146 기사

지역 업체들, 변화에 전념하다

베토스(1월 22일)—[143]**대기업 3사의 임원들이 어제 협약을 논의하기 위해 만났다.** 실행 가능성 있는 이 협약에 따르면, 프레스터 사, 앨펏 주식회사, 프로가 사는 자사 공장의 에너지 소비와 배출 수준을 제한하는 데에 전념하게 될 것이다. 이러한 변화는 각 업체의 생산 속도를 늦춤으로써 막대한 비용을 치르게 할 수 있다. [144]**그럼에도 불구하고**, 임원들은 친환경적인 방식에 집중하는 것이 장기적으로 보면 유익할 것이라는 데에 동의했다. "세 업체 모두 이 협약을 [145]**고수한다면** 아무도 손해를 많이 보지 않을 것이고, 환경은 이득을 볼 것입니다,"라고 프레스터 사의 한 임원은 주장했다. 16명의 임원 중 [146]**아무도** 계획의 실행안에 관한 어떠한 상세 내용도 자진해서 말하지 않았지만, 그들은 협약이 체결되었으며 곧 공개될 것이라고 확인해 주었다.

어휘 commit to ~에 전념하다 contract 협약(서), 계약(서) consumption 소비, 소모 emission 배출 environmentally friendly 친환경적인 beneficial 유익한 in the long run 장기적으로 보면, 결국에는 gain 이득을 얻다, 이익을 보다 volunteer 자진해서 말하다 logistics 실행 계획

143. 알맞은 문장 고르기
(A) 최근의 한 연구는 베토스의 오염 수준이 사상 최고치임을 보여 준다.
(B) 몇몇 지역 업체는 현재 신입 수준의 직원을 고용하려고 애쓰고 있다.
(C) 대기업 3사의 임원들이 어제 협약을 논의하기 위해 만났다.
(D) 태양 에너지는 수집하기 쉬운 재생 에너지의 일례일 뿐이다.

해설 빈칸 뒤에 세 개의 업체 이름을 나열하면서 이들이 이 협약에 따라 에너지 소비 제한에 동참하게 될 것이라고 하는 것으로 보아 빈칸에는 세 업체가 협약을 논의했다는 내용이 나오는 것이 자연스럽다. 따라서 정답은 (C).

144. 접속부사 nevertheless
(A) 뿐만 아니라 **(B) 그럼에도 불구하고** (C) 마찬가지로 (D) 그렇지 않으면

해설 문맥상 알맞은 접속부사를 고르는 문제이므로 빈칸 앞뒤 문장의 의미 관계를 파악해야 한다. 빈칸 앞에서 이러한 변화가 업체들로 하여

저희는 이 추가된 운영 시간을 여러분께서 누리시길 바랍니다.

체육관에서 뵙겠습니다!

베터 미 체육관, 관리자

데니스 프리머스 드림

어휘 complete (서식을) 작성하다, 완료하다; 완료된 strive to do ~하려고 노력하다 highly 대단히, 매우 valuable 소중한, 매우 유익한 individually 개별적으로, 따로따로 address (문제 등을) 다루다, 처리하다

131. 동사 자리＋과거시제
해설 빈칸은 who가 이끄는 관계사절의 동사 자리이므로 (B), (C), (D)가 정답 후보. 지문은 고객들이 과거에 설문지를 작성해 준 것에 대해 감사하다는 내용의 이메일이므로 과거시제인 (D)가 정답.

132. 형용사 자리_부사＋형용사
해설 빈칸은 주격 보어 자리이면서 빈칸 앞의 부사 highly의 수식을 받는 형용사 자리이므로 형용사인 (C)와 현재분사인 (D)가 정답 후보. 문맥상 고객의 의견이 '대단히 소중하다'는 내용이 자연스러우므로 정답은 (C). (D)는 의견이 '대단히 소중하게 여긴다'는 의미가 되어 문맥상 어색하므로 오답.

133. 명사 어휘 demand
(A) 요구 사항 (B) 일정 (C) 일상 (D) 고객
해설 문맥에 어울리는 명사 어휘를 고르는 문제로, 빈칸이 address의 목적어 자리임에 주목하자. 선택지 중 '다루다, 처리하다'를 의미하는 동사 address의 목적어이면서, 빈칸 앞 형용사 the most common과 가장 잘 어울리는 명사는 demands이므로 정답은 (A).

134. 알맞은 문장 고르기
(A) 유감스럽게도, 저희는 저희 운영 시간을 늘릴 수 없습니다.
(B) 이에 대응하여, 저희는 토요일에 저녁 9시까지 운영하기로 결정했습니다.
(C) 회원들은 원하는 만큼 오랜 시간 동안 마음껏 운동할 수 있습니다.
(D) 이것들은 여러분의 체육관 회원 약정서에 자세히 기술되어 있습니다.
해설 빈칸 앞에서 고객들이 짧은 주말 운영 시간에 대한 불만을 제기했음을 말했고 빈칸 뒤에서는 이 추가된 운영 시간을 누리길 바란다고 했다. 그러므로 빈칸에는 고객들의 불만에 대한 대응책으로 운영 시간이 늘어났음을 구체적으로 알리는 내용이 들어가야 한다. 따라서 정답은 (B).

135-138 광고

하우스가드로 여러분의 집을 지키세요! 저희의 ^{135}최신 보안 시스템은 여러분이 자신의 집에서 안전하고 편안하다고 느끼기 위해 필요한 최신의 기능들을 모두 갖추고 있습니다. 저희는 여러분의 부동산 전 구역에 걸쳐 보안 카메라, 동작 감지기, 경보 시스템을 설치할 것입니다. ^{136}게다가, 저희는 저희의 스마트 제어 로봇을 여러분의 가정에 설치해 드릴 텐데, 이것은 어떠한 위험이라도 제거하기 위해 여러분의 가전제품을 끊임없이 감시합니다. ^{137}하우스가드 로봇이 여러분의 집을 구할 수 있습니다. 예를 들면, 여러분께서 외출하실 때 가스를 켜 두셨다면, 이것이 여러분을 대신하여 ^{138}자동으로 가스를 잠가서 잠재적인 화재를 방지할 것입니다. 오늘 여러분의 댁을 더 안전하게 만드세요! 오늘 www.houseguard.com을 방문하셔서 설치 일정을 잡으세요.

어휘 secure 지키다, 안전하게 하다 feature 특징, 기능 property 건물, 부동산 equip A with B A에 B를 갖추게 하다 constantly 끊임없이 eliminate 제거하다, 없애다 prevent 방지하다 potential 잠재적인, 가능성이 있는 installation 설치

135. 형용사 어휘 state-of-the-art
(A) 중고의 (B) 장비를 제대로 갖추지 않은 (C) 구식의 **(D) 최신의**
해설 빈칸 뒤의 명사 security system을 수식하면서 문맥에 알맞은 형용사 어휘를 찾는 문제. 주어인 security system이 최신 기능을 갖추고 있다고 했으므로, 주어를 수식하는 형용사 역시 '최신의'라는 뜻을 나타내는 것이 자연스럽다. 따라서 정답은 (D).

136. 접속부사 in addition
(A) 그러므로 (B) 그렇기는 하지만 **(C) 게다가** (D) 반면에
해설 빈칸에 알맞은 접속부사를 고르는 문제. 빈칸 앞에서 업체에서 설치해 주는 다양한 기기가 나열되고 빈칸 뒤에서는 로봇 역시 설치할 것이라고 했으므로, 빈칸에는 앞 문장에 첨가의 의미를 더하는 접속부사가 알맞다. 따라서 정답은 (C).

137. 알맞은 문장 고르기
(A) 실제로, 최근 절도가 증가하고 있습니다.
(B) 하우스가드 로봇이 여러분의 집을 구할 수 있습니다.
(C) 고를 수 있는 제어 시스템이 많이 있습니다.
(D) 여러분은 이제 자신의 주방에서 굉장한 식사들을 요리할 수 있습니다.
해설 빈칸 앞에서 업체가 설치해 주는 로봇에 대해 이야기했고 빈칸 뒤에서는 로봇이 집을 지키기 위해 해 줄 수 있는 일을 예를 들어 설명하고 있으므로 빈칸에는 로봇이 집을 지키는 역할을 한다는 내용이 들어가는 것이 자연스럽다. 따라서 정답은 (B).

138. 부사 자리_동사 수식
해설 선택지를 보니 빈칸에 알맞은 품사를 고르는 문제. 빈칸 없이도 문장 성분이 완전하므로 빈칸은 수식어 자리임을 알 수 있는데, 빈칸 뒤에 동사 turn off가 있으므로 빈칸에는 이를 수식하는 부사가 들어가야 한다. 따라서 부사인 (D)가 정답.

124. 형용사 어휘 equivalent

엔지니어들은 선임 관리직에 채용이 고려되려면 석사 학위나 이와 동등한 근무 경력이 있어야 한다.

(A) 의도적인 (B) 수익성이 좋은 **(C) 동등한** (D) 체계적인

해설 빈칸 뒤의 명사구 work experience를 수식하는 형용사 어휘를 고르는 문제이다. 채용 대상자가 되기 위한 조건으로 '석사 학위나 이와 동등한 근무 경력이 있어야 한다'는 내용이 가장 자연스러우므로 정답은 (C). a degree or equivalent work experience는 채용과 관련된 주제에 자주 등장하는 어구이므로 암기하도록 하자.

어휘 master's degree 석사 학위 work experience (근무) 경력 opening 빈자리, 공석

125. 능동태 + 수 일치

도심 지역의 교통 혼잡을 완화하기 위해서 도시 계획 입안자는 일부 도로를 일방 통행로로 전환시킬 것이다.

해설 선택지를 보니 알맞은 동사 형태를 묻는 문제. 도시 계획 입안자가 일부 도로를 '전환시키는' 주체이므로 능동태인 (C)와 (D)가 정답 후보. 주어인 the city planner가 3인칭 단수이므로 정답은 (C). 현재진행형이 가까운 미래의 일을 나타내기도 한다는 것을 알아 두자.

어휘 alleviate 완화하다 traffic congestion 교통 혼잡 city planner 도시 계획 입안자 convert 전환시키다 roadway 도로, 차도 one-way street 일방 통행로

126. 명사 어휘 nomination

최종 수상자들은 비밀에 부쳐지겠지만, 탤런트 상의 최상위 후보자들은 시상식 2주 전에 밝혀질 것이다.

(A) 구독 (B) 비밀 (C) 축하 (인사) **(D) 후보자**

해설 빈칸 앞의 형용사 top 및 빈칸 뒤의 전치사구 for the talent awards의 수식을 받으면서 문맥에 알맞은 명사 어휘를 찾는 문제. 문맥상 '탤런트 상의 최상위 후보자들'이라는 의미가 가장 적절하므로 정답은 (D).

어휘 reveal 드러내다, 밝히다 ceremony 의식, 식

127. 형용사 자리_부사 + 형용사

데니 말로 씨는 면접이 진행될수록 회계직을 얻게 될 가능성에 대해 점점 더 기대하게 되었다.

해설 선택지를 보니 알맞은 품사를 고르는 문제. 빈칸은 동사 became의 주격 보어 자리이면서, 부사 more and more의 수식을 받는 형용사 자리이므로 정답은 (C).

어휘 hopeful 기대하는, 희망에 찬 chance 가능성, 기회 accounting 회계 (업무) progress 진행되다; 진보

128. 부사절 접속사 whether

내빈들은 그 행사에 참석할 계획이든 아니든 이달 말까지 초대장에 회신해야 한다.

(A) 어느 한쪽 **(B) ~이든 아니든** (C) ~한 이후로 (D) ~이긴 하지만

해설 빈칸 앞뒤로 완전한 절이 있으므로 빈칸에는 두 절을 연결하는 접속사가 와야 한다. 문장 끝에 or not이 있으므로 이와 호응하여 쓰일 수 있는 (B)가 정답. 문맥상으로도 '그 행사에 참석할 계획이든 아니든'의 의미가 자연스럽다.

어휘 be expected to do ~해야 한다, ~할 것으로 기대[예상]되다 reply 답장을 보내다 invitation 초대장, 초대

129. 소유격 관계대명사 whose

요리사 프랜시스 게일스 씨는 식당을 열었는데 그곳의 메뉴는 매일 아침 구할 수 있는 최상의 생선과 농산물에 따라 매일 바뀐다.

해설 빈칸에 알맞은 관계사를 찾는 문제이다. 빈칸 앞 선행사 restaurant와 빈칸 뒤 menu는 '식당의 메뉴'라는 의미로 소유 관계에 있으므로, 소유격 관계대명사인 (C)가 정답.

어휘 daily 매일 depending on ~에 따라 produce 농산물; 생산하다

130. 형용사 어휘 selective

헨서 주식회사의 임원들은 회사 목표를 설정하기 위한 반기 회의에 누가 들어오게 허용할지를 아주 까다롭게 고른다.

(A) 까다롭게 고르는 (B) 눈에 잘 띄는 (C) 접근 가능한 (D) 야심 있는

해설 선택지를 보니 알맞은 형용사 어휘를 고르는 문제. 문맥상 '반기 회의에 누가 들어오게 허용할지를 아주 까다롭게 고른다'는 내용이 가장 자연스러우므로 정답은 (A).

어휘 director 임원 biannual 연 2회의, 반기의 objective 목표; 객관적인

PART 6

131-134 이메일

수신: 회원 전원 〈memberlist@bettermegym.com〉
발신: 데니스 프리머스 〈dprimus@bettermegym.com〉
제목: 새로운 주말 운영 시간
날짜: 8월 4일

회원 여러분께,

베터 미 체육관에 관한 여러분의 아이디어를 공유하기 위해 저희의 설문 조사를 ¹³¹작성해 주신 모든 분께 감사드립니다. 저희는 저희 체육관을 고객들에게 가장 현대적이고 편리하게 유지하기 위해 노력하고 있기에, 여러분께서 주신 것과 같은 의견들은 저희에게 대단히 ¹³²소중합니다. 여러분 개개인에게 개별적으로 회신은 드리지 못하지만, 저희는 가장 흔한 ¹³³요구 사항들을 처리하기 위해 기꺼이 변경을 가하겠습니다. 이것들 중 첫 번째는 저희의 종료 시간에 관한 것이었습니다. 여러분 중 많은 분께서 저희의 짧은 주말 운영 시간에 대해 불만을 제기하셨습니다. ¹³⁴이에 대응하여, 저희는 토요일에 저녁 9시까지 운영하기로 결정했습니다.

어휘 patron 이용자, 후원자 renew 연장[갱신]하다 overdue fine 연체료

116. 구동사 benefit from
선임 직원들뿐만 아니라 신입 직원들도 급여 체계의 변경으로부터 혜택을 받게 될 것이다.
(A) ~의 (B) ~ 사이에 **(C) ~으로부터** (D) ~로

해설 선택지를 보니 알맞은 전치사를 찾는 문제로, 빈칸 앞 동사 benefit이 단서가 된다. 동사 benefit은 전치사 from과 함께 쓰여 '~으로부터 혜택을 받다'라는 의미를 나타낸다. 문맥상으로도 '급여 체계의 변경으로부터 혜택을 받게 될 것이다'는 의미가 자연스러우므로 정답은 (C).

어휘 not only A but also B A뿐 아니라 B 역시 revision 수정, 정정 pay scale 급여 체계

117. 접속사 vs. 전치사
지점 관리자는 눈보라가 치기 전에 직원들을 집에 보내기 위해 매장을 일찍 닫기로 결정했다.
(A) ~하기 위해서 **(B) ~하기 전에** (C) ~ 앞에 (D) ~보다는

해설 문맥에 어울리는 접속사 또는 전치사를 고르는 문제이다. to let 이하는 매장을 일찍 닫기로 결정한 목적이 되는데, '눈보라가 치기 전에 직원들을 귀가시키기 위해서'라는 의미가 자연스러우므로 접속사 (B)와 구전치사 (C)가 정답 후보. 빈칸 뒤에 절이 왔기 때문에 접속사인 (B)가 정답.

어휘 branch 지사, 분점 supervisor 관리자 snowstorm 눈보라

118. 부사 어휘 still
대회의 날짜와 장소는 선정되었지만, 프로그램은 아직도 마무리되어야 한다.
(A) 아직도 (B) 최근에 (C) 한때 (D) 정확히

해설 문맥에 어울리는 부사 어휘를 고르는 문제로, 빈칸 뒤의 동사구 needs to be finalized를 수식하면서 의미가 자연스러운 것을 고른다. but 앞의 절에 날짜와 장소가 선정되었다는 내용이 나오므로, but 이하의 절에서는 이와 대조적으로 '프로그램은 아직도 마무리되어야 한다'는 내용이 나오는 것이 자연스럽다. 따라서 정답은 (A).

어휘 venue 장소 convention 대회, 협의회 finalize 마무리 짓다, 최종적으로 승인하다

119. 지시대명사 those
동료들은 연례 야유회에 본인들을 차로 데려다주기로 자원하는 사람들에게 휘발유 비용을 주겠다고 할 것이다.
(A) 그들 **(B) 사람들** (C) 다른 (D) 누구나

해설 빈칸 뒤 who부터 picnic까지는 앞의 빈칸을 수식하는 관계대명사절이다. 이 관계대명사절의 수식을 받으면서 전치사 to의 목적어로 쓰일 수 있는 지시대명사 (B)와 부정대명사 (D)가 정답 후보. those who는 '~하는 사람들'이란 의미로 쓰이는데 문맥상으로도 '차로 데려다주기로 자원하는 사람들'이란 의미가 적절하므로 정답은 (B). 빈칸 뒤 관계대명사절의 동사 volunteer가 복수 동사이므로 단수 대명사 (D)는 오답.

어휘 colleague 동료 offer 제안하다, (기꺼이) ~해 주겠다고 하다 volunteer 자원하다, 자진해서 말하다; 자원봉사자 annual 매년의, 연례의

120. 동사 어휘 decline
금값이 몇 달 동안 꾸준히 올랐지만, 6월 말에는 하락하기 시작했다.
(A) 지연시키다 **(B) 하락하다** (C) 소비하다 (D) 제거하다

해설 두 개의 절이 접속사 but으로 연결되어 있으므로 이들은 서로 대조되는 내용이어야 한다. but 앞의 절에서 금값이 올랐다는 내용이 나왔으므로, but 뒤의 절에서는 금값이 하락했다는 반대의 내용이 나와야 자연스럽다. 따라서 정답은 (B).

어휘 steadily 꾸준히

121. 명사 자리_형용사+명사
공장의 높은 오염 수준에 관한 극심한 비판에 대한 대응으로, 그 공장은 주변 환경을 보호하기 위한 조치를 취했다.

해설 선택지를 통해 알맞은 품사를 고르는 문제임을 알 수 있다. 빈칸은 빈칸 앞 형용사 severe의 수식을 받으면서, 동시에 빈칸 뒤 concerning부터 levels까지의 전치사구의 수식을 받는 명사 자리이다. 따라서 정답은 (D).

어휘 in response to ~에 대응하여 severe 극심한 criticism 비판 concerning ~에 관한 take measures 조치를 취하다 surrounding 인근의, 주위의

122. 구전치사 based on
그 서점의 웹사이트가 업데이트되었기 때문에, 단골 고객들은 본인의 구매 내역을 바탕으로 한 도서 추천을 받을 수 있다.
(A) ~을 대표하여 (B) ~과 같은 **(C) ~을 바탕으로 한** (D) ~에도 불구하고

해설 의미상 알맞은 구전치사를 고르는 문제이다. 빈칸은 their purchase history를 목적어로 취하는 전치사구를 이루어 빈칸 앞 reading recommendations를 수식한다. '본인들의 구매 내역을 바탕으로 한 도서 추천을 받을 수 있다'는 내용이 자연스러우므로 정답은 (C).

어휘 now that ~이기 때문에 regular customer 단골손님 recommendation 추천

123. 부사 자리_동사 수식
펄리 화이트 치약은 전국의 치과 의사들로부터 강력 추천되고 있지만, 그것의 주요 경쟁 제품만큼 구매자들 사이에서 인기가 있지는 않다.

해설 though부터 nationwide까지는 주어와 be동사(it is)가 생략된 분사구문인데, 분사구문이 빈칸 없이도 완전하므로 빈칸은 빈칸 뒤의 과거분사 recommended를 수식하는 부사 자리이다. 따라서 부사인 (D)가 정답.

어휘 nationwide 전국적으로; 전국적인 competitor 경쟁자

어휘 fluent 유창한 at least 적어도, 최소한 qualification 자격, 자질 concierge (호텔의) 접객 담당자

107. 분사구문
기술자들은 전기 시스템을 수리할 때 건물 전체의 전력을 차단해야 한다.

해설 접속사 when 뒤에 절이 와야 하는데 주어와 동사가 없는 것으로 보아 주어가 생략된 분사구문임을 알 수 있다. 따라서 과거분사인 (B)와 현재분사인 (C)가 정답 후보. 빈칸 뒤에 목적어가 있고, 의미상으로도 생략된 주어인 Technicians가 시스템을 수리하는 주체이므로 능동의 의미를 가지는 현재분사 (C)가 정답.

어휘 technician 기술자, 기사 turn off 차단하다, 끄다 entire 전체의 electrical 전기의, 전기를 이용하는

108. 동사 어휘 demonstrate
영상에서는 그 소프트웨어가 사업체의 데이터를 정리하는 데 도움을 줄 수 있는 다양한 방법을 보여 준다.

(A) 문의하다 (B) 집중하다 (C) 종료하다 **(D) 보여 주다**

해설 의미상 '~에 초점을 맞추다'와 '~을 보여주다'가 적절하다. 하지만 '~에 초점을 맞추다'라는 뜻으로 쓰이려면 반드시 focus on이 되어야 하므로 정답은 (D) demonstrate.

어휘 organize 정리하다, 체계화하다

109. 소유대명사
여러분의 친구에게 저희 체육관에 가입하길 추천해 주시면, 할인된 회비를 제공해 드리겠습니다.

해설 빈칸은 전치사 of의 목적어 자리이므로 (A), (C), (D)가 정답 후보. 문맥상 '여러분의 친구들 중 한 명'이라는 뜻이 자연스러우므로 소유대명사를 써서 이중소유격이 되어야 한다. 따라서 정답은 (D). 〈관사+명사+of+소유대명사〉의 형태로 이중소유격이 쓰임을 기억하자.

어휘 recommend 추천하다 provide 제공하다 membership fee 회비

110. 부사 어휘 specifically
팀장은 니콜라 씨가 신타 사와의 협상을 이끄는 사람이어야 한다고 분명히 요구했다.

(A) 완전히 **(B) 분명히** (C) 대략 (D) 서서히

해설 문맥에 어울리는 부사 어휘를 고르는 문제. 내용상 '니콜라 씨가 협상을 이끌어야 한다고 분명히 요구했다'는 것이 가장 자연스러우므로 정답은 (B). 참고로 주절의 동사 ask는 요구를 나타내는 동사로, 목적어로 취하는 that절의 동사는 〈(should)+동사원형〉의 형태가 되어야 함을 알아 두자.

어휘 negotiation 《보통 복수형》 협상, 협의

111. 동사 자리 + 능동태
많은 후보자가 영업 사원직에 지원서를 제출해서, 그것들을 모두 검토하는 데에는 시간이 걸릴 것이다.

해설 주어 Many candidates 뒤에 동사가 없으므로 빈칸은 동사 자리이다. 따라서 동사인 (B)와 (D)가 정답 후보. 빈칸 뒤에 목적어 applications가 있고 주어인 Many candidates가 지원서를 제출하는 주체이므로 능동태인 (D)가 정답.

어휘 candidate 후보자 application 지원서, 지원 sales associate 영업 사원 go over ~을 검토하다

112. 접속사 vs. 전치사
아무런 예약 없이 공항에서 호텔로 오는 셔틀버스에 탑승하는 것은 불가능하다.

(A) ~하지 않는 한 **(B) ~ 없이** (C) ~을 제외하고는 (D) ~ 외에

해설 문맥에 어울리는 접속사 또는 전치사를 고르는 문제이다. '예약을 하지 않으면 셔틀버스를 타는 것이 불가능하다'라는 의미가 되어야 적절하므로, '~하지 않는 한'을 의미하는 접속사 (A)와 '~ 없이'를 의미하는 전치사 (B)가 정답 후보. 빈칸 뒤에 명사구가 왔기 때문에 정답은 (B).

어휘 shuttle bus 셔틀버스, 근거리 왕복 버스 reservation 예약

113. 동명사
모스 씨는 자신의 연설 역량을 향상시키는 데 도움을 줄 워크숍에 참여하는 것에 관심을 표했다.

해설 빈칸은 전치사 in의 목적어 자리이므로 명사 역할을 하는 명사 상당어구가 와야 하며 동시에 빈칸 뒤의 명사구를 목적어로 취할 수 있어야 한다. 따라서 동명사인 (C)가 정답. (D)는 to부정사로, 전치사의 목적어 자리에 올 수 없으므로 오답.

어휘 express 표현하다, 나타내다 interest 관심 public speaking 연설

114. 복합명사 baggage allowance
그 항공사의 새로운 정책에서는 국제선에 대해 수하물 허용량을 승객당 여행 가방 한 개에서 두 개로 늘렸다.

(A) 청구 (B) 개입 **(C) 허용량** (D) 습득

해설 빈칸은 동사 increases의 목적어 자리로, 빈칸 앞의 명사 baggage와 어울려 복합명사를 만드는 명사가 와야 한다. 여행 가방의 개수에 관한 내용이 나오므로 '수하물 허용량을 늘렸다'는 의미가 되어야 가장 자연스럽다. 따라서 정답은 (C). (A)도 baggage와 어울려 baggage claim(수하물 찾는 곳)이라는 복합명사를 만들 수 있지만, 문맥과 어울리지 않아 오답. baggage allowance를 하나의 덩어리로 외워 두자.

어휘 airline 항공사 suitcase 여행 가방 international flight 국제선

115. 소유격
멘서 공공 도서관의 이용자들은 온라인상에서 본인들의 대출 도서를 연장할 수 있고 그렇게 해서 연체료를 면할 수 있다.

해설 빈칸이 renew의 목적어로 쓰인 명사구 checked-out books 앞에 위치하므로, 명사구를 수식하는 한정사 역할의 소유격 (A)가 정답.

어휘 stock 재고(품) run out of ~을 다 써 버리다 significantly 상당히, 크게 profit 수익, 이익 adjust 조절하다, 조정하다 simply (부정문에서) 전혀, 단순히 profitable 수익성이 있는 hand out 나누어 주다 outline 개요, 윤곽

98. 화자에 따르면, 회사가 수익을 늘릴 수 있는 방법은?
(A) 신제품을 판매함으로써
(B) 공급업체를 변경함으로써
(C) 상품을 더 많이 구매함으로써
(D) 다른 고객을 목표로 삼음으로써

패러프레이징 [단서] by ordering more of our customer favorites → [정답] By purchasing more goods

99. 시각 자료에서, 회사가 더 적게 구매할 것은?
(A) 마스터 샤워즈
(B) 서니 레몬즈
(C) 랄라 롤리팝스
(D) 구이 거미즈

해설 단서 (99)에서 두 번째로 인기 있는 제품을 덜 주문할 것이라고 했는데, 브랜드별 판매 수량을 나타내는 막대 그래프 도표에서 서니 레몬즈가 두 번째로 매출이 많음을 알 수 있다. 따라서 정답은 (B).

100. 화자가 다음에 할 것 같은 일은?
(A) 주문하기
(B) 계획 마무리 짓기
(C) 문서 나눠 주기
(D) 가격 협상하기

패러프레이징 [단서] hand out the detailed outline of next month's order plan → [정답] Give out documents

PART 5

101. 부사 자리_동사 수식
애니타 씨는 쿠키를 구워 판매하는 것으로 늘 적극적으로 모금 행사에 참여한다.

해설 빈칸 없이도 문장의 구성 성분이 모두 갖추어져 있으므로 빈칸은 수식어 자리임을 알 수 있는데, 빈칸 뒤에 동사 participates가 있으므로 빈칸은 이를 수식하는 부사 자리이다. 따라서 부사인 (C)가 정답.

어휘 participate in ~에 참여하다 fundraiser 모금 행사

102. 관용어구 be scheduled to do
마을 축제의 퍼레이드는 내일 오후 1시에 시작할 예정이다.
(A) 예정하다 (B) 계속 ~이다 (C) 고려하다 (D) 기념하다

해설 빈칸 앞 be동사 is와 빈칸 뒤 to부정사와 함께 어울려 쓰이는 관용표현 be scheduled to do를 떠올릴 수 있어야 한다. 문맥상으로도 퍼레이드가 특정 시각에 시작하도록 '예정되어 있다'고 하는 것이 가장 적절하므로 정답은 (A). be scheduled to do(~할 예정이다)는 토익에서 자주 출제되는 to부정사 동반 관용표현이므로 반드시 기억해 두자.

어휘 parade 퍼레이드, 가두 행진

103. 형용사 자리+형용사 어휘 respective
문이 열리자, 좌석 안내원이 관객들을 그들 각자의 자리로 안내했다.
(A) 각자의 (B) 존경 (C) 경의를 표하는 (D) 존경하는; ~에 관해서

해설 전치사 to의 목적어로 쓰인 명사 seats를 수식할 수 있는 것은 형용사이므로, 형용사인 (A), (C)와 형용사 역할을 할 수 있는 현재분사 (D)가 정답 후보. 문맥상 '관객들의 자리'에 의미를 더해 줄 수 있는 것은 '각자의'라는 의미의 respective이므로 정답은 (A). (C)는 '경의를 표하는'이라는 의미이고, (D)는 '존경하는'이라는 의미이므로 문맥상 어울리지 않아 오답. 참고로 (D) respecting은 '~에 관해서'라는 의미의 전치사로도 쓰인다.

어휘 usher 좌석 안내원 show (장소로) 안내하다

104. 명사 어휘 instructions
저희 매장에서 판매되는 모든 가구에는 빠른 조립을 위한 따라 하기 쉬운 설명서가 딸려 있습니다.
(A) 추정, 견적서 **(B) 설명서** (C) 안락 (D) 환불

해설 빈칸에 알맞은 명사 어휘를 고르는 문제. 선택지 중 가구에 딸려 오는 것으로 쉽게 따라 할 수 있고 빠른 조립을 위한 용도로 사용될 수 있는 것은 instructions(설명서)뿐이므로 정답은 (B).

어휘 come with ~이 딸려 있다 easy-to-follow 따라 하기 쉬운 assembly 조립

105. 명사 자리
크롭 씨는 고객 서비스팀에 전화했을 때 답변을 듣기 위해 15분을 기다려야 했다.

해설 빈칸은 전치사 for의 목적어 자리이자 관사 an의 수식을 받는 명사 자리이므로 단수 명사인 (A)가 정답. (B)는 현재분사 또는 동명사이므로 관사의 수식을 받을 수 없고, (C)는 동사 또는 과거분사, (D)는 복수 명사 또는 단수 동사이므로 빈칸에 올 수 없다.

어휘 customer service 고객 서비스

106. 전치사 for
적어도 2개 언어에서의 유창함이 서머타임 리조트에서 접객 담당자로 일하기 위해 필요한 자격이다.
(A) ~에 대한 (B) ~을 통해 (C) ~에 의해 **(D) ~을 위해**

해설 선택지를 보니 알맞은 전치사를 고르는 문제. 문맥상 빈칸 이하는 빈칸 앞의 '필요한 자격'에 대한 목적이 되어야 한다. 따라서 '~을 위해'라는 뜻으로 목적을 나타내는 전치사 for가 적절하므로 정답은 (D). a necessary qualification for(~에 필요한 자격)는 자주 쓰이는 표현이니 기억해 두자.

Questions 95-97 refer to the following announcement and schedule.

> Good morning, visitors! We thank you for coming to explore Emerald Park. Unfortunately, ⁹⁵, ⁹⁶Sandra twisted her ankle yesterday and won't be able to give her tour today. Those of you who were scheduled to tour the park with her can join Josh's group instead, since he doesn't have that many visitors signed up. We apologize for the inconvenience. Please meet your guide at the entrance of the park at least five minutes before your departure time. ⁹⁷We would also like to kindly remind you that children under twelve must be accompanied by an adult at all times. We have noticed several children running around alone. Thank you.
>
> 안녕하세요, 방문객 여러분! 에메랄드 파크를 탐험하러 와 주셔서 감사합니다. 유감스럽게도, ⁹⁵, ⁹⁶샌드라 씨가 어제 발목을 삐어서 오늘 그녀의 투어를 제공할 수 없을 것입니다. 그녀와 함께 공원을 둘러보실 예정이었던 분들께서는 대신에 조쉬 씨의 그룹에 합류하실 수 있습니다. 그는 신청한 방문객이 그렇게 많지 않기 때문입니다. 불편을 드려 죄송합니다. 적어도 출발 시각 5분 전에는 공원 입구에서 여러분의 가이드와 만나시기 바랍니다. ⁹⁷또한 저희는 12세 이하 어린이들은 항상 어른과 동행해야 한다는 점을 다시 한번 알려 드립니다. 저희는 몇몇 어린이들이 혼자 뛰어 다니는 것을 발견했습니다. 감사합니다.

에메랄드 파크 투어 일정

출발 시각	가이드
오전 11시	신디
⁹⁶오후 12시 30분	샌드라
오후 2시	조쉬
오후 3시 30분	리처드

어휘 explore 탐험하다, 살펴보다   twist one's ankle 발목을 삐다   sign up 신청하다, 등록하다   apologize for ~에 대해 사과하다   inconvenience 불편   departure 출발, 떠남   be accompanied by ~와 동행하다, ~을 동반하다

95. 투어들 중 하나가 취소된 이유는?
(A) 기상 상태가 좋지 않다.
(B) 한 직원이 부상을 당했다.
(C) 어떤 구역에 보수 작업이 필요하다.
(D) 등록한 인원이 충분하지 않다.

패러프레이징 [단서] Sandra twisted her ankle → [정답] An employee was injured.

96. 시각 자료에서, 취소된 투어가 출발하기로 되어 있던 시각은?
(A) 오전 11시
(B) 오후 12시 30분
(C) 오후 2시
(D) 오후 3시 30분

해설 단서 (96)에서 샌드라 씨가 발목을 삐어서 그녀의 투어를 제공할 수 없을 거라고 했는데, 투어 일정표를 나타내는 도표를 보면 샌드라 씨의 투어 출발 시각이 오후 12시 30분으로 예정되어 있었다는 것을 알 수 있다. 따라서 정답은 (B).

97. 방문객들에게 금지된 것은?
(A) 아이들을 돌보는 사람 없이 두는 것
(B) 가이드 없이 들어가는 것
(C) 공원에서 뛰는 것
(D) 여러 개의 투어에 참가하는 것

Questions 98-100 refer to the following excerpt from a meeting and chart.

> Let's start by talking about our stock. We always seem to run out of the same kinds of candy. ⁹⁸I believe we can significantly increase our profits by ordering more of our customer favorites each month. So we have decided to adjust our orders and purchase more of the top-selling candy. However, ⁹⁹we are going to buy less of our second most popular item. I know this seems strange, but our supplier for that brand has raised prices by more than double, and it simply isn't as profitable for us anymore. ¹⁰⁰I will now hand out the detailed outline of next month's order plan.
>
> 우리 재고에 대해 이야기하는 것으로 시작하겠습니다. 우리는 항상 같은 종류의 사탕이 바닥나는 것 같습니다. ⁹⁸제 생각에는 우리가 매달 고객들이 가장 좋아하는 것을 더 주문함으로써 수익을 크게 늘릴 수 있을 것 같아요. 그래서 우리는 우리의 주문을 조절하여 가장 잘 팔리는 사탕을 더 구매하기로 결정했습니다. 그러나, ⁹⁹우리는 두 번째로 인기 있는 제품은 덜 주문할 예정인데요. 이게 이상해 보인다는 것은 압니다만, 그 브랜드의 공급업체가 가격을 두 배 이상 올려서, 그건 더 이상 우리에게 그만큼의 수익성이 전혀 없습니다. ¹⁰⁰이제 다음 달 주문 계획의 상세한 개요를 나눠 드리겠습니다.

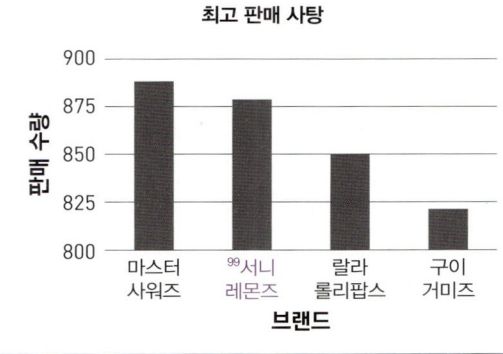

어휘 panel 패널, 토론인단　flavor 맛　soft drink 청량음료　comment 의견, 논평　pay attention to ~에 유의[주목]하다　be in disagreement 의견이 맞지 않다　identify (신원 등을) 확인하다, 알아보다

89. 청자들이 하도록 기대되는 일은?
(A) 음료 샘플들 맛보기
(B) 음악 공연들 녹화하기
(C) 광고들 검토하기
(D) 입사 지원자들 평가하기

패러프레이징 [단서] try / various flavors of our new soft drink → [정답] Taste / some beverage samples

90. 화자가 "그분들에게 신경 쓰지 마세요"라고 말한 의도는?
(A) 업체는 독립적인 의견들을 원한다.
(B) 일부 유인물에 오류가 들어 있다.
(C) 청자들은 잘못된 지시를 받았다.
(D) 일부 직원들이 활동을 감시할 것이다.

해설 화자가 한 말의 의도를 문맥을 통해 찾아내는 문제로 해당 표현의 앞뒤를 주의 깊게 들어야 한다. 해당 표현 앞에서 다른 의견을 가진 사람들이 있을 수 있다고 했고, 해당 표현 뒤에서는 생각이 다르다 해도 자유롭게 공유되길 원한다고 했다. 따라서 화자의 업체는 각자가 자신과 다른 의견을 가지고 있는 사람들에게서 영향을 받지 않고 독립적인 의견을 말해 주기를 원한다는 것을 알 수 있으므로 정답은 (A).

91. 청자들이 다음에 할 것 같은 일은?
(A) 문서 인쇄하기
(B) 질문 적어 두기
(C) 이름표 달기
(D) 소그룹 형성하기

패러프레이징 [단서] wearing the name badges → [정답] Put on name tags

Questions 92-94 refer to the following talk.

Ladies and gentlemen, ⁹²tonight we are here to recognize the winner of this year's Best Young Novelist award: Justin Lawson. Mr. Lawson's work, *Metallic Love*, has astonished critics who are all equally impressed by the beautiful writing and the intricate plot. *Metallic Love* is more than just another romance novel. The book makes powerful social statements while raising deep philosophical questions. ⁹³One thing is for sure—you will not be the same after reading this. Trust me, ⁹³it will make you rethink everything. ⁹⁴It is a great honor for me to present Mr. Lawson with this prize today. Please give him a warm welcome.

신사 숙녀 여러분, ⁹²오늘 밤 저희는 올해 최고의 젊은 소설가 상의 수상자인 저스틴 로슨 씨를 표창하기 위해 이 자리에 모였습니다. 로슨 씨의 작품인 〈메탈릭 러브〉는 아름다운 문체와 얽히고 설킨 구성에 모두 똑같이 깊은 인상을 받은 비평가들을 깜짝 놀라게 했습니다. 〈메탈릭 러브〉는 또 하나의 로맨스 소설 그 이상입니다. 그 책은 깊은 철학적 질문을 이끌어 내는 동시에 강력한 사회적 메시지를 전합니다. ⁹³한 가지 분명한 것은, 이 책을 읽은 후에 여러분은 이전의 여러분과 같지 않을 것이라는 겁니다. 저를 믿으세요, ⁹³이것은 여러분이 모든 것을 다시 생각하도록 할 것입니다. ⁹⁴제가 오늘 이 상을 로슨 씨에게 수여하는 것은 너무나 큰 영광입니다. 이분을 따뜻하게 환영해 주세요.

어휘 recognize 표창하다, 인정하다　novelist 소설가　astonish 깜짝 놀라게 하다　critic 비평가, 평론가　equally 똑같이, 동등하게　impress 깊은 인상을 주다, 감명을 주다　intricate 복잡한　plot 구성, 줄거리　statement 서술, 표현　philosophical 철학적인, 철학에 관련된

92. 담화의 목적은?
(A) 작가를 소개하기 위해
(B) 책을 광고하기 위해
(C) 의견을 비판하기 위해
(D) 후보 지명을 요청하기 위해

패러프레이징 [단서] the winner of this year's Best Young Novelist award → [정답] an author

93. 화자가 "저를 믿으세요"라고 말한 의도는?
(A) 그 책을 읽었다.
(B) 소설을 쓸 것이다.
(C) 질문에 답해 줄 계획이다.
(D) 몇 개의 상을 탔다.

해설 해당 표현 앞뒤의 단서 (93)에서 이 책을 읽은 후의 여러분은 이전의 여러분과 같지 않을 것이라고 하면서, 이 책을 읽음으로써 모든 것을 다시 생각하게 될 것이라고 말하는 화자를 믿으라고 했다. 따라서 화자는 이미 이 책을 읽었음을 유추할 수 있으므로 정답은 (A).

94. 다음에 일어날 것 같은 일은?
(A) 책에 사인을 할 것이다.
(B) 한 구절을 읽을 것이다.
(C) 몇 가지 질문을 할 것이다.
(D) 상이 수여될 것이다.

패러프레이징 [단서] present Mr. Lawson with this prize → [정답] An award will be presented.

이유를 파악해야 한다. 해당 표현의 This는 바로 앞에 언급된 새치기를 가리킨다. 새치기가 절차를 늦어지게 할 뿐이라고 말한 것이므로 새치기, 즉 무례한 행동을 방지하기 위해 한 말임을 알 수 있다. 따라서 정답은 (A).

패러프레이징 [단서] cut in line → [정답] rude behavior

85. 화자가 어린 방문객 일부에게 제공하는 것은?
(A) 우대석
(B) 무료 입장
(C) 장난감 동물
(D) 동물 사진

해설 단서 (85)에서 오늘 판다를 보지 못하는 어린이들에게 사과의 의미로 봉제 동물 인형을 준다고 했으므로 정답은 (C). 담화의 Children who are not able to see the pandas today가 문제에서는 some young visitors로 패러프레이징되었다.

패러프레이징 [단서] a free stuffed animal → [정답] A toy animal

🎧
Questions 86-88 refer to the following telephone message.

Hello. I'm calling about order number 81151. ⁸⁶·⁸⁷I received a message saying that the book I ordered, *Agents and Foes*, is out of stock and that you will send it to me at a later date. However, I need this item before April 16 because it is a birthday gift. ⁸⁶·⁸⁷I saw that *The Grand Hope* is in stock according to your Web site, so could I get that book instead? ⁸⁷It is cheaper than my original order, but rather than sending me a refund for the difference, ⁸⁸please just use an expedited delivery service. Thank you for your time.

안녕하세요. 주문 번호 81151에 관해 전화드립니다. ⁸⁶·⁸⁷저는 제가 주문한 책 〈첩보원과 적〉이 품절되어서, 이후 날짜에 그것을 저에게 보내 주시겠다는 메시지를 받았습니다. 하지만 이것은 생일 선물이라서 저는 이 물품이 4월 16일 전에 필요합니다. ⁸⁶·⁸⁷제가 귀사의 웹사이트에서 〈원대한 희망〉은 재고가 있는 것을 보아서 말인데, 대신 그 책을 받을 수 있을까요? ⁸⁷그건 제 원래 주문보다 더 저렴하지만, 차액을 저에게 환불하여 보내 주시기보다는 ⁸⁸그냥 긴급 배송 서비스를 이용해 주세요. 시간을 내주셔서 감사합니다.

어휘 be in stock 재고가 있다 original 원래의 difference 차액, 차이 expedite 더 신속히 처리하다

86. 메시지의 목적은?
(A) 주문을 변경하기 위해
(B) 사과를 하기 위해
(C) 절차를 설명하기 위해
(D) 지불을 요청하기 위해

해설 단서 (86)을 통해 화자는 자신이 주문한 책이 품절되었다는 메시지를 받았는데, 그 책을 나중에 보내 주는 대신 다른 책으로 변경해 달라고 요청하고 있음을 알 수 있다. 따라서 정답은 (A).

패러프레이징 [단서] get that book instead → [정답] modify an order

87. 〈원대한 희망〉에 대해 언급된 것은?
(A) 베스트셀러 작가가 썼다.
(B) 〈첩보원과 적〉보다 덜 비싸다.
(C) 현재 품절되었다.
(D) 생일 선물로 받았다.

패러프레이징 [단서] It is cheaper than my original order → [정답] It is less expensive than *Agents and Foes*.

88. 화자가 청자에게 하도록 요청한 일은?
(A) 환불 제공하기
(B) 신속 배송 서비스 이용하기
(C) 웹사이트 업데이트하기
(D) 회답 전화 하기

패러프레이징 [단서] use an expedited delivery service → [정답] Use a fast delivery service

🎧
Questions 89-91 refer to the following talk.

Good morning, and thank you all for being a part of this customer panel. ⁸⁹Today I'll give you various flavors of our new soft drink. After you try each one, I will record your comments. ⁹⁰Remember, some people in the group might have a widely different opinion from yours. Don't pay attention to them. ⁹⁰We want you to share your thoughts freely, even if they're in disagreement. ⁹¹Now, so that I can easily identify each of you, please make sure you're wearing the name badges I gave you before we begin. Thanks.

좋은 아침입니다. 그리고 이 고객 패널의 일원이 되어 주신 여러분 모두에게 감사드립니다. ⁸⁹오늘 저는 여러분께 다양한 맛의 저희 신제품 청량음료를 드릴 겁니다. 각 음료를 드셔 보신 후, 제가 여러분의 의견을 기록할 것입니다. ⁹⁰기억하세요, 그룹에 계신 어떤 분들은 여러분의 의견과 크게 다른 의견을 가질 수도 있다는 걸요. 그분들에게 신경 쓰지 마세요. ⁹⁰저희는 여러분의 생각이 다르다고 해도 여러분이 이를 자유롭게 공유하길 원합니다. ⁹¹이제 여러분 각각을 제가 쉽게 알아볼 수 있도록, 시작하기 전에 드린 이름표를 꼭 착용해 주세요. 감사합니다.

prepared some common customer service scenarios that I want you to act out. I've just passed out the cards explaining the various situations. You'll have some time to think because we're at a good stopping point now. ⁸²Feel free to help yourself to some refreshments or take a quick stroll outside. Let's meet back here in fifteen minutes to continue with the next session. See you then.

---

⁸⁰먼로 비치 리조트를 대표하여, 이 그룹 면접에 참석해 주신 것에 대해 여러분 모두에게 다시 한번 감사드리고자 합니다. 여러분의 이전 업무 경험을 묻는 저희의 질문에 여러분 모두 아주 잘 답변해 주셨습니다. 저희는 이제 여러분이 임기응변을 하는 방법을 보고자 합니다. ⁸¹저는 여러분이 실연해 보였으면 하는 흔히 있는 고객 서비스 시나리오를 몇 가지 준비했습니다. 여러 상황이 설명되어 있는 카드들을 제가 방금 나눠 드렸습니다. 지금 잠시 쉬었다 가기 딱 좋은 시점이니 생각해 볼 시간을 좀 갖게 되실 겁니다. ⁸²자유롭게 다과를 드시거나 밖에서 짧은 산책을 하십시오. 15분 뒤에 여기서 다시 만나서 다음 과정을 이어 갑시다. 그때 뵙겠습니다.

어휘 on behalf of ~을 대표하여 previous 이전의 think on one's feet 신속하게 결단을 내리다 act out (연극하듯) 실연해 보이다 pass out 나누어 주다 refreshments (항상 복수형) 다과 take a stroll 산책하다 continue with ~을 계속하다

80. 청자들의 신분은?
(A) 여행 가이드들
(B) 입사 지원자들
(C) 해변 방문객들
(D) 호텔 투숙객들

해설 담화의 전반적인 내용을 통해 청자들을 유추할 수 있다. 단서 (80)에서 회사를 대표해 청자들에게 그룹 면접에 참석해 줘서 감사하다고 했고, 면접 과정에 대한 설명이 이어지고 있는 것으로 보아 면접에 참가한 입사 지원자들을 대상으로 하는 담화임을 알 수 있다. 따라서 정답은 (B). Beach Resort라는 말이 들린다고 해서 (C)나 (D)를 정답으로 고르지 않도록 주의하자.

81. 청자들이 하도록 요청받은 일은?
(A) 문제를 설명하는 것
(B) 설문지를 작성하는 것
(C) 파트너를 찾는 것
(D) 역할극 활동을 하는 것

패러프레이징 [단서] act out → [정답] Do a role-play activity

82. 청자들이 다음에 할 것 같은 일은?
(A) 유인물 찾아가기
(B) 화자 따라가기
(C) 휴식 취하기

(D) 과정 등록하기

패러프레이징 [단서] help yourself to some refreshments or take a quick stroll outside → [정답] Take a break

Questions 83-85 refer to the following announcement.

Your attention, please. ⁸³Due to the recent birth of a panda cub, we have a lot of visitors today. In order to get people in as fast as possible, please queue up and be respectful. ⁸⁴Do not cut in line. This will only slow the process. There is a special line for those who wish to visit the pandas only. Proceed to this line only if you do not want to see any other animal. For safety purposes, we will not let anyone in after 3 P.M. instead of 5 P.M. today. ⁸⁵Children who are not able to see the pandas today will receive a free stuffed animal as an apology.

주목해 주십시오, 여러분. ⁸³새끼 판다의 최근 출생으로 인해, 저희는 오늘 방문객이 많습니다. 가능한 한 빨리 사람들이 입장할 수 있도록 줄을 서 주시고 실례가 되지 않도록 행동해 주십시오. ⁸⁴새치기는 하지 말아 주세요. 이것은 절차를 늦어지게 할 뿐입니다. 판다만 방문하기를 원하시는 분들을 위한 특별 줄도 있습니다. 다른 동물을 구경하고 싶지 않은 분은 이 줄로 이동해 주세요. 안전상의 이유로, 저희가 오늘은 오후 5시가 아니라 오후 3시 이후에는 누구도 입장시키지 않을 것입니다. ⁸⁵오늘 판다를 볼 수 없는 어린이들은 사과의 의미로 무료 봉제 동물 인형을 받게 될 것입니다.

어휘 birth 출생, 출산 cub (동물의) 새끼 queue up 줄을 서다 respectful 예의 바른, 공손한 cut in line 줄에 새치기하다 proceed 나아가다, 이동하다 stuffed animal 봉제 동물 인형 apology 사과, 사죄

83. 이 안내가 들릴 것 같은 장소는?
(A) 식료품점
(B) 공항
(C) 보육 시설
(D) 동물원

해설 단서 (83)에서 새끼 판다가 태어나서 오늘 방문객이 많다고 하는 것으로 보아 안내가 들리는 장소는 동물원임을 추론할 수 있다. 따라서 정답은 (D).

84. 화자가 "이것은 절차를 늦어지게 할 뿐입니다"라고 말한 이유는?
(A) 무례한 행동을 방지하기 위해
(B) 견적을 명확히 하기 위해
(C) 구매를 권장하기 위해
(D) 지연에 대해 알리기 위해

해설 문제를 먼저 읽어 화자가 This will only slow the process라고 말할 것을 예상하고, 담화에서 그 말이 나오면 앞뒤 맥락에서 말한

어휘 get by with ~으로 어떻게든 해 나가다 dress code 복장 규정 no longer 더 이상 ~ 아닌[하지 않는] manner 방식, 태도 write down ~을 적다

74. 화자가 사과하는 이유는?
(A) 좌석이 부족하다.
(B) 기계가 오작동했다.
(C) 회의가 늦게 시작할 예정이다.
(D) 장소가 변경되었다.

패러프레이징 [단서] we don't have chairs for everyone → [정답] There is a lack of seats.

75. 회의의 목적은?
(A) 직원을 소개하기 위해
(B) 단체 구성원을 선정하기 위해
(C) 새로운 정책을 설명하기 위해
(D) 프로젝트의 목표를 재검토하기 위해

패러프레이징 [단서] to discuss our company's new dress code → [정답] To explain a new policy

76. 화자에 따르면, 질문을 적어야 하는 이유는?
(A) 상사가 검토해야 한다.
(B) 녹화를 위해 소리 내어 읽을 것이다.
(C) 종류별로 분류될 필요가 있다.
(D) 한 사람당 하나로 제한되어 있다.

해설 단서 (76)에서 회의를 녹화 중이라며 질문을 적어서 건네주면 마이크에 대고 읽겠다고 했으므로 정답은 (B).

패러프레이징 [단서] read them into the microphone → [정답] They will be read aloud

호 🎧
Questions 77-79 refer to the following news report.

This is Brad Henderson reporting for *Channel 3 News* from the International Trade Expo. At this event, businesses are displaying everything from cosmetics to electronics. ⁷⁷I'm here now at the Expeedo Sports booth checking out the company's new running shoes. ⁷⁸What really sets these shoes apart is how light they are. ⁷⁷This will definitely help long-distance runners to improve their race times. But this is not the only interesting thing here. If you have a chance to visit the expo, ⁷⁹you should try all of the various samples and items. You can discover new things and try them out before you buy them.

저는 국제 무역 박람회에 나와 있는, 〈채널 3 뉴스〉의 브래드 헨더슨입니다. 이 행사에서 업체들은 화장품부터 전자 제품까지 모든 것을 전시하고 있습니다. ⁷⁷저는 지금 이곳 익스피도 스포츠 사의 부스에서 업체의 새로 나온 러닝화를 확인하고 있습니다. ⁷⁸이 신발을 정말로 돋보이게 하는 것은 이 신발이 얼마나 가벼운가입니다. ⁷⁷이것은 분명히 장거리 육상 선수들이 자신의 경주 기록을 향상시키는 데에 도움을 줄 것입니다. 하지만 이곳에서 흥미로운 것은 이뿐만이 아닙니다. 박람회를 방문할 기회가 있으시다면, ⁷⁹다양한 샘플과 물건을 모두 한번 써 보셔야 합니다. 여러분은 새로운 것들을 발견하고 그것들을 구매하기 전에 써 보실 수 있습니다.

어휘 trade expo 무역 박람회 cosmetics 화장품 electronics (항상 복수형) 전자 제품 set ~ apart ~을 돋보이게[다르게] 만들다 improve 향상시키다 discover 발견하다

77. 보도가 설명하는 제품의 종류는?
(A) 운동화
(B) 전자 기기
(C) 천연 화장품
(D) 가전제품

해설 단서 (77)에서 화자는 특정 업체의 부스에서 새로 나온 러닝화를 확인하고 있다고 했고, 이 러닝화가 장거리 선수들의 경주 기록 향상에 도움이 될 것이라고 했으므로 정답은 (A).

패러프레이징 [단서] running shoes → [정답] Athletic shoes

78. 화자에 따르면, 제품의 특별한 점은?
(A) 안전 기능
(B) 재활용 가능한 재료
(C) 작은 크기
(D) 경량 디자인

패러프레이징 [단서] how light they are → [정답] Its lightweight design

79. 화자가 하기를 권하는 것은?
(A) 가격 비교하기
(B) 제품들을 시험해 보기
(C) 웹사이트 방문하기
(D) 전화로 질문하기

패러프레이징 [단서] try all of the various samples and items → [정답] Testing products

영 🎧
Questions 80-82 refer to the following talk.

⁸⁰On behalf of Monroe Beach Resort, I'd like to thank you all once again for attending this group interview. You've all done a fantastic job answering our questions about your previous work experience. We now want to see how you think on your feet. ⁸¹I've

패러프레이징 [단서] tonight's program and the history of each piece → [정답] tonight's music

70. 시각 자료에서, 여자가 다음에 갈 것 같은 장소는?
(A) A번 방
(B) B번 방
(C) C번 방
(D) D번 방

해설 단서 (70)에서 남자가 강연은 콘서트홀의 입구와 바로 마주 보고 있는 방에서 할 것이라고 하자 여자가 알겠다고 했다. 평면도를 나타내는 도표에서 콘서트홀의 입구와 바로 마주 보고 있는 방은 D번 방이므로 정답은 (D).

PART 4

🎤 🎧
Questions 71-73 refer to the following introduction.

Welcome to the Automatic Artifacts House. ⁷¹This month's special exhibit features clocks from around the world and from every time period since the Middle Ages. ⁷²At eleven thirty, I will show you the insides of a clock and disassemble it so that you may see how these fascinating machines work. There is no better way to understand clockwork than by seeing how each piece fits together. ⁷³And make sure you stay until noon. When the clocks strike twelve, look at the cuckoo clock. It will play a beautiful song and give you a special show.

자동 공예품 하우스에 오신 것을 환영합니다. ⁷¹이달의 특별 전시회에서는 전 세계의 시계들과 중세 이후의 모든 시기의 시계들을 특별 전시하고 있습니다. ⁷²11시 30분에 제가 여러분께 시계 내부를 보여 드리고 그것을 분해해서 이 매력적인 기계들이 어떻게 작동하는지 보실 수 있게 해 드리겠습니다. 태엽 장치를 이해하는 방법으로 각 부속이 어떻게 서로 맞물려 있는지 보는 것보다 나은 방법은 없습니다. ⁷³그리고 꼭 정오까지 계시기 바랍니다. 시계들이 12시를 알릴 때, 뻐꾸기시계를 봐 주세요. 뻐꾸기시계에서 아름다운 음악이 재생되면서 여러분께 특별한 공연을 보여 드릴 것입니다.

어휘 artifact 공예품 exhibit 전시(회) disassemble 분해하다, 해체하다 fascinating 대단히 흥미로운, 매력적인 clockwork 시계[태엽] 장치 strike (시간을) 알리다, 치다 cuckoo clock 뻐꾸기시계

71. 이 담화를 들을 수 있을 것 같은 곳은?
(A) 박물관
(B) 백화점
(C) 콘서트홀
(D) 기념품점

해설 담화 도입부의 단서 (71)에서 특별 전시회에 대해 소개한 후, 관람할 내용에 관한 안내가 이어지는 것으로 보아 박물관에서 이루어지는 담화임을 추론할 수 있다. 따라서 정답은 (A).

72. 화자가 11시 30분에 할 일은?
(A) 경매 주최하기
(B) 노래 재생하기
(C) 장치 설명하기
(D) 가이드 투어 시작하기

패러프레이징 [단서] show you the insides of a clock and disassemble it so that you may see how these fascinating machines work → [정답] Explain a device

73. 화자가 청자들에게 12시에 하도록 권하는 것은?
(A) 전문가와 만나기
(B) 강의에 참석하기
(C) 특정 물품 보기
(D) 건물에서 나가기

패러프레이징 [단서] look at the cuckoo clock → [정답] Observe a specific item

🎤 🎧
Questions 74-76 refer to the following excerpt from a meeting.

Thanks for being here, and ⁷⁴I'm sorry we don't have chairs for everyone. Some of our furniture is being repaired at the moment, so we have to get by with what we have. ⁷⁵I wanted to meet with you to discuss our company's new dress code. As you may have heard, we'll no longer wear uniforms, but employees should still be dressed in a professional manner. ⁷⁶We're recording this meeting for those who cannot be here, so if you have questions, please write them down and pass them up to the front so I can read them into the microphone.

이곳에 와 주셔서 감사합니다. 그리고 ⁷⁴우리에게 모두가 앉을 수 있는 의자가 없다는 점에 대해 죄송하게 생각합니다. 지금 우리 가구 중 일부가 수리되고 있어서, 가지고 있는 것으로 어떻게든 버텨야 합니다. ⁷⁵저는 우리 회사의 새로운 복장 규정에 대해 의논하기 위해 여러분을 만나고 싶었습니다. 여러분이 들었을 수도 있지만, 우리는 더 이상 유니폼을 입지 않을 것입니다. 하지만 직원들은 그래도 전문가다운 복장을 해야 합니다. ⁷⁶우리는 이곳에 올 수 없는 사람들을 위해 이 회의를 녹화 중이니, 질문이 있으면 적어서 앞쪽으로 건네주셔서 제가 마이크에 대고 읽을 수 있게 해 주세요.

어휘 express 표현하다, 나타내다   creativity 창의성, 창조성
drop off (어디로 가는 길에) 내려 주다[가져다주다]   submission 제출(물)
speaking of which 말이 나온 김에, 얘기가 나왔으니 말인데   collect 모으다, 받다   help out 도와주다   spare 할애하다, 내다   entry 출품작

65. 남자가 내일 할 일은?
(A) 기사 작성하기
(B) 기자와 만나기
(C) 미술관 둘러보기
(D) 예술품 구매하기

패러프레이징 [단서] meeting with Theo Miller from the Stroudville Herald → [정답] Meet with a reporter

66. 시각 자료에서, 남자가 추가적으로 도움이 필요한 때는?
(A) 2월 3일
(B) 2월 5일
(C) 2월 7일
(D) 2월 20일

해설 단서 (66)에서 남자가 작품 제출 마지막 날에 인력이 필요하다고 했고, 미술 대회 안내 포스터에서 제출 기간의 마지막 날은 2월 5일이므로 정답은 (B).

67. 여자가 자신이 할 것이라고 말한 일은?
(A) 새로운 집으로 이사 가기
(B) 그림 원본 제출하기
(C) 미술관에 일찍 오기
(D) 신청서 양식 만들기

패러프레이징 [단서] moving to a new apartment → [정답] Move to a new home

🎧 **Questions 68-70** refer to the following conversation and floor plan.

W   Hello. ⁶⁸Are there any seats left for tonight's performance?

M   ⁶⁸Yes, there are. However, the only ones left are in the back of the room.

W   That's fine. I'll take one seat please.

M   Okay. That'll be $15.50. And that includes the lecture before the performance.

W   Oh, I heard about it. It's a talk by the first violinist, right?

M   That's right. ⁶⁹Mr. Rimple will give a brief introduction of tonight's program and the history of each piece.

W   That's wonderful! What time is it at?

M   It's starting in just five minutes. You'd better hurry. ⁷⁰It's in the room directly facing the entrance of the concert hall.

W   ⁷⁰Okay. Thank you very much!

여   안녕하세요. ⁶⁸오늘 밤 공연에 남은 좌석이 있나요?

남   ⁶⁸네, 있어요. 그런데 남은 것들이 뒤쪽에 있는 좌석들밖에 없어요.

여   괜찮습니다. 한 좌석으로 할게요.

남   알겠습니다. 15.50달러 되겠습니다. 그리고 거기에는 공연 전 강연도 포함되어 있어요.

여   아, 그것에 대해 들었어요. 제1 바이올린 주자가 하는 강연이죠, 그렇죠?

남   맞습니다. ⁶⁹림플 씨가 오늘 밤 프로그램과 각 작품의 역사에 대해 간단한 소개를 해 주실 거예요.

여   정말 멋지네요! 그게 몇 시에 하는 거죠?

남   딱 5분 뒤에 시작할 거예요. 서두르시는 게 좋겠어요. ⁷⁰강연은 콘서트홀 입구와 바로 마주 보고 있는 방에서 합니다.

여   ⁷⁰알겠어요. 정말 감사합니다!

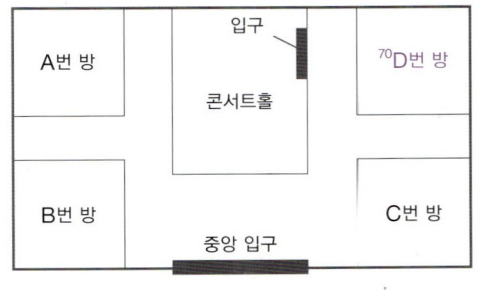

어휘 performance 공연, 연주   include 포함하다   lecture 강연, 강의   brief 간단한, 간략한   introduction 소개   directly 똑바로, 곧장   face ~을 마주 보다[향하다]   entrance (출)입구, 문

68. 남자의 신분은?
(A) 지휘자
(B) 음악가
(C) 입장권 판매원
(D) 관객

69. 남자가 강연에 대해 언급한 것은?
(A) 참석하려면 추가 비용이 든다.
(B) 더 이상 이용할 수 있는 좌석이 없다.
(C) 몇 분 전에 시작되었다.
(D) 오늘 밤에 있을 음악에 관한 것일 예정이다.

W I see. Well, I'd better let you go then.

여 네이트 씨, 벌써 퇴근하시는 거예요?

남 네. 제가 오늘 오후에 기차를 타야 한다고 프린스턴 씨께 어제 말씀드렸어요. ⁶²영양 학회 때문에 애틀랜타에 갈 예정이라서요.

여 ⁶²,⁶³아, 건강 재료 협회에서 개최하는 학회에 가시는 거예요? 저는 그게 내일이나 되어야 시작한다고 생각했는데요.

남 ⁶³맞아요. 학회가 아침 일찍 시작해서 제가 오늘 출발하는 거예요. 그래서 저는 오늘 밤에 호텔에 묵으면서 충분히 자고 싶어요. 그런데 6시 이후에는 열차가 없더라고요. ⁶⁴저는 집에 가서 제 정장을 챙긴 다음, 오늘 마지막 열차를 탈 거예요.

여 그렇군요. 음, 그럼 당신을 보내 드려야 하겠네요.

평일 열차 시간표

열차 번호	종착지	출발 시각	도착 시각
105	애틀랜타	오전 6시 20분	오전 7시 40분
207	애틀랜타	오전 10시 30분	오전 11시 50분
482	애틀랜타	오후 2시 20분	오후 3시 40분
⁶⁴553	애틀랜타	오후 5시 50분	오후 7시 10분

어휘 nutrition 영양　organize 개최하다, 조직하다　ingredient 재료, 성분　association 협회　get a good night's sleep 충분히 숙면을 취하다　had better do ~하는 편이 낫다, ~해야 하다

62. 화자들이 일할 것 같은 회사의 종류는?
(A) 여행사
(B) 의류 매장
(C) 운송 회사
(D) 식품 제조업체

해설 단서 (62)에서 남자가 영양 학회에 갈 예정이라고 했고 여자는 건강 재료 협회에서 개최하는 학회에 가는 것이냐고 묻는 것으로 보아 화자들은 모두 식품 관련 업종에서 일하고 있을 것으로 추론할 수 있다. 따라서 정답은 (D).

63. 남자가 내일 할 일은?
(A) 애틀랜타로 출발하기
(B) 행사에 참석하기
(C) 호텔 찾기
(D) 일찍 퇴근하기

패러프레이징 [단서] going to the conference → [정답] Attend an event

64. 시각 자료에서, 남자가 탈 것 같은 열차는?
(A) 105호 열차
(B) 207호 열차
(C) 482호 열차
(D) 553호 열차

해설 단서 (64)에서 남자는 오늘 마지막 열차에 탑승할 것이라고 했는데, 열차 시간표에서 오늘의 마지막 열차는 오후 5시 50분에 출발하는 553호 열차이다. 따라서 정답은 (D).

Questions 65-67 refer to the following conversation and poster.

M ⁶⁵I'm meeting with Theo Miller from the *Stroudville Herald* tomorrow to give an interview about our art contest. He's planning to write an article about it.

W That's wonderful! We want as many people as possible to know about it. I think it'll be a great way for people to express their creativity, and they can also learn more about our museum.

M Exactly. We hope that people will take a look around the museum when they drop off their submissions. ⁶⁶Speaking of which, I still need a few people to collect the art on the last day of submissions. Are you free?

W I'd love to help you out, but ⁶⁷I'm moving to a new apartment that week, and I don't have a moment to spare.

남 ⁶⁵저는 우리 미술 대회에 대한 인터뷰를 하기 위해 내일 〈스트라우드빌 헤럴드〉 지의 테오 밀러 씨와 만날 예정이에요. 그가 미술 대회에 대한 기사를 작성할 계획이라고 하네요.

여 그거 정말 좋은데요! 우리는 가능한 한 많은 사람이 그 대회에 대해 알았으면 하잖아요. 제 생각에 그것은 사람들이 자신의 창의성을 표현할 수 있는 훌륭한 방법이 될 거고, 사람들은 우리 미술관에 대해서도 더 많이 알 수 있을 거예요.

남 정확해요. 우리는 사람들이 제출물을 주고 갈 때 미술관을 한번 둘러보기를 바라고 있죠. ⁶⁶얘기가 나왔으니 말인데, 저는 제출 마지막 날에 그림을 받아 줄 사람 몇 명이 아직 필요해요. 당신은 시간이 있나요?

여 저도 도와드리고 싶지만, ⁶⁷제가 그 주에 새 아파트로 이사를 갈 예정이라, 짬을 낼 수가 없네요.

아마추어 미술 대회
출품작 모집

⁶⁶**제출 기간:** 2월 3일-5일
시상식: 2월 7일 오후 6시
일반인 전시 시작: 2월 8일
전시 종료: 2월 20일

윌로우 미술관

57. 남자가 "제가 더 분명하게 말했어야 했어요"라고 말한 의미는?
(A) 새로운 전략을 설명할 필요가 있다.
(B) 여자가 잘못된 길로 갔다고 생각한다.
(C) 상태 업데이트를 제공할 예정이다.
(D) 여자의 말에 혼란스러워 하고 있다.

해설 단서 (57)에서 남자는 길을 다시 설명하여 여자가 알고 있는 것이 틀렸음을 말하고 있으므로, 여자가 길을 잘못 가고 있다고 생각하고 있음을 알 수 있다. 따라서 정답은 (B).

58. 여자가 교차로에 대해 말한 것은?
(A) 이미 지나쳤다.
(B) 그 주변에 있는 사무실에서 일했었다.
(C) 그게 어디에 있는지 모른다.
(D) 그 옆에 있는 우체국을 찾았다.

패러프레이징 [단서] I crossed the main intersection a while ago. → [정답] She has already passed it.

Questions 59-61 refer to the following conversation.

M ⁵⁹Thanks, Ms. Carson, for taking the time to answer my questions for the *Norville Tribune*. ⁶⁰Our subscribers love to read about how local businesses found success.

W Well, ⁶⁰we decided to start offering more gluten-free options, and that strategy has helped us a great deal. My pastry chef has come up with a lot of great ideas.

M Appealing to a wider audience has certainly helped you to bring in business. What other plans do you have for the future?

W ⁶¹We plan to host a cake decorating class for beginners next month right here at the bakery.

남 ⁵⁹〈노빌 트리뷴〉지를 위해 제 질문에 답하는 시간을 내주셔서 감사합니다, 카슨 씨. ⁶⁰저희 독자들은 지역 사업체들이 성공하게 된 방법에 관해 읽고 싶어 합니다.

여 음, ⁶⁰저희는 글루텐이 들어가지 않은 선택 제품을 더 많이 제공하기 시작하기로 했고, 그 전략이 저희에게 상당히 도움이 되었습니다. 저희 페이스트리 제빵사는 훌륭한 아이디어들을 많이 내놓고 있어요.

남 더 넓은 고객층의 관심을 끈 것이 일이 들어오는 데에 확실히 도움이 되었군요. 미래를 위해 그 밖에 어떤 계획을 가지고 계신지요?

여 ⁶¹저희는 바로 이곳 제과점에서 다음 달에 초보자를 위한 케이크 장식 수업을 주최할 계획입니다.

어휘 subscriber 독자, 구독자 option 선택(할 수 있는 것) strategy 전략 a great deal 상당히, 많이 come up with ~을 내놓다[제시하다] appeal to ~의 관심을 끌다 bring in 가져오다, 들여오다 host 주최하다

59. 남자의 신분은?
(A) 페이스트리 제빵사
(B) 사업 컨설턴트
(C) 신문 기자
(D) 운동 전문가

패러프레이징 [단서] the *Norville Tribune* → [정답] newspaper

60. 화자들이 주로 이야기하고 있는 것은?
(A) 사업 전략
(B) 제품 출시
(C) 재료 부족
(D) 교육 행사

해설 단서 (60)을 보면 사업체가 성공하게 된 방법으로, 사업에 도움이 된 구체적인 전략이 언급되어 있다. 이를 통해 사업 전략에 관한 대화임을 알 수 있으므로 정답은 (A).

패러프레이징 [단서] that strategy → [정답] A business strategy

61. 여자가 다음 달에 일어날 거라고 말한 일은?
(A) 무료 다과가 제공될 것이다.
(B) 새 지점이 개업할 것이다.
(C) 수업이 제공될 것이다.
(D) 더 많은 직원이 고용될 것이다.

패러프레이징 [단서] We plan to host a cake decorating class for beginners → [정답] A class will be offered.

Questions 62-64 refer to the following conversation and schedule.

W Nate, you're leaving already?

M Yes. I told Ms. Princeton yesterday that I had a train to catch this afternoon. ⁶²I'm going to Atlanta for a nutrition conference.

W ⁶²,⁶³Oh, you're going to the conference organized by the Healthy Ingredients Association? I thought it didn't start until tomorrow.

M ⁶³That's right. I am leaving today, because it starts early in the morning. So I want to stay in a hotel tonight and get a good night's sleep. There aren't any trains after six, though. ⁶⁴I'm going home to pick up my suit, then I'm taking the last train today.

🎧 미 미
Questions 53-55 refer to the following conversation.

M   Hello, I'm calling from Verano. ⁵³, ⁵⁴Ms. Vanessa Haley left us a message to ask for a reservation for tomorrow night at six thirty. I'm sorry, but we don't have any tables available at that time. Would it be possible for your party to come at seven instead?

W   Well, that's a little late for us. ⁵⁴We're all coworkers, and we were planning on going out straight after work.

M   You are welcome to sit at the bar and even order some appetizers while you wait if you come early.

W   That sounds nice actually. All right then. ⁵⁵Put us down for seven.

남   여보세요, 베라노에서 전화드립니다. ⁵³, ⁵⁴버네사 헤일리 씨께서 저희에게 내일 저녁 6시 30분에 예약을 요청하신다는 메시지를 남기셨습니다. 죄송합니다만, 저희는 그 시간에는 예약 가능한 테이블이 없습니다. 일행분들이 대신에 7시에 오시는 것은 가능할까요?

여   음, 저희에게 그건 조금 늦어요. ⁵⁴저희는 모두 동료들이라서, 퇴근 후에 바로 나갈 계획이었거든요.

남   일찍 오신다면 기다리시는 동안 바에 앉으셔서 전채 요리를 좀 주문하셔도 좋습니다.

여   뭐 그것도 좋겠네요. 그럼 좋습니다. ⁵⁵7시로 예약해 주세요.

어휘 party 일행   coworker 동료   appetizer 전채 요리, 애피타이저
put A down for B B의 예약자[신청자]로 A의 이름을 적다[적어 두다]

53. 남자의 신분은?
(A) 호텔 지배인
(B) 식당 종업원
(C) 개인 출장 요리업자
(D) 행사 기획자

54. 여자가 내일 퇴근 후에 하려고 계획한 일은?
(A) 집으로 곧장 가는 것
(B) 동료들과 식사하는 것
(C) 식료품을 쇼핑하는 것
(D) 친구들을 만나는 것

패러프레이징 [단서] coworkers → [정답] colleagues

55. 여자가 남자에게 하도록 부탁한 것은?
(A) 여자의 요청 취소하기
(B) 여자의 주문에 항목 추가하기
(C) 여자의 사무실에서 여자와 만나기
(D) 예약하기

해설 단서 (55)에서 자신들을 7시로 적어 달라고 했으므로, 여자가 7시에 예약하려고 한다는 것을 알 수 있다. 따라서 정답은 (D). put down은 명단 등에 '적다, 적어 넣다'의 뜻으로, 예약 명단에 이름을 적어 넣어 '예약하다'라는 의미로 쓰인다는 것을 알아 두자.

패러프레이징 [단서] Put us down for seven. → [정답] Make a reservation

🎧 미 호
Questions 56-58 refer to the following conversation.

W   Hi, Elliot! ⁵⁶I'm trying to find your office, but I think I'm lost. You said to turn left after the post office, but I don't see it.

M   I'm sorry. I should have been clearer. ⁵⁷I meant to say that you will see the post office right after you turn left.

W   Well, in that case, how do I know when to turn?

M   Just take the first left after the main intersection.

W   Ah, I'm going to have to turn back. ⁵⁸I crossed the main intersection a while ago.

여   안녕하세요, 엘리엇 씨! ⁵⁶당신의 사무실을 찾으려고 하고 있는데, 제가 길을 잃은 것 같아요. 우체국을 지나면 좌회전하라고 하셨는데, 우체국이 보이질 않네요.

남   미안해요. 제가 더 분명하게 말했어야 했어요. ⁵⁷저는 좌회전하고 나면 바로 우체국이 보일 거라고 말하려던 거였어요.

여   음, 그렇다면, 언제 좌회전하는지 제가 어떻게 알죠?

남   주 교차로를 지나서 첫 번째 왼쪽 길로 가세요.

여   아, 저는 되돌아가야겠네요. ⁵⁸조금 전에 주 교차로를 건넜거든요.

어휘 say to do (= tell someone to do) ~하라고 말하다
in that case 그런 경우에는, 그렇다면   intersection 교차로   turn back 되돌아가다   a while ago 조금 전에

56. 여자가 전화를 건 목적은?
(A) 길을 물어보기 위해
(B) 회의 일정을 잡기 위해
(C) 소포에 대해 문의하기 위해
(D) 누락된 물품을 보고하기 위해

(D) 택시 운전사

해설 단서 (47)에서 남자가 아파트 임대가 가능한지 묻고 여자는 그곳의 입주자를 찾았지만 비슷한 건물이 하나 더 있다고 말하는 것으로 보아 여자는 부동산 중개업자임을 유추할 수 있다. 따라서 정답은 (C).

48. 남자가 문의한 것은?
(A) 만나는 시간
(B) 장소의 위치
(C) 건물 가치
(D) 표 가격

패러프레이징 [단서] What area is it in? → [정답] A place's location

49. 여자가 다음에 할 것 같은 일은?
(A) 남자에게 건물 찾아 주기
(B) 남자가 장소를 찾는 것 도와 주기
(C) 남자를 역까지 태워 주기
(D) 남자에게 문서 보내 주기

패러프레이징 [단서] send you a map → [정답] Send a document to the man

🎧 미 미 영

Questions 50-52 refer to the following conversation with three speakers.

> **W1** Good afternoon, Maria and Clyde. Welcome to Cozy's. ⁵⁰I'm going to show you several fireplaces today, but first, do you have anything special in mind?
>
> **M** ⁵⁰,⁵¹Well, we have a traditional house. So we are looking for a rustic style rather than something modern-looking.
>
> **W2** We still want it to have modern features, though. ⁵²The Windsor Gold model in your catalog looked like what we are looking for.
>
> **W1** ⁵²That model is our most popular item. However, before you decide, I can show you similar models that also have a wooden finish but are more energy-efficient.
>
> **M** Yes, please. We would be happy to see everything you have.
>
> **W2** We are open to other suggestions as well.

> 여1 안녕하세요, 마리아 씨, 클라이드 씨. 코지스에 오신 것을 환영합니다. ⁵⁰오늘 제가 벽난로를 몇 가지 보여 드릴 텐데요, 먼저, 특별히 염두에 두고 계신 것이 있나요?
>
> 남 ⁵⁰,⁵¹음, 저희는 전통적인 집을 가지고 있어요. 그래서 저희는 현대적인 모습의 것보다는 소박한 스타일을 찾고 있습니다.
>
> 여2 그래도, 여전히 현대적인 기능들은 가지고 있으면 좋겠어요. ⁵²귀사의 카탈로그에 있는 윈저 골드 모델이 저희가 찾고 있는 것과 비슷해 보이던데요.
>
> 여1 ⁵²그 모델이 저희의 가장 인기 있는 제품이에요. 하지만 결정하시기 전에, 역시 목재 마감으로 되어 있지만 연료 효율은 더 좋은, 비슷한 모델들도 보여 드릴 수 있어요.
>
> 남 네, 그렇게 해 주세요. 저희는 가지고 계신 모든 걸 보면 좋겠어요.
>
> 여2 저희는 다른 제안에도 마음이 열려 있습니다.

어휘 fireplace 벽난로 have ~ in mind ~을 염두에 두다 rustic 소박한, 투박한 rather than ~보다는, ~ 대신에 morden-looking 현대적인 모습의 feature 특징; ~을 특별히 포함하다 finish 표면의 마감 처리 energy-efficient 연료 효율이 좋은 suggestion 제안, 제의

50. 대화가 이루어지고 있을 것 같은 곳은?
(A) 소방서
(B) 부동산 중개업체
(C) 귀금속 매장
(D) 인테리어 디자인 업체

해설 대화가 일어나고 있는 장소에 대한 단서는 주로 대화 도입부에 나온다. 단서 (50)에서 여자가 벽난로를 보여 주겠다고 하고 남자는 본인의 집에 어울리는 스타일에 대해 말하는 것으로 보아 이들이 인테리어 디자인 업체에 있음을 유추할 수 있다. 따라서 정답은 (D).

51. 마리아 씨와 클라이드 씨가 원하는 특징은?
(A) 옛날식의 외관
(B) 현대적인 모습
(C) 전통적 시스템
(D) 높은 에너지 생산

패러프레이징 [단서] a rustic style → [정답] An old-fashioned appearance

52. 윈저 골드에 대해 언급된 것은?
(A) 품절되었다.
(B) 고객들이 가장 좋아하는 것이다.
(C) 금으로 마감이 되어 있다.
(D) 현대적인 스타일로 되어 있다.

패러프레이징 [단서] That model is our most popular item. → [정답] It's a customer favorite.

🎧

Questions 44-46 refer to the following conversation.

W Todd, ⁴⁴did you finish writing the program notes for next week's concert? The pianists want to see them before we give them out to the audience.

M Yes, I did. I was just going to send them to you. Here, you can check them right now if you'd like.

W They look nice. I like the design. ⁴⁵But it seems like a piece is missing from the timetable on the first page. The Beethoven sonata, right before intermission.

M You're right! How is that possible? ⁴⁶I know I put it in there, and I checked the program twice this morning. Anyway, I'll fix that right away.

여 토드 씨, ⁴⁴다음 주 연주회를 위한 프로그램 해설 작성을 마쳤나요? 피아노 연주자들이 우리가 그걸 청중에게 나눠 주기 전에 보고 싶어 해요.

남 네, 다 했어요. 막 보내 드리려던 참이었어요. 여기요, 원하시면 지금 바로 확인해 보세요.

여 좋아 보이네요. 디자인이 마음에 들어요. ⁴⁵그런데 첫 번째 페이지에 있는 시간표에서 한 곡이 누락된 것 같은데요. 중간 휴식 시간 바로 전에 있는 베토벤 소나타 말이에요.

남 맞네요! 어떻게 그럴 수가 있죠? ⁴⁶제가 분명 그걸 거기에 입력했고, 오늘 아침에 프로그램을 두 번이나 확인했거든요. 어쨌든, 지금 바로 고칠게요.

어휘 program note 프로그램 해설 give out ~을 나누어 주다 piece (글·미술·음악 등의 작품) 한 점 timetable 시간표 intermission (연극·영화 등의) 중간 휴식 시간 right away 곧바로, 즉시

44. 화자들이 주로 이야기하고 있는 것은?
(A) 청중 후기
(B) 음악가의 연주
(C) 광고 디자인
(D) 정보 제공 유인물

패러프레이징 [단서] the program notes for next week's concert → [정답] An informational handout

45. 여자가 언급한 문제점은?
(A) 공연의 휴식 시간이 너무 짧다.
(B) 음악 작품 하나가 형편없이 해석되었다.
(C) 연예인이 늦는다.
(D) 일정 관련 인쇄물이 불완전하다.

패러프레이징 [단서] a piece is missing from the timetable on the first page → [정답] A schedule printout is incomplete.

46. 남자가 "어떻게 그럴 수가 있죠"라고 말한 의미는?
(A) 업무를 어떻게 해야 하는지 모른다.
(B) 여자가 변경에 대해 설명해 주길 원한다.
(C) 실수를 알아채고 놀랐다.
(D) 여자의 말에 동의하지 않는다.

해설 해당 표현 바로 뒤의 단서 (46)에서 정보를 시간표에 입력했고 두 번이나 확인했다고 했으므로, 남자가 자신의 실수를 알아채고 깜짝 놀랐다는 것을 알 수 있다. 따라서 정답은 (C).

🎧

Questions 47-49 refer to the following conversation.

M Hello, ⁴⁷I'm calling about the apartment on Delaware Avenue. Is it still available for rent?

W ⁴⁷I'm sorry, I found a tenant just this morning. However, I have a similar property that is available. It's the same size and goes for the same price. If you want, you can come by and see it tomorrow.

M ⁴⁸What area is it in? Is it also close to Clarkston Station? I need to take the subway every day.

W Yes, it is very close to the station. Are you familiar with Acorn Drive? It's only a five-minute walk away. ⁴⁹I'll send you a map right now.

남 여보세요, ⁴⁷델라웨어 로에 있는 아파트 때문에 전화드렸어요. 그 아파트는 아직 임대가 가능한가요?

여 ⁴⁷죄송하지만, 제가 바로 오늘 아침에 세입자를 찾았어요. 하지만 임대 가능한 비슷한 건물이 하나 있습니다. 똑같은 크기이고 똑같은 가격에 해당합니다. 원하신다면 내일 잠깐 들르셔서 둘러보실 수 있어요.

남 ⁴⁸그건 어느 지역에 있어요? 그 아파트도 클라크스턴 역에 가깝나요? 저는 매일 지하철을 타야 하거든요.

여 네, 그 아파트는 역에서 아주 가깝습니다. 에이콘 드라이브를 잘 아시나요? 걸어서 5분 거리밖에 안 됩니다. ⁴⁹제가 지금 바로 지도를 보내 드릴게요.

어휘 tenant 세입자, 임차인 property 건물, 부동산 go for ~에 해당되다 come by 잠깐 들르다 be familiar with ~을 잘 알다, ~에 익숙하다

47. 여자의 직업일 것 같은 것은?
(A) 지하철표 판매원
(B) 인테리어 디자이너
(C) 부동산 중개업자

어휘 passport 여권   city hall 시청   in person 직접, 몸소   release (갖고 있던 것을) 내주다   make it (어떤 곳에 간신히) 시간 맞춰 가다

38. 남자가 전화를 건 이유는?
(A) 물품 배송 일정을 잡기 위해
(B) 문서가 이용 가능함을 알리기 위해
(C) 자신의 개인 정보를 업데이트하기 위해
(D) 어떤 장소로 찾아가는 길 안내를 요청하기 위해

패러프레이징 [단서] to let you know that your passport is ready → [정답] To notify of a document's availability

39. 남자가 필요하다고 말한 것은?
(A) 사진이 부착된 신분증
(B) 연락처 정보
(C) 지역 우편 주소
(D) 지불 영수증

패러프레이징 [단서] photo ID → [정답] Picture identification

40. 여자가 오늘 남자를 만나지 못하는 이유는?
(A) 자신의 여권을 잊고 안 가져왔다.
(B) 예약을 하지 않았다.
(C) 교통 체증에 갇혀 있다.
(D) 너무 멀리 살고 있다.

해설 단서 (40)에서 여자는 오늘 시청이 문을 닫기 전까지 갈 수 없을 것 같다고 말하면서 거기에 가려면 적어도 한 시간 반은 걸린다고 했으므로 정답은 (D).

패러프레이징 [단서] It takes me at least an hour and a half to get there. → [정답] She lives too far away.

미 영 호 🎧
Questions 41-43 refer to the following conversation with three speakers.

M1   Hello, ⁴¹I'm here to return some books.

W   Okay… Um… ⁴¹It says you still have one book due tomorrow.

M1   Right. Unfortunately, I left it on a train and can't return it by tomorrow. Is it possible to renew it?

W   Well, you've already extended the due date once. Hold on. ⁴²Mr. Clayton? Can we make an exception for this man?

M2   Um… Are you sure you will find the book and be able to return it?

M1   I've contacted the train station. They said they have it. I can pick it up and bring it to you on Friday.

M2   I understand your situation, but we cannot renew the item. ⁴³You will have to pay a late fee on Friday.

남1   안녕하세요. ⁴¹책을 몇 권 반납하러 왔는데요.

여   네… 음… ⁴¹회원님께서는 내일까지 반납하셔야 하는 책이 한 권 더 있다고 나오네요.

남1: 맞아요. 유감스럽게도, 제가 그걸 기차에 두고 내려서 내일까지 반납할 수가 없어요. 그것을 연장할 수 있을까요?

여   음, 회원님께서는 이미 반납일을 한 번 연장하셨네요. 잠시만요. ⁴²클레이턴 씨? 우리가 이분을 예외로 해 드릴 수 있나요?

남2   음… 그 책을 찾아서 반납할 수 있는 게 확실한가요?

남1   제가 기차역에 연락해 봤는데요. 그곳에서 그걸 가지고 있다고 했거든요. 금요일에 그걸 찾아서 가져다 드릴 수 있습니다.

남2   회원님의 상황이 이해는 갑니다만, 그 책을 연장해 드릴 수는 없어요. ⁴³금요일에 연체료를 내셔야 할 겁니다.

어휘 extend 연장하다, 넓히다   due date 만기일
make an exception 예외로 하다   contact 연락하다   renew (도서관 책의 반납 기간을) 연장하다   late fee 연체료

41. 대화가 일어나고 있을 것 같은 곳은?
(A) 기차역
(B) 서점
(C) 인쇄소
(D) 도서관

42. 여자가 클레이턴 씨에게 물어본 것은?
(A) 시설이 어디에 위치해 있는지
(B) 예외로 해 줄 수 있는지
(C) 절차가 어떻게 실행되어야 하는지
(D) 물건값이 얼마인지

해설 문제에서 Clayton이라는 고유 명사를 언급했으므로 단서를 쉽게 찾을 수 있다. 단서 (42)에서 여자가 클레이턴 씨에게 책을 반납하려는 사람을 예외로 해 줄 수 있냐고 물었으므로 정답은 (B).

패러프레이징 [단서] Can we make an exception for this man? → [정답] Whether an exception can be made

43. 금요일에 지불되어야 할 것은?
(A) 연체료
(B) 교통비
(C) 분실물 처리 요금
(D) 수하물 배송 청구 요금

패러프레이징 [단서] a late fee → [정답] An overdue fine

미 호 🎧
Questions 35-37 refer to the following conversation.

W   Hello, Mr. Robbins. This is Samantha Kelly. ³⁵Would it be okay for me to come in at ten instead of nine today? I could stay late tonight.

M   Good morning, Ms. Kelly. The company is rather strict with work hours. ³⁶As you know, our most important work is done in the morning.

W   Yes, I understand. Unfortunately, I had a dentist appointment at eight, but he is running behind schedule. It's difficult to get appointments with this doctor, so I was hoping it would be okay to be late just this once.

M   I see. Well, to be honest, things are slow this week, so it should be fine just for today. ³⁷I'll let the department head know about your situation.

여   안녕하세요, 로빈스 씨. 사만다 켈리입니다. ³⁵오늘 제가 9시 대신에 10시에 출근해도 괜찮을까요? 전 오늘 밤 늦게까지 있을 수 있어요.

남   좋은 아침이에요, 켈리 씨. 회사는 근무 시간에 대해 꽤 엄격해요. ³⁶아시다시피, 우리의 가장 중요한 업무는 오전에 이루어지잖아요.

여   네, 이해합니다. 유감스럽게도, 제가 8시에 치과 진료 예약이 되어 있었는데 의사가 일정보다 늦어지고 있어요. 이 의사와 진료 예약을 잡는 것이 어려워서, 이번 한 번만 늦어도 괜찮기를 바랍니다.

남   그렇군요. 음, 솔직히 말하면, 이번 주에는 일들이 천천히 돌아가서, 오늘만 그렇게 하는 건 괜찮을 거예요. ³⁷제가 부장님께 당신의 상황에 관해 알려 드릴게요.

어휘 come in 들어오다, 도착하다   instead of ~ 대신에   rather 꽤, 약간   strict 엄격한   unfortunately 유감스럽게도   run 진행되다   behind schedule 예정보다 늦게   situation 상황, 처지

35. 여자가 전화를 건 목적은?
(A) 예약을 하기 위해
(B) 마감을 연장하기 위해
(C) 검진 결과를 보고하기 위해
(D) 근무 시간을 변경하기 위해

해설 전화를 건 목적은 대부분 대화의 도입부에 나오므로 이 부분을 유심히 들어야 한다. 단서 (35)에서 여자는 9시 대신에 10시에 출근해도 되는지 물어보면서 오늘 밤 늦게까지 있을 수 있다고 했으므로 정답은 (D).

36. 남자가 회사에 대해 언급한 것은?
(A) 직원들의 교대 근무 일정이 유동적이다.
(B) 주요 업무가 정오 전에 이루어진다.
(C) 의무실이 오전에는 문이 열려 있지 않다.
(D) 이번 주에 생산성이 특히 높다.

패러프레이징 [단서] our most important work is done in the morning → [정답] Its major tasks are done before noon.

37. 남자가 자신이 하겠다고 말한 것은?
(A) 관리자에게 변경을 알리기
(B) 직원들을 위해 업무량 줄여 주기
(C) 치과 검진 연기하기
(D) 여자를 더 높은 직급으로 승진시키기

패러프레이징 [단서] let the department head know about your situation → [정답] Inform a manager of a change

미 미 🎧
Questions 38-40 refer to the following conversation.

M   Hello, Ms. Rivers. ³⁸This is Jason Best, calling to let you know that your passport is ready. You may pick it up at City Hall.

W   Thank you. However, I live quite far from City Hall. Would it be possible to have it mailed to my address?

M   I'm sorry, but you must pick it up in person. ³⁹I have to see another form of photo ID to release the passport.

W   I see. Well, then, I will pick it up tomorrow. ⁴⁰I wouldn't be able to make it to City Hall today before you close. It takes me at least an hour and a half to get there.

M   That's fine. I will see you tomorrow.

남   안녕하세요, 리버스 씨. ³⁸저는 제이슨 베스트라고 하며, 당신의 여권이 준비되었음을 알려 드리고자 전화드렸습니다. 시청에서 그것을 찾아가시면 됩니다.

여   감사합니다. 그런데, 제가 시청에서 꽤 멀리 살아서요. 제 주소로 그것을 부쳐 주시는 게 가능할까요?

남   죄송합니다만, 직접 찾아가셔야만 합니다. ³⁹여권을 내드리려면 사진이 부착된 다른 종류의 신분증을 제가 확인해야 하거든요.

여   알겠습니다. 음, 그러면 내일 찾아갈게요. ⁴⁰오늘은 문 닫기 전에 시청까지 시간 맞춰 갈 수 없을 것 같아요. 제가 거기 가려면 적어도 한 시간 반은 걸리거든요.

남   괜찮습니다. 내일 뵙겠습니다.

(A) 컴퓨터를 다시 시작해 보세요.
(B) 어느 파일을 말씀하시는 건가요?
(C) 서류 더미 아래에요.

해설 어느 폴더 안에 파일을 저장했는지 묻는 질문에 어느 파일을 말하는 거냐고 반문한 (B)가 정답. (C)는 file과 발음이 유사한 pile을 이용한 오답.

어휘 try doing 시험 삼아 ~해 보다   restart 다시 시작하다   pile 더미, 쌓아 올린 것

31. 미 호 🎧

When will the store restock its shoe section?
(A) Sneakers are on sale.
(B) I don't work here.
(C) I'm sorry, but they're out of stock.

매장에서 언제 신발 코너에 재고를 채울 예정인가요?
(A) 스니커즈는 할인 판매 중이에요.
(B) 저는 여기에서 일하지 않아요.
(C) 죄송하지만, 그것들은 재고가 없어요.

해설 매장의 신발 코너에 재고를 언제 채우는지 묻는 질문에 여기에서 일하지 않는다며 모른다고 우회적으로 답한 (B)가 정답.

어휘 restock 재고를 다시 채우다   section 구역, 구획   on sale 할인 판매 중인, 판매되는   out of stock 품절되어, 매진의

PART 3

미 미 🎧

Questions 32-34 refer to the following conversation.

W   Hi. ³²I need a new desktop computer. ³³I heard you're offering 20 percent off some of your items this week. Is that right?

M   ³³Yes, that is correct. But the ones on the top shelf are not on sale. Those are full price.

W   Oh, that's a shame. I was looking at the Raven-XT over there. Is there any way I can get a discount? I've bought many items from this store and have been a member for years.

M   Ah, then, ³⁴let me see your membership card. I'll take a look at your past purchases. You might be eligible to trade some points for a discount.

여   안녕하세요. ³²저는 새 데스크톱 컴퓨터가 필요한데요. ³³이번 주에 일부 제품에 20% 할인을 제공하는 중이라고 들었습니다. 그게 맞나요?

남   ³³네, 맞습니다. 하지만 맨 위 선반에 있는 것들은 할인 판매되지 않습니다. 그것들은 정가예요.

여   아, 그거 아쉽네요. 저는 저쪽에 있는 레이븐-XT를 보고 있었거든요. 제가 할인을 받을 수 있는 방법이 있을까요? 저는 이 가게에서 물건도 많이 사 왔고 몇 년째 회원이거든요.

남   아, 그렇다면, ³⁴회원 카드를 보여 주세요. 제가 고객님의 과거 구매 내역을 살펴볼게요. 고객님께서는 일부 포인트를 할인으로 교환할 자격이 되실 수도 있어요.

어휘 shame 아쉬운[애석한] 일   take a look at ~을 보다   be eligible to do ~할 자격이 있다   trade A for B A를 B로 교환하다

32. 여자가 사고 싶어 하는 것은?
(A) 카드
(B) 책상
(C) 컴퓨터
(D) 선반

패러프레이징 [단서] a new desktop computer
→ [정답] A computer

33. 남자가 제품들에 대해 말한 것은?
(A) 모든 제품이 할인되는 것은 아니다.
(B) 대부분의 제품이 재고가 없다.
(C) 많은 제품이 구식이다.
(D) 일부 제품은 라벨이 잘못 붙어 있다.

해설 단서 (33)에서 일부 제품이 할인 판매 중인지 확인하는 여자의 질문에 남자가 그렇다고 답하면서 맨 위 선반의 제품들은 할인 판매되지 않는다고 했으므로 정답은 (A).

패러프레이징 [단서] you're offering 20 percent off some of your items → [정답] Not all of them are discounted.

34. 남자가 다음에 할 것 같은 일은?
(A) 제품 가격 확인하기
(B) 관리자와 이야기하기
(C) 계정 기록 확인하기
(D) 쿠폰 출력하기

패러프레이징 [단서] take a look at your past purchases
→ [정답] Check an account history

'의자'와 '의장'이라는 서로 다른 의미를 지닌 다의어 chair를 이용한 오답.

어휘 budget 예산　committee 위원회

25.

> Do you know if the swimming pool offers classes?
> **(A) Only in the summer.**
> (B) I'm preparing for a triathlon.
> (C) The fitness center is completed.

수영장에서 강습을 제공하는지 아세요?
(A) 여름에만요.
(B) 저는 철인 3종 경기를 준비하고 있어요.
(C) 피트니스 센터가 완공되었어요.

해설　수영장에서 강습을 제공하는지 아냐고 묻는 질문에 여름에만 제공한다고 답한 (A)가 정답. (B)는 swimming에서 연상할 수 있는 triathlon을 이용한 오답.

어휘 offer 제공하다　prepare for ~을 준비하다　triathlon 철인 3종 경기, 트라이애슬론　complete 완성하다, 끝마치다

26.

> I forgot to get you a copy of the brochure.
> (A) It has a nice design.
> (B) The photocopier is out of service.
> **(C) It's okay. I've already got one.**

제가 당신에게 안내 책자를 한 부 갖다 주는 걸 잊었어요.
(A) 그건 디자인이 멋지네요.
(B) 그 복사기는 사용할 수 없어요.
(C) 괜찮아요. 저는 이미 하나 가지고 있거든요.

해설　안내 책자를 한 부 갖다 주는 걸 잊었다는 말에 괜찮다고 하면서 이미 하나를 가지고 있다고 답한 (C)가 정답.

어휘 brochure (안내·광고용) 책자　photocopier 복사기　out of service 사용이 불가능한

27.

> Aren't we supposed to turn left here?
> (A) Yes, there are a few left.
> (B) He'll be here in a minute.
> **(C) The map says to keep going.**

우리 여기에서 좌회전해야 하지 않아요?
(A) 네, 몇 개가 남아 있어요.
(B) 그가 곧 여기에 올 거예요.
(C) 지도에는 계속 가라고 되어 있어요.

해설　여기에서 좌회전해야 하지 않냐고 묻는 질문에 지도에는 계속 가라고 되어 있다며 아니라고 우회적으로 답한 (C)가 정답. (A)는 질문의 left를 반복 사용한 오답으로 질문에서는 '왼쪽으로'라는 의미의 부사로, 선택지에서는 '남겨진'이라는 의미의 과거분사로 사용되었다.

어휘 be supposed to do ~하기로 되어 있다, ~해야 하다　in a minute 곧, 즉시　keep doing 계속 ~하다

28.

> Can you print out these graphs so I can view them later?
> (A) They're probably still in the cabinet.
> **(B) The printer is malfunctioning.**
> (C) I'm curious about your views on the topic.

제가 나중에 볼 수 있도록 이 도표들을 출력해 주시겠어요?
(A) 그것들은 아마도 아직 캐비닛 안에 있을 거예요.
(B) 프린터가 제대로 작동하지 않고 있어요.
(C) 저는 그 주제에 관한 당신의 의견이 궁금해요.

해설　나중에 볼 수 있게 도표들을 출력해 주겠냐는 요청에 프린터가 제대로 작동하지 않고 있다며 요청한 일을 할 수 없다고 우회적으로 답한 (B)가 정답. (C)는 '보다'와 '의견'이라는 서로 다른 의미와 품사를 지닌 다의어 view를 이용한 오답.

어휘 print out 출력하다, 인쇄하다　probably 아마　malfunction 제대로 작동하지 않다　curious 궁금한, 호기심이 강한

29.

> Where can I renew my subscription?
> **(A) There's a link in the weekly e-mail.**
> (B) It expires in February.
> (C) Memberships start at $12.99 a month.

제 구독을 어디에서 갱신할 수 있나요?
(A) 매주 발송되는 이메일에 링크가 있어요.
(B) 2월에 만료돼요.
(C) 회비는 한 달에 12.99달러부터 시작해요.

해설　구독을 어디에서 갱신할 수 있는지 묻는 질문에 매주 발송되는 이메일에 링크가 있다며 그 링크에서 갱신할 수 있다고 우회적으로 답한 (A)가 정답. (B)와 (C)는 subscription에서 연상할 수 있는 expires와 Memberships를 각각 이용한 오답.

어휘 renew 갱신[연장]하다　subscription 구독　weekly 매주의, 주 1회의　expire 만료되다　membership 회비, 회원 자격[신분]

30.

> Which folder did you save the file in?
> (A) Try restarting the computer.
> **(B) Which file do you mean?**
> (C) Under the pile of documents.

어느 폴더 안에 그 파일을 저장하셨어요?

19. 미 미 🎧

> When will the venue for the conference be announced?
> **(A) Definitely before the weekend.**
> (B) At the Coral Convention Center.
> (C) Mr. Rose is the first speaker.

학회 장소는 언제 발표될 건가요?
(A) 주말 전에는 꼭이요.
(B) 코럴 컨벤션 센터에서요.
(C) 로즈 씨가 첫 번째 연사예요.

해설 학회 장소가 언제 발표될 것인지 묻는 질문에 주말 전에는 꼭 발표될 것이라고 답한 (A)가 정답.

어휘 venue 장소   conference 학회, 회의   announce 발표하다, 알리다   definitely 틀림없이, 분명히   speaker 연사, 발표자

20. 미 미 🎧

> Are you able to handle the negotiations on your own?
> (A) They asked for more time to decide.
> (B) We cannot sign this agreement.
> **(C) It would be nice to have some help.**

혼자서 그 협상을 처리할 수 있으세요?
(A) 그들은 결정할 시간을 더 요청했어요.
(B) 우리는 이 협정서에 서명할 수 없어요.
(C) 도움을 좀 받으면 좋겠네요.

해설 혼자서 협상을 처리할 수 있는지 묻는 질문에 도움을 좀 받으면 좋겠다고 답한 (C)가 정답. (A)와 (B)는 negotiations에서 연상할 수 있는 decide와 agreement를 각각 이용한 오답.

어휘 handle 처리하다, 다루다   negotiation (보통 복수형) 협상, 교섭   on one's own 혼자서, 단독으로   agreement 협정(서), 합의(서)

21. 영 미 🎧

> I don't know who to give these reports to.
> (A) They'll be done by five o'clock.
> (B) They are analyses of our sales figures.
> **(C) Ms. Davis usually takes care of them.**

저는 이 보고서들을 누구에게 줘야 할지 모르겠어요.
(A) 그것들은 5시까지는 완료될 거예요.
(B) 그것들은 우리 매출 수치 분석이에요.
(C) 보통 데이비스 씨가 그것들을 처리해요.

해설 보고서들을 누구에게 줘야 할지 모르겠다는 말에 보통 데이비스 씨가 그것들을 처리한다며 사람 이름으로 답한 (C)가 정답. (A)와 (B)는 reports에서 연상할 수 있는 be done과 analyses, sales figures를 각각 이용한 오답.

어휘 analysis 분석   sales figure (보통 복수형) 매출액, 매출 수치   take care of ~을 처리하다

22. 호 영 🎧

> Which department do you work for?
> (A) No. I'm still looking for a job.
> **(B) Research and development.**
> (C) I bought it at Lloyd's Department Store.

어느 부서에서 일하시나요?
(A) 아니요. 저는 아직 일자리를 찾고 있어요.
(B) 연구 개발이요.
(C) 저는 그걸 로이즈 백화점에서 샀어요.

해설 어느 부서에서 일하는지 묻는 질문에 특정 부서명으로 답한 (B)가 정답. (C)는 질문의 department를 반복 사용한 오답.

어휘 department 부서, (백화점 등의) 매장, 코너   look for ~을 찾다   research and development 연구 개발(= R&D)

23. 미 미 🎧

> Where did the author get the inspiration for her first novel?
> (A) I usually read mysteries.
> **(B) This article doesn't say.**
> (C) She finished it last year.

그 작가는 자신의 첫 소설에 대한 영감을 어디에서 얻었나요?
(A) 저는 보통 추리 소설을 읽어요.
(B) 이 기사에는 안 나와 있어요.
(C) 그녀는 그것을 작년에 탈고했어요.

해설 작가가 소설에 대한 영감을 어디에서 얻었는지 묻는 질문에 이 기사에는 안 나와 있다며 모른다고 우회적으로 답한 (B)가 정답.

어휘 author 작가   inspiration 영감   mystery 추리 소설   article 기사

24. 호 미 🎧

> There aren't enough chairs for everyone, are there?
> **(A) No, but Ms. Zoey is getting some right now.**
> (B) He's the chair of the budget committee.
> (C) Most people, but not everyone.

의자가 모두 앉을 만큼 충분하지 않아요, 그렇죠?
(A) 네, 하지만 조이 씨가 지금 몇 개를 가져오고 있어요.
(B) 그는 예산 위원회의 의장이에요.
(C) 대부분의 사람이 그렇지만, 모두가 그런 것은 아니에요.

해설 의자가 충분하지 않다는 말에 동의를 구하는 질문에 No라고 하면서 조이 씨가 지금 몇 개를 가져오고 있다고 답한 (A)가 정답. (B)는

13. 미 미 🎧

> Would you be willing to fill in for Eric when he's on vacation?
> (A) He's leaving this Friday.
> **(B) Yes, I can do that.**
> (C) He can work for me.

에릭 씨가 휴가 가 있을 때 그를 대신해 주실 의향이 있나요?
(A) 그는 이번 주 금요일에 떠날 거예요.
(B) 네, 그렇게 할 수 있죠.
(C) 그가 저 대신 일할 수 있어요.

해설 에릭 씨가 휴가를 가 있을 때 그를 대신해 줄 의향이 있는지 묻는 질문에 Yes라고 하면서 그렇게 할 수 있다고 답한 (B)가 정답. (C)는 fill in for에서 연상할 수 있는 work for를 이용한 오답.

어휘 be willing to do ~할 의향이 있다, 기꺼이 ~하다 fill in for ~을 대신하다

14. 미 미 🎧

> Why isn't the image displaying properly?
> **(A) It's in the wrong format.**
> (B) On the top left corner of the page.
> (C) Plays are more interesting than movies.

그 영상은 왜 제대로 표시되지 않고 있나요?
(A) 그건 잘못된 포맷으로 되어 있어요.
(B) 페이지 좌측 상단 구석에요.
(C) 연극이 영화보다 더 흥미롭죠.

해설 영상이 제대로 표시되지 않는 이유를 묻는 질문에 잘못된 포맷으로 되어 있어서라고 구체적인 이유로 답한 (A)가 정답. (C)는 displaying과 발음이 유사한 Plays를 이용한 오답.

어휘 display 표시되다, 전시하다 properly 제대로, 적절히 format 포맷, 서식

15. 영 미 🎧

> How would you like to serve the food?
> **(A) We can just do a buffet.**
> (B) I'm in the mood for pasta.
> (C) Yes, I'm already hungry.

음식을 어떻게 내놓길 원하세요?
(A) 우리는 그냥 뷔페식으로 할 수도 있어요.
(B) 저는 파스타를 먹고 싶어요.
(C) 네, 저는 벌써 배가 고파요.

해설 음식을 어떻게 내놓길 원하는지 묻는 질문에 그냥 뷔페식으로 할 수도 있다며 구체적인 방식 제시로 답한 (A)가 정답.

어휘 serve (음식을) 내다, 상을 차리다 in the mood for ~할 기분[생각]인

16. 미 미 🎧

> I'd like to know the library's hours.
> (A) You can check out three books at a time.
> **(B) It opens every day from nine to seven.**
> (C) Yes, it will take just a few hours.

도서관 운영 시간을 알고 싶어요.
(A) 한 번에 책을 세 권 대출할 수 있어요.
(B) 매일 9시부터 7시까지 열어요.
(C) 네, 몇 시간밖에 안 걸릴 거예요.

해설 도서관 운영 시간을 알고 싶다는 말에 매일 9시부터 7시까지 연다고 구체적인 운영 시간으로 답한 (B)가 정답.

어휘 check out (도서관 등에서) 대출하다, 확인하다 at a time 한 번에, 한꺼번에

17. 미 호 🎧

> Why are you wearing a suit and tie?
> (A) The pants are a little long.
> (B) From the new shopping center.
> **(C) I have a job interview this afternoon.**

당신은 왜 정장에 넥타이까지 차려입고 있나요?
(A) 바지가 약간 길어요.
(B) 새로 생긴 쇼핑센터에서요.
(C) 오늘 오후에 취업 면접이 있거든요.

해설 옷을 차려입은 이유를 묻는 질문에 오늘 오후에 취업 면접이 있다며 구체적인 이유로 답한 (C)가 정답. (B)는 옷을 어디에서 샀는지 묻는 질문에 적절한 답변이므로 오답.

18. 영 미 🎧

> Is rent due at the beginning or the end of the month?
> (A) I don't think I can meet that deadline.
> **(B) It should be paid a month in advance.**
> (C) I lent him some money last month.

임대료는 월초에 지불해야 하나요, 아니면 월말에 지불해야 하나요?
(A) 제가 그 기한을 못 지킬 것 같아요.
(B) 한 달 먼저 지불해야 해요.
(C) 제가 지난달에 그분에게 돈을 좀 빌려줬어요.

해설 임대료를 월초에 지불해야 하는지 월말에 지불해야 하는지 묻는 질문에 한 달 먼저 지불해야 한다고 답한 (B)가 정답.

어휘 rent 임대료, 집세 due 지불해야 하는, ~하기로 되어 있는 meet (기한 등을) 지키다 deadline 기한 in advance 미리, 사전에 lend 빌려주다

PART 2

7. 미 호 🎧

Who will pick up Mr. Mitchell from the airport?
(A) At 3:55 P.M.
(B) I'm free this afternoon.
(C) It was delayed.

미첼 씨를 공항에서 누가 모셔 올래요?
(A) 오후 3시 55분에요.
(B) 저는 오늘 오후에 한가해요.
(C) 그건 연착되었어요.

해설 미첼 씨를 공항에서 누가 데리고 올지 묻는 질문에 오늘 오후에 자신이 한가하다며 자신이 데리고 오겠다고 우회적으로 답한 (B)가 정답. (C)는 airport에서 연상할 수 있는 delayed를 이용한 오답.

어휘 pick up ~를 (차에) 태우러 가다, ~을 찾아가다   delay 지연시키다

8. 미 미 🎧

Did you enjoy the test drive?
(A) I hope you pass the test.
(B) Yes. I like this car a lot.
(C) You can park over there.

시승은 즐거우셨나요?
(A) 시험에 통과하시길 바랍니다.
(B) 네. 저는 이 차가 정말 마음에 들어요.
(C) 저쪽에 주차하시면 됩니다.

해설 시승이 즐거웠는지 묻는 질문에 Yes라고 하면서 차가 정말 마음에 든다고 답한 (B)가 정답.

어휘 test drive 시승, 시운전

9. 미 영 🎧

Have you seen the training manual?
(A) I don't know who took it.
(B) Here's the updated train schedule.
(C) It was written over a year ago.

교육 안내서를 보셨나요?
(A) 그걸 누가 가져갔는지 모르겠어요.
(B) 여기 업데이트된 열차 시간표예요.
(C) 그건 1년도 더 전에 작성되었어요.

해설 교육 안내서를 보았는지 묻는 질문에 그것을 누가 가져갔는지 모르겠다며 못 봤다고 우회적으로 답한 (A)가 정답. (B)는 training과 발음이 유사한 train을 이용한 오답.

어휘 training 교육, 훈련   manual 안내서, 설명서

10. 미 미 🎧

How far is the museum from here?
(A) I've been there once.
(B) Because it's further than expected.
(C) It's about a thirty-minute bus ride away.

여기에서 박물관이 얼마나 먼가요?
(A) 저는 거기 한 번 가 봤어요.
(B) 예상했던 것보다 더 멀어서요.
(C) 버스 타고 30분 정도 거리에 있어요.

해설 박물관까지의 거리를 묻는 질문에 버스로 30분 정도 거리에 있다고 답한 (C)가 정답.

어휘 expect 예상하다, 기대하다   ride 탑승   away 떨어져

11. 호 미 🎧

Who replaced the printer cartridge?
(A) The new intern did.
(B) It's out of ink.
(C) I placed it on the desk downstairs.

프린터 카트리지를 누가 교체했어요?
(A) 새로 온 인턴사원이 했어요.
(B) 잉크가 떨어졌어요.
(C) 제가 아래층에 있는 책상 위에 그걸 뒀어요.

해설 프린터 카트리지를 누가 교체했는지 묻는 질문에 새로 온 인턴사원이 했다고 직급으로 답한 (A)가 정답. (C)는 replaced와 발음이 유사한 placed를 이용한 오답.

어휘 replace 교체하다, 바꾸다   out of ~을 다 써 버린, ~이 떨어진

12. 영 미 🎧

A plumber will stop by between one and three this afternoon.
(A) No problem. I'll be here.
(B) It took about two hours.
(C) I'll stop it now.

배관공이 오늘 오후 1시에서 3시 사이에 들를 거예요.
(A) 문제없어요. 제가 여기에 있을게요.
(B) 그건 두 시간 정도 걸렸어요.
(C) 제가 그걸 지금 멈출게요.

해설 배관공이 오후에 들를 것이라는 말에 문제없다고 말하면서 자신이 이곳에 있겠다고 답한 (A)가 정답.

어휘 plumber 배관공   stop by (~에) 잠시 들르다

3. 미 🎧

(A) People are resting on a bench.
(B) A man is running beside a lake.
(C) A woman is taking off a jacket.
(D) **People are looking at each other.**

(A) 사람들이 벤치에서 쉬고 있다.
(B) 남자가 호수 옆에서 달리고 있다.
(C) 여자가 재킷을 벗는 중이다.
(D) 사람들이 서로를 쳐다보고 있다.

해설 두 남녀가 서로를 쳐다보고 있는 공통 동작을 바르게 묘사한 (D)가 정답.

어휘 rest 쉬다, 휴식을 취하다 beside ~의 옆에(서) take off ~을 벗다 each other 서로

4. 영 🎧

(A) Some bicycles have been left on a path.
(B) Cyclists are riding on a busy highway.
(C) Some people are resting on the grass.
(D) A bike lane runs alongside a field.

(A) 몇몇 자전거들이 길에 놓여 있다.
(B) 자전거 타는 사람들이 붐비는 고속 도로를 타고 있다.
(C) 몇몇 사람들이 잔디에서 쉬고 있다.
(D) 자전거 전용 도로가 들판을 따라 뻗어 있다.

해설 자전거를 탄 사람들만 지나가고 있는 도로가 들판을 따라 뻗어 있으므로 정답은 (D).

어휘 leave (어떤 장소에 계속) 그대로 두다, 방치하다 rest 쉬다; 휴식, 나머지 bike lane 자전거 전용 도로 alongside ~ 옆에, 나란히

5. 호 🎧

(A) A woman is writing on a notepad.
(B) A woman is gazing at a sheet of paper.
(C) A document is being stapled.
(D) A laptop has been placed on the desk.

(A) 여자가 메모장에 쓰고 있다.
(B) 여자가 종이 한 장을 응시하고 있다.
(C) 서류를 스테이플러로 철하고 있다.
(D) 노트북이 책상 위에 놓여 있다.

해설 책상 위에 노트북이 놓여 있는 모습이므로 정답은 (D). 여자가 종이 서류를 들고 있지만 이것을 응시하거나 스테이플러로 철하고 있는 것은 아니므로 (B)와 (C)는 오답.

어휘 gaze at ~을 응시하다 sheet (종이) 한 장 staple 스테이플러로 고정하다[철하다] place 놓다, 두다

6. 미 🎧

(A) Several cars are parked in a row.
(B) Snow is being shoveled off the rooftops.
(C) Windows of the houses are being closed.
(D) The road is blocked by a traffic jam.

(A) 자동차 몇 대가 일렬로 주차되어 있다.
(B) 옥상에서 눈을 삽으로 퍼내고 있다.
(C) 집들의 창문들을 닫는 중이다.
(D) 도로가 교통 체증으로 막혀 있다.

해설 길을 따라 차들이 일렬로 주차되어 있는 상태를 바르게 묘사한 (A)가 정답.

어휘 in a row 일렬로 shovel ~을 삽으로 퍼내다, 삽질하다 rooftop 옥상, 지붕 block 막다 traffic jam 교통 체증

TEST 04

LISTENING TEST

001 (A)	002 (C)	003 (D)	004 (D)	005 (D)
006 (A)	007 (B)	008 (B)	009 (A)	010 (C)
011 (A)	012 (A)	013 (B)	014 (A)	015 (A)
016 (B)	017 (C)	018 (B)	019 (A)	020 (C)
021 (C)	022 (B)	023 (B)	024 (A)	025 (A)
026 (C)	027 (C)	028 (B)	029 (A)	030 (B)
031 (B)	032 (C)	033 (A)	034 (C)	035 (D)
036 (B)	037 (A)	038 (B)	039 (A)	040 (D)
041 (D)	042 (B)	043 (A)	044 (D)	045 (D)
046 (C)	047 (C)	048 (B)	049 (D)	050 (D)
051 (A)	052 (B)	053 (B)	054 (B)	055 (D)
056 (A)	057 (B)	058 (A)	059 (C)	060 (A)
061 (C)	062 (D)	063 (B)	064 (D)	065 (B)
066 (B)	067 (A)	068 (C)	069 (D)	070 (D)
071 (A)	072 (C)	073 (C)	074 (A)	075 (C)
076 (B)	077 (A)	078 (D)	079 (B)	080 (B)
081 (D)	082 (C)	083 (D)	084 (A)	085 (C)
086 (A)	087 (B)	088 (B)	089 (A)	090 (A)
091 (C)	092 (A)	093 (A)	094 (D)	095 (B)
096 (B)	097 (A)	098 (C)	099 (B)	100 (C)

READING TEST

101 (C)	102 (A)	103 (A)	104 (B)	105 (A)
106 (D)	107 (C)	108 (D)	109 (D)	110 (B)
111 (D)	112 (B)	113 (C)	114 (C)	115 (A)
116 (C)	117 (B)	118 (A)	119 (B)	120 (B)
121 (D)	122 (C)	123 (D)	124 (C)	125 (C)
126 (D)	127 (C)	128 (B)	129 (C)	130 (A)
131 (D)	132 (C)	133 (A)	134 (B)	135 (D)
136 (C)	137 (B)	138 (D)	139 (D)	140 (A)
141 (C)	142 (C)	143 (C)	144 (B)	145 (D)
146 (C)	147 (B)	148 (C)	149 (A)	150 (C)
151 (A)	152 (B)	153 (A)	154 (B)	155 (B)
156 (D)	157 (A)	158 (D)	159 (B)	160 (A)
161 (C)	162 (C)	163 (A)	164 (A)	165 (B)
166 (D)	167 (A)	168 (D)	169 (B)	170 (D)
171 (B)	172 (D)	173 (A)	174 (C)	175 (C)
176 (B)	177 (A)	178 (C)	179 (A)	180 (C)
181 (A)	182 (B)	183 (A)	184 (B)	185 (C)
186 (D)	187 (C)	188 (D)	189 (A)	190 (C)
191 (A)	192 (B)	193 (A)	194 (D)	195 (C)
196 (D)	197 (C)	198 (A)	199 (A)	200 (C)

PART 1

1. 영 🎧

(A) A man is wearing an apron.
(B) A man is drinking from a cup.
(C) A man is filling a pot with coffee.
(D) A man is making a copy.

(A) 남자가 앞치마를 두르고 있다.
(B) 남자가 컵으로 음료를 마시고 있다.
(C) 남자가 주전자를 커피로 채우고 있다.
(D) 남자가 복사를 하고 있다.

해설 남자가 앞치마를 착용하고 있는 상태이므로 정답은 (A). 컵과 주전자가 보이지만 컵으로 음료를 마시거나 주전자를 커피로 채우고 있는 것은 아니므로 (B)와 (C)는 오답.

어휘 apron 앞치마   fill A with B A를 B로 채우다   pot 주전자   make a copy 복사하다

2. 미 🎧

(A) They are painting a wall.
(B) A woman is piling up cardboard boxes.
(C) They are taking some measurements.
(D) A man is putting a backpack next to a broom.

(A) 사람들이 벽을 페인트칠하고 있다.
(B) 여자가 판지 상자를 쌓고 있다.
(C) 사람들이 치수를 재고 있다.
(D) 남자가 빗자루 옆에 배낭을 놓고 있다.

해설 두 남녀가 벽에 줄자를 대고 치수를 재고 있는 공통 동작을 바르게 묘사한 (C)가 정답.

어휘 pile up 쌓다, 쌓이다   cardboard 판지   take measurements 치수를 재다   broom 빗자루

Answer **127**

어휘 apology 사과 verify 확인하다, 입증하다 original 원래의, 본래의 combine with ~과 결합하다 as for ~에 대해서 말하자면 kindly 죄송하지만, 부디

196. 첫 번째 웹페이지에 따르면, 키킬라 패브릭스 사가 유명한 이유는?
(A) 저렴한 가격
(B) 빠른 배송
(C) 다양한 품목
(D) 환불 정책

해설 특정 정보 확인 문제

단서 (196)에서 키킬라 패브릭스 사는 다양하게 엄선해 놓은 직물들을 갖추고 있는 것으로 유명하다고 했으므로 정답은 (C).

패러프레이징 [단서] having the widest selection of fabrics → [정답] Its variety of items

197. 플란넬 직물의 세탁 방법은?
(A) 젖은 천 조각으로 닦음으로써
(B) 드라이클리닝업자에게 맡김으로써
(C) 세탁기에 넣음으로써
(D) 찬물만 사용함으로써

해설 특정 정보 확인 문제

단서 (197)에서 플란넬 직물은 세탁기로 빨래한다고 나와 있으므로 정답은 (C).

패러프레이징 [단서] machine wash → [정답] putting it in a washing machine

198. 올센 씨가 처음에 받은 직물의 색상은?
(A) 녹색
(B) 빨간색
(C) 검은색
(D) 갈색

해설 두 지문 연계 문제_특정 정보 확인 문제

이메일의 단서 (198-1)에서 키킬라 패브릭스 사가 잘못된 색상을 배송한 것에 대해 사과하면서 올센 씨의 원래 주문인 검은색 인조 가죽을 배송했다고 했고, 두 번째 웹페이지의 단서 (198-2)에서 인조 가죽은 갈색과 검은색의 두 가지 색상이 있는 것으로 보아, 처음에 올센 씨가 받은 인조 가죽이 갈색이었다는 것을 알 수 있다. 따라서 정답은 (D).

199. 올센 씨에 대해서 암시된 것은?
(A) 구매한 상품에 대한 할인을 받았다.
(B) 잘못된 치수를 제공했다.
(C) 의류를 교환하려고 했다.
(D) 주문에 대한 배송비를 지불하지 않았다.

해설 세 지문 연계 문제_추론 문제

이메일의 단서 (199-1)에서 올센 씨가 원래 검은색 인조 가죽을 주문했다고 했고, 두 번째 웹페이지의 단서 (199-2)를 통해 검은색 인조 가죽은 재고 정리 품목에 해당된다는 것을 알 수 있다. 첫 번째 웹페이지의 단서 (199-3)을 보면 재고 정리 품목은 50% 할인 판매된다고 했으므로 올센 씨는 할인된 가격에 인조 가죽을 구매했음을 알 수 있다. 따라서 정답은 (A).

패러프레이징 [단서] 50 percent off → [정답] a discount

200. 키킬라 패브릭스 사가 사과의 의미로 올센 씨에게 제공하는 것은?
(A) 무료 직물
(B) 구매품 환불
(C) 겨울 의류 품목
(D) 추후 주문 시 무료 배송

해설 특정 정보 확인 문제

단서 (200)에서 사과의 뜻으로 빨간색 울 혼방 5미터를 함께 보내 준다고 했으므로 정답은 (A).

패러프레이징 [단서] 5 meters of red wool blend → [정답] fabric

194. 루터 씨가 하도록 요청받은 일은?

(A) 휴가 연기하기
(B) 식사 선택 변경하기
(C) 행사 일정 다시 잡기
(D) 참석자 명단에 손님 한 명 추가하기

해설 | 특정 정보 확인 문제

단서 (194)에서 멜로이 씨는 루터 씨에게 동료 직원인 스테파니 씨의 선택 요리를 변경해 줄 것을 요청하고 있으므로 정답은 (B).

패러프레이징 | [단서] switch her selection to the broccoli cream pasta → [정답] Modify a meal choice

195. 멜로이 씨가 회사 만찬에서 먹게 될 것 같은 주 요리는?

(A) 파르메산 치킨
(B) 브로콜리 크림 파스타
(C) 소고기 안심
(D) 속을 채운 버섯

해설 | 두 지문 연계 문제_추론 문제

문자 메시지의 단서 (195-1)에서 멜로이 씨와 스테파니 씨가 처음에는 같은 요리를 요청했는데 스테파니 씨의 요리를 브로콜리 크림 파스타로 변경해 달라고 요청했다. 광고의 단서 (195-2)에서 프리미엄 메뉴는 행사당 하나만 선택할 수 있다고 했기 때문에 프리미엄 메뉴 1의 파르메산 치킨 아니면 브로콜리 크림 파스타를 선택할 수 있음을 알 수 있다. 이를 통해 멜로이 씨와 스테파니 씨가 처음에 선택한 요리가 파르메산 치킨이었음을 추론할 수 있으므로 정답은 (A).

196-200 웹페이지 & 웹페이지 & 이메일

---

www.kikilafabrics.com/about

| 홈 | **기업 소개** | 제품 | 재고 정리 | 장바구니 |

¹⁹⁶키킬라 패브릭스 사는 가장 다양하게 엄선해 놓은 직물들을 갖추고 있는 것으로 유명합니다. 귀하의 모든 작업에 필요한 어떠한 질감이나 색상이라도 바로 이곳 저희 사이트에서 찾으실 수 있습니다.

¹⁹⁹⁻³재고 정리 페이지를 꼭 확인하세요. 그곳에서는 모든 제품이 50% 할인 판매되고 있습니다. 그곳에서, 귀하께서는 가격 대비 가장 가치 있는 제품을 발견하시게 될 것입니다. 게다가, 어떠한 직물이라도 10미터 이상을 주문하시면, 무료 배송을 받으실 자격이 됩니다.

직물은 주문 서식에 표시된 치수대로 재단됩니다. 잘못된 수치를 입력하시면 환불이나 교환을 해 드릴 수 없으니 치수를 주의 깊게 확인하시기 바랍니다.

어휘 | clearance (불필요한 것) 정리 fabric 직물 be eligible for ~을 받을 자격이 있다 measurement 치수, 측정 enter 입력하다, 기입하다

---

www.kikilafabrics.com/clearance

| 홈 | 기업 소개 | 제품 | **재고 정리** | 장바구니 |

¹⁹⁹⁻²9월 재고 정리 품목

¹⁹⁷플란넬 - 날염 무늬
구입 가능 무늬: 부엉이, 고양이, 곰
설명: 이 홑겹 플란넬은 퀼트와 아동복에 아주 좋습니다.
¹⁹⁷세탁: 세탁기 빨래/회전식 건조기
가격: 미터당 9.50달러

울 혼방
구입 가능 색상: 녹색, 빨간색
설명: 이것은 코트, 재킷, 담요, 그리고 기타 겨울에 즐겨 사용하는 물품에 완벽한 직물입니다.
세탁: 찬물로 세탁기 빨래/약하게 회전식 건조기 사용; 주의 사항: 다림질하지 마세요.
가격: 미터당 12.00달러

¹⁹⁸⁻² ¹⁹⁹⁻²인조 가죽
구입 가능 색상: 갈색, 검은색
설명: 이 묵직한 모조 가죽은 고급 베개와 기타 실내 장식용품에 훌륭합니다.
세탁: 젖은 천으로 닦기
가격: 미터당 6.00달러

어휘 | layer 겹, 층 apparel 의복, 의류 heavyweight 무거운 imitation 모조품, 모방 luxurious 고급이고 값비싼, 호화로운 decor 실내 장식 damp 젖은 rag 천 조각

수신: 프랜시스 올센 〈folsen@pozmail.net〉
발신: 키킬라 패브릭스 사 〈cs@kikilafabrics.com〉
제목: 주문 번호 201483
날짜: 9월 21일

올센 씨께,

저희는 구매하신 인조 가죽을 교환해 달라는 고객님의 요청을 받았습니다. ¹⁹⁸⁻¹ ¹⁹⁹⁻¹잘못된 색상을 배송해 드린 것에 대해서 정중한 사과를 드립니다. 저희는 고객님의 원래 주문을 확인했고 고객님께서 실은 검은색을 요청했다는 사실을 확인했습니다. 고객님께서 주문하신 검은색 인조 가죽 6미터가 발송되었습니다. 금요일 오후까지는 받아 보실 것으로 예상하시면 됩니다. ²⁰⁰덧붙여, 사과의 의미로 빨간색 울 혼방 5미터를 포함해 드렸습니다. 그것은 인조 가죽과 쉽게 조합하여 다양한 겨울 의류를 만들 수 있습니다.

저희가 원래 보내 드린 제품에 대해서는, 죄송하지만 귀하께서 그것을 저희에게 반송해 주실 것을 요청하는 바이며 배송 비용은 저희가 환불해 드리겠습니다.

인내심을 가지고 양해해 주셔서 감사합니다.

키킬라 패브릭스 사 드림

191-195 광고 & 이메일 & 문자 메시지

디바인 딜라이츠 출장 요리

지역 최고의 서비스와 최상의 품질의 음식을 원하신다면, 디바인 딜라이츠 출장 요리를 선택하십시오! ¹⁹¹여름이 끝났고, 저희의 가을 프리미엄 메뉴가 나왔습니다! 음료와 많은 다른 종류의 메뉴를 보시려면 저희 웹사이트 www.divinedelightscaterer.com을 참조하세요.

프리미엄 메뉴 1 (50달러/1인)	프리미엄 메뉴 2 (75달러/1인)
	와인 한 잔 포함 가격
전채 요리 (1개 선택)	전채 요리 (1개 선택)
☐ 호박 수프	☐ 양파 수프
☐ 시저 샐러드	☐ 콥 샐러드
¹⁹⁵⁻²주 요리 (1개 선택)	주 요리 (1개 선택)
☐ 파르메산 치킨	☐ 소고기 안심
☐ 브로콜리 크림 파스타	☐ 속을 채운 버섯
디저트	디저트
사과 파이	블루베리 크럼블

* 서비스가 포함된 가격입니다. ¹⁹³⁻³프리미엄 메뉴 예약은 적어도 1개월 전에 하셔야 합니다. 최소 20명의 인원이 필요합니다. ¹⁹⁵⁻²행사당 오직 한 종류의 프리미엄 메뉴만 가능합니다. 예약하실 때 각 손님의 요리 선택을 표시해 주시기 바랍니다.

어휘 appetizer 전채 요리 tenderloin 안심 stuffed 속을 채운, 배부른 reservation 예약 minimum 최소의 수[양]; 최소의 indicate 표시하다 preference 선택, 선호

발신: 루터, 필 〈prooter@glypha.com〉
수신: 스태커, 린제이 〈lstacker@glypha.com〉
날짜: 9월 15일
제목: 회사 만찬

안녕하세요. ¹⁹²저는 글리파 사와 볼러 주식회사의 합병을 기념하기 위해 회사 만찬을 열자는 당신의 제안이 훌륭한 아이디어라고 생각합니다. ¹⁹³⁻¹당신이 가능한 날짜로 10월 20일을 언급했지요. 모든 사람에게 물어보았는데, 그때가 행사를 열기에 좋은 날인 것 같습니다. 요청하신 대로, 제가 말씀드린 출장 요리업체의 전단을 첨부했습니다. 우리가 멋진 식사를 하기를 원한다는 걸 알기 때문에, 프리미엄 메뉴를 선택하면 좋을 것 같습니다. 그런데 저는 우리 예산이 어떻게 되는지 잘 모릅니다. 어느 것이 가장 좋을 것이라고 생각하시는지 제게 알려 주세요. 그러고 나서 제가 사무실에 메뉴를 돌려 모두가 자신이 원하는 요리를 선택할 수 있도록 하겠습니다.

어휘 merger 합병 budget 예산 pass ~ around ~을 돌리다 select 선택하다

발신: 트레이시 멜로이
수신: 필 루터

스테파니 씨가 이번 주에 휴가라서 없기 때문에, 제가 그녀를 대신해서 그녀의 회사 만찬 요리를 선택했습니다. ¹⁹⁵⁻¹저는 당신에게 그녀와 제가 둘 다 같은 요리로 하겠다고 말씀드렸습니다. 하지만, ¹⁹³⁻² ¹⁹⁴ ¹⁹⁵⁻¹그녀가 채식주의자라는 것을 방금 알게 되어서 말인데, 그녀의 선택 항목을 브로콜리 크림 파스타로 변경해 주시겠어요? 변경해서 죄송합니다.

어휘 find out ~을 알게 되다 vegetarian 채식주의자 selection 선택된 것, 선택

---

191. 디바인 딜라이츠 출장 요리에 대해 암시된 것은?
(A) 겨울과 봄에는 영업을 하지 않는다.
(B) 메뉴를 계절에 맞춘다.
(C) 두 종류의 메뉴만 제공한다.
(D) 온라인 예약 시스템이 있다.

해설 추론 문제

단서 (191)에서 여름이 끝났고 가을 프리미엄 메뉴가 나왔다고 했으므로 디바인 딜라이츠 출장 요리에서는 메뉴를 계절에 맞춘다고 추론할 수 있다. 따라서 정답은 (B).

192. 계획된 행사의 목적은?
(A) 동료를 축하하기 위해
(B) 성공적인 분기를 축하하기 위해
(C) 잠재 고객에게 깊은 인상을 주기 위해
(D) 새로운 동업 관계를 기념하기 위해

해설 특정 정보 확인 문제

단서 (192)에서 회사 만찬을 여는 목적이 글리파 사와 볼러 주식회사의 합병을 기념하기 위한 것이라고 했으므로 정답은 (D).

패러프레이징 [단서] to celebrate the merger of Glypha Corp. and Baller Inc. → [정답] To mark a new partnership

193. 글리파 사가 출장 요리 예약을 해야 하는 기한은?
(A) 9월 15일
(B) 9월 20일
(C) 10월 15일
(D) 10월 20일

해설 세 지문 연계 문제_추론 문제

이메일의 단서 (193-1)에서 10월 20일이 행사 날짜로 좋을 것 같다고 했고, 문자 메시지의 단서 (193-2)에서 선택 요리가 브로콜리 크림 파스타인 것으로 보아, 글리파 사가 프리미엄 메뉴 1을 예약하려 한다는 것을 알 수 있다. 그런데 광고의 단서 (193-3)에서는 프리미엄 메뉴 예약은 적어도 한 달 전에 해야 한다고 했으므로, 9월 20일까지는 출장 요리 예약을 해야 함을 추론할 수 있다. 따라서 정답은 (B).

〈포트릿 프로〉
마거릿 존스의 후기

저는 예술에 열정이 있는 누구에게나 〈포트릿 프로〉 시리즈를 적극적으로 추천합니다. 저는 지금까지 수년간 그림을 그려 왔고, 더 잘 그리기 위해서 제가 할 수 있는 일이라곤 계속해서 연습하는 것뿐이라고 생각했습니다. 저는 단지 영상을 보는 것만으로 이렇게 많이 배울 수 있을 줄은 전혀 생각지 못했습니다. 하지만, 허턴 씨의 강의 내용을 189따라 함으로써 제 실력이 열 배는 향상되었습니다. 그녀는 복잡한 기법을 쉬운 용어로 잘 설명해 내며, 저는 이 강의들을 다 봤을 때쯤에는 제가 이뤄 낸 것에 깜짝 놀랐습니다.

190-1제 유일한 불만은 아무런 사전 준비 없이 어떤 것도 참고하지 않고 작품을 창작하는 것에 관한 영상에 있습니다. 저는 그 영상을 수십 번은 봤는데도 여전히 허턴 씨의 설명을 이해할 수 없습니다. 하지만, 나머지 세 영상이 매우 도움이 되었기 때문에, 여전히 이 시리즈는 구매할 가치가 있다고 생각합니다.

어휘 passionate 열정적인 tenfold 열 배로 complicated 복잡한 be amazed by ~에 깜짝 놀라다 accomplish 이루다, 성취하다 by the time ~할 때까지(는) from scratch 아무런 사전 준비[지식] 없이 dozens of times 수십 번(이라도)

186. 개요에 의하면, 시리즈가 대상으로 하는 청중은?
(A) 전문 기술을 가진 프로 화가
(B) 그림을 그려 본 적이 없는 초보자
(C) 그림을 그려 본 경험이 있는 사람
(D) 예술 작품을 찾는 수집가

해설 특정 정보 확인 문제

단서 (186)에서 강의 시리즈가 캔버스에 그리는 유화의 기초를 이미 완전히 익힌 사람들을 대상으로 한다고 했으므로 정답은 (C).

패러프레이징 [단서] people who have already mastered the basics of oil on canvas → [정답] People with experience in painting

187. 10월 30일에 있을 세미나에서 참석자들이 하게 될 것은?
(A) 영상 촬영에 참여하기
(B) 도구를 선택하는 법을 배우기
(C) 초상화를 그리기
(D) 붓놀림을 연습하기

해설 두 지문 연계 문제_특정 정보 확인 문제

전단의 단서 (187-1)에서 10월 30일에 있을 세미나에서 〈포트릿 프로〉의 첫 번째 영상에 기초한 강연을 할 거라고 했는데, 개요의 단서 (187-2)에서 첫 번째 강의가 붓을 고르는 법에 관련된 것이라고 했다. 따라서 정답은 (B).

패러프레이징 [단서] learn how to choose the best brushes for various types of projects → [정답] Learn how to select utensils

188. 전단에 따르면, 허턴 씨가 시리즈를 제작한 이유는?
(A) 더 많은 수입이 필요했다.
(B) 자신의 수업을 홍보하고 싶었다.
(C) 자주 조언을 요청받았다.
(D) 즐거운 교수 경험을 했다.

해설 특정 정보 확인 문제

단서 (188)에서 허턴 씨는 조언과 개인 교습에 대한 요청을 반복적으로 받아서 시리즈를 출시하기로 했다고 언급되었으므로 정답은 (C). 작품으로 인한 수입이 일찍부터 있었기에 금전적인 이유에서 영상을 제작한 것은 아니었다고 했으므로 (A)는 오답.

패러프레이징 [단서] she was receiving repeated requests for tips and private lessons → [정답] She was often asked for advice.

189. 후기에서, 첫 번째 단락 네 번째 줄의 "following"과 의미상 가장 가까운 단어는?
(A) 수정하다
(B) ~의 뒤를 잇다
(C) 이용하다
(D) 시험하다

해설 동의어 문제

문맥상 '허턴 씨의 강의 내용을 따라 함으로써 실력이 열 배 향상되었다'라는 의미로, 여기에서 follow는 충고나 지시를 '따르다'는 의미로 쓰였다. 따라서 이와 가장 유사한 의미를 가지는 단어인 (C)가 정답.

190. 〈포트릿 프로〉 시리즈의 영상 중에서 존스 씨가 여러 번 봤다고 한 것은?
(A) 첫 번째
(B) 두 번째
(C) 세 번째
(D) 네 번째

해설 두 지문 연계 문제_특정 정보 확인 문제

후기의 단서 (190-1)에서 존스 씨는 아무 것도 참고하지 않고 작품을 만드는 것에 관한 영상을 수십 번은 봤다고 했는데, 개요의 단서 (190-2)에서 마지막, 즉 네 번째 영상을 통해 모델을 사용하는 대신 자신의 생각대로 그리는 법을 배우게 될 거라고 했으므로 존스 씨가 여러 번 봤다는 영상이 네 번째 영상임을 알 수 있다. 따라서 정답은 (D). 지문의 dozens of times가 문제에서는 many times로 패러프레이징되었다.

182. 스튜어트 씨가 앙굴로 씨의 불만을 조사하기 위해 이용한 것은?

(A) 거래 번호
(B) 계좌 번호
(C) 요청 날짜
(D) 적립금 잔고

해설 두 지문 연계 문제_특정 정보 확인 문제

두 지문의 내용을 모두 확인해야 하는 연계 문제로, 스튜어트 씨가 보낸 이메일을 먼저 보도록 한다. 두 번째 이메일의 단서 (182-1)에 따르면 스튜어트 씨는 앙굴로 씨가 제공한 번호를 이용하여 송금 날짜를 찾았다고 했다. 첫 번째 이메일의 단서 (182-2)에서 앙굴로 씨는 문제가 생긴 거래 건의 요청 번호를 언급하며 답변을 요청하고 있으므로 앙굴로 씨의 불만을 조사하기 위해 스튜어트 씨가 앙굴로 씨의 거래 요청 번호를 이용했음을 알 수 있다. 따라서 정답은 (A).

패러프레이징 [단서] this transaction, request #45960 → [정답] His transaction code

183. 두 번째 이메일에서, 첫 번째 단락 세 번째 줄의 "went down"과 의미상 가장 가까운 단어는?

(A) 오므라들다
(B) 오작동하다
(C) 감소하다
(D) 잃다

해설 동의어 문제

문맥상 '내부 서버의 작동이 중단되었을 때'라는 의미로, 여기에서 go down은 '작동이 중단되다'의 의미로 쓰였다. 따라서 이와 가장 유사한 의미를 가지는 단어인 (B)가 정답.

184. 앙굴로 씨가 적립금을 받았는지 확인할 수 있는 방법은?

(A) 온라인 페이지를 확인해서
(B) 인쇄된 영수증을 확인해서
(C) 종이 입출금 내역서를 요청해서
(D) 스튜어트 씨의 상사에게 이메일을 보내서

해설 특정 정보 확인 문제

단서 (184)에서 온라인 계좌의 내 잔고 링크를 클릭해서 적립 여부를 확인할 수 있다고 했으므로 정답은 (A). 지문의 verify that these amounts have been credited to you가 문제에서 confirm that a credit was received로 패러프레이징되었다.

패러프레이징 [단서] by clicking on the My Balance link after logging into your online account → [정답] By reviewing an online page

185. 앙굴로 씨에게 문제가 더 있을 경우 하도록 당부된 것은?

(A) 고객 서비스 상담 전화에 전화하기
(B) 계약 종료 요청하기
(C) 온라인으로 정식 항의 제기하기
(D) 스튜어트 씨에게 직접 연락하기

해설 특정 정보 확인 문제

단서 (185)에서 추가 문제가 있다면 고객 서비스 상담 전화 대신 스튜어트 씨 자신의 직통 번호로 전화해 달라고 했다. 즉 자신에게 직접 연락하라고 당부한 것이므로 정답은 (D).

패러프레이징 [단서] get straight through to me → [정답] Contact Ms. Stewart directly

186-190 개요 & 전단 & 후기

포트릿 프로

186〈포트릿 프로〉는 이미 캔버스에 그리는 유화의 기초를 완전히 익혔고 좀 더 고급 화법으로 넘어가고 싶은 분들을 위한 4부작 시리즈입니다. 이 영상에서 유명 디자이너 글로리아 허턴 씨는 네 단계를 통해 여러분의 그림 솜씨를 한 단계 끌어올리도록 안내해 드립니다. 187-2첫 번째 튜토리얼에서는, 다양한 종류의 작업에 가장 적합한 붓을 고르는 법을 배우게 될 것입니다. 두 번째 영상은 몇 가지 고급 기법에 중점을 둡니다. 세 번째로, 제공된 모델에 기초하여 초상화를 그리게 될 것입니다. 190-2마지막으로, 모델을 사용하는 대신 자신의 생각대로 그리는 법을 배우게 될 것입니다. 이 영상은 모든 주요 웹사이트에서 다운로드하실 수 있습니다.

어휘 portrait 초상화 master ~을 완전히 익히다 basics 기초, 기본 oil 유화 move on to ~으로 옮기다[이동하다] advanced 상급의, 고급의 renowned 유명한 tutorial 사용 지침 동영상 based on ~에 근거하여

187-1**핵스부르크 공예 박물관에서의 특별 세미나**

187-110월 30일에, 그림 그리기에 관한 특별 마스터 클래스를 들으러 핵스부르크 공예 박물관으로 오세요. 187-1화가 글로리아 허턴 씨가 그녀가 최근에 출시한 4부작 시리즈인 〈포트릿 프로〉의 첫 번째 영상에 기초한 강연을 할 것입니다.

글로리아 허턴 씨는 전 세계 박물관과 축제에서 전시되어 온 수백 점의 숨이 멎을 듯한 작품을 창작한 유명한 화가입니다. 허턴 씨는 타고난 재능 덕분에 일찍부터 자신의 작품으로 생계를 꾸릴 수 있었으므로, 금전적인 이유로 영상을 제작한 것은 아니었습니다. 188하지만 그녀는 조언과 개인 교습에 대한 반복적인 요청을 받고 있었고 정기적으로 수업을 할 시간은 없었습니다. 그래서 그녀는 마침내 자신의 튜토리얼 시리즈를 출시하기로 결정했고, 이는 즉각 베스트셀러가 되었습니다.

시간: 10월 30일, 오후 3시
장소: 핵스부르크 공예 박물관, 살란드라 룸
수업료: 35달러

이 행사는 좌석이 한정되어 있습니다. 555-8874번으로 전화하셔서 사전 등록하시기 바랍니다.

어휘 release 공개하다, 발매하다 prominent 유명한 breathtaking 숨이 멎는 듯한 make a living 생계를 꾸리다 motivation 동기 부여 tip 조언 immediately 즉시, 즉각 limited 한정된 register 등록하다

한 것으로 보아 두 부지가 서로 요금이 다르다는 것을 알 수 있다. (D)는 단서 (178D)에서 기술자를 집으로 보내 무료 상담을 받도록 해 주겠다고 했다. 그러나 (B)는 단서 (178B)에서 서비스 이용 경험이 없는 사람들도 예약 가능한 시간대가 있다고 했으므로 지문의 내용과 다르다는 것을 알 수 있다. 따라서 정답은 (B).

패러프레이징 [단서] slots are still available even if you've never used our services before → [정답] currently accepting new customers

179. 워닉 씨에 대해 암시된 것은?
(A) 첫 달에 할인을 받을 것이다.
(B) 자신의 장비를 사용하기를 원한다.
(C) 친구에게 아넷 사를 소개받았다.
(D) 평균 크기 이상의 부동산을 소유하고 있다.

해설 추론 문제

단서 (179)를 보면 고객인 비키 워닉 씨의 장비 종류와 모델명이 기입되어 있는데, 양식 하단에 고객이 자신의 장비를 사용하기를 원할 경우 이를 기입하라고 되어 있다. 따라서 워닉 씨가 자신의 장비를 사용하기를 원한다는 것을 추론할 수 있으므로 정답은 (B).

패러프레이징 [단서] the customer prefers to use his/her own equipment → [정답] She wants her own equipment to be used.

180. 워닉 씨에게 매달 청구될 금액은?
(A) 250달러
(B) 425달러
(C) 450달러
(D) 675달러

해설 두 지문 연계 문제_특정 정보 확인 문제

양식의 단서 (180-1)에서 워닉 씨가 격주로 방문하는 프리미엄 서비스를 신청했다는 것을 알 수 있는데, 전단의 단서 (180-2)에서 프리미엄 서비스는 격주 방문 시 450달러라고 했다. 따라서 정답은 (C).

181-185 이메일 & 이메일

수신: 글래드웰 금융 〈info@gladwellfinance.com〉
발신: 키스 앙굴로 〈k.angulo@irvinemail.net〉
날짜: 11월 17일
제목: 송금 문제

관계자분께:

저는 귀사의 온라인 송금 서비스를 이용해 밴쿠버에 있는 사촌에게 돈을 보내려고 했습니다. 수수료로 적립금 5달러를 사용했는데, 이는 귀사의 소식지를 신청해서 받은 것입니다. 제 사촌은 밴쿠버 지점에서 현금을 찾을 수 있었습니다. 그러나 거래가 완료된 뒤, 저는 송금 수수료가 전액 청구된 것을 알았습니다. ¹⁸¹저는 제가 이미 적립금을 사용하지 않았었다는 것을 확인하기 위해 제 계좌 내역을 살펴봤고, 제가 사용하지 않았음을 확인했습니다. 그러나 적립금은 더 이상 제 계좌에 포함되어 있지 않습니다. ¹⁸²⁻²요청 번호 45960의 이 거래와 관련해 왜 문제가 생겼는지, 그리고 이를 해결하기 위해 무엇을 할 수 있는지 제게 알려 주시기 바랍니다.

감사합니다.

키스 앙굴로 드림

어휘 money transfer 송금 credit 적립금, (계좌) 잔고; 입금하다 transaction 거래, 매매 charge (요금·값을) 청구하다 look over ~을 살펴보다 confirm 확인하다 resolve (문제 등을) 해결하다

수신: 키스 앙굴로 〈k.angulo@irvinemail.net〉
발신: 글래드웰 금융 〈info@gladwellfinance.com〉
날짜: 11월 18일
제목: 회신: 송금 문제

앙굴로 씨께,

글래드웰 금융을 대표하여, 귀하가 겪으신 불편에 대해 사과드리고자 합니다. ¹⁸²⁻¹돈을 송금하신 날짜를 언급하시지는 않았지만, 귀하가 제공해 주신 번호를 이용하여 그것을 찾을 수 있었습니다. 저희는 11월 16일에 잠깐 동안 내부 서버의 ¹⁸³작동이 중단되었을 때 일부 문제를 겪었고, 이것이 일부 고객에게 영향을 끼쳤습니다. 귀하가 받으셨어야 하는 할인을 보상해 드리기 위해 5달러 적립금을 재발행해 드렸습니다. 저희 지점장인 패트릭 오그던 씨는 또한 귀하가 불편을 겪으신 것에 대해 제가 10달러 추가 적립금을 발행하도록 재가해 주었습니다. 이 적립금은 저희 처리 수수료에 사용하실 수 있습니다. ¹⁸⁴귀하의 온라인 계좌에 로그인하신 후 내 잔고 링크를 클릭하셔서 이 금액이 적립되었음을 확인하실 수 있습니다. 귀하는 이 적립금을 언제든지 재량껏 사용하실 수 있습니다. ¹⁸⁵추가 문제가 있다면, 저희 고객 서비스 상담 전화보다는 555-3940에 내선 31번으로 전화 주세요. 그렇게 하시면 제게 곧바로 연결됩니다.

브리엘 스튜어트 드림

어휘 temporary 일시적인 internal 내부의 go down (잠시 작동이) 중단되다 reissue 재발급하다 make up for ~에 대해 보상하다 give authorization 재가하다 balance 잔고, 잔액 at one's discretion 재량에 따라 rather than ~보다는[대신에] hotline 상담[서비스] 전화, 직통 전화 get through to ~에게 닿다[전달되다]

181. 앙굴로 씨가 글래드웰 금융에 연락하기 전에 한 일은?
(A) 사촌으로부터 그 문제에 관해 들었다.
(B) 우편으로 청구서를 받았다.
(C) 자신의 과거 거래들을 확인했다.
(D) 자신의 신용 카드 청구서를 검토했다.

해설 특정 정보 확인 문제

단서 (181)에서 적립금 사용 여부를 확인하기 위해 계좌 내역을 살펴봤다고 했으므로 정답은 (C).

패러프레이징 [단서] looked over my account history → [정답] Checked his past transactions

진행 상황을 확인할 수 있다고 했으므로 정답은 (C).

패러프레이징 [단서] follow the progress of your request
→ [정답] Check the status of a claim

175. 고객이 교환 상품을 받을 수 있는 경우는?
(A) 물건을 도난당한 경우
(B) 제품에 결함이 있는 경우
(C) 소재에 얼룩이 진 경우
(D) 여행 가방이 남용된 경우

해설 특정 정보 확인 문제

단서 (175)에서 교환 상품을 발송해 주는 경우 중 하나로 제작상의 결함 또는 소재의 결함이 언급되었다. 따라서 정답은 (B). 지문의 A replacement will be sent가 문제에서는 get a replacement로 패러프레이징되었다.

패러프레이징 [단서] Flaws → [정답] defects

176-180 전단 & 양식

아넷 사

아넷 사는 지난 5년간 고품질의 서비스를 제공해 왔습니다. 5월 1일부터 10월 31일까지, 176저희는 여러분의 마당과 정원을 최상의 상태로 유지할 수 있도록 도와드리겠습니다. 저희는 잔디 깎기, 나무 가지치기, 잡초 뽑기 서비스를 매주 혹은 격주 단위로 제공해 드릴 수 있습니다. 나무, 꽃, 혹은 관목 심기에 관심이 있으시면, 177신뢰할 수 있는 지역 사업체인 파인웨이 온실의 저희 파트너들을 통해서 할인을 해 드릴 수 있습니다.

계절마다 저희를 다시 찾는 고객이 많지만, 178B저희 서비스를 전에 이용해 본 적이 없다 하더라도 예약 가능한 시간대가 아직 있습니다. 178A저희는 기업 부지에는 서비스를 제공하지 않는다는 것을 유념해 주십시오. 여러분의 마당을 관리할 수 있는 가장 좋은 방법에 대한 조언을 원하신다면, 178D저희 기술자 한 명을 댁으로 보내 드려서 무료로 상담을 받으실 수 있도록 해 드리겠습니다. 저희의 기본 서비스(잔디 깎기와 청소만)의 178C매월 요금*은 매주 방문 시 425달러 혹은 격주 방문 시 250달러입니다. 180-2또한 프리미엄 서비스(기본 서비스에 잡초 뽑기, 관목 다듬기, 비료 처리 추가)도 있는데 매주 방문 시 675달러 혹은 격주 방문 시 450달러입니다. 오늘 555-5588번으로 저희에게 전화 주세요.

*178C표준 크기의 부지에만 적용됩니다. 표준 크기 이상의 부지에 관해서는, 전화하셔서 요금을 문의해 주세요.

어휘 biweekly 격주의; 격주로 reliable 신뢰할 수 있는 slot 자리, 시간 corporate 기업의, 법인의 property 소유지, 부동산 consultation 상담 at no charge 무료로 fertilizer 비료 treatment 처리, 치료 apply to ~에 적용되다 lot 부지, 지역

아넷 사 – 신규 고객 정보

179**고객:** 비키 워닉
부지: 선버스트 드라이브 226번지, 포틀랜드, 오리건 주 97221
부지 종류: 표준
* 179**장비:** 잔디 깎는 기계(모델: 던컨-440)
요청한 서비스: [ ] 기본 180-1[X] 프리미엄
　　　　　　　　[ ] 매주 180-1[X] 격주
서비스 시작일: 6월 2일

상담 날짜: 5월 26일   **부지 평가자:** 로버트 캐스

* 179고객이 자신의 장비를 사용하기를 원한다면, 장비의 종류와 모델명을 위에 기입하세요.

어휘 assess 평가하다

176. 전단의 목적은?
(A) 소유권 변경을 알리기 위해
(B) 정원 관리 업체를 홍보하기 위해
(C) 할인 판매 행사를 광고하기 위해
(D) 신규 서비스를 소개하기 위해

해설 목적 문제

단서 (176)에서 마당과 정원 관리를 도와주겠다면서 잔디 깎기, 가지치기 등의 정원 관리와 관련된 서비스를 제공해 줄 수 있다고 한 것으로 보아 정답은 (B).

패러프레이징 [단서] mowing, tree-trimming, and weeding
→ [정답] gardening care

177. 아넷 사에 대해 시사된 것은?
(A) 온실과 협력한다.
(B) 이메일로 예약을 받는다.
(C) 각종 식물과 꽃을 판매한다.
(D) 일년 내내 서비스를 제공한다.

해설 Not/True 문제

단서 (177)에서 파인웨이 온실의 파트너들을 통해서 할인을 해 줄 수 있다고 한 것으로 보아 온실과 협력한다는 것을 알 수 있으므로 정답은 (A).

패러프레이징 [단서] our partners at the Pineway Greenhouse → [정답] It collaborates with a greenhouse.

178. 아넷 사에 대해서 언급되지 않은 것은?
(A) 주택 부지만 취급한다.
(B) 현재 신규 고객을 받고 있지 않다.
(C) 표준 크기 부지와 표준 크기 이상의 부지에 대한 가격이 다르다.
(D) 무료 상담을 제공한다.

해설 Not/True 문제

(A)는 단서 (178A)에서 이번에는 기업 부지에는 서비스를 제공하지 않는다고 했고, (C)는 단서 (178C)에서 매월 요금은 표준 크기 부지에만 적용되는 것으로 표준 크기 이상의 부지는 전화로 요금을 문의하라고

170. 기사에 따르면, 연극의 인기에 가장 크게 기여한 사람은?

(A) 마리아 델루즈
(B) 조슈아 코베트
(C) 제레미 모리아
(D) 이자벨 모턴

해설 특정 정보 확인 문제

단서 (170)에서 연극의 인기를 치솟게 한 이유로 평론가 조슈아 코베트 씨가 작성한 비평을 언급하며 이 비평이 쓰인 이후로 연극이 갑자기 유명한 작품이 되었다고 했으므로 정답은 (B).

171. [1], [2], [3], [4]번으로 표시된 위치들 중 다음 문장이 들어가기에 가장 적절한 곳은?

"이 꿈은 곧 현실이 될지도 모른다."

(A) [1]
(B) [2]
(C) [3]
(D) [4]

해설 문장 위치 찾기 문제

제시된 문장의 This dream이 지칭하는 것을 지문에서 찾아야 한다. 지문에서 무언가를 바라는 내용은 지문 후반부에서 주연 배우 모리아 씨가 한 말이 언급된 부분으로, 단서 (171)을 보면 [4]번 앞에서는 공연을 위해 해외로 나가게 되길 바란다고 했고 [4]번 뒤에서는 유럽 도처의 공연장들에서 제작 책임자에게 연락을 하고 있다고 했다. 따라서 [4]번에서 이 꿈이 이제 현실이 될지도 모른다고 하는 것이 자연스러우므로 정답은 (D).

172-175 정보문

> **랜다 굿즈 이용 약관**
>
> ¹⁷²고객님의 다음 여행에서 짐을 가지고 다니기 위해 랜다 굿즈 사를 선택해 주셔서 감사합니다. 랜다의 모든 여행 가방은 저희의 1년 보증으로 보장을 받습니다. 소포를 받는 즉시 꼼꼼히 확인하십시오. ¹⁷³ᴬ제품에 파손된 부분이 있는 경우, 제품의 어떤 부품이나 포장재도 버리지 마십시오. ¹⁷³ᴮ즉시 택배 회사에 알리십시오. 택배 회사에서 파손된 상품을 가져가고 ¹⁷³ᶜ작성해야 하는 배상 청구서와 청구 번호를 고객님께 제공할 것입니다. ¹⁷⁴그리고 나면 고객님께서는 저희 웹사이트에서 고객님 요청의 진행 상황을 확인하실 수 있습니다. ¹⁷³ᴰ청구 건을 검토하는 데에는 최대 3주까지 소요될 수 있습니다.
>
> ¹⁷⁵다음 중 어떠한 경우라도 구매 후 1년 이내에 알려 주시면 고객님께 교환 상품이 발송될 것입니다:
> – ¹⁷⁵제작상의 결함 또는 소재의 결함
> – 소재의 찢김
> – 망가진 부품
> – 바퀴 마모
> – 색 바램

> 다음과 같은 일이 발생한 경우, 해당 물품에 대한 책임은 전적으로 고객님께 있으며 고객님께서는 보상을 받을 권리가 없다는 점에 유의하십시오:
> – 무분별한 사용
> – 얼룩짐
> – 분실 또는 도난

어휘 terms and conditions 약관, 조건   cover (보험 등으로) 보장하다   warranty 보증, 보증서   claim form 배상 청구서   progress 진행, 경과   flaw 결함   workmanship 제작 솜씨, 제작 기술   be liable for ~에 대해 책임[의무]가 있다   be entitled to do ~을 할 권리가 있다

172. 정보문을 받은 사람들에 대해 암시된 것은?

(A) 물건을 반품하려 한 적이 있다.
(B) 최근에 여행 가방을 구매했다.
(C) 랜다 굿즈 사와 막 계약을 맺었다.
(D) 랜다 굿즈 사에 대한 부정적인 후기를 게시했다.

해설 추론 문제

단서 (172)에서 다음 여행에 짐을 가지고 다니기 위해 랜다 굿즈 사를 선택한 것에 대해 감사를 표하며 랜다의 여행 가방에 제공되는 보증 내용을 언급했다. 이를 통해 랜다 굿즈 사의 여행 가방을 구매한 사람들에게 제공되는 정보문임을 유추할 수 있으므로 정답은 (B).

173. 랜다 굿즈 사가 고객들이 파손된 물건을 받은 경우 하지 말 것을 요청하는 일은?

(A) 망가진 부품 폐기하기
(B) 배달 업체에 알리기
(C) 서류 작성하기
(D) 응답 기다리기

해설 Not/True 문제

Not/True 문제는 지문과 선택지를 하나하나 대조해 가며 풀어야 한다. (B)는 단서 (173B)에서 하자에 대해 즉시 택배 회사에 알리라고 했고, (C)는 단서 (173C)에서 작성해야 하는 배상 청구서가 언급되었으며, (D)는 단서 (173D)에서 청구 건 검토에 최대 3주까지 소요될 수 있다고 했다. 반면, (A)는 단서 (173A)에서 제품에 하자가 있는 경우 어떤 부품이나 포장재도 버리지 말라고 했으므로 정답은 (A).

패러프레이징 [단서] throw away any part of the product → [정답] Discard broken parts

174. 고객들이 랜다 굿즈 사의 웹사이트에서 할 수 있는 것은?

(A) 더 빠른 배달 서비스 요청하기
(B) 불만 신고 양식 작성하기
(C) 청구 상황 확인하기
(D) 제품 보증 기간 연장하기

해설 특정 정보 확인 문제

단서 (174)에서 랜다 굿즈 사의 웹사이트에서 고객이 요청한 청구 건의

165. 블라시오 씨에 대해 시사된 것은?
(A) 인기 있는 식당을 소유하고 있다.
(B) 텔레비전에 나올 것이다.
(C) 잡지에 기고하고 있다.
(D) 새로운 일자리에 지원했다.

해설 Not/True 문제

단서 (165)에서 블라시오 씨가 곧 방영될 요리 프로의 요리사라고 했으므로 정답은 (B). 나머지는 지문에 나와 있지 않은 내용이므로 모두 오답.

패러프레이징 [단서] a chef from an upcoming cooking show → [정답] He will be on television.

166. 테서 씨가 화요일에 할 일은?
(A) 광고 만들기
(B) 사진 촬영하기
(C) 기사 작성하기
(D) 메뉴 고르기

해설 다음에 할 일 문제

단서 (166)에서 테서 씨는 화요일에 블라시오 씨의 사진을 촬영하러 인터뷰 장소에 갈 거라고 했다. 따라서 정답은 (B).

패러프레이징 [단서] do the photo shoot of Mr. Blasio → [정답] Take some pictures

167. 오전 10시 48분에, 테서 씨가 "전적으로 동의해요"라고 한 것에서 그가 의도한 것은?
(A) 프로젝트 중 하나의 디자인이 마음에 들지 않는다.
(B) 사진이 가장 중요한 요소라고 생각한다.
(C) 각기 다른 부서의 사람들이 협력해야 한다고 생각한다.
(D) 인터뷰에서 어떤 주제가 다뤄질지 잘 모른다.

해설 의도 파악 문제

I couldn't agree more는 '전적으로 동의한다'는 뜻의 표현으로, 테서 씨가 해당 표현 바로 앞에 있는 모텐슨 씨의 말에서 무엇에 동의하는지 찾으면 된다. 단서 (167)에서 모텐슨 씨는 디자이너들이 기자, 사진 기자와 공동 작업을 할 때 표지가 가장 잘되는 것 같다고 했고, 테서 씨가 이 말에 동의하는 것이므로 정답은 (C).

패러프레이징 [단서] the designers collaborate with the writers and photographers → [정답] people from different departments should work together

168-171 기사

〈부서진 진주〉, 마리나 극장에서 상연되다

1월 21일—3막으로 구성된 연극 〈부서진 진주〉가 2월 13, 14, 15일에 드레스덴에 있는 마리나 극장에서 상연될 예정이다. 극본은 마리아 델루즈 씨에 의해 쓰였으며, 그녀는 이 연극의 연출도 맡았다. [168]이것은 마리나 극장에서 처음으로 상연되는 현대극이 될 것이다. — [1] —.

[169]한정된 마케팅 예산과 다소 인지도가 낮은 출연진 때문에, 헨리빌에 위치한 골든 볼케이노 극장에서 있었던 초연은 많은 관객을 끌어모으지 못했다. 그러나 공연이 매우 좋은 평을 받아서 극단은 지역 순회를 시작하여 지역의 여러 장소에서 공연을 하도록 장려되었다. — [2] —. [170]연극의 인기를 치솟게 한 것은 특히 한 비평이었는데, 악명 높은 평론가인 조슈아 코벳 씨가 작성한 것이었다. 엄격하고 종종 가차 없기까지 한 비평으로 알려져 있는 코벳 씨는 장문의 기사에서 〈부서진 진주〉를 '현대극의 보석'이라고 칭했다. [170]이리하여 이 연극은 무명의 작품에서 갑자기 유명한 작품이 되었다. — [3] —.

"우리는 〈부서진 진주〉가 이렇게 히트 작품이 되리라고는 전혀 예상치 못했습니다."라고 주연 배우인 제레미 모리아 씨가 설명했다. "모든 게 정말 흥분됩니다. 저는 새로운 장소들에서 공연하는 것을 고대하고 있습니다. [171]저는 언젠가는 공연을 위해 해외로까지 나가게 되기를 희망합니다." — [4] —. [171]실제로, 유럽 도처의 몇몇 공연장에서 제작 책임자인 이자벨 모텐 씨에게 향후 가능성이 있는 건들에 관해 연락이 오고 있다.

어휘 act (연극 등의) 막 low-profile 주목을 거의 못 받는 cast 출연진, 배역 premiere 초연, 개봉 troupe 극단 skyrocketing 치솟는 notorious 악명 높은 scathing 가차 없는, 통렬한 obscure 무명의, 잘 알려져 있지 않은

168. 마리나 극장에 대해 암시된 것은?
(A) 보통은 고전 작품들의 공연을 선보인다.
(B) 〈부서진 진주〉를 이미 여러 번 상연했다.
(C) 드레스덴에서 가장 인기 있는 극장이 되었다.
(D) 과거에 부정적인 평가를 많이 받았다.

해설 추론 문제

단서 (168)에서 〈부서진 진주〉가 마리나 극장에서 처음으로 상연되는 현대극이 될 거라고 한 것으로 보아, 마리나 극장에서 주로 상연하는 작품이 고전 작품이라는 것을 추론할 수 있다. 따라서 정답은 (A).

패러프레이징 [단서] play → [정답] performances

169. 연극의 극단에 대해 시사된 것은?
(A) 광고에 많은 돈을 썼다.
(B) 거의 알려지지 않은 배우들로 구성되어 있다.
(C) 유명한 장소에서 공연하는 것에 익숙하다.
(D) 여러 나라에서 공연해 왔다.

해설 Not/True 문제

단서 (169)에서 한정된 마케팅 예산과 인지도가 낮은 출연진 때문에 연극이 초반에 많은 관객을 끌어모으지 못했다고 한 것으로 보아, 연극의 극단이 잘 알려지지 않은 배우들로 구성되어 있음을 알 수 있다. 따라서 정답은 (B).

패러프레이징 [단서] a rather low-profile cast → [정답] little-known actors

직원이 퇴사할 때 회사가 필요한 신고서를 제출하지만, 당신의 이전 근무처는 그렇게 하지 않은 것으로 보입니다. 당신을 위해 기꺼이 이 일을 처리해 드리겠습니다만, 그러려면 [163]저는 당신이 지난 직장에서 받은 보수에 관한 정보가 필요합니다. 당신이 그 두 달 동안 받은 급여 명세서 2장을 제공해 주실 수 있다면, 제가 기꺼이 당신의 해당 과세 연도 서류를 조정해 드리겠습니다.

질문이 있으시다면 제게 알려 주십시오.

캐런 페스코 드림

어휘 go over ~을 검토하다   come to one's attention ~을 알게 되다   take ~ into account ~을 고려하다   state 명시하다   declaration 신고(서), 선언(문)   place of employment 근무처   compensation 보수, 보상(금)   pay stub 급여 명세서(= payslip)   tax year 과세 연도

161. 페스코 씨가 근무할 것 같은 부서는?

(A) 회계
(B) 마케팅
(C) 고객 서비스
(D) 연구 개발

해설 추론 문제

단서 (161)에서 직원의 세금 관련 서류를 검토하고 있다고 했고, 이메일 전체에서 납세 신고서와 관련된 이야기를 하고 있으므로 페스코 씨가 회계 부서에서 근무한다는 것을 추론할 수 있다. 따라서 정답은 (A).

162. 페스코 씨가 언급한 문제는?

(A) 일부 소득이 신고되어야 한다.
(B) 결제가 거부되었다.
(C) 세율이 올랐다.
(D) 많은 직원이 그만뒀다.

해설 특정 정보 확인 문제

단서 (162)에서 납세 신고서를 제출할 때 모셔 씨의 이전 소득이 명시되어야 한다고 했으므로 정답은 (A).

패러프레이징 [단서] your previous income must be taken into account and stated → [정답] Some income must be declared.

163. 페스코 씨가 모셔 씨에게 요청한 것은?

(A) 직무 기술서
(B) 급여 기록
(C) 재직 증명서
(D) 소득 세율표

해설 특정 정보 확인 문제

단서 (163)을 보면, 페스코 씨는 모셔 씨가 지난 직장에서 받은 보수에 관한 정보가 필요하다고 하면서 모셔 씨에게 특정 기간 동안 받은 급여 명세서 2장을 제공해 달라고 요청했다. 즉, 페스코 씨는 모셔 씨의 급여가 기록된 서류를 요청한 것이므로 정답은 (B).

패러프레이징 [단서] the two pay stubs you received for those two months → [정답] Salary records

164-167 온라인 채팅

클라이드 모텐슨 [오전 10:40]	안녕하세요, 제니퍼 그리고 헨리. [164]저는 4월호 표지 디자인을 시작하고 싶은데요. 우리가 주요 기사를 위해 누구를 인터뷰하게 될지 알고 계세요?
제니퍼 시드노 [오전 10:41]	[165]곧 방영될 요리 프로의 요리사인 셰프 블라시오 씨가 될 거예요. 실은, 제가 그 기사를 작성할 거예요. 전 다음 주 화요일에 그분을 인터뷰할 예정이에요.
헨리 테서 [오전 10:42]	그리고 제가 이 인터뷰의 사진 기자이고요. [166]그래서 저도 화요일에 블라시오 씨의 사진 촬영을 위해 그곳에 갈 거예요.
클라이드 모텐슨 [오전 10:44]	아, 다 되면 말해 주세요. 기사에서 어떤 주제가 다뤄질지, 그리고 사진들은 어떻게 보일지 알면 도움이 될 거예요.
제니퍼 시드노 [오전 10:45]	우리 모두 수요일에 만나는 건 어때요? 헨리 씨, 당신은 우리에게 당신이 찍은 사진들을 보여 줄 수 있고, 저는 두 분 모두에게 인터뷰에 대해 이야기해 줄 수 있으니까요.
클라이드 모텐슨 [오전 10:47]	전 그날 괜찮아요. [167]제 생각에 표지는 디자이너들이 기자와 사진 기자들과 공동으로 작업할 때 가장 잘되는 것 같아요.
헨리 테서 [오전 10:48]	전적으로 동의해요. 저도 수요일이 괜찮아요. 오전이요, 오후요? 저는 아무 때나 만날 수 있어요.
클라이드 모텐슨 [오전 10:49]	저한테는 오전이 훨씬 낫겠네요. 10시로 합시다.
제니퍼 시드노 [오전 10:50]	10시 좋네요. 그때 두 분을 볼게요.

어휘 issue (정기 간행물의) 호   photo shoot 사진 촬영   work 작용하다, 영향을 미치다   collaborate with ~와 공동으로 작업하다

164. 메시지 작성자들이 근무할 것 같은 곳은?

(A) 사진관
(B) 식당
(C) 디자인 업체
(D) 잡지사

해설 추론 문제

단서 (164)를 보면, 모텐슨 씨는 4월호 표지 디자인을 언급하며 제니퍼와 헨리에게 주요 기사를 위한 인터뷰의 대상에 대해 묻고 있다. 이를 통해 메시지 작성자들이 잡지사에서 근무한다는 것을 추론할 수 있으므로 정답은 (D).

156. 호텔에 대해 매닝 씨가 시사하는 바는?
(A) 무료 조식을 제공한다.
(B) 밤에 매우 시끄럽다.
(C) 도심 근처에 위치해 있다.
(D) 공항으로부터 20분 거리에 있다.

> 해설 Not/True 문제

단서 (156)을 보면, 도심 지역과의 근접성 때문에 이 호텔을 택했다고 했으므로 정답은 (C).

> 패러프레이징 [단서] its proximity to the downtown area
→ [정답] It is located near the city center.

157. [1], [2], [3], [4]번으로 표시된 위치들 중 다음 문장이 들어가기에 가장 적절한 곳은?

"제가 겪었던 유일한 문제는 제가 떠날 때였습니다."

(A) [1]
(B) [2]
(C) [3]
(D) [4]

> 해설 문장 위치 찾기 문제

제시된 문장 내에 The only issue가 쓰인 것으로 보아, 제시된 문장 앞에는 호텔에 대한 긍정적인 내용이, 제시된 문장 뒤에는 매닝 씨가 겪었던 문제에 대한 구체적인 내용이 나와야 한다. 단서 (157)을 보면 [2]번 앞에서는 호텔의 위치적 장점이 언급되었고 [2]번 바로 다음 문장부터는 매닝 씨가 겪은 문제 상황에 대한 설명이 이어지고 있다. 따라서 제시된 문장은 이 사이에 오는 것이 자연스러우므로 정답은 (B).

158. 매닝 씨가 호텔이 하기를 원하는 것은?
(A) 셔틀 서비스 추가하기
(B) 시간표 조정하기
(C) 시설 청소하기
(D) 더 많은 직원 고용하기

> 해설 특정 정보 확인 문제

단서 (158)을 보면, 매닝 씨는 호텔에서 출발하는 버스가 있었다면 자신이 겪었던 혼란을 피할 수 있었을 거라면서, 호텔에서 공항을 오가는 교통편뿐만 아니라 기차역까지 가는 교통편도 제공한다면 큰 도움이 될 거라고 했다. 이를 통해 매닝 씨는 호텔이 기차역을 오가는 셔틀 서비스를 추가로 제공하기를 원한다는 것을 알 수 있으므로 정답은 (A).

> 패러프레이징 [단서] Offering rides to the station as well → [정답] Add a shuttle service

159-160 공지

> www.mimonaartgallery.net/home
> 미모나 미술관의 웹사이트는 구축 중에 있습니다. [159]저희는 이것이 11월 1일에 작동될 것으로 예상합니다. 첫 전시회들에 관한 정보를 미술관이 개관하는 11월 21일보다 일주일 앞서 이 사이트에 게시

될 것입니다. 곧 있을 행사들에 대한 더 자세한 정보는 미술관이 개관하면 확인하실 수 있을 것입니다.

그동안에는, [160]여러분의 작품을 전시하는 것에 관한 정보를 얻으시려면 555-2937번으로 전화하시거나 elizarogers@mimonaartgallery.net으로 이메일을 보내셔서 엘리자 로저스 씨에게 연락하시기 바랍니다.

> 어휘 under construction 구축[공사] 중인   anticipate 예상하다
be up and running 작동되다   exhibit 전시회, 전시(품); 전시하다
in the meantime 그동안에

159. 공지의 목적은?
(A) 전시회 후기를 요청하기 위해
(B) 미술관의 개관을 알리기 위해
(C) 구입 가능한 미술품을 광고하기 위해
(D) 새로운 웹페이지를 위한 일정을 제공하기 위해

> 해설 목적 문제

단서 (159)를 보면 웹사이트의 운영이 시작되는 날짜와 사이트에 게시물이 올라올 날짜가 안내되고 있다. 이를 통해 새로 제작될 웹페이지와 관련된 일정들을 안내하기 위해 공지가 작성되었음을 알 수 있으므로 정답은 (D).

> 패러프레이징 [단서] this site → [정답] a new Web page

160. 엘리자 로저스 씨에게 연락해야 하는 이유는?
(A) 방문 약속을 잡기 위해
(B) 미술품을 구매하기 위해
(C) 미술품을 전시하는 것에 대해 묻기 위해
(D) 행사에 등록하기 위해

> 해설 특정 정보 확인 문제

단서 (160)에서 작품을 전시하는 것에 관한 정보를 얻으려면 엘리자 로저스 씨에게 연락하라고 했으므로 정답은 (C).

> 패러프레이징 [단서] for information about exhibiting your work → [정답] To ask about displaying artwork

161-163 이메일

> 수신: 브랜던 모셔 〈bmosher@trupal.biz〉
> 발신: 캐런 페스코 〈kpesco@trupal.biz〉
> 날짜: 3월 31일
> 제목: 납세 신고서
>
> 모셔 씨께,
>
> [161]저는 현재 당신의 세금 관련 서류를 검토하고 있습니다. 그런데 저는 당신이 작년에 두 달간 다른 회사에서 일했다는 것을 알게 되었습니다. 비록 이것이 짧은 기간일 뿐이라고 해도, [162]납세 신고서를 제출하실 때 당신의 이전 소득이 고려되고 명시되어야 합니다.

해설 의도 파악 문제

단서 (152)에서 자신이 폴리 씨를 태우고 가길 원하는지 궁금했다는 크리스토프 씨의 말에 대한 폴리 씨의 응답으로, 크리스토프 씨가 자신을 태우고 가면 좋겠다는 말을 간접적으로 표현한 것이다. 따라서 정답은 (B).

패러프레이징 [단서] to pick you up → [정답] to drive her

153-155 광고

> **클래런스 사**
>
> ¹⁵³클래런스 사는 이전을 하는 업체들에게 지역 내 최상의 서비스를 제공합니다. 저희는 새로운 장소로 여러분께서 이동하시는 것이 가능한 한 순조롭도록 다양한 선택 사항을 제공합니다.
>
> 저희의 고급 패키지를 신청하시면, 다음 서비스들을 제공해 드리겠습니다:
> - 소지품 포장용 플라스틱 상자 무제한 제공
> - 대형 장비 및 가구 포장
> - 자사 IT 전문가들의 컴퓨터 및 기타 전자 제품 특별 포장
> - 전 물품 하역
> - ¹⁵⁴자사의 자매 회사, 스파클리 클린 사의 특별 청소 서비스
>
> ¹⁵⁵오늘 553-0295번으로 저희에게 전화하셔서 저희가 여러분의 시설을 방문하여 살펴볼 시간을 정하세요. 저희 서비스의 견적을 무료로 제공해 드리겠습니다.

어휘 relocate 이전하다 transition 이동, 과도기 unlimited 무제한의 belongings 소지품 load 짐을 싣다(↔ unload 짐을 내리다) estimate 견적

153. 클래런스 사의 업종은?
(A) 기계류 제조 업체
(B) 택배 회사
(C) 이사 업체
(D) 마케팅 자문 회사

해설 특정 정보 확인 문제

단서 (153)에서 이전을 하는 업체들에게 서비스를 제공한다고 했고, 이들이 순조롭게 이동할 수 있도록 여러 선택 사항을 제공한다고 했으므로 이사를 돕는 업체임을 알 수 있다. 따라서 정답은 (C).

패러프레이징 [단서] relocating → [정답] moving

154. 클래런스 사에 대해 시사된 것은?
(A) 청소 업체와 협력 관계를 맺고 있다.
(B) 고장 난 장치를 수리할 수 있다.
(C) 여러 곳에 분점들을 갖고 있다.
(D) 현재 무료 업그레이드를 제공하고 있다.

해설 Not/True 문제

단서 (154)에서 클래런스 사의 고급 패키지에서 제공되는 서비스 중 하나로 클래런스 사의 자매 회사인 스파클리 클린 사의 청소 서비스가 언급되었다. 이를 통해 클래런스 사가 청소 서비스 업체와 협력 관계를 맺고 있음을 알 수 있으므로 정답은 (A).

패러프레이징 [단서] clean-up service from our sister company → [정답] It partners with a cleaning company.

155. 고객들이 상담을 받으면 알 수 있는 것은?
(A) 장비를 어떻게 설치하는지
(B) 자신들이 얼마를 지불해야 할지
(C) 업체를 어디로 이전시킬지
(D) 배달이 언제 이루어질지

해설 특정 정보 확인 문제

단서 (155)에서 전화로 방문 일정을 잡으라고 하면서 서비스 견적을 무료로 제공해 주겠다고 했으므로, 예약을 한 고객들은 클래런스 사의 방문 후에 서비스 비용에 대해 알 수 있을 것이다. 따라서 정답은 (B).

패러프레이징 [단서] estimate for our services → [정답] How much they will have to pay

156-158 온라인 후기

> 호텔 후기: 바시바 호텔, 허밍버드 로 1882번지
>
> 평점: ★★★★☆
>
> 이름: 스텔라 매닝
>
> 숙박 날짜: 1월 18일-20일　　객실 종류: 1인용 일반 객실
>
> 저는 바시바 호텔에서 2박을 머물렀습니다. 저는 고객 몇 분을 만나기 위해 출장 중이었습니다. 바시바 호텔은 제 목적에 가장 알맞은 곳이었습니다. 객실은 편안하며, 조식 뷔페는 훌륭하고 그 가격만큼의 가치가 충분히 있습니다. — [1] —. 가장 중요한 것은, 벽이 두껍다는 것입니다. 그래서 도시의 번화한 지역에 있었음에도 불구하고 밤에 소음이 별로 들리지 않았습니다.
>
> ¹⁵⁶저는 도심 지역과의 근접성 때문에 이 호텔을 선택했습니다. ¹⁵⁷이곳은 식당을 찾고 회의에 가기에 편리했습니다. — [2] —. ¹⁵⁷저는 이른 오후에 기차를 타기로 되어 있었습니다. 저는 프런트에 택시를 불러 달라고 부탁했습니다. 저는 그것이 도착하기까지 15분 정도를 기다려야 했습니다. — [3] —. 그리고는, 호텔 직원이 기차역에 가려면 약 20분이 걸릴 거라고 했음에도 불구하고, 45분 가까이 걸렸습니다. — [4] —. 다행히도, 제가 일찍 출발했던 덕분에 저는 간신히 제 기차 시간에 맞춰 갈 수 있었습니다. ¹⁵⁸하지만 만약 호텔에서 출발하는 버스가 있었다면 이 모든 혼란을 피할 수 있었을 겁니다. 호텔에서 이미 공항을 오가는 서비스를 제공하고 있지만, 저는 호텔의 많은 투숙객이 기차를 타고 온다고 생각합니다. 기차역까지 가는 교통편도 제공한다면 매우 도움이 될 것입니다.

어휘 ideal 가장 알맞은, 이상적인 well worth 가치가 충분히 있는 busy 번화한, 붐비는 proximity to ~와의 근접성[가까움] be supposed to do ~하기로 되어 있다 manage to do 간신히 ~하다, ~을 잘 해내다 make it 시간 맞춰 가다 hassle 혼란, 번거로운 상황

149-150 달력

머서 부동산 신입 직원 오리엔테이션 일정						
8월							
일요일	월요일	화요일	수요일	목요일	금요일	토요일
	1	2	3	¹⁴⁹4 OR	5	6
7	8	9	10	11	12	13
14	15	16	17	18	19	20
21	22	23	¹⁵⁰24 DA	25	¹⁵⁰26 PRO	27
28	29 FFD	30	31			

OR: 오리엔테이션 첫날. 구내 견학
DA: 개별 부서 배치 발표
PRO: 사진 촬영 및 웹사이트 프로필 작성
FFD: 정규직으로서 급여를 받는 첫 번째 근무일

어휘 real estate 부동산 walk-through 이동, 견학 premises (항상 복수형) 구내, 부지 individual 개인의, 각각의 assignment 배치, 배정 creation 창작(물) compensate 보수를 지불하다, 보상하다

149. 직원들이 시설을 돌아볼 날은?
(A) 8월 4일
(B) 8월 24일
(C) 8월 26일
(D) 8월 29일

해설 특정 정보 확인 문제

달력 아래 단서 (149)에서 OR에 해당되는 날에 구내 견학이 있을 거라고 했는데, 달력에서 OR은 8월 4일 칸에 기재되어 있으므로 정답은 (A). 지문의 Walk-through of premises가 문제에서는 tour the facilities로 패러프레이징되었다.

150. 회사의 웹사이트용 사진에 대해 시사된 것은?
(A) 개인의 부서를 찾는 데 필요하다.
(B) 근무 첫날에 제출되어야 한다.
(C) 부서가 배치되고 난 뒤에 촬영한다.
(D) 8월 26일에 직원들이 회사에 가져와야 한다.

해설 Not/True 문제

달력 아래 및 달력의 단서 (150)을 종합해 보면 DA, 즉 부서 배치 발표는 8월 24일에, PRO, 즉 사진 촬영 및 웹사이트용 프로필 제작은 8월 26일에 이루어진다. 이를 통해 부서가 배치되고 나서 이틀 뒤에 웹사이트용 프로필에 쓰일 사진을 촬영한다는 것을 알 수 있으므로 정답은 (C). 나머지는 지문에 나와 있지 않은 내용이므로 모두 오답.

패러프레이징 [단서] Individual department assignments → [정답] departments have been assigned

151-152 문자 메시지

지미 크리스토프 오후 3:08
레베카, 다음 주 월요일에 회의에 가기 위한 준비는 다 했나요?

레베카 폴리 오후 3:09
¹⁵¹저는 회사가 그 일을 처리하고 있는 줄 알았는데요. 회사에서 우리에게 버스를 제공해 주는 거 아니에요?

지미 크리스토프 오후 3:10
¹⁵¹아니요. 회사에서는 결국 그렇게 하지 않기로 결정했어요. 그래서 대부분의 사람은 지하철을 타거나 운전을 해서 갈 거예요.

레베카 폴리 오후 3:13
그러면 저는 운전을 해서 가야겠네요. 저희 집 근처에는 지하철역이 하나도 없거든요. 그런데 전 그 장소에 한 번도 가 본 적이 없어요. 그곳에 어떻게 가야 할지 전혀 모르겠네요.

지미 크리스토프 오후 3:14
음, 그래서 제가 당신한테 연락한 거예요. ¹⁵²제가 당신을 태워 가길 원하는지 궁금했어요.

레베카 폴리 오후 3:15
그러면 저는 훨씬 더 편하죠. 정말 괜찮으시겠어요?

지미 크리스토프 오후 3:17
물론이죠. 당신의 집은 제가 가는 길에 있잖아요. 그리고 저는 이전에 그 회의장에 여러 번 가 봤어요.

어휘 make arrangements for ~을 준비하다 take care of ~을 처리하다 after all 결국에는 contact 연락하다

151. 메시지 작성자들의 회사에 대해 시사된 것은?
(A) 직원들의 교통편 관련 업무를 처리하지 않고 있다.
(B) 지하철역 근처에 위치해 있는 사무실들이 있다.
(C) 직원들을 위한 행사를 준비하고 있다.
(D) 새로운 장소로 이전할 것이다.

해설 Not/True 문제

단서 (151)에서 회사가 직원들에게 버스를 제공하지 않는지 묻는 폴리 씨의 질문에 크리스토프 씨가 아니라고 하면서 회사에서 버스를 제공하지 않기로 결정했다고 한 것으로 보아, 회사가 직원들의 교통편과 관련된 업무를 처리하지 않고 있다는 것을 알 수 있다. 따라서 정답은 (A). 나머지는 지문에 나와 있지 않은 내용이므로 모두 오답.

패러프레이징 [단서] providing a bus for us → [정답] handling transportation for employees

152. 오후 3시 15분에, 폴리 씨가 "그러면 저는 훨씬 더 편하죠"라고 한 것에서 그녀가 의도한 것은?
(A) 버스로 가는 것을 선호한다.
(B) 크리스토프 씨가 자신을 태워 가기를 원한다.
(C) 회의 장소에서 크리스토프 씨를 태워 갈 수 있다.
(D) 지하철 타는 것을 개의치 않는다.

이라고 생각할 것이라고 했으므로 독자들이 해당 연구에 대해 알 수 있게 되는 방법에 대한 내용이 빈칸에 나와야 한다. 따라서 학술지 이름을 말하며 논문이 거기에 게재될 것이라고 하는 내용이 담긴 (D)가 정답.

144. 형용사 자리_목적격 보어

해설 빈칸은 〈find+목적어+목적격 보어〉의 구조를 취하는 5문형 동사 find의 목적격 보어 자리이다. 목적격 보어 자리에는 명사와 형용사가 올 수 있으므로 동사인 (A)와 (B)는 오답으로 제외. 명사인 (D)는 목적어인 your work와 동격을 이루어 '귀하의 연구=고무'가 되어 의미상 어색하므로 오답. 따라서 정답은 (C). 의미상으로도 '귀하의 작업이 고무적이다'가 되어야 자연스럽다.

145. 미래시제+수동태

해설 선택지가 모두 동사인 것으로 보아 동사의 알맞은 시제와 태를 묻는 문제임을 알 수 있다. 지문은 수상 사실을 알려 주는 편지로, 상금을 받는 것은 편지 수신 이후의 일이므로 미래시제인 (A)와 (D)가 정답 후보. 주어인 you가 동사 grant의 행위를 당하는 대상으로, 수동태가 쓰여야 하므로 정답은 (D). 빈칸 뒤에 목적어가 있어서 (A)를 정답으로 고르기 쉬우나, 빈칸 뒤의 $2,500는 직접목적어로, grant는 〈주어+동사+간접목적어+직접목적어〉 구조로 쓰이는 4문형 동사라서 간접목적어가 주어로 쓰이는 수동태 문장에서는 동사 뒤에 직접목적어가 그대로 남아 있다는 점을 기억하자.

146. 명사 어휘 contribution

(A) 차이 (B) 설문 조사 **(C) 기여** (D) 지식

해설 빈칸 뒤의 전치사 to와 호응하면서, 감사의 이유가 될 수 있는 명사 어휘를 찾아야 한다. 문맥상 '의약 분야에의 기여에 감사한다'는 내용이 적절하므로 정답은 (C). contribution은 뒤에 to로 시작되는 전치사구를 수반하여 '~에의 기여[공헌]'를 의미한다는 것을 기억해 두자.

PART 7

147-148 이메일

수신: 베로니카 테시에 〈v.tessier@greatinterior.com〉
발신: 루시 브래커 〈l.bracker@memail.net〉
제목: 견본 사진
날짜: 1월 18일

테시에 씨께,

[147]저희 거실에 가능한 배치의 사진들을 보내 주셔서 감사합니다. 다양한 색상과 질감이 함께 놓여 있는 사진들을 보는 것은 이것들이 어떻게 보일지를 파악하는 데 도움이 됩니다. [148]그런데 저는 귀하께서 보내신 마지막 사진을 여는 데 어려움을 겪고 있습니다. 그것은 다른 것들과는 다른 포맷으로 되어 있는 것 같은데, 제 컴퓨터는 그것을 읽지 못하는 것 같습니다. 그걸 다른 것들과 같은 포맷으로 다시 보내 주시겠습니까?

정말 감사합니다.

루시 브래커 드림

어휘 texture 질감, 결 put together 한데 모으다, 합치다
have trouble doing ~하는 데 어려움을 겪다 format 포맷, 형식

147. 테시에 씨의 신분은?

(A) 전문 사진작가
(B) 인테리어 디자이너
(C) IT 전문가
(D) 미술관 소유주

해설 추론 문제

테시에 씨는 이메일 수신자로, 단서 (147)에서 이메일 발신자인 브래커 씨는 테시에 씨가 가능한 거실 배치의 사진들을 보내 주었다고 했다. 이를 통해 테시에 씨가 인테리어 일을 맡아서 하는 사람임을 추론할 수 있으므로 정답은 (B).

148. 브래커 씨가 겪고 있는 문제는?

(A) 공간이 충분하지 않다.
(B) 색상 조합이 마음에 들지 않는다.
(C) 파일을 볼 수 없다.
(D) 이메일을 받지 못했다.

해설 특정 정보 확인 문제

단서 (148)에서 테시에 씨가 보낸 사진 하나를 여는 데 어려움을 겪고 있다고 했으므로 정답은 (C). 지문의 trouble이 문제에서는 problem으로 패러프레이징되었다.

패러프레이징 [단서] opening the last picture you sent
→ [정답] to view a file

137. 형용사 어휘 local
(A) 숙련된 (B) 의존적인 **(C) 지역의** (D) 활동적인

해설 빈칸 뒤의 명사와 어울리는 형용사 어휘를 고르는 문제. 문맥상 '지역 주민 새뮤얼 프렌디 씨가 말했다'는 내용이 가장 자연스러우므로 정답은 (C). local resident는 '지역 주민'이라는 뜻으로 자주 쓰이므로 한 단어처럼 외워 두자.

138. 알맞은 문장 고르기
(A) 누구나 이 행사에 참석할 수 있도록 초대되었다.
(B) 이것은 그날 발표될 것이다.
(C) 여러분은 그때 여러분의 책들을 가져갈 수 있다.
(D) 그는 대다수의 득표로 당선되었다.

해설 빈칸은 기사의 후반부에 있는 문장으로, 빈칸 바로 앞에서 지역 행사를 소개한 후 이 행사에 신문이 대상으로 하고 있는 지역 주민들 '누구나 참석할 수 있도록 초대되었다'는 내용이 이어지는 것이 가장 자연스러우므로 정답은 (A).

139-142 공지

> 아시다시피, 회사는 매년 F&Y 노숙자 보호소에 기부를 합니다. 올해는 기부금 대신에, 보호소에서 필요로 하는 다양한 물품을 기부하기로 결정했습니다. 여러분은 각 부서장 사무실 입구에서 통을 보게 될 것입니다. 직원들은 이 통에 양호한 상태의 물품들을 넣도록 ¹³⁹권장됩니다. 통이 ¹⁴⁰가득 차면, 홍보부 직원들이 수거하여 보호소에 전달할 것입니다. 받을 수 있는 물품들의 목록이 직원 휴게실에 게시될 예정입니다. ¹⁴¹통에 어떤 물품이든 넣기 전에 그것을 주의 깊게 참고해 주십시오. 특히, 의류는 환영이지만, 특정 ¹⁴²직물은 흔히 있을 수 있는 알레르기나 제한된 세탁 방법으로 인해 받아들여지지 않는다는 점을 유념하세요. 여러분의 기부에 미리 감사드립니다.

어휘 donate 기부하다 homeless shelter 노숙자 보호소 in need of ~을 필요로 하는 bin 통, 용기 entrance 입구, 문 acceptable 받아들여지는 in particular 특히, 특별히 due to ~ 때문에, ~에 기인하는 donation 기부

139. 수동태
해설 빈칸 앞에 be동사가 있고, 빈칸 뒤에 목적어가 없으면서 to부정사가 바로 따라오므로 수동태 문장이 아닌지 의심해 보아야 한다. 의미상으로도 직원들에게 어떤 행동이 '권장된다'는 수동의 의미가 적절하므로, 앞에 있는 are와 함께 수동태 동사구를 이루는 과거분사 (D)가 정답. 참고로, encourage는 to부정사를 목적격 보어로 취한다.

140. 형용사 어휘 full
(A) 열려 있는 **(B) 가득 찬** (C) 끝난 (D) 소비된

해설 빈칸이 있는 문장 앞에서 통에 물품들을 넣을 것을 권장했으므로, 문맥상 그 물품들로 '통이 가득 차면' 수거한다는 내용이 가장 자연스럽다. 따라서 정답은 (B).

141. 알맞은 문장 고르기
(A) 통에 어떤 물품이든 넣기 전에 그것을 주의 깊게 참고해 주십시오.
(B) 여러분에게 필요해 보이는 것은 무엇이든 가져가셔도 됩니다.
(C) 그러나, 입장은 고위 관리직으로 한정됩니다.
(D) 조건에 동의하시면 아래에 서명하시면 됩니다.

해설 빈칸 앞에 기부 가능한 물품들의 목록이 직원 휴게실에 게시될 것이라고 했고 빈칸 뒤에는 기부할 수 있는 의류 중에서도 어떤 것은 특정 이유로 받아들여지지 않는다고 했으므로, 빈칸에는 물품 목록을 주의 깊게 살펴보라고 권하는 내용이 들어가는 것이 자연스럽다. 따라서 정답은 (A).

142. 명사 어휘 material
(A) 방법 (B) 액수 **(C) 직물** (D) 지불

해설 문맥상 '의류는 기부할 수 있으나 특정 직물은 알레르기 및 세탁상의 이유로 받아들여지지 않는다'는 의미가 가장 자연스러우므로 정답은 (C).

143-146 편지

> 9월 14일
>
> 스털링 머리
> 모로코 드라이브 25번지
> 뉴타운, 펜실베이니아 주 18777
>
> 머리 씨께,
>
> 그레이퍼 과학 연구 대회에서 귀하의 '제약품의 품질 관리: 세 가지 방법론의 검증'이라는 제목의 논문으로 귀하께 1등을 수여하게 되어 기쁩니다. 귀하께서 수행하신 연구와 그 결과는 대단히 흥미로웠습니다. ¹⁴³귀하의 논문은 다음 달 〈그레이퍼 과학 뉴스〉 지에 게재될 것입니다. 저희는 과학계의 나머지 독자들도 귀하의 연구가 ¹⁴⁴고무적이라고 생각할 것임을 확신합니다. 덧붙여, 귀하는 후속 연구를 위해 2,500달러를 ¹⁴⁵수여받을 것입니다. 저희는 이것이 귀하의 추후 노력에 도움이 되길 바랍니다. 축하드립니다. 그리고 의약 분야에 ¹⁴⁶기여해 주셔서 감사드립니다.
>
> 그레이퍼 과학, 책임자
> 리처드 넬슨 드림

어휘 award 수여하다 entitle 제목을 붙이다 conduct 수행하다 finding 《보통 복수형》 (조사·연구 등의) 결과[결론] fascinating 대단히 흥미로운, 매력적인 inspirational 고무적인, 영감을 주는 grant 수여하다, 승인하다 endeavor 노력, 시도

143. 알맞은 문장 고르기
(A) 저희는 귀하께서 이 연구에 대해 읽어 보시길 강력히 추천합니다.
(B) 많은 참가자가 그 대회에 참가했습니다.
(C) 하지만, 그 정보의 대부분은 이미 잘 알려져 있었습니다.
(D) 귀하의 논문은 다음 달 〈그레이퍼 과학 뉴스〉 지에 게재될 것입니다.

해설 빈칸 뒤에서 과학계의 나머지 독자들도 머리 씨의 연구가 고무적

PART 6

131-134 이메일

수신: 마거릿 키블 〈m_keeble@tysoncomm.com〉
발신: 후안 토레스 〈j_torres@tysoncomm.com〉
날짜: 11월 18일
제목: 계속 열심히 해 주세요!

키블 씨께,

저는 당신에게 페로나 씨가 청구 오류로 인해 화가 난 채로 우리 사무실로 왔을 때의 상황을 처리해 줘서 고맙다는 말을 하고 싶습니다. 이런 상황에서 무엇을 해야 할지 아는 게 항상 쉬운 일은 아닌데, 당신이 그것을 처리한 방식은 ¹³¹적절했습니다. 우리 고객들의 기분을 맞추는 것은 업무의 중요한 부분입니다. ¹³²그렇다 해도, 우리는 고객들에게 그들이 요구하는 모든 것을 줄 수는 없습니다. 이것은 우리 재정에 해로운 영향을 줄 수 있습니다. 차분한 태도로 오류의 원인에 대해 설명함으로써 당신은 그 갈등을 빠르게 해결했습니다. ¹³³이것은 우리 하급 직원들에게도 좋은 본보기가 되어 주었습니다. 다른 팀장들과 저는 당신이 당신의 노고에 ¹³⁴보상을 받을 만한 자격이 있다는 것에 동의합니다. 그래서, 당신은 유급 휴가 하루를 추가로 받게 될 것입니다.

축하합니다!

타이슨 커뮤니케이션즈, 사무장
후안 토레스 드림

어휘 keep up (동일한 정도로) ~을 계속하다 upset 화난, 속상한 please 기쁘게 하다, 기분을 맞추다 demand 요구하다 detrimental 해로운 manner 태도, 방식 resolve (문제 등을) 해결하다 conflict 갈등, 충돌 deserve to do ~할 만한 자격이 있다 benefit from ~으로부터 혜택을 받다

131. 형용사 어휘 appropriate
(A) 실현 가능한 **(B) 적절한** (C) 꾸준한 (D) 입수 가능한

해설 빈칸은 문장의 주어를 보충하는 주격 보어 자리이고 주어는 '일을 처리한 방식'이다. 이메일이 직원의 업무 처리를 칭찬하는 내용이므로 일을 처리한 방식이 '적절했음'을 언급하는 것이 가장 자연스럽다. 따라서 정답은 (B).

132. 접속부사 nonetheless
(A) 게다가 (B) ~에도 불구하고 **(C) 그렇다 해도** (D) 예를 들면

해설 문맥에 어울리는 접속부사를 찾는 문제. 빈칸 앞 문장에서 고객의 기분을 맞추는 것이 업무의 중요한 부분이라고 했고, 빈칸 다음에 고객들이 요구하는 모든 것을 줄 수는 없다는 대조되는 내용이 나오므로 빈칸에는 '그렇다 해도'라는 양보의 접속부사가 들어가는 것이 가장 자연스럽다. 따라서 정답은 (C).

133. 알맞은 문장 고르기
(A) 페로나 씨가 지금부터 이 구역을 감독할 것입니다.
(B) 우리는 이미 변경이 반영된 당신의 새 청구서를 재인쇄했습니다.
(C) 이것은 우리 하급 직원들에게도 좋은 본보기가 되어 주었습니다.
(D) 회사는 청구 소프트웨어를 곧 업그레이드할 것입니다.

해설 빈칸 앞에서 키블 씨의 문제 해결에 대해 말하고 있고 빈칸 뒤에서는 이에 대해 보상을 받을 만한 자격이 있다고 말하고 있으므로 빈칸에는 키블 씨가 보상을 받을 만한 이유, 즉 키블 씨의 문제 해결을 칭찬하는 문장이 추가되는 것이 가장 자연스럽다. 따라서 이렇게 해결한 사례가 하급 직원들에게도 좋은 본보기가 되었다고 서술하고 있는 (C)가 정답.

134. to부정사_명사적 용법

해설 빈칸은 빈칸 앞의 동사 deserve의 목적어 자리이다. 문맥상 '보상을 받을 만한 자격이 있다'는 의미가 자연스러우므로 정답은 (A). deserve to do는 '~할 만한 자격이 있다'의 의미로 자주 쓰이므로 알아 두도록 하자.

135-138 기사

3월 16일, 나턴—소도시인 나턴 중심에 ¹³⁵위치한 새 도서관이 다음 달 문을 열 예정이다. 나턴 도서관은 온갖 주제의 도서, 잡지, 영상 모음을 보유하게 될 것이다. 게다가, 도서관은 지역 사회에 ¹³⁶기여하고자 무료 인터넷 접속을 제공하고, 정기 행사를 주최하며, 다양한 워크숍도 제공할 것이다. "제 생각에 이 도서관은 정말 도움이 될 거예요,"라고 ¹³⁷지역 주민 새뮤얼 프렌디 씨가 밝혔다. "나턴은 외진 곳에 떨어져 있어서 우리는 모든 최신 정보를 접하고 있기 어려워요." 브렌켈 시장은 4월 2일 개관식에서 연설을 하기로 예정되어 있다. ¹³⁸누구나 이 행사에 참석할 수 있도록 초대되었다. 이에 대한 더 자세한 정보를 원하면, 나턴의 공식 웹사이트를 확인하면 된다.

어휘 hold 소유하다, 보유하다 access 접속 host 주최하다 extremely 정말로, 극도로 resident 주민, 거주자 isolated 외떨어진 remote 외진, 먼 up-to-date 최신의, 최신 정보에 근거한

135. 형용사 자리+분사

해설 빈칸부터 Narton까지가 빈칸 앞의 명사 library를 수식하는 구조로, 빈칸에는 형용사가 들어가야 한다. 따라서 형용사 역할을 할 수 있는 현재분사 (B)와 과거분사 (D)가 정답 후보. locate는 '~을 (특정 위치에) 두다'라는 의미의 타동사인데 도서관은 특정 위치에 두는 주체가 아니라 대상이므로 수동의 의미를 나타내는 과거분사 (D)가 정답.

136. 동사 어휘 serve
(A) ~에 기여하다 (B) 조직하다 (C) 요청하다 (D) 방문하다

해설 빈칸은 빈칸 뒤 the community를 목적어로 취하는 to부정사의 동사 자리이다. 빈칸 앞에서 도서관이 제공할 다양한 혜택을 나열하고 있으므로, '지역 사회에 기여하기[도움이 되기] 위해서' 이러한 혜택들을 제공한다는 의미가 가장 자연스럽다. 따라서 정답은 (A).

어휘 revelation 폭로(된 사실), 적발   emission 배출, 방출   harmful 유해한   issue 쟁점, 문제

122. 명사 자리+동명사 vs. 명사
도시의 복잡한 배치를 고려해 볼 때, 포트빌 분점의 장소를 선정하는 것은 어려웠다.

해설 빈칸부터 branch까지는 문장의 주어이므로 주어 자리에 올 수 있는 동명사 (A)와 명사 (B)가 정답 후보. 빈칸 뒤에 목적어 the location을 취할 수 있는 것은 동사의 성질을 가진 동명사이므로 정답은 (A).

어휘 given ~을 고려해 볼 때   complex 복잡한   layout 배치, 설계   location 장소

123. 명사 자리
식당 지배인은 월례 점검에 대비하기 위해 직원들과 함께 식품 안전 규정을 재검토했다.

해설 빈칸은 동사 reviewed의 목적어 자리로, 빈칸 앞의 명사 safety와 어울려 '안전 규정'이라는 뜻의 복합명사를 만드는 명사가 와야 한다. 따라서 정답은 (C). safety regulations를 하나의 덩어리로 외워 두자.

어휘 review 재검토하다   prepare for ~을 준비[대비]하다   monthly 매월의   inspection 점검, 조사

124. 형용사 어휘 detailed
대선 후보 앤 라스럽 씨의 경제 계획에 관한 상세한 설명을 보시려면, 그녀의 선거 운동 웹사이트를 방문하세요.
(A) 반복된 (B) 주문 제작된 (C) 입증된 **(D) 상세한**

해설 빈칸에 알맞은 형용사 역할의 어휘를 고르는 문제. 문맥상 '경제 계획에 관한 상세한 설명'이라는 의미가 가장 자연스러우므로 정답은 (D).

어휘 explanation 설명   presidential candidate 대선 후보   economic 경제의   campaign 선거 운동, 캠페인

125. 수동태
반품한 물건에 대해 전액 환불을 받으려면 계산원에게 영수증이 제시되어야만 한다.

해설 선택지를 보니 알맞은 형태의 동사를 고르는 문제. 주어인 the receipt은 동사 present의 주체가 아니라 대상이므로 수동태가 되어야 한다. 따라서 정답은 (D).

어휘 full refund 전액 환불   return 반품하다, 돌려주다   receipt 영수증   present 제시하다, 수여하다

126. 형용사 자리 + 형용사 vs. 분사
경쟁력 있는 가격을 제공함으로써, 에르고 슈퍼마켓은 그 지역에서 가장 성공적인 식료품점 중 하나가 되었다.

해설 빈칸은 뒤의 명사 prices를 수식하는 형용사 자리이므로 형용사 역할을 하는 과거분사 (A)와 현재분사 (B), 형용사 (C)가 정답 후보. 문맥상 '경쟁력 있는 가격'이라는 의미가 가장 자연스러우므로 '경쟁력 있는'이라는 의미의 형용사인 (C)가 정답.

어휘 grocery store 식료품점

127. 접속사 vs. 전치사
애비게일 호스킨스 씨는 교육 수준을 향상시킨 공로로 시에서 준 감사장을 받았다.
(A) ~으로 (B) ~ 안으로 (C) ~ 때문에 (D) ~할 때

해설 빈칸 뒤의 내용이 빈칸 앞 절의 이유가 되므로 이유를 나타내는 전치사 (A)와 접속사 (C)가 정답 후보. 빈칸 뒤에 명사구가 왔기 때문에 이를 목적어로 취하는 전치사 (A)가 정답.

어휘 certificate of appreciation 감사장   effort 노력, 활동   improve 향상시키다   educational standards 교육 수준

128. 부사 어휘 slightly
마리아스 그릴은 도심에 약간만 더 가까운데도, 프리마베라스보다 훨씬 더 많은 손님들이 있다.
(A) 약간 (B) 압도적으로 (C) 주의 깊게 (D) 일반적으로

해설 빈칸 앞의 부사 only의 수식을 받는 동시에 빈칸 뒤의 형용사 비교급 closer를 수식하는 부사 어휘를 고르는 문제. 선택지 중 빈칸 앞뒤의 only 및 closer와 자연스러운 문맥을 이루는 것은 slightly뿐이므로, '약간만 더 가까운데도'라는 의미를 만드는 (A)가 정답.

129. to부정사_부사 역할
그 디자이너는 대회를 광고하는 안내 책자를 만들기 위해 새로운 종류의 소프트웨어를 사용했다.

해설 빈칸 앞의 문장이 완전한 것으로 보아, 빈칸 이하는 문장을 수식하는 부사 역할의 어구임을 알 수 있다. 선택지 중 빈칸 이하의 명사구를 부사구로 만들어 이끌 수 있는 것은 to부정사뿐이므로, '안내 책자를 만들기 위해'라고 목적을 나타낼 수 있는 (C)가 정답. 여기서 to부정사는 목적을 나타내는 부사적 용법으로 쓰였다.

어휘 brochure 안내 책자   advertise 광고하다   convention 대회, 총회

130. 명사 어휘 shortcomings
경영진은 에이미 볼퍼트 씨의 학력상의 결점에도 불구하고 그녀의 인턴으로서의 경력 때문에 그녀를 고용하기로 결정했다.
(A) 성취 **(B) 결점** (C) 제출 (D) 자격

해설 양보의 전치사 in spite of의 목적어인 명사를 고르는 문제. 어떤 부정적인 사항에도 불구하고 고용하기로 결정했다는 내용이 되도록 빈칸에는 부정적인 의미의 어휘가 들어가는 것이 알맞다. 따라서 '결점'이라는 의미의 (B)가 정답. 나머지 어휘는 문장의 주제인 채용과 어울리는 어휘들이지만, 문맥상 적절하지 않으므로 오답.

어휘 management 경영(진)   in spite of ~에도 불구하고   educational background 학력   experience 경력, 경험

113. 소유대명사

제 일정이 귀하의 일정보다 더 탄력적이므로 우리는 언제든 귀하가 편한 시간에 만날 수 있습니다.

해설 빈칸은 전치사 than의 목적어 자리이므로 명사 역할을 하는 (A), (B), (D)가 정답 후보. 빈칸에는 빈칸이 들어 있는 절의 주어인 my schedule과 비교하는 대상인 your schedule을 가리키는 소유대명사 yours가 와야 한다. 따라서 정답은 (D).

어휘 convenient 편리한   flexible 탄력적인, 유연한

114. 명사 자리+동명사 vs. 명사

깁슨 백화점은 고객들에게 백화점 개점 행사에 참석한 데 대한 감사를 표하기 위해 무료 샘플들이 든 작은 가방을 나눠 주었다.

해설 빈칸은 전치사 for의 목적어 자리이므로 동명사 (B)와 명사 (C), (D)가 정답 후보. 명사는 뒤에 목적어를 취할 수 없으나, 동사의 성질을 가지고 있는 동명사는 뒤에 목적어 its grand opening event를 취할 수 있으므로 동명사인 (B)가 정답.

어휘 hand out 나누어 주다   attend 참석하다   grand opening 개점, 개장

115. 전치사 of

1등석으로 여행하는 승객들은 각자 최대 3개의 여행 가방을 부치는 것이 허용된다.

(A) 위로 (B) ~을 넘어 **(C) ~의** (D) ~로

해설 빈칸 앞뒤의 명사(구)를 연결하는 알맞은 전치사를 고르는 문제이다. 빈칸 앞의 a maximum과 빈칸 뒤의 three suitcases는 의미상 동격이므로 빈칸에는 '동격'을 나타내는 전치사 of가 들어가야 한다. 따라서 정답은 (C). a maximum of는 '최대 ~'라는 의미로 쓰인다는 것을 알아 두자.

어휘 passenger 승객   permit 허용하다   check in (짐을) 부치다   maximum 최대(량), 최고(점)   suitcase 여행 가방

116. 명사 어휘 compliance

회사의 정책에 대한 엄격한 준수가 직원들에게 항상 기대된다.

(A) 적용 **(B) 준수** (C) 경영 (D) 정정

해설 빈칸 뒤의 전치사구 with the company's policies와 어울리는 명사 어휘를 골라야 한다. 빈칸에는 회사 정책과 관련된 내용이면서 직원들에게 기대되는 것이 와야 하므로 '회사 정책의 준수'라는 의미를 만들며, 전치사 with와 호응하여 쓰이는 (B)가 정답. (A)의 '적용'도 정답으로 생각할 수 있으나, 전치사 of와 호응하여 쓰이므로 오답.

어휘 strict 엄격한   policy 정책, 방침   at all times 항상, 언제나

117. 주격 관계대명사

새크라멘토 가에 위치해 있는 북문을 통해 건물에 들어오세요.

해설 선택지와 빈칸 앞의 콤마를 보니 계속적 용법으로 쓰인 관계사를 고르는 문제. 빈칸 뒤에 주어 없이 바로 동사가 이어지는 것으로 보아 빈칸은 주격 관계대명사 자리이므로 관계부사인 (C)는 오답으로 제외. 빈칸 앞에 사물 선행사 the north door가 있으므로, 사물 선행사를 취하는 주격 관계대명사인 (D)가 정답. (A)는 사람을 선행사로 취하므로 오답. (B)는 그 자체가 선행사를 포함하고 있으므로 선행사 뒤에서 선행사를 부연 설명하는 계속적 용법으로 쓸 수 없으므로 오답.

118. 부사 자리_숫자 수식

뉴스 앵커에 의하면, 그 바이러스는 단 몇 분 만에 대략 1만 대의 컴퓨터를 감염시켰다.

해설 동사 infected와 목적어 ten thousand computers 사이에 빈칸이 있는데 빈칸 없이도 문장 내용이 자연스럽게 이어지는 것으로 보아, 빈칸에는 수량 표현인 ten thousand를 수식해 주는 부사가 들어가야 한다. 따라서 정답은 (B). approximately는 뒤에 시간, 숫자 등 수량과 관련된 표현과 주로 함께 쓰인다는 것을 기억해 두자.

어휘 infect 감염시키다   approximately 대략, 거의

119. 형용사 어휘 diverse

플루코스 의류는 다양한 고객의 관심을 끌기 위해 일련의 광고들을 제작할 계획이다.

(A) 다양한 (B) 정확한 (C) 평소의 (D) 묘사하는

해설 빈칸은 목적의 의미로 쓰인 to부정사를 이루고 있는 동사 appeal to의 목적어 clientele(고객)을 수식하는 형용사 자리이다. '다양한 고객들의 관심을 끌기 위해 일련의 광고들을 제작한다'고 하는 것이 가장 자연스러우므로 정답은 (A).

어휘 clothing 《집합명사》 의류   a series of 일련의   appeal to ~의 관심을 끌다   clientele 《집합명사》 고객, 의뢰인

120. 관용어구 would rather A than B

이 연구는 고객들이 매장에서 물품을 착용하기보다는 차라리 온라인상에서 쇼핑을 하고 싶어 한다는 것을 보여 준다.

(A) 한층 더 (B) 아마 **(C) 차라리** (D) 실수로

해설 문맥에 어울리는 부사 어휘를 고르는 문제로, 빈칸 앞의 조동사 would와 빈칸 뒤쪽의 전치사 than을 보자마자 would rather A than B(B하기보다는 차라리 A하고 싶다)라는 관용표현을 떠올릴 수 있어야 한다. 따라서 정답은 (C).

어휘 indicate 보여 주다, 나타내다   try on ~을 입어 보다

121. 동사 어휘 emerge

자사 공장들의 유해 가스 배출에 대한 새로운 폭로가 그 회사의 쟁점으로 부상했다.

(A) ~이 되다 **(B) 부상하다** (C) (결과로서) 생기다 (D) 생산하다

해설 빈칸 뒤의 전치사 as와 짝을 이루어 목적어를 취하는 동사를 고르는 문제. emerge as(~으로 부상하다)를 알고 있다면 바로 답을 고를 수 있다. 어구를 몰랐더라도 as는 '~으로(서)'의 뜻이고, 이와 어울리는 동사는 자동사인 emerge뿐이므로 정답은 (B). (A)와 (C)도 자동사이지만 (A)는 전치사 없이 바로 보어를 취하고, (C)는 전치사 in 또는 from과 호응하여 목적어를 취하므로 오답. (D)는 바로 목적어를 취할 수 있는 타동사이므로 오답.

해설 선택지를 보니 문맥에 알맞은 전치사를 고르는 문제. 빈칸 앞에 행위를 나타내는 수동태 동사구가 있고 빈칸 뒤에 행위자가 나오므로, 빈칸에는 '~에 의해'라는 의미로 수동태 문장에서 행위자나 창작자를 나타낼 때 쓰이는 전치사가 들어가야 한다. 따라서 정답은 (A).

어휘 electronics 《항상 복수형》 전자 기기   device 기기, 장치   manufacture 제조[생산]하다   overseas 해외에

104. 재귀대명사_강조용법

그 팀장은 너무 바빠서 직접 공항으로 콜콧 사의 CEO를 태우러 갈 수가 없다.

해설 빈칸 앞이 완전한 문장이므로 빈칸을 생략해도 문장이 성립된다. 따라서 빈칸에는 생략 가능한 강조용법으로 쓰인 재귀대명사가 적절하므로 정답은 (D). 여기서 재귀대명사 herself는 주어인 The team leader를 강조하는 역할을 한다.

어휘 pick up ~를 태우러 가다

105. 형용사 어휘 primary

이 회의의 주된 목적은 우리의 안전 수칙을 검토하는 것이다.

(A) 주된 (B) 철저한 (C) 풍부한 (D) 때맞춘

해설 빈칸 뒤의 명사 purpose를 수식하면서 문맥에 맞는 형용사 어휘를 고르는 문제. 문맥상 '회의의 주된 목적'이라는 의미가 가장 자연스러우므로 정답은 (A).

어휘 purpose 목적   review 검토하다   safety procedure 안전 수칙

106. 부사 자리_동사 수식

연습을 했음에도 불구하고 피터 버트런드 씨는 면접관들이 자신에게 물어본 질문들에 충분히 준비되어 있지 않았다.

해설 빈칸 부분이 빠져도 문장이 완전하고, 빈칸이 〈be동사+p.p.〉 구조의 수동태 동사구 was not prepared 사이에 위치하므로, 빈칸은 수동태 동사구를 수식하는 부사 자리이다. 따라서 정답은 (D). 부사는 수동태 문장에서 be동사와 과거분사 사이에 놓인다는 것을 기억하자.

어휘 sufficiently 충분히   interviewer 면접관

107. 동사 어휘 communicate

멕시코로 출장을 가기 전에 마커스 씨는 현지인들과 의사소통할 수 있도록 스페인어를 공부했다.

(A) 말하다 **(B) 의사소통하다** (C) 예약하다 (D) 이해하다

해설 동사 어휘 문제는 뒤에 수반되는 전치사나 목적어로 쓰인 명사와의 관계를 살펴보면 쉽게 답을 찾을 수 있다. 뒤에 전치사 with를 수반하여 목적어를 취하며, '현지인들과 의사소통하다'라는 의미를 나타내는 자동사 (B)가 정답.

어휘 business trip 출장   local 현지인; 지역의

108. 수량형용사 every

모든 참석자는 진행 순서 목록과 각 발표자에 관한 정보가 들어 있는 폴더를 받게 될 것이다.

(A) 모든 (B) 거의 없는 (C) 몇몇의 (D) 모든

해설 선택지를 통해 빈칸에 알맞은 수량 표현을 찾는 문제임을 알 수 있다. 선택지 중 빈칸 뒤에 오는 가산명사의 단수형 attendee를 수식할 수 있는 것은 every뿐이므로 정답은 (A). (B)와 (C)는 가산명사의 복수형을, (D)는 가산명사의 복수형 또는 불가산명사를 수식하므로 오답.

어휘 attendee 참석자   program 진행 순서, 예정표   note (책·시디 케이스 등에 인쇄된) 관련 내용[정보]   presenter 발표자

109. 명사 어휘 development

여러 과학 분야에서의 최근의 발달은 기대 수명의 급증을 초래했다.

(A) 발달 (B) 버전 (C) 연대표 (D) 범위

해설 빈칸은 문장의 주어 자리이고, 문장의 동사로 cause가 쓰인 것으로 보아 주어에는 목적어의 원인이 될 만한 내용이 오는 것이 알맞다. '과학 분야에서의 최근의 발달'이 기대 수명 급증의 원인으로 적절하므로 정답은 (A).

어휘 recent 최근의   various 여러 가지의, 다양한   field 분야   sudden 갑작스러운   life expectancy 기대 수명

110. 형용사 자리_한정사+형용사+명사

맨더 씨가 원래의 저녁 식사 손님 명단에 이름 6개를 추가하면서, 예상되는 식사 손님의 수가 23명으로 늘어났다.

해설 빈칸 앞에 정관사 the가 있고 빈칸 뒤에 명사구 dinner guest list가 있으므로 빈칸은 명사(구)를 수식할 수 있는 형용사 자리이다. 따라서 정답은 형용사인 (C).

어휘 original 원래의   bring A up to B A를 B까지 올리다   expect 예상하다, 기대하다   diner 식사하는 사람[손님]

111. 동사 어휘 unveil

비비 패션 하우스에서 나온 가죽 핸드백의 봄 상품 라인이 지난주에 있었던 패션쇼에서 발표되었다.

(A) 참고하다 (B) 완화하다 (C) 시도하다 **(D) 발표하다**

해설 문장의 주어가 '봄 상품 라인'이므로 주어를 고려하면 '발표되었다, 출시되었다'라는 의미가 되어야 가장 적절하다. 따라서 정답은 (D).

어휘 line (상품의) 종류   leather 가죽   runway (패션쇼장의) 무대

112. 미래진행시제

자원봉사자들은 모금 행사를 준비하기 위해 다음 주 토요일 오전 11시에 건물 로비에 모일 것이다.

해설 선택지가 모두 동사인 것을 보아 동사의 시제를 묻는 문제임을 알 수 있다. 알맞은 시제를 찾기 위한 단서로 시간을 나타내는 부사구 next Saturday에 주목해야 한다. 미래의 일을 말해야 하므로 미래시제인 (C)와 (D)가 정답 후보. 전치사 at으로 '다음 주 토요일 오전 11시'라는 미래 시점에 일어날 일에 대해 이야기하고 있으므로 정답은 미래진행시제인 (C). 미래완료진행시제는 기간을 나타내는 시간 표현과 함께 쓰이므로 (D)는 오답.

어휘 volunteer 자원봉사자   gather 모이다   fundraising 모금

Questions 98-100 refer to the following introduction and list.

Good afternoon, everyone. ⁹⁸My name is Fannie Willis, and I'm the head of the quality control team here at Nexxon Manufacturing. ⁹⁹I'll be giving you a tour of our facilities so that you understand our production process before making an investment in our company. We make a wide range of furniture using various materials, and you will see each type today. ¹⁰⁰We'll spend about twenty minutes in each section except for where we're producing metal items. That area is very hot, so we'll only stay there for ten minutes. Please wear your safety gear at all times, and feel free to ask questions throughout the tour.

안녕하세요, 여러분. ⁹⁸제 이름은 패니 윌리스이고, 저는 이곳 넥슨 제조사의 품질 관리팀장입니다. ⁹⁹여러분이 저희 회사에 투자하시기 전에 저희 생산 과정을 이해하실 수 있도록, 제가 저희 시설을 견학시켜 드리겠습니다. 저희는 여러 가지 재료를 이용해 다양한 가구를 만드는데, 여러분은 오늘 각각의 종류를 보시게 될 겁니다. ¹⁰⁰금속 제품을 생산하는 곳을 제외하고 우리는 각 구역에 20분 정도 있을 예정입니다. 그 구역은 매우 뜨거우므로, 우리는 그곳에 10분만 머물 겁니다. 항상 안전 장비를 착용하시고, 견학하시는 동안 자유롭게 질문해 주세요.

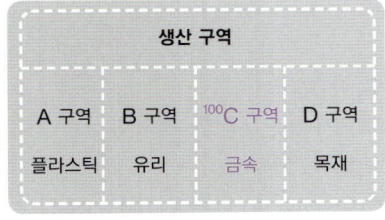

어휘 quality control 품질 관리 production process 생산 과정 make an investment 투자하다 a wide range of 다양한, 광범위한 various 여러 가지의, 다양한 except for ~을 제외하고 produce 생산하다 safety gear 안전 장비 feel free to do 마음대로[거리낌 없이] ~하다 throughout ~ 동안 내내

98. 화자가 담당하는 일은?
(A) 제품 품질 보장하기
(B) 채용 절차 감독하기
(C) 업체 제품 홍보하기
(D) 생산 장비 수리하기

패러프레이징 [단서] quality control → [정답] Assuring the quality of goods

99. 청자들의 신분은?
(A) 안전 검사관들
(B) 신입 사원들
(C) 잠재 투자자들
(D) 부서장들

100. 시각 자료에서, 청자들이 가장 짧은 시간을 보낼 구역은?
(A) A 구역
(B) B 구역
(C) C 구역
(D) D 구역

해설 단서 (100)에서 금속 제품을 생산하는 곳은 10분, 나머지 구역은 20분 동안 머물 거라고 했다. 생산 구역을 나타내는 도표에서 금속을 다루는 구역은 C 구역이므로 정답은 (C).

PART 5

101. 등위접속사 or
귀하께서는 5월 11일 연주회의 입장권을 사전에 또는 입구에서 구입하실 수 있습니다.
(A) ~이니까 (B) 그래서 **(C) 또는** (D) ~도 아닌

해설 선택지를 보니, 문맥에 알맞은 등위접속사를 고르는 문제. 문장을 수식하는 역할의 전치사구가 빈칸 앞뒤에 대등하게 나열되어 있으므로 빈칸에는 '선택'의 의미를 나타내는 등위접속사가 들어가야 한다. 따라서 (C)와 (D)가 정답 후보. 그런데 수식을 받는 문장이 긍정문이므로 정답은 (C). 문장에 not이나 neither와 같은 부정어가 없으므로 (D)는 오답. (A)는 '이유', (B)는 '결과'의 의미를 나타내는 등위접속사로, 문맥상 적절하지 않으므로 오답.

어휘 in advance 사전에, 미리

102. 명사 자리 + 사람명사 vs. 사물/추상명사
자신의 강의에서 브리짓 콜먼 씨는 법정에서 흔히 사용되는 생소한 용어들의 번역을 제공했다.

해설 빈칸은 문장의 목적어 역할을 하면서 빈칸 뒤의 전치사구 of foreign terms의 수식을 받는 명사 자리이므로 명사인 (C)와 (D)가 정답 후보. '생소한 용어들의 번역'이라는 의미가 자연스러우므로 정답은 (D). '번역가'라는 의미의 명사 (C)는 가산명사의 단수형으로 관사 없이 쓰일 수 없고, 또한 문맥에도 맞지 않으므로 오답.

어휘 translation 번역 foreign 생소한, 이질적인 term 용어, 말 commonly 흔히, 일반적으로 court 법정

103. 전치사 by
마고스 전자의 기기들 대부분은 해외에 있는 공장들에 의해 제조된다.
(A) ~에 의해 (B) ~에 대한 (C) ~을 지나서 (D) ~을 따라

Answer **107**

92. 화자가 다음 주에 면접 볼 것 같은 사람은?
(A) 컴퓨터 수리 기사들
(B) 영업 이사들
(C) 그래픽 디자이너들
(D) 실험실 연구원들

패러프레이징 [단서] people for our graphic design team
→ [정답] Graphic designers

93. 화자가 "우리가 예상한 것의 두 배였다"라고 말한 의미는?
(A) 일자리에 많은 지원자가 몰렸다.
(B) 업체의 시장 점유율이 크게 늘어났다.
(C) 후보자가 더 높은 봉급을 요구했다.
(D) 채용 절차가 계획보다 오래 걸렸다.

해설 단서 (93)에서 지원자들이 충분히 많지 않을까 봐 염려했다는 걸 알고 있다고 했으므로, 예상한 것의 두 배였다는 것은 일자리에 지원한 사람들이 예상보다 많았다는 의미임을 알 수 있다. 따라서 정답은 (A).

94. 화자에 따르면, 티머시 씨가 할 일은?
(A) 면접을 위해 회의실 예약하기
(B) 지원자들의 이력서 재검토하기
(C) 팀의 휴가 일정 만들기
(D) 업무 공간을 양보해 줄 자원자들 찾기

패러프레이징 [단서] to give up your desks → [정답] to give up their workspaces

🔊 🎧
Questions 95-97 refer to the following radio broadcast and map.

Good morning. You're listening to *Melville Traffic News*. ⁹⁵The new department store at the intersection of Cane Street and First Avenue is still under construction, making the area particularly dangerous and congested. ⁹⁶Although the project was supposed to be finished last night, the end date has been pushed back another week due to budget issues. The projected end date is now October 12. Until then, we recommend taking a detour on Pearson Road. Despite the disturbance, ⁹⁷the annual arts and crafts market will still be held on Chestnut Street this afternoon. Come check out some amazing items by local artists.

안녕하세요. 여러분께서는 〈멜빌 교통 뉴스〉를 청취하고 계십니다. ⁹⁵케인 가와 퍼스트 로의 교차로에 있는 새 백화점이 아직 건설 중에 있어서, 그 구역을 특히 위험하고 혼잡하게 하고 있습니다. ⁹⁶그 프로젝트는 어젯밤에 완료되기로 되어 있었지만, 예산 문제로 인해 완료일이 일주일 더 미뤄졌습니다. 예상 완료일은 이제 10월 12일입니다. 그때까지는 피어슨 로로 우회하는 것을 추천합니다. 소란스러운 상황에도 불구하고 ⁹⁷매년 열리는 미술 공예 시장은 여전히 오늘 오후에 체스넛 가에서 열릴 예정입니다. 오셔서 지역 예술가들이 만든 멋진 물건들을 확인해 보세요.

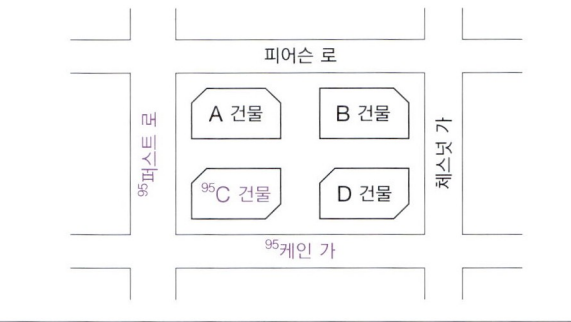

어휘 under construction 건설[공사] 중인 congested 혼잡한, 붐비는 project 프로젝트; 예상하다 be supposed to do ~하기로 되어 있다 push back 미루다 take a detour 우회하다 disturbance 소란, 방해 arts and crafts 미술 공예

95. 시각 자료에서, 건설 중인 건물은?
(A) A 건물
(B) B 건물
(C) C 건물
(D) D 건물

해설 단서 (95)에서 케인 가와 퍼스트 로의 교차로에 있는 백화점이 아직 건설 중이라고 했다. 지도를 나타내는 도표에서 케인 가와 퍼스트 로가 교차하는 지점에 있는 건물은 C 건물이므로 정답은 (C).

96. 건설 프로젝트가 지연된 이유는?
(A) 자재 부족
(B) 자동차 사고
(C) 기상 조건
(D) 재정적 문제

패러프레이징 [단서] budget issues → [정답] Financial problems

97. 오늘 오후에 일어날 일은?
(A) 개업식
(B) 할인 판매 행사
(C) 기념일 파티
(D) 공예가 풍물 장터

패러프레이징 [단서] the annual arts and crafts market
→ [정답] An artisan fair

Questions 89-91 refer to the following talk.

[89]Welcome to F&U Manufacturer. We are excited to start working with you. Before we begin, [90]let's go over some of our general safety guidelines. First, you must wear a hard hat at all times. This includes when you are on break. As long as you are on factory premises, you must not be seen without a hard hat. [91]Please also wear safety glasses when you are doing work, no matter what the task is. We work in close proximity to one another. [91]Even if you're not doing anything threatening to the eyes, the person next to you might be. Finally, although they close automatically, always check that doors are shut properly.

[89]F&U 제조사에 오신 것을 환영합니다. 여러분과 함께 일을 시작하게 되어 기쁩니다. 시작하기 전에, [90]우리의 전반적인 안전 지침 몇 가지를 살펴보겠습니다. 먼저, 여러분은 항상 안전모를 착용해야만 합니다. 이는 여러분이 휴식 중인 때도 포함합니다. 여러분이 공장 부지에 있는 한 여러분은 안전모를 쓰고 있지 않은 모습을 보여서는 안 됩니다. [91]또한 작업을 할 때에는 그 작업이 무엇이든 간에 보안경을 착용하십시오. 우리는 서로 아주 가까운 거리에서 작업을 합니다. [91]여러분이 눈에 위협이 되는 어떤 일도 하지 않고 있다 하더라도 여러분의 옆에 있는 사람은 하고 있을 수도 있습니다. 마지막으로, 문이 자동으로 닫히기는 하지만, 제대로 닫혀 있는지 늘 확인하십시오.

어휘 manufacturer 제조 회사, 제조업자 go over ~을 잘 살펴보다 general 전반적인 safety guideline 안전 지침 hard hat 안전모 premises (항상 복수형) 부지 safety glasses 보안경 task 작업, 일 in close proximity to ~에 아주 근접하여 threatening 위협하는, (나쁜 일이) 닥칠 듯한 automatically 자동으로

89. 청자들의 신분은?
(A) 방문 중인 고객들
(B) 은퇴한 직원들
(C) 지점 관리자들
(D) 새로 온 근로자들

해설 단서 (89)에서 제조사에 온 것을 환영한다면서 청자들과 함께 일하게 되어 기쁘다고 했고, 담화 전반에 걸쳐 공장의 안전 지침들이 언급되고 있다. 따라서 청자들이 새로 온 공장 근로자들임을 유추할 수 있으므로 정답은 (D).

90. 담화의 목적은?
(A) 몇 가지 규칙을 간략히 이야기하기 위해
(B) 휴식 시간을 알리기 위해
(C) 새로운 관리자를 소개하기 위해
(D) 성과를 평가하기 위해

패러프레이징 [단서] go over some of our general safety guidelines → [정답] outline some rules

91. 화자가 "우리는 서로 아주 가까운 거리에서 작업을 합니다"라고 말한 이유는?
(A) 규정의 타당함을 보여 주기 위해
(B) 길 안내를 해 주기 위해
(C) 배치를 설명하기 위해
(D) 존중을 요구하기 위해

해설 화자가 한 말의 이유를 묻는 문제로, 해당 표현의 앞뒤 문맥을 잘 살펴야 한다. 해당 표현 앞뒤의 단서 (91)을 보면 작업 중에 보안경을 착용하라고 하면서, 그 규정의 근거로 청자들이 아니더라도 청자들 옆에 있는 사람이 눈에 위협이 되는 일을 하고 있을 수도 있다고 했다. 따라서 해당 표현은 규정의 근거를 제시하기 위해 한 말임을 알 수 있으므로 정답은 (A).

패러프레이징 [단서] wear safety glasses when you are doing work → [정답] a policy

Questions 92-94 refer to the following excerpt from a meeting.

Next on the agenda, I'd like to let you know that [92]next week I'm going to be interviewing people for our graphic design team. We are not a well-known company, so [93]I know that some of you were concerned that the applicant pool for the job opening wouldn't be large enough. Well, I'm pleased to say that it was twice what we expected. Now, [94]I'll need some of you to give up your desks to allow applicants to do a computer-based exercise as part of the interview. Timothy will be asking you about this, so if you're able to work from a laptop, or if you'll be out of the office next week, please talk to him.

다음 안건으로, [92]제가 다음 주에 우리 그래픽 디자인팀을 위해 사람들을 면접 볼 예정임을 알려 드리고자 합니다. 우리가 잘 알려진 회사가 아니라서 [93]여러분 중 일부는 그 자리에 지원한 사람들이 충분히 많지 않을까 봐 염려했다는 걸 알고 있습니다. 음, 우리가 예상한 것의 두 배였다는 걸 말씀드리게 되어 기쁩니다. 이제, [94]여러분 중 몇 분은 지원자들이 면접의 일환으로 컴퓨터를 이용한 연습 문제를 풀 수 있도록 책상을 양보해 주셔야 합니다. 티머시 씨가 이것에 대해 여러분에게 물어볼 테니, 노트북으로 일하실 수 있거나 다음 주에 사무실에 안 계실 거라면, 그에게 말씀해 주세요.

어휘 agenda 안건 concerned 염려하는 applicant 지원자 pool 이용 가능 인력

점이 매우 성공일 것임을 확신하게 합니다. 그는 오늘 늦게 우리와 합류하여 이곳에서 일들이 어떻게 운영되는지 지켜볼 것입니다. 그는 오후 4시쯤 이곳에 도착할 예정입니다. ⁸⁵지금 그는 새로운 장소의 시설을 방문 중입니다.

어휘 graduate (대학의) 졸업생 culinary art 요리법 specialize in ~을 전공하다 cuisine 요리(법) obtain 획득하다, 얻다 master's 석사 학위(=master's degree) business administration 경영학 combination 결합 corporate 기업의, 법인의 confident 확신하는 run 운영하다 facilities 〈항상 복수형〉 시설

83. 화자에 따르면, 최근에 일어난 일은?
(A) 지점이 개점했다.
(B) 두 회사가 합병했다.
(C) 제품이 출시되었다.
(D) 식당이 메뉴를 변경했다.

패러프레이징 [단서] The second Stella's Kitchen has finally opened its doors → [정답] A branch was opened.

84. 보일 씨가 대학원에서 공부한 것은?
(A) 요리
(B) 경영학
(C) 이탈리아어
(D) 미술

85. 보일 씨가 현재 하고 있는 것은?
(A) 식당 둘러보기
(B) 메뉴판 디자인하기
(C) 음식 주문하기
(D) 강좌 참석하기

패러프레이징 [단서] visiting the facilities of the new location → [정답] Touring a restaurant

Questions 86-88 refer to the following recorded message.

⁸⁶You have reached Hannon Telecom. Thank you for contacting us. ⁸⁶˙⁸⁷We have received a number of calls regarding slow Internet connections in the past few hours. We are working on fixing the issue and trust that the problem will be resolved soon. Internet speed should be back to normal for all customers by this evening. However, ⁸⁸if you are unable to connect to the Internet at all, please press 0 to explain the issue to the next available customer service representative.

⁸⁶고객님께서는 해넌 텔레콤 사에 연락하셨습니다. 저희에게 연락해 주셔서 감사합니다. ⁸⁶˙⁸⁷지난 몇 시간 동안 저희는 느린 인터넷 접속과 관련해 많은 전화를 받았습니다. 저희는 문제를 바로잡기 위해 애쓰고 있으며 문제가 곧 해결될 것이라고 믿고 있습니다. 모든 고객의 인터넷 속도가 오늘 저녁까지는 다시 정상화될 것입니다. 하지만 ⁸⁸인터넷 접속이 아예 안 되신다면, 0번을 누르셔서 다음으로 연결 가능한 고객 서비스 상담원에게 문제를 설명해 주시기 바랍니다.

어휘 reach 연락하다, 닿다 a number of 많은, 다수의 connection 접속, 연결 fix 바로잡다, 고치다 resolve 해결하다 normal 정상, 보통 connect 접속하다, 연결하다

86. 전화 발신자가 연락한 업체의 종류는?
(A) 통신 서비스 제공업체
(B) 전자 제품 제조사
(C) 웹 디자인 회사
(D) 장치 수리점

해설 단서 (86)에서 업체명에 Telecom이 있고, 인터넷 접속 관련 전화를 많이 받았다는 것으로 보아 통신 서비스 제공업체임을 알 수 있다. 따라서 정답은 (A).

패러프레이징 [단서] Hannon Telecom → [정답] A communications provider

87. 화자가 언급한 문제점은?
(A) 서비스가 느리다.
(B) 기계에 결함이 있다.
(C) 배달이 지연되었다.
(D) 웹사이트가 다운되었다.

패러프레이징 [단서] slow Internet connections → [정답] A service is slow.

88. 전화 발신자들이 0번을 눌러야 하는 이유는?
(A) 요금제를 업그레이드하기 위해
(B) 문제를 알리기 위해
(C) 주문을 취소하기 위해
(D) 환불을 요청하기 위해

패러프레이징 [단서] to explain the issue to the next available customer service representative → [정답] To report an issue

두어야 한다고 했으므로 청자들이 인사 업무를 담당한다는 것을 알 수 있다. 따라서 정답은 (A).

78. 청자들이 화자가 지난주에 보낸 문서에서 찾을 수 있는 것은?
(A) 계약 조건
(B) 혜택 선택 항목
(C) 직원 정보
(D) 자격 요건

패러프레이징 [단서] each person's department and status → [정답] Employee information

79. 청자들이 수요일까지 해야 하는 일은?
(A) 몇몇 업무에 관해 읽기
(B) 입사 지원서 검토하기
(C) 구인 광고하기
(D) 웹사이트 업데이트하기

패러프레이징 [단서] familiarize yourselves with the job descriptions we currently have for each position → [정답] Read about some occupations

🎧
Questions 80-82 refer to the following telephone message.

Hello, ⁸⁰this is Jonas Bolder calling from Valaca Systems regarding the workshop you will be leading next week. We want to make sure everything is ready. ⁸¹I've confirmed with each person that will be attending. The total is fourteen. We've reserved a room equipped with a projector and a whiteboard. If you need anything else, please let us know. ⁸²I was also wondering whether you need a ride from the airport. We'd be happy to call a limo service so that you don't have to worry about finding your way to our office. I look forward to hearing back from you.

여보세요, ⁸⁰저는 발라카 시스템즈 사의 조너스 볼더이며 귀하께서 다음 주에 진행하실 워크숍에 관해 전화를 드립니다. 저희는 모든 것이 준비되었는지 확인하고 싶습니다. ⁸¹저는 참석할 사람들을 각각 확인했습니다. 총 인원은 14명입니다. 저희는 프로젝터와 화이트보드를 갖춘 방을 예약했습니다. 그밖에 필요하신 게 있다면 저희에게 알려 주십시오. ⁸²저는 또한 귀하께서 공항에서 타고오실 것이 필요하신지 궁금합니다. 저희 회사로 오는 길을 찾는 것에 대해 걱정하실 필요가 없도록 저희가 기꺼이 리무진 서비스를 불러 드리겠습니다. 귀하의 답변을 기다리겠습니다.

어휘 regarding ~에 관하여 lead 이끌다, 지도하다 confirm 확인하다 equipped with ~을 갖춘 ride 탈것 limo 리무진(= limousine)

80. 화자가 준비하고 있는 것은?
(A) 행사를 주최하는 것
(B) 대회에 참석하는 것
(C) 새로운 장소로 이사하는 것
(D) 새 장비를 설치하는 것

패러프레이징 [단서] the workshop → [정답] an event

81. 화자가 "총 인원은 14명입니다"라고 말한 이유는?
(A) 지불을 요청하기 위해
(B) 예상되는 참석자 수를 알려 주기 위해
(C) 정책을 설명하기 위해
(D) 강의 수를 알려 주기 위해

해설 화자가 한 말의 이유를 문맥을 통해 찾아내는 문제로 해당 표현의 앞뒤를 주의 깊게 들어야 한다. 해당 표현 바로 앞에 있는 단서 (81) 에서 참석할 사람들 각각을 확인했다고 했으므로, 워크숍에 총 몇 명이 참석할 것으로 예상되는지 확인하여 알려 주려 했음을 알 수 있다. 따라서 정답은 (B).

82. 화자가 해 주겠다고 제안한 것은?
(A) 할인 적용하기
(B) 태우러 갈 차편 준비하기
(C) 회의 연기하기
(D) 길 안내 정보 보내기

패러프레이징 [단서] call a limo service → [정답] Arrange a pickup

🎧
Questions 83-85 refer to the following talk.

Hello, everyone. ⁸³, ⁸⁵The second Stella's Kitchen has finally opened its doors in Chesterfield. Colin Boyle will be the manager at this new restaurant. Mr. Boyle is a graduate of Millaty School of Culinary Arts, where he specialized in Italian cuisine. In addition, ⁸⁴he recently obtained a master's in business administration, and is thus perfect for this job. The combination of his cooking knowledge and corporate know-how makes me confident that the Chesterfield branch will be highly successful. He will be joining us later today to watch how things are run here. He'll be here around 4 P.M. ⁸⁵Right now, he is visiting the facilities of the new location.

안녕하세요, 여러분. ⁸³, ⁸⁵스텔라스 키친 2호점이 마침내 체스터필드에 문을 열었습니다. 콜린 보일 씨가 이 새로운 식당의 지배인이 될 것입니다. 보일 씨는 밀러티 요리 학교의 졸업생으로, 그곳에서 그는 이탈리아 요리를 전공했습니다. 뿐만 아니라 ⁸⁴그는 최근에 경영학 석사 학위를 획득했고, 따라서 이 일에 적임입니다. 그가 겸비한 요리 지식과 기업 관련 노하우는 저로 하여금 체스터필드 지

Questions 74-76 refer to the following telephone message.

Hello. ⁷⁴This is Adam Hayes from Corco Legal Group. We were pleased with your interview last week, and ⁷⁴we'd like to offer you a job as a legal consultant. First, however, I want to make sure you are able to start work on August 15 at the latest. During your interview, you had mentioned that you would prefer to start in September. Unfortunately, because of some urgent cases we have, ⁷⁵the start date is not negotiable. We hope you understand and are still interested in the position despite the tight time frame. ⁷⁶Please call me back and let me know whether you wish to accept our offer.

안녕하세요. ⁷⁴저는 코르코 법률 그룹의 애덤 헤이즈입니다. 저희는 지난주에 있었던 귀하와의 면접이 만족스러웠으며, ⁷⁴귀하께 법률 고문으로서의 자리를 제의하고자 합니다. 하지만 먼저, 저는 귀하께서 늦어도 8월 15일에는 일을 시작하실 수 있는지를 확인하고 싶습니다. 면접 중에 귀하께서는 9월에 일을 시작하고 싶다고 말씀하셨습니다. 유감스럽게도, 저희에게 몇 가지 긴급한 소송들이 있어서 ⁷⁵업무 시작일은 협상이 불가합니다. 귀하께서 이해해 주시길 바라며 빠듯한 기간에도 불구하고 여전히 이 자리에 관심이 있으시길 바랍니다. ⁷⁶저에게 다시 전화를 주셔서 저희의 제의를 받아들일 의향이 있으신지 알려 주십시오.

어휘 legal 법률과 관련된 consultant 컨설턴트, 고문 at the latest 늦어도 urgent 긴급한 case 소송, 사건 negotiable 협상의 여지가 있는 time frame 기간

74. 화자가 근무하는 업체의 종류는?
(A) 보험 회사
(B) 부동산 중개소
(C) 법률 사무소
(D) 회계 사무소

패러프레이징 [단서] Legal Group → [정답] A law firm

75. 화자가 일자리에 관해 언급한 것은?
(A) 급여는 협상될 수 있다.
(B) 소재지가 바뀌었다.
(C) 업무 시작일이 정해져 있다.
(D) 업무에 고급 기술이 필요하다.

패러프레이징 [단서] the start date is not negotiable → [정답] Its start date is fixed.

76. 청자가 하도록 요청받은 일은?
(A) 면접 보러 방문하기
(B) 회신 전화하기
(C) 입사 지원서 제출하기
(D) 일정 변경하기

패러프레이징 [단서] call me back → [정답] Return a phone call

Questions 77-79 refer to the following excerpt from a meeting.

Before we end this meeting, ⁷⁷I'd like to remind you that several part-timers will start working full-time next week. That means that all of the files for those employees must be updated by Friday, including their benefits packages. If you're not sure which package a person qualifies for, ⁷⁸consult the document I sent you last week. It lists each person's department and status. It is important that no mistake is made. Finally, ⁷⁹remember our staff meeting on Wednesday. Several department heads will be attending to give us information about new positions. ⁷⁷,⁷⁹Please familiarize yourselves with the job descriptions we currently have for each position before then.

이 회의를 마치기 전에, ⁷⁷다음 주에 시간제 근무 직원 몇 명이 정규직으로 일을 시작한다는 것을 여러분께 다시 한번 알려 드리고자 합니다. 이는 복지 혜택을 포함한 해당 직원들의 모든 파일이 금요일까지는 업데이트되어야 한다는 것을 의미합니다. 만약 직원이 어떤 혜택을 받을 자격이 되는지 잘 모르겠으면, ⁷⁸제가 지난주에 보내 드린 문서를 참고하세요. 거기에 각 직원의 부서와 직위가 명단으로 나와 있습니다. 어떠한 실수도 발생하지 않는 게 중요합니다. 마지막으로, ⁷⁹수요일에 있을 우리의 직원 회의를 기억하세요. 부서장 몇 명이 참석해서 새로 뽑는 자리들에 대한 정보를 제공할 것입니다. ⁷⁷,⁷⁹그 전에 우리가 현재 가지고 있는 각 자리의 직무 기술서를 익혀 두시기 바랍니다.

어휘 remind 다시 한번 알려 주다, 상기시키다 including ~을 포함하여 benefits package 복지 혜택, 복리 후생 제도 qualify for ~의 자격이 있다 consult 참고하다, 찾아보다 status 지위 familiarize oneself with ~을 익히다, ~에 익숙해지다 job description 직무 기술서

77. 청자들이 일할 것 같은 부서는?
(A) 인사
(B) 마케팅
(C) 회계
(D) 고객 서비스

해설 단서 (77)에서 일부 직원들의 정규직 전환과 관련된 파일 업데이트 업무가 언급되었고, 현재 가지고 있는 각 자리의 직무 기술서를 익혀

68. 남자가 기차를 타는 것보다 차를 빌리는 것을 선호하는 이유는?
(A) 더 저렴하다.
(B) 더 편리하다.
(C) 더 빠르다.
(D) 더 믿을 만하다.

> 패러프레이징 [단서] less of a hassle → [정답] more convenient

69. 시각 자료에서, 여자가 예약할 것 같은 차량은?
(A) 1번 차량
(B) 2번 차량
(C) 3번 차량
(D) 4번 차량

> 해설 단서 (69)에서 남자는 자신이 수동 차량을 운전하지 못하며 7명을 태울 수 있는 차량이 필요하다고 했고, 여자는 그 기준에 맞는 밴이 하나 있다며 그것을 예약하겠다고 했다. 각 대여 차량의 특징을 나타내는 도표에서, 7명 이상을 태울 수 있으면서 수동이 아닌 것은 4번 차량이므로 정답은 (D).

70. 남자가 여자에게 묻는 것은?
(A) 그들이 어디에 주차를 할지
(B) 몇 명이 운전을 할지
(C) 대여료가 얼마가 될지
(D) 그들이 언제 출발해야 하는지

> 패러프레이징 [단서] What's the total price going to be for three days? → [정답] How much the rental will cost

---

PART 4

영 🎧

Questions 71-73 refer to the following excerpt from a meeting.

> ⁷¹I've called this meeting because our newest clothing line is not performing well. Staff at our retail stores reported that customers often grab the dresses off the shelves to try them on but rarely buy them. Many return them, too. The design is visually appealing, but customers complain that the dresses are itchy and too tight in the shoulders. Thus, ⁷²I think we need to concentrate more on making our items pleasant to wear rather than just attractive to look at. To start with, ⁷³here are the fabrics used by some of our competitors. Let's talk about the advantages and disadvantages of each.
>
> ⁷¹우리의 최신 의류 라인이 성과가 좋지 않아 이 회의를 소집했습니다. 우리 소매점의 직원들이 알려 온 바로는 손님들이 자주 선반에서 옷을 꺼내어 입어 보지만 그 옷을 사는 일은 드물다고 합니다. 많은 손님들이 반품도 합니다. 디자인은 눈으로 볼 때 매력적이지만, 손님들은 옷이 피부를 가렵게 하고 어깨 부분이 너무 꽉 조인다고 불평합니다. 따라서 ⁷²저는 우리가 우리 제품들을 단순히 보기에 매력적이기보다는 입었을 때 쾌적하도록 만드는 데 더 집중해야 한다고 생각합니다. 우선, ⁷³여기 우리의 경쟁사들 몇 군데에서 사용되는 옷감이 있습니다. 각각의 강점과 약점에 대해 이야기해 봅시다.

> 어휘 call a meeting 회의를 소집하다 perform 해내다, 공연하다 retail store 소매점 grab 움켜쥐다, 낚아채다 rarely 드물게, 좀처럼 ~않고 visually 시각적으로 appealing 매력적인 itchy 가렵게 하는 concentrate on ~에 집중하다 pleasant 쾌적한 rather than ~보다는 to start with 우선 fabric 옷감, 직물 advantage 강점 (↔disadvantage 약점)

71. 화자가 일하는 업계는?
(A) 연예
(B) 패션
(C) 자동차
(D) 마케팅

> 패러프레이징 [단서] clothing line → [정답] Fashion

72. 화자에 따르면, 회사가 주력해야 하는 것은?
(A) 더 편안한 제품
(B) 더 좋은 고객 서비스
(C) 더 경쟁력 있는 가격
(D) 더 안전한 디자인

> 해설 단서 (72)에서 매력적인 디자인의 옷보다는 쾌적한 착용감의 옷을 만드는 데 더 집중해야 한다고 했으므로 정답은 (A). 담화의 concentrate more on이 문제에서는 focus on으로 패러프레이징되었다.

> 패러프레이징 [단서] pleasant to wear → [정답] comfortable

73. 청자들이 다음에 할 것 같은 일은?
(A) 디자인 보기
(B) 차량 시운전하기
(C) 옷 입어 보기
(D) 직물 살펴보기

> 해설 단서 (73)에서 경쟁사들이 사용하는 옷감을 보면서 각각의 강점과 약점에 대해 이야기해 보자고 했으므로 청자들이 옷에 쓰인 직물들을 살펴볼 것임을 유추할 수 있다. 따라서 정답은 (D).

> 패러프레이징 [단서] talk about the advantages and disadvantages of each / the fabrics used by some of our competitors → [정답] Review / some materials

W Oh! I had no idea. ⁶⁷What a nice surprise!

여 더블라떼 작은 사이즈로 한 잔 주세요. ⁶⁵그리고 페이스트리는 어떤 종류가 있나요?

남 음, ⁶⁶특별 메뉴에 있는 커피를 주문하시면 커피와 함께 무료로 간식을 받으실 수 있어요. 여기 특별 메뉴가 있습니다.

여 맞네요. 그 메뉴에 대해 잊고 있었어요. 어디 봅시다… ⁶⁶그럼 대신에 모카로 특별 메뉴를 주문할게요.

남 네. 3.50달러입니다.

여 ⁶⁷여기가 너무 일찍 문을 닫는 게 아쉬워요.

남 ⁶⁷실은, 저희 영업시간이 바뀌었어요. 저희는 오늘 밤 11시까지 문을 열어요.

여 아! 전혀 몰랐어요. ⁶⁷뜻밖에 반가운 소식이네요!

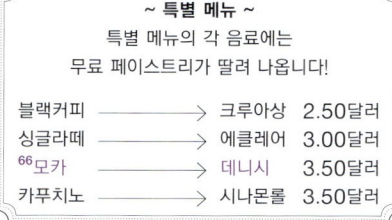

어휘 shame 아쉬운[애석한] 일

65. 여자가 문의한 것은?

(A) 어떤 음식을 먹을 수 있는지
(B) 물품의 가격이 얼마인지
(C) 어떤 커피가 가장 좋은지
(D) 메뉴가 어디에 위치해 있는지

패러프레이징 [단서] what kinds of pastries do you have
→ [정답] What food is available

66. 시각 자료에서, 여자가 받을 페이스트리는?

(A) 크루아상
(B) 에클레어
(C) 데니시
(D) 시나몬롤

해설 단서 (66)에서 남자가 특별 메뉴의 커피를 주문하면 무료로 간식을 받을 수 있다고 했고, 여자는 모카로 특별 메뉴를 주문하겠다고 했다. 음료와 각 음료에 딸려 나오는 무료 페이스트리가 나타나 있는 도표에서, 모카에 딸려 나오는 페이스트리는 데니시이므로 정답은 (C).

67. 여자가 놀란 이유는?

(A) 가격이 인하되었다.
(B) 가게가 늦게 문을 닫는다.
(C) 메뉴에서 선택 가능한 것들이 바뀌었다.

(D) 커피가 진하다.

패러프레이징 [단서] We're open until 11 P.M. tonight.
→ [정답] The shop closes late.

Questions 68-70 refer to the following conversation and list.

W Hey, Ryan. If we're taking the train to the symposium next weekend, we should reserve tickets now.

M I'd rather rent a car. ⁶⁸I know taking the train there sounds cheaper, but getting around while we're there will be less of a hassle if we have a car.

W Okay. As long as you don't mind driving, I'm fine with that. Hold on one second... Um... Okay... I found a list of vehicles.

M Well, ⁶⁹I can't drive manual. And we need a vehicle that can carry seven passengers.

W ⁶⁹There's a van that fits those criteria. I'll reserve it.

M ⁷⁰What's the total price going to be for three days?

여 저기요, 라이언 씨. 다음 주말에 있을 심포지엄에 우리가 기차를 타고 갈 예정이라면, 우리는 지금 표를 예매해야 해요.

남 저는 차라리 차를 빌리고 싶어요. ⁶⁸기차를 타고 그곳에 가는 게 더 저렴할 것 같다는 건 알지만, 우리에게 차가 있다면 그곳에 있는 동안 돌아다니기가 덜 번거로울 거예요.

여 알겠어요. 당신이 운전하는 걸 꺼리지만 않는다면, 저는 그렇게 해도 괜찮아요. 잠시만요… 음… 네… 제가 차량 목록을 찾았어요.

남 음, ⁶⁹저는 수동으로는 운전을 못해요. 그리고 우리는 7명의 승객을 태울 수 있는 차량이 필요해요.

여 ⁶⁹그 기준들에 맞는 밴이 하나 있네요. 제가 그걸 예약할게요.

남 ⁷⁰3일 동안이면 가격이 총 얼마가 되는 거죠?

	최대 승객 수	변속기
1번 차량	5	수동
2번 차량	5	자동
3번 차량	8	수동
⁶⁹4번 차량	8	자동

어휘 symposium 심포지엄, 학술 토론회 get around 돌아다니다 hassle 번거로운[귀찮은] 일 as long as ~하기만[이기만] 하면 drive manual 수동 변속 차량을 운전하다 criterion 기준

61. 남자가 여자에게 하도록 추천한 것은?

(A) 개인 위생 일과 따르기
(B) 의사와 진료 예약 잡기
(C) 단 음료 마시는 것 피하기
(D) 직장에서 휴가 얻기

패러프레이징 [단서] staying away from sugary drinks
→ [정답] Avoid drinking sweet beverages

Questions 62-64 refer to the following conversation and schedule.

M	⁶²Did you read the e-mail Mr. Porter just sent? The company is building another store in Weston.
W	I just saw that. And ⁶³it looks like they're looking for someone to be the manager there. Are you going to go for it?
M	⁶³I'm not sure. It's a great opportunity, but I don't know if I'd enjoy being a manager.
W	I think you should see what the job would be and make a final decision later. They have the interview hours listed here.
M	You're right. Well, ⁶⁴it looks like there's only one time slot I can sign up for since I work Monday through Friday until 4 P.M.

남	⁶²포터 씨가 방금 보낸 이메일을 읽었나요? 회사가 웨스턴에 또 다른 매장을 짓고 있대요.
여	방금 그걸 봤어요. 그리고 ⁶³그들은 그곳에서 관리자를 맡을 사람을 찾고 있는 것 같네요. 당신은 그 자리에 도전해 볼 건가요?
남	⁶³잘 모르겠어요. 정말 좋은 기회이긴 하지만, 제가 관리자 역할을 즐기면서 할 수 있을지 모르겠어요.
여	전 당신이 그 일이 어떨지 알아보고 그 후에 최종 결정을 내려야 한다고 생각해요. 여기에 면접 시간을 목록으로 만들어 놓았네요.
남	당신 말이 맞아요. 음, ⁶⁴제가 월요일부터 금요일까지는 오후 4시까지 근무를 하니 제가 신청할 수 있는 시간대는 하나밖에 없는 걸로 보이네요.

면접 시간

시간대	요일	시간
1	월요일	오후 3:00
2	수요일	오전 10:30
⁶⁴3	수요일	오후 5:00
4	금요일	오후 1:45

어휘 go for ~을 얻으려고 애쓰다[노리다]   opportunity 기회   list 목록을 작성하다, 명단에 기재하다   time slot 시간대

62. 이메일에서 발표된 것은?

(A) 직원이 승진되었다.
(B) 새 지점이 문을 열 것이다.
(C) 기한이 연장되었다.
(D) 회사가 이전할 것이다.

패러프레이징 [단서] The company is building another store in Weston. → [정답] A new branch is opening.

63. 남자가 하기를 망설이고 있는 것은?

(A) 제안 수락하기
(B) 자리에 지원하기
(C) 후보자 선택하기
(D) 관리자에게 이야기하기

패러프레이징 [단서] go for / the manager → [정답] Apply for / a position

64. 시각 자료에서, 남자가 참석할 수 있는 시간대는?

(A) 1번 시간대
(B) 2번 시간대
(C) 3번 시간대
(D) 4번 시간대

해설 가능한 면접 시간대를 나타내는 도표가 주어져 있으므로 요일 및 시간과 관련된 내용이 나올 것임을 예상하며 듣는다. 단서 (64)에서 남자는 자신이 주중에 오후 4시까지 근무를 하므로 신청 가능한 시간대가 하나밖에 없는 것 같다고 했다. 면접 시간을 나타내는 도표에서 오후 4시 이후로 설정되어 있는 시간대는 3번 시간대밖에 없으므로 정답은 (C).

Questions 65-67 refer to the following conversation and menu.

W	I'd like a small double latte, please. ⁶⁵And what kinds of pastries do you have?
M	Well, ⁶⁶if you order a coffee from the special menu, you can get a free snack with it. Here is the special menu.
W	That's right. I forgot about that menu. Let's see… ⁶⁶I'll get a special then, please, with a mocha instead.
M	Okay. That will be $3.50 please.
W	⁶⁷It's a shame you close so early.
M	⁶⁷Actually, we changed our hours. We're open until 11 P.M. tonight.

어휘 sign up for ~에 등록하다, ~을 신청하다 healthcare 건강 관리, 의료 presenter 발표자 send in 제출하다, 내보내다 review 보고서, 논평 relevant 유의미한, 적절한 shut down 문을 닫다

56. 여자가 최근에 한 일은?
(A) 연속 강의에 참석했다
(B) 행사에 등록했다
(C) 조사 연구를 검토했다
(D) 발표를 했다

패러프레이징 [단서] signed up for the Haya Corp. healthcare conference → [정답] Registered for an event

57. 남자가 해야 한다고 여자가 생각한 것은?
(A) 연사 만나기
(B) 기한 연장하기
(C) 연구 제출하기
(D) 주제 고르기

패러프레이징 [단서] send in the study you did last month → [정답] Submit a study

58. 여자가 자신이 작성한 보고서에 대해 암시한 것은?
(A) 최신 정보가 아니다.
(B) 곧 게재될 것이다.
(C) 만드는 데 오랜 시간이 걸렸다.
(D) 학회에서 발표되었다.

해설 단서 (58)에서 여자는 자신이 6개월 전에 작성한 보고서가 더 이상 유의미하지 않다면서, 보고서에 작성된 업체들 중 두 곳이 문을 닫았다고 했다. 이를 통해 보고서가 최신 정보를 담고 있지 않다는 것을 유추할 수 있으므로 정답은 (A).

패러프레이징 [단서] that review is not relevant anymore → [정답] It is outdated.

🇺🇸🇬🇧 🎧
Questions 59-61 refer to the following conversation.

M Hello. [59]Before I start the checkup, do you feel any pain anywhere?

W [59, 60]Sometimes my teeth in the bottom right feel sensitive. But overall, there is no specific problem.

M [60]Do they feel like that all of the time?

W No, not all of the time. Drinking cold water causes it.

M I see. Let me take a look. Um… well, you do have a cavity. It's a small one, but that is probably what is causing the problem. You're going to need a filling.

W Oh. Does that mean I should brush more often?

M Not necessarily. But [61]I recommend staying away from sugary drinks.

남 안녕하세요. [59]검진을 시작하기에 앞서, 어디든 통증이 느껴지는 곳이 있나요?

여 [59, 60]때때로 오른쪽 아래에 있는 치아들이 시려요. 하지만 전반적으로 특별한 문제는 없어요.

남 [60]그 치아들이 항상 그런 느낌이 나요?

여 아니요, 항상 그런 건 아니에요. 찬물을 마시면 그렇게 돼요.

남 그렇군요. 어디 한번 보죠. 음… 손님께 충치가 하나 있긴 하네요. 작은 것이긴 한데, 아마도 그게 문제를 일으키고 있는 것 같습니다. 손님께서는 때우는 작업이 필요하시게 될 거예요.

여 아. 그 말씀은 제가 양치를 더 자주 해야 한다는 뜻인가요?

남 반드시 그런 건 아니에요. 하지만 [61]설탕이 든 음료를 멀리하시는 걸 추천해요.

어휘 checkup 건강 진단, 검사 sensitive 민감한 overall 전반적으로; 전체의 specific 특별한, 구체적인 cavity 충치(의 구멍) filling (치과의) 충전재 necessarily 반드시, 필연적으로 stay away from ~을 멀리하다 sugary 설탕이 든

59. 남자의 신분은?
(A) 비서
(B) 치과 의사
(C) 배관공
(D) 영양사

해설 단서 (59)에서 checkup과 pain이 언급되었고, 여자가 겪고 있는 치아 문제에 관한 대화가 이어지는 것으로 보아 남자의 직업이 치과 의사임을 알 수 있다. 따라서 정답은 (B).

60. 여자가 "찬물을 마시면 그렇게 돼요"라고 말한 이유는?
(A) 가능한 치료법을 제안하기 위해
(B) 건강한 습관을 설명하기 위해
(C) 자신의 식습관에 대해 상세히 설명하기 위해
(D) 문제가 언제 발생하는지 설명하기 위해

해설 여자가 한 말의 이유를 문맥을 통해 찾아내는 문제로 해당 표현의 앞뒤를 주의 깊게 들어야 한다. 해당 표현의 앞에 있는 단서 (60)에서 여자가 가끔 치아가 시리다고 하자 남자는 항상 그 증상이 느껴지냐고 물었다. 해당 표현은 이에 대한 여자의 응답이므로 치아 문제가 어떤 경우에 발생하는지 설명하기 위해 한 말임을 알 수 있다. 따라서 정답은 (D).

패러프레이징 [단서] my teeth in the bottom right feel sensitive → [정답] a problem

호 미 🎧
Questions 53-55 refer to the following conversation.

> M ⁵³Jeremy Billings has agreed to come to our bookstore on August 8. He will be signing copies of his bestseller, *The Confession*.
>
> W Oh, that's great news. I think it will be a big event. It's a really popular book these days.
>
> M Yes. I expect a lot of people will come. So we need to prepare the space to make it an ideal venue for a large crowd.
>
> W Right. There will be a long line. Perhaps ⁵⁴we can rearrange the shelves in the children's section to make some room for people to line up.
>
> M Good idea. ⁵⁵I'll start working on designing a flyer to publicize the event.
>
> 남 ⁵³제레미 빌링스 씨가 8월 8일에 우리 서점에 오는 것에 합의했어요. 그는 자신의 베스트셀러인 〈고백〉 책에 사인을 할 거예요.
>
> 여 아, 그거 아주 좋은 소식이네요. 제 생각에 그건 큰 행사가 될 거예요. 그건 요즘 정말 인기 있는 책이잖아요.
>
> 남 네. 전 많은 사람이 올 것으로 예상하고 있어요. 그래서 우리는 공간을 준비해서 그곳이 많은 사람을 받기에 이상적인 장소가 되도록 만들어야 해요.
>
> 여 맞아요. 긴 줄이 생길 거예요. 어쩌면 ⁵⁴우리가 아동 코너의 책장들을 다시 배치해서 사람들이 줄을 설 공간을 좀 만들 수도 있겠네요.
>
> 남 좋은 생각이에요. ⁵⁵저는 그 행사를 홍보할 전단의 디자인 작업을 시작할게요.

어휘 ideal 이상적인 crowd 사람들, 군중 perhaps 어쩌면, 아마 rearrange 재배치하다 line up 줄을 서다 publicize 홍보[광고]하다, 알리다

53. 8월 8일에 일어날 일은?
(A) 업체가 이전할 것이다.
(B) 작가를 인터뷰할 것이다.
(C) 계약이 체결될 것이다.
(D) 책 사인회가 열릴 것이다.

패러프레이징 [단서] He will be signing copies of his bestseller, *The Confession*. → [정답] A book signing will be held.

54. 여자가 하기를 제안한 것은?
(A) 물품들을 치우는 것

(B) 행사에 등록하는 것
(C) 줄을 서서 기다리는 것
(D) 가구를 옮기는 것

패러프레이징 [단서] rearrange the shelves → [정답] Moving some furniture

55. 남자가 하겠다고 말한 일은?
(A) 광고 준비하기
(B) 입장권 예매하기
(C) 개요 작성하기
(D) 장소 방문하기

패러프레이징 [단서] working on designing a flyer to publicize the event → [정답] Prepare an advertisement

미 미 🎧
Questions 56-58 refer to the following conversation.

> W Hi, Michael. ⁵⁶I've just signed up for the Haya Corp. healthcare conference. Are you going?
>
> M Yes, I plan on going. It will be an interesting conference.
>
> W Actually, I heard they're looking for more presenters. ⁵⁷You should send in the study you did last month. People would be interested in hearing about it.
>
> M Um … Maybe I will. I'm not sure I have time, though. I've got a deadline coming up. What about the review you did on healthcare companies? That could be an interesting topic.
>
> W I'm afraid ⁵⁸that review is not relevant anymore. I did it six months ago, and two of the companies I wrote about have shut down since then.
>
> 여 안녕하세요, 마이클 씨. ⁵⁶저는 하야 사의 건강 관리 학회에 막 등록했어요. 당신도 가세요?
>
> 남 네, 갈 계획이에요. 흥미로운 학회가 될 거예요.
>
> 여 실은, 그들이 발표자들을 더 구하고 있다고 들었어요. ⁵⁷당신이 지난달에 한 연구를 제출해 보세요. 사람들은 그것에 대해 듣는 데 관심이 있을 거예요.
>
> 남 음… 어쩌면 제출할지도요. 그렇지만 제가 시간이 있는지는 잘 모르겠네요. 다가오는 마감 일자가 있어서요. 당신이 건강 관리 업체들에 대해 작성한 보고서는 어때요? 흥미로운 주제가 될 수 있을 텐데요.
>
> 여 유감스럽게도 ⁵⁸그 보고서는 더 이상 유의미하지 않아요. 저는 6개월 전에 그걸 작업했는데, 제가 작성한 업체들 중 두 곳이 그 이후에 문을 닫았어요.

어휘 carton 종이 용기, 판지 상자 font 서체 silly 우스꽝스러운, 유치한 obviously 분명히 appeal to ~의 관심을 끌다 target 목표의; 목표 demographic (상품의) 고객층, 구매층 go too far 도를 넘다 ultimately 결국, 궁극적으로 make a decision 결정을 내리다

47. 화자들이 주로 이야기하고 있는 것은?
(A) 기사 내용
(B) 강좌 난이도
(C) 제품 포장
(D) 음료 가격

패러프레이징 [단서] the new juice cartons → [정답] A product's packaging

48. 남자가 "그들은 약간 도를 넘었어요"라고 말한 이유는?
(A) 디자인이 유치하다고 생각한다.
(B) 제품이 비싸다고 생각한다.
(C) 지사를 이전시키고 싶어 한다.
(D) 정책에 동의하지 않는다.

해설 남자가 한 말의 이유를 문맥을 통해 찾아내는 문제로 해당 표현의 앞뒤를 주의 깊게 들어야 한다. 해당 표현 앞에 있는 단서 (48)에서 여자는 디자이너들이 분명 아이들의 관심을 끌려고 했던 것 같다고 했고 남자는 아이들이 그들의 목표 고객층이라고 했다. 그럼에도 불구하고 디자이너들이 약간 도를 넘었다고 한 것은 남자가 디자인이 지나치게 유치하다고 생각하고 있음을 의미하므로 정답은 (A).

49. 여자가 하겠다고 말한 일은?
(A) 물품 반납하기
(B) 선택된 것 전하기
(C) 광고 만들기
(D) 고객들에게 연락하기

패러프레이징 [단서] tell the designers we'd like the first design with a different font → [정답] Report a choice

미 영 🎧
Questions 50-52 refer to the following conversation.

M Hey, ⁵⁰I heard you're transferring to another department. Is that true? Where are you going?

W Yeah. ⁵⁰I'm going to be working in customer service. ⁵¹I'm looking forward to interacting with our customers face-to-face.

M Really? To me, that sounds so stressful. I prefer working in the back. I would hate to listen to complaints all day.

W Well, it's not all complaints. You get some positive feedback as well. But to be honest, I am a little bit nervous.

M Oh, ⁵²you should talk to Marty. He's worked in customer service for years. ⁵²I'm sure he'll have some great tips.

남 저기, ⁵⁰당신이 다른 부서로 이동한다고 들었어요. 그게 진짜예요? 어디로 가시는데요?

여 네. ⁵⁰저는 고객 서비스팀에서 일할 거예요. ⁵¹저는 우리 고객들과 대면하여 소통하기를 고대하고 있어요.

남 정말요? 저한테는, 그게 굉장히 스트레스가 많을 것 같아요. 전 뒤쪽에서 일하는 게 더 좋거든요. 온종일 항의를 듣는 건 싫을 것 같네요.

여 음, 그게 다 항의인 건 아니에요. 긍정적인 의견 역시 받거든요. 하지만 솔직히 말해서, 전 약간 긴장이 돼요.

남 아, ⁵²마티 씨와 이야기해 보세요. 그는 수년간 고객 서비스팀에서 일해 왔거든요. ⁵²그가 분명 좋은 조언을 해 줄 거예요.

어휘 transfer 이동하다, 옮기다 look forward to doing ~하기를 고대[기대]하다 interact 소통하다, 상호 작용하다 face-to-face 대면하여, 정면으로 맞서서 stressful 스트레스가 많은 complaint 항의, 불평 positive 긍정적인 to be honest 솔직히 말하면 nervous 긴장되는, 불안해하는

50. 화자들이 주로 이야기하고 있는 것은?
(A) 새로운 공석
(B) 직무 변경
(C) 고객 항의
(D) 사무실 배치

패러프레이징 [단서] transferring to another department → [정답] A job change

51. 여자가 고대하고 있다고 말한 것은?
(A) 사람들과 직접 이야기하는 것
(B) 남자와 함께 일하는 것
(C) 논평을 읽는 것
(D) 새로운 회사에 들어가는 것

패러프레이징 [단서] interacting with our customers face-to-face → [정답] Talking to people directly

52. 남자가 여자에게 하도록 제안한 것은?
(A) 항의 제기하기
(B) 동료와 상담하기
(C) 다른 일자리 찾기
(D) 조언해 주기

패러프레이징 [단서] talk to Marty → [정답] Consult a coworker

W	Oh, really? I should read the reviews.
M1	Yes, you should. ⁴⁵I think Gulliver Travel is worth the extra money. Anyway, I'm guessing we have a lot of work to do.
W	We do. ⁴⁶While you were away, Fiona quit. So we have to cover for her.
M2	That's a surprise. I hope we find a replacement soon.

여 안녕하세요, 찰스 씨, 월터 씨. 유람선 여행은 어땠어요?
남1 굉장했어요. 저는 걸리버 여행사의 유람선 여행을 정말로 추천해요.
여 ⁴⁴,⁴⁵제가 실은 블루 그린 여행사를 통해서 유람선 여행을 가는 것에 대해 생각 중이거든요. 아시다시피, 우리는 이 회사에 근무하기 때문에 그곳에서 할인을 받잖아요.
남2 알아요. 하지만 블루 그린 사의 고객 서비스는 평판이 형편없어요. ⁴⁵그래서 저희가 그 대신 걸리버 여행사를 통해 간 거예요. 저희는 차라리 돈을 더 내고 형편없는 서비스를 상대하지 않으면 좋겠다 싶었어요.
여 아, 정말요? 후기들을 읽어봐야겠네요.
남1 네, 그러셔야 해요. ⁴⁵저는 걸리버 여행사가 추가 금액을 낼 만한 가치가 있다고 생각해요. 그건 그렇고, 우리는 해야 할 일이 많은 것 같네요.
여 그래요. ⁴⁶여러분이 없는 동안 피오나 씨가 그만뒀거든요. 그래서 우리가 그녀의 일을 대신 처리해야 해요.
남2 그거 뜻밖이네요. 우리가 빨리 후임자를 찾으면 좋겠어요.

어휘 cruise 유람선 여행 terrible 형편없는, 끔찍한 reputation 평판 would rather (차라리) ~하고 싶다 deal with ~을 상대하다[처리하다] worth ~의 가치가 있는 quit 그만두다 cover for ~의 일을 대신 처리하다 replacement 후임자, 대체

44. 여자가 할 계획이라고 말한 것은?
(A) 유람선 여행 가기
(B) 부정적인 후기 작성하기
(C) 초과 근무하기
(D) 본인의 자리에서 사임하기

45. 남자들이 걸리버 여행사에 대해 암시한 것은?
(A) 고객 서비스가 형편없다.
(B) 자사 직원들에게 할인을 제공한다.
(C) 시중에서 가장 저렴한 유람선 여행 상품이 있다.
(D) 블루 그린 여행사보다 더 비싸다.

해설 단서 (45)에서 여자가 블루 그린 여행사를 통해서 여행을 가는 것에 대해 생각 중이라고 하자, 남자들은 자신들이 돈을 더 내고 걸리버 여행사를 통해 여행을 갔으며 그곳이 추가 금액을 낼 가치가 있다고 했다. 이를 통해 걸리버 여행사가 블루 그린 여행사보다 더 비싸다는 것을 유추할 수 있으므로 정답은 (D).

46. 여자에 따르면, 남자들이 없는 동안 회사에서 일어난 일은?
(A) 동료가 직장을 그만뒀다.
(B) 고객이 항의를 제기했다.
(C) 새로운 사람이 고용되었다.
(D) 설문 조사가 실시되었다.

패러프레이징 [단서] Fiona quit → [정답] A coworker left her job.

Questions 47-49 refer to the following conversation.

W	Hi, Danny. I wanted to show you these. ⁴⁷They are two possible designs for the new juice cartons. What do you think?
M	I like the first one because it has nice colors. But... Um... The font is strange. It's too large, and it looks a bit silly.
W	I agree. ⁴⁸I think the designers obviously wanted to appeal to children.
M	Well, ⁴⁸that is our target demographic. But they went a little too far.
W	Right. Even if we are selling to kids, the parents are the ones ultimately making the purchase decision. ⁴⁹So I'll tell the designers we'd like the first design with a different font.

여 안녕하세요, 대니 씨. 당신에게 이것들을 보여 드리고 싶었어요. ⁴⁷이것들은 새 주스 종이 용기에 쓸 수 있는 두 가지 디자인이에요. 어떻게 생각하세요?
남 저는 첫 번째 디자인이 색상이 멋져서 마음에 들어요. 그런데… 서체가 이상하네요. 너무 크고, 조금 우스꽝스러워 보여요.
여 동의해요. ⁴⁸제 생각에는 디자이너들이 분명 아이들의 관심을 끌고 싶어 했던 것 같아요.
남 음, ⁴⁸그게 우리가 목표로 하는 고객층이니까요. 하지만 그들은 약간 도를 넘었어요.
여 맞아요. 우리가 아이들에게 판매하는 거라고 하더라도, 결국에 구매 결정을 내리는 사람들은 부모들이니까요. ⁴⁹그럼 제가 디자이너들에게 우리가 다른 서체로 된 첫 번째 디자인을 원한다고 말할게요.

39. 처음 온 고객들이 받게 되는 것은?
(A) 할인
(B) 무료 물품
(C) 상품권
(D) 회원증

해설 단서 (39)에서 남자가 염색 가격이 70달러라고 하자 여자가 새로 온 손님들은 첫 염색에 40달러만 지불하면 된다고 했다. 즉 이곳을 처음 방문한 고객들은 염색 서비스에서 30달러 할인을 받을 수 있음을 유추할 수 있으므로 정답은 (A). 대화의 Newcomers가 문제에서는 first-time customers로 패러프레이징되었다.

40. 남자가 다음에 할 것 같은 일은?
(A) 구매하기
(B) 머리 감기기
(C) 색상 선택하기
(D) 환불해 주기

패러프레이징 [단서] start your shampoo → [정답] Wash some hair

미 미 🎧
Questions 41-43 refer to the following conversation.

> **M** Hello. I recently purchased an item from your Parson branch, and ⁴¹I'd like to talk about an issue I have with your policy.
> **W** Yes, sir. What is the problem?
> **M** ⁴²I bought a lawn mower. But when I got home, it wouldn't start.
> **W** I'm sorry to hear that. Did you try to return it?
> **M** Of course. However, the manager told me I could not return it because it was on sale when I bought it.
> **W** They must have misunderstood our policy. We accept returns for defective items, even if they were on sale. I'm very sorry about this, sir. ⁴³I will contact the Parson branch manager immediately. Someone will call you back shortly.

남 여보세요. 제가 최근에 귀사의 파슨 지점에서 물건을 하나 구매했는데, ⁴¹귀사의 방침과 관련해 제가 겪고 있는 문제에 대해 이야기하고 싶어서요.
여 네, 고객님. 무엇이 문제인가요?
남 ⁴²저는 잔디 깎는 기계를 샀어요. 그런데 집에 와 보니, 그게 시동이 걸리지 않더라고요.
여 그랬다니 유감이네요. 그걸 반품하려고 하셨나요?
남 물론이죠. 하지만 제가 그걸 샀을 당시에 그게 할인 판매 중이었기 때문에 그걸 반품할 수 없다고 지점장이 말했어요.

여 그들이 저희의 방침을 잘못 이해한 게 틀림없어요. 저희는 물건이 할인 판매 중이었다고 해도, 결함이 있는 물건에 대해서는 반품을 받습니다. 이 일에 대해 정말로 죄송합니다, 고객님. ⁴³제가 즉시 파슨 지점의 지점장에게 연락하겠습니다. 누군가가 곧 고객님께 다시 전화를 드릴 거예요.

어휘 issue 문제, 사안 lawn mower 잔디 깎는 기계 misunderstand 오해하다 accept 받아들이다, 받다 defective 결함이 있는 contact 연락하다 immediately 즉시 shortly 곧, 얼마 안 되어

41. 남자가 전화를 건 이유는?
(A) 규정에 대해 항의하기 위해
(B) 주문을 하기 위해
(C) 서비스를 설명하기 위해
(D) 가격에 대해 묻기 위해

패러프레이징 [단서] to talk about an issue I have with your policy → [정답] To complain about a rule

42. 남자가 잔디 깎는 기계에 대해 언급한 문제점은?
(A) 제때 배달되지 않았다.
(B) 제대로 작동하지 않는다.
(C) 잘못된 모델이다.
(D) 가격이 잘못 매겨졌다.

패러프레이징 [단서] it wouldn't start → [정답] It doesn't work properly.

43. 여자가 하겠다고 말한 것은?
(A) 관리자에게 연락하기
(B) 환불해 주기
(C) 할인 판매 행사 준비하기
(D) 장치 수리하기

미 호 미 🎧
Questions 44-46 refer to the following conversation with three speakers.

> **W** Hi, Charles and Walter. How was the cruise?
> **M1** It was amazing. I really recommend Gulliver Travel's cruises.
> **W** ⁴⁴,⁴⁵I'm actually thinking about going on one with Blue Green Travel. You know, we get a discount with them for working at this company.
> **M2** I know, but Blue Green's customer service has a terrible reputation. ⁴⁵So we went with Gulliver Travel instead. We'd rather pay more and not deal with bad service.

M That's fine. I have thought about your offer, and ³⁷I just want to discuss a few details in your proposal so we can reach an agreement. Tuesday at 10 A.M. is the best time for me.

남 안녕하세요, 루니 씨. 저는 베카 산업의 제이슨 트래퍼입니다. ³⁵몇 주 전에 저희 두 회사의 합병 제안에 관해 제 비서와 통화하셨죠. 혹시 저희가 직접 만나서 이것에 관해 이야기를 나눌 수 있을까 해서요.

여 안녕하세요, 트래퍼 씨. 그거 좋은 생각인 것 같네요. 유감스럽게도, ³⁶제가 이번 주는 내내 협의회에 와 있어요. 하지만 다음 주에는 어느 요일이든 시간을 낼 수 있습니다.

남 좋습니다. 당신의 제안에 대해 생각해 봤는데, ³⁷우리가 합의에 도달할 수 있도록 당신의 제안에서 몇 가지 세부 사항들을 좀 논의하고 싶어서요. 저는 화요일 오전 10시가 가장 좋습니다.

어휘 assistant 비서, 조수   a couple of 몇 개의, 두서너 개의   proposal 제안   wonder ~할까 생각하다, 궁금하다   in person 직접   unfortunately 유감스럽게도   convention 협의회, 대회   make time 시간을 내다   offer 제안, 제의   detail 세부 사항   reach an agreement 합의에 도달하다

35. 남자의 신분은?
(A) 관리자의 비서
(B) 보조금 신청자
(C) 회사의 임원
(D) 협의회의 기조 연설자

해설 단서 (35)에서 남자는 여자가 두 회사의 합병 제안에 관해 남자의 비서와 통화를 했다고 했고, 이것에 대해 직접 만나 이야기를 나누고 싶다고 했다. 합병에 대한 논의를 직접 하려는 것으로 보아 남자가 회사의 중책을 맡은 임원임을 유추할 수 있으므로 정답은 (C).

36. 여자가 이번 주에 할 일은?
(A) 제안서 작성하기
(B) 협의회 참석하기
(C) 후보자들 면접하기
(D) 새로운 회사에서 교육받기

패러프레이징 [단서] I am at a convention → [정답] Attending a conference

37. 남자가 여자를 만나고 싶어 하는 이유는?
(A) 거래를 협상하기 위해
(B) 발표를 준비하기 위해
(C) 취업 기회를 논의하기 위해
(D) 동료를 소개하기 위해

패러프레이징 [단서] to discuss a few details in your proposal so we can reach an agreement → [정답] To negotiate a deal

미 영 호

Questions 38-40 refer to the following conversation with three speakers.

W1 Hello. ³⁸I'd like a haircut. I'm also thinking about dyeing my hair, but I'm not sure.

W2 Okay. Well, how about taking a look at our colors? Jack! Can you bring the color catalog over, please?

M Here it is. Our most popular color right now for your hair type is this strawberry blond.

W1 That is a nice color. How much does dyeing cost?

M ³⁹It would be $70.

W2 Not for her. It's your first time here, right? ³⁹Newcomers pay only $40 for their first dyeing.

W1 Oh, that's a really good price! Let's do it!

M Great! ⁴⁰If you come over here, I'll start your shampoo.

여1 안녕하세요. ³⁸저는 머리를 자르고 싶어요. 머리를 염색하는 것에 대해서도 생각 중인데, 확실하지는 않네요.

여2 알겠습니다. 음, 저희 색상들을 한번 보시는 게 어떠세요? 잭! 색상 카탈로그를 가져와 주시겠어요?

남 여기 있어요. 고객님의 모발 종류에 맞는 저희의 현재 가장 인기 있는 색은 이 붉은색이 도는 금발이에요.

여1 그거 멋진 색이네요. 염색은 비용이 얼마나 드나요?

남 ³⁹70달러가 되겠습니다.

여2 그분은 아니에요. 여기 오신 게 이번이 처음이죠, 그렇죠? ³⁹새로 오신 분들은 첫 염색에 40달러만 지불하시면 됩니다.

여1 아, 그거 정말 괜찮은 가격이네요! 그렇게 하죠!

남 좋습니다! ⁴⁰이쪽으로 오시면 샴푸를 시작해 드리겠습니다.

어휘 haircut 이발   dye 염색하다   take a look at ~을 보다   newcomer 새로 온 사람   shampoo 샴푸 하기, 머리 감기

38. 화자들이 있을 것 같은 곳은?
(A) 의류 매장
(B) 식료품점
(C) 미용실
(D) 페인트 소매점

로 다른 의미와 품사를 지닌 다의어 process를 이용한 오답.

어휘 be in charge of ~을 담당하다   hire 고용하다

31. 미영 🎧

> Did the tenant renew his lease?
> (A) Because the rent is too high.
> (B) It's due on the fifth of each month.
> **(C) He hasn't decided yet.**

세입자가 임대차 계약을 갱신했나요?
(A) 임대료가 너무 높아서요.
(B) 매달 5일에 지불해야 해요.
(C) 그는 아직 결정하지 않았어요.

해설 세입자가 임대차 계약을 갱신했는지 묻는 질문에 아직 결정하지 않았다며 갱신하지 않았다고 우회적으로 답한 (C)가 정답.

어휘 tenant 세입자   renew 갱신[연장]하다   lease 임대차 계약   rent 임대료   due (돈을) 지불해야 하는

PART 3

영 미 🎧

Questions 32-34 refer to the following conversation.

> W Hello, this is Dr. Martha Collins. ³²I'm a history professor, and I would like to bring two of my classes to your museum next month.
>
> M Hello, Dr. Collins. We would be happy to welcome you and your students. ³³Which day would you like to visit?
>
> W A Wednesday or Friday morning would be best for us.
>
> M Fridays are usually quite busy. However, if you come on a Wednesday, we can let you in some of the rooms that are normally closed to the public. So how about Wednesday, May 4?
>
> W That sounds good. ³⁴I'll call again next week to let you know exactly how many we will be.

여 여보세요, 저는 마사 콜린스 박사입니다. ³²저는 역사학 교수인데, 다음 달에 귀하의 박물관에 제가 맡은 수업 두 개의 학생들을 데려가고 싶습니다.

남 안녕하세요, 콜린스 박사님. 저희는 박사님과 박사님의 학생들을 기꺼이 환영합니다. ³³무슨 요일에 방문하길 원하세요?

여 저희는 수요일이나 금요일 오전이 가장 좋을 것 같습니다.

남 금요일은 대개 꽤 붐빕니다. 하지만 수요일에 오신다면, 보통은 일반인들에게 개방되지 않는 방들 중 일부에 들어가게 해드릴 수 있어요. 그러니 5월 4일 수요일이 어떠신가요?

여 그게 좋겠네요. ³⁴제가 다음 주에 다시 전화해서 저희가 정확히 몇 명이나 될지 알려 드릴게요.

어휘 let in ~을 들어오게 하다   normally 보통은, 일반적으로   the public 일반 사람들, 대중   exactly 정확히

32. 여자가 일할 것 같은 곳은?
(A) 병원
(B) 대학교
(C) 박물관
(D) 식당

33. 남자가 문의한 것은?
(A) 서비스에 비용이 얼마나 드는지
(B) 어떤 수업들을 가르치고 있는지
(C) 무슨 요일이 편한지
(D) 장소가 얼마나 붐비는지

34. 여자가 다음 주에 제공할 정보는?
(A) 업체 운영 시간
(B) 자세한 일정
(C) 강의 주제
(D) 방문객 수

해설 여자가 다음 주에 제공할 정보를 묻고 있으므로 next week가 언급되는 부분을 주의해서 듣는다. 단서 (34)에서 다음 주에 다시 박물관에 전화해서 박물관을 방문할 정확한 인원을 알려 주겠다고 했으므로 정답은 (D).

패러프레이징 [단서] exactly how many we will be → [정답] The number of visitors

---

미 미 🎧

Questions 35-37 refer to the following conversation.

> M Hello, Ms. Rooney. This is Jason Trapper from Becca Industries. ³⁵You spoke to my assistant a couple of weeks ago about a proposal for the merger of our two companies. I was wondering if we could meet in person to talk about it.
>
> W Hello, Mr. Trapper. I think that's a good idea. Unfortunately, ³⁶I am at a convention all of this week. However, I can make time any day next week.

25. 미 호 🎧

Have you reserved the venue for Mr. Allen's retirement party?
(A) The new restaurant that opened last week.
(B) I'm still searching for a place.
(C) He's retiring at the end of May.

앨런 씨의 퇴직 기념 파티를 위한 장소를 예약하셨나요?
(A) 지난주에 개업한 새로운 식당이요.
(B) 저는 아직 장소를 찾고 있어요.
(C) 그는 5월 말에 퇴직할 거예요.

해설 파티를 위한 장소를 예약했는지 묻는 질문에 아직 장소를 찾고 있다며 예약하지 않았다고 우회적으로 답한 (B)가 정답. (C)는 retirement와 retire의 파생어를 이용한 오답.

어휘 reserve 예약하다 retirement 퇴직, 은퇴 search for ~을 찾다 retire 퇴직하다, 은퇴하다

26. 미 미 🎧

When does the conference end?
(A) I haven't seen the schedule.
(B) Why don't you come with me?
(C) It's at Carlton Center.

학회가 언제 끝나나요?
(A) 저는 일정표를 보지 못했어요.
(B) 저와 함께 가는 게 어때요?
(C) 그건 칼턴 센터에서요.

해설 학회가 언제 끝나는지 묻는 질문에 일정표를 보지 못했다며 모른다고 우회적으로 답한 (A)가 정답. (B)와 (C)는 학회가 어디서 열리는지 묻는 질문에 적절한 답변이므로 오답.

어휘 conference 학회, 회의

27. 영 미 🎧

I can't refill this prescription without a doctor's note, can I?
(A) She works at Lakewood Hospital.
(B) Sorry, it's against our policy.
(C) I hope you feel better soon.

저는 의사의 확인증 없이는 이 약을 다시 조제할 수 없지요, 그렇죠?
(A) 그녀는 레이크우드 병원에서 근무해요.
(B) 죄송합니다만, 그건 저희 정책에 위배됩니다.
(C) 빨리 회복되기를 바라요.

해설 의사의 확인증 없이 약을 다시 조제할 수 없다는 말을 확인하는 질문에 죄송하지만 그것은 정책에 위배된다며 조제할 수 없다고 우회적으로 답한 (B)가 정답. (C)는 refill과 발음이 유사한 feel을 이용한 오답.

어휘 (re)fill a prescription 처방전대로 약을 (재)조제하다 note (특정한 목적의) 증서, ~장 policy 정책, 방침

28. 미 미 🎧

Why did the customer return the shirt?
(A) How much does it cost?
(B) Actually, she just exchanged it.
(C) At the counter over there.

그 고객은 셔츠를 왜 반품한 건가요?
(A) 그건 가격이 얼마인가요?
(B) 사실, 그녀는 그걸 교환한 것뿐이에요.
(C) 저쪽에 있는 계산대에서요.

해설 고객이 셔츠를 반품한 이유를 묻는 질문에 사실은 그것을 교환한 거라고 답한 (B)가 정답. (C)는 물건을 어디서 반품할 수 있는지 묻는 질문에 적절한 답변이므로 오답.

어휘 return 반품하다; 반품 cost (값이) ~이다 exchange 교환하다

29. 호 미 🎧

Could you make fifty copies of this flyer?
(A) I was just about to leave.
(B) My flight has been delayed.
(C) Thank you. That should be enough.

이 전단을 50부 복사해 주시겠어요?
(A) 저는 막 나가려던 참이었는데요.
(B) 제 항공편이 지연되었어요.
(C) 고마워요. 그거면 충분할 거예요.

해설 전단을 복사해 달라는 요청에 막 나가려던 참이었다며 해 줄 수 없다고 우회적으로 답한 (A)가 정답. (C)는 fifty copies에서 연상할 수 있는 enough를 이용한 오답.

어휘 make a copy of ~을 복사하다 flyer 전단 be about to do 막 ~하려는 참이다 flight 항공편, 비행

30. 미 호 🎧

Who is in charge of the hiring process?
(A) The payment has been processed.
(B) Interviews start next week.
(C) I thought you were.

누가 채용 절차를 담당하나요?
(A) 결제가 처리되었습니다.
(B) 면접은 다음 주에 시작돼요.
(C) 당신인 줄 알았는데요.

해설 누가 채용 절차를 담당하는지 묻는 질문에 당신인 줄 알았다며 모른다고 우회적으로 답한 (C)가 정답. (A)는 '절차'와 '처리하다'라는 서

19. 미 호

The art museum closes early on Mondays, doesn't it?
(A) It just opened last month.
(B) Tuesday works better for me.
(C) Yes. We should hurry.

그 미술관은 월요일에 문을 일찍 닫죠, 그렇죠?
(A) 그곳은 지난달에 막 개관했어요.
(B) 저에게는 화요일이 더 나아요.
(C) 네. 우리는 서둘러야 해요.

해설 특정 미술관이 월요일에 문을 일찍 닫는다는 말에 동의를 구하는 질문에 Yes라고 하면서 서둘러야 한다고 답한 (C)가 정답.

20. 미 미

How did you get Ms. Brandon's business card?
(A) I met her at a networking event.
(B) Any form of photo ID will be okay.
(C) Turn right at the next intersection.

당신은 브랜든 씨의 명함을 어떻게 얻었나요?
(A) 인맥을 쌓는 행사에서 그녀를 만났어요.
(B) 사진이 부착된 신분증이면 어떤 형태이든 괜찮을 거예요.
(C) 다음 교차로에서 우회전하세요.

해설 브랜든 씨의 명함을 얻게 된 경로를 묻는 질문에 그녀를 어떤 행사에서 만났다고 답한 (A)가 정답. (C)는 How did you get에서 길을 묻는 질문을 연상하여 길 안내로 답한 오답.

어휘 business card 명함 networking 인맥 구축 form 종류, 형태 intersection 교차로

21. 미 영

I'm not sure which color scheme to use for the Web site.
(A) Just click on "log in" in the top right corner.
(B) Didn't you register online?
(C) I personally prefer the blue version.

웹사이트에 어떤 색채 배합을 사용해야 할지 잘 모르겠어요.
(A) 그냥 우측 상단 모서리에 있는 '로그인'을 클릭하세요.
(B) 온라인으로 등록하지 않으셨나요?
(C) 저는 개인적으로 파란색 버전이 더 좋아요.

해설 어떤 색채 배합을 사용해야 할지 잘 모르겠다는 말에 자신은 파란색 버전이 더 좋다고 답한 (C)가 정답. (A)와 (B)는 Web site에서 연상할 수 있는 click on "log in"과 online을 각각 이용한 오답.

어휘 color scheme 색채의 배합 register 등록하다 personally 개인적으로

22. 미 호

Can't you stay a little longer?
(A) The shorter one would be better.
(B) I have a doctor's appointment.
(C) Yes, you can if you want.

조금 더 오래 머무실 수 없나요?
(A) 더 짧은 것이 낫겠네요.
(B) 저는 진료 예약이 있어요.
(C) 네, 원하신다면 그러셔도 돼요.

해설 조금 더 오래 머물라는 제안에 진료 예약이 있다며 더 머무를 수 없다고 우회적으로 답한 (B)가 정답. (C)는 you로 물어본 질문에 I가 아닌 you로 답했으므로 오답.

23. 미 미

Which newspaper do you get your news from?
(A) Your subscription expires on May 20.
(B) A huge company merger.
(C) I usually listen to the radio.

어느 신문으로 뉴스를 받아 보세요?
(A) 당신의 구독은 5월 20일에 만료됩니다.
(B) 거대 기업 합병이요.
(C) 저는 보통 라디오를 들어요.

해설 어느 신문으로 뉴스를 받아 보는지 묻는 질문에 보통은 라디오를 듣는다고 답한 (C)가 정답. (B)는 news에서 연상할 수 있는 merger를 이용한 오답.

어휘 subscription 구독, 구독료 expire 만료되다 merger 합병

24. 영 미

Where will the festival be held?
(A) At Willowbrook Park.
(B) Local artists and musicians will attend.
(C) Sometime next month.

축제가 어디서 열릴 예정인가요?
(A) 윌로우브룩 파크에서요.
(B) 지역 예술가들과 음악가들이 참석할 거예요.
(C) 다음 달 언젠가요.

해설 축제가 열리는 장소를 묻는 질문에 특정 장소로 답한 (A)가 정답.

13. 호 미 🎧

How do I enter the parking garage after hours?
(A) The security director can give you a pass.
(B) Is there a fee to do so?
(C) It has room for three hundred cars.

근무 시간 후에는 어떻게 주차장 건물에 들어가나요?
(A) 보안 책임자가 당신에게 출입증을 줄 수 있어요.
(B) 그렇게 하는 데 요금이 있나요?
(C) 그곳에는 차 300대를 위한 공간이 있어요.

해설 근무 시간 후에 주차장 건물에 들어가는 방법을 묻는 질문에 보안 책임자가 출입증을 줄 수 있다고 답한 (A)가 정답.

어휘 parking garage 주차장 건물 after hours 근무 시간 후에 pass 출입증; 통과하다 fee 요금, 수수료 room 공간, 자리

14. 미 미 🎧

Should we cancel the employee picnic or just postpone it?
(A) Larry will bring food.
(B) To let the entire staff relax.
(C) There's time to do it next week.

직원 야유회를 취소해야 할까요, 아니면 그냥 연기해야 할까요?
(A) 래리 씨가 음식을 가져올 거예요.
(B) 모든 직원이 휴식을 취하게 하려고요.
(C) 다음 주에 그것을 할 시간이 있어요.

해설 직원 야유회를 취소해야 할지 연기해야 할지 묻는 질문에 다음 주에 그것을 할 시간이 있다며 연기하자고 우회적으로 답한 (C)가 정답.

어휘 cancel 취소하다 postpone 연기하다 entire 전체의

15. 미 영 🎧

Our profits increased dramatically last year, didn't they?
(A) I hope they will.
(B) No. They were about the same.
(C) That doesn't sound profitable.

우리 수익이 지난해에 급격히 증가했어요, 그렇죠?
(A) 그들이 그러기를 바라요.
(B) 아니요. 거의 똑같았어요.
(C) 그건 수익성이 있을 것 같지 않네요.

해설 수익이 지난해에 크게 증가했냐는 질문에 No라고 하면서 거의 똑같았다고 답한 (B)가 정답. (A)는 과거의 일을 묻는 질문에 미래의 일을 바란다고 답했으므로 오답.

어휘 profit 수익 increase 증가하다 dramatically 급격하게, 극적으로 profitable 수익성이 있는

16. 미 미 🎧

Are you sure you can pick me up from the airport?
(A) Yeah, I don't have anything to do that day.
(B) I'm landing at 6:55 P.M. in Detroit.
(C) Probably by taxi.

정말로 공항으로 저를 태우러 와 주실 수 있으세요?
(A) 네, 저는 그날 할 일이 아무것도 없어요.
(B) 저는 저녁 6시 55분에 디트로이트에 도착해요.
(C) 아마 택시로요.

해설 확실히 공항으로 태우러 와 줄 수 있는지 묻는 질문에 Yeah라고 하면서 그날 할 일이 아무것도 없다고 답한 (A)가 정답.

어휘 pick up ~를 (차에) 태우러 가다 land 도착하다, 착륙하다 probably 아마

17. 영 호 🎧

Why are there signs all over the building?
(A) They are likely to sign the sales contract.
(B) For the new employees.
(C) The construction work is going smoothly.

왜 건물 곳곳에 표지판들이 있는 거죠?
(A) 그들이 판매 계약서에 서명할 것 같아요.
(B) 신입 사원들을 위해서요.
(C) 공사 작업은 순조롭게 진행되고 있어요.

해설 건물 곳곳에 표지판들이 있는 이유를 묻는 질문에 신입 사원들을 위해서라고 답한 (B)가 정답. (A)는 '표지판'과 '서명하다'라는 서로 다른 의미와 품사를 지닌 다의어 sign을 이용한 오답.

어휘 be likely to do ~할 것 같다 contract 계약(서) construction 공사, 건설 smoothly 순조롭게

18. 미 미 🎧

Didn't the organizers change the program?
(A) No, they decided to keep the original.
(B) Someone on the IT team.
(C) It's a charitable organization.

주최자들이 프로그램을 변경하지 않았나요?
(A) 아니요, 그들은 원래의 것을 유지하기로 결정했어요.
(B) IT팀에 있는 누군가요.
(C) 그건 자선 단체예요.

해설 주최자들의 프로그램 변경 여부를 묻는 질문에 No라고 하면서 원래의 것을 유지하기로 했다고 답한 (A)가 정답. (C)는 organizers와 organization의 파생어를 이용한 오답.

어휘 organizer 주최자, 조직자 original 원본; 원래의 charitable 자선의 organization 단체, 조직

PART 2

7. 미 영 🎧

What's the venue for the concert?
(A) April 2.
(B) March Hall.
(C) A piano recital.

콘서트 장소가 어디인가요?
(A) 4월 2일이요.
(B) 마치 홀이요.
(C) 피아노 연주회요.

해설 콘서트가 열리는 장소를 묻는 질문에 특정 장소로 답한 (B)가 정답.

어휘 venue 장소　recital 연주회, 발표회

8. 호 미 🎧

Should I record the speech?
(A) Twenty-five questions in total.
(B) The recent elections.
(C) Yes, if possible.

제가 연설을 녹화해야 하나요?
(A) 총 25개의 질문이요.
(B) 최근의 선거들이요.
(C) 네, 가능하다면요.

해설 연설을 녹화해야 하냐는 질문에 Yes라고 하면서 가능하다면 그렇게 하라고 답한 (C)가 정답. (B)는 speech에서 연상할 수 있는 elections를 이용한 오답.

어휘 speech 연설　recent 최근의　election 선거

9. 미 미 🎧

Where do we store the client files?
(A) There's a cabinet near the back door.
(B) I have a meeting with him tomorrow.
(C) In alphabetical order.

우리는 고객 파일을 어디에 보관하나요?
(A) 뒷문 근처에 캐비닛이 있어요.
(B) 저는 내일 그와 회의가 있어요.
(C) 알파벳순으로요.

해설 고객 파일을 어디에 보관하는지 묻는 질문에 파일을 보관하는 캐비닛을 언급하며 구체적인 위치로 답한 (A)가 정답. (C)는 파일을 보관하는 방식을 묻는 질문에 적절한 답변이므로 오답.

어휘 store 보관하다; 상점　client 고객　alphabetical 알파벳순의　order 순서; 주문하다

10. 미 미 🎧

It looks like it's going to rain.
(A) Why did you bring an umbrella?
(B) The forecast said it would.
(C) No, this lane is closed.

비가 올 것 같아요.
(A) 왜 우산을 가져오셨어요?
(B) 예보에서 그럴 거라고 했어요.
(C) 아니요, 이 차선은 폐쇄되었어요.

해설 비가 올 것 같다는 말에 예보에서 그럴 거라고 답한 (B)가 정답. (C)는 rain과 발음이 유사한 lane을 이용한 오답.

어휘 forecast 예보, 예측　lane 차선

11. 영 미 🎧

When was the last time you talked to Mark?
(A) Of course I did.
(B) Three days ago.
(C) We talked for two hours.

마크 씨와 마지막으로 이야기한 게 언제예요?
(A) 물론 제가 했죠.
(B) 사흘 전에요.
(C) 우리는 두 시간 동안 이야기했어요.

해설 마크 씨와 마지막으로 이야기를 나눈 시점을 묻는 질문에 정확한 시점으로 답한 (B)가 정답. (A)는 마크 씨와 이야기를 했는지를 묻는 질문에 적절한 답변이므로 오답.

12. 미 미 🎧

Who is the guest speaker on today's show?
(A) It was a great performance.
(B) A best-selling author.
(C) It starts at 10 A.M.

오늘 프로그램의 초청 연사는 누구인가요?
(A) 아주 멋진 공연이었어요.
(B) 한 베스트셀러 작가요.
(C) 그건 오전 10시에 시작해요.

해설 오늘 프로그램의 초청 연사가 누구인지 묻는 질문에 베스트셀러 작가라고 직업으로 답한 (B)가 정답. (C)는 프로그램이 언제 시작하는지 묻는 질문에 적절한 답변이므로 오답.

어휘 performance 공연　best-selling 베스트셀러의　author 작가

어휘 lecturer 강사 audience (집합명사) 청중 arrange 배치[배열]하다 auditorium 강당 distribute 나누어 주다

3. 미 🎧

(A) They are typing on a keyboard.
(B) The woman is pointing at a computer monitor.
(C) They are examining some documents.
(D) The man is writing on a clipboard.

(A) 사람들이 키보드를 타이핑하고 있다.
(B) 여자가 컴퓨터 모니터를 가리키고 있다.
(C) 사람들이 서류를 검토하고 있다.
(D) 남자가 클립보드에 적고 있다.

해설 두 남녀가 서류를 검토하고 있는 모습이므로 정답은 (C).

어휘 type on a keyboard 키보드를 타이핑하다 point at ~을 가리키다 examine 검토하다 clipboard 클립보드

4. 호 🎧

(A) He's hanging a painting on a building.
(B) He's closing the windows of a house.
(C) A ladder is placed against a wall.
(D) A bucket is being emptied onto the ground.

(A) 남자가 건물에 그림을 걸고 있다.
(B) 남자가 집의 창문들을 닫고 있다.
(C) 사다리가 벽에 기대어 놓여 있다.
(D) 양동이를 땅바닥에 비우고 있다.

해설 사다리가 벽에 기대어 놓여 있는 모습을 바르게 묘사한 (C)가 정답. 사진상에 집의 창문들은 보이지만, 남자가 창문들을 닫고 있는 것은 아니므로 (B)는 오답.

어휘 hang 걸다, 매달다 ladder 사다리 bucket 양동이 empty 비우다; 비어 있는

5. 미 🎧

(A) Some umbrellas are being opened.
(B) Some tables are located in front of some buildings.
(C) An open space is crowded with pedestrians.
(D) A section of a plaza is being paved.

(A) 몇몇 파라솔들을 펴고 있다.
(B) 몇몇 테이블들이 건물들 앞에 위치해 있다.
(C) 공터가 보행자들로 붐비고 있다.
(D) 광장의 한 구획이 포장되고 있다.

해설 테이블들이 건물들 앞에 위치해 있는 상태이므로 정답은 (B).

어휘 be located 위치해 있다 be crowded with ~으로 붐비다 pedestrian 보행자 section 구획, 구역 plaza 광장 pave 포장하다

6. 영 🎧

(A) A boat is arriving at the dock.
(B) Luggage is being unloaded.
(C) Passengers are buying tickets.
(D) A walkway has been set up.

(A) 배가 부두에 도착하고 있다.
(B) 수하물을 내리고 있다.
(C) 승객들이 표를 사고 있다.
(D) 통로가 설치되어 있다.

해설 배와 지면 사이에 통로가 설치되어 있는 모습이므로 정답은 (D). 승객들은 표를 사고 있는 게 아니라 배에 오르고 있는 것이므로 (C)는 오답.

어휘 dock 부두 luggage (집합명사) 수하물, 짐 unload 짐을 내리다 (↔load 짐을 싣다) walkway 통로, 보도 set up ~을 설치하다[세우다]

TEST 03

LISTENING TEST

001 (A) 002 (B) 003 (C) 004 (C) 005 (B)
006 (D) 007 (B) 008 (C) 009 (A) 010 (B)
011 (B) 012 (B) 013 (A) 014 (C) 015 (B)
016 (A) 017 (B) 018 (A) 019 (C) 020 (A)
021 (C) 022 (B) 023 (C) 024 (A) 025 (B)
026 (A) 027 (B) 028 (B) 029 (A) 030 (C)
031 (C) 032 (B) 033 (C) 034 (D) 035 (C)
036 (B) 037 (A) 038 (C) 039 (A) 040 (B)
041 (A) 042 (B) 043 (A) 044 (A) 045 (D)
046 (A) 047 (C) 048 (A) 049 (B) 050 (B)
051 (A) 052 (B) 053 (D) 054 (D) 055 (A)
056 (B) 057 (C) 058 (A) 059 (B) 060 (D)
061 (C) 062 (B) 063 (B) 064 (C) 065 (A)
066 (C) 067 (B) 068 (B) 069 (D) 070 (C)
071 (B) 072 (A) 073 (D) 074 (C) 075 (C)
076 (B) 077 (A) 078 (C) 079 (A) 080 (A)
081 (B) 082 (B) 083 (A) 084 (B) 085 (A)
086 (A) 087 (A) 088 (B) 089 (D) 090 (A)
091 (A) 092 (C) 093 (A) 094 (D) 095 (C)
096 (D) 097 (D) 098 (A) 099 (C) 100 (C)

READING TEST

101 (C) 102 (D) 103 (A) 104 (D) 105 (A)
106 (D) 107 (B) 108 (A) 109 (A) 110 (C)
111 (D) 112 (C) 113 (D) 114 (B) 115 (C)
116 (B) 117 (D) 118 (B) 119 (A) 120 (C)
121 (B) 122 (A) 123 (C) 124 (D) 125 (D)
126 (C) 127 (A) 128 (A) 129 (C) 130 (B)
131 (B) 132 (C) 133 (C) 134 (A) 135 (D)
136 (A) 137 (C) 138 (A) 139 (D) 140 (B)
141 (A) 142 (C) 143 (D) 144 (C) 145 (D)
146 (C) 147 (B) 148 (C) 149 (A) 150 (C)
151 (A) 152 (B) 153 (C) 154 (A) 155 (B)
156 (C) 157 (B) 158 (A) 159 (D) 160 (C)
161 (A) 162 (A) 163 (B) 164 (D) 165 (B)
166 (B) 167 (C) 168 (A) 169 (B) 170 (B)
171 (D) 172 (B) 173 (A) 174 (C) 175 (B)
176 (B) 177 (A) 178 (B) 179 (B) 180 (C)
181 (C) 182 (A) 183 (B) 184 (A) 185 (D)
186 (C) 187 (B) 188 (C) 189 (C) 190 (D)
191 (B) 192 (D) 193 (B) 194 (B) 195 (A)
196 (C) 197 (C) 198 (D) 199 (A) 200 (A)

PART 1

1. 미 🎧

(A) She's pouring an ingredient into a bowl.
(B) She's tying an apron around her waist.
(C) She's mixing some food with a spoon.
(D) She's cleaning a kitchen counter.

(A) 여자가 그릇에 재료 하나를 붓고 있다.
(B) 여자가 허리에 앞치마를 둘러서 묶고 있다.
(C) 여자가 숟가락으로 음식을 섞고 있다.
(D) 여자가 부엌 조리대를 닦고 있다.

해설 여자가 그릇에 요리 재료로 보이는 것을 붓고 있는 모습이므로 정답은 (A). 여자는 이미 앞치마를 착용한 상태이므로 (B)는 오답.

어휘 ingredient 재료, 성분 tie 묶다, 매다 apron 앞치마 kitchen counter 부엌 조리대

2. 영 🎧

(A) A lecturer is walking towards a projector screen.
(B) Audience members are listening to a speaker.
(C) Some chairs are being arranged in an auditorium.
(D) Some papers are being distributed to people.

(A) 강사가 프로젝터 스크린을 향해 걸어가고 있다.
(B) 청중이 연사의 말을 듣고 있다.
(C) 몇몇 의자들이 강당에 배치되고 있다.
(D) 사람들에게 서류를 나눠 주고 있다.

해설 청중이 앞에 있는 연사의 말을 듣고 있는 모습이므로 정답은 (B). 의자들은 이미 강당에 배치되어 있는 상태이므로 (C)는 오답.

- 월터 반스, 동화 시간
- [200-2]엘리자베스 랭커스터, 숙제 지원
- 하리티 나약, 유아 독서

[198-2]우리는 모집 인원을 완전히 채우지는 못했습니다. 하지만 저는 그래도 단체의 규모에 만족합니다. 이번 주 후반에 자원봉사자 명단을 보내 드리겠습니다.

어휘 overview 개관, 개요 indicate 명시하다, 나타내다 guarantee 보장하다 match with ~과 짝을 맞추다 coordinator 책임자, 진행자 recruitment 신규 모집, 채용

수신: 미리엄 자르밀로 〈m.jarmillo@richmondpl.org〉
발신: 원 랭 〈w.lang@richmondpl.org〉
날짜: 4월 29일
제목: 프로그램들에 관한 최근 정보

자르밀로 씨께,

도서관 프로그램들이 어떻게 진행되고 있는지에 관한 최신 정보를 알려 드리고자 합니다. 신규 자원봉사자들은 그들의 역할에 잘 적응해 가고 있으며, 우리는 프로그램에 참가한 사람들로부터 많은 긍정적인 피드백을 받았습니다. [200-1]특히나 중학생들 사이에서 숙제 지원 프로그램에 대한 수요가 높아서, 그 프로그램의 책임자는 자원봉사자를 몇 명 더 찾아 볼 계획입니다. 저는 각 프로그램의 주간 참가 현황을 추적하고 있으며 다음 달에 더 자세한 수치를 보여 드리겠습니다.

리치먼드 공공 도서관 프로그램 책임자
원 랭 드림

어휘 settle into ~에 자리를 잡다[익숙해지다] participate in ~에 참가하다 track 추적하다, 탐지하다 detailed 상세한, 자세한

196. 자원봉사자들에게 기대되는 것이 아닌 것은?
(A) 매주 일정 시간 이상 근무하기
(B) 현장에서 진행되는 교육 과정 참석하기
(C) 최소 연령 요건 충족하기
(D) 추천서 제출하기

해설 Not/True 문제

공고의 자원봉사자 지원 요건과 선택지를 비교해 보자. (A)는 단서 (196A)에서 일주일에 최소 4시간은 일해야 한다고 했고, (B)는 단서 (196B)에서 도서관에서 진행되는 오리엔테이션 워크숍에 참석해야 한다고 했으며, (C)는 단서 (196C)에서 적어도 18세는 되어야 한다고 했다. 그러나 추천서에 대한 내용은 언급되지 않았으므로 (D)가 정답.

197. 공고에서, 첫 번째 단락 다섯 번째 줄의 "reach"와 의미상 가장 가까운 단어는?
(A) 맞먹다
(B) 뻗다

(C) 성취하다
(D) 다가가다

해설 동의어 문제

문맥상 '더 많은 사람에게 다가간다'라는 의미로, 여기에서 reach는 '~에 달하다'의 의미로 쓰였다. 따라서 이와 가장 유사한 '다가가다, 접근하다'의 의미를 지닌 (D)가 정답.

198. 4월 7일에 진행된 교육에 대해 암시된 것은?
(A) 총 두 시간 동안 진행되었다.
(B) 자원봉사자들의 문해력을 평가했다.
(C) 참가 인원이 30명 미만이었다.
(D) 자원봉사자들로부터 긍정적인 피드백을 받았다.

해설 두 지문 연계 문제_추론 문제

공고의 단서 (198-1)에서 최소 30명의 신규 봉사자들을 받고 싶다고 했고, 회람의 단서 (198-2)에서 교육 과정이 4월 7일에 열릴 것인데 모집 인원을 다 채우지는 못했다고 했으므로, 최종 결정된 자원봉사자 인원이 30명 미만이라는 것을 알 수 있다. 이를 토대로 4월 7일에 진행된 교육 과정에 30명 미만의 인원이 참가했음을 추론할 수 있으므로 정답은 (C).

199. 자원봉사자들이 교육 과정에서 양식을 작성하게 될 이유는?
(A) 선호하는 것을 나타내기 위해
(B) 연사들의 수행을 채점하기 위해
(C) 자신의 일정을 확정하기 위해
(D) 신규 프로그램을 제안하기 위해

해설 특정 정보 확인 문제

단서 (199)를 보면 교육 과정에서 자원봉사자들은 봉사하기를 원하는 프로그램을 명시할 수 있는 양식을 받게 된다. 즉, 어떤 프로그램을 선호하는지 나타내기 위해 양식을 작성할 것이므로 정답은 (A).

패러프레이징 [단서] indicate which programs they would like to assist with → [정답] express their preferences

200. 자원봉사자들을 더 모집하려고 계획 중인 사람은?
(A) 마르케시 씨
(B) 반스 씨
(C) 랭커스터 씨
(D) 나약 씨

해설 두 지문 연계 문제_특정 정보 확인 문제

이메일의 단서 (200-1)에서 숙제 지원 프로그램의 책임자가 자원봉사자를 더 찾아 볼 계획이라고 했는데, 회람의 단서 (200-2)를 보면 숙제 지원 프로그램의 책임자는 엘리자베스 랭커스터 씨로 되어 있다. 즉, 자원봉사자들을 더 모집할 계획인 사람이 랭커스터 씨라는 것을 알 수 있으므로 정답은 (C). 지문의 plans to find a few more volunteers가 문제에서는 plans to recruit more volunteers로 패러프레이징되었다.

191. 기사의 목적은?
(A) 제품 라인의 신제품을 홍보하기 위해
(B) 소비자에게 제품 리콜을 알리기 위해
(C) 업체의 성과를 기념하기 위해
(D) 제품의 단종을 알리기 위해

해설 목적 문제
기사 서두의 단서 (191)에서 맥케이브 가전제품이 특정 공기 청정기의 생산을 중단할 예정임을 언급했고, 이에 대한 내용이 이어지고 있으므로 정답은 (D).

패러프레이징 [단서] to halt production of its PrimeAir-60 air purifier → [정답] the discontinuation of a product

192. 기사에서, 두 번째 단락 두 번째 줄의 "accounts for"와 의미상 가장 가까운 단어는?
(A) 사용하다
(B) 상당하다
(C) 발생하다
(D) 설명하다

해설 동의어 문제
문맥상 '프라임에어-60은 업체 수익의 2% 미만을 차지하고 있다'의 의미이므로 여기에서 account for는 '차지하다'의 의미로 사용되었음을 알 수 있다. 따라서 이와 가장 유사한 '상당하다'란 의미를 지닌 (B)가 정답.

193. 웹페이지에 따르면, 고객들이 10월에 받을 수 있는 것은?
(A) 보증 기간 연장
(B) 무료 교체용 필터
(C) 업데이트된 카탈로그
(D) 무료 배송

해설 특정 정보 확인 문제
10월에 고객들이 받을 수 있는 것을 묻는 질문이므로 10월(October)이 명시된 부분에서 단서를 찾는다. 단서 (193)에서 모든 주문은 10월 1일부터 10월 31일까지 무료 배송 대상이 된다고 했으므로 정답은 (D).

패러프레이징 [단서] free delivery → [정답] Complimentary shipping

194. 덴스모어 씨가 프라임에어-60에 대해 암시하는 것은?
(A) 낮 시간 동안에만 사용한다.
(B) 보다 최신 모델로 교체할 것이다.
(C) 제품이 너무 시끄러웠다고 생각하지 않는다.
(D) 제품에 대해 업체에 항의했다.

해설 두 지문 연계 문제_추론 문제
덴스모어 씨는 온라인 후기의 단서 (194-1)에서 가장 흔히 제기되는 불만 사항을 자신은 한 번도 겪은 적이 없다고 했는데, 기사의 단서 (194-2)에서 기기를 구매한 고객 대다수가 작동 소음에 대해 불만을 제기했다고 했다. 이를 통해 덴스모어 씨는 기기의 작동 소음을 경험한 적이 없다는 것을 추론할 수 있으므로 정답은 (C).

패러프레이징 [단서] its loud operation → [정답] it was too noisy

195. 덴스모어 씨에 대해 사실일 것 같은 것은?
(A) 프라임에어-60을 75.99달러에 샀다.
(B) 그녀의 거실은 1,500입방피트보다 작다.
(C) 교체용 필터에 55.99달러를 썼다.
(D) 그녀가 구매한 것은 속달 우편으로 배송되었다.

해설 두 지문 연계 문제_추론 문제
덴스모어 씨는 자신이 쓴 온라인 후기의 단서 (195-1)에서 재고 정리 세일로 교체용 필터 5개들이 팩을 하나 구매했다고 했는데 웹페이지의 단서 (195-2)에서 교체용 필터 5개들이 팩의 가격이 재고 정리가로 55.99달러임을 확인할 수 있다. 따라서 정답은 (C). 덴스모어 씨는 프라임에어-60을 작년에 구매했다고 했는데 75.99달러는 현재 재고 정리 가격이므로 (A)는 오답.

196-200 공고 & 회람 & 이메일

> **자원봉사자 모집**
>
> 리치먼드 공공 도서관은 필수적인 교육 서비스를 지역 사회에 제공하고 있으며, 저희는 저희 프로그램에 도움을 줄 자원봉사자들을 찾고 있습니다. [196C]적어도 18세는 되어야 하며 [196A]일주일에 최소 4시간은 일할 수 있어야 합니다. 자원봉사자로 지원하려면, 3월 20일까지 안내 데스크에 있는 양식을 작성해 주십시오. [196B]모든 봉사자는 자원봉사를 시작하기 전에 도서관에서 진행되는 오리엔테이션 워크숍에 참석해야 한다는 점을 유념해 주시기 바랍니다. 지역 사회 구성원들의 도움이 있으면 저희는 더 많은 사람에게 [197]다가가 그들이 문해력 목표를 달성하도록 도울 수 있습니다. [198-1]저희는 저희 프로그램들에 적어도 30명의 신규 봉사자들을 받게 되기를 희망하므로, 가족과 친구들에게도 자원하도록 권해 주시기 바랍니다.

어휘 volunteer 자원봉사자; 자원하다   educational 교육의   minimum 최소한도   fill out 작성하다   reach ~에 닿다[이르다]   attain 달성하다, 이루다   literacy 읽고 쓰는 능력

> **회람**
>
> 직원 여러분께,
>
> 우리의 새로운 도서관 자원봉사자들을 교육하기 위해 바쁜 일정 중에 시간을 내 주신 여러분, 감사합니다. [198-2]교육은 4월 7일에 열릴 것이며 오후 1시에 시작됩니다. 2시간 동안 도서관에 대한 일반 정보를 살펴본 후, 이어서 아래와 같이 각 프로그램의 책임자에 의해 개별 프로젝트에 대한 개관이 (각 30분씩) 진행될 것입니다. [199]오리엔테이션이 끝날 때쯤 자원봉사자들은 어떤 프로그램을 돕고 싶은지 명시할 수 있는 양식을 받을 것입니다. 모든 봉사자들이 그들이 처음 선택한 대로 배정될 거라고 보장할 수는 없지만, 최선을 다해 보겠습니다.
>
> 프로그램 책임자:
>
> – 실바노 마르케시, 성인 문해 교육

(C) 〈시합에서〉
(D) 〈비매품〉

해설 두 지문 연계 문제_특정 정보 확인 문제

두 번째 이메일의 단서 (188-1)에서 스틸트너 씨가 요청한 영화의 특별 초대 손님이 변경될 것이라고 했다. 첫 번째 이메일의 단서 (188-2)에서 스틸트너 씨가 입장권 추가 구매를 요청한 영화가 〈시합에서〉임을 알 수 있으므로 정답은 (C).

189. 두 번째 이메일에서, 첫 번째 단락 첫 번째 줄의 "enjoys"와 의미상 가장 가까운 단어는?

(A) 경험하다
(B) 보유하다
(C) 감상하다
(D) 환영하다

해설 동의어 문제

문맥상 '널찍한 좌석 공간을 갖추고 있다'라는 의미로, 여기에서 enjoy는 '(좋은 것을) 가지고 있다'의 의미로 쓰였다. 따라서 이와 가장 유사한 의미를 가지는 단어인 (B)가 정답.

190. 란 씨에 따르면, 스틸트너 씨가 매표소에 전화해야 하는 이유는?

(A) 변경을 확인하기 위해
(B) 업데이트된 시간표를 얻기 위해
(C) 구매를 취소하기 위해
(D) 지불 정보를 제공하기 위해

해설 특정 정보 확인 문제

단서 (190)에서 입장권을 원한다면 매표소로 전화해 신용 카드 정보를 알려 줘야 한다고 했으므로 정답은 (D).

패러프레이징 [단서] to give us your credit card details
→ [정답] To provide payment information

191-195 기사 & 웹페이지 & 온라인 후기

맥케이브 가전제품이 자사 제품 라인을 정리하다

8월 27일—191맥케이브 가전제품은 9월 중으로 프라임에어-60 공기 청정기의 생산을 중단할 계획이고, 해당 제품을 취급하고 있는 매장들은 품절될 때까지만 이것을 판매할 예정이다. 현재 프라임에어-60을 보유하고 있는 고객들은 필터를 비축해 두도록 장려되고 있는데, 이는 다른 맥케이브 공기 청정기용 필터들은 모양이 달라서 그 기기에는 호환이 될 수 없기 때문이다.

맥케이브 가전제품의 대변인은 이 결정은 더 잘 팔리는 제품에 주력하기 위해 내려졌다고 언급했다. 프라임에어-60은 업체 수익의 2% 미만을 192차지하고 있어서, 맥케이브 사의 의사 결정자들은 이제 다른 디자인을 홍보할 때라고 생각한다. 194-2게다가 해당 기기를 구매한 고객들 대다수는 기기의 작동 소음에 대해 불만을 표했다. 맥케이브 가전제품의 전체 제품 목록을 확인하려면 www.mccabehomeapp.com을 방문하면 된다.

어휘 trim 잘라 내다   halt 중단시키다   air purifier 공기 청정기   be encouraged to do ~하도록 장려되다   stock up on ~을 비축하다   account for (부분·비율을) 차지하다   decision-maker 의사 결정자   majority 대다수   operation 작동

---

www.mccabehomeapp.com

홈 〉〉 카탈로그 〉〉 세일 품목 〉〉 재고 정리

다음 제품들은 모든 제품이 판매될 때까지 할인 판매됩니다.
10월 1일 갱신

프라임에어-60   장바구니에 담기

정상가: 169.99달러   재고 정리가: 75.99달러

프라임에어-60은 1,500입방피트까지의 공간에서 사용할 수 있는 공기 청정기입니다. 이것은 전력 사용량이 적고 현재 시중에 나와 있는 대부분의 공기 청정기보다 더 효율적으로 작동합니다. 프라임에어-60의 주기적인 사용으로 여러분의 집에 존재하는 박테리아, 바이러스, 알레르기 유발 항원을 줄일 수 있습니다. 이 기기는 알레르기 환자와 호흡기 질환이 있는 분들에게 적극 추천됩니다. 필터는 손으로 세척할 수 있고 10번까지 재사용할 수 있습니다.

프라임에어-60 교체용 필터 3개들이 팩   장바구니에 담기

정상가: 59.99달러   재고 정리가: 39.99달러

195-2**프라임에어-60 교체용 필터 5개들이 팩**   장바구니에 담기

정상가: 89.99달러   재고 정리가: 55.99달러

193재고 정리 품목을 포함한 모든 주문은 10월 1일부터 10월 31일까지 무료 배송 대상이 됩니다.

어휘 clearance (재고) 정리   cubic foot 입방피트   efficiently 효율적으로   presence 존재   allergen 알레르기 유발 항원   sufferer 환자   respiratory 호흡기의, 호흡의   reuse 재사용하다   replacement 교체, 대체   qualify for ~의 자격이 있다, ~의 대상이 되다

---

www.mccabehomeapp.com

홈 〉〉 후기 〉〉 프라임에어-60

작성자: 올리비아 덴스모어   게시: 10월 5일

저는 이 제품이 단종되는 것을 보게 되어 안타까울 것 같습니다. 저는 제 것을 작년에 구매했는데 그때 이후로 계속 즐겨 사용하고 있습니다. 194-1회사가 가장 흔히 제기되는 불만 사항에 관해 조치를 취해야만 한다는 것을 이해는 합니다만, 저는 그 문제를 한 번도 경험한 적이 없습니다. 필터를 손으로 세척하고 재사용할 수 있긴 하지만, 저는 꼭 이 제품을 오랫동안 사용할 수 있도록 195-1오늘 재고 정리 세일로 5개들이 팩 하나를 샀습니다.

어휘 constantly 끊임없이, 계속   take action 조치를 취하다

186-190 전단 & 이메일 & 이메일

엘즈버리 홀의 수요일 밤 다큐멘터리 상영

엘즈버리 홀은 다큐멘터리 수상작들과, 그 뒤를 이어 목록상의 특별 초대 손님들과 함께하는 질의응답 시간을 여러분에게 제공하게 되어 기쁩니다.

6월 7일: 〈모래시계〉 / **상영 시간:** 2시간 21분
특별 초대 손님: 올랜도 브리그스 (감독)
이 영화는 [186]관광 사업이 작은 섬 키호아에 지난 50년간 어떤 영향을 미쳐 왔는지를 탐구합니다.

6월 14일: 〈북쪽으로 맹렬히 나아가며〉 / **상영 시간:** 2시간 18분
특별 초대 손님: 브루스 모리슨 (캔-일렉 사 부사장)
이 영화는 [186]캐나다의 에너지 회사인 캔-일렉 사가 몇십 년 전 회사가 창립된 이래로 어떻게 자사의 사업 모델을 조정해 왔는지를 탐구합니다.

6월 21일: 〈시합에서〉 / **상영 시간:** 2시간 5분
특별 초대 손님: 샴바 메타 (감독)
[186]19세기의 영국에서 보잘것없이 시작하여 오늘날 세계에서 가장 인기 있는 스포츠가 되기까지 축구의 발전을 시청해 보세요.

6월 28일: 〈비매품〉 / **상영 시간:** 1시간 48분
특별 초대 손님: 에린 핸슨 (감독)
[186]정치인 벤자민 트리블 씨의 이력이 1982년 자신의 첫 선거에서부터 오늘날에 이르기까지 어떻게 펼쳐져 왔는지 확인해 보세요.

많이 절약하시려면 미리 예약하세요! [187-2]5월 중에 입장권을 구매하셔서 입장료에서 5달러를 할인받으세요.

어휘 screening 상영 hourglass 모래시계 tourism 관광 산업 power (특정 방향으로) 맹렬히 나아가다 adapt 조정하다, 맞추다 inception (단체·기관 등의) 시작, 개시 humble 보잘것없는, 겸손한 unfold 펼쳐지다, 펴다 entrance fee 입장료

수신: 엘즈버리 홀 〈bookings@elsberryhall.com〉
발신: 로지 스틸트너 〈r_stiltner@ravenpost.com〉
날짜: 6월 15일, 오전 10:33
제목: 입장권

관계자분께:

저는 어젯밤 있었던 〈북쪽으로 맹렬히 나아가며〉의 상영회에 참석했고, 그것이 재미있는 동시에 유익하다고 생각했습니다. [188-2]저는 아직 〈시합에서〉 입장권들을 구할 수 있는지 궁금합니다. 이미 한 장을 가지고 있는데, 가능하다면 세 장을 더 사고 싶습니다. [187-1]이번에는 입장권 가격이 처음 제 주문에서 제가 지불했던 11달러 대신에 16달러가 될 거라는 것은 알고 있습니다.

로지 스틸트너 드림

어휘 entertaining 재미있는 informative 유익한 original 최초의, 본래의

수신: 로지 스틸트너 〈r_stiltner@ravenpost.com〉
발신: 엘즈버리 홀 〈bookings@elsberryhall.com〉
날짜: 6월 15일, 오후 1:41
제목: 회신: 입장권

스틸트너 씨께,

엘즈버리 홀은 거의 500명의 인원을 수용할 수 있는 널찍한 좌석 공간을 [189]갖추고 있어, [188-1]요청하신 영화에 대해 이용 가능한 입장권들이 아직 남아 있음을 알려 드리게 되어 기쁩니다. 하지만 감독이 계획대로 참석하지는 못하게 되어 그 날짜의 특별 초대 손님은 시나리오 작가인 케빈 드러먼드 씨가 될 거라는 점에 유의해 주십시오. 이러한 변동에도 불구하고 [190]여전히 입장권을 원하신다면, 555-3866번으로 저희 매표소에 전화하셔서 귀하의 신용 카드 정보를 다시 알려 주셔야 합니다. 저희는 이전 거래의 정보를 저장하지 않기 때문입니다.

엘즈버리 홀, 고객 서비스 담당자
마일스 란 드림

어휘 enjoy (좋은 것을) 가지고 있다 spacious 널찍한 accommodate 수용하다 screenwriter 시나리오 작가

---

186. 모든 영화가 공유하는 특징은?
(A) 2시간 이상 계속된다.
(B) 주제를 시간의 흐름에 따라 탐구한다.
(C) 사업과 관련된 문제들에 초점을 맞춘다.
(D) 잘 알려진 감독들에 의해 제작되었다.

해설 특정 정보 확인 문제

단서 (186)을 종합해 보면, 상영되는 모든 영화가 시간의 흐름에 따른 각 주제의 변화 양상을 보여 준다는 것을 알 수 있다. 따라서 정답은 (B).

187. 스틸트너 씨에 대해 암시된 것은?
(A) 자신의 입장권을 다른 영화의 입장권으로 교환하고 싶어 한다.
(B) 혼자서 다큐멘터리 영화를 만들었다.
(C) 6월 1일 이전에 원래의 입장권을 예매했다.
(D) 극장의 회원 프로그램에 가입했다.

해설 두 지문 연계 문제_추론 문제

첫 번째 이메일의 단서 (187-1)에서 스틸트너 씨는 이번에 구매하는 입장권의 가격이 자신이 처음 입장권을 주문할 때 지불했던 11달러가 아닌 16달러가 될 것임을 알고 있다고 했는데, 전단의 단서 (187-2)에서 5월 중에 입장권을 구매하면 5달러를 할인해 준다고 나와 있다. 이로 미루어 보아 스틸트너 씨는 원래 입장권을 6월 1일보다 이전인 5월 중에 구매했음을 추론할 수 있으므로 정답은 (C).

188. 특별 초대 손님이 변경된 영화는?
(A) 〈모래시계〉
(B) 〈북쪽으로 맹렬히 나아가며〉

우리는 이사 전문 업체인 게라 사를 고용했고, [183]그곳의 직원들이 3월 17일 금요일에 우리 건물을 방문할 것입니다. 그날 여러분은 출근하지 않아도 됩니다. 이사에 앞서 직원들은 첨부된 일정에 따라 회사의 가구와 장비, 비품의 목록을 작성하는 것을 돕게 될 것입니다. [184-2]여러분이 개인 소지품을 모아 놓을 수 있도록 인사부장이 상자와 테이프, 라벨을 지급할 것입니다.

어휘 incorporated 주식회사(= Inc.) immediate 즉각적인 attention 관심, 주목 attachment 첨부 merger 합병 downsize 줄이다, 축소하다 overhead cost 간접비 underground 지하의 report to work 출근하다 prior to ~에 앞서 assist with ~을 돕다 take inventory of ~의 목록을 만들다

물품 목록 작성 일정

날짜	장소	부서	부서장
3월 13일 월요일	2층	회계	나오토 코다마
[185]3월 14일 화요일	3층	영업	트로이 콩코드
		마케팅	제시 마테오 *
3월 15일 수요일	4층	[184-1]인사	알라나 템플턴
		연구 개발	카말 박시
3월 16일 목요일	1층	경영	조앤 패퍼드

* [185]제시 마테오 씨가 그 주에 결근할 예정이므로, 그의 부서가 배정된 날에는 경영 부서의 조앤 패퍼드 씨가 그를 대신할 것입니다.

어휘 R&D 연구 개발(= research and development) administration 경영, 관리 absent 결근한, 결석한 fill in for ~을 대신하다 assign 배정하다, 맡기다

181. 딕슨 씨가 회람을 보낸 이유는?
(A) 회사 합병을 발표하기 위해
(B) 이전 절차를 설명하기 위해
(C) 건설 프로젝트에 대한 최신 상황을 알려 주기 위해
(D) 직원들에게 지출을 줄일 것을 부탁하기 위해

해설 목적 문제

메모 전체의 맥락과 단서 (181)로 보아, 직원들에게 회사의 사무실 이전 절차에 대해 설명하고자 보낸 메모임을 알 수 있으므로 정답은 (B).

패러프레이징 [단서] moving our offices next month from the Rinehart Building to the Werner Building → [정답] relocation

182. 라인하트 빌딩에 대해 시사된 것은?
(A) 전용 주차 공간을 가지고 있다.
(B) 세르반테스 주식회사의 본사가 될 것이다.
(C) 3월 중에 철거될 것이다.
(D) 워너 빌딩보다 크다.

해설 Not/True 문제

단서 (182)를 종합해 보면 새로 이사 갈 워너 빌딩도 현재 사무실이 위치해 있는 라인하트 빌딩처럼 직원들만 이용할 수 있는 주차장이 있다고 했으므로, 라인하트 빌딩이 전용 주차 공간을 가지고 있음을 알 수 있다. 따라서 정답은 (A).

패러프레이징 [단서] an underground parking lot for employees only → [정답] a private parking area

183. 세르반테스 주식회사의 직원들에 대해 암시된 것은?
(A) 다른 부서로 재배치될 것이다.
(B) 임시로 재택근무를 해야 한다.
(C) 3월 중에 하루 휴가를 얻게 될 것이다.
(D) 딕슨 씨에게 물품 목록 작성상의 문제를 보고해야 한다.

해설 추론 문제

단서 (183)에서 이사 업체 직원들이 건물을 방문하는 3월 17일 금요일에 직원들은 출근하지 않아도 된다고 했으므로 직원들이 3월 중에 하루 휴가를 얻게 될 것임을 추론할 수 있다. 따라서 정답은 (C).

패러프레이징 [단서] You do not need to report to work on that day → [정답] They will be given a day off

184. 템플턴 씨에 대해 암시된 것은?
(A) 워너 빌딩을 둘러보았다.
(B) 3층에서 근무한다.
(C) 딕슨 씨에게 제안을 했다.
(D) 포장용품을 나눠 줄 것이다.

해설 두 지문 연계 문제_추론 문제

일정표를 보면 단서 (184-1)에서 템플턴 씨가 인사부장임을 확인할 수 있는데, 회람의 단서 (184-2)에서 직원들이 소지품을 모아 놓을 수 있도록 인사부장이 상자, 테이프 등을 지급할 거라고 했다. 이를 통해 인사부장인 템플턴 씨가 이사를 위한 포장용품을 나눠 줄 것임을 추론할 수 있으므로 정답은 (D).

패러프레이징 [단서] The head of HR will supply boxes, tape, and labels for you to gather your personal belongings → [정답] She will distribute packing supplies

185. 3월 14일에 일어날 것으로 예정된 일은?
(A) 한 회사가 새 건물로 이전할 것이다.
(B) 패퍼드 씨가 자기 부서가 아닌 부서를 도울 것이다.
(C) 게라 사의 직원들이 회사를 방문할 것이다.
(D) 콩코드 씨가 회사에 결근할 것이다.

해설 다음에 할 일 문제

일정표의 단서 (185)에서 3월 14일은 마케팅 부서가 물품 목록을 작성하는 날이며 마케팅부장이 제시 마테오 씨라는 것을 알 수 있는데, 일정표 아래 참고 설명을 보면 제시 마테오 씨가 결근할 예정이므로 마케팅 부서가 배정된 날에는 경영 부서의 조앤 패퍼드 씨가 그를 대신할 거라고 했다. 즉 패퍼드 씨가 3월 14일에 마케팅부장의 업무를 대행할 예정임을 알 수 있으므로 정답은 (B).

패러프레이징 [단서] Joan Pafford from administration will fill in for him → [정답] Ms. Pafford will assist a department that is not hers

2. 트리보 렌탈스를 선택한 이유는 무엇입니까?
트리보 렌탈스에서는 신차 대신에 몇 년 된 차를 사용함으로써 가격을 낮춘다는 점이 아주 마음에 듭니다. [180]회사가 정말 차별화되는 점은 직원을 저희 집으로 보내 트리보 렌탈스 사무소까지 저를 태워다 준다는 것입니다. 이는 매우 편리한데, 저는 주차 문제를 일으키지 않고는 직접 그곳까지 차를 몰고 갈 수 없기 때문입니다.

3. 저희가 서비스를 개선할 수 있는 방법에는 무엇이 있겠습니까?
보험 및 부가 서비스에 대한 추가 요금을 처음부터 좀 더 명확하게 설명해 주어야 한다고 생각합니다.

4. [179-2]저희 서비스를 친구 또는 가족에게 추천하시겠습니까? [네] / 아니요

이름: 클리프 바우어　이메일 주소: c.bower@ferrel.com

어휘　matter 중요하다, 문제가 되다　duration (지속) 기간, 지속
fuel-efficient 연비가 좋은　set ~ apart ~을 돋보이게 만들다
give ~ a ride ~를 태워 주다　convenient 편리한　up front 미리, 처음부터

176. 편지의 목적은?
(A) **고객의 경험에 대한 정보를 요청하기 위해**
(B) 신제품에 대한 의견을 모으기 위해
(C) 고객에게 의견에 대해 감사하기 위해
(D) 연구 결과를 요청하기 위해

해설　목적 문제

단서 (176)에서 자사의 서비스 개선을 위해 스타인 씨로부터 대여 건에 관한 의견을 받고 싶다고 했으므로 정답은 (A).

패러프레이징　[단서] to get your feedback → [정답] To request information about a customer's experience

177. 트리보 렌탈스에 대해 암시된 것은?
(A) 사업 전문가들에게 특별 패키지를 제공한다.
(B) 전국에 지점을 운영한다.
(C) 매우 다양한 보험 선택 사항을 제공한다.
(D) **예약을 위한 스마트폰 애플리케이션을 가지고 있다.**

해설　추론 문제

단서 (177)에서 스타인 씨가 트리보 렌탈스의 휴대폰 앱을 통해 차량 대여 예약을 했다고 했으므로, 트리보 렌탈스가 대여 예약 기능이 있는 스마트폰 애플리케이션을 갖추고 있음을 추론할 수 있다. 따라서 정답은 (D).

패러프레이징　[단서] the Trivo Rentals mobile phone app / booked a vehicle rental → [정답] a smartphone application / reservations

178. 편지에서, 첫 번째 단락 세 번째 줄의 "find"와 의미상 가장 가까운 단어는?
(A) 제안하다
(B) 발견하다
(C) **생각하다**
(D) 습득하다

해설　동의어 문제

문맥상 '가장 좋은 방법이라고 생각하기 때문입니다'라는 의미로, 여기에서 find는 '~이라고 여기다, 생각하다'의 의미로 쓰였다. 따라서 이와 유사한 의미를 가지는 단어인 (C)가 정답.

179. 스타인 씨에 대해 사실인 것은?
(A) 대여에 대해 보상 포인트를 적립할 수 있다.
(B) 이메일로 10% 할인 쿠폰을 받게 될 것이다.
(C) GPS 장치 추첨에 응모될 것이다.
(D) **무료 장비 대여를 받을 수 있다.**

해설　두 지문 연계 문제_Not/True 문제

편지의 단서 (179-1)에서 친구에게 서비스를 소개하는 사람에게는 GPS 무료 대여 쿠폰이 주어진다고 했는데, 설문 조사의 단서 (179-2)에서 스타인 씨가 친구에게 서비스를 추천했음을 확인할 수 있다. 따라서 스타인 씨가 GPS 무료 대여 쿠폰을 받게 될 것임을 알 수 있으므로 정답은 (D).

패러프레이징　[단서] you will be given a voucher for a free GPS rental → [정답] She can receive a free equipment rental

180. 스타인 씨가 트리보 렌탈스에 대해 마음에 들어 하는 것 하나는?
(A) 편리한 위치
(B) 신차
(C) 저렴한 보험
(D) **태우러 오는 서비스**

해설　특정 정보 확인 문제

단서 (180)에서 직원을 보내 고객을 사무소까지 태워다 주는 트리보 렌탈스의 서비스를 장점으로 꼽으며 이 서비스가 매우 편리하다고 평했다. 따라서 정답은 (D).

패러프레이징　[단서] it sends a representative to my home to give me a ride to the Trivo Rentals office → [정답] Its pick-up service

181-185 회람 & 일정표

수신: 세르반테스 주식회사 직원
발신: 총무부장, 아르만도 딕슨
제목: 즉각적인 관심 바람
첨부: 물품 목록 작성 일정

2월 23일

지난해 합병 이후, 우리는 계속해서 직원 수를 줄이고 있으며 간접비를 줄일 방법들을 찾고 있습니다. 그 결과, [181, 182]우리는 다음 달에 라인하트 빌딩에서 임대료가 더 저렴한 워너 빌딩으로 사무실을 이전할 것입니다. 차를 가지고 다니시는 분들은 [182]워너 빌딩 역시 현재 우리 건물처럼 직원 전용의 지하 주차장을 갖고 있다는 사실을 알게 되어 기쁘실 겁니다.

어휘 extensive 대규모의 underway 진행 중인 obstacle 장애(물) bid 입찰 contaminated 오염된 hydraulic 유압식의 dredge 준설선 sediment 침전물 diameter 직경, 지름 draw 인기를 끄는 것 enthusiast 열광적인 팬 downward trend 하락세 councilperson 시의회 의원 revenue 수익

172. 기사의 주제는?
(A) 프로젝트 경과
(B) 기계 이용 가능성
(C) 정책 변경
(D) 관광업 동향

해설 주제 문제

기사의 주제는 대개 기사의 앞부분에서 드러난다. 기사 첫 번째 문장의 단서 (172)에서 호수 정화 프로젝트의 계획이 마침내 진행 중이라고 언급한 뒤, 프로젝트의 진행 경과를 설명하는 내용이 이어지고 있다. 따라서 정답은 (A).

173. 클리프턴 씨가 프로젝트에 대해 갖고 있을 것 같은 생각은?
(A) 연초에 시작되었어야 했다.
(B) 담당자들은 경험이 충분하지 않다.
(C) 높은 비용에도 불구하고 지역 사회에 유익할 것이다.
(D) 최종 비용은 뱃놀이를 하는 사람들과 낚시꾼들이 지불해야 한다.

해설 추론 문제

단서 (173)에서 클리프턴 씨는 이 프로젝트에 큰 비용이 들어가고 있지만 프로젝트가 완료되면 지역의 경제와 환경 모두에 득이 될 거라고 말했다. 따라서 정답은 (C).

패러프레이징 [단서] it's a win-win situation for everyone / This project is costing taxpayers tens of millions of dollars → [정답] It will benefit the community / its high costs

174. 캐리지 호수에 대해 사실이 아닌 것은?
(A) 현재는 수영하기에 적합하지 않다.
(B) 방문객 수가 꾸준히 감소해 왔다.
(C) 마을 식수의 주요 공급원이다.
(D) 야외 공연 구역의 부지가 될 것이다.

해설 Not/True 문제

(A)는 단서 (174A)에서 지난 수십 년간 호수에서 수영하는 것을 허용하지 않았다고 했고, (B)는 단서 (174B)에서 수년간 방문객 수가 하락세라고 했으며, (D)는 단서 (174D)에서 캐리지 호수에 야외 무대를 지어 음악회 등을 열 것이라고 했다. 그러나 식수에 관한 내용은 지문에서 언급되지 않았으므로 정답은 (C).

175. [1], [2], [3], [4]번으로 표시된 위치들 중 다음 문장이 들어가기에 가장 적절한 곳은?

"가능성이 있는 업체들 중 제안된 예산 내에서 사업의 범위를 완결 지을 수 있는 회사는 없었다."

(A) [1]
(B) [2]
(C) [3]
(D) [4]

해설 문장 위치 찾기 문제

주어진 문장은 예산 내에서 사업 범위를 완성할 수 있는 회사는 없었다며 입찰 단계에서의 문제를 언급하는 내용이므로 지문에서 입찰 관련 내용이 언급된 부분을 살펴봐야 한다. 단서(175)에서 '다행히도'를 의미하는 부사 Fortunately가 나오고 이어서 한 회사와 계약을 합의할 수 있었다는 내용이 나오므로, 그 앞에는 어떤 회사와도 계약을 하지 못했다는 문제 상황이 나오는 것이 자연스럽다. 따라서 정답은 (B).

176-180 편지 & 설문 조사

7월 3일

앤 스타인
풀턴 가 414번지
윈체스터, 켄터키 주 40391

스타인 씨께,

¹⁷⁷고객님께서는 최근 트리보 렌탈스의 휴대폰 앱을 통해 차량 대여를 예약하셨습니다. 저희 회사를 이용해 주셔서 감사드리며 ¹⁷⁶저희 서비스를 더 개선하기 위하여 동봉된 서식에 대여에 관한 고객님의 의견을 받고 싶습니다. 저희는 이와 같은 조사를 정기적으로 실시하는데, 이것이 저희가 고객님들을 이해할 수 있는 가장 좋은 방법이라고 ¹⁷⁸생각하기 때문입니다.

¹⁷⁹⁻¹저희는 또한 고객님에서 저희 서비스에 관심을 가질 만한 친구분께 저희를 소개해 주시기를 바랍니다. 만약 그렇게 해주신다면, 고객님의 친구분께서는 어떤 대여 서비스라도 10%를 할인받을 수 있는 할인권을 이메일로 받으실 것이며, ¹⁷⁹⁻¹고객님께는 다음에 저희 대여 서비스를 이용하실 때 사용하실 수 있는 GPS 무료 대여 쿠폰이 주어질 것입니다.

참여해 주셔서 감사합니다!

트리보 렌탈스 팀 일동 드림

어휘 enclose 동봉하다 conduct 실시하다, 수행하다 regularly 정기적으로 voucher 할인권, 쿠폰 participation 참여, 참가

트리보 렌탈스

이 설문 조사를 작성하기 위해 시간을 내 주셔서 감사합니다. 여러분의 의견은 저희에게 중요합니다!

이름: 앤 스타인   최근 대여 날짜: 6월 25일
대여 장소: 윈체스터   대여 기간: 1주

1. 트리보 렌탈스를 얼마나 자주 이용하시며, 그 이유는 무엇입니까?
제 개인 차량은 밴이기 때문에, 저는 1년에 몇 차례 다른 주로 출장을 가기 위해 연비가 좋은 차를 대여합니다.

기 때문에 고객님께서는 회사까지 걸어가실 수 있을 것입니다. — [3] —. 현 세입자가 6월 20일에 이사를 나가므로, 고객님께서는 6월 21일에 이사를 오실 수 있습니다. 관심이 있으시다면 170제가 임대 계약서를 보내 드릴 수 있습니다만, 계약서는 늦어도 6월 14일까지는 서명해서 다시 보내 주셔야 합니다. 171그때 저희는 200달러의 예약금을 받을 것입니다. — [4] —. 이 아파트는 인기 있는 건물 안에 있으므로, 고객님께서 기회를 놓치시지 않도록 고객님에게서 답변을 빨리 들을 수 있기를 바랍니다.

리 장 드림

어휘 realty 부동산 neighborhood 지역, 근처 move out 이사를 나가다(↔ move in 이사 오다) lease agreement 임대 계약(서) no later than 늦어도 ~까지는 collect 징수하다, 모으다 holding fee 예약금

168. 장 씨가 이메일을 보낸 이유는?
(A) 제안을 수락하기 위해
(B) 둘러보는 일정을 잡기 위해
(C) 주택 임대 계약서를 보내기 위해
(D) 최신 부동산 정보를 알려 주기 위해

해설 목적 문제

단서 (168)에서 장 씨는 아파트 중 일부가 임대되었음을 알리며 한 아파트는 아직 임대가 가능하다고 말하고 있다. 이를 통해 부동산과 관련된 현재의 상황, 즉 최신 부동산 정보를 알려 주기 위해 이메일을 보냈음을 알 수 있으므로 정답은 (D).

169. 이메일에 암시된 것은?
(A) 마잔티 씨는 침실 2개짜리 주택을 선호한다.
(B) 장 씨는 마잔티 씨의 사무실에서 그녀를 만날 것이다.
(C) 마잔티 씨의 직장은 알레타에 위치해 있다.
(D) 메트로 부동산은 설문 조사 정보를 모으고 있다.

해설 추론 문제

단서 (169)에서 HSW 빌딩의 아파트가 알레타 지역 내에 위치하고 있어 회사까지 걸어갈 수 있을 거라고 한 것으로 보아, 마잔티 씨의 회사 역시 알레타 지역 내에 위치하고 있음을 추론할 수 있으므로 정답은 (C).

패러프레이징 [단서] your office → [정답] Ms. Mazzanti's workplace

170. 장 씨에 따르면, 마잔티 씨가 서류를 제출해야 하는 기한은?
(A) 6월 10일
(B) 6월 14일
(C) 6월 20일
(D) 6월 21일

해설 특정 정보 확인 문제

단서 (170)에서 장 씨는 늦어도 6월 14일까지는 계약서에 서명을 하여 다시 보내 달라고 했으므로 정답은 (B). 지문의 a lease agreement가 문제에서는 some paperwork로 패러프레이징되었다.

171. [1], [2], [3], [4]번으로 표시된 위치들 중 다음 문장이 들어가기에 가장 적절한 곳은?

"게다가 고객님께서는 이사를 들어오실 때 한 달 치 임대료만큼의 보증금을 지불하셔야 할 것입니다."

(A) [1]
(B) [2]
(C) [3]
(D) [4]

해설 문장 위치 찾기 문제

제시된 문장에 추가를 나타내는 연결어 Additionally가 쓰였으므로, 이 문장과 같은 맥락을 갖고 있는 문장을 지문에서 찾아야 한다. 제시된 문장은 보증금 지불에 대한 내용이므로 보증금처럼 지불과 관련된 문장 뒤에 오는 것이 자연스러운데, 단서 (171)에서 예약금 지불에 대한 내용이 나오므로 해당 문장은 이 뒤에 이어서 나오는 것이 자연스럽다. 따라서 정답은 (D).

172-175 기사

캐리지 호수에서 정화 작업이 시작되다
제레미 트리그 작성

9월 9일—172시 당국이 몇 가지 장애물에 맞닥뜨린 끝에 마침내 캐리지 호수의 대규모 정화 프로젝트를 위한 계획이 진행 중에 있다. — [1] —. 호수 환경 개선의 필요성에 관한 논의가 올해 초 시작되었고, 필요한 대중의 지지를 모으는 데는 오랜 시간이 걸리지 않았다. 시 당국은 3월 말에 업체들이 응할 수 있도록 프로젝트를 입찰에 부쳤다. — [2] —. 175다행히도, 2차 입찰의 결과로 모리스 기업과 적절한 계약 합의가 이루어졌다.

지난주에 시작된 작업에는 호수 바닥에서 오염된 토양을 제거하는 일이 포함된다. — [3] —. 모리스 기업의 작업반은 프레스턴-680 유압식 준설선을 사용하여 침전물을 제거하고 있다. 이 장비는 직경이 24인치인 펌프를 갖추고 있는데, 모리스 기업은 이 프로젝트에 사용하기에는 힘이 충분하지 않았 카라밀로-55를 대체하고자 이 장비를 구입했다.

"과거에는 캐리지 호수가 뱃놀이 팬들과 낚시 팬들 사이에서 굉장한 인기를 끌었지만, 174B수년간 방문객 수가 하락세에 있었습니다,"라고 173시 의회 의원인 제인 클리프턴 씨는 말했다. "이 프로젝트에 납세자들이 낸 수천만 달러가 들고 있지만, 완성된 결과물은 관광객들과, 그들이 함께 가져올 수익을 끌어오게 될 것입니다. 환경에 미치는 영향도 고려한다면, 이것은 모두에게 득이 되는 상황입니다."

일단 작업이 완료되면 물속의 수은 함량은 97%만큼이나 감소될 것으로 예상된다. — [4] —. 이 때문에, 174A당국에서는 지난 수십 년간 허용하지 않았던 호수에서의 수영을 다시 한 번 허용할 계획이다. 174D또한 시에서는 그곳에 야외 무대를 지을 예정인데, 이곳에서 음악회, 시상식, 그리고 그 밖에 많은 것들을 개최할 것이다. 정화 작업의 경과를 확인하려면 www.carriagelakecleanup.org를 방문하면 된다.

라다 파이 오후 1:18	소장품의 규모가 방대해서, 전부 다 보려면 미리 계획을 세워야 해요.	
클라라 스탠스 오후 1:42	미술관의 일부 구역에서는 방문객들에게 사진 촬영이 허용되지 않는다고 들었어요.	
조이스 가르사 오후 1:46	당신 말이 맞아요, 클라라. 일부 구역에서 사진이 허용되지 않는데, 방문객들에게 알리기 위해 표지판이 눈에 띄게 놓여 있어요.	
클라라 스탠스 오후 1:59	¹⁶⁵그곳이 주말에는 정말 붐빌 것 같아서 평일에 가려고 해요. 어떤 요일이 가장 좋을까요?	
조이스 가르사 오후 2:16	그곳은 항상 만원이에요. 하지만 제 경험상, ¹⁶⁵많은 관광객과 학교 단체에 둘러싸이고 싶지 않다면 화요일이 가기에 가장 좋은 요일이에요.	
클라라 스탠스 오후 2:25	¹⁶⁵그렇다면 화요일에 그곳에 가야겠네요.	
알리사 베르디 오후 2:37	¹⁶⁶웹사이트, 안내 데스크, 미술관 곳곳에 세워진 표지판을 통해서 그곳의 규정에 대한 정보를 얻을 수 있어요.	
라다 파이 오후 2:51	¹⁶⁶맞아요. 라파예트는 제가 지난주에 방문한 곳인 팀버 미술관보다 더 나아요. 팀버 미술관은 그곳을 본받아야 해요.	
알리사 베르디 오후 2:55	¹⁶⁷한 번 이상 갈 계획이라면, 회원 가입을 해 볼 만해요. 1년 회원권은 20달러가 드는데, 방문할 때마다 7달러를 절약하게 되거든요.	
클라라 스탠스 오후 3:39	조언해 주셔서 감사해요, 여러분.	

어휘 collection 수집품, 소장품 enormous 막대한, 거대한 plan ahead 미리 계획하다 inform 알리다, 통지하다 assume (사실일 것으로) 추정하다 follow one's example ~을 본받다 sign up for ~을 신청[가입]하다 appreciate 고맙게 생각하다, 감사하다

164. 스탠스 씨가 요청하는 것은?
(A) 관광지 추천
(B) 장소 방문에 관한 조언
(C) 전시회를 열기 위한 조언
(D) 일정에 관한 설명

해설 특정 정보 확인 문제

단서 (164)에서 스탠스 씨가 라파예트 미술관에 관해 전시회 비평을 쓸 예정이라며 그 미술관에 가 본 적이 있는 사람들에게 조언을 요청한 것으로 보아 조언이 미술관 방문에 관한 것임을 알 수 있다. 따라서 정답은 (B).

패러프레이징 [단서] any advice / the Lafayette Art Museum → [정답] Tips / a place

165. 스탠스 씨가 화요일에 방문하기로 결정한 이유는?
(A) 인파를 피하고 싶어서.
(B) 특별 강의를 들을 수 있어서.

(C) 입장료가 할인되어서.
(D) 안내원이 딸린 견학이 제공되어서.

해설 특정 정보 확인 문제

단서 (165)에서 스탠스 씨는 미술관이 주말에 붐빌 것 같아서 평일에 가려고 한다면서 어떤 요일이 가장 좋을지 물어봤고, 이에 가르사 씨가 인파를 피하기 위한 요일로 화요일을 추천하자 화요일에 가야겠다고 했다. 이를 통해 스탠스 씨는 많은 사람을 상대하는 것을 피하고 싶어 함을 알 수 있으므로 정답은 (A).

패러프레이징 [단서] you don't want to be around a lot of tourists and school groups → [정답] she wants to avoid the crowds

166. 오후 2시 51분에, 파이 씨가 "팀버 미술관은 그곳을 본받아야 해요"라고 한 것에서 그녀가 의도한 것은?
(A) 팀버 미술관의 관람객 수가 현저히 감소했다.
(B) 팀버 미술관의 입장료는 관광객들에게 너무 비싸다.
(C) 팀버 미술관의 규정은 분명히 설명되어 있지 않다.
(D) 팀버 미술관의 소장품은 규모가 별로 크지 않다.

해설 의도 파악 문제

단서 (166)을 보면, 라파예트 미술관에서는 규정에 대한 정보를 다양한 방법으로 얻을 수 있다는 말에 대해 파이 씨가 동의하며 이전에 자신이 방문한 팀버 미술관보다 라파예트가 더 낫다고 한 것이므로, 팀버 미술관의 규정이 분명히 설명되어 있지 않다는 의미임을 알 수 있다. 따라서 정답은 (C).

167. 베르디 씨가 회원권에 대해 암시하는 것은?
(A) 온라인으로 구매해야 한다.
(B) 매년 갱신해야 한다.
(C) 매년 20달러의 할인을 제공한다.
(D) 회원들이 이틀짜리 입장권을 사도록 허용해 준다.

해설 추론 문제

단서 (167)에서 베르디 씨는 회원 가입을 추천하며 1년 회원권의 가격을 언급했다. 이를 통해 회원권이 1년 단위로 돌아간다는 것, 즉 매년 갱신해야 한다는 것을 추론할 수 있으므로 정답은 (B).

168-171 이메일

수신: 아이다 마잔티 〈a.mazzanti@smindustries.net〉
발신: 리 장 〈zhangli@metrorealty99.com〉
날짜: 6월 10일
제목: 메트로 부동산으로부터

마잔티 씨께,

지난주에 저를 만나 저희 회사를 통해 구할 수 있는 아파트 몇 군데를 돌아봐 주셔서 감사합니다. ¹⁶⁸엘리엇 타워의 아파트들과 지오 스위츠의 아파트는 임대되었음을 알아 두시기 바랍니다. — [1] —. ¹⁶⁸ ¹⁶⁹HSW 빌딩의 침실 2개짜리 아파트는 아직 임대가 가능합니다. 이곳이 고객님께서 원하셨던 것보다 더 크다는 것은 알고 있습니다. — [2] —. 하지만 ¹⁶⁹이곳은 알레타 지역 내에 위치하고 있

159. 리브스 씨의 신분은?
(A) 아이스 스케이팅 코치
(B) 패션 디자이너
(C) 영화 제작자
(D) 프로 선수

해설 추론 문제

단서 (159)에서 디자이너인 프레드릭 씨가 디자인 학교 졸업 후 처음 근무했던 곳으로 리브스 씨의 디자이너 의상실이 언급되었다. 이를 통해 리브스 씨 역시 패션 디자이너임을 유추할 수 있으므로 정답은 (B).

160. 하트 씨에 대해 암시된 것은?
(A) 프레드릭 씨와 몇몇 프로젝트에서 함께 일한 적이 있다.
(B) 최근에 영화 개봉 행사에 참석했다.
(C) 기념일 파티에서 프레드릭 씨를 만났다.
(D) 개인적으로 리브스 씨를 알고 있다.

해설 추론 문제

단서 (160)에서 프레드릭 씨가 이번 주 초에 영화 개봉 행사에 참석했는데 하트 씨가 이 행사에 그녀와 동행했다고 했으므로 하트 씨 역시 영화 개봉 행사에 참석했음을 유추할 수 있다. 따라서 정답은 (B). 기념일 파티에서 프레드릭 씨를 만난 사람은 하트 씨가 아니라 올리에로 씨이므로 (C)는 오답.

패러프레이징 [단서] the debut event for *Golden Galaxy* earlier this week → [정답] recently attended a movie premiere

161-163 편지

3월 8일
매장 관리자 숀 보이드
아웃도어즈 플러스, 술라드 지점
애시 로 1009번지
세인트루이스, 미주리 주 63146

보이드 씨께,

아시다시피, ¹⁶¹캠핑 스피어 주식회사에서 자사 제품 라인에 신제품 경량 배낭을 내놓을 계획입니다. 4월과 5월 두 달 내내 저희는 특별 판촉 행사를 열어 권장 소비자가에서 30% 할인된 가격에 그 제품을 내놓을 것입니다. 저희는 2주 앞서 할인 판매를 광고하기 시작할 것입니다. 공식 출시일은 4월 1일이 될 예정이며, ¹⁶²매킨리 하이츠 지점에서 특별 출시 행사가 있을 것입니다. 당신도 술라드 지점에서 이 행사를 개최하겠다고 신청했다는 것을 알고 있습니다만, ¹⁶²저희는 이미 이번과 같은 대규모 행사를 담당해 본 적이 있는 매장으로 하기로 결정했습니다. ¹⁶³다음 주에 제가 이 신제품 배낭을 위한 진열품들을 갖다 드리러 귀하의 매장에 방문할 것입니다. 이 진열대들은 눈에 잘 띄는 공간에 배치되어야 하며, ¹⁶³그때 제가 배치에 관해 조언해 드릴 수 있습니다.

저스틴 도슨 드림

어휘 introduce 내놓다, 도입하다 lightweight 경량의 promotion 판촉 (활동) in advance 앞서, 사전에 official 공식적인 large-scale 대규모의 drop off 내려 주다, 갖다 주다 prominent 눈에 잘 띄는 arrangement 배치

161. 신제품에 할인이 제공될 기간은?
(A) 1주
(B) 2주
(C) 1개월
(D) 2개월

해설 특정 정보 확인 문제

단서 (161)에서 신제품 출시 계획을 밝힌 후, 4월과 5월 두 달 내내 그 제품을 할인된 가격에 내놓을 거라고 했으므로 정답은 (D).

패러프레이징 [단서] for the entire months of April and May → [정답] Two months

162. 편지에 따르면, 행사를 위해 매킨리 하이츠 지점이 선택된 이유는?
(A) 매출액 향상이 가장 많이 필요하다.
(B) 직원들이 비슷한 행사를 주최한 적이 있다.
(C) 회사의 가장 큰 매장이다.
(D) 고객들이 그곳에서 행사를 여는 데 투표했다.

해설 특정 정보 확인 문제

단서 (162)에서 매킨리 하이츠 지점에서 행사가 있을 거라면서 이전에 이번과 같은 행사를 담당해 본 적이 있는 매장에서 행사를 주최하기로 했다고 했다. 즉, 매킨리 하이츠 지점의 직원들이 이전에 이와 비슷한 행사를 주최한 적이 있음을 알 수 있으므로 정답은 (B).

패러프레이징 [단서] had already been in charge of large-scale events such as this → [정답] have hosted similar events

163. 다음 주에 일어날 일은?
(A) 한 지점장이 홍보용 자료를 인쇄할 것이다.
(B) 도슨 씨가 몇몇 진열 전략을 추천해 줄 것이다.
(C) 한 매장에서 신제품 배낭을 판매하기 시작할 것이다.
(D) 보이드 씨가 제품 출시 행사를 감독할 것이다.

해설 다음에 할 일 문제

단서 (163)에서 다음 주에 신제품 배낭을 위한 진열품들을 매장에 가져다 주겠다고 하면서, 이때 배치에 관해 조언해 주겠다고 했으므로 정답은 (B).

패러프레이징 [단서] I can advise you on the arrangement → [정답] Mr. Dawson will recommend some display strategies

164-167 온라인 채팅

클라라 스탄스 안녕하세요. ¹⁶⁴저는 제 다음 전시회 비평으로 라
오후 1:09 파예트 미술관에 관해 쓸 예정이에요. 여러분 모두 전에 거기 가 본 적이 있는 걸 알아요. 제게 조언해 주실 만한 게 있나요?

도널드 그레이엄 [오전 9:15]
네, 예산을 약간 초과하긴 하지만, 그럴 만한 가치가 있다고 생각해요.

웨이 루 [오전 9:16]
그렇게 생각하세요? 거기엔 심지어 가구 비용은 포함되지도 않았잖아요.

도널드 그레이엄 [오전 9:18]
157로비는 사람들이 도착했을 때 처음으로 보게 되는 거라는 걸 이해하셔야 해요. 사람들이 맨 처음부터 우리 회사에 대해 긍정적인 생각을 갖는 것이 가장 중요하니까요.

웨이 루 [오전 9:19]
일리가 있네요. 그게 사람들로 하여금 우리 서비스에 더 많은 신뢰를 갖게 해 줄 거라고 봐요.

어휘 estimate 견적 slightly 약간 budget 예산 worth ~을 할 가치가 있는 include 포함하다 essential 가장 중요한, 필수적인 have a good opinion of ~을 좋게 생각[평가]하다 business 회사 have a point 일리가 있다 confidence 신뢰, 자신감

156. 메시지 작성자들이 주로 이야기하고 있는 것은?
(A) 호텔 숙박 시설
(B) 예산 한도
(C) 개조 비용
(D) 고객 후기

해설 주제 문제

단서 (156)에서 로비 리모델링 견적이 언급되고, 리모델링 비용에 관한 내용이 이어지고 있으므로 정답은 (C). budget이라는 말 때문에 (B)를 정답으로 고르지 않도록 주의하자.

패러프레이징 [단서] the estimate from the interior designer for remodeling our lobby → [정답] Renovation costs

157. 오전 9시 19분에 루 씨가 "일리가 있네요"라고 한 것에서 그녀가 의도한 것은?
(A) 신규 고객들을 유치하는 것은 쉽지 않다.
(B) 회사는 지출에 주의해야 한다.
(C) 좋은 인상을 주는 것이 중요하다.
(D) 로비는 곧 확장되어야 한다.

해설 의도 파악 문제

단서 (157)에서 그레이엄 씨는 사람들이 회사에 도착해서 처음 보게 되는 것이 로비이고, 그들이 처음부터 회사에 대해 긍정적인 생각을 갖도록 하는 게 가장 중요하다고 했다. 루 씨는 이에 대한 동의의 표현으로 '일리가 있네요'라고 말한 것이므로 그레이엄 씨의 말을 달리 표현한 (C)가 정답.

패러프레이징 [단서] It's essential that they have a good opinion of our business → [정답] Making a good impression is important

158-160 기사

뉴욕 (9월 10일)—폴라 프레더릭 씨는 패션쇼 무대 위와 무대 아래 모두에서 최신 유행의 세련된 패션으로 알려져 있다. 그녀는 자신의 소매 사업뿐만 아니라 158다수의 영화를 위해 상을 받은 의상들을 만들어 왔는데, 그중 최신작으로는 SF 블록버스터 〈골든 갤럭시〉가 있다. 이제 프레더릭 씨는 국가 대표 아이스 스케이팅팀의 준비 운동용 유니폼과 경기용 의상을 디자인하는 새로운 프로젝트에 자신의 재능을 보탤 것이다. 그 팀은 1월 3일부터 1월 16일까지 개최되는 국제 아이스 스케이팅 토너먼트에서 이 의상들을 입을 것이다.

159프레더릭 씨는 샬럿 리브스 씨의 기념일 행사에서 그 팀의 코치인 빈스 올리에로 씨를 만나 이 프로젝트를 제안받았는데, 샬럿 리브스 씨의 디자이너 의상실은 프레더릭 씨가 디자인 학교를 졸업하고 나서 처음으로 고용되었던 곳이었다. 올리에로 씨가 팀의 외양을 최신식으로 바꿀 필요가 있다고 언급하면서 이 프로젝트에 대한 아이디어가 탄생했다.

업계 관계자들은 프레더릭 씨의 정교한 스타일이 스포츠계에서 어떻게 변화할지 지켜보는 것에 관심을 가지고 있다. "저는 그 도전을 고대하고 있어요."라고 160이번 주 초 〈골든 갤럭시〉의 개봉 행사에서 프레더릭 씨는 말했다. "이 영화에서 저는 과장된 디자인과 호화로운 장식을 이용해 작업할 수 있었어요. 새 프로젝트에서는 선택할 수 있는 천 소재도 제한적이고 편안함과 실용성에 우선순위를 두어야겠죠." 160행사에 프레더릭 씨와 동행한 〈골든 갤럭시〉의 제작자 리엄 하트 씨 역시 프레더릭 씨의 무한한 창조성이 프로젝트를 성공으로 이끄는 데 도움을 줄 것을 확신한다고 말하면서 프로젝트에 대한 견해를 밝혔다.

프레더릭 씨 작품의 팬들은 영화관 및 그녀의 웹사이트에서 〈골든 갤럭시〉의 의상들을 볼 수 있다. 그러나 유니폼을 보려면 토너먼트를 직접 또는 TV 생중계로 봐야 할 것이다.

어휘 sophisticated 세련된 outfit 복장 fashion house 디자이너 의상실 insider 관계자, 내부자 elaborate 정교한 translate (다른 형태로) 바꾸다[바꾸다] over-the-top 정도가 지나친 lavish 호화로운, 풍성한 embellishment 장식(물) prioritize 우선순위를 매기다 practicality 실용성 accompany 동행하다, 동반하다 big screen 영화(관)

158. 〈골든 갤럭시〉 의상에 대해 사실인 것은?
(A) 프레더릭 씨의 첫 프로젝트였다.
(B) 실용적이고 편안하다.
(C) 상을 받았다.
(D) 온라인에서 구매할 수 있다.

해설 Not/True 문제

단서 (158)을 통해 프레더릭 씨가 만든 영화 의상들이 상을 받았음을 알 수 있는데, 그중 최신작이 〈골든 갤럭시〉라고 나와 있다. 따라서 정답은 (C).

패러프레이징 [단서] award-winning costumes → [정답] They received an award

(C) 생산 효율이 높아졌다.
(D) 고객들이 다른 직물들을 선호하기 시작했다.

해설 특정 정보 확인 문제

단서 (151)에서 비단 공급 업체들이 비단을 모아 비축해 오고 있으며 이로 인해 비단의 가격이 상승했다고 했다. 따라서 정답은 (A). China and India가 언급되었다고 해서 (B)를 정답으로 고르지 않도록 주의하자.

패러프레이징 [단서] Silk suppliers have been accumulating large quantities of the product at cheap prices and storing it → [정답] Some dealers are stocking up on the material

152. 의류 제조 업체들이 변화에 대처하고 있는 방법은?
(A) 공급 업체들과 직접 협상을 함으로써
(B) 대체 직물로 제품을 개발함으로써
(C) 공급품을 대량으로 구매함으로써
(D) 상품이 광고되는 방식을 바꿈으로써

해설 특정 정보 확인 문제

단서 (152)에서 많은 의류 생산 업체들이 비단 시장의 예측 불가능성을 피하기 위해 인조 직물로 만든 의류를 디자인하고 있다고 했으므로 정답은 (B). 지문의 many such producers가 문제에서는 clothing manufacturers로 패러프레이징되었다.

패러프레이징 [단서] designing clothing made from man-made fabric, such as nylon and rayon → [정답] developing products with alternative materials

153-155 이메일

수신: 니나 이젤 〈n.ezell@prime-cleaning.net〉
발신: 아카시 바달 〈a.badal@prime-cleaning.net〉
날짜: 4월 4일
제목: 청소 용역

니나 씨께,

우리가 4월 10일부터 길버트 앤드 어소시엇츠 사에 제공할 전문 청소 용역에 관해 메일을 드립니다. 제가 검토해 보길 원하셨던 계약서를 살펴보던 중이었는데, 153유감스럽게도 잘못된 주소가 사용되어 우리는 현재의 계약서 양식에 서명할 수 없습니다. 154당신이 4월 1일에 길버트 앤드 어소시엇츠 사의 담당자와 만나 계약 조건을 논의했다는 것을 알고 있습니다. 그러나 그 사람은 당신에게 회사가 이틀 뒤 사무실을 이전할 예정이었다는 말을 해 줬어야만 합니다. 계약서에는 새 건물의 주소가 반영되어야 합니다. 당신이 이 고객을 맡아 온 사람이므로, 155당신이 그들에게 전화를 걸어 정확한 새 주소를 알아내는 것이 최선일 것 같습니다. 우리는 서명된 버전의 계약서를 내일 택배로 발송해야 하므로, 155이 일을 오늘 처리해서 우리가 서류 작업에서 예정보다 뒤처지지 않게 해 주세요.

아카시 드림

어휘 regarding ~에 관하여 associate (일·사업 등의) 제휴자, 동료 contract 계약(서) representative 대표자, 담당자 terms (항상 복수형) 조건, 조항 relocate 이전하다 reflect 반영하다 find out ~을 알아내다 behind schedule 예정보다 늦게 paperwork 서류 작업

153. 바달 씨가 이메일을 보낸 이유는?
(A) 업체를 추천하기 위해
(B) 청소 일정을 변경하기 위해
(C) 업데이트된 계약서를 보내기 위해
(D) 오류를 지적하기 위해

해설 목적 문제

단서 (153)에서 계약서에 잘못된 주소가 사용되어 서명을 할 수 없다는 문제를 언급했다. 이를 통해 계약서상의 오류를 알리기 위해 이메일을 보냈음을 알 수 있으므로 정답은 (D).

패러프레이징 [단서] the wrong address was used → [정답] an error

154. 길버트 앤드 어소시엇츠 사가 새 건물로 이사한 때는?
(A) 3월 28일
(B) 3월 30일
(C) 4월 1일
(D) 4월 3일

해설 특정 정보 확인 문제

단서 (154)를 보면 4월 1일에 있었던 미팅에서 길버트 앤드 어소시엇츠 사의 담당자가 자신의 회사가 이틀 뒤 사무실을 이전한다는 이야기를 하지 않았음을 알 수 있다. 4월 1일에서 이틀 뒤는 4월 3일이므로 정답은 (D). 지문의 relocate their offices가 문제에서는 move to a new building으로 패러프레이징되었다.

155. 이젤 씨가 오늘까지 해야 하는 일은?
(A) 일부 계약 조건 협상하기
(B) 길버트 앤드 어소시엇츠 사무실에 연락하기
(C) 바달 씨에게 고객 추천서 보내기
(D) 프라임 클리닝 사에 우편으로 서류 보내기

해설 특정 정보 확인 문제

단서 (155)에서 이젤 씨에게 길버트 앤드 어소시엇츠 사에 전화하여 새 주소를 알아낼 것을 요청하면서 일정에 뒤처지지 않도록 오늘 이 일을 처리해 달라고 했으므로 정답은 (B).

패러프레이징 [단서] call them → [정답] Contact the Gilbert & Associates office

156-157 문자 메시지

도널드 그레이엄 [오전 9:12]
156인테리어 디자이너에게서 받은 우리 로비의 리모델링 견적을 당신에게 이메일로 보냈어요.

웨이 루 [오전 9:14]
제가 예상하던 것보다 비싸네요. 특히나 우리 변호사들은 그 공간을 많이 이용하지도 않으니까요.

147. 이 공지를 찾을 수 있을 것 같은 곳은?

(A) 제품 카탈로그
(B) 공공 게시판
(C) 지하철 승차권 영수증
(D) 수공예 설명서

해설 출처 문제

단서 (147)에서 멜빌 지역 단체에서 활동할 회원을 모집한다고 한 것으로 보아 멜빌 지역의 주민들을 대상으로 하는 공지임을 추론할 수 있다. 이러한 지역 주민 대상 공지는 지역의 공공 게시판에서 찾을 수 있을 것으로 유추할 수 있으므로 정답은 (B).

148. 공지에 따르면, 사람들이 웹사이트를 방문해야 하는 이유는?

(A) 지난 프로젝트들의 사진을 보기 위해
(B) 행사 등록을 확정하기 위해
(C) 이메일로 설명서를 요청하기 위해
(D) 자신이 선택한 재료를 알리기 위해

해설 특정 정보 확인 문제

단서 (148)에서 웹사이트에 글을 남겨 뚜껑 재료로 무엇을 가져올 것인지 알려 달라고 했으므로 정답은 (D). 지문의 commenting in the forum at warmhandswh.org/forum이 문제에서는 visit the Web site으로 패러프레이징되었다.

패러프레이징 [단서] let us know what you plan to bring for your project → [정답] report their choices of materials

149-150 청구서

월러스 공구

청구서 날짜: 10월 25일
청구서 번호: 8395
이름: 딘 모네트
주소: 캐리지 드라이브 805번지, 알링턴 하이츠, 일리노이 주 60005
연락처: 555-6950
1주 대여료: 49.99달러

[내용물]
하드론-360 전기 드릴
¹⁴⁹ᴰ플라스틱 휴대용 케이스
¹⁴⁹ᴮ장치 배터리용 충전기
¹⁴⁹ᶜ1주간의 보험 보장 (보험 증권 정보 관련 인쇄물)

세금 및 운송료: 8.95달러
총액: 58.94달러

위 서비스의 대금은 모두 지불되었습니다. ¹⁵⁰물건을 더 오래 가지고 계시길 원하신다면, 555-2900번으로 저희에게 전화해 주십시오. ¹⁴⁹ᴬ기구의 사용 설명서는 저희 웹사이트인 www.wallacetools.net에서 다운로드하실 수 있습니다.

어휘 invoice 청구서, 송장   rental 대여료, 임대   unit (작은) 기구, 장치

coverage (보험) 보장 범위   policy 보험 증권   printout 인쇄(물)
in full 전부   user manual 사용 설명서

149. 대여 물품과 함께 발송되지 않은 것은?

(A) 사용 설명서
(B) 배터리 충전기
(C) 보험 세부 정보
(D) 휴대용 용기

해설 Not/True 문제

Not/True 문제는 지문과 선택지를 하나하나 대조해 가며 풀어야 한다. 단서 (149B), (149C), (149D)를 통해 대여 물품인 전기 드릴과 함께 배터리 충전기, 보험 증권 관련 인쇄물, 휴대용 케이스가 발송되었음을 알 수 있다. 하지만 단서 (149A)에서 사용 설명서는 웹사이트에서 다운로드할 수 있다고 했으므로 정답은 (A).

150. 모네트 씨가 주어진 번호로 전화해야 하는 이유는?

(A) 서비스에 대한 피드백을 하기 위해
(B) 지불을 하기 위해
(C) 사용 설명서를 요청하기 위해
(D) 대여 기간을 연장하기 위해

해설 특정 정보 확인 문제

단서 (150)에서 대여 물품을 더 오래 가지고 있으려면 주어진 번호로 전화해 달라고 했다. 따라서 정답은 (D).

패러프레이징 [단서] to keep the item longer → [정답] To extend a rental period

151-152 기사

베이징 (7월 5일)—생사의 가격이 지난 분기에 4년 만에 최저치를 기록한 이후로 다시 상승세에 있다. 이는 부분적으로는 세계 최대의 비단 생산국인 중국과 인도에서의 동향 때문이다. ¹⁵¹비단 공급 업체들은 많은 양의 생산물을 낮은 가격에 모아 그것들을 시장에 내놓는 대신에 비축해 오고 있다. 이는 가격 상승으로 이어졌으며, 이러한 현상은 다음 몇 분기 동안 계속될 것으로 예상된다. 의류 생산 업체들은 비단의 낮은 가격을 누려 왔으나, 이제 더 높은 원자재 비용이 예상됨에 따라 해당 직물은 매력이 크게 떨어졌다. 그 결과, ¹⁵²이러한 생산 업체들 다수가 비단 시장의 예측 불가능성을 피하기 위해 나일론이나 레이온과 같은 인조 직물로 만든 의류를 디자인하고 있다.

어휘 raw silk 생사(生絲), 생 명주실   on the rise 상승 추세에 있는
hit a low 최저치를 기록하다   in part 부분적으로는   supplier 공급자, 공급 회사   accumulate 모으다, 축적하다   store 비축하다, (창고에) 보관하다
lead to ~으로 이어지다   now that ~이므로   project 예상하다   fabric 직물   man-made 인조의   unpredictability 예측 불가능

151. 기사에 따르면, 비단의 가격에 영향을 미친 것은?

(A) 일부 취급 업자들이 직물을 비축하고 있다.
(B) 중국과 인도의 통화 가치가 떨어졌다.

141. 소유격

해설 선택지를 통해 인칭대명사의 알맞은 격과 수를 고르는 문제임을 알 수 있다. 빈칸은 구전치사 due to의 목적어인 modern facilities and proximity를 수식해 주는 한정사 자리로, 선택지 중 한정사로 쓰일 수 있는 것은 소유격이므로 (A)와 (C)가 정답 후보. 내용상 소유격이 앞 문장에 나오는 단수 명사 Boulevard Hall을 가리키므로 단수 대명사 it의 소유격 its가 적절하다. 따라서 정답은 (C).

142. 알맞은 문장 고르기

(A) 저희는 귀하께서 넓은 공간에 깊은 인상을 받으실 거라고 생각합니다.
(B) 그렇다 할지라도, 많은 사람이 사무실에서부터 걸어갈 수 있습니다.
(C) 이 요금은 저희의 예상 예산 범위 안에 있습니다.
(D) 만약 그렇지 않다면, 저희는 다른 가능한 날짜도 몇 개 염두에 두고 있습니다.

해설 빈칸 앞에서 특정 날짜에 불러바드 홀을 이용할 수 있기를 바란다고 했으므로 빈칸에서는 그 날짜에 홀을 이용할 수 없는 경우에 대해 언급하는 것이 자연스럽다. If not을 이용하여 앞 문장과 대조되는 경우를 언급하며 특정 날짜 외에 다른 날짜들도 염두에 두고 있다고 한 (D)가 정답.

143-146 이메일

수신: 트래블 타임즈 〈info@traveltimes-magazine.com〉
발신: 크리스토퍼 벤 〈c.venn@frequenx.com〉
제목: 구독 번호 28571
날짜: 9월 3일

관계자분께:

저는 현재 2월 말까지 유효한 〈트래블 타임즈〉지 구독을 하고 있습니다. 다음 호가 나오기 전에 우편 주소를 변경하는 것이 ¹⁴³가능한지 궁금합니다. ¹⁴⁴귀사의 웹사이트를 통해서는 이렇게 하는 것에 관한 어떤 정보도 찾을 수 없었습니다. 저는 현재 직장에서 잡지를 받고 있는데, 새로운 부장님이 우리가 더 이상 그곳으로 개인 우편물이 배달되지 않도록 할 것을 ¹⁴⁵요청하셨거든요. ¹⁴⁶제 집 주소는 트렐로니 로 798번지, 피닉스, 애리조나 주 85010입니다. 이 변경과 관련해 수수료가 있다면, 제게 이메일을 보내 주시기 바랍니다.

감사합니다.

크리스토퍼 벤 드림

어휘 subscription 구독 valid 유효한 wonder 궁금하다 mailing address 우편 주소 come out (책이) 출판되다, 나오다 no longer 더 이상 ~ 아닌 residential address 집 주소 fee 수수료 associated with ~과 관련된

143. 명사절 접속사 if

(A) 무엇 **(B) ~인지 아닌지** (C) ~하는 동안 (D) ~이니까

해설 빈칸 이하는 동사 am wondering의 목적어이므로 명사절을 이끌 수 있는 의문대명사 (A)와 명사절 접속사 (B)가 정답 후보. 빈칸 뒤에 완전한 절이 나오고, 의미상으로도 '변경하는 것이 가능한지' 궁금한 것이므로 정답은 (B).

144. 알맞은 문장 고르기

(A) 스페인에 관한 정보가 특히 흥미로웠습니다.
(B) 월별 청구서에서 제게 두 건의 구독에 대한 요금을 청구했습니다.
(C) 귀사의 웹사이트를 통해서는 이렇게 하는 것에 관한 어떤 정보도 찾을 수 없었습니다.
(D) 제가 제출한 기사를 게재해 주셔서 감사합니다.

해설 빈칸 앞에서 주소 변경 가능 여부를 물었고 빈칸 뒤에서는 주소 변경 이유를 설명하고 있으므로, 빈칸에도 역시 주소 변경과 관련된 내용이 들어가야 한다. 따라서 정답은 (C). 선택지의 doing this는 바로 앞 문장의 to change the mailing address를 가리킨다.

145. 동사 어휘 request

(A) 요청하다 (B) 가능하게 하다 (C) 인정하다 (D) 취소하다

해설 문맥에 알맞은 동사 어휘를 고르는 문제. 새로운 부장님이 '개인 우편물이 배달되지 않도록 할 것을 요청했다'고 하는 것이 우편 주소를 변경하려는 이유로 가장 적절하므로 정답은 (A). 요구를 나타내는 동사 request의 목적어로 쓰인 that절의 동사는 《(should)+동사원형》의 형태가 되어야 함을 알아 두자.

146. 소유격

해설 빈칸 뒤의 residential address를 수식하기에 알맞은 한정사 역할의 어휘를 고르는 문제. 문맥상 잡지를 받을 '자신의 집 주소'를 의미하므로 정답은 (D).

PART 7

147-148 공지

따뜻한 손 따뜻한 마음(WHWH)에서는 ¹⁴⁷멜빌 지역 단체의 신규 회원들을 모집하고 있는데, 그 단체는 노숙자들에게 기부할 벙어리장갑과 손가락장갑을 뜹니다. 저희의 다음 모임은 11월 2일 토요일 오후 1시부터 4시까지 린데일 커피숍에서 있을 예정입니다. 그곳에 오시려면, 지하철 5호선을 타고 킹스타운 경기장 역으로 오셔서 5번 출구를 이용하십시오.

참여자들은 본인의 뜨개실과 뜨개질바늘을 가지고 와야 합니다. 또한 저희는 여러 가지 색상과 뜨개실 종류를 원하므로, ¹⁴⁸warmhandswh.org/forum의 포럼 게시판에 글을 남겨서 본인의 뜨개 작업을 위해 무엇을 가져올 계획인지 저희에게 알려 주세요.

어휘 knit 뜨다, 짜다 mitten 벙어리장갑 donate 기부하다 the homeless 노숙자들 yarn 뜨개실 knitting needle 뜨개질바늘 a variety of 여러 가지의 comment 의견을 말하다, 주석을 달다

었으므로 빈칸에는 독자에게 선착순 판매 및 할인 행사 시작일과 관련하여 요청하는 내용이 나오는 것이 자연스럽다. 따라서 인과를 나타내는 연결사 So를 이용하여 할인 혜택을 놓치지 않도록 빨리 올 것을 요청하는 (B)가 정답이다.

135-138 공지

노라 데번스 씨와의 공공 세미나
5월 14일 목요일 저녁 7시

프레드릭 시에서 노숙 문제를 없애는 것에 대한 유명 135옹호자인 노라 데번스 씨가 레너 컨벤션 센터에서 2시간짜리 세미나를 진행할 예정입니다. 데번스 씨는 300명이 넘는 회원이 있는 단체인 사회 복지사 협회의 회장입니다. 그녀는 지난 8년간 노숙자 공동체를 후원하는 활동을 136이끌어 왔습니다. 세미나 동안, 그녀는 청중에게 노숙자 문제의 심각성에 관해 이야기할 것입니다. 137그녀는 또한 그것의 해결을 도울 방법도 언급할 것입니다.

강연은 모든 연령의 청중에게 열려 있고, 입장료는 없습니다. 138그러나, 마리골드 노숙자 쉼터를 후원하기 위해 입구에서 기부금을 걷을 것입니다. 더 자세한 정보를 원하시면 www.assocofsw.org를 방문해 주세요.

어휘 prominent 유명한, 현저한 eliminate 없애다, 제거하다 homelessness 노숙자임 present 진행하다, 수여하다 association 협회, 연상 social worker 사회 복지사 support 후원하다 homeless 노숙자의 seriousness 심각함 entrance fee 입장료 donation 기부(금) shelter 쉼터, 피난처

135. 명사 어휘 advocate

(A) 설립자 **(B) 옹호자** (C) 후보자 (D) 검사

해설 콤마 앞의 고유 명사 Nora Devons와 동격을 이루면서 빈칸 뒤의 전치사구 of eliminating homelessness in Fredrick City의 수식을 받을 수 있는 명사를 찾아야 한다. 문맥상 '노숙 문제를 없애는 것에 대한 유명 옹호자'라는 의미가 가장 자연스러우므로 정답은 (B).

136. 현재완료시제

해설 단서로 기간을 나타내는 부사구 for the past eight years를 빠르게 찾아야 한다. 문맥상 '지난 8년간 노숙자 공동체를 후원하는 활동을 이끌어 왔다'는 의미이므로 현재완료시제가 적절하다. 따라서 정답은 (B). 이처럼 기간을 나타내는 표현은 특정 시점까지 지속되는 상태를 나타내는 완료시제와 잘 어울려 쓰인다는 점을 기억하자.

137. 알맞은 문장 고르기

(A) 그녀는 또한 그것의 해결을 도울 방법도 언급할 것입니다.
(B) 휴식 시간 동안 청중이 질문을 했습니다.
(C) 그 당시에, 그녀는 시 의회 의원으로 일했습니다.
(D) 그녀는 석사 학위를 따기 위해 그레이슨 대학으로 돌아갈 계획입니다.

해설 빈칸 앞에서 세미나에서 이야기할 주제인 노숙자 문제의 심각성을 언급했으므로 빈칸에는 이와 관련된 내용이나 세미나에서 다뤄질 또 다른 내용이 들어가야 자연스럽다. 따라서 정답은 (A). 선택지의 it은 바로 앞 문장의 the homeless problem을 가리킨다.

138. 접속부사 however

(A) 따라서 (B) 구체적으로 말하면 (C) 분명히 **(D) 그러나**

해설 문맥상 알맞은 접속부사를 고르는 문제이므로 빈칸 앞뒤 문장의 의미 관계를 파악해야 한다. 빈칸 앞의 '강연 입장료가 없다'는 내용과 빈칸 뒤의 '기부금을 걷을 것이다'는 내용은 의미상 대조 관계이므로 대조를 나타내는 접속부사 (D)가 정답이다.

139-142 이메일

수신: 나타샤 시모어 〈nseymour@vicivenues.com〉
발신: 로버트 손턴 〈r.thornton@hvelectronics.net〉
날짜: 10월 3일
제목: 불러바드 홀에서의 행사

시모어 씨께,

저는 HV 일렉트로닉스 사의 제 동료들 중 한 명의 은퇴 기념 만찬 139준비를 맡은 위원회의 일원입니다. 귀사의 장소들 중 몇 군데가 140고려되었습니다만, 불러바드 홀이 가장 높은 지지를 받았습니다. 이는 141그곳의 현대적인 시설과 브레이클리 타워스에 위치한 저희 사무실과의 근접성 때문이었습니다.

저희가 불러바드 홀에서 행사를 진행하는 것은 이번이 처음이 될 것입니다. 11월 중에 어느 날짜가 이용 가능한지 확인해 주시겠습니까? 저희는 11월 20일을 선호하므로 그날 저녁이 아직 비어 있기를 바랍니다. 142만약 그렇지 않다면, 저희는 다른 가능한 날짜도 몇 개 염두에 두고 있습니다.

로버트 손턴 드림

어휘 committee 위원회 be in charge of ~을 맡다[담당하다] retirement 은퇴 coworker 동료 electronics 《항상 복수형》 전자 기기 consider 고려하다 support 지지 due to ~ 때문에 facility 시설 proximity 근접성, 가까움

139. 동사 어휘 arrange

(A) 고무하다 **(B) 준비하다** (C) 기여하다 (D) 방문하다

해설 문맥상 '은퇴 기념 만찬 준비를 맡은 위원회'라는 의미가 가장 자연스러우므로 정답은 (B).

140. 동사 자리_수동태+과거시제

해설 빈칸에 들어갈 알맞은 태와 시제를 가진 동사를 고르는 문제. consider가 타동사임에도 빈칸 뒤에 목적어가 없고, 내용상 문장의 주어인 '몇 군데의 장소들'은 고려되는 주체가 아니라 고려받는 대상이므로 수동태인 (A)와 (C)가 정답 후보. 문맥상 '몇 군데 장소들이 고려되었는데 가장 높은 지지를 받은 장소가 있었다'는 의미가 되어야 자연스러우므로 과거시제인 (C)가 정답이다.

해설 문맥상 '다른 스피커들에 비해 눈에 띄게 우수하다'는 의미가 가장 자연스러우므로 정답은 (A).

어휘 superior 우수한 compared to ~과 비교하여 on the market 시중에 나와 있는 afford (~을 살) 여유가 되다

129. 관계대명사

객석의 맨 앞 두 줄은 VIP 내빈을 위해 특별히 지정되어 있는데, 그들 대부분이 발표자들이다.

해설 빈칸에는 콤마 앞뒤로 위치해 있는 두 개의 절을 이어 주면서 빈칸 뒤의 동사 are의 주어 역할을 하는 관계대명사가 들어가야 한다. 목적격 관계대명사 앞에 most of가 붙어 '선행사의 대부분'을 의미하는 (C)가 정답.

어휘 row 줄, 열 auditorium 객석, 강당 reserve 지정하다, 예약해 두다 presenter 발표자 as a matter of fact 사실상 on the contrary 반대로

130. 형용사 어휘 enjoyable

많은 견학 참가자들이 시의 역사에 대해 배우는 것이 얼마나 재미있을 수 있는지 알고 매우 기뻐했다.

(A) 상당한 (B) 책임이 있는 **(C) 재미있는** (D) 이동할 수 있는

해설 빈칸을 포함하는 to부정사구 앞에 감정을 나타내는 형용사인 delighted가 나왔으므로 to부정사구는 감정의 원인을 설명해 주는 부사 역할을 하고 있음을 알 수 있다. '배우는 것이 얼마나 재미있을 수 있는지 알게 되는 것'이 delighted의 원인으로 가장 자연스럽다. 따라서 정답은 (C).

어휘 delighted 아주 기뻐하는 discover 깨닫다, 발견하다

PART 6

131-134 광고

7월 첫 주 동안 트윙클 주얼리에서 1주년을 기념하기 위한 특별 행사가 열릴 예정입니다. 단 일주일간, 제품 두 개를 사시면 저희가 한 개의 ¹³¹**값만 청구할 것입니다**. 예를 들어, 만약 여러분이 목걸이 하나와 팔찌 하나를 구매하신다면, 더 저렴한 제품의 값만 지불하시게 됩니다! 여러분은 다양하게 ¹³²**구비된** 저희의 보석류 중 어느 것이든 마음에 드시는 것 두 개를 고르실 수 있습니다. 이 할인은 저희의 모든 제품에 적용됩니다! ¹³³**게다가**, 한 사람이 받을 수 있는 할인 혜택의 횟수에는 제한이 없습니다. 하지만 보석류는 재고가 남아 있는 동안 선착순으로 제공될 것입니다. ¹³⁴**그러니 빨리 오셔서 절대 이 기회를 놓치지 마세요**. 행사는 7월 1일에 시작됩니다.

어휘 charge (요금·값을) 청구하다, 충전하다 pay for 대금을 지불하다 a wide selection of 다양하게 구비된 offer 할인, 제안 apply to ~에 적용되다 limit 제한 benefit from ~의 혜택을 받다 give out ~을 나누어 주다 on a first come, first served basis 선착순으로 supply 재고(량), 공급(량)

131. 동사 자리_미래시제+능동태

해설 앞으로 있을 행사에 대한 안내이므로, 미래시제인 (A)와 (B)가 정답 후보. 주어인 we는 값을 청구하는 주체이고 빈칸 뒤에 목적어가 있으므로 능동태인 (A)가 정답.

132. 명사 자리_형용사+명사

해설 빈칸은 빈칸 앞에 있는 〈소유격+형용사〉 구조인 our wide의 수식을 받으면서, 동시에 빈칸 뒤 전치사구 of jewelry의 수식을 받는 명사 자리이다. 따라서 정답은 명사인 (C).

133. 접속부사 in addition

(A) 게다가 (B) 그 결과 (C) 그러므로 (D) 따라서

해설 빈칸 앞 문장에서 모든 제품이 할인 대상임을 언급했고, 빈칸 뒤에서는 그 할인을 받을 수 있는 횟수에 제한이 없다고 했다. 할인 혜택이 나열되고 있으므로, 빈칸에는 추가의 의미를 나타내는 접속부사가 오는 것이 적절하다. 따라서 정답은 (A).

134. 알맞은 문장 고르기

(A) 그래서 저희가 고객님의 구매에 대해 환불을 해 드리기로 동의한 겁니다.
(B) 그러니 빨리 오셔서 절대 이 기회를 놓치지 마세요.
(C) 요청하시는 물건들은 저희가 고객님을 위해 따로 챙겨 놓겠습니다.
(D) 가능한 한 빨리 지불을 완료해 주세요.

해설 빈칸 앞에서 보석류는 재고가 남아 있는 동안 선착순으로 제공될 거라는 내용이 나오고 빈칸 뒤에서는 할인 행사의 시작일이 언급되

사가 와야 하므로 전치사인 (B)와 (D)가 정답 후보. fluctuation은 전치사 in을 동반하여 '어떤 분야나 특징의 변동'을 의미하므로 정답은 (B). fluctuation in을 하나의 덩어리로 외워 두자.

어휘 take ~ into account ~을 고려하다, 계산에 넣다
currency rate (보통 복수형) 환율   make a projection 예측하다

120. 부사 자리_형용사 수식
많은 잠재적 고객이 플레처 모바일 사의 혼란스러울 정도로 비슷한 휴대 전화 요금제들 때문에 의욕을 잃었다.

해설 빈칸 없이도 문장이 완전하므로 빈칸은 빈칸 뒤의 형용사 similar를 수식해 주는 부사 자리이다. 따라서 부사인 (B)가 정답. 빈칸 앞의 전치사 by만 보고 전치사의 목적어를 고르는 문제로 착각하여 동명사인 (A)나 명사인 (C)를 정답으로 고르지 않도록 주의하자.

어휘 potential 잠재적인   discouraged 의욕을 잃어버린, 낙담한
confusingly 혼란스럽게   plan (특정 연금·보험료 등을 위한) 제도, 요금제

121. 명사 자리+명사 어휘 signature
쳉 씨는 그 협약의 증인 자격으로 계약서에 자신의 서명을 추가했다.

해설 빈칸은 소유격 her의 수식을 받는 자리이므로 명사인 (C) signature가 정답. (B) signs를 명사 sign의 복수형으로 볼 수도 있지만, sign이 명사로 쓰이면 '징후, 신호'라는 뜻이므로 문맥에 어울리지 않는다.

어휘 add 추가하다, 덧붙이다   contract 계약(서)   witness 증인, 목격자
agreement 협약, 협정, 계약

122. 부정대명사 another
탑승권을 분실 또는 훼손하셨다면, 탑승구 직원에게 이야기하세요. 그러면 그걸 확인하고 또 하나를 인쇄해 드릴 것입니다.
(A) 또 하나 (B) (둘 사이에서) 서로 (C) 다른 것들 (D) (셋 이상 사이에서) 서로

해설 빈칸은 동사 print의 목적어인 동시에, 앞에서 언급한 boarding pass의 또 다른 한 개를 의미해야 한다. 따라서 '또 (다른) 하나'를 가리키는 부정대명사 (A)가 정답. '서로'를 의미하는 (B)와 (D)는 의미상 print의 목적어가 되기에 어색하므로 오답. 빈칸이 가리키는 것은 한 개의 boarding pass이므로 '다른 것들'을 의미하는 복수형 부정대명사인 (C)도 오답.

어휘 boarding pass 탑승권   gate 탑승구, 문   agent 직원, 대리인
verify 확인하다, 입증하다

123. 동사 어휘 specify
직원들은 수리를 필요로 하는 기기의 모델 번호를 명시하도록 요구된다.
(A) 강화하다 **(B) 명시하다** (C) 통합하다 (D) 증언하다

해설 빈칸에 알맞은 동사 어휘를 고르는 문제. 문맥상 '모델 번호를 명시하도록'이라는 의미가 가장 자연스러우므로 정답은 (B).

124. 전치사 throughout
루시 버먼은 프로 수영 선수로서 지난 8년간의 선수 생활 내내 다수의 수영 기록을 세웠다.
(A) ~보다 위에 (B) ~에 관하여 **(C) ~ 내내** (D) ~의

해설 빈칸 뒤에 기간을 나타내는 her eight-year career가 나오므로 빈칸에는 기간을 나타내는 전치사가 와야 한다. 문맥상 '8년간의 선수 생활 내내'가 되어야 자연스러우므로 빈칸에는 '~ 내내'의 의미를 지닌 전치사 throughout이 들어가야 한다. 따라서 정답은 (C).

어휘 set a record 기록을 세우다   a number of 다수의   career 경력
professional 프로의, 전문적인

125. 동명사+수동태
디아즈 씨는 회의에 늦어서, 주목받는 것을 피하기 위해 회의실 뒤쪽에 있는 자리에 앉았다.

해설 동사 avoid의 목적어 자리에 알맞은 것을 고르는 문제. avoid는 목적어로 동명사를 취하므로 (B)와 (D)가 정답 후보. 문맥상 디아즈 씨는 주목하는 주체가 아니라 주목받는 대상이므로 동명사의 수동형인 (B)가 정답. 능동형인 (D)가 쓰이려면 빈칸 뒤에 목적어가 있어야 하므로 오답.

어휘 take a seat 자리에 앉다   notice 주목하다, 알아채다

126. 형용사 자리+분사
그 마을의 독립 기념일 퍼레이드는 새로 선출된 시장의 짧은 연설로 시작될 것이다.

해설 빈칸은 앞에 있는 부사 newly의 수식을 받으면서 뒤에 있는 명사 mayor를 수식하는 형용사 자리이므로, 형용사 역할을 하는 과거분사 (A)와 현재분사 (C)가 정답 후보. mayor는 선출하는 주체가 아니라 선출된 대상이므로 수동의 의미를 가진 과거분사 (A)가 정답.

어휘 Independence Day 독립 기념일   commence 시작되다   brief 짧은   speech 연설   elect 선출하다   mayor 시장

127. 형용사 어휘 ambitious
카를라 스텐턴 씨는 전국적으로 빠르게 확장된 신규 업체를 시작한 야심 있는 기업가이다.
(A) 당황한 (B) 받아들일 만한 **(C) 야심 있는** (D) 불안해하는

해설 빈칸 뒤의 명사 entrepreneur를 수식하는 형용사 어휘를 고르는 문제. who 이하는 선행사인 entrepreneur를 수식하는 주격 관계대명사절로, 선택지 중 '전국적으로 빠르게 확장된 신규 업체를 시작한 기업가'를 묘사하기에 가장 적절한 어휘는 ambitious이므로 정답은 (C).

어휘 entrepreneur 기업가, 사업가   launch 시작하다, 착수하다; 출시, 발매   start-up 신규 업체   expand 확장하다

128. 부사 어휘 markedly
비비코 스피커의 음질은 시중에 나와 있는 다른 스피커들에 비해 눈에 띄게 우수하지만, 많은 사람이 그것을 살 여유가 되지 않는다.
(A) 눈에 띄게 (B) 각각 (C) 단호하게 (D) 허용되어

110. 명사 어휘 enrollment

지역 문화 회관의 직원들은 강좌 등록자 수가 15% 증가하여 기뻤다.
(A) 서술 **(B) 등록자 수** (C) 재고품 목록 (D) 태도

해설 빈칸은 that절의 주어 자리로, 명사 course와 어울려 쓰이면서 문맥에 적절한 명사 어휘를 찾아야 한다. 문맥상 '강좌 등록자 수가 증가했다'는 의미가 가장 자연스러우므로 정답은 (B).

어휘 community center 지역 문화 회관   official 공무원, 직원

111. 접속사 provided that

이용자들은 도서관장으로부터 특별 허가를 받았다면 도서관에서 참고 도서를 가지고 나갈 수 있다.
(A) 그렇지 않으면 (B) 그래서 (C) ~하는 반면에 **(D) 만약 ~이라면**

해설 문맥에 어울리는 접속사를 고르는 문제. 빈칸 뒤의 '도서관장의 특별 허가'는 참고 도서를 가지고 나갈 수 있는 조건이 되므로, '만약 ~이라면'이라는 뜻으로 조건을 나타내는 접속사 (D)가 정답.

어휘 patron (도서관의) 이용자, 고객   take out 가지고 나가다, 꺼내다   reference book 참고 도서   permission 허가   head librarian 도서관장

112. 형용사 자리_주격 보어

발권기가 설치된 후, 역에서 더 많은 승객을 처리하는 것이 가능했다.

해설 빈칸은 주어 it을 보충 설명하는 주격 보어 자리로, was 앞의 it은 가주어, 빈칸 뒤의 to handle 이하는 진주어임을 재빨리 알아채야 한다. 보어 자리에는 명사나 형용사가 올 수 있으므로 (A), (B), (D)가 정답 후보. 문맥상 '더 많은 승객을 처리하는 것이 가능했다'의 의미가 자연스러우므로 '가능한'의 의미를 지닌 형용사 (A)가 정답. 명사인 (B)와 (D)는 진주어인 to 이하와 동격을 이루어 '더 많은 승객을 처리하는 것은 가능성이다'라는 의미가 되어 문맥상 어색하므로 오답.

어휘 ticketing 매표   install 설치하다   handle 처리하다, 다루다

113. 부사 어휘 regularly

드윗 커뮤니케이션즈 사는 자사 직원들에게 고객 서비스 교육을 정기적으로 제공하여, 우수성에 대한 명성을 쌓아 왔다.
(A) 정기적으로 (B) 확고히 (C) 최근에 (D) 신속히

해설 문맥상 '고객 서비스 교육을 정기적으로 제공한다'는 의미가 가장 자연스러우므로 정답은 (A). (C) recently는 오래 되지 않은 과거를 나타내는 표현으로 현재시제와 함께 사용될 수 없으므로 오답.

어휘 build a reputation 명성을 쌓다   excellence 우수성

114. 부사 자리_형용사 수식

규정에 따라, 우리는 그 문제에 직접적으로 관련된 사람들에게 최신 정보를 제공할 것이다.

해설 빈칸 없이도 문장이 완전하므로 빈칸은 빈칸 뒤의 형용사 involved를 수식해 주는 부사 자리이다. 따라서 부사인 (B)가 정답.

어휘 in compliance with ~에 따라   regulation 규정   update 최신 정보   directly 직접적으로   involved in ~에 관련[연루]된

115. 관용어구 a wealth of

자이론 제약이 관리하는 연구 데이터베이스는 내과 의사들에게 풍부한 정보를 제공한다.
(A) 품질 (B) 유사성 **(C) 풍부한 양** (D) 언급

해설 빈칸 앞뒤의 a 및 of와 어울려 쓰이면서 자연스러운 문맥을 이루는 명사 어휘를 찾는 문제. 문맥상 '내과 의사들에게 풍부한 정보를 제공한다'고 하는 것이 자연스러우므로 정답은 (C). a wealth of는 '풍부한'이라는 의미로 종종 등장하므로 하나의 어구로 외워 두도록 한다.

어휘 research 연구   maintain 유지하다, 관리하다   pharmaceuticals 약, 제약   physician 내과 의사

116. 형용사 자리+분사

거래가 완료되면, 이체를 요청한 사람은 입금을 확인해 주는 메시지를 받을 것이다.

해설 빈칸은 빈칸 앞의 message를 수식해 주는 형용사 자리이다. 따라서 형용사 역할을 하는 현재분사 (A)와 과거분사 (C)가 정답 후보. 빈칸 뒤의 the deposit을 목적어로 취하여 '입금을 확인해 주는 메시지'라는 능동의 의미를 나타내는 것이 자연스러우므로 (A)가 정답.

어휘 transaction 거래, 매매   complete 완료된, 완전한   transfer 이체   deposit 예금, 입금

117. 접속사 now that

링컨 씨는 상용 승객 우대 제도에 가입했기 때문에 늘 같은 항공사를 이용한다.
(A) ~하기 위해서 (B) ~할지라도 (C) ~하지 않는 한 **(D) ~이기 때문에**

해설 빈칸에 알맞은 접속사를 찾는 문제로, 빈칸 앞뒤의 의미 관계를 따져 보아야 한다. 빈칸 뒤의 우대 제도 가입은 링컨 씨가 같은 항공사를 이용하는 이유가 되므로, '~이기 때문에'라는 뜻으로 이유를 나타내는 접속사 (D)가 정답.

어휘 join 가입하다   frequent flyer (항공사의) 상용[단골] 고객

118. 동사 자리+능동태

세차를 한 후, 하워드 씨는 표면에서 광이 나게 하기 위해 왁스를 얇게 칠해 발랐다.

해설 빈칸은 a thin coat of wax를 목적어로 가지는 동사 자리로, 준동사인 (A)와 (B)는 오답으로 제외. 주어인 Mr. Howard가 동사 apply의 주체이므로 빈칸에는 능동태 동사가 와야 한다. 따라서 정답은 (D).

어휘 apply 바르다, 신청하다   coat 칠, 도금   surface 표면   shine 광을 내다, 빛나다

119. 전치사 in

메이스 씨는 예측을 할 때 환율의 변동에 대해 고려하는 것을 깜박했다.
(A) 자주 **(B) ~에서** (C) 마침내 (D) ~에 관하여

해설 빈칸부터 rates까지는 take ~ into account의 목적어인 명사 fluctuations를 수식하는 수식어구이다. 따라서 빈칸에는 명사구인 currency rates를 목적어로 취해 수식어구를 구성할 수 있는 전치

PART 5

101. 인칭대명사_주격
학회 참석자 대부분은 그들이 유용한 정보를 많이 배웠음을 확인해 주었다.
해설 선택지를 보니 인칭대명사의 알맞은 격을 고르는 문제. 빈칸은 접속사 that이 이끄는 명사절의 동사 learned 앞 주어 자리이므로 주격 인칭대명사인 (D)가 정답.
어휘 attendee 참석자 conference 학회, 회의 confirm 확인해 주다, 확증하다 useful 유용한

102. 명사 자리+동명사 vs. 명사
배달 수요를 충족시키는 데 있어서의 신뢰성은 어떤 택배 업체에서도 중요한 부분이다.
해설 빈칸은 주어 자리이므로 주어 자리에 올 수 있는 동명사 (B)와 명사 (D)가 정답 후보. 동명사 Relying은 전치사 on이나 upon과 호응하여 쓰이는데, 빈칸 뒤에는 in으로 시작되는 전치사구가 오고 의미상으로도 '신뢰하는 것'이 되어 어색하므로 (B)는 오답. 따라서 정답은 (D).
어휘 reliability 신뢰성, 신뢰할 수 있음 meet 충족시키다 demand 수요 courier 택배 회사, 배달원

103. 부정대명사 one
켈러 자동차 사의 소형 하이브리드 자동차는 국내에서 판매되는 소형 하이브리드 자동차들 중 가장 가격이 저렴한 것이다.
(A) 그러한 것 **(B) 것** (C) ~하는 것 (D) 각자
해설 빈칸 앞에 정관사 the와 최상급 형용사 most affordable이 있는 것으로 보아 빈칸에는 형용사의 수식을 받는 명사나 대명사가 와야 한다. 문맥상 앞서 나온 mini hybrid와 동일한 종류를 가리키면서 형용사의 수식을 받을 수 있는 (B)가 정답. (A)와 (D) 또한 앞서 나온 것을 대신하는 대명사이지만 형용사의 수식을 받을 수 없어서 오답이고, (C)는 선행사를 포함하는 관계대명사로 뒤에 불완전한 명사절이 와야 하므로 오답.
어휘 automotive 자동차의 affordable (가격이) 알맞은, 저렴한

104. 동사 어휘 change
에머슨 철도 회사는 돈을 절약하기 위해 자사의 보험 공급 업체를 바꾸는 것에 관심이 있다.
(A) 보장하다 (B) 나타내다 **(C) 바꾸다** (D) 얻다
해설 문맥상 '보험 공급 업체를 바꾸는 것'이라는 의미가 가장 자연스러우므로 정답은 (C).
어휘 insurance 보험 provider 공급자 in order to do ~하기 위하여

105. 전치사 along
마라톤 참가자들은 네스 강을 따라 달려서 윌로우 공원에서 경주를 마칠 것이다.
(A) ~을 따라 (B) ~ 위로 (C) 떨어져 (D) ~ 외에는
해설 빈칸 뒤에 the Ness River라는 장소를 나타내는 명사구가 나오므로 빈칸에는 장소나 방향을 나타내는 전치사가 들어가야 한다. 따라서 (A)와 (B)가 정답 후보. 문맥상 '네스 강을 따라 달려서'가 되어야 자연스러우므로 '~을 따라'라는 방향의 의미를 지닌 (A)가 정답. (B)는 '네스 강 위로 달린다'는 의미가 되어 어색하므로 오답.
어휘 participant 참가자

106. to부정사_부사 역할
치플리 가전에서 나온 신형 건조기는 옷이 건조되는 때를 감지하도록 설계되어 있다.
해설 문맥상 '옷이 건조되는 때를 감지하도록 설계되어 있다'는 의미로, 빈칸 이하는 형용사 역할을 하는 과거분사 designed를 수식하는 부사 역할을 한다. 선택지들 중 부사 역할을 할 수 있는 것은 to부정사 뿐이므로 정답은 (A).
어휘 appliance 가전제품, 기기 sense 감지하다

107. 부사 어휘 barely
출장 요리업자는 손님들이 해산물 전채 요리에 거의 손대지 않은 것 같아 놀랐다.
(A) 편리하게 (B) 외관상으로는 **(C) 거의 ~ 아니게** (D) 약간
해설 출장 요리업자가 놀란 원인을 설명하는 that절의 빈칸에 알맞은 부사 어휘를 고르는 문제. 요리에 거의 손대지 않은 것 같아서 놀랐다고 하는 것이 가장 적절하므로 정답은 (C).
어휘 caterer 출장 요리업자 appetizer 전채 요리, 식욕을 돋우는 것

108. 형용사 어휘 imperative
겨울 의류의 성수기가 다가오고 있으므로 우리는 반드시 버카 지점의 새로운 지점장을 빨리 찾아야 한다.
(A) 반드시 해야 하는 (B) 즉각 반응하는 (C) 독점적인 (D) 설득력 있는
해설 문맥상 '우리는 반드시 버카 지점의 새로운 지점장을 빨리 찾아야 한다'는 의미가 가장 자연스러우므로 정답은 (A). imperative와 같이 의무나 필수의 의미를 가진 형용사가 뒤에 that절을 이끌 때 that절의 동사는 《(should)+동사원형》의 형태를 취한다는 점을 알아 두자.
어휘 peak season 성수기 come up 다가오다 branch 지점

109. 접속사 vs. 전치사
27번 고속 도로에 차선을 추가하는 공사는 자재 부족 때문에 지연되었다.
(A) ~ 때문에 (B) ~ 때문에 (C) ~할 경우에 대비해서 (D) 결과적으로
해설 공사가 지연된 것은 자재 부족 때문이라는 의미가 자연스러우므로 이유를 나타내는 전치사 (A)와 접속사 (B)가 정답 후보. 빈칸 뒤에 명사구가 왔기 때문에 전치사인 (A)가 정답.
어휘 construction 공사, 건설 additional 추가의 lane 차선 shortage 부족 material 자재, 재료

95. 전화의 목적은?
(A) 예약을 변경하기 위해
(B) 주문을 확인하기 위해
(C) 배달상의 실수를 알리기 위해
(D) 지불을 요청하기 위해

패러프레이징 [단서] to check a quantity on the order you placed → [정답] To verify an order

96. 시각 자료에서, 화자가 언급한 수량은?
(A) 35
(B) 30
(C) 15
(D) 6

해설 단서 (96)에서 장미 덤불의 주문 수량이 너무 많은 것 같다고 했다. 주문서를 나타내는 도표에서 장미 덤불의 주문 수량은 15개이므로 정답은 (C).

97. 화자가 필립 씨에 대해 말한 것은?
(A) 환불을 해 줄 수 있다.
(B) 메시지를 적을 수 있다.
(C) 정원을 설계할 수 있다.
(D) 식물을 찾아올 수 있다.

패러프레이징 [단서] He can write down your comments and leave them on my desk. → [정답] He can take a message.

Questions 98-100 refer to the following excerpt from a meeting and chart.

Here at Florence Inc., ⁹⁸we're dedicated to maintaining a pleasant work environment for our staff as well as providing customers with the insurance they need. That's why we asked for your suggestions at last week's meeting. You'll see on this chart the most popular ones. The managers have already started reassessing the company dress code, and we'll have more news on that in May. ⁹⁹Then in June, we'll consider the second-most-common suggestion. Also, although we can't provide free lunches like some of you suggested, ¹⁰⁰I'm pleased to say there's coffee and doughnuts in the staff lounge today, so help yourselves.

이곳 플로렌스 주식회사에서 ⁹⁸우리는 고객들에게 그들이 필요로 하는 보험을 제공하는 것뿐만 아니라 직원들을 위해 쾌적한 근무 환경을 유지하는 것에도 전념하고 있습니다. 그것이 바로 저희가 지난주 회의 때 여러분에게 제안을 요청한 이유입니다. 이 도표에서 가장 인기 있는 제안들을 보실 수 있을 겁니다. 부장들은 이미 회사의 복장 규정을 다시 평가하기 시작했고, 5월 중에 그것에 대한 소식이 더 있을 것입니다. ⁹⁹그 다음 6월에는, 두 번째로 많이 나온 제안을 검토할 것입니다. 또한, 여러분 중 일부가 제안한 것처럼 무료 점심을 제공해 드리지는 못하지만, ¹⁰⁰오늘 직원 휴게실에 커피와 도넛이 있다는 말씀을 드리게 되어 기쁘네요. 마음껏 드시기 바랍니다.

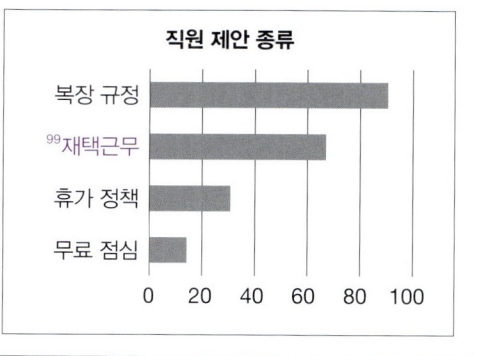

어휘 be dedicated to ~에 전념하다 maintain 유지하다 pleasant 쾌적한, 기분 좋은 environment 환경 provide A with B A에게 B를 제공하다 insurance 보험 suggestion 제안 reassess 재평가하다

98. 청자들이 일할 것 같은 곳은?
(A) 보험 회사
(B) 법률 사무소
(C) 잡지사
(D) 환경 기관

99. 시각 자료에서, 회사가 6월에 다룰 의제는?
(A) 복장 규정
(B) 재택근무
(C) 휴가 정책
(D) 무료 점심

해설 단서 (99)에서 6월에는 두 번째로 많이 나온 제안을 검토할 거라고 했는데, 직원들이 내놓은 제안들을 보여 주는 도표에서 두 번째로 많이 나온 제안은 재택근무이므로 정답은 (B). 담화의 consider가 문제에서는 address로 패러프레이징되었다.

100. 화자에 따르면, 오늘 직원 휴게실에서 이용 가능한 것은?
(A) 정책 설명서
(B) 설문지 양식
(C) 다과
(D) 고객 명단

패러프레이징 [단서] coffee and doughnuts → [정답] Some refreshments

Questions 92-94 refer to the following announcement.

Good morning. ⁹²It's wonderful to see so many people here for our hospital's free annual health screening. You'll be given a complete checkup by me or one of my colleagues. We are also happy to answer any questions about specific concerns you may have. Although it's not required, ⁹³there is a survey form to fill out regarding amenities you'd like to see at the hospital. This is really valuable information. ⁹³Without it, we have difficulty knowing our areas of weakness. ⁹⁴Please remember to bring your coat, handbag, and other belongings with you when you come into the exam room. We won't be monitoring this area, so it's best not to leave them unattended.

안녕하세요. ⁹²이렇게 많은 분이 저희 병원의 연례 무료 건강 검진을 위해 와 주신 것을 보니 기쁩니다. 여러분은 저나 제 동료들 중 한 명으로부터 종합 건강 검진을 받게 될 것입니다. 또한 저희는 여러분이 가지고 계실 수도 있는 구체적인 걱정에 관한 어떠한 질문에도 기꺼이 답해 드릴 것입니다. 필수는 아니지만, ⁹³저희 병원에 있었으면 하는 편의 시설에 관해 작성하는 설문지가 있습니다. 이것은 매우 귀중한 정보입니다. ⁹³이것이 없으면, 저희는 저희가 취약한 부분을 알기가 어렵습니다. ⁹⁴검사실로 들어오실 때 외투와 핸드백, 그리고 다른 소지품을 같이 가지고 오시는 것을 기억하세요. 저희는 이 구역을 감시하지 않을 것이므로, 그것들을 방치해 두지 않는 것이 가장 좋습니다.

어휘 screening 검사, 심사 specific 구체적인 concern 걱정, 관심사 fill out ~을 작성하다 regarding ~에 관하여 amenity (보통 복수형) 편의 시설 valuable 귀중한 have difficulty doing ~하는 데 어려움을 겪다 weakness 약점 belongings 소지품 unattended 방치된

92. 화자의 신분은?
(A) 경비원
(B) 대학 강사
(C) 여행 가이드
(D) 의료 전문가

해설 단서 (92)에서 화자는 무료 건강 검진을 받으러 온 청자들을 환영하면서, 화자 또는 화자의 동료가 청자들의 종합 건강 검진을 진행할 것이라고 했으므로 정답은 (D).

93. 화자가 "이것은 매우 귀중한 정보입니다"라고 말한 의미는?
(A) 청자들이 설문지를 작성하도록 장려한다.
(B) 일부 서류가 분실될까 봐 걱정한다.
(C) 일부 자료가 주의 깊게 보호되기를 원한다.
(D) 많은 정보가 수집된 것에 기뻐하고 있다.

해설 단서 (93)을 보면 편의 시설에 관해 작성하는 설문지가 있다고 했고, 이것이 없으면 자신들의 취약점을 파악하기가 어렵다고 했으므로 설문지를 작성해 달라고 장려하고 있음을 알 수 있다. 따라서 정답은 (A).

패러프레이징 [단서] a survey form to fill out → [정답] complete a survey

94. 청자들에게 하도록 상기시키는 일은?
(A) 개인 물품을 소지하고 있기
(B) 검사 결과를 위해 나중에 전화하기
(C) 신분증 제시할 준비를 하기
(D) 신청서를 미리 작성하기

패러프레이징 [단서] bring your coat, handbag, and other belongings with you → [정답] Keep their personal items with them

Questions 95-97 refer to the following telephone message and order form.

Good morning, Ms. Segura. This is Jason from Summertime Landscaping. ⁹⁵I wanted to check a quantity on the order you placed. Um ... ⁹⁶There seem to be too many rose bushes for the size of your property. Please call me back at 555-5928 to let me know how many you need. I'll be doing some planting at a customer's house this afternoon, so it would be better to call before lunch, if possible. ⁹⁷If I'm not here, just ask for Phillip. He can write down your comments and leave them on my desk.

안녕하세요, 세구라 씨. 서머타임 조경의 제이슨입니다. ⁹⁵귀하께서 하신 주문의 수량 하나를 확인하려고요. 음… ⁹⁶귀하의 부지 크기에 비해 장미 덤불의 수량이 너무 많은 것 같습니다. 555-5928번으로 제게 다시 전화해 주셔서 얼마나 많이 필요한지 알려 주세요. 저는 오늘 오후에 다른 고객님의 집에서 식재 작업을 할 것이므로, 가능하면 점심 전에 전화를 주시는 것이 좋을 것 같습니다. ⁹⁷만약 제가 여기 없다면, 필립 씨를 찾으세요. 그가 고객님의 의견을 적어 제 책상에 남겨 놓으면 되니까요.

고객: 페이 세구라	
주문 번호: 1223389	
종류	수량
수선화 구근	35
튤립 구근	30
⁹⁶장미 덤불	15
라벤더 덤불	6

어휘 quantity 수량, 양 place an order 주문하다 bush 덤불 planting 심기, 식재(植栽) write down ~을 적어 두다 comment 의견, 논평

어휘 facilities (항상 복수형) 시설 production 생산 process 과정 from start to finish 처음부터 끝까지 technician 기술자 in action 작동[활동]을 하는 go through ~을 살펴보다 in detail 상세히 remind 다시 한번 알려 주다, 상기시키다 wander off (일행으로부터) 떨어져 나가다 by oneself 혼자서

86. 소개가 이루어지고 있는 곳은?
(A) 제조 공장
(B) 자동차 정비소
(C) 건설 현장
(D) 컨벤션 센터

패러프레이징 [단서] production → [정답] manufacturing

87. 구스타브 파머 씨의 신분은?
(A) 경영주
(B) 엔지니어
(C) 기자
(D) 내과 의사

88. 화자가 청자들에게 하도록 요청한 것은?
(A) 디자인 아이디어 제안하기
(B) 보호 장비 착용하기
(C) 사진 찍지 않기
(D) 단체로 모여 있기

해설 청자들에게 요청하는 내용은 주로 담화의 마지막 부분에 나온다. 단서 (88)에서 you must not이라는 표현을 써서 혼자 떨어져서 돌아다니면 안 된다고 했으므로, 견학 중에 일행에서 이탈하지 않고 단체로 모여 있을 것을 요청하고 있음을 알 수 있다. 따라서 정답은 (D).

패러프레이징 [단서] not wander off by yourselves → [정답] Stay together as a group

🎧 **Questions 89-91** refer to the following excerpt from a meeting.

> Good afternoon, everyone. ⁸⁹Thank you for coming to support our efforts to launch an adult literacy program here in Selby. Registration for our first session is higher than expected, so we're looking forward to getting started. We had planned on conducting the session at the public library, but unfortunately, ⁹⁰its conference room is closed following damage from yesterday's storm. I'm worried about what we're going to do without a venue. ⁹¹If you know of any sites that might be free, please e-mail me. I'll need to know the size of the building, where it is, and how many people it can accommodate. Thank you.

안녕하세요, 여러분. ⁸⁹이곳 셀비에서 성인 대상 읽고 쓰기 프로그램을 시작하려는 저희의 노력을 지원해 주시고자 이렇게 와 주셔서 감사합니다. 저희 첫 번째 과정의 등록자 수가 예상보다 많아서, 시작하게 되기를 고대하고 있습니다. 저희는 해당 과정을 공립 도서관에서 진행하기로 계획했었습니다만, 유감스럽게도 ⁹⁰어제 있었던 폭풍우의 피해로 인해 도서관의 회의실이 폐쇄되었습니다. 장소 없이 우리가 어떻게 해야 할지 걱정이 됩니다. ⁹¹비어 있을 것 같은 어떤 장소든 알고 계신다면, 제게 이메일을 보내 주십시오. 건물 크기와 위치, 그리고 수용 가능한 인원을 제가 알아야 할 것입니다. 감사합니다.

어휘 support 지원[지지]하다 launch 시작하다 literacy 읽고 쓰는 능력 registration 등록자 수, 등록 following ~의 결과로 venue 장소 accommodate 수용하다

89. 화자가 주로 이야기하고 있는 것은?
(A) 교육 프로그램
(B) 등록비
(C) 도서관 모금 행사
(D) 지역 단위 소풍

패러프레이징 [단서] an adult literacy program → [정답] An educational program

90. 화자가 걱정하는 이유는?
(A) 자금이 부족하다.
(B) 모임 공간을 이용할 수 없다.
(C) 곧 날씨가 나빠질 것으로 예상된다.
(D) 프로젝트에 대한 관심이 줄었다.

해설 단서 (90)에서 과정을 진행하기로 했던 도서관의 회의실이 폐쇄되었다면서, 진행 장소 없이 어떻게 해야 할지 걱정이라고 했으므로 정답은 (B). 담화의 worried가 문제에서는 concerned로 패러프레이징 되었다.

패러프레이징 [단서] its conference room is closed → [정답] A meeting space is not available.

91. 화자가 청자들에게 하도록 요청한 것은?
(A) 행사에 등록하기
(B) 화자에게 건물 정보 보내기
(C) 건물 앞에서 만나기
(D) 재정적 기부하기

패러프레이징 [단서] please e-mail me / the size of the building, where it is, and how many people it can accommodate → [정답] Send her / property information

해설 단서 (81)에서 화자는 자신이 다른 주에서 일자리를 제안받았기 때문에 이번 학년도에는 프로그램에 참여할 수 없다고 했다. 이를 통해 더 이상 자원봉사를 할 수 없게 되었다는 소식을 전하게 된 것에 대해 본인이 안타까워하고 있음을 나타내고자 한 말임을 알 수 있으므로, 정답은 (A).

82. 화자가 청자에게 하도록 요청한 것은?
(A) 자선 단체에 자원하기
(B) 문서 제공하기
(C) 직원 추천하기
(D) 새로운 프로그램 이끌기

패러프레이징 [단서] e-mail me your advertising flyer → [정답] Provide a document

Questions 83-85 refer to the following excerpt from a meeting.

> [83]I regret to inform you that our CEO, Michael Hoskins, has decided to step down. Mr. Hoskins is responsible for the enormous growth of our company, [84]helping us to become the top producer of hybrid cars in the country. We will miss him greatly. As board members, you will be expected to select a replacement. To assist you with this task, [85]Ms. Melville has already put together a list of current staff members who may be qualified enough to take on the role.
>
> [83]우리 CEO인 마이클 호스킨스 씨가 사직하기로 결정하였음을 알려 드리게 되어 유감입니다. 호스킨스 씨로 인해 우리 회사는 거대한 성장을 이루었고, [84]그는 우리가 국내 최고의 하이브리드 차량 생산 업체가 되는 데 도움을 주었습니다. 우리는 그가 대단히 그리울 겁니다. 이사진으로서, 여러분은 후임자를 선정해야 할 것입니다. 여러분이 이 일을 하는 것을 도와드리기 위해, [85]멜빌 씨가 그 직책을 맡을 자격을 충분히 갖췄을 만한 현 직원들의 명단을 이미 만들어 놓았습니다.

어휘 step down 사직하다, 물러나다 be responsible for ~에 책임이 있다, ~의 계기가 되다 enormous 거대한, 막대한 select 선정하다 replacement 후임자 assist A with B A가 B하는 것을 도와주다 put together (이것저것을 모아) 만들다 qualified 자격이 있는 take on (일을) 맡다

83. 회의의 목적은?
(A) 경쟁사의 계획을 보고하기 위해
(B) 대표직의 변경을 알리기 위해
(C) 새 회사 정책을 설명하기 위해
(D) 상과 관련해 청자들을 축하하기 위해

패러프레이징 [단서] to inform you that our CEO, Michael Hoskins, has decided to step down → [정답] To announce a leadership change

84. 청자들이 근무할 것 같은 회사의 종류는?
(A) 에너지 발전소
(B) 차량 제조사
(C) 통신 회사
(D) 건설 업체

패러프레이징 [단서] the top producer of hybrid cars in the country → [정답] A vehicle manufacturer

85. 화자에 따르면, 멜빌 씨가 한 일은?
(A) 대체 부품을 주문했다.
(B) 상을 받았다.
(C) 경쟁사를 분석했다.
(D) 직원 명단을 준비했다.

패러프레이징 [단서] put together a list of current staff members → [정답] Prepared an employee list

Questions 86-88 refer to the following introduction.

> Hello, everybody! [86]Welcome to the tour of the B&U facilities. Today you'll learn about the production process of our popular line of bicycles from start to finish. You'll watch our technicians and machines cutting the aluminum frame, assembling the parts, adding tires, and more. You'll even see the testing process in action. Once we've gone through the entire process, [87]you'll get to meet Gustav Palmer, one of our senior engineers who helps to design new products for our line. He'll answer your questions in detail. Now, before we get started, I just want to remind you all that, for safety reasons, [88]you must not wander off by yourselves.
>
> 안녕하세요, 여러분! [86]B&U 시설 견학에 오신 것을 환영합니다. 오늘 여러분은 저희의 인기 있는 자전거 라인의 생산 과정에 대해 처음부터 끝까지 배우게 되실 겁니다. 여러분은 저희 기술자들과 기계들이 알루미늄 틀을 자르고, 부품을 조립하고, 타이어를 장착하고, 그 외의 것들을 하는 모습을 보실 텐데요. 심지어 여러분은 테스트 과정이 진행되는 것도 보시게 될 겁니다. 전 과정을 살펴보고 나면 [87]여러분은 구스타브 파머 씨를 만나게 되실 텐데, 그분은 저희 라인의 신제품 디자인을 돕는 수석 엔지니어들 중 한 분입니다. 그분이 여러분의 질문에 상세히 답해 줄 겁니다. 자, 시작하기 전에, 여러분 모두에게 다시 한번 알려 드립니다. 안전상의 이유로, [88]혼자 떨어져서 돌아다니시면 안 됩니다.

패러프레이징 [단서] assistance in transporting their bags
→ [정답] Help to move luggage

패러프레이징 [단서] the six-digit code for the side door
→ [정답] An access code

미 🎧
Questions 77-79 refer to the following telephone message.

Hi, Mr. Shaw. This is Henry calling. ⁷⁷,⁷⁸I got your message saying that you'd like me to set up new displays for the windows of our department store. It's no problem for me to do this. We've had the same ones for quite a while. Tourist season is starting soon, so ⁷⁸we'd better get ready. Since I'll be coming in early, ⁷⁹please text me the six-digit code for the side door. Thanks!

안녕하세요, 쇼 씨. 저 헨리예요. ⁷⁷,⁷⁸우리 백화점 쇼윈도의 새 전시품을 제가 놔 줬으면 한다는 당신의 메시지를 받았어요. 제가 이 작업을 하는 건 문제없습니다. 우리는 꽤 오랫동안 똑같은 전시품을 진열했잖아요. 휴가철이 곧 시작되니 ⁷⁸준비를 하는 것이 좋겠어요. 일찍 갈 테니까 ⁷⁹옆문 비밀번호 6자리를 저에게 문자로 보내 주세요. 고마워요!

어휘 set up ~을 놓다[설치하다] for a while 잠시 동안 tourist season 휴가[관광]철 digit 자릿수, 숫자 code 암호, 부호

77. 화자가 전화한 이유는?
(A) 업무를 수락하기 위해
(B) 불만을 처리하기 위해
(C) 감사를 표하기 위해
(D) 도움을 요청하기 위해

패러프레이징 [단서] to set up new displays for the windows of our department store → [정답] a task

78. 화자가 "휴가철이 곧 시작되니"라고 말한 의도는?
(A) 일손이 부족한 것에 대해 걱정한다.
(B) 수익이 낮은 이유를 이해하지 못한다.
(C) 청자의 제안에 동의한다.
(D) 매장이 광고를 더 자주 해야 한다고 생각한다.

해설 화자가 한 말의 의도를 문맥을 통해 찾아내는 문제이다. 단서(78)에서 언급된, 쇼윈도의 전시품을 새로 놓자는 청자의 제안에 대한 화자의 답변으로, 화자는 이어서 준비를 하는 게 좋겠다고 했다. 이를 통해 청자의 제안에 화자 역시 동의하고 있음을 알 수 있으므로 정답은 (C).

79. 화자가 요청한 것은?
(A) 출입 비밀번호
(B) 평면도
(C) 승인 양식
(D) 동료의 전화번호

미 🎧
Questions 80-82 refer to the following telephone message.

⁸⁰Hello, this is Walter Freeman from Practon Middle School. I volunteered as a tutor at your library this past year. It was an incredibly rewarding experience. ⁸¹However, I was just offered a job at a school in a different state and cannot participate in your program for the upcoming school year. It truly saddens me to say this. I realize that finding a replacement on such short notice is difficult. So I would like to help you in any way I can. ⁸²Please e-mail me your advertising flyer so that I may distribute it to my former colleagues. I am sure some of them would be interested in helping out.

⁸⁰여보세요, 저는 프랙턴 중학교의 월터 프리먼입니다. 저는 지난해 귀 도서관에서 개인 지도 교사로 자원봉사를 했습니다. 그것은 엄청나게 보람 있는 경험이었습니다. ⁸¹그런데, 제가 다른 주에 있는 학교에서 일자리를 막 제안받아서 돌아오는 학년도에는 당신의 프로그램에 참여할 수 없게 되었습니다. 이런 말씀을 드리게 되어 정말 안타깝습니다. 이렇게 갑작스럽게 후임자를 찾는 것이 어렵다는 걸 알고 있습니다. 그래서 저는 제가 할 수 있는 어떤 방법으로든 도움을 드리고 싶습니다. ⁸²제가 제 이전 동료들에게 배포할 수 있도록 광고 전단을 저에게 이메일로 보내 주세요. 그들 중 일부는 도움을 주는 것에 관심이 있을 거라 확신합니다.

어휘 volunteer 자원봉사로 하다; 자원봉사자 tutor 개인 지도 교사 incredibly 믿을 수 없을 정도로, 엄청나게 rewarding 보람 있는 participate in ~에 참여하다 sadden 슬프게 하다 replacement 후임자, 대체(물) on short notice 갑자기, 충분한 예고 없이 distribute 나누어 주다, 배포하다

80. 화자의 신분은?
(A) 사서
(B) 인사 관리자
(C) 마케팅 담당자
(D) 교사

81. 화자가 "이런 말씀을 드리게 되어 정말 안타깝습니다"라고 말한 이유는?
(A) 본인의 안타까움을 표현하기 위해
(B) 본인의 이견을 강조하기 위해
(C) 신청을 거절하기 위해
(D) 본인의 기분 변화를 보여 주기 위해

안녕하세요. 여러분께서는 벤저민 펠덤의 〈컬처 아워〉를 듣고 계십니다. ⁷¹첫 번째 문화계 소식은 곧 있을 알바라도 미술관의 경축 행사입니다. 운영비를 위한 기금을 모으고자 준비되고 있는 이 행사에 모든 분을 초대합니다. 티켓을 가지신 분들께는 운영 시간 이후 본관에서 열릴 연회에 입장하실 수 있는 독점적 권한이 주어집니다. ⁷²그리고 등록하시는 첫 50분의 손님께는 유명 미술가 보리스 노도바의 사인이 되어 있는 무료 포스터 역시 주어집니다. ⁷³이어서 이 방송에서 진행될 미술관 큐레이터 알리시아 콜먼 씨와의 인터뷰를 들으시면서 더 많은 정보를 알아보세요.

어휘 gala 경축 행사 organize 준비[조직]하다 raise funds 기금을 모으다 operating expense (보통 복수형) 운영비 exclusive 독점적인 access 입장, 접근(권) after-hours 영업시간 후의 register 등록하다 station 방송 (프로), 방송국

71. 방송의 주제는?
(A) 미술관 견학
(B) 미술 경연 대회
(C) 회화 수업
(D) 모금 행사

패러프레이징 [단서] the gala, which is being organized to raise funds → [정답] A fundraiser

72. 참가자들이 무료 선물을 받을 수 있는 방법은?
(A) 우편물 수신자 명단에 이름을 올려서
(B) 정기적으로 기부를 해서
(C) 등록한 첫 50명 중 한 명이 되어서
(D) 티켓을 한 장 이상 구매해서

해설 단서 (72)에서 등록을 하는 첫 50명에게는 무료 포스터가 주어진다고 했으므로 정답은 (C). 담화의 be given a free poster가 문제에서는 receive a free gift로 패러프레이징되었다.

패러프레이징 [단서] the first fifty guests to register → [정답] the first fifty people to enroll

73. 화자가 청자들에게 하도록 권장한 일은?
(A) 라디오 방송국에 전화하기
(B) 콜먼 씨에게 연락하기
(C) 프로그램 청취하기
(D) 웹사이트 방문하기

패러프레이징 [단서] listening to the interview with museum curator Alicia Coleman → [정답] Listen to a program

---

Questions 74-76 refer to the following announcement.

May I have your attention, please? This announcement is for passengers traveling to Manchester. ⁷⁴The departure track has changed, so you should now board at platform 6, not 3. ⁷⁵You will have to exit the area and present your ticket again at the platform 6 entrance, so please have your ticket ready. You need to take the stairs to get to platform 6, so ⁷⁶those who require assistance in transporting their bags can speak to a staff member. They can be found throughout the area and can be easily identified by their orange vests.

주목해 주십시오, 여러분. 이 안내는 맨체스터로 가시는 승객들을 위한 안내입니다. ⁷⁴출발 선로가 변경되어, 여러분은 이제 3번 플랫폼이 아니라 6번 플랫폼에서 탑승하셔야 합니다. ⁷⁵지금 있는 구역에서 나가셔서 6번 플랫폼 입구에서 승차권을 다시 보여 주셔야 하오니, 승차권을 준비해 주십시오. 6번 플랫폼으로 가려면 계단을 이용하셔야 하므로, ⁷⁶짐을 옮기는 데 도움이 필요하신 분들은 직원에게 말씀하시면 됩니다. 직원들은 이 구역 도처에서 찾으실 수 있으며 주황색 조끼로 쉽게 알아보실 수 있습니다.

어휘 departure 출발 track 선로 board 탑승하다; 이사회 exit 나가다 present 보여 주다 require 필요로 하다 assistance 도움 transport 이동시키다, 실어 나르다 throughout 도처에 identify (신원 등을) 알아보다, 확인하다

74. 화자가 일할 것 같은 곳은?
(A) 택시 회사
(B) 공항
(C) 기차역
(D) 여행사

75. 청자들이 하도록 요청받을 일은?
(A) 영수증 보여 주기
(B) 좌석에 앉기
(C) 다음 지시 기다리기
(D) 승차권 제시하기

76. 화자가 직원들이 할 것이라고 말한 것은?
(A) 새 승차권 발부하기
(B) 짐 옮기는 것 도와주기
(C) 안전 절차 업데이트하기
(D) 공고문 걸기

해설 단서 (76)에서 짐을 옮기는 데 도움이 필요한 사람들은 직원에게 말하라고 했으므로 정답은 (B). 담화의 a staff member가 문제에서는 employees로 패러프레이징되었다.

Questions 68-70 refer to the following conversation and chart.

M Ms. Peterson, ⁶⁸I'm sure you heard the news about last night's awards ceremony. Unfortunately, our company did not win the prestigious Horton Prize.

W Yes, it was a disappointment. I was just looking over the market share figures since I was so surprised about the company that was chosen as the winner.

M Well, ⁶⁹they may only have the third-largest market share, but they've been making a name for themselves since Jesse Dominguez, the new CEO, took over.

W Right. ⁷⁰That could be a problem for us if some of our clients want to switch to their firm.

M Yes. We have to find a way to market ourselves better.

W Let's bring this up at the next meeting.

남 피터슨 씨, ⁶⁸어젯밤 시상식에 대한 소식을 분명 들으셨을 거예요. 안타깝게도, 우리 회사는 명망 있는 호턴 상을 타지 못했어요.

여 네, 실망스러운 일이었죠. 수상자로 선정된 회사를 알고 너무 놀라서, 시장 점유율 수치를 살펴보던 중이었어요.

남 음, ⁶⁹그 회사는 겨우 세 번째로 높은 시장 점유율을 차지하고 있을지 몰라도, 새로운 CEO인 제시 도밍게스가 회사를 인수한 이후로 유명해지고 있어요.

여 맞아요. ⁷⁰우리 고객 일부가 그 회사로 옮기고 싶어 하게 된다면 이는 우리에게 문제가 될 수 있어요.

남 네. 우리는 우리 스스로를 더 잘 광고할 수 있는 방법을 찾아야 해요.

여 다음 회의 때 이 이야기를 꺼내 봅시다.

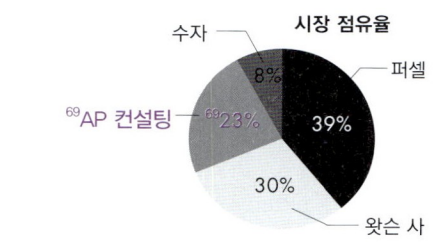

어휘 prestigious 명망 있는 disappointment 실망스러운 것, 실망 look over ~을 살펴보다 market share 시장 점유율 make a name for oneself 유명해지다 take over (기업 등을) 인수하다 market (상품을) 광고하다[내놓다] bring up (화제를) 꺼내다

68. 남자가 어제 일어났다고 말한 일은?
(A) 예산안이 제출되었다.
(B) 새 지점이 개점했다.
(C) 마케팅 캠페인이 시작되었다.
(D) 상이 수여되었다.

69. 시각 자료에서, 최근에 CEO가 바뀐 회사는?
(A) 퍼셀
(B) 왓슨 사
(C) AP 컨설팅
(D) 수자

해설 단서 (69)에서 남자는 시장 점유율이 세 번째로 높은 회사가 새로운 CEO에게 인수된 이후로 유명해지고 있다고 말했다. 네 회사의 시장 점유율을 나타내는 도표에서 세 번째로 시장 점유율이 높은 회사는 AP 컨설팅이므로 정답은 (C). 대화의 Jesse Dominguez, the new CEO, took over가 문제에서는 changed its CEO로 패러프레이징되었다.

70. 여자가 걱정하는 것은?
(A) 경쟁사에 고객을 빼앗기는 것
(B) 마케팅에 너무 많은 돈을 쓰는 것
(C) 수요를 따라잡지 못하는 것
(D) 불만을 느끼는 직원들이 있는 것

패러프레이징 [단서] if some of our clients want to switch to their firm → [정답] Losing customers to a competitor

PART 4

Questions 71-73 refer to the following radio broadcast.

Good morning. You're listening to *Culture Hour* with Benjamin Feldom. ⁷¹First up in culture news is the Alvarado Art Museum's upcoming gala. Everyone is invited to the gala, which is being organized to raise funds for operating expenses. Your ticket gives you exclusive access to an after-hours banquet in the main hall. ⁷²And the first fifty guests to register will also be given a free poster signed by famous artist Boris Nodova. ⁷³Find out more by listening to the interview with museum curator Alicia Coleman, coming up next on this station.

해설 좌석 배치도를 나타내는 도표가 주어져 있으므로 좌석과 관련된 내용이 나올 것임을 예상하며 듣는다. 단서 (63)에서 여자는 남자가 C 구역으로 들어가는 입구에 있는데, 남자의 좌석은 반대편에 있다면서 4번 출입구로 갈 것을 제안했다. 도표에서 C 구역 반대편에 있으면서 4번 출입구와 연결되는 구역은 D 구역이므로 남자의 좌석이 D 구역에 있음을 알 수 있다. 따라서 정답은 (D).

64. 남자가 다음에 할 것 같은 일은?
(A) 메시지 보내기
(B) 여자에게 자기 자리 주기
(C) 티켓 교환하기
(D) 밖에서 친구 기다리기

패러프레이징 [단서] text → [정답] Send a message

미 호 🎧
Questions 65-67 refer to the following conversation and schedule.

> **W** Richard, the head of the city's planning department called me this morning, and he informed me that ⁶⁵we need a permit to build the fence at the Crowley Street property.
>
> **M** We've built fences for clients before without a permit.
>
> **W** Yes, but ⁶⁵this one will be over eight feet tall, so the regulations are different. It'll take about a week to get the permit.
>
> **M** Okay. ⁶⁶Since we were supposed to work on the fence next week, let's switch that task with the following week's so we don't get behind schedule.
>
> **W** ⁶⁶Good idea. And ⁶⁷the client, Ms. Kenmore, has been asking for some pictures of the progress so far. I'll take care of that today.

여 리처드 씨, 오늘 아침에 제게 시의 기획 부서 책임자가 전화해서, ⁶⁵크라울리 가에 있는 부지에 울타리를 세우려면 허가증이 필요하다는 사실을 알려 줬어요.

남 우리는 이전에는 허가증 없이도 고객들에게 울타리를 세워 주었잖아요.

여 네, 하지만 ⁶⁵이번 것은 높이가 8피트 이상이 될 거라 규정이 달라요. 허가증을 받는 데에는 일주일 정도 걸릴 거예요.

남 알겠어요. ⁶⁶다음 주에 울타리를 작업하도록 되어 있었으니, 예정보다 늦어지지 않도록 그 작업을 그 다음 주 작업과 바꿉시다.

여 ⁶⁶좋은 생각이에요. 그리고 ⁶⁷우리 고객인 켄모어 씨가 지금까지의 진행 상황을 보여 주는 사진들을 요청하고 있어요. 그건 제가 오늘 처리할게요.

크라울리 가 778번지: 작업 일정	
1주차	나무 손질하기
2주차	관개 시스템 설치하기
⁶⁶3주차	나무 울타리 세우기
⁶⁶4주차	화단 파기

어휘 inform 알리다, 통지하다 property 토지, 부동산 regulation 규정 switch A with B A와 B를 바꾸다 behind schedule 예정[계획]보다 늦은 progress 진행, 진척

65. 여자가 허가증에 대해 언급한 것은?
(A) 이미 시에서 승인받았다.
(B) 울타리의 높이 때문에 요구된다.
(C) 처리하려면 몇 주 걸릴 것이다.
(D) 8개월 동안 유효할 것이다.

해설 단서 (65)에서 울타리를 지으려면 허가증이 필요한데, 이 울타리의 높이가 8피트 이상이 될 거라 규정이 다른 것이라고 했으므로 정답은 (B).

패러프레이징 [단서] this one will be over eight feet tall → [정답] the fence's height

66. 시각 자료에서, 화자들이 다음 주에 할 일은?
(A) 나무 손질하기
(B) 관개 시스템 설치하기
(C) 나무 울타리 세우기
(D) 화단 파기

해설 단서 (66)에서 남자는 다음 주로 예정되어 있던 울타리 작업을 그 다음 주의 작업과 바꾸자고 했고 여자도 이에 동의했다. 작업 일정을 나타내는 도표에서 '나무 울타리 세우기'는 3주차 일정으로 나와 있고 그 다음 주인 4주차 일정은 '화단 파기'이므로, 다음 주에 울타리 작업 대신에 하게 될 일은 화단 파기 작업임을 알 수 있다. 따라서 정답은 (D).

67. 여자가 켄모어 씨에게 보낼 것은?
(A) 한 벌의 사진들
(B) 업데이트된 일정
(C) 최종 청구서
(D) 자재 목록

패러프레이징 [단서] some pictures of the progress so far → [정답] A set of photographs

남 ⁶¹이번 한 번만 허용해 주시면 안 될까요? 제 차를 옮기기는 번거로울 것 같은데요.

여 이게 엄격한 정책이라는 것을 알고 있습니다. 특히나 주차장에 아직 자리가 남아 있는 경우에는요. 하지만 저는 손님을 도와드릴 수가 없어요. ⁶¹그건 제가 결정할 수 있는 사안이 아닙니다.

어휘 check out of ~에서 체크아웃하다 fly out 비행기를 타고 떠나다 pass 패스, 통행증 valid 유효한 hassle 번거로운[귀찮은] 일 strict 엄격한 make a decision 결정을 내리다

59. 화자들이 있을 것 같은 곳은?
(A) 공항
(B) 공공 도서관
(C) 컨벤션 센터
(D) 호텔 로비

60. 여자가 주차장에 대해 언급한 것은?
(A) 투숙객용으로 제한되어 있다.
(B) 현재 꽉 찬 상태이다.
(C) 공사 중이다.
(D) 저녁에는 폐쇄된다.

패러프레이징 [단서] our parking lot is for guests only → [정답] It is restricted to guests.

61. 여자가 "저는 손님을 도와드릴 수가 없어요"라고 말한 의도는?
(A) 어떤 장소까지 찾아가는 길을 모른다.
(B) 예외를 두는 것이 허용되지 않는다.
(C) 추천을 하는 데 어려움이 있다.
(D) 정책의 세부 사항을 설명하지 못한다.

해설 여자가 한 말의 의도를 문맥을 통해 찾아내는 문제로 해당 표현의 앞뒤를 주의 깊게 들어야 한다. 단서 (61)의 이번만 허용해 달라는 남자의 요청에 대한 여자의 답변으로, 여자는 이것이 자신이 결정할 수 있는 사안이 아니라고 했다. 이를 통해 여자에게는 정책상 예외를 두는 것이 허용되지 않는다는 것을 알 수 있으므로 정답은 (B).

패러프레이징 [단서] allow it just this once → [정답] make exceptions

🎧 미 미
Questions 62-64 refer to the following conversation and seating chart.

W ⁶²Welcome to the Lyndale Theater. I hope you enjoy Andrew Livonia's concert this evening. May I see your ticket?

M Of course. Here you are. I'm really looking forward to the show. The critics have been giving it excellent reviews.

W Yes, we're pleased about that. But it looks like you're at the wrong entrance for your section, sir. ⁶³This entrance is for Section C, but your seat is on the other side. You need to go to Door 4.

M Oh, I see. ⁶⁴I guess I'd better text my friend. She's sitting with me and will probably try to come in this way too.

여 ⁶²린데일 극장에 오신 것을 환영합니다. 오늘 저녁 앤드루 리보니아의 콘서트를 즐겁게 관람하시길 바랍니다. 티켓을 보여주시겠어요?

남 그럼요. 여기 있습니다. 공연이 정말 기대되네요. 비평가들이 극찬을 하더라고요.

여 네, 그 점에 대해 기쁘게 생각하고 있습니다. 하지만 고객님께서는 지금 고객님의 구역으로는 갈 수 없는 입구에 계시는 것 같네요. ⁶³이 입구는 C 구역으로 가는 곳인데, 고객님의 좌석은 반대편에 있습니다. 4번 출입구로 가셔야 해요.

남 아, 그렇군요. ⁶⁴친구에게 문자를 보내야겠어요. 친구도 저랑 같이 앉을 거라 아마도 이쪽으로 들어가려고 할 거라서요.

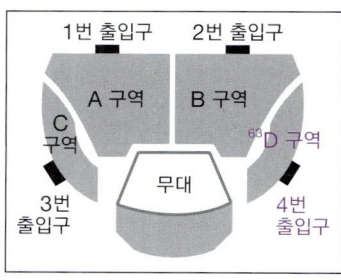

어휘 look forward to ~을 기대[고대]하다 critic 비평가 review 비평 section 구역, 구획 text (휴대 전화로) 문자를 보내다

62. 여자의 신분은?
(A) 극장 직원
(B) 미디어 비평가
(C) 음악 공연인
(D) 무대 감독

63. 시각 자료에서, 남자가 앉을 것 같은 구역은?
(A) A 구역
(B) B 구역
(C) C 구역
(D) D 구역

영미 🎧
Questions 56-58 refer to the following conversation.

W Hi. My name is Sienna Talbot. I bought a rug from your store earlier this week, and it was supposed to be delivered yesterday. ⁵⁶I'm wondering what's going on with my order.

M I'm sorry about the delay, ma'am. Someone should have contacted you.

W Oh, so then you're aware of the problem?

M Yes. Unfortunately, ⁵⁷there was some kind of trouble with our delivery truck's engine. It's being repaired now.

W So what should I do?

M Our delivery schedule will be back on track soon, so ⁵⁸I suggest waiting another twenty-four hours. You'll almost certainly have your item by then.

W All right. I guess I have no choice.

여 안녕하세요. 제 이름은 시에나 탤벗입니다. 이번 주 초에 귀하의 매장에서 양탄자를 하나 샀고, 그게 어제 배달되기로 되어 있었거든요. ⁵⁶제 주문이 어떻게 되고 있는지 알고 싶어요.

남 지연에 대해 사과드립니다. 고객님. 고객님께 누군가 연락을 드렸어야 했는데 말입니다.

여 아, 그럼 그 문제에 대해 알고 계신 건가요?

남 네. 유감스럽게도, ⁵⁷저희 배달 트럭의 엔진에 문제가 좀 생겼습니다. 현재 그것을 수리 중이고요.

여 그럼 제가 어떻게 해야 하죠?

남 곧 저희 배달 일정이 다시 정상 복구될 테니, ⁵⁸24시간 더 기다려 주시기 바랍니다. 그때까지는 거의 틀림없이 물건을 받으실 거예요.

여 알겠어요. 선택의 여지가 없는 것 같네요.

어휘 rug 양탄자, 깔개 wonder 궁금하다 contact 연락하다 be aware of ~을 알다 unfortunately 유감스럽게도 back on track 다시 정상 궤도에 들어선 have no choice 선택의 여지가 없다

56. 전화의 목적은?
(A) 파손된 물건에 대해 항의하기 위해
(B) 지연에 대해 사과하기 위해
(C) 주문 상태를 확인하기 위해
(D) 할인에 대해 문의하기 위해

해설 전화의 목적에 대한 단서는 주로 대화 앞부분에 나온다. 단서 (56)에서 여자는 I'm wondering이라는 표현을 써서 주문의 진행 상황에 대해 알고 싶다고 했으므로, 주문 상태를 확인하기 위해 건 전화임을 알 수 있다. 따라서 정답은 (C). 지연에 대해 사과하는 사람은 전화를 받은 남자이므로 (B)는 오답.

패러프레이징 [단서] what's going on with my order
→ [정답] the status of an order

57. 남자에 따르면, 문제를 일으킨 것은?
(A) 엔진 오작동
(B) 컴퓨터 오류
(C) 직원 결근
(D) 심각한 폭풍우

패러프레이징 [단서] some kind of trouble with our delivery truck's engine → [정답] An engine malfunction

58. 남자가 하기를 추천한 것은?
(A) 온라인상으로 정보 확인하기
(B) 나중에 다시 전화하기
(C) 하루 더 기다리기
(D) 추적 번호 제공하기

패러프레이징 [단서] waiting another twenty-four hours
→ [정답] Waiting another day

호미 🎧
Questions 59-61 refer to the following conversation.

M Good morning. ⁵⁹I'd like to check out of room 304. Here is my keycard. And is it possible for me to leave my car here for the day? I've got some business at the Woodbridge Convention Center before flying out this evening.

W Unfortunately, ⁶⁰our parking lot is for guests only, so your pass is not valid after you check out.

M ⁶¹Couldn't you allow it just this once? It would be a hassle to move my car.

W I know it's a strict policy, especially when we still have space in the lot. But I can't help you. ⁶¹I don't make those decisions.

남 안녕하세요. ⁵⁹304호에서 체크아웃하려고요. 여기 제 키 카드입니다. 그리고 제가 오늘 하루 동안 제 차를 여기 두는 게 가능한가요? 오늘 저녁 비행기를 타고 떠나기 전에 우드브리지 컨벤션 센터에서 일이 좀 있거든요.

여 유감스럽게도 ⁶⁰저희 주차장은 투숙객들만 쓰실 수 있기 때문에, 손님의 주차권은 체크아웃하신 후에는 사용이 불가합니다.

(C) 제품 출시
(D) 고객 항의

패러프레이징 [단서] our online store's / The photographs
→ [정답] a Web site / images

51. 여자가 프로젝트에 대해 언급한 것은?
(A) 직원들이 충분하지 않다.
(B) 취소되었다.
(C) 예산 조정이 필요하다.
(D) 아직 진행 중이다.

해설 단서 (51)에서 여자의 팀에서 아직 테스트를 하면서 조정 중이며, 이 작업을 완료하기까지는 사흘이 더 남아 있다고 했으므로 정답은 (D).

패러프레이징 [단서] running the tests and making adjustments
→ [정답] in progress

52. 남자가 다음 주에 하려고 계획한 것은?
(A) 서비스 평가하기
(B) 이미지 교체하기
(C) 새로운 업무 배정하기
(D) 장비 수리하기

패러프레이징 [단서] my evaluation of the service → [정답] Assess a service

미 영 미 🎧

Questions 53-55 refer to the following conversation with three speakers.

> M Hello. My name is Martin Hardy. ⁵³I was here yesterday for a dental appointment, and I accidentally left my credit card behind.
>
> W1 Do you know who found it?
>
> M Yes, ⁵⁴it was Ms. Michaels. She left a message on my phone this morning saying it was here.
>
> W1 Just a moment, sir. Ms. Michaels? Mr. Hardy is here.
>
> W2 Oh, hello, Mr. Hardy. I'm glad we were able to get in touch with you.
>
> M Yes, I'm very lucky. Thank you for finding my card.
>
> W2 No problem. I have it here, but ⁵⁵I'll need to see a photo ID to give it back to you.
>
> M ⁵⁵Of course.

남 안녕하세요. 제 이름은 마틴 하디입니다. ⁵³어제 치과 진료 예약이 있어서 여기에 왔다가, 실수로 신용 카드를 두고 갔어요.

여1 누가 그것을 발견했는지 아세요?

남 네, ⁵⁴마이클스 씨였어요. 그분이 오늘 아침에 제 전화에 그것이 이곳에 있다는 메시지를 남겨 놓았어요.

여1 잠시만요, 손님. 마이클스 씨? 여기 하디 씨가 오셨어요.

여2 아, 안녕하세요, 하디 씨. 당신과 연락이 돼서 다행입니다.

남 네, 제가 정말 운이 좋네요. 제 카드를 찾아 주셔서 감사해요.

여2 천만에요. 여기 제게 카드가 있습니다만, ⁵⁵이걸 돌려드리려면 제게 사진이 있는 신분증을 보여 주셔야 합니다.

남 ⁵⁵물론이죠.

어휘 accidentally 잘못하여, 우연히   leave behind ~을 두고 가다
get in touch with ~와 연락하다

53. 남자가 업체를 방문한 이유는?
(A) 치과 검진을 받기 위해
(B) 영수증을 받기 위해
(C) 물건을 찾기 위해
(D) 예약을 하기 위해

해설 단서 (53)에서 남자가 어제 이곳에 왔다가 실수로 신용 카드를 두고 갔다고 했고, 그 뒤로 이 카드를 돌려받는 것에 대한 이야기가 이어지고 있으므로 정답은 (C). dental appointment라는 표현이 들린다고 해서 (A)나 (D)를 정답으로 고르지 않도록 주의한다.

패러프레이징 [단서] my credit card → [정답] an item

54. 마이클스 씨가 아침에 한 일은?
(A) 신용 카드 결제를 처리했다.
(B) 청구상의 오류를 알아챘다.
(C) 서류를 작성했다.
(D) 전화 메시지를 남겼다.

패러프레이징 [단서] left a message on my phone → [정답] Left a telephone message

55. 남자가 다음에 할 것 같은 일은?
(A) 치과 의사와 이야기하기
(B) 일정 확인하기
(C) 신분증 보여 주기
(D) 검사실로 가기

패러프레이징 [단서] a photo ID → [정답] an ID card

영미

Questions 47-49 refer to the following conversation.

W   Hi, Mr. Ritter. You wanted to speak to me?

M   Yes. Ever since we released the new delivery schedule last week, ⁴⁷a lot of the delivery drivers have been telling me how upset they are.

W   Oh, really? What's causing them to feel that way?

M   ⁴⁸Previously, drivers were expected to make ten deliveries in a day, and now that number has been changed to fifteen. Since they have to install the items too, it's a lot to ask.

W   I see what you mean. Hmm... ⁴⁹we could buy more vans and hire more people, and then start charging a higher installation fee.

여   안녕하세요, 리터 씨. 저와 이야기하고 싶어 하셨다고요?

남   네. 지난주에 우리가 새 배달 일정을 발표한 이후로 ⁴⁷많은 배달 기사들이 자신들이 얼마나 당황해하고 있는지 제게 말하고 있어요.

여   아, 정말요? 무엇이 그들에게 그런 식으로 느끼게 하고 있는 거죠?

남   ⁴⁸이전에는 기사들이 하루에 10건의 배달을 하도록 되어 있었는데, 이제는 그 수가 15건으로 바뀌었어요. 그분들은 제품 설치까지 해야 하기 때문에, 요구하기에 많은 양이죠.

여   무슨 말씀이신지 알겠어요. 음… ⁴⁹우리는 밴을 더 구입하고 사람들을 더 고용할 수 있어요. 그렇게 하면 설치 수수료를 더 많이 청구하기 시작할 수 있겠네요.

어휘   upset 당황한, 화난   previously 이전에   expect (어떤 일을 하기를) 요구하다, 기대하다   make a delivery 배달하다   charge 청구하다   installation 설치

47. 남자가 최근에 한 일은?
(A) 새로운 직위로의 승진을 받아들였다.
(B) 회사에 새로운 제품들을 도입했다.
(C) 직원들로부터 부정적인 피드백을 받았다.
(D) 사업주에게 더 많은 밴을 구입하도록 권했다.

패러프레이징   [단서] a lot of the delivery drivers have been telling me how upset they are → [정답] Received negative feedback from employees

48. 남자가 "요구하기에 많은 양이죠"라고 말한 의미는?
(A) 작업량이 불합리하다고 생각한다.
(B) 큰 부탁을 해야 하는 것에 대해 마음이 불편하다.
(C) 기한을 맞출 수가 없다.
(D) 결정에 대해 생각할 시간이 좀 필요하다.

해설   남자가 한 말의 의미를 문맥을 통해 찾아내는 문제로, 단서 (48)에서 배달 건수가 늘었을 뿐만 아니라 제품 설치까지 해야 한다고 했다. 즉, 기사들에게 요구되는 작업량이 너무 많다는 의미임을 알 수 있으므로 정답은 (A).

49. 여자가 하기를 제안한 것은?
(A) 운영 시간 연장하기
(B) 기사들 채용하기
(C) 새로운 공급자 찾기
(D) 서비스 수수료 낮추기

패러프레이징   [단서] hire more people → [정답] Recruiting some drivers

호미

Questions 50-52 refer to the following conversation.

M   Melissa, ⁵⁰I was looking at our online store's catalog, and there seems to be a problem when it's viewed on a mobile device. The photographs are too big, so I think that's going to make it difficult for customers to make purchases.

W   ⁵¹My team is still running the tests and making adjustments, so you're not looking at the final version. ⁵¹We have three more days to complete the work.

M   I see. In that case, ⁵²I'll hold off my evaluation of the service until next week. I'm sure you've got everything under control.

남   멜리사 씨, ⁵⁰우리 온라인 매장의 카탈로그를 보다 보니, 이걸 모바일 기기로 볼 때 문제가 있는 것 같네요. 사진들이 너무 큰데, 이 때문에 고객들이 구매를 하기가 어려울 것 같아요.

여   ⁵¹저희 팀에서 아직 테스트를 하면서 조정을 하고 있어서, 지금 최종 버전을 보고 계시는 건 아니에요. ⁵¹이 작업을 완료하려면 사흘이 더 남아 있어요.

남   알겠어요. 그렇다면, ⁵²그 서비스에 대한 제 평가는 다음 주까지 연기할게요. 당신이 모두 알아서 잘 하고 있으리라 확신해요.

어휘   make a purchase 구매하다   run (테스트·검사 등을) 하다   make an adjustment 조정하다   complete 완료하다; 완전한   hold off 연기하다   under control 통제[제어]되는

50. 대화의 주된 내용은?
(A) 카탈로그상의 인쇄 오류들
(B) 웹사이트의 이미지들

41. 남자들이 하도록 권장되는 일은?
(A) 회사 차 빌리기
(B) 워크숍에 등록하기
(C) 차 함께 타고 출근하기
(D) 주차 공간 예약하기

> 패러프레이징 [단서] a carpool program at our office
> → [정답] Share rides to work

42. 여자가 오후에 할 일은?
(A) 관리자들과 만나기
(B) 이메일로 계획안 보내기
(C) 변경 사항 공지하기
(D) 프로그램 시작하기

> 해설 단서 (42)에서 여자가 점심 식사 후에 부서장들을 만날 거라고 했으므로 정답은 (A). 대화의 after lunch가 문제에서는 in the afternoon으로 패러프레이징되었다.

> 패러프레이징 [단서] get together with the department heads
> → [정답] Meet with managers

43. 여자가 에이든 씨에게 고마워하는 이유는?
(A) 일정보다 먼저 일을 끝마쳤다.
(B) 여자 대신 회의에 참석하는 것에 동의했다.
(C) 제안들을 내놓겠다고 자원했다.
(D) 신입 사원들이 자리 잡는 것을 도울 것이다.

> 패러프레이징 [단서] to brainstorm a few ideas → [정답] to provide suggestions

🎧 **Questions 44-46** refer to the following conversation.

M Amy, could you help me with something this afternoon? ⁴⁴I'm overseeing the company's efforts to hire new employees, and I need help screening the résumés that we've received.

W I would love to help, but ⁴⁵Anthony, who works in my department, is out sick today. So I have to finish some of his assignments. I'm already on a tight schedule, and ⁴⁵I'm worried I won't even be able to handle that.

M I understand. ⁴⁶I can take care of it myself as long as Ms. Hendricks extends the deadline for my other project.

W I'm sure she will, but ⁴⁶you'd better talk to her soon.

남 에이미 씨, 오늘 오후에 저 좀 도와주시겠어요? ⁴⁴제가 회사의 신입 사원 채용 활동을 감독하고 있는데요, 우리가 받은 이력서들을 거르는 작업에 도움이 필요해요.

여 도와드리고 싶지만, ⁴⁵저희 부서에서 근무하는 앤소니 씨가 오늘 아파서 결근했어요. 그래서 저는 그분에게 배정된 업무 중 일부를 끝내야 해요. 이미 일정이 빠듯해서, ⁴⁵그 일조차도 처리하지 못할까 봐 걱정이에요.

남 알겠어요. ⁴⁶제가 맡은 다른 프로젝트의 기한을 헨드릭스 씨가 연장해 주기만 한다면, 그 일은 저 혼자서 처리할 수 있어요

여 그분은 분명 그렇게 해 주시겠지만, ⁴⁶그분께 빨리 말씀드리는 게 좋겠네요.

> 어휘 oversee 감독하다 effort (특정 목적을 위한) 활동 screen 거르다, 가려내다 be out sick 아파서 결근하다 assignment 임무, 과제 handle 처리하다 take care of ~을 처리하다 as long as ~하기만 하면 extend 연장하다 deadline 기한

44. 남자가 도움을 필요로 하는 일은?
(A) 영화 상영
(B) 퇴직 기념 파티
(C) 교육 과정
(D) 채용 절차

> 패러프레이징 [단서] screening the résumés that we've received
> → [정답] A recruiting process

45. 여자가 남자를 도와줄 수 없는 이유는?
(A) 고객을 만나야 한다.
(B) 지원자들과 면접이 있다.
(C) 동료의 일을 끝마쳐야 한다.
(D) 진료 예약이 있다.

> 해설 단서 (45)에서 같은 부서에 근무하는 앤소니 씨가 결근을 해서 그의 일을 대신 끝내야 하는데, 그 일조차도 처리하지 못할까 봐 걱정이라고 했으므로 정답은 (C).

> 패러프레이징 [단서] I have to finish some of his assignments → [정답] She has to complete a coworker's tasks.

46. 남자가 헨드릭스 씨와 논의할 것 같은 것은?
(A) 마감일을 변경하는 것
(B) 다른 사업장으로 전근 가는 것
(C) 임시 직원을 고용하는 것
(D) 회사 정책을 업데이트하는 것

> 패러프레이징 [단서] extends the deadline → [정답] Changing a due date

여 알겠습니다. 귀하는 저희 중앙 출입구에서 작업하시게 될 테니, 고객들에게 프랭클린 가로 나 있는 옆문을 이용해야 한다는 것을 알리는 ³⁹공고문을 붙여 놓을게요.

남 좋습니다. 그렇게 해 주시면 도움이 되겠네요. 또, ⁴⁰귀하의 부지를 이용하려면 특별한 허가증이 있어야 하나요?

여 ⁴⁰아니요. 아무 자리에나 주차하시면 됩니다. 모든 자리가 일반 대중을 위한 것이기 때문에, 마음대로 골라서 이용하시면 돼요.

어휘 be scheduled to do ~할 예정이다 security camera 보안 카메라 monitoring system 감시 시스템 on schedule 예정대로 entrance (출)입구 permit 허가(증) lot (특정 용도의) 부지 general public 일반 대중 take one's pick ~의 마음대로 고르다

38. 남자가 방문하는 목적은?
(A) 배달을 하기 위해
(B) 건물을 점검하기 위해
(C) 회사를 소개하기 위해
(D) 보안 장비를 설치하기 위해

패러프레이징 [단서] to install a security camera and a monitoring system → [정답] To install security equipment

39. 여자가 하려고 계획한 일은?
(A) 남자에게 다시 전화하기
(B) 계속해서 출입구 잠가 놓기
(C) 방문 일정 다시 잡기
(D) 표지판 내붙이기

패러프레이징 [단서] post a notice → [정답] Put up a sign

40. 남자가 문의한 것은?
(A) 회사 송장
(B) 주차 상황
(C) 시간당 요금
(D) 도로 폐쇄

해설 단서 (40)에서 부지를 이용하려면 허가증이 필요한지 묻는 남자의 질문에 여자는 아니라고 답하면서 아무 자리에나 주차하면 된다고 했다. 이를 통해 남자가 건물의 주차 상황에 대해 물었음을 알 수 있으므로 정답은 (B).

Questions 41-43 refer to the following conversation with three speakers.

W Aiden, Bernard, you both usually drive to work, right? ⁴¹We're starting a carpool program at our office. Why don't you join?

M1 That's a good idea. The parking lot here is so small.

M2 Yeah, and about half of the spots are reserved for customers.

W I hope this plan will help. We're also going to offer some kind of benefit to employees who take part in the program.

M1 Oh, really? Like what?

W I'm not sure yet. ⁴²I'm going to get together with the department heads after lunch to discuss it.

M2 Let us know what you come up with.

M1 You know, ⁴³I'd be happy to brainstorm a few ideas that I think the staff might like.

W ⁴³Thanks, Aiden. That would be helpful.

여 에이든 씨, 버나드 씨, 두 분 다 평소에 자가용으로 출근하시죠, 그렇죠? ⁴¹회사에서 카풀 프로그램을 시작하기로 했는데요. 동참하시는 게 어때요?

남1 그거 좋은 생각이네요. 여기 주차장은 정말 작잖아요.

남2 맞아요, 그리고 주차 공간의 절반 정도가 고객용으로 지정되어 있고요.

여 이 계획이 도움이 되기를 바라요. 또한 우리는 프로그램에 참여하는 직원들에게 혜택 같은 것도 제공할 거예요.

남1 아, 정말요? 예를 들면요?

여 아직은 잘 모르겠어요. ⁴²점심 식사 후에 부서장들과 만나서 그것에 대해 논의할 거예요.

남2 생각해 낸 것들에 대해 저희에게 알려 주세요.

남1 있잖아요, ⁴³제가 직원들이 좋아할 만하다고 생각되는 아이디어들을 몇 개 브레인스토밍해 볼게요.

여 ⁴³고마워요, 에이든 씨. 그래 주시면 도움이 될 거예요.

어휘 reserve (~용으로) 지정하다, (자리 등을) 따로 남겨 두다 take part in ~에 참여하다 get together with ~와 만나다 department head 부서 책임자 come up with ~을 생각해 내다

34. 여자가 전화를 걸고 싶어 하는 이유는?
(A) 예산을 늘리기 위해
(B) 의견을 얻기 위해
(C) 주소를 확인하기 위해
(D) 다른 매장을 확인하기 위해

해설 단서 (34)에서 여동생에게 전화를 걸어 선호하는 색상이 있는지 알아보겠다고 했으므로 정답은 (B).

패러프레이징 [단서] to see if there's a certain color she prefers → [정답] To get an opinion

Questions 35-37 refer to the following conversation.

M Hi. ³⁵I need to have my laptop fixed, and my friend recommended you. How long does it usually take? I need it for a presentation tomorrow.

W Well, that depends on the kind of problem you're having and whether or not we need to order additional components. What seems to be the issue?

M ³⁶I was coming home from a business trip yesterday, and during the flight, the entire screen suddenly went black.

W That could be caused by a number of factors. Actually, we're supposed to close in about fifteen minutes. ³⁷However, since you're in a hurry, I can work overtime to make sure it's ready as soon as possible.

남 안녕하세요. ³⁵노트북을 수리받아야 하는데, 친구가 귀사를 추천했습니다. 수리하는 데 보통 얼마나 걸리나요? 내일 있을 프레젠테이션을 위해 그것이 필요하거든요.

여 음, 그건 귀하가 겪고 있는 문제의 종류와 저희가 추가 부품을 주문해야 하는지 아닌지의 여부에 따라 결정됩니다. 무엇이 문제인 것 같으세요?

남 ³⁶어제 제가 출장에서 돌아오는 길이었는데, 비행기를 타고 오는 중에 전체 화면이 갑자기 까매졌어요.

여 그건 여러 요인에 의해 발생했을 수 있어요. 사실, 저희는 15분 정도 뒤에 문을 닫기로 되어 있습니다. ³⁷하지만 손님께서는 급하시니, 제가 초과 근무를 해서 가능한 한 빨리 이 노트북이 준비될 수 있도록 하겠습니다.

어휘 additional 추가의 component 부품, 구성 요소 issue 문제, 쟁점 entire 전체의 a number of 여러, 다수의 factor 요인 be supposed to do ~하기로 되어 있다 work overtime 초과 근무를 하다 as soon as possible 가능한 한 빨리

35. 화자들이 있을 것 같은 곳은?
(A) 회의장
(B) 차량 대여 업체
(C) 컴퓨터 수리점
(D) 공항

패러프레이징 [단서] to have my laptop fixed → [정답] computer repair

36. 남자가 자신이 어제 했다고 말한 일은?
(A) 비행기로 이동했다.
(B) 개업했다.
(C) 부품을 주문했다.
(D) 프레젠테이션을 했다.

해설 단서 (36)에서 어제 비행기를 타고 출장에서 돌아오던 중 노트북에 문제가 발생했다고 했으므로 정답은 (A).

패러프레이징 [단서] coming home from a business trip yesterday, and during the flight → [정답] Traveled by airplane

37. 여자가 남자를 위해 해 주겠다고 제안한 것은?
(A) 남자에게 카탈로그 보여 주기
(B) 환불해 주기
(C) 전문가와 상담하기
(D) 초과 근무하기

패러프레이징 [단서] work overtime → [정답] Work extra hours

Questions 38-40 refer to the following conversation.

M Hello. I'm calling from Oshea Inc. My name is Gregory, and ³⁸I'm scheduled to visit your building at 1 P.M. to install a security camera and a monitoring system. I just wanted to let you know that I'm still on schedule.

W All right. You'll be working at our main entrance, so ³⁹I'll post a notice letting customers know that they should use our side entrance on Franklin Street.

M Good. That would be helpful. Also, ⁴⁰do I need a special permit to use your lot?

W ⁴⁰No. You can park in any spot. They're all for the general public, so you can take your pick.

남 안녕하세요. 오셔 주식회사에서 전화드립니다. 제 이름은 그레고리이고, ³⁸오후 1시에 보안 카메라 및 감시 시스템 설치를 위해 귀하의 건물을 방문할 예정입니다. 제가 예정대로 간다는 것을 알려 드리려고요.

(B) 그것이 너무 어렵지는 않다고 생각하신다면요.
(C) **보통은요, 하지만 그는 가벼운 부상을 입었어요.**

해설 커티스 씨가 요가 고급반을 가르치냐는 질문에 보통은 그가 가르치지만 부상을 입었다며 현재는 가르치고 있지 않다고 우회적으로 답한 (C)가 정답. (B)는 advanced에서 연상할 수 있는 difficult를 이용한 오답.

어휘 advanced 고급[상급]의 strongly 강(경)하게 minor 가벼운, 심각하지 않은 injury 부상

30. 미 미 🎧

Can you calculate the departmental spending for the past week?
(A) I'll try to cut back, if possible.
(B) Adam has all the figures.
(C) When will we get corporate cards?

지난주의 부서별 지출을 계산해 주시겠어요?
(A) 가능하면 줄여 보도록 할게요.
(B) 애덤 씨가 모든 수치를 보유하고 있어요.
(C) 우리는 언제 법인 카드를 받죠?

해설 부서별 지출을 계산해 달라는 요청에 애덤 씨가 모든 수치를 보유하고 있다며 우회적으로 요청을 거절한 (B)가 정답. (A)는 spending에서 연상할 수 있는 cut back을 이용한 오답.

어휘 calculate 계산하다 departmental 부서(별)의 cut back 줄이다, 삭감하다 figure (보통 복수형) 수치 corporate 법인의, 기업의

31. 영 미 🎧

I can proofread the document by Wednesday.
(A) So did I. It's a great article.
(B) I didn't notice any big mistakes.
(C) Is it possible to have it done sooner?

저는 수요일까지 그 문서를 교정볼 수 있어요.
(A) 저도 그랬어요. 그건 훌륭한 기사예요.
(B) 저는 어떤 심각한 오류도 발견하지 못했어요.
(C) 그것을 더 일찍 끝내는 게 가능할까요?

해설 수요일까지 교정을 볼 수 있다는 말에 그보다 더 일찍 끝낼 수 있냐고 반문한 (C)가 정답. (B)는 proofread에서 연상할 수 있는 mistakes를 이용한 오답.

어휘 proofread 교정보다 article 기사, 논설 notice 알아채다; 공고문, 통지

PART 3

미 미 🎧
Questions 32-34 refer to the following conversation.

W Good morning. ³²Your store sent me a flyer a few days ago saying that you were having a sale in some of your departments. I'd like to buy a microwave for my apartment.

M All right. We have plenty of models to choose from. ³³I also suggest getting some pots and pans if you need any. The Warner brand is seventy-five percent off because the products will be discontinued.

W Really? I don't need any, but my sister does. ³⁴Let me call her to see if there's a certain color she prefers. Just a moment.

여 안녕하세요. ³²며칠 전 귀하의 가게에서 제게 일부 코너에서 세일을 하고 있다는 전단을 보내 왔습니다. 제 아파트에 둘 전자레인지를 하나 사고 싶어요.

남 알겠습니다. 저희에게는 고르실 수 있는 모델들이 많이 있습니다. ³³혹시 취사도구가 필요하시다면 그것들을 구매하시는 것도 권해 드려요. 워너 브랜드는 제품 생산이 중단될 예정이라 75% 할인 중이거든요.

여 정말요? 저는 전혀 필요하지 않지만, 제 여동생은 필요해요. ³⁴여동생에게 전화해서 혹시 선호하는 특정 색상이 있는지 알아볼게요. 잠시만 기다려 주세요.

어휘 flyer 전단 department (백화점·시장의) 매장, 코너 microwave 전자레인지 pots and pans 취사도구 discontinue (생산을) 중단하다 certain 특정한, 일정한

32. 여자가 세일에 대해 알게 된 경로는?
(A) 현수막을 보고
(B) 인터넷 검색을 하고
(C) 우편으로 전단을 받고
(D) 신문에서 광고를 보고

33. 남자가 구매하기를 추천한 것은?
(A) 전자 장치
(B) 취사도구
(C) 가구 한 점
(D) 옷

패러프레이징 [단서] some pots and pans → [정답] Some cookware

연상할 수 있는 agreement를 이용한 오답.

어휘 translate 번역하다　trade agreement 무역 협정

24.

> The bed frame is easy to assemble without any special tools.
> (A) Let's take it apart.
> **(B) That's a relief.**
> (C) The instructions are on the table.

그 침대의 틀은 특별한 도구 없이도 조립하기 쉬워요.
(A) 그걸 분해합시다.
(B) 그거 다행이네요.
(C) 설명서는 테이블 위에 있어요.

해설 침대의 틀이 조립하기 쉽다는 말에 다행이라고 답한 (B)가 정답. (A)는 assemble의 반의어인 take apart를 이용한 오답.

어휘 frame 틀, 뼈대　assemble 조립하다　take apart 분해하다　relief 안도, 안심　instructions 《항상 복수형》 (사용) 설명서

25.

> Where can I get a charger for my phone?
> (A) Probably around 7 P.M.
> **(B) Why don't you just borrow mine?**
> (C) Its battery is completely dead.

제 전화기에 쓸 충전기를 어디서 구할 수 있을까요?
(A) 아마 저녁 7시쯤요.
(B) 그냥 제 것을 빌리는 게 어때요?
(C) 그것은 배터리가 완전히 닳았어요.

해설 충전기를 어디서 구할 수 있는지 묻는 질문에 자신의 것을 빌리는 게 어떠냐고 반문한 (B)가 정답. (A)는 충전기를 구할 수 있는 시점을 묻는 질문에 적절한 답변이므로 오답.

어휘 charger 충전기　probably 아마도　dead 다 닳은, 더 이상 사용할 수 없는

26.

> The manager approved my vacation request, didn't she?
> **(A) Yes, a few days ago.**
> (B) We need her approval to conduct the study.
> (C) I hope you had fun.

부장님이 제 휴가 신청을 승인하셨죠, 그렇죠?
(A) 네, 며칠 전에요.
(B) 그 연구를 수행하려면 그녀의 승인이 필요해요.
(C) 즐거운 시간을 보냈기를 바라요.

해설 부장님이 휴가 신청을 승인했는지 확인하는 질문에 Yes라고 하면서 며칠 전에 승인했다고 답한 (A)가 정답. (C)는 미래에 있을 휴가에 대한 질문에 과거로 답했으므로 오답.

어휘 approve 승인하다　request 신청, 요구; 요청하다　approval 승인　conduct 수행하다, 실시하다　have fun 즐거운 시간을 보내다

27.

> Did the package arrive without any broken contents?
> (A) I checked the arrival time.
> (B) Glasses and flower vases.
> **(C) It's still in transit.**

소포가 깨진 내용물 없이 도착했나요?
(A) 제가 도착 시간을 확인했어요.
(B) 유리잔들과 꽃병들이요.
(C) 그건 아직 운송 중이에요.

해설 소포가 깨진 내용물 없이 도착했는지 묻는 질문에 그것이 아직 운송 중이라고 답한 (C)가 정답. (B)는 broken에서 연상할 수 있는 Glasses와 vases를 이용한 오답.

어휘 package 소포, 포장한 상품　contents 《항상 복수형》 내용물　arrival 도착　in transit 운송 중에

28.

> Who requested repairs to the air conditioner?
> (A) Half an hour, probably.
> **(B) Mr. Lambert should know.**
> (C) It will be repaired tomorrow.

누가 에어컨 수리를 요청했나요?
(A) 아마도 30분이요.
(B) 램버트 씨가 알고 있을 거예요.
(C) 그건 내일 수리될 거예요.

해설 에어컨 수리를 요청한 사람이 누구인지 묻는 질문에 램버트 씨가 알고 있을 거라며 자신은 모른다고 우회적으로 답한 (B)가 정답. (C)는 질문의 repairs를 반복 사용한 오답으로 질문에서는 '수리'라는 의미의 명사로, 선택지에서는 '수리하다'라는 의미의 동사로 쓰였다.

29.

> Doesn't Curtis teach the advanced yoga class?
> (A) No, I strongly recommend jogging.
> (B) If you think it's not too difficult.
> **(C) Usually, but he has a minor injury.**

커티스 씨가 요가 고급반을 가르치지 않나요?
(A) 아니요, 저는 조깅을 강력 추천해요.

새 실험용 장비를 보셨어요?
(A) 우리는 무엇을 주문해야 하죠?
(B) 저는 출장을 가 있었어요.
(C) 화학 실험이요.

[해설] 새 실험용 장비를 보았냐는 질문에 출장을 가 있느라 보지 못했다고 우회적으로 답한 (B)가 정답. (A)는 new laboratory equipment에서 연상할 수 있는 order를 이용한 오답.

[어휘] laboratory 실험용, 실험실 be out of town (출장 등으로) 도시를 떠나 있다 chemical 화학의 experiment 실험

19.

Would you prefer a seminar on marketing techniques or budget management?
(A) It depends on who is presenting.
(B) No, I haven't given any lectures lately.
(C) I didn't know the budget proposal was due today.

마케팅 기법에 관한 세미나를 선호하세요, 아니면 예산 관리에 관한 세미나를 선호하세요?
(A) 그건 누가 발표를 하느냐에 달려 있어요.
(B) 아니요, 저는 최근에 어떤 강연도 한 적이 없어요.
(C) 저는 예산안이 오늘 마감인 줄 몰랐어요.

[해설] 두 세미나 중 어느 것을 선호하는지 묻는 질문에 발표자에 달려 있다고 답한 (A)가 정답. (B)는 seminar에서 연상할 수 있는 lectures를 이용한 오답으로, 선택 의문문에 No라고 답했으므로 우선적으로 소거한다.

[어휘] budget 예산 management 관리 depend on ~에 달려 있다, ~에 의해 결정되다 present 발표하다, 보여 주다 give a lecture 강연하다 proposal 제안, 신청 due ~하기로 되어 있는[예정된]

20.

What was Dale's reaction to the news of his raise?
(A) Yesterday morning.
(B) He got a bonus.
(C) He couldn't believe it.

자신의 임금 인상 소식에 대한 데일 씨의 반응은 어땠나요?
(A) 어제 아침에요.
(B) 그는 보너스를 받았어요.
(C) 그는 믿기지 않아 했어요.

[해설] 임금 인상 소식에 대한 데일 씨의 반응을 묻는 질문에 그가 믿기지 않아 했다고 답한 (C)가 정답. (A)는 임금 인상 소식이 알려진 시점을 묻는 질문에 적절한 답변이므로 오답.

[어휘] reaction 반응

21.

How often does the lawn need to be mowed?
(A) About twice a month.
(B) With a gas-powered device.
(C) No, a landscaping company.

잔디를 얼마나 자주 깎아야 하나요?
(A) 한 달에 두 번 정도요.
(B) 가스 추진식 장치로요.
(C) 아니요, 조경 회사요.

[해설] 잔디를 깎아야 하는 빈도를 묻는 질문에 대략적인 빈도로 답한 (A)가 정답. (C)는 lawn과 mowed에서 연상할 수 있는 landscaping을 이용한 오답.

[어휘] mow (잔디를) 깎다 gas-powered 가스로 작동하는 device 장치 landscaping 조경

22.

Are you moving to a new apartment or renewing your current lease?
(A) I haven't seen that movie.
(B) It was released last month.
(C) I'm planning to stay here.

새 아파트로 이사를 갈 건가요, 아니면 현재의 임대차 계약을 갱신할 건가요?
(A) 저는 그 영화를 본 적이 없어요.
(B) 그것은 지난달에 발매되었어요.
(C) 저는 계속 이곳에 있을 계획이에요.

[해설] 이사를 갈지 현재의 임대차 계약을 갱신할지 묻는 질문에 계속 이곳에 있을 거라며 계약을 갱신할 것임을 우회적으로 밝힌 (C)가 정답.

[어휘] renew 갱신하다, 연장하다 current 현재의 lease 임대차 계약 release 발매하다, 발표[공개]하다

23.

Do you know who will translate these documents for our German partners?
(A) By Thursday afternoon.
(B) Mainly the trade agreement.
(C) Let me check with my supervisor.

우리의 독일 협력사를 위해 누가 이 문서를 번역할지 아세요?
(A) 목요일 오후까지요.
(B) 주로 무역 협정이요.
(C) 제 상사에게 확인해 볼게요.

[해설] 문서를 번역할 사람이 누구인지 묻는 질문에 상사에게 확인해 보겠다며 모른다고 우회적으로 답한 (C)가 정답. (B)는 partners에서

해설 목표액을 달성했다는 말에 동의를 구하는 질문에 No라고 하면서 몇백 달러가 부족하다고 답한 (A)가 정답. (C)는 모금의 목적을 묻는 질문에 적절한 답변이므로 오답.

어휘 reach (목적 따위를) 달성하다, ~에 이르다 fundraising 모금 charity 자선 short 부족한, 모자란 restore 재건[복구]하다

13.

These sales figures need to be accurate.
(A) I'll be sure to double-check them.
(B) The past quarter, I think.
(C) They need the sales report for a meeting.

이 판매 수치는 정확해야 합니다.
(A) 제가 그것들을 꼭 재확인할게요.
(B) 지난 분기인 것 같아요.
(C) 그들은 회의를 위해 그 판매 보고서가 필요해요.

해설 수치가 정확해야 한다는 말에 수치를 꼭 재확인하겠다고 답한 (A)가 정답. (B)는 sales figures에서 연상할 수 있는 quarter를 이용한 오답.

어휘 sales figure (보통 복수형) 판매 수치 accurate 정확한 double-check 재확인하다

14.

When will we have the monthly fire evacuation drill?
(A) For everyone's safety.
(B) No, I finished my evaluation.
(C) The alarm will sound at three.

우리는 월례 화재 대피 훈련을 언제 할 건가요?
(A) 모두의 안전을 위해서요.
(B) 아니요, 저는 평가를 끝냈어요.
(C) 3시에 경보가 울릴 거예요.

해설 화재 대피 훈련을 언제 할 것인지 묻는 질문에 3시에 경보가 울릴 거라며 정확한 시점으로 답한 (C)가 정답. (B)는 evacuation과 발음이 유사한 evaluation을 이용한 오답으로, 의문사 의문문에 No로 답했으므로 우선적으로 소거한다.

어휘 monthly 한 달에 한 번의 evacuation drill 대피 훈련 safety 안전 evaluation 평가 alarm 경보, 경보기

15.

Do you mind ending the meeting a bit early?
(A) I'm sending it right now.
(B) But we have a lot to cover.
(C) Do you want me to come in early?

회의를 조금 일찍 끝내도 될까요?
(A) 제가 지금 그걸 보내고 있어요.
(B) 하지만 우리는 다뤄야 할 게 많아요.
(C) 제가 일찍 오기를 원하세요?

해설 회의를 일찍 끝내도 되냐는 요청에 다룰 내용이 많다며 안 된다고 우회적으로 답한 (B)가 정답.

어휘 cover 다루다, 포함시키다 come in 들어오다, 도착하다

16.

Will you be ready in time for the speech?
(A) I just need to practice a few more times.
(B) It started at two o'clock.
(C) She's a very good public speaker.

연설을 제시간에 준비할 수 있겠어요?
(A) 몇 번만 더 연습하면 돼요.
(B) 그것은 2시에 시작했어요.
(C) 그녀는 매우 훌륭한 대중 연설가예요.

해설 연설이 시간 맞춰 준비되겠냐는 질문에 몇 번만 더 연습하면 된다고 긍정적으로 답한 (A)가 정답.

어휘 in time 제시간에, 시간 맞춰 speech 연설, 담화 public speaker 대중 연설가

17.

Which pharmacy do you use to fill your prescriptions?
(A) I'm taking one pill a day.
(B) No, I'm not a pharmacist.
(C) The one across the street.

처방 약 조제를 위해 어느 약국을 이용하시나요?
(A) 하루에 한 알씩 복용하고 있어요.
(B) 아니요, 저는 약사가 아니에요.
(C) 길 건너에 있는 곳이요.

해설 어느 약국을 이용하는지 묻는 질문에 특정 약국의 위치로 답한 (C)가 정답. (A)는 fill과 발음이 유사한 pill을 이용한 오답.

어휘 pharmacy 약국 fill a prescription (처방) 약을 조제하다 pill 알약 pharmacist 약사

18.

Did you see the new laboratory equipment?
(A) What should we order?
(B) I've been out of town.
(C) A chemical experiment.

PART 2

7. 미 미 🎧

Where is the nearest gas station?
(A) Yes, for my new car.
(B) On the other side of the park.
(C) The train is departing soon.

가장 가까운 주유소가 어디에 있나요?
(A) 네, 제 새 차를 위해서요.
(B) 공원 반대편이에요.
(C) 기차가 곧 출발해요.

해설 가장 가까운 주유소의 위치를 묻는 질문에 특정 위치로 답한 (B)가 정답.

어휘 on the other side of ~의 반대편에   depart 출발하다, 떠나다

8. 미 영 🎧

This hotel is more spacious than the last one we stayed in, isn't it?
(A) I'd be happy to recommend one.
(B) It's booked for the next three nights.
(C) Yes, we've got plenty of room this time.

이 호텔은 우리가 지난번에 묵었던 호텔보다 널찍하네요, 그렇죠?
(A) 기꺼이 하나 추천해 드릴게요.
(B) 앞으로 3박 동안 예약되어 있어요.
(C) 네, 이번에는 공간이 넉넉하네요.

해설 호텔이 널찍하다는 말에 동의를 구하는 질문에 Yes라고 하면서 공간이 넉넉하다고 답한 (C)가 정답. (A)와 (B)는 hotel에서 연상할 수 있는 recommend와 booked를 각각 이용한 오답.

어휘 spacious 널찍한   recommend 추천하다   book 예약하다   plenty of 넉넉한, 많은   room 공간, 방

9. 미 미 🎧

Isn't this sweater twenty-five percent off?
(A) No, the sale has ended.
(B) This is the only size we have.
(C) I think it fits you perfectly.

이 스웨터는 25% 할인되지 않나요?
(A) 아니요, 세일은 끝났어요.
(B) 이것이 저희가 가지고 있는 유일한 치수예요.
(C) 당신에게 딱 맞는 것 같아요.

해설 스웨터의 할인 여부를 묻는 질문에 No라고 하면서 세일이 끝났다고 답한 (A)가 정답. (B)와 (C)는 sweater에서 연상할 수 있는 size와 fits를 각각 이용한 오답.

어휘 fit (꼭) 맞다, 적합하다   perfectly 더할 나위 없이, 완벽하게

10. 호 미 🎧

Who does the manager plan to promote to assistant marketing director?
(A) It's our sales promotion.
(B) Yes, it happened quite suddenly.
(C) Rachel, from the Westland branch.

부장님이 누구를 마케팅 차장으로 승진시킬 계획인가요?
(A) 그게 저희 판촉 활동이에요.
(B) 네, 그 일은 꽤나 갑작스럽게 일어났어요.
(C) 웨스틀랜드 지사의 레이첼 씨요.

해설 마케팅 차장으로 누구를 승진시킬지 묻는 질문에 사람 이름으로 답한 (C)가 정답. (A)는 promote와 promotion의 파생어를 이용한 오답.

어휘 promote 승진시키다, 촉진하다   assistant director 차장   promotion 촉진, 승진   branch 지사, 분점

11. 미 미 🎧

Why is the vending machine in the break room unplugged?
(A) Let's take a break.
(B) It was having electrical problems.
(C) Can I get you something to drink?

휴게실에 있는 자동판매기의 플러그가 왜 뽑혀 있죠?
(A) 잠시 쉬죠.
(B) 전기 관련 문제가 있었어요.
(C) 마실 것을 좀 가져다 드릴까요?

해설 자동판매기의 플러그가 뽑혀 있는 이유를 묻는 질문에 전기 관련 문제가 있었다고 답한 (B)가 정답. (C)는 vending machine에서 연상할 수 있는 something to drink를 이용한 오답.

어휘 vending machine 자동판매기   unplug (전기) 플러그를 뽑다   take a break 잠시 휴식을 취하다   electrical 전기의

12. 영 호 🎧

We reached our fundraising goal at the charity event, right?
(A) No, we're a few hundred dollars short.
(B) Yes, it'll be a lot of fun.
(C) To help restore the museum.

우리는 자선 행사에서 모금 목표액을 달성했죠, 그렇죠?
(A) 아니요, 몇백 달러가 부족해요.
(B) 네, 그건 매우 재미있을 거예요.
(C) 박물관 재건을 돕기 위해서요.

3. 미 🎧

(A) A customer is reaching for an item.
(B) Some plants are on display.
(C) A woman is arranging a bouquet.
(D) Flowers are being watered.

(A) 손님이 물건을 향해 손을 뻗고 있다.
(B) 몇몇 식물들이 진열되어 있다.
(C) 여자가 부케를 만들고 있다.
(D) 꽃들에 물을 주고 있다.

해설 꽃집으로 보이는 곳에 식물들이 진열되어 있는 모습이므로 정답은 (B). 손님들이 보이지만 아무도 물건을 향해 손을 뻗고 있지는 않으므로 (A)는 오답.

어휘 reach for (~을 향해) 손을 뻗다　on display 진열된　arrange 정리[정돈]하다, 배열하다

4. 호 🎧

(A) Some people are attending a presentation.
(B) Some people are raising their hands.
(C) A man is drawing a graph.
(D) A woman is writing on a whiteboard.

(A) 몇몇 사람들이 프레젠테이션에 참석하고 있다.
(B) 몇몇 사람들이 손을 들고 있다.
(C) 남자가 그래프를 그리고 있다.
(D) 여자가 화이트보드에 쓰고 있다.

해설 회의실로 보이는 곳에서 사람들이 프레젠테이션에 참석하고 있는 모습이므로 정답은 (A).

어휘 attend 참석하다　raise 들다, 들어 올리다; 임금[가격] 인상

5. 미 🎧

(A) He's repairing some safety glasses.
(B) He's putting away some equipment.
(C) He's operating a machine.
(D) He's removing a hard hat from his head.

(A) 남자가 보안경을 고치고 있다.
(B) 남자가 장비를 치우고 있다.
(C) 남자가 기계를 조작하고 있다.
(D) 남자가 머리에 쓴 안전모를 벗고 있다.

해설 공장으로 보이는 곳에서 남자가 기계를 조작하고 있는 모습이므로 정답은 (C). 남자는 안전모를 착용한 채로 작업하고 있으므로 (D)는 오답.

어휘 safety glasses 보안경　put away ~을 치우다　operate 조작하다, 가동하다　remove 벗다, 없애다　hard hat 안전모

6. 영 🎧

(A) Several chairs are lined up in a row.
(B) Furniture has been left on the lawn.
(C) A barbecue is being installed on a terrace.
(D) A sitting area is unoccupied.

(A) 의자 몇 개가 일렬로 줄지어 있다.
(B) 가구가 잔디 위에 놓여 있다.
(C) 바비큐용 그릴을 테라스에 설치하고 있다.
(D) 앉는 공간이 비어 있다.

해설 의자들이 모두 비어 있으므로 정답은 (D). 바비큐용 그릴은 이미 설치된 상태이므로 (C)는 오답.

어휘 be lined up 줄지어 있다　in a row 일렬로　lawn 잔디(밭)　install 설치하다　unoccupied 비어 있는

TEST 02

LISTENING TEST

001 (B)	002 (C)	003 (B)	004 (A)	005 (C)
006 (D)	007 (B)	008 (C)	009 (A)	010 (C)
011 (B)	012 (A)	013 (A)	014 (C)	015 (B)
016 (A)	017 (C)	018 (B)	019 (A)	020 (C)
021 (A)	022 (C)	023 (C)	024 (B)	025 (B)
026 (A)	027 (C)	028 (B)	029 (C)	030 (B)
031 (C)	032 (C)	033 (B)	034 (B)	035 (C)
036 (A)	037 (D)	038 (D)	039 (D)	040 (B)
041 (C)	042 (A)	043 (C)	044 (D)	045 (C)
046 (A)	047 (C)	048 (A)	049 (B)	050 (B)
051 (D)	052 (A)	053 (C)	054 (D)	055 (C)
056 (C)	057 (A)	058 (C)	059 (D)	060 (A)
061 (B)	062 (A)	063 (D)	064 (A)	065 (B)
066 (D)	067 (A)	068 (D)	069 (C)	070 (A)
071 (D)	072 (C)	073 (C)	074 (C)	075 (D)
076 (B)	077 (A)	078 (C)	079 (A)	080 (D)
081 (A)	082 (B)	083 (B)	084 (B)	085 (D)
086 (A)	087 (B)	088 (D)	089 (A)	090 (B)
091 (B)	092 (D)	093 (A)	094 (A)	095 (B)
096 (C)	097 (B)	098 (A)	099 (B)	100 (C)

READING TEST

101 (D)	102 (D)	103 (B)	104 (C)	105 (A)
106 (A)	107 (C)	108 (A)	109 (A)	110 (B)
111 (D)	112 (A)	113 (A)	114 (B)	115 (C)
116 (A)	117 (D)	118 (D)	119 (B)	120 (B)
121 (C)	122 (A)	123 (B)	124 (C)	125 (B)
126 (A)	127 (C)	128 (A)	129 (C)	130 (C)
131 (A)	132 (C)	133 (A)	134 (B)	135 (B)
136 (B)	137 (A)	138 (D)	139 (B)	140 (C)
141 (C)	142 (D)	143 (B)	144 (C)	145 (A)
146 (D)	147 (B)	148 (D)	149 (A)	150 (D)
151 (A)	152 (B)	153 (D)	154 (D)	155 (B)
156 (C)	157 (C)	158 (C)	159 (B)	160 (B)
161 (D)	162 (B)	163 (B)	164 (B)	165 (A)
166 (C)	167 (B)	168 (D)	169 (C)	170 (B)
171 (D)	172 (A)	173 (C)	174 (C)	175 (B)
176 (A)	177 (D)	178 (C)	179 (D)	180 (D)
181 (B)	182 (A)	183 (C)	184 (D)	185 (B)
186 (B)	187 (C)	188 (C)	189 (B)	190 (D)
191 (D)	192 (B)	193 (D)	194 (C)	195 (C)
196 (D)	197 (D)	198 (C)	199 (A)	200 (C)

PART 1

1. 미 🎧

(A) She is putting fruit into a basket.
(B) She is standing behind a counter.
(C) She is placing products on a shelf.
(D) She is buying some groceries.

(A) 여자가 과일을 바구니 안에 넣고 있다.
(B) 여자가 카운터 뒤에 서 있다.
(C) 여자가 선반 위에 제품들을 놓고 있다.
(D) 여자가 식료품을 사고 있다.

해설 여자가 카운터 뒤에 서 있는 모습을 바르게 묘사한 (B)가 정답. 과일은 이미 바구니 안에 들어 있는 상태이므로 (A)는 오답.

어휘 place 놓다, 두다   product 제품   groceries (항상 복수형) 식료품류

2. 미 🎧

(A) One of the men is strolling past a bench.
(B) One of the men is jogging along the water.
(C) One of the men is riding a bicycle in the park.
(D) One of the men is pushing a stroller.

(A) 한 남자가 벤치를 지나 거닐고 있다.
(B) 한 남자가 물가를 따라 조깅을 하고 있다.
(C) 한 남자가 공원에서 자전거를 타고 있다.
(D) 한 남자가 유모차를 밀고 있다.

해설 사람들이 공원에서 산책을 하고 있는 모습으로, 자전거를 타고 있는 한 남자의 개별 동작을 바르게 묘사한 (C)가 정답.

어휘 stroll 거닐다, 산책하다   stroller 유모차

Answer **045**

수신: 월터 빈슨
발신: 에린 솔버그
날짜: 4월 4일
제목: 업데이트된 직무 설명서

안녕하세요, 월터

최고 재무 담당자 직책의 직무 설명서에 대한 조언에 감사드립니다. 당신이 제안한 정보를 추가했어요. [199]지난 회의에서 이사회에 또 다른 일원을 추가하기로 표결했으므로 우리는 그 사람도 찾기 시작해야 해요. 내규에 따르면, [200-2]선정 절차는 3인의 위원회에 의해 수행되어야 하고 이사회의 고위급 임원, 즉 의장이나 부의장이 이끌어야 합니다. 어떻게 생각하시는지 제게 알려주세요.

밀러브룩 이사회, 간사
에린 솔버그 드림

어휘 bylaw 내규, 규칙   carry out 수행하다   committee 위원회   head 이끌다   high-ranking 고위직의   officer 사무관   chair 의장   vice chair 부의장

196. 보도 자료에서 톨렌티노 씨에 대해 시사된 것은?
(A) 회사로부터 상을 받을 것이다.
(B) 자신만의 사업을 시작하기 위해 퇴사할 것이다.
(C) 모든 이사진의 지지를 받았다.
(D) 자신의 후임자를 교육시킬 계획이다.

해설 추론 문제

톨렌티노 씨는 기사에서 새로운 대표이사로 언급된 인물인데, 단서 (196)에서 이사회의 만장일치로 선택되었다고 했으므로 정답은 (C).

패러프레이징 [단서] unanimously selected → [정답] had the support of all board members

197. 촘리 씨에 대해 암시된 것은?
(A) 새로운 도시로 이주할 계획이다.
(B) 강력한 의사소통 기술을 가지고 있다.
(C) 빈슨 씨의 이전 동료이다.
(D) 전에 소프트웨어 프로그램을 설계했었다.

해설 두 지문 연계 문제_추론 문제

촘리 씨는 첫 번째 이메일에서 빈슨 씨가 최고 재무 담당자 직책에 추천한 사람으로, 단서 (197-2)에서 그 직책에 요구되는 모든 자격요건을 갖추고 있다고 했다. 기사의 단서 (197-1)에서 이 직책의 자격요건으로 의사소통 능력에 대해 언급했으므로 정답은 (B).

패러프레이징 [단서] clearly communicate to the board and investors → [정답] has strong communication skills

198. 빈슨 씨에 따르면, 촘리 씨가 그 직책에 대해 확신하지 못하는 이유는?
(A) 직무가 너무 전문적이다.
(B) 예상 근무 시간이 너무 길다.
(C) 복리 후생을 포함한 보수가 충분히 설명되어 있지 않다.
(D) 회사의 면접 절차가 길다.

해설 특정 정보 확인 문제

단서 (198)에서 촘리 씨가 최고 재무 담당자 직책에 확신을 가지지 못하는 이유가 직무 설명에 급여 외의 혜택에 대한 정보가 빠져 있기 때문이라고 했으므로 정답은 (C).

패러프레이징 [단서] does not include information → [정답] is not fully described

199. 두 번째 이메일에서, 밀러브룩 이사회에 대해 암시된 것은?
(A) 규모를 늘릴 것이다.
(B) 더 자주 모일 것이다.
(C) 더 많은 급여를 받을 것이다.
(D) 내규를 업데이트할 것이다.

해설 추론 문제

단서 (199)에서 이사회에 또 다른 임원을 추가하기로 표결했다고 했으므로 이사회 규모를 늘릴 것임을 알 수 있으므로 정답은 (A).

패러프레이징 [단서] add another member → [정답] increase in size

200. 빈슨 씨에 대해 암시된 것은?
(A) 이사회에 새로 들어온 위원이다.
(B) 제안된 변경사항에 반대했다.
(C) 자신의 친구를 감독할 것이다.
(D) 위원회를 이끌 자격이 있다.

해설 두 지문 연계 문제_추론 문제

첫 번째 이메일의 단서 (200-1)에서 빈슨 씨가 이사회의 부의장임을 알 수 있고, 두 번째 이메일의 단서 (200-2)에서 의장 또는 부의장이 선정 절차를 위한 위원회를 이끌어야 한다고 했다. 따라서 빈슨 씨에게 위원회를 이끌 자격이 있으므로 정답은 (D).

(C) 회사 프로그램의 규정을 설명하기 위해
(D) 부서 운영에 대한 개선사항을 제안하기 위해

해설 목적 문제

이메일의 단서 (192)를 통해 지오다노 씨가 브라이트 쇼핑 단지에 소규모 일반 매장을 열자는 의견을 제출한 것을 알 수 있는데, 이 제안과 관련하여 검토가 필요한 사항들을 열거한 후에 같은 문단 마지막 부분에서 최종 결정 전에 조금 더 알아보고 싶다고 한 것으로 보아 추가 정보를 요청하기 위해 쓴 이메일임을 유추할 수 있다. 따라서 정답은 (B).

패러프레이징 [단서] explore this matter further → [정답] request further information

193. 콘웨이 사가 종사하는 업계는?
(A) 신발 제조
(B) 부동산 개발
(C) 일자리 알선
(D) 미디어 서비스

해설 두 지문 연계 문제_특정 정보 확인 문제

이메일의 단서 (193-1)에서 아카디아 사를 언급하며 콘웨이 사의 경쟁업체라고 했고, 기사의 단서 (193-2)에서 아카디아 사는 운동화 제조업체라고 했으므로 콘웨이 사 역시 신발 제조업체임을 알 수 있다. 따라서 (A)가 정답.

패러프레이징 [단서] the maker of high-end athletic shoes → [정답] Footwear manufacturing

194. 브라이튼 쇼핑 단지에서 아카디아 사가 위치하게 될 점포는?
(A) 101호
(B) 104호
(C) 106호
(D) 107호

해설 두 지문 연계 문제_특정 정보 확인 문제

기사의 단서 (194-1)에서 아카디아 사의 매장이 골든 어패럴 옆에 위치하게 될 것이라고 했으므로 웹페이지의 평면도에서 해당 위치를 찾으면 106호다. 따라서 정답은 (C).

195. 기사에서 아카디아 제품의 어떤 측면이 강조되고 있는가?
(A) 다양한 종류의 선택권
(B) 저렴한 가격
(C) 유명인사의 이용
(D) 친환경 디자인

해설 특정 정보 확인 문제

기사의 단서 (195)에서 아카디아 사의 인기가 높아지는 이유로 유명한 운동선수들이 이 회사의 제품을 입는 것을 들었으므로 (C)가 정답.

패러프레이징 [단서] famous athletes → [정답] celebrities

196-200 기사 & 이메일 & 이메일

긴급 보도용

토론토 (3월 15일)—밀러브룩 엔터프라이즈 사의 대변인은 퇴임하는 대표이사 메리 길허스트 씨를 대신해 살바도르 톨렌티노 씨가 대표이사로 승진되었다고 발표했다. 196그는 밀러브룩 엔터프라이즈 사의 이사회의 만장일치로 선택되었으며 길허스트 씨와의 교육 후에 5월 25일부터 그의 새로운 역할을 맡게 될 것이다.

밀러브룩 엔터프라이즈 사는 최첨단 인공지능 소프트웨어를 공급한다. 그곳의 제품과 연구가 지난 10년간 업계를 선도했으며 향후 수년간 몇몇 해외 지사를 열 계획이다. 197-1톨렌티노 씨가 이전에 회사의 최고 재무 담당자로 근무했기 때문에 회사는 이 직책에 충원할 사람을 신속히 찾고 있는 중이다. 업무에는 재무 자료를 분석하고 회사 지출을 감독하는 것이 포함된다. 이 역할은 서면과 구두 형태 두 방식 모두로 이사회 및 투자자들과 명확히 의사소통 하는 능력이 요구된다. 이 직책에 대한 보다 자세한 사항과 채용 절차는 www.millerbrook.com에 게시되어 있다.

어휘 immediate 즉각적인 release 보도 spokesperson 대변인 be promoted to ~로 승진되다 replace 교체하다, 대신하다 outgoing 떠나는 unanimously 만장일치로 board 이사회 take on ~을 떠맡다 cutting-edge 최첨단의 artificial intelligence 인공 지능 formerly 이전에 CFO 최고 재무 담당자 analyze 분석하다 financial 재무의, 재정적인 monitor 감독하다, 감시하다 expenditure 지출, 경비 require 요구하다 further 추가적인 post 게시하다

수신: 밀러브룩 엔터프라이즈 이사회
발신: 월터 빈슨
날짜: 4월 4일
제목: 최고 재무 담당자 후보

이사회 동료 위원들께,

저는 공석인 최고 재무 담당자 직책에 브리아나 촘리 씨를 후보자로 제안하고 싶습니다. 그녀는 저와 랄스턴 대학 동문이며, 197-2그 직책에 요구되는 모든 자격요건을 갖추고 있습니다. 저는 그 직책에 지원하는 것에 대해 그녀와 이야기를 나눴습니다. 하지만, 198그녀는 그것이 자신에게 맞을지 확신하지 못하고 있습니다. 이것은 우리 웹사이트에 있는 직무 설명에는 급여만 언급되어 있고 우리가 제공하는 분기별 보너스, 스톡 옵션, 그리고 주택 수당에 대한 정보가 포함되어 있지 않기 때문입니다. 다른 후보자들도 아마 같은 오해를 하고 있을지 모르기 때문에 저는 우리가 이를 업데이트 해야 한다고 생각합니다.

200-1밀러브룩 이사회, 부의장
월터 빈슨 드림

어휘 put forth 제시하다 candidate 후보자 meet 맞추다, 충족시키다 qualification 자격요건 apply for ~에 지원하다 job description 직무 설명 list 나열하다, 목록화하다 quarterly 분기별의 housing allowance 주택 수당 misconception 오해

아 크레스 씨가 본관 홀의 부스에서 일했을 것임을 유추할 수 있으므로 (B)가 정답이다.

190. 바움 씨가 하고자 계획하는 것은?
(A) 주제에 대한 추가 조사 착수하기
(B) 또 다른 온라인 평가서 작성하기
(C) 그녀의 일상 식습관 바꾸기
(D) 건강과 관련된 사업 시작하기

해설 특정 정보 확인 문제
바움 씨는 세 번째 지문인 박람회 참가 후기의 작성자로, 단서 (190)에서 채식주의 식단으로 변경하기로 결정했다고 했으므로 (C)가 정답이다.

패러프레이징 [단서] transition to a completely vegetarian diet → [정답] Change her daily eating habits

191-195 이메일 & 기사 & 웹페이지

수신: 아르미나 지오다노 〈a.giordano@conway-co.com〉
발신: 라시드 파델 〈r.fadel@conway-co.com〉
날짜: 8월 21일
주제: 제출

지오다노 씨께,

우리 콘웨이 사의 '콘웨이 미래 성장 계획'에 참여해주신 데 감사드립니다. ¹⁹¹우리가 사업 확장을 위해 제안을 요청한 것은 이번이 처음이며, 매우 많은 아이디어들을 전사의 직원들과 공유하게 되어 기뻤습니다.

¹⁹²브라이튼 쇼핑 단지에 소규모로 우리의 일반 매장을 여는 것에 관해 당신이 주신 의견은 매우 흥미롭습니다. 위원회 위원들은 고객들을 가장 인기 있는 우리 제품에 노출시키는 아이디어를 매우 좋아했지만 우리에게 큰 그림이 그려지지는 않는 것 같습니다. 예를 들면, 그 장소에 어떤 종류의 유동 인구가 오갈지 궁금합니다. 월 임대료가 꽤 높다고 알고 있으므로 그만한 가치가 있는지 확실히 해야 할 것 같습니다. 또한, 어떤 다른 사업체들이 그곳에서 운영을 하고 있거나, 혹은 사업을 할 계획인가요? ¹⁹³⁻¹아카디아 사가 10월에 브라이튼 쇼핑 단지에서 대규모 개점을 한다는 광고를 한 것으로 알고 있습니다. 그곳은 우리의 주요 경쟁업체이고 우리와 매우 비슷한 물품들을 취급하고 있으므로 이것이 주요 쟁점이 될 수도 있습니다. ¹⁹²최종 결정을 하기 전에 이 문제에 대해 보다 더 알아보고 싶습니다.

콘웨이 미래 성장 계획, 위원장
라시드 파델 드림

어휘 submission 제출, 제안 appreciate 감사하다 initiative 계획 expand 확장하다 throughout ~ 도처에 regarding ~에 관하여 usual 흔한 complex (건물) 단지 intriguing 매우 흥미로운 committee 위원회 expose 노출하다 big picture 큰 그림, 전체적인 상황 foot traffic 도보 인파 lease fee 임대료 worth ~의 가치가 있는 in addition 게다가, 또한 in operation 운영 중인 advertise 광고하다

competitor 경쟁업체[체] carry (가게에서 품목을) 취급하다 inventory 물품 목록 explore 탐구하다 further 보다 더 make a decision 결정하다

롱뷰 (10월 3일)—이번 달 하순, ¹⁹³⁻²농구, 달리기 등을 위한 고급 운동화 제조업체인 아카디아 사가 브라이튼 쇼핑 단지에 최신 지점을 여는 개점 행사를 가질 것이다. 행사에 참여하는 고객들은 5,000달러 상당의 아카디아 제품이 상품으로 걸린 추첨에 참여할 기회를 가지게 될 것이다.

¹⁹⁴⁻¹매장은 골든 어패럴 옆에 위치하게 될 것이며, 회사에서 가장 높은 수익을 올리는 지점들 중 하나가 될 것으로 예상된다. ¹⁹⁵농구 선수인 스콧 애킨슨과 마라톤 선수인 캐롤라인 홈즈 같은 유명한 운동선수들이 그곳의 제품을 착용하고 있기에, 아카디아 사가 지난 몇 년 동안 인기가 높아진 것은 놀라운 일이 아니다.

어휘 high-end 고급의, 고가의 athletic (운동) 경기의; 체육의 drawing 추첨 merchandise 제품, 물건 be located 위치하다 be expected to do ~할 예정이다 earn (돈을) 벌다, (수익을) 올리다 popularity 인기

191. 콘웨이 미래 성장 계획에 대해 암시된 것은?
(A) 새로운 직원들을 타깃으로 한다.
(B) 한 달 동안 지속될 것이다.
(C) 파델 씨에 의해 제안되었다.
(D) 전 직원들에게 열려 있었다.

해설 추론 문제
'미래 성장 계획'은 첫 번째 지문인 이메일에 언급된다. 단서 (191)에서 이 계획을 통해 전 직원들과 많은 아이디어들을 공유하게 되어 기뻤다는 것으로 보아 전 직원에게 개방된 계획이었음을 유추할 수 있으므로 정답은 (D).

패러프레이징 [단서] shared by staff throughout the entire company → [정답] open to all employees

192. 파델 씨가 이메일을 보냈던 이유는?
(A) 경쟁업체와 합병을 제안하기 위해
(B) 제안에 대한 추가 정보를 요청하기 위해

어휘 preparation 준비 underway 진행 중인 expo 박람회 take place 개최되다 feature 특징으로 삼다 a variety of 다양한 related 관련된 goods 제품 additionally 게다가, 또한 local 지역의 physician 의사 screening 검사 blood pressure 혈압 contain 포함하다 vendor 상인, 판매 회사 supplement 보충(물) therapist 치료사 representative 대표자, 담당자 wing 부속 건물

연례 헬스 앤 웰빙 박람회
판매 업체 의견 설문조사

이름: 안나 피어슨
업체/회사: 선라이즈 스파

187-2 저는 오크데일 비즈니스 협회의 제 회원 자격을 통해 행사에 대해 통보를 받았습니다. 이번이 제가 판매 업체로서 처음 참여한 것이었고, 기대했던 것보다 더 많은 사람들에게 다가갔습니다. 하지만, 188 저는 현장에서 마사지를 제공하기 위해 부스가 좀 더 컸더라면 좋았겠다고 생각했고, 더 작은 부스를 필요로 했던 몇몇 다른 판매 업체들과도 이야기를 나눴습니다. 모든 사람들이 똑같은 요구를 가지고 있는 것이 아니므로 앞으로는 이 점을 고려하는 것이 좋을 것 같습니다.

어휘 be informed 통보 받다 association 협회 on-site 현장의 address 고심하다, 다루다

---

http://www.rtgoakdale.com/reviews

귀하의 경험에 대해 저희에게 말씀해주세요.

평가자 (선택): 셰릴 바움

RTG 오크데일에 대해 어떻게 처음 알게 되었나요?
오크데일 헬스 앤 웰빙 박람회에 방문함으로써

귀하의 경험에 대해 얼마나 만족하셨나요? (0=매우 실망, 5=매우 만족) 5

의견: 저는 채식주의 생활방식이 환경에 이로운 영향을 주기 때문에 최근에 이에 더욱 관심을 가지게 되었습니다. 190 저는 곧 완전히 채식주의 식단으로 변경하기로 결정했으나 단백질, 철분 그리고 부족할지 모르는 그 밖의 다른 것을 충분히 섭취하는 것에 대해 우려하고 있었습니다. 하지만, 189-2 제게 어떤 종류의 비타민 보충제가 필요할지 잘 몰랐습니다. 앤서니 크레스 씨의 회사 부스에서 그와 이야기를 나눈 후 저는 제대로 알게 된 것 같은 느낌이 들었습니다. 크레스 씨는 아는 것이 많았고 저의 특정한 상황에 대해 아주 좋은 추천을 해주었습니다. 전반적으로 제게는 매우 긍정적인 경험이었습니다.

어휘 vegetarian 채식주의의 beneficial 이로운 transition 이행[변천]하다; 변경 be concerned about ~에 대해 걱정하다 lack 부족하다 knowledgeable 아는 것이 많은, 잘 아는 specific 특정한, 구체적인 circumstance 상황, 환경 overall 전반적으로

---

186. 기사에 따르면, 행사 기획자들이 올해 다른 장소를 사용한 이유는 무엇인가?
(A) 더 많은 공간을 확보하기 위해
(B) 교통 문제를 최소화하기 위해
(C) 새로운 건물을 홍보하기 위해
(D) 출장 시간을 줄이기 위해

해설 특정 정보 확인 문제

단서 (186)에서 박람회 장소가 바뀌었음을 언급하며, 그 이유가 참여하려는 업체들의 수가 증가하고 있기 때문이라고 한 것으로 보아 더 넓은 장소가 필요했기 때문에 장소를 변경한 것임을 알 수 있으므로 정답은 (A).

패러프레이징 [단서] contain the number of vendors
→ [정답] ensure more space

187. 피어슨 씨에 대해 암시된 것은?
(A) 조기 등록할 자격이 있었다.
(B) 최근에 사업을 시작했다.
(C) 이전 행사에 참여한 적이 있다.
(D) 할인을 받을 자격이 있었다.

해설 두 지문 연계 문제_추론 문제

피어슨 씨는 두 번째 지문인 설문조사에 응한 사람으로, 단서 (187-2)에서 오크데일 비즈니스 협회 회원임을 밝혔는데, 첫 번째 지문인 기사의 단서 (187-1)에서 오크데일 비즈니스 협회의 회원은 20% 할인을 받을 수 있다고 했으므로 피어슨 씨는 할인 받을 자격이 있음을 알 수 있다. 따라서 정답은 (D).

패러프레이징 [단서] get a twenty percent discount
→ [정답] eligible for a discount

188. 피어슨 씨가 다음 박람회를 위해 제안한 것은?
(A) 소음에 대한 일부 불만을 처리하는 것
(B) 더 많은 전기 콘센트를 제공하는 것
(C) 다양한 크기의 부스를 제공하는 것
(D) 더 많은 사람들에게 행사를 광고하는 것

해설 특정 정보 확인 문제

단서 (188)에서 피어슨 씨가 자신은 더 큰 부스가 필요했던 반면 더 작은 부스를 원했던 업체들도 있었다며, 부스 크기에 대한 다양한 요구를 반영하는 것이 좋겠다는 바람을 나타냈으므로 정답은 (C).

189. 크레스 씨에 대해 암시된 것은?
(A) 오랫동안 오크데일에 살아 왔다.
(B) 본관 홀 부스에서 일했다.
(C) 박람회를 위한 행사 기획자였다.
(D) 바움 씨를 고용하는 것을 고려 중이다.

해설 두 지문 연계 문제_추론 문제

크레스 씨는 세 번째 지문에서 언급된다. 단서 (189-2)에서 크레스 씨가 비타민 보충제에 대해 잘 알고 있다고 했고, 단서 (189-1)에서 비타민과 건강 보조제 판매 회사들을 본관 홀에서 만날 수 있다고 한 것으로 보

청소업체를 고용하는 데 어려움을 겪어온 것을 알고 있으므로 제가 매우 운이 좋다고 느낍니다. ¹⁸⁴⁻²귀사가 저희 회사에서 작업을 시작한 지 벌써 4년이 되었다는 게 믿어지지 않습니다. ¹⁸³재정적인 조언을 받기 위해 저희를 방문하시는 분들 모두가 저희 사무실에 깊은 인상을 받아오셨고 귀사가 그러한 긍정적인 첫인상을 만드는 데 중요한 역할을 해주셨습니다.

귀사의 탁월함에도 불구하고 저희는 조금 있으면 더 이상 귀사의 서비스가 필요하지 않게 되어서 ¹⁸⁵⁻²마지막 청소 날짜는 2월 28일로 하고 싶습니다. 저희는 오하이오 가 579번지의 새로운 사무실 건물로 이전할 것이며, 그 건물의 유지보수 팀이 월 사용료의 일부로 청소를 해줍니다. 상황이 된다면 귀사를 다른 사람들에게 기꺼이 추천하겠습니다.

완다 밀번 드림

어휘 upcoming 곧 있을 have trouble doing ~하는 데 어려움을 겪다 reliable 믿을 만한 financial 재정적인, 재무의 impressed 깊은 인상을 받은 play a role 역할을 하다 first impression 첫인상 in spite of ~에도 불구하고 excellence 탁월함, 뛰어남 no longer 더 이상 ~ 않는 maintenance 유지보수 arise 생기다, 발생하다

181. 편지에 따르면, 서비스 비용이 인상되는 때는?
(A) 1월 5일
(B) 1월 31일
(C) 3월 4일
(D) 3월 5일

해설 특정 정보 확인 문제

단서 (181)을 보면, 편지의 도입부에서 청소 서비스 요금이 인상된다고 알리면서, 현재 요금이 3월 4일까지 유효하다고 했고, 마지막 문단에서는 변경 사항이 3월 5일에 발효된다고 직접적으로 밝혔으므로 정답은 (D).

182. 버그 씨와 밀번 씨의 의견이 일치하는 지점은?
(A) 청소가 정기적으로 이루어져야 한다는 것
(B) 좋은 청소업자를 찾기 힘들다는 것
(C) 규정이 엄격해지고 있다는 것
(D) 청소 서비스 비용이 오르고 있다는 것

해설 두 지문 연계 문제_특정 정보 확인 문제

단서 (182)를 보면, 버그 씨가 쓴 편지에서 완벽하고 꼼꼼한 청소 서비스를 하는 곳이 드물다고 했고, 밀번 씨가 쓴 이메일에서는 믿을 만한 청소 업체를 찾는 데 어려움을 느끼는 사업주들이 있다고 했으므로 두 사람은 모두 괜찮은 청소업자를 찾는 것이 어렵다고 생각하고 있음을 알 수 있다. 따라서 (B)가 정답.

183. 밀번 씨가 근무할 것 같은 업종은?
(A) 그래픽 디자인 회사
(B) 소프트웨어 개발 회사
(C) 상업 건설 회사
(D) 재무 컨설팅 회사

해설 추론 문제

단서 (183)에서 재정적인 조언을 얻기 위해 방문하는 사람들이 있다고 한 것으로 보아 밀번 씨의 회사는 재무 컨설팅과 관련된 일을 하는 업체임을 유추할 수 있으므로 (D)가 정답.

패러프레이징 [단서] financial advice → [정답] financial consulting

184. 샤인타임 커머셜 클리닝 사에 대해 시사된 것은?
(A) 4년간 운영해오고 있다.
(B) 3월에 본사를 이전할 것이다.
(C) 최근에 경쟁사에 매각되었다.
(D) 추가 직원을 고용할 계획이다.

해설 두 지문 연계 문제_Not/True 문제

단서 (184-1)에서 샤인타임 커머셜 클리닝이 개업한 첫 달에 밀번 씨의 회사가 고객이 되었다고 했고, 단서 (184-2)에서 이 업체가 밀번 씨의 회사에 서비스를 제공한 지 4년이 되었다고 했다. 이를 종합하면, 샤인타임 커머셜 클리닝 사는 4년간 운영되어 왔음을 알 수 있으므로 정답은 (A).

185. 밀번 씨는 버그 씨가 요청한 것을 어떻게 제공하는가?
(A) 서비스에 대한 의견을 제공함으로써
(B) 일부 새로운 계약 조건에 동의함으로써
(C) 원하는 종료 날짜를 확정함으로써
(D) 새로운 회사 주소를 알려줌으로써

해설 두 지문 연계 문제_특정 정보 확인 문제

단서 (185-1)에서 버그 씨가 계약을 종료하고 싶다면 원하는 마지막 서비스 날을 알려달라고 했는데, 단서 (185-2)에서 밀번 씨가 마지막 청소 날짜를 2월 28일로 원한다고 했으므로 정답은 (C).

패러프레이징 [단서] your desired final day of service → [정답] the desired termination date

186-190 기사 & 양식 & 양식

오크데일(4월 9일)—6월 19일 일요일에 개최될 제8회 연례 오크데일 헬스 앤 웰빙 박람회의 준비가 진행 중이다. 박람회는 다양한 건강 관련 제품과 서비스를 제공하는 사업체들을 선보일 것이다. 또한, 지역의 의사들과 간호사들이 혈압과 콜레스테롤 수치뿐만 아니라 기본 시력 검사도 무료로 제공할 것이다.

수년간 주니퍼 홀에서 열린 데 이어, 올해는 박람회가 베이리지 컨벤션 센터로 옮겨졌다. ¹⁸⁶"높아지는 행사의 인기 때문에, 주니퍼 홀은 더 이상 박람회 참가에 관심이 있는 판매 회사의 수를 수용할 수가 없습니다"라고 행사 기획자 중 한 명인 켄 엑슬리 씨가 말했다. "¹⁸⁹⁻¹본관 홀에는 비타민과 건강 보조제 판매 회사들, 동관에는 마사지 치료사와 스파 담당자들, 서관에는 체육관 직원들 및 스포츠 관련 사업체들이 있어서, 방문객들은 찾고 있는 것을 쉽게 구할 수 있습니다."

등록하려면 www.oakdalehealthexpo.com에 방문해야 한다. ¹⁸⁷⁻¹오크데일 비즈니스 협회의 회원들은 20% 할인을 받을 수 있다.

나 추위를 막아주는 대형 텐트를 이용하여 행사를 진행할 수도 있다고 했지만, 소유권에 관해서는 언급된 바가 없으므로 (A)가 정답.

패러프레이징 [단서] doubled the size of our parking lot
→ [정답] expanded its parking area / [단서] bands or singers
→ [정답] musicians / [단서] protects against rain can be heated in cold weather → [정답] can accommodate different types of weather

177. 에드젤 가든스에서 음식을 제공할 수 있는 때는?

(A) 월요일 오전 10시
(B) 수요일 새벽 1시
(C) 토요일 오전 11시
(D) 일요일 오전 9시

해설 특정 정보 확인 문제

단서 (177)에서 식사 및 음료를 주중에는 오전 11시부터 자정까지, 주말에는 오전 10시부터 새벽 1시까지 제공한다고 했으므로 이 시간대에 해당하는 (C)가 정답.

패러프레이징 [단서] 10 A.M. to 1 A.M. on weekends
→ [정답] Saturday at 11 A.M.

178. 광고에서 웹사이트에 방문할 것을 추천하는 이유는?

(A) 가격 목록을 보기 위해
(B) 고객 의견을 읽기 위해
(C) 영감을 얻기 위해
(D) 예약을 하기 위해

해설 특정 정보 확인 문제

단서 (178)에서 웹사이트 주소를 제시하면서 사진 갤러리에 방문해서 영감 받으라고 하고 있으므로 (C)가 정답.

패러프레이징 [단서] get inspired → [정답] get some inspiration

179. 프레드 워런 씨에 대해 암시된 바는?

(A) 텐트 안에서만 사진을 찍었다.
(B) 웹사이트에서 좋은 평가를 받았다.
(C) 머피 씨의 부모님과 친구이다.
(D) 에드젤 가든스에 직접 고용되어 있다.

해설 두 지문 연계 문제_추론 문제

단서 (179)를 보면, 광고 두 번째 문단에서 프리미엄 패키지를 이용하면 회사 내부의 사진작가를 이용할 수 있다고 했는데, 이메일에서 프리미엄 패키지를 이용했으며, 전문 사진작가인 프레드 워런 씨가 사진을 찍어주었다고 했다. 이로 보아 프레드 워런은 에드젤 가든스 사에 고용된 전문 사진작가임을 유추할 수 있으므로 정답은 (D).

패러프레이징 [단서] in-house → [정답] employed

180. 이메일에서, 첫 번째 단락 네 번째 줄의 "fit"과 의미상 가장 가까운 단어는?

(A) 직책
(B) 맞춤
(C) 개발
(D) 각색

해설 동의어 문제

fit은 동사로는 '~에 맞다, 적합하다', 명사로는 '어울림, 조화'라는 의미로 쓰인다. 해당 문장에서는 명사로 쓰였으므로 이와 가장 비슷한 의미의 단어인 (B)가 정답.

181-185 편지 & 이메일

완다 밀번
코빗 엔터프라이즈
라딘 가 4443
내슈빌, 테네시 주 37210
1월 5일

밀번 씨께,

저희는 상기 주소의 코빗 엔터프라이즈 사에 실시하는 [181]청소 서비스의 요금 인상에 대해 귀하께 알리기 위해 편지를 씁니다. 귀하께서 지불하고 계신 현재 요금은 3월 4일까지 유효합니다. [184-1]귀하께서는 저희가 개업한 바로 그 첫 달에 저희 고객이 되어주신 분 중 한 명이기 때문에 저희는 가능한 한 오래 저렴한 가격으로 요금을 유지해 왔습니다.

[182-1]저희는 저희 작업자들에게 공정하게 보상하고자 이러한 변경을 시행하려고 하는데요, 그들은 항상 완벽하고 꼼꼼한 청소 서비스를 수행하기 때문입니다. 이렇게 하는 것은 저희 업계에서는 드문 일입니다. 새로운 요금 명세서를 동봉합니다.

[181]변경 사항은 3월 5일에 발효될 것입니다. [185-1]계약을 종료하고 싶으시면 귀하께서 원하시는 마지막 서비스 날을 알려주십시오. 앞으로도 여러 해 동안 귀하를 계속 모실 수 있기를 희망합니다.

샤인타임 커머셜 클리닝 사 관리자
그랜트 버그 드림

어휘 inform A of B A에게 B에 대해 알리다   perform 시행하다, 실시하다   current 현재의   valid 유효한   rate 비율   as ~ as possible 가능한 ~ 하게   implement 수행하다   ensure that ~을 보장하다   compensate 보상하다   fairly 공정하게   complete 완전한   rare 드문, 희귀한   enclosed 첨부된   breakdown 명세서   go into effect 효력이 발생하다   terminate 끝내다, 종료하다   contract 계약(서)

수신: 그랜트 버그 〈grant@shinetimecommcleaning.com〉
발신: 완다 밀번 〈w.milburn@corbittenterprises.com〉
날짜: 1월 11일
제목: 청소 계약

버그 씨께,

곧 있을 변경 사항에 대해 알려주셔서 감사합니다. 제공받은 관리 수준에 저희는 만족합니다. [182-2]저는 많은 사업주들이 믿을 만한 있으며, 대화 전반에서 홍보와 관련된 내용이 계속 언급되고 있으므로 이들은 마케팅 부서 소속임을 알 수 있다. 따라서 가오 씨의 직업에 가장 가까운 것은 (C)이다.

174. 메이페어 네트워크에 대해 사실인 것은?
(A) 연례 행사를 주최하고 있다.
(B) 메시지 작성자들의 회사와 제휴를 맺을 것이다.
(C) 직원들이 많은 경력을 가지고 있다.
(D) 요금이 메시지 작성자들의 회사에 너무 비싸다.

해설 Not/True 문제

단서 (174)에서 팀코 씨가 언급한 메이페어 네트워크에서의 TV 캠페인에 대해 가오 씨가 해당 방송국에서 요구하는 가격을 감당할 여력이 안 된다고 하는 것으로 보아, 메이페어 네트워크에서 요구하는 금액이 메시지 작성자들의 회사에는 너무 비싸다는 것을 알 수 있으므로 (D)가 정답.

패러프레이징 [단서] We can't afford the prices the station was charging → [정답] Its fees are too high for the writers' company.

175. 오전 9시 28분에, 풀커슨 씨가 "별거 아니에요"라고 한 것에서 그가 의도한 것은?
(A) 팀코 씨가 문제를 해결해 줄 것에 기쁘다.
(B) 기꺼이 등록 절차를 빠르게 완료할 것이다.
(C) 이용 가능한 정보가 부족한 것에 놀랐다.
(D) 팀을 위한 행사를 발견하게 되어 기쁘다.

해설 의도 파악 문제

"It's nothing"은 '별거 아니다'라는 뜻으로, 단서 (175)에서 풀커슨 씨가 퇴근 전까지 행사 등록을 하겠다고 하자 팀코 씨가 신속한 일처리에 고맙다고 한 데 대한 응답이다. 즉, 풀커슨 씨가 흔쾌히 등록 절차를 빠르게 완료하겠다는 의미로 한 말임을 알 수 있으므로 (B)가 정답.

패러프레이징 [단서] register our company for the event by the end of the day → [정답] complete a registration process quickly

176-180 광고 & 이메일

에드젤 가든스와 함께 여러분의 행사를 아주 멋지고 기억에 남는 것으로 만들어 보세요!

스톡턴 근처에 위치하고 있으며 4에이커의 식물원으로 이루어진 에드젤 가든스는 정말로 독특하고 낭만적인 장소라는 점이 특징입니다. 여러분은 저희 장소에서 제공되는 평화로운 주위 환경과 멋진 경치, 최신 편의 시설들을 좋아하실 것입니다. 저희는 결혼식과 기념일 파티를 전문으로 하며, 더 큰 규모의 단체를 수용하기 위해 ¹⁷⁶ᴮ최근 주차장의 크기를 두 배로 늘렸습니다. ¹⁷⁶ᴰ여러분은 전적으로 야외에서 행사를 개최할 수도 있고 저희의 대형 텐트를 이용할 수도 있는데, 이것은 비를 막아주고 추운 날씨에는 난방을 할 수도 있습니다. 저희 텐트는 하객을 최대 180명까지 수용하며, ¹⁷⁷주중에는 오전 11시부터 자정까지, 주말에는 오전 10시부터 새벽 1시까지 식사 및/또는 음료를 제공하도록 허용하는 식품 및 주류 면허증을 가지고 있습니다.

저희 팀은 반드시 모든 것이 정확히 여러분이 원하시는 그대로가 되도록 여러분과 함께 노력할 것입니다. ¹⁷⁹⁻¹저희 프리미엄 패키지로, 계획하는 일을 쉽게 만들어줄 내부 사진작가와 출장 뷔페를 이용하실 수 있습니다. 라이브 음악을 원하시면, ¹⁷⁶ᶜ밴드와 가수들을 추천해드릴 수 있습니다.

일을 시작하시려면 555-8790번으로 저희에게 오늘 전화주세요. ¹⁷⁸행사의 주제를 어떤 종류로 할지 잘 모르시겠다면 www.edselgardens.com의 저희 사진 갤러리에 방문하셔서 영감을 얻으세요. 여러분의 행사를 주최하길 고대합니다!

어휘 memorable 기억할 만한 comprise ~로 구성되다 botanical garden 식물원 feature ~의 특징을 이루다 unique 독특한 gorgeous 멋진 amenity ((보통 복수형)) 편의 시설 specialize in ~을 전문으로 하다 double 두 배가 되다 parking lot 주차장 accommodate 수용하다 hold 개최하다 completely 완전히, 전적으로 protect 보호하다 up to ~까지 permit A to do A가 ~하는 것을 허가하다 exactly 정확히 in-house (회사) 내부의 caterer 출장 뷔페 inspired 영감을 받는

수신: 에드젤 가든스 〈info@edselgardens.com〉
발신: 라모나 머피 〈rmurphy@haven-mail.com〉
날짜: 4월 11일
제목: 감사합니다!

관계자 분께,

최근에 귀사의 장소에서 저희 부모님을 위한 기념일 파티를 열었고, 멋진 경험을 하게 해주셔서 감사 드리고 싶었습니다. ¹⁷⁹⁻²저는 프리미엄 패키지를 이용했는데, 편리하고 가격이 저렴했습니다. 저는 전문 사진작가인 프레드 워런 씨가 찍어준 사진들에 매우 깊은 인상을 받았습니다. 또한 제가 고용했던 밴드에 대해 많은 칭찬을 받았습니다. 아름다운 장소는 저희 부모님 스타일에 딱 맞는 것이었습니다. 저는 행사를 개최할 장소를 찾고 있는 제 모든 친구들과 가족들에게 에드젤 가든스를 강력 추천할 계획입니다.

라모나 머피 드림

어휘 affordably priced 저렴한 가격의 be impressed with ~에 깊은 인상을 받다 compliment 칭찬 hire 고용하다 venue 장소 fit 어울림, 조화

176. 에드젤 가든스에 대해 사실이 아닌 것은?
(A) 현재 새로운 소유주가 운영하고 있다.
(B) 최근에 주차 구역을 확장했다.
(C) 음악가들을 추천해 줄 수 있다.
(D) 다양한 종류의 날씨에 맞출 수 있다.

해설 Not/True 문제

단서 (176B), (176C), (176D)에서 에드젤 가든스는 최근에 주차 구역을 두 배로 확장했으며, 원하는 경우 밴드나 가수를 추천해 줄 수 있고, 비

170. 아메드 씨에 대해 사실일 것 같은 것은?
(A) 도기 전문가이다.
(B) 알딘 대학을 졸업했다.
(C) 베를린에서 자랐다.
(D) 책을 출간할 계획이다.

해설 추론 문제

단서 (170)을 종합해 보면 복원 프로젝트의 대상은 화병과 그릇 조각, 즉 도기류이며, 자밀라 아메드 씨는 이 도기 복원 프로젝트에 딱 맞는 전문 지식과 경험을 가지고 있다. 이를 통해 아메드 씨가 도기에 대한 지식과 경험이 많은 전문가임을 유추할 수 있으므로 정답은 (A). 나머지 선택지들은 언급되지 않은 내용이므로 모두 오답이다.

패러프레이징 [단서] her specialized knowledge and extensive experience → [정답] an expert

171. 유물들에 대해 암시된 것은?
(A) 개인 수집가들에 의해 기부되었다.
(B) 운송 전에 몇 주간 검사를 받을 것이다.
(C) 10월 2일부터 전시될 것이다.
(D) 운송 중에 약간의 손상이 있었다.

해설 추론 문제

먼저 기사 맨 앞의 단서 (171)을 통해 기사가 작성된 날짜가 9월 7일임을 확인한다. 기사 후반부에서 유물들이 10월 2일에 베를린으로 운송될 수 있도록 현재 유물들의 검사 작업이 시작되었다고 했으므로, 한 달이 조금 안 되는 시간 동안 알딘 대학에서 유물들을 검사할 것임을 알 수 있다. 따라서 정답은 (B).

패러프레이징 [단서] to be shipped → [정답] transportation

172-175 온라인 채팅

유한 가오 [오전 9:18]
안녕하세요, 여러분. 제가 어제 팀 회의를 취소해서, 173일들이 어떻게 진행되고 있는지 확인하고 싶어요. 리사, 무역 박람회 조사는 어떻게 되어가고 있어요?

리사 팀코 [오전 9:19]
예상했던 것보다 훨씬 잘 되어가고 있어요! 174'전국 뷰티 박람회'라는 8월에 있을 박람회 하나를 찾았는데요, 우리의 천연 스킨케어 제품을 홍보하기에 안성맞춤일 것 같아요. 등록비도 1,500달러밖에 안 하고요.

유한 가오 [오전 9:21]
아주 좋네요! 그렇게 진행해 주세요.

조지 라이네스 [오전 9:22]
그거 잘됐네요! 이목을 끄는 행사들이야말로 우리에게 필요한 것이죠.

론 풀커슨 [오전 9:23]
잘했어요, 리사! 175저에게 세부 사항을 보내주시면 제가 오늘 퇴근 전까지 우리 회사를 행사에 등록할게요.

리사 팀코 [오전 9:24]
174제 생각엔 메이페어 네트워크에서 하는 우리의 대대적인 TV 캠페인과 이것을 함께 준비하려면 바쁠 것 같아요.

유한 가오 [오전 9:25]
안타깝게도 그건 불발되었어요. 174우리는 방송국에서 요구하던 가격을 감당할 여력이 안 돼서, 172다른 방식으로 새로운 로션 제품을 홍보해야 할 거예요.

리사 팀코 [오전 9:27]
알겠어요. 그리고 175이 일을 그렇게 신속하게 처리해 줘서 고마워요, 론.

론 풀커슨 [오전 9:28]
별거 아니에요.

유한 가오 [오전 9:29]
173계속 수고해 주세요, 여러분!

어휘 check in with (상태 확인 또는 정보 획득을 위해) ~와 접촉하다   come along (원하는 대로) 되어가다   promote 홍보하다, 판매를 촉진하다   registration 등록   fee 요금   high-profile 세간의 이목을 끄는   register for ~에 등록하다   be busy doing ~하느라 바쁘다   along with ~와 함께   extensive 대규모의, 광범위한   fall through 불발되다, 실패로 돌아가다   afford (금전적·시간적) 여유가 [형편이] 되다   station 방송국, 방송 (프로)   charge 청구하다, 값을 매기다   appreciate 감사하다   Keep up the good work. 앞으로도 계속해서 잘해 주세요.

172. 메시지 작성자들이 종사할 것 같은 업계는?
(A) 여행
(B) 기술
(C) 의류
(D) 화장품

해설 추론 문제

단서 (172)를 보면, 9시 19분에 팀코 씨는 자신이 찾아낸 박람회가 회사의 천연 스킨케어 제품을 홍보하기에 안성맞춤일 것 같다고 했고, 9시 25분에 가오 씨는 새로운 로션 제품에 대해 언급했다. 이를 통해 메시지 작성자들이 화장품 업계 종사자들임을 알 수 있으므로 정답은 (D).

패러프레이징 [단서] our natural skincare products / Lotions → [정답] cosmetics

173. 가오 씨의 직업일 것 같은 것은?
(A) 보안 고문
(B) 인사부장
(C) 마케팅 관리자
(D) 연구 조수

해설 추론 문제

가오 씨가 업무 진행 상황을 묻는 말로 대화가 시작되어, 모두에게 수고해 달라는 말로 마무리되고, 나머지 사람들은 가오 씨에게 관련 사항을 보고하고 있는 것으로 보아 가오 씨가 관리자 위치에 있음을 유추할 수

165. 팔라치 씨에 따르면, 사람들이 브라이어힐 사의 제품을 직접 본 곳은?

(A) 호주
(B) 인도네시아
(C) 노르웨이
(D) 스웨덴

해설 특정 정보 확인 문제

단서 (165)에서 브라이어힐 사는 인도네시아에서 가정용품 무역 박람회에 참가했다고 했으므로, 해당 박람회에서 사람들이 제품들을 직접 볼 수 있었다는 것을 알 수 있다. 따라서 정답은 (B).

166. 팔라치 씨가 사업 증대로 이어질 것으로 예상하는 것은?

(A) 고객 로열티 프로그램
(B) TV 프로그램과 제휴
(C) 호텔 체인들과의 계약
(D) 온라인 광고 캠페인

해설 특정 정보 확인 문제

단서 (166)에서 팔라치 씨는 페트로 리드 씨의 제안이 매출을 확대할 것으로 확신한다고 했는데, 그 제안은 체인을 가지고 있는 호텔들을 대상으로 한 것이므로 (C)가 정답.

패러프레이징 [단서] the proposal made by Pedro Reid, which

167. [1], [2], [3], [4]번으로 표시된 위치들 중 다음 문장이 들어가기에 가장 적절한 곳은?

"다음은 우리의 해외 진출 성과에 대한 개요입니다."

(A) [1]
(B) [2]
(C) [3]
(D) [4]

해설 문장 위치 찾기 문제

주어진 문장이 Here is로 시작하는 것으로 보아, 이 문장 뒤에는 이와 관련된 세부적인 내용이 이어져야 한다. 주어진 문장에서 '해외 진출 성과'를 언급했으므로 나라별 매출 실적을 열거하는 두 번째 단락 앞에 와서 해외 진출 성과를 소개하는 도입 문장으로서의 역할을 하는 것이 적절하다. 따라서 정답은 (B).

168-171 기사

베를린([171]9월 7일)—역사 보존 재단(HPF)은 지속적인 연구를 위한 지원을 제공할 뿐만 아니라 역사적 유물을 대중이 볼 수 있도록 하는 것을 목표로 한다. HPF는 1940년대 서아시아에서 발굴된 유물 수집품에 대한 작업을 할 계획이다. [168, 170]알딘 대학은 2세기까지 거슬러 올라가는 화병과 그릇 조각들을 입수했다. [168, 169]이것들은 베를린에 있는 HPF의 주요 시설에서 복원될 것이다. [169]"이러한 물품들을 저희가 관리하게 되어 영광입니다"라고 책임자인 마티아스 보겔 씨는 말했다. "부서지기 쉬운 유물들을 다뤄온 저희의 실적은 타의 추종을 불허하며, 저희는 그것들이 마땅히 받아야 할 세심한 관리를 제공할 수 있는 자원을 보유하고 있습니다."

HPF의 직원들은 도구, 무기, 그리고 장신구와 같은 금속 물건을 대상으로 작업하는 데는 능숙하지만, 점토로 된 물건, 특히 틀로 찍어낸 물건을 대상으로 하는 작업은 그들에게 다소 생소하다. "저희는 작업이 제대로 수행될 수 있도록 알딘 대학과 파트너십을 맺고 있습니다"라고 보겔 씨는 말했다. "[170]저희는 자밀라 아메드 씨가 베를린에 있는 저희 현장으로 와서 작업 과정을 감독하게 되어 매우 기쁩니다. 이 프로젝트는 그녀의 전문적인 지식 및 폭넓은 경험과 완벽하게 들어맞습니다."

유물들은 현재 알딘 대학에서 소장하고 있다. [171]이 대학의 팀은 유물들을 베를린으로 운송할 준비를 하기 위해 그것들을 검사하기 시작했으며, 운송은 10월 2일로 예정되어 있다. 이 물건들의 공개 전시 날짜는 아직 정해지지 않았다.

어휘 historical 역사적인 preservation 보존 foundation 재단 artifact 인공 유물, 공예품 the public 일반 사람들, 대중 ongoing 계속 진행 중인 excavation 발굴 fragment 조각 date back to ~까지 거슬러 올라가다 acquire 얻다, 획득하다 restore 복원하다 facility 시설 track record 실적 deal with ~을 다루다 fragile 부서지기 쉬운 unmatched 타의 추종을 불허하는 resource 자원 attention 보살핌, 돌봄 deserve ~을 받을 만하다 proficient 능숙한 somewhat 다소 form 형성하다 ensure 확실히 하다 carry out ~을 수행하다 oversee 감독하다 operation 작업 (과정), 공정 line up 한 줄로 서다, 줄을 이루다 specialized 전문적인 knowledge 지식 extensive 폭넓은 house 소장하다 examine 검사하다 determine 결정하다

168. 기사의 주요 주제는?

(A) 박물관 개관
(B) 발굴을 위한 모금 행사
(C) 일부 유물의 새로운 발견
(D) 도기 복원 프로젝트

해설 주제 문제

기사 전반에서 유물 복원 프로젝트에 대해 설명하고 있으며, 단서 (168)을 통해 해당 유물이 화병 및 그릇 조각들, 즉 도기류임을 알 수 있으므로 정답은 (D).

패러프레이징 [단서] fragments of vases and bowls
→ [정답] pottery

169. 보겔 씨의 직책은?

(A) 유지보수 관리자
(B) 보조 연구원
(C) 알딘 대학 총장
(D) HPF 책임자

해설 특정 정보 확인 문제

지문에서 'Vogel'이라는 이름이 언급된 부분을 찾아 확인한다. 단서 (169)를 보면 유물들은 HPF의 주요 시설에서 복원될 것이며, 보겔 씨는 이 HPF의 책임자(director)임을 알 수 있으므로 정답은 (D).

어휘 agreement 동의, 협정   enter into a contract 계약을 체결하다   original 독창적인, 창작의   representative 대리인, 대표자   headquarters 본사   intended 의도된   appearance 외관, 모양   reimburse 변제하다, 배상하다   expense 비용   provided ~라는 조건으로   receipt 영수증   spending 지출   additional 추가의   round 한 차례   revision 수정   selected 선택된   completion 완성, 완료

161. 라스콘 씨에 대해 계약서에 암시된 것은?
(A) 4월 22일까지 프로젝트를 완료할 것이다.
(B) 노리스 씨와 일했었다.
(C) 에이드리엔 세일즈 사의 영업 사원이다.
(D) 디자인을 만들어 보수를 받을 것이다.

해설   추론 문제
계약서 전반에 걸쳐 라스콘 씨에 대한 내용이 언급되어 있으므로 해당 부분을 각 선택지와 꼼꼼히 대조해야 한다. 단서 (161)의 내용을 종합해 보면, 그래픽 디자이너인 라스콘 씨는 에이드리엔 세일즈 사를 위해 로고를 디자인해야 하며 이에 대해 보수를 받기로 했으므로 (D)가 정답.

패러프레이징   [단서] create an original logo → [정답] create a design

162. 첫 번째 단락 다섯 번째 줄의 어휘 "presents"와 의미상 가장 가까운 단어는?
(A) 발행하다
(B) 제출하다
(C) 선물로 주다
(D) 전시하다

해설   동의어 문제
presents가 포함된 부분은 문맥상 '비용 지출 영수증을 제출하다'라는 의미이므로, presents가 '제출하다'라는 의미로 쓰였다. 선택지 중 이와 의미상 가장 유사한 의미인 (B)가 정답. present는 동사로 쓰였을 때 '보여주다', '증정하다'라는 의미 외에 '제출하다, 건네주다'라는 의미도 있음을 기억하자.

163. 계약서에 따르면, 라스콘 씨에게 하도록 요구되는 일은?
(A) 발표하기
(B) 업계 동향 조사하기
(C) 요청된 수정 진행하기
(D) 직업 관련 추천서 제공하기

해설   특정 정보 확인 문제
단서 (163)에서 에이드리엔 세일즈 사가 라스콘 씨에게 최대 세 차례의 로고 수정 요청을 할 수 있다고 했으므로 (C)가 정답.

패러프레이징   [단서] ask for up to three additional rounds of revisions → [정답] make some requested adjustments

164-167 이메일

발신: 니콜라 팔라치
수신: 브라이어힐 사 전 직원
날짜: 7월 2일
제목: 참고 사항

브라이어힐 사 직원들께,

직원 여러분이 정보를 보다 잘 알고 계실 수 있도록, 회사의 진행 상황에 대해 정기적으로 최신 정보를 보내 드리겠습니다. — [1] —. 작년 이번 분기와 비교하여, 우리의 국내 매출은 15퍼센트 증가했습니다. 몇몇 우리 상품이 TV 프로그램 <패밀리 펀>의 세트장의 일부로 나오게 한 것이 큰 차이를 만들어낸 것 같지는 않지만, 이는 그래도 우리 웹사이트에 쓸 흥미로운 사진들을 제공했습니다.

— [2] —. ¹⁶⁴ ¹⁶⁵인도네시아에서, 우리는 자카르타 가정용품 무역 박람회에 참여한 후 63퍼센트의 놀라운 매출 증가를 경험했습니다. 호주에서는 매출이 고정적이어서, 0.5퍼센트 증가에 그쳤습니다. — [3] —. ¹⁶⁴우리의 신제품인 면직물 커튼이 엇갈린 평가를 받고 있기 때문에 이는 놀라운 일이 아니었습니다. 스웨덴과 노르웨이에서는 매출이 부진하여 각각 8퍼센트와 6퍼센트 하락했습니다. 이는 다른 업체들과의 치열한 경쟁 때문입니다.

— [4] —. 보시다시피 개선이 필요한 지역도 있고 잘하고 있는 지역도 있습니다. ¹⁶⁶저는 호텔들을 직접 겨냥하여 그들의 전 체인들을 상대로 판매하자는 페트로 리드 씨의 제안이 희망적인 결과를 낳아 우리의 매출을 더욱 증가시킬 것이라고 확신합니다.

니콜라 팔라치 드림

어휘   keep ~ informed ~에게 계속해서 알려 주다   regular 정기적인, 규칙적인   progress 진행, 경과   compared to ~와 비교하여   quarter 분기   domestic 국내의   goods 상품   make difference 차이를 만들다   boost 증가   houseware 가정용품   steady 변함없는, 고정적인   cotton 면직물   mixed 엇갈리는   sluggish 부진한   respectively 각각   competition 경쟁   target 겨냥하다, 대상으로 삼다   directly 직접적으로   entire 전체의   yield (결과를) 내다   promising 유망한, 전망이 좋은

164. 브라이어힐 사의 업종으로 보이는 것은?
(A) 슈퍼마켓 체인
(B) 가정용품 소매업체
(C) 책 출판사
(D) 전자기기 제조사

해설   추론 문제
단서 (164)에서 가정용품 무역 박람회에 참가한 후로 매출이 늘었다고 한 점과 신제품 커튼을 언급한 것으로 보아, 브라이어힐 사가 커튼과 같은 가정용품을 판매하는 업체임을 유추할 수 있다. 따라서 정답은 (B).

패러프레이징   [단서] housewares / cotton curtains → [정답] home furnishings

158-160 이메일

수신: 안젤라 클라인 〈kleina@rtinternet.net〉
발신: 호세 다미코 〈jose@sapphire-yoga.com〉
날짜: 6월 12일
제목: 3급 인증

클라인 씨께,

사파이어 요가 스튜디오의 곧 있을 3급 인증 과정을 위한 요가 강사 교육 과정에 대해 귀하가 지불한 예치금을 받았습니다. — [1] —. 이 과정은 6월 29일부터 시작하여 4주 동안 진행되는 풀타임 집중 과정입니다.

— [2] —. ¹⁵⁸베로니카 클라크 씨에게 veronica@sapphire-yoga.com으로 이메일을 보내 귀하가 이 과정에서 요구되는 것들을 수행할 수 있을 만큼 건강하다는 것을 보여주는 의사의 건강 검진 기록을 제출하십시오. 이는 귀하의 안전을 위한 것이며 저희 측 보험사가 요구하는 것입니다.

¹⁵⁹ ¹⁶⁰요가 매트 및 블록은 모든 수업 시 현장에서 이용 가능합니다. — [3] —. ¹⁶⁰따라서, 그것들을 믿고 사용하실 수 있습니다. 그러나 ¹⁵⁹대부분의 수강생들은 집에서 개인 물품을 가져오는 것을 선호한다고 알고 있습니다. 그렇게 하셔도 됩니다만, 저희는 그 어떤 것도 다음 날까지 보관해 드릴 수 없다는 것을 알아두시기 바랍니다.

과정에 대해 궁금한 점이 있다면 알려 주십시오. — [4] —.

사파이어 요가 스튜디오 매니저
호세 다미코 드림

어휘 certification 증명, 인증 deposit 예치금, 예금 payment 지불, 납입 upcoming 곧 있을 intensive 집중적인 submit 제출하다 fit 건강한 take on (일 등을) 맡다 demand 요구(되는 일들) safety 안전 insurance 보험 provider 제공자, 제공 기관 on site 현장에서 confidence 신뢰 personal 개인의 be aware that ~을 알고 있다 store 보관하다 overnight 하룻밤 동안

158. 클라인 씨가 클라크 씨에게 이메일을 보내야 하는 이유는?
(A) 의사 추천서를 받기 위해
(B) 보험에 가입하기 위해
(C) 자신의 신체 건강을 확인해 주기 위해
(D) 과정에 대한 정보를 더 얻기 위해

해설 특정 정보 확인 문제

단서 (158)에 따르면 클라인 씨는 자신이 교육 과정을 따라갈 수 있다는 것을 보여주는 건강 검진 기록을 클라크 씨에게 이메일로 제출해야 한다. 즉, 이메일로 건강 검진 기록을 보내는 것은 자신의 신체적 건강 상태를 확인해 주기 위한 것이므로 정답은 (C).

패러프레이징 [단서] fit to take on the demands of the course → [정답] physical health

159. 다미코 씨가 수강생들에 대해 암시하는 것은?
(A) 자신의 장비를 사용하는 것을 선호한다.
(B) 과정 중 일부를 집에서 할 것이다.
(C) 무료로 수업에 참여할 수 있다.
(D) 다른 시작 시간을 선택할 수 있다.

해설 추론 문제

단서 (159)를 보면 모든 수업에서 요가 매트와 블록이 제공되지만, 수강생 대부분이 집에서 개인 물품을 가져오는 것을 선호한다고 했다. 이를 통해 수강생들이 집에 있는 자신의 개인 요가 장비를 가져와 사용하는 것을 선호한다는 것을 알 수 있으므로 정답은 (A).

패러프레이징 [단서] personal items → [정답] their own equipment

160. [1], [2], [3], [4]번으로 표시된 위치들 중 다음 문장이 들어가기에 가장 적절한 곳은?

"저희는 사용할 때마다 위생 처리 작업을 실행합니다."

(A) [1]
(B) [2]
(C) [3]
(D) [4]

해설 문장 위치 찾기 문제

주어진 문장은 위생 처리 작업에 관한 내용이므로, 요가 매트와 블록 등의 요가 장비를 언급한 다음인 [3] 자리에 와서, 인과관계를 나타내는 접속사 so와 자연스럽게 연결되어 이렇게 위생 처리가 되었기 때문에 믿고 사용할 수 있다는 내용으로 이어지는 것이 알맞다. 따라서 정답은 (C).

161-163 계약서

계약 동의서

이 계약은 에이드리엔 세일즈 사와 프리랜서 그래픽 디자이너인 오스카 라스콘이 4월 22일에 체결한 것이다. ¹⁶¹라스콘 씨는 에이드리엔 세일즈 사를 위한 창작 로고를 만드는 데 동의한다. 라스콘 씨는 회사 본사에서 에이드리엔 세일즈 사의 담당자들과 만나 의도하는 로고 형태에 대해 논의한다. ¹⁶²에이드리엔 세일즈 사는 라스콘 씨가 비용 지출 영수증을 제출하는 경우, 회의를 위한 출장 관련 비용으로 최대 25파운드까지 변제한다. 라스콘 씨는 5월 20일까지 세 가지 버전의 로고를 만들어 제출한다. ¹⁶³에이드리엔 세일즈 사는 채택된 로고에 대해 최대 세 차례의 추가 수정을 요구할 수 있다. ¹⁶¹에이드리엔 세일즈 사는 최종 이미지가 완성되는 대로 라스콘 씨에게 750파운드를 지불하는 데 동의한다.

계약자:

오스카 라스콘	4월 22일
그래픽 디자이너	날짜

엘리자베스 노리스	4월 22일
에이드리엔 세일즈 사	날짜

어휘 gear 복장, 장비 dome 반구형 모양의 것 be supposed to do ~하기로 되어 있다 issue 문제 warehouse 창고 be scheduled to do ~할 예정이다 originally 원래 overnight shipping 익일 배송 refund 환불하다 take care of ~을 처리하다 account 계정

153. 하퍼 씨가 아웃도어 기어 사에 메시지를 보낸 이유는?
(A) 텐트 파손을 알리기 위해
(B) 제품 카탈로그를 요청하기 위해
(C) 원치 않는 제품을 교환하기 위해
(D) 상품이 언제 도착하는지 확인하기 위해

해설 목적 문제

단서 (153)에서 하퍼 씨는 주문한 텐트를 아직 받지 못했으며 그것이 언제 도착하는지 궁금하다고 했으므로 정답은 (D).

패러프레이징 [단서] when it will get here → [정답] when an item will arrive

154. 오전 9시 31분에, 로스 씨가 "물론입니다"라고 한 것에서 그녀가 의도한 것은?
(A) 빠른 서비스가 필요하다는 것을 알고 있다.
(B) 하퍼 씨의 새 계정을 만들어 줄 수 있다.
(C) 문제를 해결하는 것을 즐겼다.
(D) 하퍼 씨에게 환불해 주는 것에 동의한다.

해설 의도 파악 문제

의도 파악 문제는 제시된 문장의 앞뒤 문장에서 단서를 찾는다. 제시된 문장은 배송료가 환불되어야 할 것 같다는 하퍼 씨의 말에 동의함을 나타내는 것이므로, 정답은 (D). 지금 바로 환불 처리를 해주겠다는 말을 덧붙이고 있는 것에서도 이를 확인할 수 있다.

패러프레이징 [단서] I should be refunded for the shipping fee → [정답] issue Mr. Harper a refund

155-157 웹페이지

---

www.cincinnaticommunitycenter.com

| 홈 | 사진 갤러리 | 행사 | 연락처 |

게시일: 1월 19일

신시내티 만남

155 3월 12일 토요일 오전 9시–오전 11시
155 강사: 다이앤 로빈슨

신시내티에 처음 오셨나요? 이 도시가 제공하는 다음과 같은 것들에 대해 알아보세요:

- 156C 지역 업체의 일자리를 찾는 곳과 찾는 방법
- 156A 통근자들이 이용할 수 있는 버스 및 시내 전차 노선
- 156D 자선 단체와 함께하는 자원봉사 기회 및 참여 방법

이 강좌는 해외에서 신시내티로 이주하신 분들께 특히 도움이 될

것입니다. 등록은 1월 25일에 시작하여 3월 5일에 끝납니다. 자리는 선착순으로 배정됩니다. 본 강좌는 인원이 빨리 찰 것으로 예상되므로 조기 등록을 권장합니다.

정부 보조금 덕분에 157 "신시내티 만남"은 신시내티에 거주하는 모든 분께 무료로 제공되지만, 등록은 필수입니다.

어휘 encounter 뜻밖의 만남 instructor 강사 streetcar 시내 전차 route 노선, 길 commuter 통근자 volunteer 자원봉사자 opportunity 기회 charity 자선 단체 participate (in) (~에) 참여하다 especially 특히 overseas 해외에 registration 등록 assign 배정하다 on a first-come, first-served basis 선착순으로 fill up (사람으로) 만원이 되다 thanks to ~ 덕분에 government 정부 grant 보조금 required 필수인

155. 로빈슨 씨가 강좌를 가르칠 때는?
(A) 1월 19일
(B) 1월 25일
(C) 3월 5일
(D) 3월 12일

해설 특정 정보 확인 문제

단서 (155)에 행사가 진행되는 3월 12일의 강사로 다이앤 로빈슨이 명시되어 있으므로 정답은 (D). 지문의 instructor를 질문에서 teach a class로 바꾸어 표현했다.

156. "신시내티 만남"의 주제로 시사되지 않은 것은?
(A) 대중교통 이용하기
(B) 지방 자치 단체에 입후보하기
(C) 지역에서 일자리 구하기
(D) 비영리 단체 돕기

해설 Not/True 문제

단서 (156A), (156C), (156D)를 통해 (A), (C), (D)에 대한 내용을 확인할 수 있으나, 지방 자치 단체나 입후보에 관한 내용은 제시되어 있지 않으므로 정답은 (B).

157. "신시내티 만남"에 대해 언급된 것은?
(A) 주민들에게 무료로 제공된다.
(B) 세 시간 동안 진행될 것이다.
(C) 한 사업가에 의해 개발되었다.
(D) 진행 중인 시리즈의 일부이다.

해설 Not/True 문제

단서 (157)에 "신시내티 만남"은 신시내티에 거주하는 모든 사람에게 무료로 제공된다고 했으므로 (A)가 정답. "신시내티 만남"은 오전 9시부터 11시까지 진행된다고 나와 있으므로 (B)는 본문 내용과 다르며, (C)와 (D)는 언급되지 않은 내용이다.

패러프레이징 [단서] provided for free to anyone living in Cincinnati → [정답] offered to residents at no cost

(D) 자기 사업체를 설립했다.

해설 추론 문제

단서 (149)의 내용을 종합해보면, 잭슨 씨는 왓킨스 은행의 새로운 홍보 담당 이사로서 전에 CHK 은행에서 약 20년간 근무했으므로, 최근에 왓킨스 은행으로 회사를 옮겼음을 추론할 수 있다. 따라서 정답은 (B).

150. 초대받은 사람들이 미리 할 수 있는 것은?
(A) 따뜻한 음료 주문하기
(B) 몇몇 이미지 보기
(C) 자리 예약하기
(D) 질문 제출하기

해설 특정 정보 확인 문제

단서 (150)에서 잭슨 씨에게 질문이 있으면 행사 전에 인사팀으로 보내 달라고 했으므로 정답은 (D). 지문의 prior to the event가 질문에서는 in advance로 패러프레이징되었다.

패러프레이징 [단서] send it to the HR team → [정답] Submit their questions

151-152 이메일

수신: 타마라 앳우드
발신: 시립 수영 센터
날짜: 11월 14일
제목: 요청 사항

앳우드 씨께,

귀하의 이메일을 받았음을 알려 드리고자 이메일을 보냅니다. ¹⁵¹귀하의 요청 사항을 처리했으며, 귀하의 회원 자격은 한 해 더 연장될 것입니다. 귀하의 회원 자격의 새로운 종료 날짜는 내년 11월 30일이 될 것입니다. 귀하는 무료 사물함 업그레이드 자격이 되십니다. ¹⁵²11월 30일 이후 언제든지 안내 데스크로 오셔서 현재 사용 중인 사물함 열쇠를 새 열쇠로 교환하십시오.

애용해 주셔서 감사합니다.

시립 수영 센터, 고객 서비스팀
데릭 슈렛 드림

어휘 request 요청 (사항) acknowledge (편지·소포 등을) 받았음을 알리다 receipt 수령, 받음 process 처리하다 continue 연장하다, 계속하다 be eligible for ~에 대한 자격이 있다 swap 맞바꾸다, 교환하다 current 현재의 patronage (상점 등의) 단골, 애용

151. 슈렛 씨가 이메일을 보낸 이유는?
(A) 오류에 대해 사과하기 위해
(B) 새로운 서비스를 소개하기 위해
(C) 갱신을 확정하기 위해
(D) 일자리를 제안하기 위해

해설 목적 문제

글의 목적은 대개 지문 도입부에 제시된다. 단서 (151)에서 앳우드 씨의 요청 사항이 처리되어 회원 자격이 연장될 것이라고 알리고 있으므로, 회원 자격 갱신을 확정하기 위한 이메일임을 알 수 있다. 따라서 정답은 (C).

패러프레이징 [단서] your membership will be continued for another year → [정답] confirm a renewal

152. 앳우드 씨가 11월 30일 이후에 할 수 있는 것은?
(A) 슈렛 씨에게 연락하기
(B) 환불받기
(C) 수업에 출석하기
(D) 열쇠 교환하기

해설 특정 정보 확인 문제

단서 (152)에서 11월 30일 이후 언제든지 현재 사용 중인 사물함 열쇠를 새 열쇠로 교환하러 오라고 했으므로 정답은 (D).

패러프레이징 [단서] swap → [정답] Exchange

153-154 문자 메시지

모니크 로스 [오전 9:21]
안녕하세요, 아웃도어 기어 고객 서비스팀의 모니크입니다. 어떻게 도와드릴까요?

에릭 하퍼 [오전 9:22]
안녕하세요. ¹⁵³어제 도착하기로 되어 있었던 반구형 텐트를 8월 2일에 주문했는데요. 그런데 아직 그것을 못 받았어요. 그게 언제 도착하는지 궁금해요.

모니크 로스 [오전 9:23]
그건 제가 도와드릴 수 있습니다. 주문 번호가 어떻게 되나요?

에릭 하퍼 [오전 9:24]
주문번호 034587입니다.

모니크 로스 [오전 9:25]
감사합니다. 잠시만 기다려 주세요.

모니크 로스 [오전 9:28]
물류 창고에 문제가 있었던 것 같은데요, 현재 내일 상품이 발송되는 것으로 일정이 잡혀 있습니다. 따라서, 원래 예상됐던 것보다 이틀 더 늦게, 목요일에 도착할 거예요.

에릭 하퍼 [오전 9:29]
제가 익일 배송료를 지불했으니, ¹⁵⁴배송료는 환불되어야 할 것 같네요.

모니크 로스 [오전 9:31]
물론입니다. ¹⁵⁴제가 지금 바로 처리해 드릴 테니, 몇 시간 이내에 고객님 계정에 표시될 겁니다. 다른 도움이 필요하신가요?

에릭 하퍼 [오전 9:32]
지금은 그게 다예요. 감사합니다.

해설 빈칸에 알맞은 명사 어휘를 고르는 문제로 전반적인 내용을 살펴보아야 한다. 마지막 부분에서 새로운 소프트웨어의 사용으로 직원 모두가 가장 중요한 업무에 집중할 수 있게 되었다고 했으므로, 스펜서 씨가 개선하고자 했던 것으로 가장 적합한 것은 '효율성'이다. 따라서 정답은 (B).

144. 목적격 대명사

해설 give는 '주어+동사+간접목적어+직접목적어' 구조로 쓰이는 4형식 동사로, 빈칸은 동사 give의 간접목적어 자리이다. 선택지의 대명사 모두 목적어 역할을 할 수 있으나, 문맥상 빈칸은 앞의 the software를 가리키므로 사물을 가리키는 3인칭 단수대명사 it이 가장 적절하다. 따라서 정답은 (D). give it a try는 '한번 해보다, 시도하다'라는 뜻으로 자주 쓰이는 표현이니 암기해두자.

145. 부사 자리

해설 빈칸 없이도 문장이 완전하므로 빈칸은 수식어 자리임을 알 수 있다. 빈칸 앞에 동사 wasn't가 있는 것으로 보아 빈칸에는 이를 수식하는 부사가 들어가 '원래는 ~가 아니었다'라는 의미를 만드는 것이 자연스럽다. 따라서 부사인 (B)가 정답.

146. 알맞은 문장 고르기

(A) 그녀는 자신의 노트북용으로도 그 프로그램을 구입했다.
(B) 그녀는 몇 개의 다른 사업체를 설립했다.
(C) 그녀는 그들을 만날 것을 고대한다.
(D) 그녀는 그 기능들을 이해할 수 없었다.

해설 빈칸 앞에서 소프트웨어를 '모든 직원들의 컴퓨터에 사용할' 용도로 구입했다고 했고, 빈칸 뒤에서는 '우리(we) 모두가 중요한 업무에 집중할 수 있게 되었다'고 했으므로, 구성원 중 한 명인 사업주 본인 역시 해당 소프트웨어를 구입해 업무에 집중할 수 있게 되었다는 내용으로 연결되는 것이 자연스럽다. 따라서 (A)가 정답.

PART 7

147-148 기사

새로운 도서관 프로그램이 열광적 관심을 불러일으키다

4월 30일—이번 여름, 147시러큐스 도서관이 지역 꿀벌들을 돕기 위한 프로그램을 시작한다. 지역 꿀벌 수가 급격히 감소했는데, 도서관은 이 생물들을 돕는 것을 목표로 하고 있다. 그들은 꿀벌에 관한 책이 있는 특별 서가를 만들 것이며 꿀벌이 환경에 어떻게 유익한지에 대한 강의를 주최할 것이다. 148강의에 참석하는 누구나 꿀벌을 유인하는 꽃들의 씨앗 한 포를 무료로 받게 될 것이다.

어휘 buzz 열광, 흥분; (벌 등의) 윙윙거리는 소리 launch 시작하다 local 지역의 sharply 급격히 decline 감소하다, 하락하다 creature 생물 host 주최하다 benefit ~에게 도움이 되다, 이롭다 environment 환경 anyone who ~하는 사람 누구나 attend 참석하다 pack 꾸러미, 묶음 seed 씨앗 attract 유인하다, 끌어들이다

147. 프로그램의 목적은?

(A) 꿀벌 개체군을 유지하기 위해
(B) 사람들에게 새로운 기술을 가르치기 위해
(C) 신규 도서관 회원을 유치하기 위해
(D) 자선 단체를 위해 모금하기 위해

해설 목적 문제

목적 문제의 단서는 대개 지문 도입부에 제시된다. 단서 (147)에서 지역 꿀벌을 돕기 위한 프로그램을 시작한다고 했고, 지역 내 꿀벌 수가 감소한 상황에서 꿀벌들을 돕는 것을 목표로 한다고 했으므로, 프로그램의 목적이 꿀벌 개체군을 유지하는 것이라는 것을 알 수 있다. 따라서 정답은 (A).

148. 참가자들이 무료 선물을 받을 수 있는 방법은?

(A) 설문 조사를 작성함으로써
(B) 강연에 참석함으로써
(C) 기부를 함으로써
(D) 도서관 카드를 보여줌으로써

해설 특정 정보 확인 문제

단서 (148)에서 강의에 참석한 사람 모두에게 씨앗 한 포를 무료로 준다고 했으므로 정답은 (B).

패러프레이징 [단서] attends a lecture → [정답] attending a talk

149-150 초청장

149왓킨스 은행의 신임 홍보 담당 이사인 애덤 잭슨 씨와 만나 이야기를 나누는 자리에 함께해 주십시오.

12월 12일 월요일 오후 1시-2시
콘퍼런스룸 A

149애덤 잭슨 씨는 거의 20년간 CHK 은행에서 홍보 업무를 담당했습니다. 그는 왓킨스 은행의 브랜드 이미지를 쇄신하고 우리 고객과 더 긴밀한 관계를 구축하기 위한 자신의 계획에 대해 간략하게 발표할 것입니다. 150잭슨 씨에게 질문이 있다면 행사 전에 인사팀으로 보내 주십시오.

커피와 따뜻한 차가 제공될 예정입니다.

어휘 meet-and-greet 만남과 대화의 행사 public relations 홍보 (활동) handle 처리하다, 다루다 nearly 거의 decade 10년 brief 간단한, 짧은 rebrand 브랜드 이미지를 새롭게 하다 connection 관계, 관련 prior to ~에 앞서

149. 잭슨 씨에 대해 암시된 것은?

(A) 현재 CHK 은행에 근무한다.
(B) 최근에 고용주가 바뀌었다.
(C) 12월 12일에 상을 받을 것이다.

137. 동사 자리
해설 첫 문장이 미래시제인 will be on display(전시될 것이다)로 쓰인 것으로 보아 전시회는 아직 시작하지 않은 상태이다. 따라서 현재진행형인 (A)나 현재완료시제인 (C), 과거시제인 (D)는 모두 답이 될 수 없으며, 방문객들이 조언을 얻을 수 있다는 '가능성'을 나타낸 (B)가 가장 적절하다.

138. 알맞은 문장 고르기
(A) 여러분이 어떻게 긍정적인 변화를 만들 수 있는지 확인해 보세요.
(B) 회원이 되시려면 저희 웹사이트를 방문하세요.
(C) 다행히도, 시간이 연장되었습니다.
(D) 유리는 대부분의 장소에서 재활용이 가능합니다.

해설 빈칸 앞의 문장에서 전시회 방문객들은 바다에 미치는 영향을 줄이기 위한 조언을 얻을 수 있다고 했다. 따라서 '그들이 바다에 미치는 영향을 줄이는 것(reducing their impact on the oceans)'을 '긍정적인 변화(a positive change)'로 바꾸어 표현해 전시회에 방문할 것을 권유하는 (A)가 빈칸에 가장 적절하다.

139-142 광고

> 존과 제레미 로블스 형제에 의해 설립된 버던트 조경 회사는 주택용 토지를 위한 최고급 조경 서비스를 ¹³⁹제공합니다. 저희는 아예 처음부터 정원에 식물을 심고, 기존의 잔디와 화단을 정비하고, 나무를 다듬고, 불필요한 정원 쓰레기를 치워 드릴 수 있습니다.
>
> ¹⁴⁰그 결과, 여러분의 야외 공간은 여러분이 즐길 수 있는 아름답고 편안한 장소가 될 것입니다. ¹⁴¹너무 큰 규모라서, 혹은 너무 작은 규모라서 못할 작업은 없습니다. 저희는 단 1인 규모인 경우도 포함하여 어떠한 규모의 작업반이든 보내 드릴 수 있습니다. 전문가들을 고용하는 것이 여러분의 예산 내에서 가능할지 잘 모르시겠다면, 555-4433번으로 저희에게 전화 주셔서 무료 비용 ¹⁴²견적을 받아 보세요. 여러분께 서비스를 제공하게 되기를 고대합니다!

어휘 landscaping 조경 found 설립하다 residential 주거의, 주택용의 property 건물, 소유지 from scratch 맨 처음부터 existing 기존의 flowerbed 화단 trim 다듬다 remove 치우다, 제거하다 unwanted 원치 않는, 불필요한 debris 잔해, 쓰레기 crew (함께 일하는) 조, 반 including ~을 포함하여 unsure 확신이 없는 professional 전문가 budget 예산 look forward to doing ~하기를 고대하다

139. 동사 자리 + 현재시제
해설 빈칸은 Verdant Landscaping을 주어로 하는 문장의 동사 자리이다. 글의 전반에 걸쳐 업체에서 제공하는 서비스를 소개하고 있으므로, 반복적인 일을 나타낼 때 쓰는 현재시제가 적절하다. 따라서 정답은 (B). (A)는 미래시제로, 앞으로의 서비스 계획을 설명할 때 알맞고, (C)는 과거 이전의 시점을 나타내는 과거완료로 현재도 서비스를 제공하고 있는 상황에는 적절하지 않다. (D)는 동명사 또는 현재분사로, 동사 자리에 올 수 없다.

140. 접속부사 as a result
(A) 예를 들어 (B) 그와는 반대로 **(C) 그 결과** (D) 비교해 보면

해설 빈칸 앞의 내용에서 조경 회사가 제공하는 서비스를 언급하고 있으며, 이러한 서비스를 바탕으로 '그 결과' 야외 공간이 아름답고 편안한 장소가 될 것이라는 내용이므로, 결과를 나타내는 접속부사 (C)가 정답이다.

141. 알맞은 문장 고르기
(A) 다른 사업체들은 우리와 경쟁이 안 됩니다.
(B) 이러한 기술들은 친환경적입니다.
(C) 저희는 기꺼이 교육을 해드리고자 합니다.
(D) 너무 큰 규모라서, 혹은 너무 작은 규모라서 못할 작업은 없습니다.

해설 빈칸 뒤에 이어지는 문장에서 작업자 한 명이 필요한 경우를 포함하여 어떤 규모의 작업반이든 보내 줄 수 있다고 했으므로, 빈칸에는 작업 규모에 구애받지 않는다는 내용이 오는 것이 적절하다. 따라서 작업이 크든 작든 상관없이 서비스 제공이 가능하다는 내용인 (D)가 정답이다.

142. 명사 어휘 estimate
(A) 휴가 **(B) 견적(서)** (C) 설치 (D) 좁은 길

해설 빈칸 뒤의 전치사구 of the costs와 어울려 자연스러운 문맥을 이루는 명사가 와야 한다. 문맥상 예산 부분이 확실하지 않다면 업체에 전화하여 '무료 비용 견적'을 받아 보라는 내용이 자연스러우므로 (B)가 정답.

143-146 기사

> 소규모 사업주로서 켈리 스펜서 씨는 ¹⁴³효율성을 개선하는 가장 좋은 방법을 연구하는 데 많은 시간을 할애한다. 그녀의 직원들은 그녀의 이전 방식에 잘 대응하지 못했지만, 그녀는 바로 그때 흥미로운 소프트웨어인 포즈-프로를 찾아냈다. "처음에는 높은 비용 때문에 저도 망설였어요. 하지만 업체에서 30일 동안 소프트웨어를 무료로 사용할 수 있게 해주고 있었기 때문에, ¹⁴⁴그것을 한번 해봐야겠다는 생각이 들었죠."
>
> 포즈-프로를 사용하면 고용주들이 소셜 미디어 페이지와 같은 주의를 산만하게 하는 웹사이트로의 접근을 차단할 수 있으므로, 직원들이 시간을 허비하지 않게 된다. 그것은 ¹⁴⁵원래 스펜서 씨가 찾던 것은 아니었지만, 그녀는 그 결과를 부정할 수 없었다. 그녀는 모든 직원들의 컴퓨터에 사용할 소프트웨어의 정식 버전을 구입했다. ¹⁴⁶그녀는 자신의 노트북용으로도 그 프로그램을 구입했다. "포즈-프로의 도움으로, 저희 모두는 가장 중요한 업무에 집중할 수 있습니다"라고 그녀는 말했다.

어휘 research 연구하다 improve 개선하다 respond to ~에 대응하다 previous 이전의 method 방식, 방법 hesitant 망설이는 block 막다, 차단하다 distracting 주의를 산만하게 하는 waste 낭비하다 deny 부정하다 purchase 구입하다 focus on ~에 집중하다

143. 명사 어휘 efficiency
(A) 임금 **(B) 효율성** (C) 경쟁 (D) 교육

해설 빈칸은 뒤의 동사 closed를 수식하는 부사 자리로, 문맥상 '일주일간 임시로 수영장을 폐쇄했다'라는 의미가 자연스러우므로 (D)가 정답. temporarily close(임시 폐쇄하다)는 자주 쓰이는 표현이니 덩어리로 외워두자.

어휘 main 주요한, 가장 큰   while ~하는 동안

PART 6

131-134 편지

조지나 해리슨
워너 가 962
케이프 지라도, 미주리 주 63703

해리슨 씨께,

웨스트사이드 호텔 단체 예약에 관심을 가져 주셔서 감사합니다. 귀하의 편의를 위해 저희의 편의 시설에 대한 포괄적인 131설명을 첨부했습니다. 저희는 투숙객들의 경험에 개별적으로 맞춰 드리는 것을 목표로 하고 있습니다. 저희는 촉박하게 통보해 주시는 대부분의 투숙객들의 요구에 맞춰 드릴 준비가 되어 있습니다. 하지만 만약 귀하께서 132특이한 요청사항이 있으시다면, 그 부분을 맞춰 드릴 수 있도록 사전 통지를 주셔야 합니다. 일단 예약이 되고 나면, 저희의 취소 정책에 따라 요금이 청구될 수 있습니다. 133이에 대한 조항들은 저희 웹사이트에 포함되어 있습니다. 예약을 확정하시기 전에, 지불에 대한 세부사항 한 부를 다운로드하여 자세히 134검토하시기 바랍니다.

웨스트사이드 호텔 팀 드림

어휘 attach 첨부하다   comprehensive 포괄적인   amenity ((보통 복수형)) 편의 시설   for one's convenience ~의 편의를 위해   personalize (개인의 필요에) 맞추다   meet the needs 요구를 충족시키다   short notice 촉박한 통보   advance notice 사전 통고, 예고   in order to do ~하기 위해서   fulfill (요구, 조건 등을) 만족시키다   charge (요금을) 청구하다   fee 요금   cancellation 취소   policy 정책

131. 명사 자리

해설 빈칸 앞에 관사 a와 형용사 comprehensive가 있으므로 빈칸에는 이 둘의 수식을 동시에 받으면서 동사 have attached의 목적어 역할을 하는 명사가 와야 한다. 따라서 명사인 (D)가 정답.

132. 형용사 어휘 unusual

(A) 흔치 않은, 이례적인 (B) 부재한 (C) 명백한 (D) 융통성 있는

해설 빈칸 앞의 문장에서 투숙객이 촉박하게 통보해도 투숙객의 요구를 맞출 준비가 되어 있다고 했으나 However 이하 문장에서는 사전에 미리 통지해 달라고 했으므로, 예상치 못한 '흔치 않은' 요청일 경우 준비 시간이 걸릴 수 있음을 암시하는 내용이 되어야 자연스럽다. 따라서 빈칸 뒤의 requests를 수식하기에 문맥상 가장 적합한 것은 (A)이다.

133. 알맞은 문장 고르기

(A) 프런트는 하루 24시간 열려 있습니다.
(B) 솔직한 의견을 서식에 작성해 주셔야 합니다.
(C) 귀하의 지속적인 애용에 감사드립니다.
(D) 이에 대한 조항들은 저희 웹사이트에 포함되어 있습니다.

해설 빈칸 앞의 문장에서 예약 취소 시 청구되는 요금 정책에 대해 언급하고 있으므로, 이 취소 정책(cancellation policy)을 this로 받아 '이 취소 정책의 조항들이 웹사이트에 포함되어 있다'는 내용이 이어지는 것이 자연스럽다. 따라서 정답은 (D).

134. 동사 자리

해설 빈칸 앞의 등위접속사 and로 보아 빈칸에는 download와 병렬 구조를 이루는 동사가 와야 한다. please로 시작하는 명령문의 본동사로 동사원형 download가 쓰였으므로, 빈칸 역시 동사원형이 되어야 한다. 따라서 정답은 (B).

135-138 정보

킴볼 박물관의 환경적 책임

〈웨이브즈 오브 원더〉가 킴볼 박물관에서 여름 내내 전시됩니다. 이번 135전시는 해변의 유리로 만든 조각 작품들을 특징으로 합니다. 작품들은 해양 오염으로 인해 개체군이 심각한 피해를 입은 해양 136동물에 중점을 둡니다. 각 동물에 대한 흥미로운 사실들이 작품 옆에 게시될 것입니다. 방문객들은 지역적으로나 전 세계적으로 그들이 바다에 미치는 영향을 줄이기 위한 조언 137또한 얻을 수 있습니다. 138여러분이 어떻게 긍정적인 변화를 만들 수 있는지 확인해 보세요. 〈웨이브즈 오브 원더〉는 6월 10일부터 9월 5일까지 관람하실 수 있습니다.

어휘 environmental 환경의   responsibility 책임   on display 전시 중인   throughout ~ 내내   feature 특징으로 삼다   sculpture 조각품   marine 해양의   population (전) 개체군   severely 심하게   impact 영향   locally 지역적으로   worldwide 전 세계적으로   available 이용 가능한

135. 명사 어휘 exhibit

(A) 상 (B) 원고 (C) 전시 (D) 영화

해설 빈칸 앞의 문장에서 〈웨이브즈 오브 원더〉가 박물관에서 전시된다고 했고, 빈칸이 포함된 문장에서 여기서 소개되는 조각 작품들에 대해 설명하고 있으므로, '특별히 선보이다'라는 의미의 동사 feature의 주어 자리인 빈칸에 가장 적합한 것은 '전시(회)'를 뜻하는 (C)이다.

136. 전치사 on

해설 빈칸 앞의 동사 focuses는 전치사 on과 함께 focus on(~에 중점을 두다)이라는 표현으로 쓰인다. 정답은 (C).

122. 명사 자리
지난 몇 년간의 유리한 시장 상황은 대부분의 산업에 걸쳐 더 많은 사업 투자라는 결과를 낳았다.

해설 빈칸은 전치사 in의 목적어 자리로, 빈칸 앞의 명사 business와 어울려 복합명사를 이루는 명사가 와야 한다. 유리한 시장 상황이 더 많은 '사업 투자'로 이어졌다는 자연스러운 문맥을 만드는 (B)가 정답. (A)는 동사 또는 과거분사, (C)는 to부정사로 전치사의 목적어 자리에 올 수 없다. (D)의 investor(투자자)도 명사이나 문맥상 어색할 뿐만 아니라, more 뒤에 오려면 복수 형태인 investors가 되어야 한다.

어휘 favorable 유리한, 순조로운　condition ((보통 복수형)) 상황, 사정　result in ~의 결과를 낳다　industry (특정 분야의) 산업

123. 동사 어휘 equip
VC 콘퍼런스 홀의 모든 회의실은 내장형 스피커와 영사기를 갖추고 있다.
(A) 실행된 **(B) 장비를 갖춘** (C) 활성화된 (D) 드러낸

해설 빈칸 앞 be동사 are, 빈칸 뒤 전치사 with와 함께 어울려 be equipped with(~을 갖추고 있다)로 쓰이는 (B)가 정답. 문맥상으로도 회의실이 스피커와 영사기를 '갖추고 있다'고 하는 것이 가장 적절하다. be equipped with를 하나의 표현으로 기억해두자.

어휘 built-in 붙박이의, 내장의　projector 영사기

124. 형용사 자리
새 쇼핑 센터는 지역 경제에 유익한 영향을 미칠 것이다.

해설 관사 a와 명사 effect 사이에 빈칸이 온 것으로 보아 빈칸은 뒤의 명사 effect를 수식하는 형용사 자리이다. 따라서 정답은 형용사인 (C). (A)와 (D)는 둘 다 명사 또는 동사로 형용사 자리에 적절하지 않다. (B)는 부사이므로 오답.

어휘 have an effect on ~에 영향을 미치다　local 지역의　economy 경제

125. 복합관계부사 however
직원들은 모든 할당된 업무들이 아무리 어려워 보여도 완수할 것으로 기대된다.
(A) 아무리 ~해도 (B) 마찬가지로 (C) 사실은 (D) 오히려

해설 콤마 앞뒤로 두 개의 절이 있는 것으로 보아, 빈칸에는 두 절을 연결하는 접속사 역할을 하면서 빈칸 뒤의 형용사 difficult를 수식하는 품사가 와야 함을 알 수 있다. 문맥상 '할당된 업무들이 아무리 어려워 보여도'라는 뜻이 되어야 자연스러우므로, '아무리 ~해도'라는 의미의 복합관계부사 (A)가 정답. however는 접속부사와 복합관계부사 두 가지 쓰임이 있는데, 복합관계부사로 쓰이는 경우 'however+형용사/부사+주어+동사' 구조로 쓰인다. 나머지 선택지는 모두 접속부사로 절과 절을 연결할 수 없다.

어휘 be expected to do ~할 것으로 기대[예상]되다　complete 완료하다　assign 할당하다, 배정하다　task 과업　seem (~인 것처럼) 보이다

126. 부사 자리
후보자가 질문에 얼마나 창의적으로 대답하는지가 해당 역할에 고려되는 중요한 요소이다.

해설 How부터 questions까지는 How가 이끄는 명사절로, 의문부사 How 뒤에는 완전한 절이 온다. 빈칸 뒤에 '주어+동사+목적어(a candidate ~ the questions)'를 갖춘 완전한 절이 왔으므로, 빈칸에는 부사가 와서 동사를 수식하는 역할을 하는 동시에 의문부사 How의 수식을 받는 것이 적절하다. 따라서 정답은 (D).

어휘 candidate 후보자　component 구성 요소　role 역할

127. 접속사 given that
산길이 위험할 수 있음을 고려하면 국립 공원 방문객들은 가이드를 동반해야만 한다.
(A) ~보다 **(B) ~을 고려하면** (C) 비록 ~일지라도 (D) ~이긴 하지만

해설 빈칸은 빈칸 앞뒤의 절을 연결하는 접속사 자리로, 문맥상 '산길이 위험할 수 있음을 고려하면'이라는 의미가 되어야 자연스럽다. 따라서 '~을 고려하면'이라는 의미의 접속사인 (B)가 정답. (A)는 전치사와 접속사 모두 가능하나, than 앞에는 반드시 비교급 표현이 와야 한다. (C)와 (D)는 둘 다 양보의 의미를 나타내는 접속사로 문맥상 적절하지 않다.

어휘 accompany 동반하다　trail 오솔길, 산길

128. 전치사 in
법인 체인에 의한 그 식당의 매입은 음식 질의 하락으로 이어졌다.
(A) ~보다 아래에 (B) ~에서 **(C) ~의** (D) ~로서

해설 문맥에 어울리는 전치사를 고르는 문제이다. 빈칸에는 앞의 명사 decline과 함께 decline in으로 쓰여 '~의 하락'이란 의미를 나타내는 in이 들어가는 것이 알맞다. 따라서 정답은 (C).

어휘 purchase 매입, 구입　corporate 법인의　lead to ~로 이어지다　decline in ~의 하락

129. 명사 어휘 competition
매크레이 씨는 두 회사 간의 경쟁이 혁신적인 제품들을 만들어냈다고 설명했다.
(A) 확인 (B) 결과, 중요성 **(C) 경쟁** (D) (위임된) 임무

해설 빈칸은 that절의 주어 자리로, between the two companies의 수식을 받으면서 문맥에 적절한 명사 어휘를 찾아야 한다. 문맥상 '두 회사 간의 경쟁이 혁신적인 제품들을 만들어냈다'는 내용이 가장 자연스러우므로 정답은 (C).

어휘 create 만들어내다, 창작하다　innovative 혁신적인

130. 부사 어휘 temporarily
사우스필드 피트니스 센터는 가장 큰 수영장이 청소되는 동안 일주일간 임시로 그곳을 폐쇄했다.
(A) 현재 (B) 완벽하게 (C) 단호하게 **(D) 임시로**

113. 전치사 despite
추운 날씨에도 불구하고 토요일의 지역사회 야유회의 참석률은 높았다.
(A) ~에 관해서 (B) ~ 맞은편에 (C) **~에도 불구하고** (D) ~을 가로질러

해설 문맥에 알맞은 전치사를 고르는 문제이다. '야유회 참석률이 높았다'는 빈칸 앞의 내용과 '추운 날씨'라는 빈칸 뒤의 내용이 서로 대조되므로, 빈칸에는 양보의 의미를 지닌 전치사가 오는 것이 적절하다. 따라서 정답은 (C).

어휘 attendance 참석(률)   picnic 야유회

114. 형용사 어휘 mandatory
오염 여부 확인을 위한 의무적인 실험을 실행하기 위해 토양 표본이 채취되었다.
(A) 좁은 **(B) 의무적인** (C) 썩기 쉬운 (D) 명백한

해설 빈칸 뒤의 명사 testing을 수식하는 형용사 어휘를 고르는 문제이다. 문맥상 '오염 여부 확인을 위한 의무적인 실험'이라는 뜻이 되어야 자연스러우므로 정답은 (B).

어휘 soil 토양   sample 표본   carry out ~을 실행[수행]하다   pollution 오염

115. 동명사
에어컨을 수리하기 전에 퍼킨스 씨는 그 작업을 위해 몇 가지 교체 부품을 주문했다.

해설 빈칸에 알맞은 동사 형태를 고르는 문제이다. before는 전치사와 접속사로 모두 쓰이지만 이 문장에서는 뒤에 주어가 없으므로 전치사로 쓰인 것을 알 수 있다. 따라서 빈칸 뒤의 명사 the air conditioner를 목적어로 취하는 동시에 그 자체로 전치사 before의 목적어 역할을 할 수 있는 동명사 형태가 와야 하므로 정답은 (A).

어휘 fix 수리하다, 고치다   replacement 대체, 교체   part 부품   task (부과된) 일

116. 동사 자리 + 현재완료시제
제품 매출이 최근에 차질을 겪었고 추가 조치 없이는 개선되지 않을지도 모른다.

해설 빈칸 앞 문장의 주어이고 빈칸은 a setback을 목적어로 갖는 동사 자리이므로 (B) have suffered와 (D) suffer가 정답 후보이다. 뒤에 과거시제 또는 완료시제와 어울려 쓰이는 시간 부사 recently(최근에)가 있으므로, 현재완료시제인 (B)가 정답. (A)는 to부정사, (C)는 동명사 또는 현재분사로 동사 자리에 올 수 없다. (D)는 현재시제로 recently와 어울려 쓰이지 않는다.

어휘 suffer 겪다   setback 차질   improve 개선되다   further 더 이상의, 추가의   action 조치

117. 동사 어휘 prefer
사업차 출장을 다니는 사람들은 큰 책상이 있는 호텔 객실을 선호하는 경향이 있다.
(A) 신청하다, 적용하다 (B) 포함하다 **(C) 선호하다** (D) 믿다

해설 문맥상 출장을 다니는 사람들은 '특정 객실을 선호하는 경향이 있다'고 하는 것이 자연스러우므로 (C)가 정답. (A)는 apply for(~을 신청하다) 또는 apply to(~에 적용하다) 등으로 쓰인다.

어휘 tend to do ~하는 경향이 있다

118. 비교급
예상보다 더 빠름에도 불구하고, 그 배송 서비스는 비싼 비용을 들일 가치가 없었다.

해설 빈칸 뒤에 than(~보다)이 있는 것으로 보아 빈칸에는 비교급 표현이 와야 하므로 (B)가 정답. (A)는 형용사의 원급, (C)는 형용사의 최상급, (D)는 부사의 원급이다.

어휘 even though ~에도 불구하고   than expected 예상보다   delivery 배송   worth ~의 가치가 있는

119. 명사 어휘 structure
도시에서 가장 높은 세 개의 건축물인 고급 아파트 단지는 시내의 대부분 지역에서 볼 수 있다.
(A) 지역 사회 (B) 거리 (C) 거주자 **(D) 건축물**

해설 빈칸 앞의 관사 및 형용사(The three tallest)의 수식을 받으며 luxury apartment complexes와 동격을 이루는 명사 어휘를 골라야 한다. '고급 아파트 단지'는 '건축물'에 해당하므로 (D)가 정답.

어휘 luxury 사치스러운, 호화로운   complex (건물) 단지

120. 전치사 beyond
그 차고는 폭풍우 때문에 수리할 수 없을 정도로 훼손되어 다시 지어야 했다.
(A) ~의 (B) (~되고 있는) 중인 **(C) ~을 넘어서, ~할 수 없는** (D) ~의 위에

해설 알맞은 전치사를 고르는 문제가 나오면 일단 전치사의 목적어를 확인하여 문맥에 맞는 전치사를 고르도록 한다. 빈칸 뒤의 명사 repair와 어울려 '수리할 수 없을 정도로 훼손되었다'라는 내용이 되는 것이 자연스러우므로 '(능력·한계 등을) 넘어서는, ~할 수 없는'이라는 의미의 전치사인 (C)가 정답. beyond repair(수리할 수 없을 정도로)를 하나의 표현으로 기억해두자.

어휘 garage 차고   damage 피해를 주다, 훼손하다   rebuild 다시 짓다, 재건하다

121. 동사 자리
부서장들은 직원들의 업무 성과를 공식적으로 평가하기 위해 6월 4일에서 8일 사이에 만날 것이다.

해설 빈칸은 주어 Department managers 뒤에 오는 동사 자리이므로 미래진행시제의 동사 형태인 (A)가 정답. (B)와 (C)는 동명사 또는 현재분사로 동사 자리에 올 수 없고, (D)는 to부정사로 역시 동사 자리에 올 수 없다.

어휘 department 부서   formally 공식적으로   assess 평가하다   performance 성과

어휘 manufacturing 제조업　develop 개발하다　method 방식, 방법　cardboard 판지

104. 전치사 for
그 건물의 소유주는 주차장 이용을 위한 요금을 인상했다.
(A) ~을 위한 (B) ~에 대한 (C) ~에 (D) ~ 사이에

해설 문맥상 '주차장 이용을 위한 요금'이라는 의미가 되어야 자연스러우므로, '~을 위한'이라는 뜻의 전치사로 쓰이는 (A)가 정답. (D)는 '(셋 이상의) 사이에'라는 뜻의 전치사로 뒤에 복수 명사가 오므로 오답.

어휘 increase 증가시키다, 늘리다　fee 요금　parking lot 주차장　access 이용, 접근

105. 부사 어휘 correctly
그 공장의 폐쇄가 산업에 미치는 영향에 대해 정확하게 예측한 시장 분석가는 거의 없었다.
(A) 장소상으로 (B) 끊임없이 (C) 친절하게 **(D) 정확하게**

해설 빈칸은 뒤의 동사 predicted를 수식하기에 적합한 부사가 들어갈 자리이다. 문맥상 '산업 관련 영향을 정확하게 예측한 분석가가 거의 없었다'는 의미가 되어야 가장 자연스러우므로 (D)가 정답.

어휘 few 거의 없는　analyst 분석가　predict 예측하다　industry (특정 분야의) 산업　effect 영향　closure 폐쇄

106. 동사 어휘 give
소셜 미디어에서 우리에게 평가를 제공하고자 하는 고객들은 그렇게 할 것을 권장합니다.
(A) 설명하다 (B) 말하다 **(C) 제공하다** (D) 가지다

해설 빈칸은 뒤의 us와 a review를 각각 간접목적어와 직접목적어로 갖는 동사가 올 자리이다. 선택지 중 뒤에 간접목적어와 직접목적어를 취하는 4형식 동사는 give뿐이므로 정답은 (C).

어휘 customer 고객　review 평가, 비평　be encouraged to do ~하도록 권장되다

107. 전치사 during
8월 한 달 동안 매주 주말마다 그 호텔 레스토랑은 라이브 음악 공연을 선보인다.
(A) ~조차 **(B) ~ 동안** (C) ~할 때 (D) ~하는 동안

해설 빈칸 뒤에 명사구(the month of August)가 온 것으로 보아 빈칸은 전치사 자리이므로 (B)가 정답. 의미상으로도 '8월 한 달 동안'이라는 뜻이 되어 알맞다. (A)는 부사, (C)와 (D)는 접속사로 명사구를 이끌 수 없다.

어휘 feature 특별히 포함하다, 특징으로 삼다　performance 공연

108. 소유격
포틀랜드 보험사의 직원들은 그들의 희망 휴가 날짜를 포함한 서식을 작성해야 한다.

해설 형용사(desired)의 수식을 받는 복합 명사(vacation days) 앞에 올 수 있는 것은 소유격이므로 (A) their와 (B) its가 정답 후보. 빈칸에 들어갈 말은 의미상 앞의 employees를 가리키므로 복수 형태인 (A)가 정답. (B)는 단수 명사를 가리키는 소유격으로 쓰이며, (C)는 재귀대명사로서 목적격으로 쓰이고, (D)는 주격과 목적격으로 쓰이므로 오답.

어휘 complete (서식을 빠짐없이) 작성하다　form 서식　desired 원하는, 바라는

109. 명사 자리
많은 건설 업체들이 건축 자재의 수입에 대한 새로운 규제에 대해 긴장하고 있다.

해설 빈칸 앞에 관사 a와 형용사 new가 있으므로 빈칸에는 이 둘의 수식을 동시에 받으면서 전치사 about의 목적어 역할을 하는 명사가 와야 한다. 따라서 명사인 (D)가 정답.

어휘 construction 건설　business 사업체　restriction 제한, 규제　importation 수입　material 재료, 자재

110. 접속사 even though
몇 주간 행사 광고를 아주 많이 했음에도 불구하고 콘서트 표가 잘 팔리지 않고 있다.
(A) ~ 때문에 (B) ~하지 않는 한 (C) ~일 뿐 아니라 **(D) ~에도 불구하고**

해설 빈칸은 앞뒤의 절을 연결해 주는 접속사 자리로, 문맥상 '행사 광고를 많이 했음에도 불구하고 표가 잘 팔리지 않고 있다'라는 의미가 되어야 자연스러우므로 양보의 의미를 나타내는 접속사 (D)가 정답. (A)는 이유를 나타내는 접속사, (B)는 조건을 나타내는 접속사로 문맥상 적절하지 않다. (C)는 구전치사이므로 뒤에 절이 올 수 없다.

어휘 advertise 광고하다　heavily 심하게, 아주 많이

111. 부사 자리
상점의 여름 세일을 위해 가격이 상당히 인하되었다.

해설 빈칸은 수동태를 이루는 be동사 were와 과거분사 reduced 사이에서 동사를 수식하는 부사 자리이므로 (A)가 정답. (B)는 명사, (C)는 형용사, (D)는 동사로 모두 수동태 구문의 be동사와 과거분사 사이에 들어갈 수 없다.

어휘 significantly 상당히　reduce 줄이다, (가격 등을) 낮추다

112. 형용사 어휘 accurate
자영업을 하는 사람들은 그들 사업의 이익과 비용에 대해 정확한 기록을 해둬야 한다.
(A) 정확한 (B) 불공평한 (C) 시각적인 (D) 넓은

해설 빈칸 뒤의 명사 records를 수식하기에 적합한 형용사 어휘를 고르는 문제이다. 문맥상 '정확한 기록을 해둬야 한다'는 내용이 되어야 자연스러우므로 정답은 (A).

어휘 self-employed 자영업을 하는　keep a record 기록해두다　profit 이익, 수익　cost 비용

다음 안건 항목으로 넘어가기 전에 ⁹⁸여러분 모두에게 큰 감사를 드리고 싶습니다. 일정 변경으로 인해 갑작스럽게 웨비나 용 콘텐츠를 완료하느라 힘들었다는 걸 알고 있습니다. 여러분의 노고가 없었다면 우리는 그것을 할 수 없었을 것입니다. ⁹⁹우리의 새로운 프로젝트인 연례 무역 박람회가 내일 시작됩니다. 고려해야 할 요소들이 상당수 있기에, 이에 대한 계획을 세우기 시작하려고 합니다. 하지만 ¹⁰⁰최종 예산이 확정될 때까지는 우리가 할 수 있는 게 많지 않을 겁니다. 패트릭이 목요일에 그렇게 할 것이므로, 그동안에는 여러분이 할 수 있는 일을 해주십시오. 다음 회의에서 주요 업무에 대해 좀 더 상세히 다루도록 하겠습니다.

프로젝트 A	기업 후원
프로젝트 B	화상 대회
프로젝트 C	무료 웨비나
⁹⁹프로젝트 D	연례 무역 박람회

어휘 move on to ~으로 넘어가다 agenda 안건 item 항목, 사항 webinar 웨비나 (웹사이트에서 진행되는 세미나) warning 예고, 통지 annual 연례의 trade expo 무역 박람회 quite a few 상당수 component (구성) 요소 consider 고려하다 budget 예산 in the meantime 그동안에 task (부과된) 일, 직무 in detail 상세히

98. 화자가 팀에게 고마워하는 이유는?
(A) 갑작스러운 요청에도 프로젝트를 완수했다.
(B) 인기 있는 제품을 만들었다.
(C) 몇몇 신규 고객들을 찾았다.
(D) 신입 직원들을 교육하는 것을 도왔다.

해설 화자가 청자들에게 고마워하는 이유를 묻는 문제로, 담화 초반부에서 감사를 표하는 부분에 주목한다. 단서 (98)에서 청자들에게 감사를 표하며 일정이 변경되어 갑작스럽게 콘텐츠를 완료했다고 했으므로 정답은 (A).

패러프레이징 [단서] finish the contents for the webinar with little warning → [정답] finished a project on short notice

99. 시각 자료에서, 내일 시작될 프로젝트는?
(A) 프로젝트 A
(B) 프로젝트 B
(C) 프로젝트 C
(D) 프로젝트 D

해설 특정 시점에 시작될 프로젝트를 묻는 문제로, 제시된 시각 자료와 함께 tomorrow가 언급되는 부분에 주목한다. 단서 (99)에서 새로운 프로젝트인 연례 무역 박람회가 내일 시작된다고 했으므로, 시각 자료에서 여기에 해당하는 프로젝트를 찾으면 (D)가 정답임을 알 수 있다.

100. 패트릭이 목요일에 할 일은?
(A) 상 받기
(B) 연설하기
(C) 고객 방문하기
(D) 예산 마무리짓기

해설 특정 인물이 특정 시점에 할 일을 묻는 문제로, 질문의 키워드인 Patrick과 Thursday가 언급된 담화 후반부에 주목한다. 단서 (100)에서 패트릭이 목요일에 그 일을 할 것이라고 했는데, 여기서 '그 일(that)'은 '최종 예산을 확정하는 것'을 가리키므로 정답은 (D).

패러프레이징 [단서] have our final budget → [정답] Finalize a budget

PART 5

101. 부사 자리
일부 임원들은 법인세 체계의 변경 사항에 대해 개인적으로 우려를 표했다.

해설 빈칸을 제외해도 문장의 필수 성분이 모두 갖춰져 있으므로 빈칸은 수식어 자리임을 알 수 있는데, 빈칸 뒤에 동사 expressed가 온 것으로 보아 빈칸에는 이를 수식하는 부사가 와야 한다. 따라서 부사인 (D)가 정답.

어휘 official 임원, 공무원 express 표현하다 concern 우려, 걱정 corporate 기업의, 법인의 tax 세금 structure 구조, 체계 privately 개인으로서, 비공식적으로

102. 형용사 자리
베일러 모터스의 새로운 전기차는 도시 환경 내에서의 짧은 이동을 위해 만들어졌다.

해설 전치사 for의 목적어로 쓰인 명사 journeys를 수식할 수 있는 것은 형용사이므로 (B)가 정답. short는 부사로 쓰이기도 한다는 것도 알아두자.

어휘 electric car 전기차 be intended for ~을 위해 만들어지다[의도되다] journey 여행, 이동 within ~ 이내에 urban 도시의 environment 환경

103. 동사 자리+수 일치
아메스 매뉴팩처링 사는 판지를 훨씬 덜 사용하는 포장 방식을 개발했다.

해설 빈칸이 포함된 that 이하는 선행사 a packaging method를 수식하는 관계대명사절로, 빈칸은 관계대명사절의 동사 자리이므로 동사 형태인 (A) uses와 (D) use가 정답 후보. 주격 관계대명사절의 동사는 앞의 선행사에 수를 일치시켜야 하므로, 단수 명사 a packaging method와 수가 일치하는 단수 동사 (A)가 정답. (B)는 동명사/분사, (C)는 to부정사로 동사 자리에 올 수 없으므로 오답.

패러프레이징 [단서] good for the environment
→ [정답] environmentally friendly

94. 스테파니 루츠 씨의 신분은?
(A) 기자
(B) 시 공무원
(C) 농부
(D) 라디오 프로 진행자

해설 특정 인물의 직업을 묻는 문제로, Stephanie Lutz라는 이름이 언급된 담화 후반부에 주목한다. 단서 (94)에서 스테파니 루츠 씨가 최근 자신의 딸기 농장에 과일 따기 활동을 추가했다고 한 것으로 보아 그녀가 농부임을 알 수 있다. 따라서 정답은 (C).

Questions 95-97 refer to the following talk and map.

⁹⁵Welcome, applicants. We're pleased that you are interested in working here at Collins International. Today will be the group interview, and those of you who pass that stage will be invited back. We're here in the staff room now, but ⁹⁶most of your time today will be spent in the HR office. It's at the end of the hallway, across from the storage room. ⁹⁷And at four-thirty, I'll show you how to get to the computer lab, where you'll be taking a series of personality tests.

⁹⁵환영합니다, 지원자 여러분. 이곳 콜린스 인터내셔널 사에서 일하는 것에 관심을 가져 주셔서 기쁩니다. 오늘은 단체 면접이 있을 것이고, 그 단계를 통과하는 분들은 다시 모실 것입니다. 지금 우리는 이곳 직원 휴게실에 있지만, ⁹⁶여러분은 오늘 대부분의 시간을 인사팀 사무실에서 보내게 될 것입니다. 그곳은 복도 끝, 창고 맞은편에 있습니다. ⁹⁷그리고 4시 30분에는 제가 컴퓨터실에 가는 방법을 알려 드릴 것이며, 그곳에서 여러분은 일련의 인성 검사를 받을 것입니다.

201호	202호	⁹⁶204호
엘리베이터		
직원 휴게실	203호	창고

어휘 applicant 지원자, 신청자 be interested in ~에 관심이 있다 pass 통과하다 stage 단계 invite 초대[초청]하다 hallway 복도 across from ~의 맞은편에 storage room 창고 get to ~에 도착하다 a series of 일련의 personality 인성, 성격

95. 화자가 말하고 있는 대상은?
(A) 잠재적 투자자들
(B) 회사 매니저들
(C) 입사 지원자들
(D) 정부 조사관들

해설 청자가 누구인지 묻는 문제로, 담화 초반부에서 청자에 대한 정보가 드러나는 곳을 잘 듣는다. 단서 (95)에서 청자들이 화자가 소속된 회사, 즉 콜린스 인터내셔널 사에 입사 지원을 한 사람들임을 알 수 있으므로 정답은 (C).

96. 시각 자료에서, 청자들이 이날 대부분의 시간 동안 이용할 사무실은?
(A) 201호
(B) 202호
(C) 203호
(D) 204호

해설 제시된 시각 자료와 함께 사무실의 위치에 대해 언급하는 부분에 주목한다. 단서 (96)에서 화자는 청자들이 인사팀 사무실에서 대부분의 시간을 보낼 것이라고 했고, 인사팀 사무실이 복도 끝, 창고 맞은편에 있다고 했으므로 정답은 (D).

97. 청자들이 4시 30분에 갈 곳은?
(A) 회의실
(B) 컴퓨터실
(C) 구내식당
(D) 경비실

해설 특정 시점에 있을 일을 묻는 문제로, 4시 30분이라는 시각이 언급된 담화 후반부에 주목한다. 단서 (97)에서 화자는 4시 30분에 청자들에게 컴퓨터실로 가는 방법을 알려줄 것이며 그곳에서 청자들이 인성 검사를 받게 될 것이라고 했으므로 정답은 (B).

Questions 98-100 refer to the following excerpt from a meeting and list.

Before we move on to the next agenda item, ⁹⁸I'd like to give you all a big thank you. I know it was difficult to finish the contents for the webinar with little warning because of our schedule change. We couldn't have done it without your hard work. ⁹⁹Our new project, the annual trade expo, starts tomorrow. There are quite a few components to consider, so I'd like to start planning for this. However, ¹⁰⁰we won't be able to do much until we have our final budget. Patrick is doing that on Thursday, so please do what you can in the meantime. At the next meeting, we'll cover the main tasks in more detail.

여름철에 휴가를 냈습니다. 이는 우리가 일손이 모자랐다는 걸 의미했고, 그래서 고객들을 응대하느라 매우 바빴습니다. 안타깝게도, 이는 우리가 제공할 수 있는 서비스의 수준에 부정적인 영향을 미쳤습니다. 따라서, 이제부터는 휴가 신청을 위한 새로운 시스템을 갖추도록 하겠습니다. 90여러분은 회사 웹사이트에서 서식을 작성해야 할 것입니다. 여러분이 선호하는 날짜들 중 적어도 일부라도 휴가로 주고자 노력하겠지만 이것을 보장하지는 못합니다. 91변경 사항에 대해 질문이 있다면 올리비아에게 이메일을 보내 주세요. 그녀가 즉시 처리해 줄 겁니다.

어휘 agenda 안건 policy 정책 take time off 휴가를 내다 short-staffed 직원이 부족한, 일손이 모자란 be busy doing ~하느라 바쁘다 serve (손님을) 접대[응대]하다 from now on 이제부터 request 요청 fill out 작성하다 form 서식 at least 최소한 preferred 선호하는 guarantee 보장하다 address 다루다, 처리하다 promptly 즉시

89. 화자가 주로 이야기하고 있는 것은?
(A) 고객 불만 사항
(B) 직원 승진
(C) 결제 시스템
(D) 회사 정책

해설 담화의 주제를 묻는 문제로, 담화 초반부에 집중한다. 단서 (89)에서 화자는 회사의 새 휴가 정책에 대해 설명하고자 한다고 했으므로 정답은 (D).

패러프레이징 [단서] our new vacation policy → [정답] A company policy

90. 청자들에게 하도록 요청되는 것은?
(A) 온라인 서식 작성하기
(B) 파트너와 함께 일하기
(C) 유인물 읽기
(D) 교육 과정에 참여하기

해설 청자가 해야 할 일을 묻는 문제로, 담화 중반부에 나오는 요청 사항에 주목한다. 단서 (90)에서 앞으로는 휴가 신청을 하려면 회사 웹사이트에서 서식을 작성해야 할 것이라고 했으므로 정답은 (A).

패러프레이징 [단서] fill out the form on our company's Web site → [정답] Complete an online form

91. 화자에 따르면, 올리비아가 할 일은?
(A) 일부 장비 반납하기
(B) 일부 자료 출력하기
(C) 질문에 답하기
(D) 일정 짜기

해설 질문의 키워드인 Olivia가 언급된 부분에 주목한다. 단서 (91)에서 변경 사항에 대한 질문이 있으면 올리비아에게 이메일을 보내라면서, 그러면 그녀가 즉시 처리해 줄 거라고 했으므로 정답은 (C).

패러프레이징 [단서] address them → [정답] Answer questions

Questions 92-94 refer to the following broadcast.

You're listening to *Time for the Town,* the show that keeps you up to date on local activities that may interest you. 92Today we're looking at a fairly new trend, picking fresh fruit. Many farms and orchards are opening their sites to tourists to harvest their own fruits and vegetables. 93It's becoming popular because getting food locally is good for the environment. Our guest today is 94Stephanie Lutz, whose strawberry farm has recently added this activity. She's here to tell us how it works.

여러분은 여러분이 관심을 가질 만한 지역 활동들에 대한 최신 정보를 알려주는 〈타임 포 더 타운〉을 듣고 계십니다. 92오늘은 상당히 새로운 경향인 신선한 과일 따기 활동을 살펴보겠습니다. 많은 농장과 과수원에서 여행객들이 직접 과일과 채소를 수확할 수 있게 장소를 개방하고 있습니다. 93먹거리를 현지에서 얻는 것은 환경에 이롭기 때문에 이것은 인기가 높아지고 있습니다. 오늘의 초대 손님은 94최근 본인의 딸기 농장에 이 활동을 추가한 스테파니 루츠 씨입니다. 그녀는 진행 상황에 대해 저희에게 이야기해 주고자 이곳에 와 있습니다.

어휘 show (텔레비전·라디오의) 프로[프로그램] keep A up to date A에게 최신 소식을 알려주다 interest ~의 관심을 끌다 fairly 상당히, 꽤 trend 추세, 경향 pick (과일 등을) 따다 orchard 과수원 harvest 수확하다, 거둬들이다 locally 지역에서, 현지에서 environment 환경 recently 최근에 work (계획 따위가) 잘 되어 가다

92. 방송 중에 논의될 것은?
(A) 온라인 배달
(B) 과일 따기
(C) 가정 원예
(D) 농산물 직판장

해설 방송에서 다뤄질 주제를 묻는 문제로, 지역 활동에 대한 최신 정보를 제공하는 방송이라면서, 단서 (92)에서 오늘 살펴볼 것은 신선한 과일 따기 활동이라고 했으므로 정답은 (B).

패러프레이징 [단서] picking fresh fruit → [정답] Fruit picking

93. 화자에 따르면, 활동이 인기가 있는 이유는?
(A) 사람들의 건강을 유지한다.
(B) 모든 세대에게 재미가 있다.
(C) 참가자들의 돈을 절약한다.
(D) 친환경적이다.

해설 과일 따기 활동이 인기가 있는 이유를 묻는 문제로, 질문의 키워드인 popular가 언급된 부분에 주목한다. 단서 (93)에서 먹거리를 현지에서 얻는 것이 환경에 좋기 때문에 과일 따기 활동의 인기가 높아지고 있다고 했으므로 정답은 (D).

85. 화자가 할 계획이라고 말한 것은?
(A) 고용 계약서 보내기
(B) 면접 시간 잡기
(C) 일부 서류 보관하기
(D) 청자의 추천서 확인하기

해설 화자가 할 일을 묻는 문제로, 담화 후반부에 주목한다. 화자의 회사는 이미 해당 직책에 다른 후보자를 선발했으나, 단서 (85)에 따르면 추후에 대비하여 헨쇼 씨의 자기소개서와 이력서 파일을 보관하겠다고 했으므로 정답은 (C).

패러프레이징 [단서] your cover letter and résumé on file
→ [정답] some documents

호 🎧
Questions 86-88 refer to the following telephone message.

Hi, Jessica. It's Luis Garza. [86]Thank you so much for agreeing to be interviewed for *World Fashions Magazine.* I'm sure our readers will love getting a behind-the-scenes look at your studio and how you develop your lovely dresses. [87]I appreciate that you volunteered to have someone from your office take photos. However, our photographer works full time. The next step would be a phone meeting so we can discuss the details of my visit. [88]Please let me know when you are available. I am happy to work around your schedule.

안녕하세요, 제시카. 저는 루이스 가르자입니다. [86]〈월드 패션스 매거진〉과 인터뷰를 하기로 해주셔서 대단히 고맙습니다. 저는 저희 독자들이 무대 뒤의 당신의 스튜디오와 당신이 아름다운 드레스들을 만들어내는 방법을 보고 싶어 할 것이라고 확신합니다. [87]자진해서 당신의 사무실 직원에게 사진을 찍게 하시겠다고 해주셔서 감사드립니다. 하지만 저희 사진작가는 전임으로 일합니다. 다음 단계는 저의 방문에 대한 세부 사항을 논의할 수 있도록 전화로 회의를 하는 겁니다. [88]언제 시간이 되는지 알려 주세요. 기꺼이 당신의 일정에 맞추도록 하겠습니다.

어휘 reader 독자 behind-the-scenes 무대 뒤의 develop 개발하다, 만들어내다 appreciate 고마워하다 volunteer to do 자진[자원]하여 ~하다 take photos 사진을 찍다 photographer 사진작가 work full time 풀타임[전임]으로 일하다 discuss 논의하다 details 세부 사항 visit 방문 available 시간이 있는 around (특정한 사람 등에) 맞춰

86. 화자가 일할 것 같은 곳은?
(A) 마케팅 회사
(B) 지역 신문사
(C) 화장품 회사
(D) 패션 잡지사

해설 화자가 근무하는 업종을 묻는 문제로, 담화 초반부에 주목한다. 단서 (86)에서 화자가 청자에게 〈월드 패션스 매거진〉과의 인터뷰에 응해준 데 감사를 표하는 것으로 보아 화자가 패션 잡지사에서 근무함을 알 수 있다. 따라서 정답은 (D). 보통 회사 이름에 그 업종이 드러나는 경우가 많다.

87. 화자가 "저희 사진작가는 전임으로 일합니다"라고 말한 이유는?
(A) 문제점을 설명하기 위해
(B) 제안을 거절하기 위해
(C) 오해를 바로잡기 위해
(D) 도움을 요청하기 위해

해설 화자의 의도를 묻는 문제로, 제시된 문장 앞뒤 문맥에 주목한다. 제시된 문장 바로 앞에 있는 단서 (87)을 보면 청자가 자발적으로 자신의 직원에게 사진을 찍게 하겠다고 했으나 화자가 자사의 사진작가가 전임으로 일하고 있으므로 그럴 필요가 없다고 거절하는 맥락임을 알 수 있다. 따라서 정답은 (B).

88. 화자가 청자에게 하도록 요청한 일은?
(A) 남자에게 언제 시간이 가능한지 알려주기
(B) 남자에게 몇몇 서류 보내주기
(C) 최종 납부 확인하기
(D) 몇몇 사진 선택하기

해설 화자의 요청 사항을 묻는 문제로, 담화 후반부에 주목한다. 단서 (88)에서 전화로 회의하기에 가능한 시간이 언제인지를 알려 달라고 했으므로 정답은 (A).

패러프레이징 [단서] let me know when you are available
→ [정답] Inform him of her availability

미 🎧
Questions 89-91 refer to the following excerpt from a meeting.

Good morning, everyone. First on today's agenda, [89]I'd like to explain our new vacation policy. Last year, too many people took time off in the busy summer months. This meant we were short-staffed, so we were very busy serving customers. Unfortunately, this negatively affected the level of service we could provide. So, from now on, we will have a new system for making vacation requests. [90]You'll need to fill out the form on our company's Web site. We will try to give you at least some of your preferred dates, but this is not guaranteed. [91]If you have any questions about the change, please e-mail Olivia. She will address them promptly.

모두들 좋은 아침입니다. 오늘의 첫 번째 안건으로, [89]우리의 새 휴가 정책을 설명하고자 합니다. 작년에 너무 많은 사람들이 바쁜

operate 운영하다   current 현재의   condition 상태   due to ~ 때문에
direct 직행의   no longer 더 이상 ~ 아닌   indirect route 우회 경로
simply 단지   present 제시하다, 보여 주다   valid 유효한

80. 버스 출발이 지연된 이유는 무엇인가?
(A) 청소 중이다.
(B) 수리 중이다.
(C) 지역에 교통 정체가 있다.
(D) 일정에 오류가 있었다.

해설   버스 출발이 지연된 이유를 묻는 문제로, 질문의 키워드인 departure와 delayed가 언급된 부분에 주목한다. 단서 (80)에서 현재 수리 중인 깨진 창문이 있다고 했으므로 정답은 (B).

패러프레이징   [단서] is being fixed → [정답] is undergoing repairs

81. 화자가 "저희는 일부 우회 노선이 있습니다"라고 말한 이유는?
(A) 새로운 일정을 확정하기 위해
(B) 정책을 설명하기 위해
(C) 대안을 제시하기 위해
(D) 불평을 하기 위해

해설   화자의 의도를 묻는 문제로, 제시된 문장의 앞뒤 문맥에 주목한다. 단서 (81)에서 화자는 이제 잉글우드 행 직행 버스가 빠른 옵션이 아닐 수 있다며 다른 우회 노선을 이용하는 방법을 설명하고 있다. 즉, 수리 중인 직행 버스의 대안을 제시하고 있으므로 정답은 (C).

82. 청자들이 하도록 요청받은 것은?
(A) 화자와 이야기하기
(B) 티켓 보여 주기
(C) 나중에 다시 오기
(D) 영수증 보여 주기

해설   요청 사항이 제시되는 담화의 후반부에 주목한다. 화자는 우회 노선 버스를 이용하는 방법을 설명하면서, 단서 (82)에서 운전기사에게 티켓을 제시하면 된다고 했으므로 정답은 (B).

패러프레이징   [단서] presenting your valid ticket → [정답] Show a ticket

🎧 **Questions 83-85** refer to the following telephone message.

Good afternoon. This message is for Victor Henshaw. My name is Tessa Baxter, and [83]I'm calling from Duncan Realty. We've received your application for our realtor position. [84]We were impressed that you have so much experience in a sales role. That is an essential skill to have in this field. Unfortunately, we did not receive your application until after the deadline, and we had already selected another candidate. However, [85]I'll keep your cover letter and résumé on file in case a similar job becomes available in the future, as I think you'd be a good fit for our company's needs. I hope we get a chance to work together in the future.

안녕하세요. 이 메시지는 빅터 헨쇼 씨에게 남기는 것입니다. 제 이름은 테사 백스터이고, [83]덩컨 부동산에서 전화 드립니다. 저희 부동산 중개인 직책에 대한 귀하의 지원서를 받았습니다. [84]저희는 귀하가 영업직 경력이 그렇게 많다는 것에 깊은 인상을 받았습니다. 그것은 이 분야에서 반드시 갖추어야 할 능력입니다. 안타깝게도, 저희는 귀하의 지원서를 마감일이 지난 후에야 받았고, 저희는 다른 후보자를 이미 선발했습니다. 하지만 저는 귀하가 저희 회사의 요구에 적임자라고 생각하기 때문에, [85]향후 비슷한 업무에 자리가 있을 때를 대비하여 귀하의 자기소개서와 이력서를 파일로 보관하겠습니다. 향후 우리가 함께 일할 수 있는 기회가 생기기를 바랍니다.

어휘   realty 부동산   application 지원서   realtor 부동산 중개인   position 직책   impressed 깊은 인상을 받은   essential 필수의, 없어서는 안 될   unfortunately 안타깝게도   not A until B B가 되어서야 A하다   deadline 마감일   candidate 후보자   cover letter 자기 소개서   résumé 이력서   in case ~할 경우에 대비해서   fit 맞는 것

83. 화자가 전화하고 있을 것 같은 장소는?
(A) 부동산 중개소
(B) 치과
(C) 건축 회사
(D) 제조 시설

해설   화자가 근무하는 곳을 묻는 문제로, 담화 초반부에 주목한다. 단서 (83)에서 화자가 자신의 이름을 말한 후 덩컨 부동산에서 전화한다며 소속을 밝혔으므로 정답은 (A).

패러프레이징   [단서] Duncan Realty → [정답] A real estate agency

84. 화자가 언급한 자격 조건은?
(A) 탄력적인 일정
(B) 대학 학위
(C) 국가 인증
(D) 영업 경력

해설   화자가 언급한 자격 조건을 묻는 문제로, 빅터 헨쇼의 경력을 언급한 부분에 주목한다. 단서 (84)에서 헨쇼 씨의 풍부한 영업 경력이 이 분야에서 필수적인 능력이라고 했으므로 정답은 (D).

패러프레이징   [단서] so much experience in a sales role → [정답] Sales experience

76. 화자가 "이런 것은 다시는 보실 수 없을 겁니다"라고 말한 의도는?
(A) 가입 절차가 헷갈릴 수 있다.
(B) 발표를 볼 가치가 있다.
(C) 사업은 성공적일 것으로 기대된다.
(D) 청자들은 할인을 이용해야 한다.

해설 화자의 의도를 묻는 문제로, 제시된 문장의 바로 앞부분에 주목한다. 단서 (76)에서 화자는 오늘 등록하면 특가 상품이 제공된다며 상품의 가격을 언급했다. 그런 다음 그 가격이 다시는 없을 특별한 가격이라고 강조하는 것으로 보아, 이는 청자들이 할인된 특가(offer)를 이용해야 한다는 의미로 한 말임을 알 수 있다. 따라서 정답은 (D).

패러프레이징 [단서] offering a special deal → [정답] an offer

Questions 77-79 refer to the following speech.

Good morning, everyone. ⁷⁷I know it is a challenge to keep up with the demands of the medical industry while still providing the proper care to your patients, and you've done that beautifully. As you may know, we've hired Judy Arnold as a consultant to inspect our site and help make improvements. ⁷⁸I feel reassured that she will be the one carrying out this task because I know how thorough and meticulous she is. As she is doing her work, ⁷⁹please feel free to ask her for guidance on how to do things efficiently. You'll see that she's very knowledgeable.

모두들 좋은 아침입니다. ⁷⁷환자들에게 적절한 보살핌을 제공하면서 의료계의 요구를 따르는 것이 어려운 일이라는 것과, 여러분이 그것을 아주 멋지게 해냈다는 것을 알고 있습니다. 아시다시피, 우리는 현장을 점검하고 개선을 도와줄 컨설턴트로 주디 아놀드 씨를 고용했습니다. ⁷⁸저는 그녀가 얼마나 빈틈없고 세심한지 알기 때문에 그녀가 이번 업무를 수행할 사람이라는 데 마음이 놓입니다. 그녀가 업무 중일 때, ⁷⁹부담 갖지 말고 그녀에게 일을 효율적으로 하는 방법에 대해 지도해 달라고 요청하세요. 여러분은 그녀가 매우 박식하다는 것을 알게 될 것입니다.

어휘 challenge 도전, 난제 keep up with ~을 따르다 demand 요구 medical 의료의 proper 적절한 care 보살핌, 주의 consultant 컨설턴트, 고문 inspect 점검하다 improvement 개선 feel reassured 마음이 놓이다 carry out 수행하다 task 업무 thorough 빈틈없는 meticulous 세심한 feel free to do 마음껏 ~하다 guidance 지도 efficiently 효율적으로 knowledgeable 아는 것이 많은

77. 청자들이 근무할 것 같은 사업체의 종류는?
(A) 건설 회사
(B) 국제 배송 서비스
(C) 신문사
(D) 의료 시설

해설 단서 (77)에서 청자들이 하는 일이 환자들에게 적절한 보살핌을 제공하는 동시에 의료계의 요구를 따르는 일이라는 것을 알 수 있으므로, 이들이 의료계 종사자임을 유추할 수 있다. 따라서 정답은 (D).

78. 화자가 안심이 된다고 말하는 것은?
(A) 직원의 세부적인 것에 대한 주의
(B) 투자자의 향후 계획
(C) 고객 설문 조사의 답변
(D) 검사 점수

해설 화자가 안심하는 부분을 묻는 문제로, 질문의 키워드인 reassured가 언급되는 부분에 주목한다. 화자는 컨설턴트로 주디 아놀드 씨를 고용했다고 한 후, 단서 (78)에서 그녀가 빈틈없고 세심한 사람이기 때문에 안심이 된다고 했으므로 정답은 (A).

패러프레이징 [단서] how thorough and meticulous she is → [정답] A worker's attention to detail

79. 청자들이 하도록 권장받은 것은?
(A) 아놀드 씨에게 이메일 보내기
(B) 조언 구하기
(C) 교육 행사에 참석하기
(D) 신제품 시도해 보기

해설 청자들에게 권장하는 것을 묻는 문제로, 담화의 후반부에 주목한다. 단서 (79)에서 일을 효율적으로 하는 방법에 대해 아놀드 씨에게 언제든지 지도를 요청하라고 했으므로 정답은 (B).

패러프레이징 [단서] guidance → [정답] advice

Questions 80-82 refer to the following announcement.

May I have your attention, please? ⁸⁰The departure of the 1:35 bus to Englewood has been delayed to approximately 3:20. There is a broken window that is being fixed now, and we cannot operate the bus in its current condition. Due to this delay, ⁸¹the direct bus to Englewood may no longer be the faster option. We do have some indirect routes. ⁸¹,⁸²You can use any of those simply by presenting your valid ticket to the driver.

주목해 주시겠습니까? ⁸⁰잉글우드로 향하는 1시 35분 버스의 출발이 대략 3시 20분쯤으로 연기되었습니다. 현재 수리 중인 깨진 창문이 있으며, 현재 상태로는 버스를 운행할 수 없습니다. 이번 지연으로 ⁸¹잉글우드 행 직행 버스는 이제 더 빠른 옵션이 아닐지도 모릅니다. 저희는 일부 우회 노선이 있습니다. ⁸¹,⁸²여러분은 운전기사에게 유효한 티켓을 제시하기만 하면 그것들 중 어떤 것이라도 이용할 수 있습니다.

어휘 attention 집중, 주목 departure 출발 delay 연기하다, 지연시키다; 연기, 지연 approximately 대략, 거의 fix 수리하다, 고치다

똑같은 오래된 관광지가 지겨우신가요? 무언가 새로운 것을 시도해 보세요, 그리고 로지빌 주얼리 작업장을 둘러보세요. 여러분은 보석 제작 공정의 각 단계를 보실 수 있습니다. 또, 71마지막에는 저희의 재능 있는 보석 제작자 중 한 명으로부터 여러분의 질문에 답변을 받을 수 있는 기회를 갖게 되실 겁니다. 72각 참가자에게는 소속된 투어 그룹을 식별하기 위한 아름다운 팔찌가 제공되며, 이 선물은 여러분이 가지시면 됩니다. 저희는 매일 문을 엽니다. 작업장 내부는 온도 차이가 크다는 것을 유념해 주시고, 그러므로 73쉽게 입고 벗을 수 있는 여분의 재킷이나 스웨터를 반드시 가져오시기 바랍니다.

어휘 be tired of ~에 질리다 tourist site 관광지 workshop 작업장 process 과정, 절차 at the end 마지막에 address 다루다, 처리하다 talented 재능 있는 participant 참가자 bracelet 팔찌 identify 확인하다, 식별하다 keep 보관하다 daily 매일 note 유념하다 temperature 온도 be sure to do 반드시 ~하다 extra 여분의, 추가의 put on ~을 입다 take off ~을 벗다

71. 각 작업장 투어가 끝나는 방식은?
(A) 직원이 질문에 답변한다.
(B) 유용한 정보를 주는 영상을 보여준다.
(C) 단체 사진을 찍는다.
(D) 장비 한 대가 시연된다.

해설 작업장 투어가 마무리되는 방법에 대해 묻는 문제로, 질문의 키워드인 end에 해당하는 at the end가 언급된 부분을 집중해서 듣는다. 단서 (71)에서 마지막에는 보석 제작자 중 한 명이 청자들의 질문에 답을 해준다고 했으므로 정답은 (A).

패러프레이징 [단서] one of our talented jewelry makers → [정답] an employee

72. 각 투어 참가자들이 받는 것은?
(A) 보석 한 점
(B) 할인권
(C) 현장 지도
(D) 음료

해설 투어 참가자들이 받는 것을 묻는 문제로, 질문의 키워드인 receive에 해당하는 is given이 언급된 부분에 주목한다. 단서 (72)에서 각 참가자에게 팔찌가 제공된다고 했으므로 정답은 (A).

패러프레이징 [단서] a beautiful bracelet → [정답] A piece of jewelry

73. 청자들이 주의를 받는 것은?
(A) 어떤 출입구를 이용해야 하는지
(B) 어디서 만나야 하는지
(C) 어떤 옷을 가져와야 하는지
(D) 어떻게 사전 예약하는지

해설 청자들에게 당부한 것을 묻는 문제로, 담화 후반부에 집중한다. 화자는 작업장 내부의 온도 차이가 크다며, 단서 (73)에서 재킷 또는 스웨터를 가져오라고 했으므로 정답은 (C).

패러프레이징 [단서] an extra jacket or sweater → [정답] clothing

Questions 74-76 refer to the following speech.

74I'm delighted to see so many people here for Herold Gym's membership drive. We have a variety of exercise equipment to help you reach your fitness goals. 75You'll see from the class list you received when you arrived that there's something for everyone. 76You don't have to sign up today, but if you do, we're offering a special deal—a one-year membership for just fifteen dollars a month. You won't see anything like it again.

74헤럴드 체육관 회원 모집에 이렇게 많은 분들이 와주셔서 기쁩니다. 저희는 여러분의 건강 목표 달성을 돕기 위한 다양한 운동 장비를 갖추고 있습니다. 75도착했을 때 받으신 수업 목록을 보시면 모든 분들을 위한 것들이 있다는 걸 알 수 있으실 겁니다. 76오늘 등록하실 필요는 없지만 만약 하시면, 저희가 특가 상품으로 월회비 15만 원에 일 년 회원권을 제공해 드립니다. 이런 것은 다시는 보실 수 없을 겁니다.

어휘 be delighted to do ~해서 기쁘다 membership 회원 자격[신분] drive (조직적인) 운동 a variety of 다양한 equipment 장비 reach a goal 목표를 달성하다 fitness 건강 sign up ~에 신청하다, 등록하다 special deal 특가 상품

74. 화자의 신분은?
(A) 공장 직원
(B) 운전 강사
(C) 체육관 매니저
(D) 은행 직원

해설 화자가 누구인지 묻는 문제로, 담화 초반부에 주목한다. 단서 (74)에서 화자는 헤럴드 체육관의 회원 모집 운동을 언급했고, 담화 전반에 걸쳐 체육관의 운동 장비와 수업, 회원권 등에 대해 소개하고 있으므로 이런 일을 하는 직업에 가장 가까운 (C)가 정답이다.

75. 청자들이 받은 것은?
(A) 제품 샘플
(B) 직원 명부
(C) 일일 입장권
(D) 수업 목록

해설 청자들이 받은 것을 묻는 문제로, 질문의 키워드인 have been given이 received로 표현된 부분에 주목한다. 단서 (75)에서 화자가 체육관에 도착했을 때 받은 수업 목록을 언급했으므로 정답은 (D).

M We've been consistently meeting our sales quotas, and ⁶⁹our staff just finished their quarterly safety training yesterday.

W Wonderful! Now, summer is the time when most people work on home projects. Did you get the display plan I e-mailed you?

M Yes, but ⁷⁰I'm wondering if we could move the paints closer to the entrance. I'd like people to see them right when they enter the store.

W Sure. ⁷⁰You can swap those with the batteries.

남 ⁶⁸저희 웨스트체스터 지점 철물점에 방문해 주셔서 기쁩니다, 에이브럼스 씨.

여 이곳에 오게 되어 기쁩니다. 지역 매니저로서 모든 지점이 순조롭게 운영되도록 하고 싶어요. 일들은 어떻게 되어가고 있나요?

남 저희는 꾸준히 판매 할당량을 달성하고 있고, ⁶⁹저희 직원들은 어제 막 분기별 안전 교육을 마쳤어요.

여 훌륭하네요! 자, 여름은 대부분의 사람들이 집을 보수하고 단장하는 데 노력을 들일 때죠. 제가 이메일로 보내 드린 진열 계획안을 받으셨나요?

남 네, 그런데 ⁷⁰혹시 페인트들을 입구에 더 가까운 쪽으로 옮길 수 있는지 궁금해요. 저는 사람들이 매장에 들어서자마자 그것들을 봤으면 좋겠어요.

여 그럼요. ⁷⁰그것들을 배터리들과 자리를 바꾸시면 돼요.

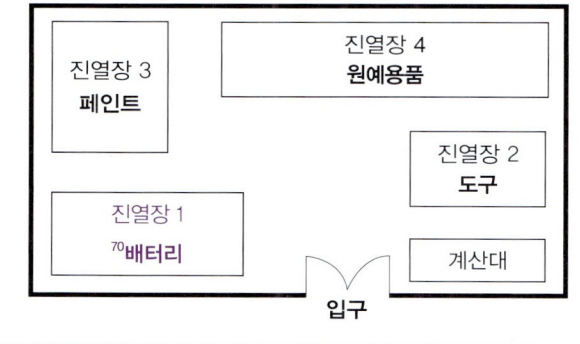

어휘 branch 지점, 지사　hardware store 철물점　regional 지역의　make sure 확실히 하다　operation 운영　run 운영하다　smoothly 순조롭게　consistently 지속적으로, 끊임없이　meet 충족시키다　quota 할당량　quarterly 분기별　work on ~에 노력을 들이다　entrance 입구　swap 바꾸다

68. 화자들이 있는 곳은?
(A) 미술 학회
(B) 수리점
(C) 철물점
(D) 장난감 가게

해설 화자들이 있는 장소를 묻는 문제로, 대화 초반부에 주목한다. 단서 (68)에서 남자가 여자에게 '우리 철물점(our hardware store)'의 지점에 방문해 줘서 기쁘다고 한 것으로 보아 두 사람은 철물점에서 대화를 하고 있음을 알 수 있다. 따라서 정답은 (C).

69. 남자에 따르면, 직원들이 어제 한 일은?
(A) 영상을 녹화했다.
(B) 교육을 완료했다.
(C) 신제품을 내렸다.
(D) 안전 장비를 설치했다.

해설 직원들이 어제 한 일에 대해 묻는 질문으로, 질문의 키워드인 yesterday가 언급된 부분에 주목한다. 단서 (69)에서 남자가 여자에게 어제 직원들이 안전 교육을 마쳤다고 알리고 있으므로 정답은 (B).

패러프레이징 [단서] finished their quarterly safety training
→ [정답] Completed some training

70. 시각 자료에서, 일부 페인트 통이 옮겨질 곳은?
(A) 진열장 1
(B) 진열장 2
(C) 진열장 3
(D) 진열장 4

해설 시각 자료와 함께 질문의 키워드인 paint가 언급된 부분에 주목한다. 남자가 페인트를 입구에 더 가까운 쪽으로 옮길 수 있는지 묻자 여자가 배터리와 자리를 바꾸면 된다고 했으므로 시각 자료에서 배터리의 위치를 확인하면 (A)가 정답이다.

PART 4

Questions 71-73 refer to the following advertisement.

Are you tired of the same old tourist sites? Try something new and tour the Lodgevile Jewelry Workshop. You'll get to see each step of the jewelry-making process. And, ⁷¹at the end, you'll have the chance to get your questions addressed by one of our talented jewelry makers. ⁷²Each participant is given a beautiful bracelet to identify their tour group, and this gift is yours to keep. We're open daily. Please note there are big temperature differences inside the workshop, so ⁷³be sure to bring an extra jacket or sweater that can easily be put on and taken off.

(D) 댄스 수업 가르치기

해설 남자의 여동생이 금요일에 할 일을 묻는 문제로, 대화의 후반부에 여동생에 대해 언급된 부분에 주목한다. 단서 (64)에서 남자는 여동생이 금요일에 다른 지역에서 취업 면접이 있다고 했으므로 정답은 (C).

미 미 🎧

Questions 65-67 refer to the following conversation and price list.

M	Hello. I reserved a vehicle online. My name is Doug Lambert.
W	Let me just find your information, Mr. Lambert. Yes, ⁶⁵you selected a standard sedan.
M	That's right. ⁶⁶I'm here in Atlanta to be shown around the new Hamilton Apartment Tower.
W	That sounds great. Oh, and you have earned enough loyalty points for a free upgrade. So, ⁶⁵I can give you a luxury sedan at the standard sedan price. Would you like to do that this time?
M	⁶⁵Sure! Thank you.
W	It's our pleasure. And, ⁶⁷if you're not familiar with the city, there's a great driving app you can get for your smartphone. Downloading it is free.

남	안녕하세요. 온라인으로 차량을 예약했어요. 제 이름은 더그 램버트입니다.
여	고객님의 정보를 찾아볼게요, 램버트 씨. 네, ⁶⁵일반 세단을 선택하셨네요.
남	맞아요. ⁶⁶저는 이곳 애틀랜타에 새로 지은 해밀턴 아파트 타워를 둘러보러 왔어요.
여	잘됐네요. 아, 그리고 고객님께서는 무료 업그레이드를 할 수 있는 충분한 포인트를 적립하셨어요. 그래서, ⁶⁵저희가 일반 세단 가격에 고급 세단을 드릴 수 있습니다. 이번에 그렇게 하시겠어요?
남	⁶⁵그럼요! 감사합니다.
여	별말씀을요. 그리고, ⁶⁷이 도시에 친숙하지 않으시다면 스마트폰에 깔 수 있는 좋은 운전 앱이 있어요. 다운로드는 무료입니다.

차량 종류	일일 요금
⁶⁵일반 세단	65달러
프리미엄 세단	70달러
고급 세단	85달러
엘리트 세단	110달러

어휘 reserve 예약하다 vehicle 차량 select 선택하다 standard 일반적인, 보통의 sedan 세단(형 자동차) earn 얻다, 벌다 loyalty point (상점의) 고객 적립 포인트 luxury 고급의 be familiar with ~에 익숙하다

65. 시각 자료에서, 남자에게 하루에 부과될 요금은?
(A) 65달러
(B) 70달러
(C) 85달러
(D) 110달러

해설 남자가 하루에 지불할 요금을 묻는 문제로, 제시된 시각 자료와 함께 비용이 언급된 부분에 주목한다. 단서 (65)에서 남자가 일반 세단을 예약했다고 했지만, 적립 포인트가 있어 고급 세단을 이용할 수 있다는 여자의 제안을 수락했으므로 도표에서 일반 세단 요금을 확인하면 정답은 (A).

66. 남자가 애틀랜타에 방문한 이유는?
(A) 계약을 맺기 위해
(B) 집단 토론을 이끌기 위해
(C) 학회에 참석하기 위해
(D) 건물을 둘러보기 위해

해설 남자가 애틀랜타에 방문한 이유를 묻는 문제로, 질문의 키워드인 Atlanta가 언급된 부분에 주목한다. 단서 (66)에서 새로 지은 아파트 타워를 둘러보러 애틀랜타에 왔다고 했으므로 정답은 (D).

패러프레이징 [단서] to be shown around the new Hamilton Apartment Tower → [정답] To tour a building

67. 여자가 하기를 권하는 것은?
(A) 붐비는 도로 피하기
(B) 영수증 보관하기
(C) 앱 다운로드하기
(D) 인기 있는 식당 방문하기

해설 여자가 권하는 일을 묻는 문제로, 대화의 후반부에 주목한다. 단서 (67)에서 여자는 괜찮은 운전 앱이 있다며 무료로 다운로드할 수 있다고 했다. 즉, 해당 앱을 다운로드할 것을 권하는 것이므로 정답은 (C)이다.

미 영 🎧

Questions 68-70 refer to the following conversation and display plan.

M	⁶⁸We're glad you had time to visit the Westchester branch of our hardware store, Ms. Abrams.
W	I'm glad to be here. As regional manager, I like to make sure operations are running smoothly at all branches. How are things going?

패러프레이징 [단서] the answers we got on our latest survey of customers → [정답] Some customer survey responses

60. 클레어가 언급한 문제점은?
(A) 한 재료가 건강에 해롭다고 여겨진다.
(B) 제품 선택량이 충분히 많지 않다.
(C) 일부 영업 시간이 불편하다.
(D) 몇몇 직원들이 완전히 교육받지 않았다.

해설 세 명의 화자 중 한 명인 클레어가 언급한 문제점을 묻는 문제로, 단서 (60)에서 설문조사에서 많은 사람이 짧은 영업 시간이 불편하다는 불만을 드러냈다고 말했다. 따라서 정답은 (C).

패러프레이징 [단서] how inconvenient our short business hours are → [정답] Some business hours are inconvenient.

61. 여자들이 하도록 요청받은 것은?
(A) 광고 캠페인 감독하기
(B) 추가 교대 근무하기
(C) 요약 보고서 작성하기
(D) 새로운 직원 채용하기

해설 두 명의 여자들이 요청받은 것을 묻는 문제로, 대화 후반부에 주목한다. 단서 (61)에서 남자가 두 여자에게 새로운 직원을 채용하는 업무를 부탁하고 있으므로 정답은 (D).

패러프레이징 [단서] take care of hiring someone → [정답] Hire a new employee

호 미 🎧
Questions 62-64 refer to the following conversation and map.

> M Allison, are you doing anything on Friday night? I've got an extra ticket to the 7 P.M. show for the Vancouver Ballet Company. ⁶²The group added Friday and Sunday shows because tickets for the original date sold out.
>
> W ⁶²Oh, really? I didn't know they were offering more shows. I'd love to go!
>
> M Great! ⁶³The seats are near the back, but they're in the center, so I think the view will be fine.
>
> W That sounds good to me. Why do you have an extra ticket?
>
> M ⁶⁴I was planning on taking my sister, but she now has an out-of-town job interview on Friday.
>
> 남 앨리슨, 금요일 밤에 뭐 할 일 있어요? 제게 밴쿠버 발레단의 저녁 7시 공연 티켓 여유분이 생겼어요. ⁶²본 공연 날짜의 티켓이 매진되어서 발레단에서 금요일과 일요일 공연을 추가했대요.

여 ⁶²오, 정말요? 그들이 추가 공연을 하는 줄은 몰랐어요. 가고 싶어요!

남 좋아요! ⁶³좌석은 뒤쪽 근처이긴 한데, 중앙에 있으니 잘 보일 거예요.

여 괜찮을 것 같네요. 그런데 여유분 티켓이 왜 생긴 거예요?

남 ⁶⁴제 여동생을 데려갈 계획이었는데, 동생이 지금 금요일에 다른 지역에서 취업 면접이 있어요.

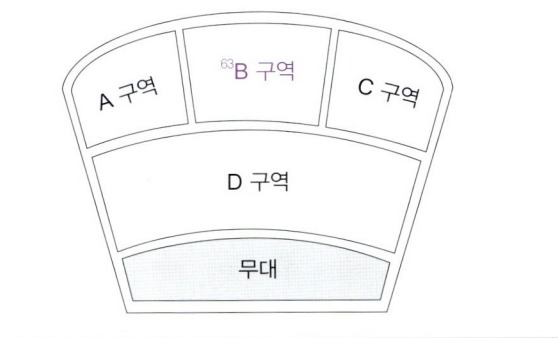

어휘 extra 추가의, 여분의   add 추가하다   original 원래의
sell out 다 팔리다   offer 제공하다   plan on ~할 계획이다
out-of-town 다른 도시의, 다른 시에서 하는   job interview 취업 면접

62. 여자가 놀라움을 표현하는 이유는?
(A) 일부 티켓 가격이 인상되었다.
(B) 몇몇 새로운 공연 날짜가 추가되었다.
(C) 무용단이 상을 탔다.
(D) 남자가 발레 보는 것에 관심이 있다.

해설 여자가 놀랍다는 반응을 보이기 직전에 남자가 한 말에 주목한다. 단서 (62)에서 남자가 발레 공연이 추가되었다고 하자 여자가 정말이냐며 되물었으므로 정답은 (B).

패러프레이징 [단서] The group added Friday and Sunday shows → [정답] Some new performance dates have been added.

63. 시각 자료에서, 남자의 티켓이 해당하는 구역은?
(A) A 구역
(B) B 구역
(C) C 구역
(D) D 구역

해설 남자가 가지고 있는 공연 티켓이 어느 구역의 티켓인지 묻는 문제로, 제시된 시각 자료와 함께 좌석의 위치가 언급된 부분에 주목한다. 단서 (63)에서 남자가 좌석은 뒤쪽이지만 중앙에 있다고 했으므로 시각 자료에서 해당 구역을 찾으면 (B)가 정답임을 알 수 있다.

64. 남자의 여동생이 금요일에 할 일은?
(A) 파티에 가기
(B) 다른 곳으로 이사하기
(C) 면접에 참여하기

남	저도요. ⁵⁶여기 재무팀 모두 그 일로 들떠 있어요. 그녀는 아주 잘 해낼 거예요. 있잖아요, 이번 성과를 축하하기 위해 점심 회식을 해야겠어요.
여	여기 사무실에서 하는 거 어때요? ⁵⁷우리에게 음식을 제공할 출장 요리 업체에 제가 전화할게요.
남	좋아요! ⁵⁸그녀에게 선물도 해줄까 해요.
여	사실, 티나가 같은 생각을 했어요. ⁵⁸그녀가 각 팀원들에게 돈을 걷고 있으니 돈을 보태고 싶으면 그녀에게 이야기해 보세요.

어휘 thrilled 아주 흥분한   be promoted to ~로 승진하다
department 부서   finance 재무, 재정   fantastic 환상적인, 엄청난
accomplishment 성과, 성취   caterer 출장 요리 업체
be willing to do 기꺼이 ~하다   chip in (돈을) 조금씩 내다, 끼어들다

56. 화자들이 근무하는 부서는?
(A) 인사 부서
(B) 재무 부서
(C) 마케팅 부서
(D) 배송 부서

해설 화자들이 근무하는 부서를 묻는 문제로, 대화 초반부에 주목한다. 단서 (56)에서 남자가 '여기 재무팀(here on the finance team)'이라고 언급했으므로 정답은 (B)이다.

57. 여자가 하겠다고 제안하는 것은?
(A) 회사 정책 검토하기
(B) 이 씨의 고객들 중 한 명에게 전화하기
(C) 업무 일정 짜기
(D) 식사를 위한 준비하기

해설 여자가 하겠다고 한 일을 묻는 문제로, 남자의 점심 회식 제안에 대한 여자의 응답에 주목한다. 단서 (57)에서 여자가 출장 요리 업체에 전화하겠다고 했으므로 정답은 (D).

패러프레이징 [단서] call a caterer to provide the food
→ [정답] Make preparations for a meal

58. 여자에 따르면, 남자가 티나와 이야기해야 하는 이유는?
(A) 선물에 보탬이 되기 위해
(B) 상을 받기 위해
(C) 선호하는 것을 표현하기 위해
(D) 보고서를 확인하기 위해

해설 질문의 키워드인 Tina가 언급된 부분에 집중하며 듣는다. 단서 (58)에서 남자가 이 씨에게 선물도 해주고 싶다고 하자, 여자는 티나가 선물 준비를 위해 돈을 걷고 있으니 돈을 보태고 싶다면 그녀에게 이야기를 해보라고 했다. 즉, 선물에 보탬이 되고 싶으면 연락을 하라는 의미이므로 정답은 (A).

패러프레이징 [단서] chip in → [정답] contribute to a gift

미 영 미 🎧
Questions 59-61 refer to the following conversation with three speakers.

M	Thanks for coming to this meeting, Claire and Eleanor. I scheduled it because ⁵⁹I want to talk about the answers we got on our latest survey of customers.
W1	We've both looked over your summary report. Overall, it seems that people are pleased with the new breads and cakes we're offering at our bakery. ⁶⁰Right, Claire?
W2	Yes. Especially the low-sugar options. However, ⁶⁰a lot of people complained about how inconvenient our short business hours are.
M	Right, so we should extend them. ⁶¹But to do so, we'll need another employee. Could you two please take care of hiring someone?

남	클레어, 엘리너, 이 회의에 와 줘서 고마워요. ⁵⁹최근 우리 고객 설문 조사에서 받은 답변들에 대해 이야기하고 싶어서 회의를 잡았어요.
여1	우리 둘 다 당신이 준 요약 보고서를 훑어보았어요. 전반적으로, 제과점에서 우리가 제공하고 있는 새로운 빵과 케이크에 만족해하는 것 같아요. ⁶⁰그렇죠, 클레어?
여2	네. 특히 당분이 적은 메뉴들을요. 하지만 ⁶⁰우리의 짧은 영업 시간이 얼마나 불편한지에 대해 많은 사람들이 불평했어요.
남	맞아요, 그래서 영업 시간을 늘려야 해요. ⁶¹하지만 그렇게 하기 위해서는 또 다른 직원이 필요해요. 두 분이 채용을 좀 맡아주실 수 있을까요?

어휘 schedule 일정을 잡다   latest 최근의, 최신의   survey 설문 조사
look over ~을 훑어보다, 살펴보다   overall 전반적으로   be pleased
with ~에 만족하다, 기쁘다   especially 특히   low-sugar 당분이 적은
complain about ~에 대해 불평하다   inconvenient 불편한
business hours 영업 시간   extend 연장하다   take care of ~을 처리하다, 다루다   hire 채용하다

59. 남자가 회의에서 이야기하고 싶어한 것은?
(A) 몇몇 고객 설문 조사 답변들
(B) 몇몇 직원 불만 사항
(C) 새로운 재료 공급업체
(D) 곧 있을 판촉 활동

해설 남자가 회의에서 말하고 싶어한 것을 묻는 문제로, 회의 안건을 밝힌 대화 초반부에 주목한다. 단서 (59)에서 남자는 최근 실시한 고객 설문 조사 답변들에 대해 이야기하고 싶다고 했으므로 answers를 responses로 바꿔 표현한 (A)가 정답이다.

Questions 53-55 refer to the following conversation.

W: ⁵³Thank you for visiting Augusta Furniture. How may I help you?

M: Hello. ⁵⁴I will open a small hotel next month, and I need some items for the lobby. There's room for two sofas and a few armchairs.

W: What kind of style did you have in mind?

M: I've renovated a historic building, so I'd like items that have a classic style. But as for the color combinations, I have no idea.

W: Well, ⁵⁵you might find it helpful to check out the photo gallery on our Web site.

M: Wouldn't that just be pictures of the merchandise I can see here in the store?

W: Yes, but it shows the items in different settings, so it can help you to get some decorating ideas.

여 ⁵³오거스타 가구점에 방문해 주셔서 감사합니다. 무엇을 도와드릴까요?

남 안녕하세요. ⁵⁴제가 다음 달에 작은 호텔을 개업할 건데요, 로비에 둘 몇 가지 제품이 필요해요. 소파 두 개와 몇 개의 안락의자를 둘 공간이 있어요.

여 어떤 종류의 스타일을 생각하고 계신가요?

남 저는 역사적인 건물을 개조했어요. 그래서 고전적인 스타일의 제품들이면 좋겠어요. 하지만 색상 조합에 관해서는 잘 모르겠어요.

여 음, ⁵⁵저희 웹사이트의 사진 갤러리를 확인해 보시면 도움이 될지도 몰라요.

남 그건 그냥 이곳 매장에서 볼 수 있는 상품들의 사진이 아닌가요?

여 맞아요, 하지만 다양한 배경에서 제품을 보여 주는 거라서 장식에 대한 아이디어를 좀 얻는 데 도움이 될 거예요.

어휘 room 공간 armchair 안락의자 have ~ in mind ~을 염두에 두다, 생각하다 renovate 개조하다 as for ~에 관해서는 combination 조합 check out 확인하다 merchandise 제품 setting 배경, 설정 decorate 장식하다

53. 여자의 신분은?
(A) 여행사 직원
(B) 배송 기사
(C) 가구 판매원
(D) 호텔 매니저

해설 여자의 직업을 묻는 문제로, 여자의 말을 집중해서 듣는다. 대화 초반의 단서 (53)에서 여자가 오거스타 가구점에 방문해 주어서 감사하다고 했으므로 정답은 (C). 회사 이름이 언급되는 경우 이름에서 업종을 알 수 있는 경우가 많다.

54. 남자가 다음 달에 할 일은?
(A) 도시를 떠나 여행을 갈 것이다.
(B) 새로운 업체를 열 것이다.
(C) 행사에서 연설을 할 것이다.
(D) 새 집으로 이사를 할 것이다.

해설 남자가 다음 달에 할 일을 묻는 문제로, 질문의 키워드인 next month가 언급되는 부분에 주목한다. 단서 (54)에서 남자는 다음 달에 작은 호텔을 개업할 것이라고 했으므로 정답은 (B).

패러프레이징 [단서] open a small hotel → [정답] open a new business

55. 여자가 제안하는 것은?
(A) 웹사이트에서 광고하는 것
(B) 온라인에서 몇몇 이미지를 보는 것
(C) 전문 장식가를 고용하는 것
(D) 스마트폰 앱을 다운로드하는 것

해설 제안 사항은 주로 대화의 후반부에 나온다. 단서 (55)에서 여자는 남자에게 회사 웹사이트의 사진 갤러리를 확인해서 아이디어를 얻으라고 제안하고 있으므로 정답은 (B).

패러프레이징 [단서] check out the photo gallery on our Web site → [정답] Viewing some images online

Questions 56-58 refer to the following conversation.

W: I'm thrilled that Ms. Lee has been promoted to the head of our department.

M: Me, too. ⁵⁶Everyone here on the finance team is excited about it. She'll do a fantastic job. You know, we should have a team lunch to celebrate this accomplishment.

W: How about we do it here at the office? ⁵⁷I can call a caterer to provide the food for us.

M: Perfect! ⁵⁸Maybe we should get her a gift as well.

W: Actually, Tina had the same idea. ⁵⁸She's collecting money from each team member, so talk to her if you're willing to chip in.

여 이 씨가 우리 부서장으로 승진해서 너무 좋아요.

47. 문제는 무엇인가?
(A) 일부 장비가 손상되었다.
(B) 회사가 믿을 만하지 않다.
(C) 몇몇 신입 직원이 경험이 부족하다.
(D) 업무 공간이 너무 좁다.

해설 대화에서 언급된 문제점을 묻는 문제로, 대화 첫 부분에 주목한다. 단서 (47)에서 여자는 신입 직원들을 배치해야 하는데 현재 공간이 충분하지 않다고 했으므로 정답은 (D).

패러프레이징 [단서] out of office space → [정답] A workspace is too small.

48. 남자가 "제 친구 펠릭스가 부동산에서 일을 해요"라고 말한 이유는?
(A) 추천을 받을 것을 제안하기 위해
(B) 사업 제안서를 거절하기 위해
(C) 오해를 바로잡기 위해
(D) 결정에 대한 이유를 설명하기 위해

해설 화자의 의도를 묻는 문제로, 제시된 문장의 앞뒤 문맥에 주목한다. 단서 (48)에서 여자가 어떤 동네가 가장 좋을지 모르겠다고 하자 남자가 친구 펠릭스가 부동산에서 일을 한다고 한 것은 그에게 조언을 요청하자는 의미이다. 따라서 정답은 (A).

49. 여자가 하겠다고 말한 것은?
(A) 동네 방문하기
(B) 몇몇 평가 읽어보기
(C) 전화하기
(D) 몇몇 서류 준비하기

해설 여자가 앞으로 할 일을 묻는 문제로, 대화 후반부를 집중해서 듣는다. 단서 (49)에서 여자가 유인물을 인쇄하겠다고 했으므로 정답은 (D)이다.

패러프레이징 [단서] print the handouts → [정답] Prepare some documents

미 미 🎧
Questions 50-52 refer to the following conversation.

M Okay, ⁵⁰the total for these hiking boots and high heels is ninety-seven fifty.
W Alright. And do you know when you're getting the new line of Cartright products?
M I'm very sorry, but ⁵¹our inventory program on the computer is not working at the moment.
W Oh, that's too bad. I wanted to get those as soon as they were in stock.
M We should have the system working again soon. ⁵²If you give me your phone number, I can give you a call this afternoon.

남 네, ⁵⁰이 등산화와 하이힐의 총 금액은 97.50달러입니다.
여 알겠어요. 그리고 카트라잇의 신제품 라인이 언제 들어오는지 아시나요?
남 대단히 죄송합니다만, ⁵¹현재 저희 컴퓨터의 재고 관리 프로그램이 작동하지 않고 있어요.
여 아, 아쉽네요. 그것들이 재고가 들어오자마자 구입하고 싶었어요.
남 곧 시스템을 복구할 거예요. ⁵²전화번호를 제게 주시면 제가 오늘 오후에 전화를 드릴게요.

어휘 total 합계, 총액 hiking boots 등산화 line (상품의) 종류 inventory 재고 work 작동하다 at the moment 바로 지금 in stock 재고가 있는

50. 남자가 일할 것 같은 곳은?
(A) 커피숍
(B) 은행
(C) 자동차 대여 회사
(D) 신발 가게

해설 남자가 근무하는 곳을 묻는 문제로, 남자의 대화에서 단서가 될 표현들에 주목한다. 대화 초반부의 단서 (50)에서 등산화와 하이힐의 총 금액을 언급한 것으로 보아 남자가 신발 가게에서 일한다는 것을 알 수 있다. 따라서 정답은 (D).

패러프레이징 [단서] hiking boots and high heels → [정답] shoe

51. 남자에 따르면, 무엇이 문제인가?
(A) 일부 제품들이 매진되었다.
(B) 배송품이 도착하지 않았다.
(C) 일부 소프트웨어가 제대로 작동하지 않고 있다.
(D) 직원이 실수를 했다.

패러프레이징 [단서] our inventory program on the computer is not working → [정답] Some software is malfunctioning.

52. 남자가 여자를 위해 해주겠다고 제안하는 것은?
(A) 나중에 전화해 주기
(B) 상사 불러 주기
(C) 환불해 주기
(D) 카탈로그 보내 주기

해설 남자가 하겠다고 제안하는 일을 묻는 문제로, 대화의 후반부를 집중해서 듣는다. 남자는 시스템이 곧 다시 작동하도록 할 거라고 한 후, 단서 (52)에서 여자에게 오늘 오후에 전화해 주겠다고 했다. 따라서 정답은 (A).

패러프레이징 [단서] give you a call this afternoon → [정답] Call her later

남	웨스턴 씨, ⁴⁴마샬 회계 사무소에 오신 걸 환영하며 이번 면접에 와 주셔서 감사합니다. ⁴⁵이 자리에 대해 어떻게 알게 되셨나요?
여	⁴⁵일자리 웹사이트에서 이메일 알림을 신청했어요. 이 직책에 대해 메시지를 받았을 때, 제게 아주 잘 맞을 거라는 걸 알았어요.
남	왜 그렇게 생각하시나요?
여	귀사는 개인보다는 주로 기업 고객들에게 서비스를 제공하시죠. 저는 8년간 다국적 기업에서 일을 했고, 그래서 그런 종류의 고객들에 꽤 익숙해요.
남	그렇다니 잘됐네요. 그리고 당신의 이력서에는 올해의 직원상을 받았다고 쓰여 있더군요. 그건 무엇 때문이었나요?
여	저희는 고객 기반을 구축하는 데 주력했는데 ⁴⁶제가 가장 많은 신규 고객들을 등록시켰어요.
남	대단하네요!

어휘 job opening (직장의) 빈자리 sign up for ~을 신청하다 alert 알림, 경보 position (일자리, 직위) fit 맞는 것 firm 회사 serve (제품이나 서비스를) 제공하다 corporate 기업의 rather than ~보다는 individual 개인 multinational 다국적의 corporation 기업 quite 꽤, 상당히 résumé 이력서 focus A on B A를 B에 집중시키다 base 기반 register 등록하다

44. 화자들이 있을 것 같은 곳은?
(A) 경영 대학원
(B) 회계 법인
(C) 보험 회사
(D) 관공서

해설 화자들이 있는 장소를 묻는 문제로, 대화의 초반부에 집중해서 듣는다. 단서 (44)에서 남자가 언급한 자신의 회사 이름 Marshall Accounting과 가장 관련 깊은 업종인 (B)가 정답이다.

패러프레이징 [단서] Marshall Accounting → [정답] an accounting firm

45. 여자는 구인 중인 일자리에 대해 어떻게 알게 되었는가?
(A) 잡지를 읽음으로써
(B) 이메일을 받음으로써
(C) 동료와 이야기함으로써
(D) 취업 박람회에 참석함으로써

해설 여자가 일자리에 대해 알게 된 경로를 묻는 문제로, 질문의 키워드인 job opening이 언급된 부분에 주목한다. 단서 (45)에서 남자가 이 자리에 대해 어떻게 알았는지 묻자 여자가 웹사이트에서 이메일 알림을 신청했다고 했다. 즉, 이메일을 받고 알았음을 알 수 있으므로 정답은 (B).

패러프레이징 [단서] e-mail alerts → [정답] receiving an e-mail

46. 여자가 언급한 성과는?
(A) 다른 직원들을 교육시킨 것
(B) 가장 높은 직원 평가를 받은 것
(C) 새로운 소프트웨어 프로그램을 개발한 것
(D) 가장 많은 신규 고객들을 데려온 것

해설 여자의 성과를 묻는 문제로, 여자의 경력 사항을 언급한 부분에 주목한다. 올해의 직원상을 받은 이유를 묻는 질문에 단서 (46)에서 자신이 가장 많은 신규 고객들을 등록시켰다고 했으므로 정답은 (D).

패러프레이징 [단서] registered the most new clients → [정답] Bringing in the most new customers

Questions 47-49 refer to the following conversation.

W	We have three new employees starting here next month. ⁴⁷I have no idea where we're going to put them.
M	Oh, ⁴⁷we're out of office space?
W	Yes, ⁴⁷our current unit just isn't enough anymore. Fortunately, our lease is up soon, so we could move to another site. But ⁴⁸I have no idea which neighborhood would be best.
M	Well, my friend Felix works in real estate.
W	Perfect! Would you mind calling him? While you're doing that, ⁴⁹I can print the handouts we need for this afternoon's meeting.
M	Of course. I'll try him now.

여	다음 달부터 이곳에서 세 명의 신입 직원들이 일을 시작할 거예요. ⁴⁷그들의 자리를 어디에 배치해야 할지 모르겠어요.
남	아, ⁴⁷사무실 공간이 부족한가요?
여	네, ⁴⁷우리 현재 공간의 크기만으로는 더 이상 충분치가 않아요. 다행히, 우리 임대 계약이 곧 끝날 거라서 다른 장소로 옮길 수 있어요. 하지만 ⁴⁸어떤 동네가 가장 좋을지 모르겠어요.
남	음, 제 친구 펠릭스가 부동산에서 일을 해요.
여	잘됐네요! 그에게 전화해 줄래요? 그러는 동안 ⁴⁹제가 오늘 오후 회의에 필요한 유인물을 인쇄할게요.
남	그럼요. 제가 지금 전화해 볼게요.

어휘 be out of ~을 다 써서 없다, 바닥나다 current 현재의 unit (하나의 전체를 구성하는) 일정량, 일정한 크기 fortunately 다행히 lease 임대차 계약 move to ~로 이사하다 site 장소 neighborhood 동네, 이웃 real estate 부동산 handout 유인물

미 영 호 🎧
Questions 41-43 refer to the following conversation with three speakers.

> **W1** Tommy and Jennifer, the two of you have been so much help in promoting Ruth Taylor's new novel. ⁴¹I think it's going to be one of our publishing firm's best sellers. I appreciate your taking charge of the book launch event. Jennifer, how did it go?
>
> **W2** It was great! ⁴²I didn't expect so many people to be there. There was a line outside the store just to get in.
>
> **W1** I'm so glad to hear that! I guess the advertisements we made really worked. Tommy, ⁴³did you take a lot of pictures at the launch?
>
> **M** Yes, and ⁴³I'll upload them to the Web site this afternoon.
>
> 여1 토미, 제니퍼, 두 사람이 루스 테일러 씨의 새로운 소설 홍보에 많은 도움이 되었어요. ⁴¹그것은 우리 출판사의 베스트셀러 중 하나가 될 것 같아요. 책 출간 행사를 담당해 준 것에 감사드려요. 제니퍼, 행사가 어떻게 되었나요?
>
> 여2 훌륭했어요! ⁴²그렇게 많은 사람들이 올 줄은 예상하지 못했어요. 들어오려고 상점 밖에까지 줄을 섰었어요.
>
> 여1 그랬다니 정말 기쁘군요! 우리가 만든 광고가 정말 효과가 있었던 것 같아요. 토미, ⁴³출간 행사에서 사진은 많이 찍었나요?
>
> 남 네, 그리고 ⁴³오늘 오후에 그것들을 웹사이트에 올려놓을게요.

어휘 promote 홍보하다 publishing firm 출판사 appreciate 고마워하다 take charge of ~을 담당하다 launch 출간, 출시 expect A to do A가 ~할 것을 기대하다 get in ~에 들어가다 advertisement 광고 work 효과가 있다

41. 화자들이 일하는 곳은?
(A) 사업 협회
(B) 도서관
(C) 출판사
(D) 신문사

해설 화자들의 직장을 묻는 문제로, 화자들이 하는 일이 드러나는 부분을 잘 듣는다. 단서 (41)에서 첫 번째 여자가 '우리 출판사'라고 회사의 업종을 밝히고 있으므로 정답은 (C).

패러프레이징 [단서] our publishing firm → [정답] a publishing company

42. 제니퍼가 놀란 것은?
(A) 행사 참석률
(B) 일부 부정적인 평가
(C) 제안된 계약
(D) 동료의 전근

해설 제니퍼를 놀라게 한 일에 대해 묻는 문제로, 첫 번째 여자가 제니퍼에게 일의 진행 상황을 확인하는 부분에 주목한다. 단서 (42)에서 제니퍼가 행사에 그렇게 많은 사람들이 올 줄은 예상하지 못했다고 했으므로 높은 참석률에 놀랐음을 알 수 있다. 따라서 정답은 (A).

패러프레이징 [단서] so many people to be there → [정답] Attendance at an event

43. 오늘 오후에 일어날 일은?
(A) 몇몇 고객들이 피드백을 줄 것이다.
(B) 새로운 배송품이 도착할 것이다.
(C) 남자가 면접을 할 것이다.
(D) 사진들이 웹사이트에 추가될 것이다.

해설 특정 시점에 일어날 일을 묻는 문제로, 질문의 키워드인 this afternoon이 나온 부분에 집중한다. 단서 (43)에서 남자가 책 출간 행사에서 찍은 사진들을 오늘 오후에 웹사이트에 업로드하겠다고 했으므로 정답은 (D).

패러프레이징 [단서] I'll upload them to the Web site → [정답] Photos will be added to a Web site.

미 미 🎧
Questions 44-46 refer to the following conversation.

> **M** ⁴⁴Welcome to Marshall Accounting, Ms. Weston, and thanks for coming to this interview. ⁴⁵How did you find out about this job opening?
>
> **W** ⁴⁵I signed up for e-mail alerts on a job Web site. When I got the message about this position, I knew it'd be a great fit for me.
>
> **M** What makes you say that?
>
> **W** Your firm mainly serves corporate clients, rather than individuals. I worked at a multinational corporation for eight years, so I'm quite comfortable with that kind of client.
>
> **M** That's great to hear. And your résumé says you won an Employee of the Year Award. What was that for?
>
> **W** We were focused on building our customer base, and ⁴⁶I registered the most new clients.
>
> **M** Fantastic!

해설 여자가 주문한 것을 묻는 문제로, 질문의 키워드인 order가 언급된 부분에 주목한다. 단서 (36)에서 여자는 재택근무를 원하는 남자를 위해서 노트북을 주문했다고 했으므로 (D)가 정답.

37. 여자가 남자에게 하도록 상기시키는 것은?
(A) 워크숍 신청하기
(B) 사용 설명서 읽기
(C) 제품을 주의해서 옮기기
(D) 고객에게 연락하기

해설 여자가 남자에게 상기시키는 일을 묻는 문제로, 대화의 후반부에 집중해서 듣는다. 단서 (37)에서 회사 노트북 컴퓨터에 손상이 생길 경우 남자가 책임져야 하니 여기저기 옮길 때 보호 케이스를 사용하라고 당부했으므로 정답은 (C).

패러프레이징 [단서] use a protective case when moving it from place to place → [정답] Transport an item carefully

영 미 🎧
Questions 38-40 refer to the following conversation.

W Welcome to the Seabreeze Café. ³⁸Would you like a table in our dining room or on our patio?

M ³⁸I'm not sure what my friend would like. He'll be here in a minute, so I'll wait and ask him.

W That's no problem. You can see here on our specials board that ³⁹we have six different fresh soups to choose from today.

M That's more than I expected.

W Well, we try to make sure there's something for everyone.

M ³⁹That's great. Oh, and ⁴⁰are you still accepting this coupon from the newspaper for ten percent off any meal?

W Yes, that's valid until the end of the month.

여 시브리즈 카페에 오신 걸 환영합니다. ³⁸식당 내 테이블이 좋으신가요, 아니면 테라스 테이블이 좋으신가요?

남 ³⁸제 친구가 어디를 좋아할지 모르겠어요. 그가 곧 올 테니, 기다렸다가 물어볼게요.

여 좋습니다. 여기 저희 특선 요리 게시판을 보시면 ³⁹오늘은 선택하실 수 있는 6가지의 다양한 신선한 수프가 있습니다.

남 제가 기대했던 것 이상이네요.

여 음, 저희는 반드시 모든 분들을 위한 무언가가 있도록 하려고 노력합니다.

남 ³⁹훌륭하네요. 아, 그리고 ⁴⁰모든 식사에 10% 할인을 해주는 이 신문 쿠폰을 아직 받으시나요?

여 네, 그건 이번 달 말까지 유효해요.

어휘 dining room 식당 patio 테라스 in a minute 곧, 즉시 accept 받다, 수락하다 meal 식사 valid 유효한

38. 남자는 무엇에 대해 그의 친구의 의견을 원하는가?
(A) 지불 방식
(B) 예약 시간
(C) 음식 주문
(D) 좌석 선택

해설 질문의 키워드인 friend가 언급된 부분에 주목하면, 단서 (38)에서 여자가 식당 내 자리와 테라스 자리 중 어디가 더 좋은지 묻자 남자가 친구에게 물어보겠다고 했으므로 정답은 (D).

패러프레이징 [단서] a table in our dining room or on our patio → [정답] A seating option

39. 남자가 "제가 기대했던 것 이상이네요"라고 말한 이유는?
(A) 항의를 하기 위해
(B) 제안을 거절하기 위해
(C) 변명을 하기 위해
(D) 기분 좋음을 표현하기 위해

해설 화자의 의도를 묻는 문제로, 제시된 문장의 앞뒤 문맥에 주목한다. 단서 (39)에서 선택 가능한 신선한 수프 6가지가 제공된다고 하자 남자가 기대 이상이라며 긍정적인 반응을 보인 것은 다양한 선택권이 주어진 것에 대해 흡족해 하고 있음을 나타내는 것이므로 정답은 (D).

40. 남자가 문의하는 것은?
(A) 할인 제공
(B) 주방장의 추천
(C) 운영 시간
(D) 주차 상황

해설 남자가 문의한 내용을 묻는 문제로, 대화의 후반부에 집중해서 듣는다. 단서 (40)에서 남자가 10% 할인 쿠폰을 받는지 물었으므로 정답은 (A).

패러프레이징 [단서] accepting this coupon from the newspaper for ten percent off any meal → [정답] A discount offer

남 음… 맞네요, 12 사이즈가 여기서는 가장 큰 사이즈예요. 그래도 그 브랜드에서 다른 사이즈들도 만들긴 해요.

여 다른 지점에서 하나 구입할 수 있을까요?

남 ³⁴저희 웹사이트를 방문하시면, 거기서 구입할 수 있는지 아실 수 있을 거예요.

어휘 wonder 궁금하다 shelf 선반 carry (가게에서 품목을) 취급하다 look up 찾아보다 branch 지점, 지사

32. 대화가 이루어지는 곳은?
(A) 서점에서
(B) 세탁소에서
(C) 백화점에서
(D) 우체국에서

해설 화자들이 이야기를 나누는 장소를 묻는 문제로, 대화의 초반부에 주목한다. 대화 시작 부분의 단서 (32)에서 남자가 매디슨 백화점에 오신 걸 환영한다고 했으므로 정답은 (C).

33. 남자가 확인하는 것은?
(A) 구입 가능한 사이즈
(B) 판매 가격
(C) 배송료
(D) 발송 날짜

해설 남자가 확인하는 것을 묻는 문제로, 단서 (33)을 보면, 여자가 14 사이즈가 있는지 묻자 남자가 컴퓨터로 찾아보겠다고 했다. 즉, 남자가 매장에서 구입할 수 있는 청바지의 사이즈를 확인했으므로 정답은 (A).

34. 남자가 하기를 권하는 것은?
(A) 온라인에서 제품을 확인하는 것
(B) 긴급 주문을 하는 것
(C) 다른 지점을 방문하는 것
(D) 다른 브랜드를 구입하는 것

해설 남자가 권하는 일을 묻는 문제로, 대화의 후반부를 집중해서 듣는다. 여자가 찾는 사이즈가 현재 매장에 없자 단서 (34)에서 웹사이트에서 확인해 보라고 했으므로 (A)가 정답.

패러프레이징 [단서] our company's Web site → [정답] online

Questions 35-37 refer to the following conversation.

W I'm glad you got my message about stopping by, Rick.

M I came as soon as I read it. Is anything the matter?

W Not at all. ³⁵The head of marketing is very pleased with the designs you've made for us so far. And since you said you'd like to work from home some days, ³⁶I've ordered you a company laptop. Here it is.

M Oh, that's great. Thanks! Now I won't have to keep any company files on my personal computer anymore.

W Right. But you will be responsible for any damage to this device. So, ³⁷don't forget to use a protective case when moving it from place to place.

여 릭, 잠깐 들러 달라는 제 메시지를 받아서 다행이에요.

남 그걸 읽자마자 왔어요. 무슨 문제가 되는 거라도 있나요?

여 전혀 없어요. ³⁵마케팅 부장님이 지금까지 당신이 해준 디자인에 매우 만족해하세요. 그리고 당신이 며칠은 재택근무를 하고 싶다고 했기 때문에 ³⁶제가 당신을 위해서 회사 노트북 컴퓨터를 주문했어요. 여기 있어요.

남 오, 잘됐네요. 고마워요! 이제 더 이상 제 개인 컴퓨터에 회사 파일을 저장할 필요가 없겠네요.

여 맞아요. 하지만 이 기기에 대한 손상에는 책임을 지셔야 해요. 그러니 ³⁷여기저기 옮길 때 보호 케이스를 사용하는 걸 잊지 마세요.

어휘 stop by (~에) 잠시 들르다 as soon as ~하자마자 matter 문제 so far 지금까지 work from home 재택근무를 하다 order 주문하다 laptop 노트북 컴퓨터 personal 개인의 be responsible for ~을 책임지다 damage 손상, 피해 device 기기, 장치 protective 보호하는 from place to place 여기저기

35. 남자의 직업은 무엇일 것 같은가?
(A) 마케팅 부장
(B) 그래픽 디자이너
(C) 수리공
(D) 인사부장

해설 남자의 직업을 묻는 문제로, 남자의 업무를 언급한 부분에 주목한다. 단서 (35)에서 마케팅 부장이 남자가 한 디자인을 마음에 들어 했다는 것으로 보아 디자인이 남자의 업무임을 알 수 있으므로 정답은 (B).

36. 여자가 남자를 위해 주문한 것은?
(A) 유니폼
(B) 책상
(C) 파일 캐비닛
(D) 노트북 컴퓨터

Answer **009**

(A) 주로 도보 여행자들을 위해서요.
(B) 네, 저는 하나 가져오기로 결정했어요.
(C) 그것들은 텐트 옆에 있어요.

해설 경량 배낭을 둔 장소를 묻는 Where 의문문에, 텐트 옆에 있다며 구체적인 장소로 답변한 (C)가 정답. (B)는 의문사 의문문에 Yes로 답변한 오답.

어휘 keep 두다, 유지하다 | lightweight 가벼운, 경량의 | backpack 배낭 | hiker 도보 여행자, 하이커

29. 호 미 🎧

Don't you have to turn in your portfolio today?
(A) I'm putting the finishing touches on it.
(B) Please turn left at the corner.
(C) Yes, it is a portable device.

당신의 포트폴리오를 오늘 제출해야 하지 않나요?
(A) 마무리 작업을 하는 중이에요.
(B) 모퉁이에서 왼쪽으로 도세요.
(C) 네, 그건 휴대용 기기예요.

해설 포트폴리오를 오늘 제출해야 되지 않냐고 묻는 부정 의문문에 직접적인 Yes/No 답변 대신 마무리 작업을 하고 있는 중이라며 거의 완료되었음을 간접적으로 나타낸 (A)가 정답. (C)는 질문의 portfolio(포트폴리오)와 발음이 유사한 portable(휴대용의)을 이용해 혼동을 준 오답.

어휘 turn in 제출하다 | put the finishing touches (on) (~에) 마무리 작업을 하다 | portable 휴대용의 | device 기기, 장치

30. 미 호 🎧

Who was selected to give the opening speech at the awards ceremony?
(A) At the end of the year.
(B) She did a wonderful job.
(C) It hasn't been announced yet.

누가 시상식에서 개막 연설을 하도록 선정되었나요?
(A) 연말에요.
(B) 그녀는 훌륭하게 해냈어요.
(C) 아직 발표되지 않았어요.

해설 시상식에서 연설할 사람을 묻는 Who 의문문에 아직 발표가 되지 않았다고 답변한 (C)가 정답. (B)는 대명사 she로 지칭할 만한 인물이 질문에서 언급되지 않았으므로 오답.

어휘 select 선정하다 | give a speech 연설하다 | awards ceremony 시상식 | announce 발표하다

31. 호 영 🎧

Which item can I use this coupon for?
(A) It expired last month.
(B) Yes, I shop here often.
(C) Three would be enough.

이 쿠폰은 어떤 제품에 사용할 수 있나요?
(A) 그건 지난달에 만료되었어요.
(B) 네, 저는 여기서 자주 쇼핑을 해요.
(C) 세 개면 충분할 것 같아요.

해설 쿠폰을 사용할 수 있는 제품이 어떤 것인지 묻는 Which 의문문에, 이미 만료가 되었다는 말로 사용할 수 없는 쿠폰임을 나타낸 (A)가 정답. 어떤 제품에 쿠폰을 사용할 수 있는지 묻는 질문에 세 개면 충분하다는 대답은 맥락에 맞지 않으므로 (C)는 오답.

어휘 expire 만료되다 | shop 쇼핑을 하다 | enough 충분한

PART 3

미 영 🎧

Questions 32-34 refer to the following conversation.

M   ³²Welcome to Madison Department Store. Can I help you find anything today?

W   ³³I'm wondering if these jeans come in a size fourteen. I didn't see any on the shelf.

M   ³³I think twelve is the largest size we carry, but let me look it up on the computer.

W   Thanks. I really like this style.

M   Hmm... yes, twelve is the largest size here, though the brand does make other sizes.

W   Could I buy one at another branch?

M   ³⁴If you visit our company's Web site, you should be able to see if you can get it there.

남   ³²매디슨 백화점에 오신 걸 환영합니다. 오늘 뭐 찾으시는 거라도 있으세요?

여   ³³이 청바지가 14 사이즈로 나오는지 궁금해요. 선반에서는 못 봤거든요.

남   ³³12 사이즈가 저희가 취급하는 가장 큰 사이즈인 것 같아요, 하지만 컴퓨터에서 찾아볼게요.

여   고마워요. 저는 이 스타일이 정말 마음에 들거든요.

23. 미 호 🎧

Why don't we make comment cards for our customers?
(A) Yes, I think she's a new customer.
(B) That would streamline our feedback process.
(C) Did you drive to work by yourself?

우리 고객들을 위해 의견 카드를 만드는 게 어때요?
(A) 네, 그녀는 신규 고객인 것 같아요.
(B) 그러면 우리 피드백 절차가 간소화될 거예요.
(C) 직접 운전해서 출근했나요?

해설 고객들을 위해 의견 카드를 만드는 게 어떠냐는 Why don't you 제안 의문문에, 그렇게 하면 피드백 절차가 간소화될 거라는 말로 긍정적인 의견을 제시한 (B)가 정답. (C)는 질문의 cards를 cars로 잘못 들었을 경우 연상되는 drive(운전하다)를 이용하여 혼동을 준 오답.

어휘 comment 논평, 의견 streamline 간소화하다 process 절차 by oneself 혼자, 스스로

24. 영 미 🎧

Where can I get this month's copy of the magazine?
(A) No, I haven't had much time.
(B) There's a newsstand around the corner.
(C) Because of an interesting article.

그 잡지의 이번 달 호 한 부를 어디서 얻을 수 있나요?
(A) 아니요, 저는 시간이 많지 않았어요.
(B) 모퉁이를 돌면 잡지 가판대가 있어요.
(C) 흥미로운 기사 때문에요.

해설 이번 달 잡지 한 부를 구할 수 있는 장소를 묻는 Where 의문문에 구체적인 장소로 답변한 (B)가 정답. (A)는 의문사 의문문에 No로 답변한 오답.

어휘 copy (신문·책의) 한 부 magazine 잡지 newsstand 신문·잡지 가판대 article 기사

25. 미 영 🎧

Doesn't the office seem extra quiet today?
(A) Yes, a lot of employees took the day off.
(B) Sorry, I'll try to keep it down.
(C) I think tomorrow is fine.

오늘 유독 사무실이 조용한 것 같지 않아요?
(A) 네, 많은 직원들이 휴가를 냈어요.
(B) 죄송해요, 조용히 하도록 할게요.
(C) 내일이 괜찮을 것 같아요.

해설 오늘 유독 사무실이 조용한 것 같지 않냐며 부정 의문문으로 묻는 질문에, Yes로 그렇다고 동의한 후 휴가를 낸 직원들이 많다고 부연 설명한 (A)가 정답. (B)는 질문의 quiet(조용한)에서 연상되는 keep it down(조용히 하다, 목소리를 낮추다)을 이용하여 혼동을 주는 오답.

어휘 extra 여분으로, 특별히; 추가의 take a day off 하루 쉬다, 휴가를 내다 keep ~ down (소리 등을) 약하게 하다

26. 미 미 🎧

Can we meet by video conference, or do we need to do it in person?
(A) Yes, I enjoyed the conference.
(B) Face-to-face would be better.
(C) To discuss employee performance.

우리 화상 회의로 만날 수 있을까요, 아니면 직접 만나서 회의를 해야 할까요?
(A) 네, 저는 학회가 즐거웠어요.
(B) 얼굴을 맞대고 하는 게 나을 거 같아요.
(C) 직원 성과를 논의하기 위해서요.

해설 화상 회의와 직접 만나서 하는 회의 중 무엇이 나을지 묻는 선택 의문문에, 얼굴을 맞대고 하는 게 나을 것 같다는 말로 후자를 선택하여 답변한 (B)가 정답. (C)는 질문의 conference(학회)에서 연상되는 discuss(논의하다)를 이용하여 혼동을 주는 오답.

어휘 video conference 화상 회의 in person 직접 conference 학회, 회의 face-to-face 마주보는 performance 성과

27. 미 호 🎧

Why is the door to the side entrance locked?
(A) No, you can leave it open.
(B) For a few more hours.
(C) I heard it was being repaired.

측면 출입구 문이 왜 잠겨 있나요?
(A) 아니요, 열어 놓으셔도 돼요.
(B) 몇 시간 더요.
(C) 수리 중이라고 들었어요.

해설 측면 출입구가 잠겨 있는 이유를 묻는 Why 의문문에 수리 중이라고 그 이유를 설명한 (C)가 정답. (B)는 이유를 묻는 Why 의문문에 소요 시간으로 답변한 오답.

어휘 side entrance 측면의 출입구 lock 잠그다 repair 수리하다

28. 미 영 🎧

Where do you keep your lightweight backpacks?
(A) Mainly for hikers.
(B) Yes, I decided to bring one.
(C) They're next to the tents.

경량 배낭들을 어디에 두시나요?

을 대명사 them으로 칭하며 재활용하라고 해결책을 제시한 (C)가 정답. (A)는 질문의 promotional(홍보의)과 파생 관계인 promotion(승진)을 이용해 혼동을 준 오답.

어휘 leftover 남은   promotional 홍보의   congratulations ((항상 복수형)) 축하 (인사)   promotion 승진   recycle 재활용하다

18. 영 미 🎧

I forgot the code to enter the laboratory.
(A) She'll show you some experiments.
(B) It's five-seven-seven-one.
(C) He is our top scientist.

실험실에 들어가는 암호를 잊어버렸어요.
(A) 그녀가 몇몇 실험을 당신에게 보여 줄 거예요.
(B) 5-7-7-1이에요.
(C) 그는 우리의 최고의 과학자예요.

해설 실험실의 암호를 잊어버렸다는 말에 직접적으로 암호를 알려준 (B)가 정답. (A)와 (C)는 각각 질문의 laboratory(실험실)에서 연상되는 experiments(실험)와 scientist(과학자)를 이용하여 혼동을 준 오답.

어휘 code 암호   laboratory 실험실   experiment 실험

19. 미 호 🎧

Would you like me to e-mail you a summary of the meeting?
(A) Thanks, but I took notes.
(B) The entire management team.
(C) Approximately two hours.

제가 회의 요약본을 당신께 이메일로 보내 드릴까요?
(A) 고맙지만, 제가 메모했어요.
(B) 경영팀 전체요.
(C) 약 2시간이요.

해설 회의 요약본을 이메일로 보내 주겠다고 제안하는 Would 의문문에 고맙지만 이미 메모했다는 말로 제안을 거절한 (A)가 정답. (C)는 회의가 진행된 시간 등 소요 시간을 묻는 How long 의문문에 적합한 답변이므로 오답.

어휘 summary 요약, 개요   take notes 메모하다, 필기하다   entire 전체의   management 경영, 운영   approximately 약, 대략

20. 미 영 🎧

Where do I send the completed application?
(A) A full-time position, I think.
(B) Details are on the Web site.
(C) No later than July 1.

작성된 지원서는 어디로 보내나요?
(A) 제 생각에는 정규직이에요.
(B) 자세한 사항은 웹사이트에 있어요.
(C) 늦어도 7월 1일까지요.

해설 지원서를 보내야 하는 곳을 묻는 Where 의문문에 세부 사항은 웹사이트에 있다는 말로 간접적으로 질문자가 원하는 정보를 제시한 (B)가 정답. (C)는 지원서 제출 마감일 등을 묻는 When 의문문에 적절한 답변이므로 오답.

어휘 completed 작성된   application 지원서, 신청서   full-time position 정규직   details 세부 정보   no later than 늦어도 ~까지

21. 영 미 🎧

I can bring two bags onto the plane, can't I?
(A) No, you'll have to check one.
(B) The flight will depart shortly.
(C) Yes, I've put them in a bag.

제가 가방을 두 개 가지고 비행기를 탈 수 있죠, 그렇죠?
(A) 아니요, 하나만 부쳐야 할 거예요.
(B) 비행기가 곧 출발할 거예요.
(C) 네, 제가 그것을 가방에 넣었어요.

해설 비행기에 가방 두 개를 가지고 탈 수 있는지 여부를 묻는 부가의문문에 No라고 안 된다고 답한 후 하나만 부칠 수 있다고 덧붙인 (A)가 정답. (B)는 질문의 plane(비행기)에서 연상되는 동의어 flight(비행기)을 이용하여 혼동을 주는 오답.

어휘 check (수하물을) 부치다   depart 출발하다   shortly 곧

22. 미 미 🎧

I'll let the manufacturer know about this safety issue.
(A) I work at a manufacturing facility.
(B) We can save some for later.
(C) That's the right move. Thanks.

제가 제조업체에 이번 안전 문제에 대해 알릴게요.
(A) 저는 제조 시설에 근무합니다.
(B) 나중을 위해 일부를 남겨둘 수 있어요.
(C) 그게 맞는 조치네요. 고마워요.

해설 제조업체에 직접 문제를 알리겠다는 평서문에 그게 맞는 조치라며 긍정적으로 답변한 (C)가 정답. (A)는 manufacturer(제조업체)와 manufacturing(제조의; 제조)의 파생 관계를 이용해 혼동을 준 오답이며, (B)는 save와 safety의 발음상의 유사점을 이용한 오답.

어휘 manufacturer 제조업자, 제조업체   safety 안전   issue 문제, 사안   manufacturing facility 제조 시설   save 저축하다, 남겨 두다   move 조치, 행동

공항까지 태워다 줘서 고마워요.
(A) 가능하다면, 직항이요.
(B) 별말씀을요.
(C) 저는 출장을 갔어요.

해설 공항에 태워다 줘서 고맙다는 감사 인사에 적절한 응답 표현으로 답변한 (B)가 정답. (A)는 질문의 airport(공항)에서 연상되는 direct flight(직항)을 이용하여 혼동을 준 오답.

어휘 appreciate 감사하다　give a ride 태워 주다　direct flight 직항　go on a business trip 출장을 가다

13. 미 미 🎧

Do you need me to check the copy machine?
(A) Press the green button on the front.
(B) The quarterly report for investors.
(C) Oh, I got it working again.

제가 복사기를 확인해 드릴까요?
(A) 앞에 있는 초록색 버튼을 누르세요.
(B) 투자자들을 위한 분기별 보고서요.
(C) 아, 다시 작동돼요.

해설 복사기를 확인해 줄 필요가 있는지 묻는 Do 일반 의문문에 다시 작동되게 만들었다고 한 (C)가 정답. (A)는 질문의 copy machine(복사기)에서 연상되는 Press(누르세요)와 green button(초록색 버튼)을 이용하여 혼동을 준 오답.

어휘 copy machine 복사기　press 누르다　quarterly 분기별의　investor 투자자　get it working 그것이 작동하게 만들다　work 작동하다

14. 호 영 🎧

When will the crew finish trimming the bushes?
(A) Probably around noon.
(B) In the front yard.
(C) Pink and white roses.

언제 작업반이 관목을 다듬는 것을 끝내나요?
(A) 아마 정오쯤이요.
(B) 앞뜰에서요.
(C) 분홍색과 흰색 장미들이요.

해설 관목 다듬기를 마치는 시간을 묻는 When 의문문에 대략적인 시점(around noon)으로 답변한 (A)가 정답. (B)는 시간을 묻는 When 의문문에 장소(front yard)로 답변한 오답.

어휘 crew 작업반　trim 다듬다　bush 관목　probably 아마

15. 미 미 🎧

Is there a fee to park in this lot?
(A) I appreciate the help.
(B) Yes, according to the sign.
(C) To get to the Bennington Building.

이 구역에 주차 요금이 있나요?
(A) 도움에 감사드립니다.
(B) 네, 표지판에 따르면요.
(C) 베닝턴 빌딩에 도착하기 위해서요.

해설 주차 요금이 있는지 여부를 묻는 Be동사 일반 의문문에 Yes라고 답한 후, 표지판에 쓰여 있다며 그 근거를 덧붙인 (B)가 정답. (C)는 질문의 park를 '공원'으로 알아들었을 경우, park(공원)와 lot(구역)에서 연상되는 장소 명사(Bennington Building)를 이용하여 혼동을 주는 오답.

어휘 fee 요금　park 주차하다; 공원　lot 지역, 부지　appreciate 감사하다　sign 표지판, 간판　get to ~에 도착하다

16. 호 미 🎧

I can arrive late to the presentation, right?
(A) No, the presents have not arrived.
(B) Please feel free to use mine.
(C) Yes, but you'll have to stand at the back.

제가 발표에 늦게 도착해도 되죠, 그렇죠?
(A) 아니요, 선물들은 도착하지 않았어요.
(B) 제 것을 마음껏 사용하세요.
(C) 네, 하지만 뒤에 서 있어야 할 거예요.

해설 발표에 늦어도 괜찮은지 여부를 묻는 질문에 Yes로 괜찮다고 답한 후, 대신에 뒤에 서 있어야 할 거라고 부연 설명한 (C)가 정답. (A)는 질문의 presentation(발표)과 부분적으로 발음이 유사한 presents(선물)를 사용하여 혼동을 주는 오답.

어휘 arrive 도착하다　presentation 발표　present 선물　feel free to do 마음대로 ~하다

17. 미 영 🎧

What can I do with the leftover promotional posters?
(A) Congratulations on your promotion!
(B) By five o'clock.
(C) Just recycle them.

제가 남은 홍보 포스터로 무엇을 할 수 있을까요?
(A) 승진 축하해요!
(B) 5시까지요.
(C) 그것들은 그냥 재활용하세요.

해설 남은 포스터로 할 수 있는 일을 묻는 What 의문문에 포스터들

PART 2

7. 호 미 🎧

When will the landlord inspect the property?
(A) No, it failed the inspection.
(B) I'll e-mail him about it.
(C) Do you like the apartment?

집주인이 건물을 언제 점검할까요?
(A) 아니요, 그것은 점검을 통과하지 못했어요.
(B) 제가 그에게 그것에 대해 이메일을 보낼게요.
(C) 당신은 아파트가 마음에 드나요?

해설 집주인이 건물을 점검하는 시기를 묻는 When 의문문에 구체적인 시점을 제시하는 대신 이메일로 물어보겠다고 우회적으로 답변한 (B)가 정답. (C)는 질문의 landlord(집주인)와 property(건물)에서 연상되는 apartment(아파트)를 이용하여 혼동을 준 오답.

어휘 landlord 집주인, 임대인 inspect 점검하다, 검사하다 property 건물, 부동산 inspection 점검, 검사

8. 미 호 🎧

Who's giving the new employees a tour tomorrow?
(A) I'll be at another branch.
(B) Let's visit the most famous sites.
(C) Our team has reached the goal.

누가 내일 신입 사원들에게 견학을 시켜 주나요?
(A) 저는 다른 지점에 있을 거예요.
(B) 가장 유명한 곳들을 방문합시다.
(C) 저희 팀은 목표에 도달했어요.

해설 내일 신입 사원들을 견학시켜 줄 사람을 묻는 Who 의문문에 자신(I)은 다른 지점에 있을 거라며 다른 사람이 할 것이라고 우회적으로 답변한 (A)가 정답. (B)는 질문의 tour(견학)에서 연상되는 visit(방문하다)과 sites(장소)를 이용해 혼동을 준 오답.

어휘 new employee 신입 직원 give a tour 견학[구경]을 시켜 주다 branch 지점 site 장소, 현장 reach ~에 이르다, 도달하다 goal 목표

9. 미 영 🎧

Would you prefer coffee or a soft drink with your lunch set?
(A) A cup of black coffee, please.
(B) I'll show you our menu.
(C) He said he was thirsty.

런치 세트와 함께 커피로 하시겠어요, 아니면 탄산음료로 하시겠어요?
(A) 블랙커피 한 잔 주세요.
(B) 저희 메뉴를 보여 드릴게요.
(C) 그는 목이 마르다고 했어요.

해설 커피나 탄산음료 중 무엇이 좋을지 묻는 선택 의문문에 블랙커피를 달라며 둘 중 하나를 선택하여 답변한 (A)가 정답. (C)는 질문의 주어 you와 답변의 주어 He가 일치하지 않으며, drink(음료)에서 연상되는 thirsty(목이 마른)를 이용하여 혼동을 준 오답.

어휘 prefer 선호하다 soft drink 탄산음료 thirsty 목이 마른, 갈증이 나는

10. 미 호 🎧

Isn't this leather jacket on sale?
(A) No, I like the other one.
(B) Yes, it's half off today.
(C) Some cold weather.

이 가죽 재킷은 할인 중 아닌가요?
(A) 아니요, 저는 다른 것이 좋아요.
(B) 네, 오늘 반값이에요.
(C) 추운 날씨요.

해설 가죽 재킷이 할인 중이 아닌지 묻는 부정 의문문에 Yes로 할인 중이라고 답한 후, 오늘은 반값 할인을 한다며 구체적인 정보를 덧붙인 (B)가 정답. (A)는 가죽 재킷의 할인 여부를 묻는 질문에 다른 것이 좋다는 맥락에 맞지 않는 답변을 한 오답.

어휘 leather 가죽 on sale 할인 중인 half off 반값의, 50% 할인의

11. 영 호 🎧

How many people will attend the lecture?
(A) A talk on sustainable energy.
(B) Professor Franklin starts at seven o'clock.
(C) Nearly fifty have signed up.

얼마나 많은 사람들이 강의를 들을 건가요?
(A) 지속 가능한 에너지에 대한 연설이에요.
(B) 프랭클린 교수가 7시 정각에 시작할 거예요.
(C) 약 50명이 신청했어요.

해설 강의를 들을 사람들의 수를 묻는 How many 의문문에 약 50명이 신청을 했다고 한 (C)가 정답. (B)는 질문의 lecture(강의)에서 연상되는 professor(교수)를 이용하여 혼동을 준 오답.

어휘 attend 출석하다, 참석하다 lecture 강의 talk 연설 sustainable 지속 가능한 nearly 약, 거의 sign up 신청하다, 등록하다

12. 호 영 🎧

I appreciate your giving me a ride to the airport.
(A) A direct flight, if possible.
(B) It's my pleasure.
(C) I went on a business trip.

어휘 water 물을 주다   potted plant 화분   pile (물건을 차곡차곡) 쌓다   put away 치우다

3. 영 🎧

(A) They're folding a piece of paper.
(B) One of the men is cutting some wood.
(C) A toolbox has been set on the floor.
(D) A brick wall is being painted.

(A) 사람들이 종이 한 장을 접고 있다.
(B) 남자들 중 한 명이 목재를 자르고 있다.
(C) 공구 상자가 바닥에 놓여 있다.
(D) 벽돌 벽을 페인트칠하고 있다.

해설 바닥에 공구 상자가 놓여 있는 상태를 적절하게 묘사한 (C)가 정답. (A)는 남자들 중 한 명이 종이를 접고 있는(folding) 것이 아니라 종이를 들고 있으므로 오답.

어휘 fold 접다   toolbox 공구 상자   set ~을 놓다

4. 호 🎧

(A) A piano has been positioned under a window.
(B) Some cushions have been stacked in the corner.
(C) A seating area has been arranged on a rug.
(D) A carpet is being installed.

(A) 피아노 한 대가 창문 아래 위치해 있다.
(B) 몇몇 쿠션들이 구석에 쌓여 있다.
(C) 앉는 자리가 깔개 위에 마련되어 있다.
(D) 카펫을 깔고 있다.

해설 깔개 위에 앉는 자리가 준비되어 있는 상태를 적절하게 묘사한 (C)가 정답. (B)는 쿠션들이 구석에 쌓여 있지(have been stacked) 않고 소파 위에 놓여 있으므로 오답.

어휘 position ~에 두다, 배치하다   stack 쌓다   area 지역, 구역   arrange 정리하다, 배열하다   rug 깔개, 양탄자

5. 영 🎧

(A) One of the men is entering a music store.
(B) One of the men is repairing a guitar.
(C) The men are waiting in line at a bus stop.
(D) The men are playing instruments.

(A) 남자들 중 한 명이 음반 가게에 들어가고 있다.
(B) 남자들 중 한 명이 기타를 수리하고 있다.
(C) 남자들이 버스 정류장에서 줄 서서 기다리고 있다.
(D) 남자들이 악기를 연주하고 있다.

해설 남자들이 악기를 연주하고 있는 모습을 적절하게 묘사한 (D)가 정답. (B)는 사진에 보이는 기타(guitar)로 혼동을 주는 오답으로, 기타를 수리하고 있는(repairing) 사람은 없다.

어휘 music store 음반 가게   repair 수리하다   wait in line 줄을 서서 기다리다   instrument 악기, 도구

6. 미 🎧

(A) A woman is signing copies of a book.
(B) A ladder is being stored in a closet.
(C) Some documents have fallen on the floor.
(D) Some books have been placed on shelves.

(A) 여자가 책 여러 권에 서명을 하고 있다.
(B) 사다리를 벽장에 보관하고 있다.
(C) 일부 서류가 바닥에 떨어졌다.
(D) 몇몇 책들이 책장에 놓여 있다.

해설 책들이 책장에 놓여 있는 상태를 적절하게 묘사한 (D)가 정답. (A)는 사진에 보이는 책들로 혼동을 주는 오답으로, 여자가 책에 서명을 하는(signing) 중은 아니다.

어휘 sign 서명하다, 사인하다   copy (책·신문 등의) 한 부, 사본   store 저장하다, 보관하다   closet 벽장   document 서류   place 두다, 놓다

TEST 01

LISTENING TEST

001 (B)	002 (A)	003 (C)	004 (C)	005 (D)
006 (D)	007 (B)	008 (A)	009 (A)	010 (B)
011 (C)	012 (B)	013 (C)	014 (A)	015 (B)
016 (C)	017 (C)	018 (B)	019 (A)	020 (B)
021 (A)	022 (C)	023 (B)	024 (B)	025 (A)
026 (B)	027 (C)	028 (C)	029 (A)	030 (C)
031 (A)	032 (C)	033 (A)	034 (A)	035 (B)
036 (D)	037 (C)	038 (D)	039 (D)	040 (A)
041 (C)	042 (A)	043 (D)	044 (B)	045 (B)
046 (D)	047 (D)	048 (A)	049 (D)	050 (D)
051 (C)	052 (A)	053 (C)	054 (D)	055 (B)
056 (B)	057 (D)	058 (A)	059 (A)	060 (C)
061 (D)	062 (B)	063 (B)	064 (C)	065 (A)
066 (D)	067 (C)	068 (C)	069 (D)	070 (A)
071 (A)	072 (A)	073 (C)	074 (C)	075 (D)
076 (D)	077 (D)	078 (A)	079 (B)	080 (B)
081 (C)	082 (B)	083 (A)	084 (D)	085 (C)
086 (D)	087 (B)	088 (A)	089 (D)	090 (A)
091 (C)	092 (B)	093 (D)	094 (C)	095 (C)
096 (D)	097 (B)	098 (A)	099 (D)	100 (D)

READING TEST

101 (D)	102 (B)	103 (A)	104 (A)	105 (D)
106 (C)	107 (B)	108 (A)	109 (D)	110 (D)
111 (A)	112 (A)	113 (C)	114 (B)	115 (A)
116 (B)	117 (C)	118 (B)	119 (D)	120 (C)
121 (A)	122 (B)	123 (B)	124 (C)	125 (A)
126 (D)	127 (B)	128 (C)	129 (C)	130 (D)
131 (D)	132 (A)	133 (D)	134 (B)	135 (C)
136 (C)	137 (B)	138 (A)	139 (B)	140 (C)
141 (D)	142 (B)	143 (B)	144 (D)	145 (B)
146 (A)	147 (A)	148 (B)	149 (B)	150 (D)
151 (C)	152 (D)	153 (D)	154 (D)	155 (D)
156 (B)	157 (A)	158 (C)	159 (A)	160 (C)
161 (D)	162 (B)	163 (C)	164 (B)	165 (B)
166 (C)	167 (B)	168 (D)	169 (D)	170 (A)
171 (B)	172 (D)	173 (C)	174 (D)	175 (B)
176 (A)	177 (C)	178 (C)	179 (D)	180 (B)
181 (D)	182 (B)	183 (D)	184 (A)	185 (C)
186 (A)	187 (D)	188 (C)	189 (B)	190 (C)
191 (D)	192 (B)	193 (A)	194 (C)	195 (C)
196 (C)	197 (B)	198 (C)	199 (A)	200 (D)

PART 1

1. 미 🎧

(A) He's staring at a vase.
(B) He's pouring a beverage.
(C) He's spreading out a tablecloth.
(D) He's sipping from a coffee cup.

(A) 남자가 꽃병을 응시하고 있다.
(B) 남자가 음료를 따르고 있다.
(C) 남자가 식탁보를 깔고 있다.
(D) 남자가 커피 잔으로 조금씩 마시고 있다.

해설 남자가 차를 따르고 있는 모습을 적절하게 묘사한 (B)가 정답. (D)는 사진에 찻잔이 보이기는 하지만, 잔으로 음료를 마시는(sipping) 중은 아니므로 오답.

어휘 stare at ~을 응시하다 pour 따르다, 붓다 beverage 음료 spread out 깔다, (접힌 것을) 펼치다 sip (음료를) 조금씩 마시다

2. 미 🎧

(A) The woman is wearing glasses.
(B) The woman is watering some potted plants.
(C) Some books are being piled on a shelf.
(D) A laptop computer is being put away.

(A) 여자가 안경을 쓰고 있다.
(B) 여자가 화분에 물을 주고 있다.
(C) 몇몇 책들을 선반 위에 쌓고 있다.
(D) 노트북 컴퓨터를 치우고 있다.

해설 여자가 안경을 쓴 모습을 적절하게 묘사한 (A)가 정답. wear와 put on은 둘 다 '입다/신다'라는 뜻이지만 wear는 이미 착용한 상태를 나타내는 반면, put on은 착용하는 동작에 초점을 맞춘 표현이다.

에듀윌 토익
실전 LC+RC
정답 및 해설